THE
MAKING OF AMERICA
SERIES

MOSCOW
LIVING AND LEARNING ON THE PALOUSE

This landscape, close to where the Nez Perce harvested the camas bulb, is representative of the rolling hills of the Palouse. (Courtesy Mara Lei Monroe.)

THE
MAKING OF AMERICA
SERIES

MOSCOW

LIVING AND LEARNING ON THE PALOUSE

JULIE R. MONROE

ARCADIA

Published by Arcadia Publishing,
an imprint of Tempus Publishing, Inc.
2 Cumberland Street
Charleston, SC 29401

Printed in Great Britain.

Library of Congress Catalog Card Number: 2003100304

For all general information contact Arcadia Publishing at:
Telephone 843-853-2070
Fax 843-853-0044
E-Mail sales@arcadiapublishing.com

For customer service and orders:
Toll-Free 1-888-313-2665

Visit us on the Internet at http://www.arcadiapublishing.com

Front cover: *One of the major attractions of Moscow's gala Fourth of July celebrations was the race to determine who was the town's fastest fat man. This race down Main Street took place on July 4, 1911.*

CONTENTS

ACKNOWLEDGMENTS

Moscow: Living and Learning on the Palouse came about through the efforts of many people—past and present—and I wish to thank all those who made it possible for me to write this history. Special thanks go to Erika Kuhlman, who thought of me when her destiny led her beyond Moscow and to Mary Reed of the Latah County Historical Society and Terry Abraham of the University of Idaho's Special Collections, for generously granting me permission to use the historic photographs that appear in this book. I would also like to acknowledge all of the Latah County historians—amateur and professional—whose love of local history, with its stories of everyday people, created a legacy of which the residents of our area should be truly proud.

The images that appear in this book were provided by a number of organizations and individuals. Credit for these images is provided at the end of captions and those from the Latah County Historical Society are abbreviated "LCHS."

A candy lovers heaven! Ray Hunter and Eileen Condell proudly display a super-sized serving of Hunter's Candy, c. 1950.

INTRODUCTION

Moscow, Idaho is a community of surprising contrasts. It is a small town of less than 22,000 that offers cultural and educational opportunities found only in major metropolitan areas. It is the home of the University of Idaho, the state of Idaho's land-grant institution that is one of the most "connected" universities in the nation. Yet many of its residents are as deeply connected to the land as they are to their personal computers. Moscow is located in the uniquely beautiful Palouse, one of the most productive agricultural areas not just in the nation, but also in the world. And its nickname (or epithet, depending upon your politics) "Berkeley of Idaho" speaks volumes in a state as conservative as Idaho.

Perhaps these contrasts are the result of Moscow's history as a city of crossroads. Before history, in fact, two major Native American trails, the Greater Nez Perce Trail and the Red Wolf Trail, intersected in the northeastern part of Paradise Valley, the present-day name of the area in which Moscow is located. In succession, white men followed these same trails in search of fur, gold, souls, and finally land. In this regard, Moscow was established in much the same way as were other communities located in the Inland Northwest, the last American frontier. Initially, Americans moving westward to fulfill their manifest destiny ignored the interiors of what would become the states of Washington, Oregon, and Idaho, preferring the golden opportunities to be found along the Pacific Ocean. Only after discovering that the opportunities were somewhat tarnished, or when they simply grew restless, did permanent white settlers begin moving into the Inland Northwest.

In 1871, one such American was Almon Lieuallen, who, with his brother Noah, left the area around Walla Walla, Washington, to homestead in a valley called "Tatkinmah" by the Nez Perce Indians. Each year, the Nez Perce, along with the Palouse and Coeur d'Alene Indians, temporarily camped in the valley where Moscow now stands to dig the root of the blue-flowered camas plant. That same year, other permanent settlers, including George Tomer, John Russell, James Deakin, William Taylor, and Henry McGregor, also homesteaded in the valley. In 1873, when the first post office was established, the settlement was called Paradise; by 1876, the name had been changed to Moscow. In 1888, Moscow became the seat of Latah County, the only county in the nation to have been formed by an act of the United States Congress.

Thirteen years later, in January 1889, the University of Idaho was created by an act of the legislature of the Territory of Idaho. The placement of the state's university in Moscow was the single most significant event in the community's history. Simply put, without the university, it is unlikely that the fledgling community would have had the means to grow beyond its original role as a retail center for the area's farmers and ranchers. For this reason, the history of Moscow and the history of the university are closely linked, as are the histories of the Palouse and wheat farming.

From the day the University of Idaho opened its door on October 3, 1892, the destinies of thousands of people from throughout the state, the nation, and the world have crossed with that of Moscow. As these talented individuals with their diversity of cultural and personal experience pass through Moscow, they leave their mark. But the gesture is often reciprocated because it is difficult to forget a community where it is still possible to hear the cry of a hawk amid the clatter of contemporary life. Moscow is a place where many pause to learn how they can achieve the life they wish to lead.

Moscow's 1934 American Legion parade was held on Main Street, and this drum and bugle corps pauses during the event to pose for their photograph. (Courtesy LCHS.)

1. The Beginning

The community of Moscow is nestled within an area called the Palouse, a region of northern Idaho and eastern Washington that encompasses approximately 4,000 square miles. Within the expanse of the Palouse are several counties, including Latah County, in which Moscow is located. The topography of the Palouse, with its vast contour of low, rolling hills, is striking. It is a landscape that provides its residents with a living backdrop of colors, ranging from velvet brown to vibrant spring green to golden amber. The Palouse inspires deep affection in those who live within its borders, and much of what forms the identity of Moscow is its location within this unique landscape.

The singular topography of the region is the result of cataclysmic natural events that occurred millions of years ago. The Palouse is located on the eastern edge of the Columbia River Plateau, the area situated between the Cascade Mountains on the west and the Rocky Mountains on the east. The plateau rests upon layers of basalt formed during a period from 6 million to 17 million years ago. Known as the Columbia River Basalts, a series of lava spills covered parts of Washington, Oregon, and Idaho at speeds of 20 to 30 miles per hour. Latah County historian John B. Miller has compared the lava to melted wax that was slowly poured into a large, irregular mold.

Upon this layer of basalt sit the dune-like hills of the Palouse, which were formed over 100,000 years ago by fierce windstorms loaded with massive amounts of silt. Coming from the southwest, the winds deposited the silt, also known as loess, on the bedrock of basalt and molded it into a landscape of rolling, curving ridges and slopes. The source of the loess is a topic of debate among geologists; some theorize it is volcanic ash from the eruptions of the Cascade Mountains, while others say it is glacial flour from the regions once covered in glaciers to the north of the Palouse . The prevailing belief is that the loess came from the western side of the Columbia Plateau near the Cascade Mountains.

During the present epoch, the loess developed into an extremely fertile soil due in large part to its ability to retain moisture. This characteristic is the result of the high volume of volcanic ash in Palouse loess. Over the eons, the erupting volcanoes of the Cascade Mountains have repeatedly dusted the region. One such eruption occurred, not in the distant past, but only two decades ago. On May 18,

This amazing view reveals the unique beauty of a Moscow area wheat field during harvest. (Courtesy LCHS.)

1980, Mount St. Helens erupted, and residents of the Palouse found themselves caught in a blizzard of ash that literally blocked out the sun. Contrary to fears that the ash would ruin crops, farmers harvested a bumper crop that year.

In some places, the fertile Palouse topsoil is 250 feet deep, which partly explains why the Palouse is so well-suited to the production of grains and legumes. Because the soil retains moisture so well, Palouse farmers are able to practice dry land farming with much success; it is the most common method of crop cultivation used in the region. Wheat is the predominant Palouse crop, but other crops, especially dry edible peas and lentils, are grown as well. In fact, nearly all of the nation's commercially-grown dry peas and lentils are raised in Moscow's Latah County and its neighbor to the west, Washington's Whitman County.

Just as there are multiple theories regarding the origin of Palouse loess, the source of the word Palouse is also a subject of debate. Some say French trappers used the word *pelouse*, or "grassy spot," to describe the area; however, the more likely explanation is that the name comes from the Sehaptin word Palus, the name of a major village of the Palouse Indians. Sehaptin is a linguistic group to which the Palouse and their neighbors to the south, the Nez Perce, belong. The village of Palus was located at the confluence of the Palouse and Snake Rivers in what is now Whitman County, Washington. At a spot near the village, a great rock extended from far below the surface of the water to far above it, and the word Palus is interpreted to mean "something sticking down in the water." The Palouse Indians believed this rock was the solidified heart of Beaver, an important figure in their religious beliefs. The Nez Perce, on the other hand, believed the rock to be the canoe of Coyote, the trickster who outwitted the monster whose body filled the homeland of the Nez Perce.

According to legend, Coyote created the Nez Perce people when he outwitted Its-welks, the monster who had swallowed all the other Animal Persons, including Grizzly Bear, Fox, Rattlesnake, and Muskrat. Although Coyote tricked Its-welks into swallowing him, Coyote had a plan and vanquished the monster by cutting out its heart. Coyote then cut Its-welks into pieces and threw them in each of the four directions. From the many parts of the monster's body came the human people who would be neighbors of the Nez Perce, such as the Blackfoot, Shoshone, and Flatheads. And from the blood of the heart of the monster came a good, strong, and brave people who would lead good lives, and they were the Nez Perce.

When Coyote created the Nez Perce, he placed them in a large country. The original territory of the Nez Perce has been estimated at nearly 27,000 square miles, and it extended into parts of northern Idaho, eastern Montana, and western Oregon. Theirs was a territory marked by a diverse natural environment, with steep river canyons in the south, vast grasslands in the middle, and mountains to the north and east. Included within this territory was a valley the Nez Perce called Tatkinmah, "place of the spotted deer." This is the valley of the south fork of the Palouse River, and it is the valley in which Moscow is situated.

The Nez Perce were not the only Native Americans to visit Tatkinmah, but before the coming of the white man, they were its primary inhabitants. The Coeur d'Alenes, whose territory was and remains centered near present-day Lake Coeur d'Alene north of Moscow, ventured into the valley but generally went no farther south. The Palouse Indians also visited the valley, but their original territory lay to the west. Although none of the tribes who inhabited the Palouse River Valley established permanent settlements there, it was nonetheless an important place for several reasons.

Two ancient north-south trails, which came to be know as the Greater Nez Perce Trail or Lapwai Trail and the Red Wolf Trail or Stevens Trail, passed through Tatkinmah, intersecting at a point 2.5 miles northeast of present-day Moscow. The Greater Nez Perce Trail, used most frequently, began near the Clearwater River and branched west to Spokane Falls and north to Lake Coeur d'Alene. The Nez Perce, Coeur d'Alenes, and Palouse Indians followed these trails in their seasonal searches for food, moving north to the mountains in the summer to fish, hunt, and pick berries, especially huckleberries. In the fall, they again passed through Tatkinmah on their return trip to the region's warm river canyons. And during the spring, the valley became the site of a large temporary campground because it was itself a significant source of food.

The root of the camas plant, a blue-flowered wild lily, grew in such abundance that members of many tribes camped in Tatkinmah annually in late spring to harvest it. Joseph M. Cataldo was one of several Jesuit missionaries to the Northwest during the middle part of the nineteenth century. Sometime around 1924, in a letter written to Father Nicholas F. Wirtzberger, pastor of Moscow's Catholic church, Father Cataldo recalled seeing the camas harvest on one of his journeys from the Jesuit missions in northern Idaho to the Catholic mission in present-day Lewiston, Idaho: "The root of the camas was an essential food source for the native people, and it was versatile. The roots were eaten fresh, dried in the sun, cooked into mush in underground pits, or ground into flour to make biscuits or loaves of bread." Moscow and Latah County pioneer Clara Ransom Davis recalled seeing Indian women make flour from the roots. In a note written for the records of the Latah County Pioneer Association, Davis wrote, "After the drying and curing was completed, the squaws rubbed off the husks of the camas and pounded the roots to a flour in stone jars. They could turn out a surprising amount of flour in a day. The flour was baked into flat pancakes and sometimes a bit of fine ashes was added by way of soda or baking powder."

More than the harvest of camas took place at Tatkinmah; it was also important as a location where the Native Americans traded goods and supplies and, after the introduction of the horse, formed intertribal groups to hunt buffalo on the Great Plains during the late summer. Long before the introduction of the horse, however, Tatkinmah was a significant site within the Nez Perce culture, an ancient

A Nez Perce woman pounds camas roots after they have been baking in the sun on a tule mat. This photo was taken either at the upper Clearwater River or at the South Fork of the Clearwater, c. 1890. (#ID 38-1062, Historical Photograph Collection, University of Idaho Library.)

A member of the Nez Perce tribe posed for this postcard wearing the full regalia representative of his tribe around 1900. (Courtesy LCHS.)

culture that is over 10,000 years old. In fact, Nez Perce villages discovered along Idaho's Snake River have been dated to 11,000 years ago. Besides the Snake River, the Nez Perce also lived in the canyons of the Clearwater and Salmon Rivers. The term Nez Perce is French in derivation. According to tribal accounts, a French-Canadian interpreter with the Lewis and Clark expedition named the tribe Nez Perce, or "pierced nose," in 1805, even though nose piercing was not common among the tribe. The Nez Perce people call themselves Nimi'ipuu (noo-me-poo), which means the "real people" or "we the people."

It is believed the horse reached the Nez Perce sometime between 1690 and the early 1700s, and the tribe soon became the most renowned horsemen among the native peoples of Idaho. One reason for their success as horsemen was the nature of their homeland. Its plateaus of grasslands and deep, protected valleys proved to be perfect country for raising horses, and the Nez Perce produced large numbers of fast horses with much endurance. By the nineteenth century, Nez Perce horses were famous throughout the western part of the nation and as far east as the Dakotas. The Nez Perce used selective breeding techniques to raise superior horses and were especially fond of spotted horses, which early fur traders called Nez Perce horses. We now call these spotted horses Appaloosas, an ancient breed that may have had its origins in the plains of eastern Asia.

The superiority of Nez Perce horses, which Meriwether Lewis once described in his journals as "fat as seals," was due also to the high nutritional value of the grass upon which they fed. Before widespread farming of the Palouse, it was covered in vast grasslands, consisting mainly of a family of grasses we now call bunchgrass. Growing out of the fertile loessal soil, bunchgrass more than adequately met the nutritional requirements of horses and helps explain the large herds the Nez Perce were able to maintain.

Two of the first white men in the area, fur traders David Thompson and Alexander Ross, both commented on the great quantity of horses on the Palouse. In 1811, Thompson wrote, "The country was literally covered with horses, of which there could not have been less than four thousand in sight of camp." In 1814, Alexander Ross described a gathering of Palouse Indians as having "three thousand people and treble that number of horses."

In less than a century, the immense herds of horses were gone from the Palouse. Thomas B. Keith writes in his history of the use of horses on the Palouse, *The Horse Interlude*:

> Unfortunately, many of the spotted Indian horses were destroyed by armies sent in to move the Nez Perce tribes to a reservation in 1877. In order to prevent the soldiers from taking their horses, the Indians tried to swim them across the Snake River, during flood stage, from Wallowa Valley, Oregon. Most of the foals drowned. Many horses were killed during battles of the Nez Perce War while others were confiscated as war loot and moved to Fort Keogh, Montana, where they were sold at auction and scattered to many parts of the U.S.

In fact, after the area's earliest inhabitants, including the Nez Perce, were defeated in the Indian wars of the late 1870s and subsequently segregated onto reservations to the north and south of Moscow, there was little visible proof that a culture thousands of years old had once inhabited the area. In an attempt to discover evidence of the valley's earliest inhabitants, Cornelius J. Brosnan, professor of history at the University of Idaho, led an expedition of students in 1937 to determine the locations of the ancient trails used by the Nez Perce in the area of present-day Moscow.

The members of the expedition were successful in identifying remnants of the trails in Latah County. The Greater Nez Perce Trail originated in what is now Lapwai, Idaho, a small community south of Lewiston that serves as the headquarters of the Nez Perce Tribe. This trail crossed the eastern edge of Moscow at several places, including the present site of the Moscow Cemetery and Moscow's first post office, which is no longer standing. A branch of this trail, known by several names, including the Red Wolf Trail (in honor of a Nez Perce chief whose camp was located near present-day Lewiston and Clarkston, Washington) as well as Stevens Trail (after Washington Territorial Governor Isaac Stevens), was also discovered a few miles to the east of Moscow's current city limits.

In his account of the expedition, Professor Brosnan and his students urged the residents of Moscow to erect a series of historic markers at the sites the expedition has discovered for "the boys and girls of Moscow, now studying history in their classrooms." Among the several sites identified, Professor Brosnan suggested a marker be placed:

> near the East end of the Camas Fields commemorating a historic camas ground and the eastern end of a five mile Indian race course used by the Indians since about 1600 A.D., or since the introduction of Spanish ponies which followed the bunch grass northward from Mexico.

A letter written in 1872 corroborates Professor Brosnan's conclusion that a race track was located in Tatkinmah. On July 1, 1872, John B. Monteith, Indian agent for the Nez Perce, wrote to F.A. Walker, commissioner of Indian affairs in Washington, D.C., that the Nez Perce as well as the:

> Coeur d'Alenes, Spokanes and Umatillas and others from the Columbia River annually gathered on this ground [Tatkinmah] for the purpose of digging Camas. An interchange of friendly feeling and to have a general good time racing horses and other amusements [sic]. They had made a race course in the valley nearly two miles long where they were wont to run their horses.

The members of Professor C.J. Brosnan's expedition to discover remnants of Nez Perce trails in the Moscow area posed for this photograph in 1937. Neither the tree nor the sign are still standing. (Courtesy LCHS.)

THIS MARKS THE JUNCTION OF
STEVENS TRAIL WITH THE
GREATER NEZ PERCE INDIAN TRAIL
USED OVER 1,000 YRS.
ARRIVING HERE JUNE 21, 1855,
GOV. I. I. STEVENS RECORDED
THE FIRST HISTORY OF MOSCOW AREA.
ERECTED BY THE WORTHWHILE CLUB 1938

The boulder on which this plaque sits is the only existing commemoration of the early history of the Moscow area. (Courtesy LCHS.)

Unfortunately, with the exception of a little-known monument at the intersection of the Greater Nez Perce Trail and the Red Wolf Trail about 4 miles east of Moscow, little physical evidence of Moscow's earliest inhabitants can be found. In 1938, the Worthwhile Club, a club founded in 1929 by women from rural Latah County for the purpose of promoting friendship and worthy community projects, placed a large boulder at the intersection of the two trails. On the boulder, they placed a commemorative plaque noting the historically significant site.

As late as 1976, Rudolph Carlson, one of Moscow's earliest historians, claimed that "the ridge trail [Greater Nez Perce Trail] is etched to a depth of four feet, giving evidence of its extensive use." Sections of these trails have not been preserved, so it is fortunate that amateur local historians, often the children or grandchildren of Moscow's pioneer white settlers, took it upon themselves to record family stories that document the presence of native peoples in the area.

Prior to her death in 1985, Alma Lauder Keeling, granddaughter of William Taylor and Priscilla Mitchell Taylor, one of Moscow's earliest pioneer families, collected the stories her mother told her about growing up on the Moscow frontier. In *The Un-Covered Wagon*, Keeling wrote that her mother Minnie was a child when the family moved to Moscow from Chicago in 1871. As recorded by Keeling, Minnie recalled that when her family first saw what is now the southern part of Moscow, where her grandfather had homesteaded, the area was "covered with Indian teepees, a sight these curious children from the city had never seen before. It was camas-digging time and the Indians as usual were laying in their supply of camas for the winter."

Minnie, who married Wylie A. Lauder, also recalled the often unexpected visits from Native Americans during meal times:

> Often, about the time the food was on the table, and hungry men washed up and about to sit down, the kitchen door would open and in would walk a string of braves, preceded by their obvious leader, and, amid grunts of approval, seat themselves at the long table. They evidently enjoyed Grandmother's Pennsylvania Dutch cooking. . . . when they had cleared the table of anything eatable, they would solemnly rise and seat themselves in a circle on the floor, beckoning Grandfather to join them. Then, the pipe of peace would be passed around the circle. When each had taken a puff, they would as solemnly rise again and march out.

Incidents such as the one recalled by Minnie Taylor Lauder became less and less common as white settlers increasingly encroached upon land that once belonged

Many thanks are due Alma Lauder Keeling for celebrating the early history of Moscow in her collection of family history, The Un-Covered Wagon. (Courtesy LCHS.)

to the area's native people. In his July 1, 1872 letter, John B. Monteith explained that the camas ground that is now the site of Moscow was "outside the Reserve and open to settlement." Beginning in 1855 with the Stevens Treaty of June 11, the Nez Perce were forced to cede major portions of their original territory to the United States government. The Stevens Treaty reduced their territory by nearly 13 million acres, and the treaty of June 9, 1863, signed shortly after the discovery of gold in northern and north-central Idaho, reduced it yet further. A significant area that the Nez Perce were forced to relinquish with this treaty was that at the confluence of the Snake and Clearwater Rivers, where the cities of Lewiston, Idaho, and Clarkston, Washington now stand.

Not all of the Nez Perce had signed the treaty of 1863. Several bands of Nez Perce, namely those led by Joseph, White Bird, and Looking Glass, resisted the demands of the United States government. In 1877, however, General Oliver O. Howard issued an ultimatum demanding that the non-treaty Nez Perce relocate to the reservation centered at present-day Lapwai. Before they could comply with the

Wylie Lauder married Minnie Taylor, the daughter of William Taylor, one of Moscow's earliest pioneers, in 1886. Wylie, Minnie, and their two children, Alma and Ralph, posed for friend and photographer Henry Erichson in 1895. (Courtesy LCHS.)

demand, a band of young men killed a few white settlers living along the Clearwater River. In response, Howard organized 500 soldiers and civilian volunteers to pursue the Nez Perce, who had fled over the Lolo Pass into Montana.

After a series of skirmishes, the War of 1877, as the conflict came to be called, ended on October 5, 1877 when Chief Joseph surrendered to General Howard and Colonel Nelson Miles at Bear Paw Mountain in Canada. Although the War of 1877 took place miles away from Moscow, then generally referred to as Paradise Valley by its residents, residents had nonetheless taken measures to defend themselves against an attack by the Nez Perce. After word of the settlers' deaths along the Clearwater River reached Paradise Valley, residents built three stockades in the Moscow area: Fort Russell, Fort Howard, and Fort Crumerine. Fort Howard was built northeast of Moscow, and Fort Crumerine at the eastern end of what is now Sixth Street. Fort Russell, the largest stockade, was built north of Main Street in the area now known as the Fort Russell neighborhood on land then owned by pioneer settler John Russell. According to Alma Lauder Keeling, "Men hastily felled and hauled logs from the mountains, six miles distant, and these logs, from six to ten inches in diameter, were set upright in the ground close together with just enough room between them for a rifle to point."

She adds that the "site of the stockade was near Russell's own home" and that a "narrow platform was built along the inside of the four walls, where men on guard could stand during the night. Bedding and camping equipment were brought from each home, and, of course, food. Here the settlers with their wives and families spent the night." Lillie Lieuallen Woodworth, the daughter of Almon Asbury Lieuallen, the man who has been called the founder of Moscow, told Keeling that while the children of the settlers "had a wonderful time playing together inside the fort," their parents were genuinely alarmed and fearful of attack; however, it never came. The closest Paradise Valley came to the War of 1877 was when a group of Nez Perce traveled through the valley on its way north to recruit members of the Coeur d'Alene tribe into the conflict. According to Keeling, "The head of the Coeur d'Alene tribe had always been in cordial relations with the white man, and through his influence and that of Father Cataldo of the Catholic Mission, the Coeur d'Alenes were held in check, and the Nez Perce Indians returned disappointed."

Keeling also recorded the following:

> the settlers had thought their time had come when they saw a great cloud of dust rapidly approaching in their direction. Men hurried to the fort to be ready for the emergency. Suddenly the cloud of dust veered off in another direction, and it was discovered that this was not a band of painted warriors on the kill, but a bunch of happy horses on the loose!

The "war scare" of 1877 is commemorated by a large boulder bearing a bronze plaque located near the curbing of the house at 810 East B Street in Moscow. Eliza Spalding Warren of the Moscow Daughters of the American

Revolution chapter erected the monument in 1930. Prior to that time, according to local historian Lillian Otness, remnants of Fort Russell could still be found in the neighborhood.

After their defeat in the War of 1877, Chief Joseph and over 400 other Nez Perce were relocated to Oklahoma. In 1885, the non-treaty Nez Perce were allowed to return to the Northwest, but not to the reservation at Lapwai. Instead, they were relocated to the Colville Indian Reservation in northeastern Washington state. Chief Joseph died on the Colville Reservation in 1904.

The final blow to the solidarity of the Nez Perce, and that of most of the nation's indigenous people, was the Dawes Severalty Act of 1895. Reservation lands, under this act, became eligible for sale after they were divided into allotments. For the Nez Perce, allotment led to the loss of most of the land reserved for the tribe by the treaty of 1863. By 1975, the Nez Perce owned less than 80,000 acres. In the 1980s, however, as part of an economic, social, and cultural initiative to celebrate and revive the Nez Perce culture, the tribe began a land acquisition program that has since expanded the reservation by 20,000 acres.

With melancholic sensitivity, longtime University of Idaho English professor William Banks summed up the consequences of the interaction of native culture with European-American culture in a letter to a friend dated March 6, 1945. The centuries of digging camas roots and racing horses in the area the Nez Perce called Tatkinmah, he explains, came to an end after "the white men came and made a store and houses, and the Indians returned, and the white boys played with the Indian boys and traded ponies for guns and watches, and the camas meadows were plowed and fenced, and the trout died in the muddy stream. And the Indians came a last summer and came no more."

The first white men to enter the valley of the south fork of the Palouse River came via the same trails the Nez Perce and the area's other native peoples had traversed for centuries. As was common throughout the American West, the first white men to explore the Moscow area were fur trappers. They entered the valley as early as 1805. While the populations of such animals as beaver were not high enough to warrant large-scale trapping, fur trappers did travel through the valley, which would become known as Paradise Valley, for the next 25 years. The valley lay between two trading posts, the North West Company's Fort Nez Perce at the mouth of the Walla Walla River and Spokane House, near the present city of Spokane, Washington.

Beginning in the 1840s, Catholic and Protestant missionaries appeared, searching not for fur but for the souls of the Northwest's Indians. According to local historian Father Kenneth Arnzen, two of the region's most famous missionaries, Jesuit priest Father Joseph Cataldo and Presbyterian minister Henry Spalding, once met at a spring north of Moscow to discuss means of pacifying the Native Americans. Father Arnzen adds that Father Cataldo's journal mentions the two men sharing potatoes. Spalding established a mission near Lapwai, Idaho, and several Catholic missions were founded by Cataldo and other Jesuit missionaries north of Moscow; however, no missions were established in Paradise Valley.

According to the doctor at the time of his death in 1904, Chief Joseph, a Nez Perce leader in the 1870s, died from a broken heart for having been exiled from his home in Oregon's Wallowa Valley, part of the original territory of his people. (Courtesy LCHS.)

The 1850s saw the groundwork laid for the permanent settlement of the area surrounding present-day Moscow. In 1855, Isaac I. Stevens was the 37-year-old governor of the Territory of Washington, which had been created in 1853. Stevens was the territory's first governor, and as territorial governor, he was responsible for both Indian affairs and for identifying a northern transcontinental route for the Northern Pacific Railroad. His task in regard to the territory's native people was not only to negotiate for land cessions as far east as Nebraska and as far west as the Pacific Ocean, but also to remove the Indians from the land they ceded.

To that end, in May 1855, Stevens and Joel Palmer, commissioner of Indian affairs, conducted negotiations with the Northwest Indians at the mission

This lithograph illustrates the Pacific Railroad Reports written by Washington Territorial Governor Isaac Stevens, following his survey of the Palouse country in 1853 and 1854. (Courtesy LCHS.)

established by Marcus and Narcissa Whitman in 1836, near present-day Walla Walla. The Walla Walla Council, as the meeting came to be known, was attended by nearly 6,000 Native Americans, including Walla Wallas, Yakimas, Cayuses, Umatillas, Palouses and Nez Perces. When the meeting had ended, Stevens had fulfilled his gubernatorial obligation in regard to Indian affairs. In separate treaties, the tribes ceded much of their land and agreed to be moved to reservations. The Nez Perce reservation, while containing much of the Nez Perce's original territory in western Oregon and central Idaho, did not extend as far north as Paradise Valley.

In addition to his role as representative of the United States government to the Northwest Indians, Stevens also was responsible for conducting a survey to identify possible railroad routes to the Pacific. The Pacific railroad surveys, conducted between 1854 and 1861, were extremely important, not only as a reconnaissance for possible intercontinental transportation routes, but because they also were sources of accurate information about the western United States. This information was essential for the future exploitation of the resources of the Northwest.

After the victory of the Walla Walla Council, Stevens turned his attention to the identification of railroad routes. On June 16, 1855, Stevens, accompanied by a packmaster, fifteen teamsters, two Indian guides, and four assistants, rode out of the Walla Walla area to survey the watershed of the Palouse River as a possible railroad route over the Bitterroot Mountains. From Red Wolf's Camp near Lewiston and

Clarkston, at the confluence of the Snake and Clearwater Rivers, Stevens and his crew followed ancient Native American trails northward. After journeying five days, Stevens would "discover" Moscow. From a hill southeast of present-day Moscow now known as Paradise Ridge, where he had stopped to camp for the night, Stevens looked down into the valley where Moscow now rests and wrote, "We have been astonished today at the luxuriance of the grass and the richness of the soil. The whole view presents to the eye a vast bed of flowers in all their varied beauty." The beautiful flowers Stevens saw were the blue-flowered camas.

Five years after Stevens's reconnaissance, in 1860, Captain Elias Pierce, a soldier and lawyer, entered the Paradise Valley seeking gold. Finding none, he traveled south to what is now Clearwater County where he found what he was looking for. News of Pierce's gold strike spread and soon thousands of prospectors rushed into Idaho's creeks and streams, hoping to make their fortunes as gold diggers. One such prospector was Ben Hoteling from Walla Walla. In the fall of 1860, Hoteling and eight other men were on their way to the gold fields of Clearwater County when they were caught in an early snowstorm several miles north of Moscow, near the present-day town of Potlatch.

With their travel completely restricted by snow, the men decided to prospect right where they were and—Ureka!—they discovered gold. During the next two decades, prospectors would mine the precious metal from the land surrounding the tributaries of the Palouse River throughout the northeastern part of what is now Latah County. Three significant mining districts located within Latah County were the Blackfoot or Gold Hill, the Mica Mountain, and the Hoodoo mining districts. The gold taken from these districts was said to be of high quality; in fact, during one rush in 1880, miners working claims in the Hoodoo district extracted over $1 million worth of gold.

As would be expected, new towns sprung up around the sites where gold was discovered and these upstart settlements gave the residents of Moscow cause for concern. According to a report in a Lewiston newspaper in 1875, "A new town, called Paradise City, has been started in opposition to Moscow. The rivalry is said to be very acrimonious. One is the St. Louis and the other the Chicago of the Northwest." The rivalry was not long-lived, as Paradise City quickly became one of the many Latah County communities that vanished over the decades.

During its mining era, a variety of minerals and gems were extracted from Latah County's creeks and gulches. In addition to gold, opals, copper, mica, vermiculite, and asbestos were also discovered and removed from the land. While the deposits were nowhere near the magnitude of those in other parts of Idaho, mining did contribute to the development of Latah County and Moscow. News of strikes brought people into the area and they, in turn, paved the way for permanent settlers. But it wasn't just gold seekers who came to the area. Stories of treasure buried in Latah County, including caches of Chinese valuables and stashed gold nuggets, probably attracted more people to the area than did veins of ore.

Where there was a strike, a town like Paradise City would spring up, but such settlements as Eldorado Gulch and Mizpah Creek would eventually vanish from existence as deposits dwindled and another group of people discovered that the area was bountiful in something just as valuable as gold: land. Beginning in the early 1870s, the unclaimed expanses of the Paradise Valley would be discovered by land-hungry homesteaders, and as the area's first permanent settlers, they would transform the wilderness into the community we now call Moscow.

The most famous mining camp in Latah County was the Hoodoo Mining District's Grizzle Camp, located in what is now Laird Park. (Courtesy LCHS.)

2. Founding and Settlement

Gold fever had propelled prospectors toward the Hoodoo mining district in northern Latah County, and in the early 1870s, something just as intangible— dreams—led homesteaders to the valley of the south fork of the Palouse River. Most of the immigrants who eventually settled in Paradise Valley were backtracking, having ignored the interior of the Pacific Northwest on their migrations to the Oregon Country. Dissatisfied with what lay unclaimed in such places as Oregon's Willamette Valley, Moscow's early pioneers entered the Paradise Valley seeking acres of fertile soil, vast grasslands, and husky stands of timber.

Under the provisions of the Homestead Act of 1862, anyone who had $10 in his pocket and an enterprising nature could lay claim to 160 acres of public domain. After residing on or cultivating the claim for five years, homesteaders could then gain title to the land. Because the majority of homesteaders initially bypassed the Inland Northwest, homesteading on the Palouse, including Paradise Valley, did not begin until the 1870s.

The majority of homesteaders who came to the Palouse were native-born Americans from the Midwest and Northeast who had immigrated to the Oregon country following the Civil War. Unlike fur trappers and gold prospectors—single men unencumbered by wives and children—most of the homesteaders were family men. Many of Moscow's early pioneers migrated as a family unit, moving northeast from the Oregon country as a group, traveling in wagons. Most of the homesteaders, too, came to the Moscow area via Walla Walla in the Washington Territory. Located on the Oregon Trail, Walla Walla was the hub of the Inland Northwest; it was where travelers gathered their resources before heading off into unexplored territory, which included Paradise Valley in the early 1870s.

From Walla Walla, it is likely the homesteaders followed the Greater Nez Perce Trail from the Lewiston area to Paradise Valley, where the Nez Perce were still harvesting camas each spring. The first homesteaders arrived in Paradise Valley in 1871 when approximately two dozen families arrived in what would later become Moscow and Latah County to stake a claim to the dream that had uprooted them in the first place.

One of the homesteaders who arrived in Moscow in 1871 was William Taylor, the grandfather of Alma Lauder Keeling. According to Keeling, her grandfather, who had left his native Ireland as an adolescent, was over 50 years old when he left the "outskirts of Chicago" having "heard the call of the Far West":

> Grandfather came west with a caravan of wagons in the spring of 1871, seeking a location for his future home. Some of the caravan left them in northern California, but others, obviously not interested in what was then an arid-looking country, pressed on. They passed through what is now our southern Idaho, and here others of the caravan remained. But, William Taylor was still not satisfied. Although from his boyhood a builder and stonemason, he must also have had some "farmer blood" coursing through his veins, for a farmer he turned out to be! So, with a few other seeking souls he went on until he came via Walla Walla to what is now our Moscow.

Keeling recalled hearing her grandfather say:

> that when he looked on this fertile valley with its two-foot high bunch grass waving in the breeze, its beautiful purple mountains in the distance, and its two crystal streams flowing through the valley, he was intrigued by it all. But when he put down his shovel and turned up this rich, black loam, he said to his fellow-travellers, "This is the place for me!"

William Taylor, a native of Ireland, left Chicago when he was over 50 years old and arrived in Paradise Valley in 1871. (Courtesy LCHS.)

After William Taylor had built a log cabin to shelter himself and his family, he sent for his wife Priscilla and their seven children. (An eighth child was on the way!) Priscilla and the children took the train from Chicago as far west as Ogden, Utah, where William and his oldest daughter's husband met them. From there, the family journeyed to Moscow by wagon, via Walla Walla, which Keeling pointed out was "still over one hundred and thirty-five miles from what was to be their future home!" Keeling explained that William and Priscilla's oldest daughter Elizabeth "was then a recent bride of 21, so she and her young husband came along to look after Priscilla and her other six children. At Ogden the groom bought a large wagon and team of work horses, and the journey began."

While William Taylor's homestead claim lay adjacent to the southern city limits of present-day Moscow, other homesteading families settled to the north, west, and east. One such family was the Lieuallen family. Brothers Almon and Noah, along with approximately 20 other families, arrived in Latah County in 1871 and took out homestead claims on land roughly 3 miles to the east of present-day Moscow. If anyone can legitimately be called the founder of Moscow, it is Almon Asbury Lieuallen.

Almon Asbury Lieuallen was typical of the individuals who homesteaded the Palouse. He was a native American, born in Tennessee, who migrated west to the Oregon Country in 1867, and then moved eastward again until he stopped, apparently liking what he found in Paradise Valley. He, wife Sarah, and their children settled in Paradise Valley in the summer of 1871, bringing with them a herd of cattle, reportedly worth $40,000. Like other immigrants attracted to the Palouse by its vast vistas of bunchgrass, Lieuallen intended to raise cattle; however, his dreams of achieving prosperity by raising stock were soon dashed by a series of severe winters. In fact, Lieuallen lost his entire stock and a small financial fortune during the harsh winters of the mid-1870s. Not only were the winters colder than usual, so much snow fell that journeys to Walla Walla to purchase feed were impossible. Lieaullen's stock either froze to death or died of starvation.

When Almon and Sarah first arrived in Paradise Valley, they homesteaded in the area north of what is now the Elks Golf Course, about 3 miles northeast of Moscow. According to local historian Lillian W. Otness, Lieuallen's original homestead was the first land claimed in Paradise Valley. This area came to be known as Haskins Flat, having been named after another of Moscow's original homesteaders, Lorettus Haskins, Sarah's stepfather. Haskins was believed to have been a prospector before settling down to homesteading. Moscow's first school was erected on the Haskins homestead—a log cabin with a dirt floor built in 1871. The teacher was Almon's brother Noah, who had homesteaded near his brother.

In 1873, near Almon Lieuallen's homestead, another homesteader, Samuel Miles Neff, opened the first general merchandise store in Paradise Valley. It was located on the southeast corner of what is now Mountain View Road and Hillcrest Drive. At that time, the store was little more than a stage stop for the route from Lewiston to Spokane, Washington. In the log cabin that housed the store was the

The first apple tree planted in the Moscow area was on the 1871 homestead of Almon Asbury Lieuallen, shown here with his family. (Courtesy LCHS.)

area's first post office; it had been established on March 19, 1873. Reportedly, Neff's establishment had faced some stiff competition for the location of the post office. A saloon south of present-day Moscow was also considered until Neff convinced the settlers that a saloon was no place for respectable citizens to retrieve their mail.

The name of the post office was Paradise, and according to longtime Moscow resident Elsie Nelson in her memoir *Today is Ours*, it consisted of nothing more than "a shoe box on one shelf" of Neff's store. A carrier delivered the mail weekly, traveling by horseback and following the Greater Nez Perce Trail. Homesteaders generally called this trail the Spokane Falls Trail, leading as it did from Lewiston to Spokane Falls in the Washington Territory. According to local historian Homer David, the first postmaster was Vanison Craig, who served from 1873 to 1874. Samuel Edwards followed Craig, serving from 1874 to 1876, when Sarah Edwards (perhaps Samuel's wife) became Moscow's first postmistress. Sarah served from 1876 to 1877 and was postmistress when the community's new post office was opened in 1876.

In 1875, Almon Lieuallen had bought a homestead claim to land comprising what is now northeastern Moscow, a claim originally filed by Samuel Neff. On a section of that property, now the southwest corner of First and Main Streets, Lieuallen opened a general merchandise store, Moscow's first successful commercial enterprise. This building may have been the very same one that had housed Samuel Neff's store on the outskirts of Moscow. Perhaps believing he would attract more customers with "one-stop shopping," Lieuallen also sought control of the community's post office, and he had succeeded by November 1876. Not only was the post office operating out of his store (which was also the Lieuallen family home), Lieuallen had become postmaster, succeeding Sarah Edwards. Also, by the time Lieuallen became postmaster, the name of the post office had been changed from Paradise to Moscow.

There are nearly as many theories about how Moscow got its name as there are communities in the United States named Paradise. The Nez Perce, the area's earliest inhabitants, believe Moscow's real name is "Tatkinmah" or "Taxt-hinma." For the Nez Perce, Moscow was a special place for its abundant fields of camas and according to Tribal Elder Allen Slickpoo in a local history paper in the archives of the Latah County Historical Society:

> [It] was also a favorite place because of the mule deer who summered there, and the taxt, the mule deer fawns. The people would look up from digging and—poof!—a little taxt would leap out of the bushes. A few more roots in the basket, another look up to rest the back and—poof!—another little taxt would pop up. Every summer it went like that, and soon the Nimipu [Nez Perce] knew the name for this place—Taxt-hinma—the place of the mule deer fawns.

But with the coming of homesteaders, the mule deer fawns would be displaced by another four-legged animal: the hog. To survive the cold and snowy winters of Paradise Valley, cattle required feed, which had to be transported from Walla Walla. Hogs, on the other hand, instinctively discovered the bulbs of the abundant camas and "came through the winter in fine fettle," said Alma Lauder Keeling in *The Un-Covered Wagon*. Thus, with tongue in cheek, Moscow's first residents called their fledgling community "Hog Heaven." Keeling reports that when it came time to establish the first post office, the men "rather facetiously" suggested retaining the name of Hog Heaven, but the "ladies, upon hearing this, rose up in arms." Keeling goes on to explain that a traveler passing through the area remarked on its similarity to a Paradise Valley he knew in his home state, and thus was the name of Paradise Valley adopted for the community.

When Almon Lieuallen moved the post office to his store on what is now Moscow's Main Street, the community's name had been officially changed. As Lalia Boone explains in her book *Idaho Place Names*, the U.S. Postal Service had requested that the citizens of Paradise Valley change the name of its post office to avoid confusion with other communities named "Paradise" in the Idaho Territory. But why "Moscow" was selected as the community's new name is a subject of debate. Clara Ransom Davis, one of the founders of the Latah County Pioneer Association, which with the Moscow Historical Club would evolve into the Latah County Historical Society, recorded in a reminiscence that George Northrup, "who came to Moscow with the first white family in 1871," claimed that "a man named 'Neymer' " suggested the name of Moscow. According to Northrup, "A shaggy group of German-Russians from Moscow had spent a few months during a previous summer in the settlement while scouting around for a proper location." While it is true that Russian Germans were one of the largest European immigrant groups in neighboring Whitman County, Washington by the end of the nineteenth century, there was never a large German-Russian community in Latah County. Moreover, the German Russians did not arrive in the Palouse until after the construction of the Northern Pacific Railroad in 1882. Interestingly, though, the man named Neymer could be a reference to Bart Neumayer, a surveyor who reportedly bought his homestead from a Russian settler.

Even though it is unlikely that Moscow got its name from its Russian citizens, several theories have been put forth claiming that the Russian city of Moscow was the direct inspiration for the naming of Moscow, Idaho. Almon Lieuallen's daughter Lillie stated in an interview that her father and Samuel Neff selected the name "Moscow" because, at that time, Moscow, Russia seemed a "far-away glamorous sort of city." Mickey Aitken in his article "How Moscow Got that Name," in the *Inland Empire Magazine*'s September 30, 1951 edition, wrote that Moscow, Idaho, was indeed named for Moscow, Russia, by none other than Samuel Neff. According to Aitken, the founding of Moscow, Idaho, reminded Neff of the founding of a community in Russia during the time of Peter the Great. In his book *Idaho for the Curious*, Cort Conley presents yet another connection to the history of Russia; he writes that Moscow's name stems from Almon Lieuallen's belief that the problems of isolation confronting the community were

Annually, the Nez Perce came to the area north of the present Elks golf course, now known as Haskins Flat, to harvest camas bulbs. (Courtesy LCHS.)

All that remains to document Moscow's first post office near the intersection of Mountain View and Hillcrest Streets is a small row of Lombardy poplars. (Courtesy LCHS.)

comparable to those in Russia during the reign of Ivan the Terrible. In a letter he wrote to Clara Ransom Davis, Samuel Neff's son Miles explained that his father "named the place Moscow on account of the root meaning of the word, which in Russian is 'Holy City,' a good name for the city of Paradise Valley."

All of these theories probably contain a kernel of truth, and the most plausible theory—the one most fully researched and documented—does give Samuel Neff credit for naming Moscow. Place names historian Lalia Boone asserts that Moscow, Idaho, was named by Samuel Neff in cooperation with the men who were responsible for establishing the municipal center of Moscow. Neff, although never an official postmaster, "managed the mail," according to Boone. He, Lieuallen, and three homesteaders with substantial land claims in the valley—James Deakin, John Russell, and Henry McGregor—met to select a name. Boone explains that while the men wanted a prestigious name for the community, they could not agree on a choice. Therefore, they selected Neff to complete the post office application papers, and it was Neff who chose the name. According to Boone, Neff selected the name Moscow because "its favorable meaning 'city of brotherly love', met the desired requirements." Perhaps a more significant factor in Neff's decision was the fact that he had been born near Moscow, Pennsylvania, and had later lived in Moscow, Iowa.

Henry Erichson took this photograph at the unveiling of the William Headington monument in the Moscow Cemetery, c. 1889. (Courtesy LCHS.)

With Neff's help, within a span of just five years, a tribe of homesteaders had transformed Paradise Valley into a growing community named Moscow. Lola Clyde, a longtime Latah County resident and local historian, told Alma Lauder Keeling that the grandmother of her husband Earl Clyde had arrived in Paradise Valley in 1877 as a member of a large immigrant group. As recorded by Keeling in *The Un-Covered Wagon*, Clyde recalled, "One of the large wagon trains into Moscow was the one of 1877. It originated in Kansas, leaving there in May and arriving here in early September." She also recalled:

> how Earl's grandmother had often spoken of her arrival here in an immigrant train, and how thrilled these new pioneers were when they arrived at the William Taylor home after a long and weary trip, and saw Grandmother Taylor and the other women relatives standing on the long veranda of the Taylor home, waiting there to greet them as their wagon train rolled in.

While the period between 1877 and 1880 was a time of optimism as immigrants swept into Paradise Valley buoyed by dreams of golden opportunities, it was also a time of sorrow for many families. As Alma Lauder Keeling writes, "Black diphtheria had been sweeping the country from 1877 to 1880, and one chronicler says that fifty percent of Moscow's children died in this epidemic! The L. [Lorettus] Haskins family buried three small children in less than three weeks! Almost every family here lost one or more." Keeling's mother Minnie lost her brother to the disease and was herself a survivor of it.

Many of the victims of the diphtheria epidemic were laid to rest in the Moscow Cemetery, which was established as early as 1871. At the request of her mother who was in ill health, Mrs. George Tomer, as well as Mrs. Julia Summerfield and Belle Haskins, "prepared a lunch, and saddled up their horses," and began searching for a suitable site for a cemetery. They considered two other locations, but selected the present site of the cemetery, a gentle hill on the eastern edge of Moscow, near the original homesteads of the Lieuallen brothers. After making their selection, the three women dedicated it with a prayer, and later the men of the young community built a crude rail fence to form the boundaries of the cemetery.

Despite the hardships of pioneer life, and perhaps because of them, the early residents of Moscow dedicated themselves to building their community, and it was built in much the same way permanent settlers had built other cities on the American frontier. Sometimes in advance of settlement and sometimes afterwards, the American frontier was surveyed according to a platting scheme that divided the land into squares or townships. Each township was 6 miles square and was divided into 36 sections, each section containing 640 acres. As early as July 8, 1871, U.S. Deputy Surveyor Henry Meldrum had run the boundaries of the township that now contains Moscow.

Agricultural homesteaders claimed land in quarter sections, or plats of 160 acres. The claims of four of Moscow's early pioneers—Almon Lieuallen, James Deakin, Henry McGregor, and John Russell—met at the current intersection of Sixth and Main Streets. At this point in the mid- to late 1870s, probably 1876, the four men each agreed to donate 30 acres of their land as the basis for a commercial district, a city center. Their donations were significant; through their sacrifice, they made a commitment to the future of their fledgling community by providing the foundation from which it could grow into a commercial center. It was their intention that Moscow would become the Walla Walla of the Paradise Valley, the place where residents went to buy supplies, goods, and services.

For the area's earliest pioneers, Walla Walla was the only place to purchase supplies, and the trip from Moscow to Walla Walla was nearly 150 miles long and treacherous. Alma Lauder Keeling writes of her grandfather William Taylor taking:

> those long, hard trips to Walla Walla by team and wagon, often over almost impassable, muddy roads, to lay in necessities for his large family—flour, salt, sugar, the many things we find it hard to live without. Also the needed equipment for his growing farming operations. Mother once told me that often for weeks at a time they lived on practically nothing but boiled wheat and milk while he was away.

The need for a local source of supplies was acute, and to that end, Almon Lieuallen opened a general merchandise store in 1875; according to Keeling, Lieuallen's "stock consisted of two wagon loads of general merchandise from Walla Walla." Interestingly, another of Moscow's earliest commercial enterprises was the dental practice of James McCallie, who opened his doors in 1877. Moscow's first physician, Dr. Henry B. Blake, a graduate of Oxford University in England, also began his practice in 1877. Dr. Blake married into the Lorettus Haskins family and would go on to become one of Moscow's most respected citizens.

Also in 1877, Robert H. Barton, Samuel J. Langdon, and Hiram Epperly began operating the area's first permanent sawmill. Robert Barton had moved to Moscow in 1877, bringing with him the machinery for a sawmill on wagons pulled by oxen. Barton's sawmill was located 6 miles east of Moscow, at the south foot of Moscow Mountain where the area's first sawmill had been constructed in 1876 by an informal group of Paradise Valley residents. After six months, the owners of that mill had relocated to Colfax, Washington. According to Kenneth B. Platt in *Some Pioneer Glimpses of Latah County*, Barton's mill provided the lumber for most of the buildings in early Moscow. Among this construction was Moscow's first hotel, built and operated by Barton until it was destroyed by fire in 1890.

In addition to sawmills, another business essential to pioneer Palouse residents was harness making. In the days before railroads and the combustion engine, goods (and people) got from one place to the next on wagons. Because oxen, mules, and horses powered wagons and farm equipment, harnesses were needed to strap the animals to the gear. It is believed that Gottfried Weber, a native of Germany, was the first harness maker in the Palouse; he is also credited with being its finest. Weber, who also made saddles, established his business in 1879 on Moscow's Main Street.

Just as essential to animal-powered transportation as the harness maker was the blacksmith. Fred Zumhof established a blacksmithing business in Moscow

The dental office of Dr. James McCallie was located at 106 North Main Street. Living quarters for his family were on the building's upper floor. (Courtesy LCHS.)

A stagecoach ran between the Hotel Moscow and the railroad depot; both were located on Main Street. When the coach wasn't wheel-deep in mud, it was engulfed in a storm of dust. (Courtesy LCHS.)

sometime before 1885, serving individuals and the community's numerous livery stables. One of the earliest stables was the Lone Star, owned by the Stewart brothers, who also operated horse-drawn stage lines between Palouse, Washington, and the community of Juliaetta in southern Latah County. Southwest of the Stewart's Main Street stable was another early stable; its last owner was Kerallah Jabbora, a Syrian immigrant.

According to the January 1, 1892 edition of the *Moscow Mirror*, an early Moscow newspaper, after Lieuallen's store, "the next business started in Moscow was a trading post by H.H. Maguire and Charles Curtis." The use of the term trading post implies a diversity of goods, but in actuality Maguire and Curtis sold only eyeglasses, and on a commission basis to boot. Furthermore, Maguire's first name did not start with an "H." His first name was James.

The partnership of Curtis and Maguire did not last long in Moscow. In the spring of 1879, Maguire went into partnership with William J. McConnell, who would go on to become one of Moscow's most influential early residents. Maguire and McConnell, who later became the third governor of Idaho and its first United States senator, respectively, formed the McConnell-Maguire Company and opened a general merchandise store on the southeast corner of Main and First Streets. According to W.G. Emery in his 1897 history of Moscow:

> The people of the surrounding country were greatly encouraged at the sight of the then mammoth store, and from that time on the town

This is an interior view of the harness shop of Gottfried Weber taken around 1883. The two men in the photo are Henry Ryrie and Weber, who is believed to be on the right. (Courtesy LCHS.)

commenced to grow. When this store was completed Moscow had the immense population of 25. The news of the great store at Moscow spread everywhere, and people from all parts of the Potlatch and Palouse countries flocked to Moscow to do their trading, and it is no exaggeration to say that to no men living in Moscow is the town so much indebted for its present size and flourishing condition than to ex-Senator McConnell and J.H. Maguire.

Like Almon Lieuallen, William J. McConnell was a native-born American who left home to seek his fortune in the West. McConnell was born in 1829 in Michigan, left there at the age of 21, and eventually settled in the gold fields of California. After a decade there, McConnell uprooted himself again to investigate the gold strike in southwestern Idaho. But he got no further than Portland, Oregon before he heard that the Idaho fields were disappointing. McConnell then decided to accept a position teaching school in Yamhill, Oregon. There he stayed until 1863 when he could no longer resist the lure of the Idaho gold mines.

After two years in Idaho's Payette Valley, McConnell left Idaho and returned to Yamhill where he became a well-respected member of the community, operating a general merchandise store and serving as state senator until 1878, the year he left Oregon for Moscow. According to Ed Burke in *The Rest of the Story: A Brief Sketch of McConnell's Background*, McConnell had predicted that Moscow and the Palouse would become "a great agricultural area and he wanted to be a part of its development." Between 1878 and 1886, McConnell divided his time between Yamhill and Moscow, and on Christmas Eve, 1886, McConnell moved his family of wife Louisa and their four children, William, Benjamin, Mary, and Olive, into their impressive new home on the corner of Adams and Second Streets. Since 1968, McConnell's home has served Latah County as its museum.

Another of Moscow's early builders was Michael J. Shields who, like McConnell, came to Moscow in 1878 and was a merchant. Shields also contributed significantly to the development of Moscow. More importantly, though, Shields was a contractor who literally built many of Moscow's buildings and established the basic utilities, such as electricity. In March 1879, Shields established the M.J. Shields Company on Main Street and, during the

William J. McConnell came to Moscow in 1878 and later served as the governor of Idaho from 1893 to 1897. (Courtesy LCHS.)

next decade, built a "flourishing business in hardware, stoves, carriages, and wagon stock," according to local historian Lillian Otness in her book, *A Great Good Country*.

Shields was born in Lockport, New York in 1852 of Irish immigrant parents, and in 1878, with money earned by towing rafts of lumber between Tonawanda and Troy, New York, he migrated westward to the Oregon Country. After a brief stay in Dayton, Washington, near Walla Walla, Shields moved to Moscow where he opened an implement store with its initial inventory of six plows and two wagons; his business would grow to become one of the largest in the Palouse. Shields's original business was housed in a two-story wooden building. The second floor was used as a meeting hall and, until 1887 when Moscow's first Catholic church was built, was where the community's Catholics gathered to receive Mass.

By 1880, with impetus from enterprising individuals like Shields and McConnell, Moscow was shaping up as a retail center. Its population stood at a grand total of 300. By 1881, Moscow had three general merchandise stores, two

At the height of his career, Michael J. Shields was worth over $300,000. He died at the age of 57 in 1909. His funeral mass was said by the pastor of Moscow's Holy Trinity parish, Father Remi Pecoul. (Courtesy LCHS.)

Members of the Moscow unit of the Grand Army of the Republic pause in front of the Moscow Brewery during a parade, c. 1890. (Courtesy LCHS.)

hotels, one hardware store, and a variety of butcher shops, saloons, blacksmith shops, farm implement stores, and even a few professional offices of doctors, dentists, and lawyers. According to an 1881 account in the *Nez Perce News*, Moscow was "a lively thriving, enterprising, progressive place, and will take a boom this summer. The people are never tired of talking of the Palouse Country and they are right, for if there is a better country in the world, we have never seen it."

The period of Moscow's history between 1880 and 1885 can be described as an era of firsts. On north Main Street, Charles and Miles Moore established the first flourmill, the Peerless Flour Mill, in 1881. In an apparent attempt to cover all their bases, the residents of Moscow built their first church, the Zion Baptist Church, in 1881 as well as their first brewery, the Moscow Brewery, in 1882. As a member of its congregation, Almon Lieuallen had donated land for the Zion Baptist Church and it was ecumenical in nature. The members of several other denominations worshipped within its walls until they were able to build churches of their own. Moscow Brewery, like Peerless Flour Mill, was located on Main Street; Otto Fries and Joseph Niederstadt were partners in the business until 1886 when the partnership was dissolved.

The *Moscow Mirror*, the first newspaper, began in 1883, and Henry Erichson opened the first photography studio in 1884. That same year, John Russell donated yet more land to Moscow—more precisely to the school district—with

Frank L. White opened the first drugstore in Moscow and later served as office manager for the McConnell-Maguire store. This photo of Main Street was taken c. 1885. (Courtesy LCHS.)

the condition that the district spend $1,000 to construct a school building. The school district built a wooden structure on a block of land northeast of Main Street and named the school in honor of Russell. It was the first building in Moscow dedicated for use as a public school. Sadly, later in his life following some financial difficulties, John Russell was reduced to working as a janitor in the very same school that bore his name.

To replace the log cabin housing his store, Almon Lieuallen built a frame structure and to replace that, in 1885, he built Moscow's first brick building. This building also housed the Baker-Clark Bank, one of Moscow's first banks. Dr. Dorsey Syng Baker, who had made his fortune building the "rawhide railroad" from the west coast to Walla Walla, started the Baker-Clark Bank. That same year, Frank L. White opened Moscow's first drugstore, the Post Office Drug Store.

By 1885, Moscow was well on its way to becoming a commercial force to be reckoned with on the Palouse, and people new to the area liked what they saw. One such newcomer was Charles J. Munson. Arriving in Moscow in 1884, after a five-year journey westward from his native Indiana, Munson would go on to become one of Moscow's—and Idaho's—most respected citizens. In his autobiography *Westward to Paradise*, Munson describes his first sighting of the Paradise Valley in 1884:

Dotted over the beautiful hills and valleys were log houses and cabins, and here and there a frame house. The fields were not large, for two thirds of the area still was in bunch grass. Half of the acreage was in flax, and it was in full bloom. About four miles northwest were a few houses and sheds huddled together, and that was the village of Moscow, Nez Perce County, Idaho Territory. I knew I had come to the place where I could "grow up with the country." Here I would stay: here I would have a home, if ever so humble. Here I would raise my family of boys and girls, and here I would be buried when I died.

Charles J. Munson, shown here with his family, purchased the farm originally owned by Almon Lieuallen. Munson christened his home Cozy Cove Farm. (Courtesy LCHS.)

3. Agriculture and Transportation

Charles Munson kept his pledge to make Moscow his home; in fact, such was his devotion to his adopted community and state that he served as a state legislator from Latah County from 1898 to 1909. Munson also served Idaho as its lands commissioner from 1906 to 1909. His home in Moscow was the homestead originally owned by Almon Asbury Lieuallen, which Munson named Cozy Cove Farm. Munson's was the first farm to be officially recorded in Latah County.

Perhaps Lieuallen relinquished control of his original homestead because he had no interest in farming. After all, like other early pioneers on the Palouse, he had come to the region not to farm, but to raise cattle, intending to graze them on the plentiful and nutritious native bunchgrass. For nearly a decade, raising cattle proved to be a lucrative way to earn a living on the Palouse. There was a market for cattle (the mining camps of Idaho and Montana), but the business of raising cattle on the Palouse was not long-lived for several reasons. By the late 1870s, overgrazing and overproduction (despite a series of hard winters) had seriously weakened the industry, and the loss of open range due to the encroachment of sheep ranching and homesteading simply made cattle raising unprofitable.

For the most part, the earliest settlers in Paradise Valley were not ranchers but homesteaders who wanted nothing more than to "live off the land." They were subsistence farmers who fenced their land and raised enough vegetables, fruit, and livestock to sustain themselves and their families. In addition to their hogs, which grew fat on camas bulbs, Paradise Valley homesteaders also grew beef and dairy cattle, chickens, fruit trees, and large vegetable gardens. Settlers also harvested the bounty of the natural world, gathering wild currants, huckleberries, gooseberries, and serviceberries; fishing for trout; and hunting doves, grouse, and waterfowl.

Self-sufficiency was not a choice but a requirement to which everyone in the family contributed. Alma Lauder Keeling recalled watching her grandmother Priscilla, the "official milker of the Taylor household," milk the Taylor family cow:

> I can still almost smell the warm milk from the foaming pails as I trotted
> along beside her to the house, and then watched her strain those pails of

milk into the big, flat, tin pans that found their way to the shelves in the underground dirt cellar. What luscious yellow cream rose to the top of every pan! I also remember doing my small bit at running the wooden dasher up and down in the big stone churn which turned out such beautiful golden butter.

The earliest homesteaders also cultivated crops—oats, barley, wheat, and flax—using primitive techniques and equipment. The process of preparing ground for cultivation was lengthy and backbreaking. Initially, the sod was broken with a "breaking" plow, generally pulled by several horses and guided by a farmer holding the handles. After the plot had been left to winter over, it was plowed again with a walking plow, sometimes referred to as a foot burner. Crops were then sown by hand. In his autobiography, Carl Olson recalled his mother sowing wheat by hand on his family's Latah County farm. "I used to watch her," he wrote. "She would hold the bag of wheat in one hand and throw out a handful with the other. Then she would change hands and throw the seed to the other side."

Although subsistence farming was never completely deposed, by the late 1870s the fertility of the Palouse hills had become obvious to its farmers. The region's earliest pioneers had settled in "bottomlands" near water sources, such as streams or springs, because that is what farmers had done in the East; however, what worked best in the East turned out not to work best in the West, especially on the Palouse. In this area, it was the steep hills that contained the most fertile soil and it did not take Palouse farmers long to discover this fact. As early as 1877,

Palouse wheat was originally cut by hand and the process of farming was extremely difficult. This photo was taken c. 1880. (Courtesy LCHS.)

Whitman County, Washington farmer A.J. Calhoun Sr. had discovered the richness of the hills following an experiment in which he had sewn crops on both the flatlands and hills of his farm. He had reasoned that if crops couldn't grow well on the hilltops, there wasn't much of anywhere else they could grow.

By 1879, what had once been experimental was routine. The *Palouse Gazette* reported the following:

> Our own observations have been confirmed by the experience of farmers that the hill lands prove to be best for all kinds of grain. While being about the country for the last ten days, it was noticed that grain is looking unusually well for this time of year, many hills so high that it would seem impossible to cultivate, being covered with a fine stand of wheat.

It is not surprising that the reporter writing for the *Palouse Gazette* would find wheat in his survey of the Palouse country. Farmers had rapidly discovered that wheat grew especially well on the tops of the Palouse hills. A type of wheat known as "soft white wheat" is particularly well suited to the Palouse; it produces a soft, white kernel low in protein and high in starch that makes excellent flour.

In this age of mechanization and automation, it is difficult to comprehend agricultural production before the invention of machines, much less before the use of oxen, horses, and mules to power those machines. On the Palouse, as in agricultural areas throughout the world, wheat was originally harvested and threshed by hand. Settlers used the traditional hand implements, the cradle and the flail. A cradle was used to harvest wheat; it consisted of a scythe with long wooden tines attached above and parallel to the blade. A flail was used to beat the harvested grain to separate the kernels from the heads. It was a wooden pole with a shorter stick at one end that swung freely. Grain was placed on the floor or ground and then flailed.

Another threshing technique involved men or horses, or little girls, stepping on the crop to break down its hard protective covering. Elizabeth Deobald grew up on a farm in Latah County south of Moscow, and she recalled riding a horse in a circle over dry beans so that its hooves would break down the pods. She and her siblings would then separate the beans from the pods and pieces of dirt.

In 1831, American agriculture was transformed with the appearance of the McCormick horse-drawn reaper. The reaper cut ten times as much grain as had traditional methods, and in 1844, the Case thresher was yet another major technological advancement. When a farmer had use of a thresher, a typical harvest began with the farmer cutting his own grain and gathering it in small bundles. A threshing crew would then drive wagons around the field to retrieve the bundles and transport them to the thresher, which replaced the age-old technique of trampling the grain to remove the kernels from the stalks. On the thresher, the grain was swept through a pipe where it fell into sacks to be stored.

Among the most skilled workers in threshing crews were the sewers who sewed the sacks of grain shut with as few as 11 or 12 stitches. Working in pairs, the sewers

The men who sewed shut sacks of grain weighing an average of 140 pounds were some of the highest paid harvest workers. (Courtesy LCHS.)

could sew as many as 900 sacks individually each day. Sack sewers had to be both skilled and physically strong because they were expected to carry the full sacks of grain, which generally weighed an average of 140 pounds, to a central transport location. Sack sewers were rewarded for their expertise, receiving between $5 and $7 per day in comparison to cooks who received $2 per day.

Despite the disparity in wages, cooks were certainly important to the hard-working crews. Cooks served breakfast before dawn, generally around 3 a.m., lunch at 9 a.m., dinner at noon, second lunch at 4 p.m., and supper at 8 p.m. Perhaps the wage difference was based on gender. Many of the cooks were women. Oral histories from the collection of the Latah County Historical Society reveal that much was demanded of threshing and harvesting cooks. The days were long and hot and the conditions primitive. The cook's workplace was a small wooden building set on wheels and pulled by a team of horses. The cook started work before sunrise and quit after sunset, and in between she cooked, baked, set and cleared tables, washed dishes and pans, and secured the contents of the cookhouse for when it was moved to the next farm.

Palma Hanson Hove was 17 years old when she and her older sister worked for her uncle's threshing crew. She recalls, "We always had meals ready on time, believe you me. We baked bread twice a day, eight loaves of bread, twice a day . . . and we baked pies. For every dinner we had pie or pudding. And we had cookies. We baked cookies, probably . . . every day if not twice a day. We usually averaged

Young women often worked as cooks during harvest season. The woman on the left is Hilda Olson and on the right is Anna Frantzich. (Courtesy LCHS.)

about maybe four-and-a-half hours of sleep, sometimes five." The sisters slept on the floor of the cookhouse, in between the benches.

Hove also recalled the roustabout, the man who "bought all the meat and vegetables and everything. So often the farmers where we were stationed would give us vegetables, fresh vegetables. But we really bought most of it in tin cans, though, because it was quicker to prepare." When it was time to move the cookhouse, everything had to be tied down. "You had cupboards for the dishes and you just had to wire the cupboard door shut so they wouldn't fall out."

In her oral history, Hove explained that harvest began on the rim of the field, which was called the rimrock. The crew began there because that's where the crops reached maturity first. Harvest would go on "for weeks and weeks. And then, of course, if there was a rain, why then they'd have to stop and that was always a terrible thing." Despite the grueling nature of the work, Hove said those were "good days. We were young and happy and strong. We could take it."

The use of hand implements to harvest wheat might have been acceptable for subsistence farming, but Palouse farmers needed equipment that would make large-scale, single-crop farming possible. That is one reason they quickly adopted new horse-drawn reapers and threshers. From the period beginning in the late 1870s until the appearance of gasoline-powered engines after World War I,

Palouse farmers literally relied on horsepower (and mule power) to conduct the business of farming. Even as late as the early 1930s, 6-horse teams, 20-horse teams, even 36-horse teams, perched on steep hillsides, powered the wide variety of equipment farmers used to sow and harvest their crops.

Thomas B. Keith, in his book *The Horse Interlude: A Pictorial History of Horse and Man in the Inland Northwest*, recalls his experience as a young man in 1929 traveling on the train near Walla Walla:

> My fellow passengers in the observation car became fascinated with a spectacle that came into view on a steep hillside overlooking the track. A combine pulled by 33 horses had almost reached the top of the hill. As we looked up, the driver began making a 90-degree turn. With a big team, this was a complicated maneuver even on level land. Passengers near me were excited—and the excitement must have been felt elsewhere on the train. The engineer brought the train to a sudden halt and an enthralled audience of travelers watched intently as the driver skillfully executed the turn with the big team.

Had he been traveling through the Palouse that year, it would have been very likely that Keith would have seen a similar sight on Moscow's hills because Palouse farmers, like those throughout the Northwest, became very proficient in handling multiple-hitch teams. Their skill in handling large teams of horses or

Palouse farmers were well known for their skill in handling large teams of horses and mules. (Courtesy LCHS.)

mules, or sometimes oxen, made the best use possible of mechanized harvesting, which in turn made large-scale wheat farming possible.

With the combine, Palouse farmers had found a way to reduce the cost of harvesting wheat dramatically, but innovation did not end there. Traditional farming methods and equipment had been developed for cultivating and harvesting on lowlands, not the abrupt Palouse hills. In 1904, two Moscow blacksmiths, Cornelius Quesnell and Andrew Anderson, had designed a push combine that was specifically suited to the sort of hillsides with which Moscow area farmers were well acquainted. Quesnell and Anderson joined with a local implement dealer, Gainford "Gub" Mix, to secure financing for the development of their combine.

With backing from mining magnate Jerome J. Day, who happened to be Mix's brother-in-law, the Idaho National Harvester Company was formed. Between 1905 and 1917, in its plant on north Main Street, the company produced a combine known as the "Little Idaho" because it was lighter in weight and less expensive than other combines. The 1905 model was sold for $700, whereas larger combines sold for as much as $2,000. The difference in weight between the Little Idaho and other harvesters was phenomenal. For example, the 1908 model, at 2,240 pounds, weighed one-tenth of the next lightest combine, which weighed 22,000 pounds.

Another decided advantage to the Idaho Harvester was that it was pushed rather than pulled. Because the horses or mules providing the power were stationed at the rear of the machine, they did not tread on the uncut grain. Lighter, less expensive, and with its design as a push combine, response to the Idaho Harvester was enthusiastic. By 1912, the company was overwhelmed with requests,

This is a photograph of the 1908 model of the Idaho National Harvester. This combine, known as the "Little Idaho," was manufactured in Moscow from 1906 to 1918. (Courtesy LCHS.)

receiving as many as 20 each day from throughout the United States and abroad, including Russia; however, the company was capable of producing only two machines per day. Farmers who were fortunate enough to purchase the combine were impressed with its results for one reason: they were able to cut more acres of wheat than with other combines. For example, with one Idaho Harvester, W.H. and F.E. Carpenter of Florence, Arizona cut 600 acres in a period of 32 days. William Weimerskirch, also of Arizona, cut 723 acres with another Little Idaho.

The first Idaho Harvesters had been built in a blacksmith's shop on the northwest corner of Main and A Streets. Beginning in 1907, however, production was shifted to the Rhodes Iron Works on south Main Street. It continued there until 1909. Willis M. Rhodes had established the Rhodes Iron Works in 1898, and in 1912, he designed and developed his own harvester. Like the Little Idaho, it was lightweight and was purposefully designed for use on Palouse hills.

To keep up with requests for the Little Idaho, the Idaho National Harvester Company built a new plant in 1909. Located at the north end of Main Street, the plant consisted of three buildings of reinforced concrete and glass, which housed a foundry, a machine shop, and an assembly building with attached paint shop. Despite its popularity and success, the Idaho Harvester, powered as it was by mules and horses, became a historical artifact after World War I and the advent of gasoline-powered engines.

In the years before the invention of the Idaho Harvester, during the late 1880s and through the first decade of the 1900s, many Palouse farmers augmented the production of grain with the production of fruit. After the arrival of the railroad in the mid- to late 1880s, farmers suddenly had an accessible and affordable means of getting their crops to market and orchard centers developed throughout the region. The September 12, 1912 edition of the *Palouse Republic* reported on the profitability of fruit-growing on the Palouse:

> Fruit raising has been demonstrated a success and there are now right in the heart of the Palouse country commercial orchards that are paying big money. The varieties of fruit that have proven best adapted to the conditions of that country are apples, pears, peaches, cherries, prunes, and plums.

In his autobiography, Moscow pioneer Charles J. Munson writes of the "thousands of acres" planted in fruit trees. In Latah County alone there were 22,739 apple trees in 1890. "Apples, pears, prunes, and cherries," Munson wrote, "had a ready sale and were shipped in carload quantities, taking premiums at all fairs and apple shows." In her memoir *The Un-Covered Wagon*, Alma Lauder Keeling writes, "I was interested in reading in *History of North Idaho* that it was William Taylor and two other men who first got the idea that fruit trees should grow in this wonderfully fertile soil, and planted experimental orchards."

In the early 1900s, Moscow businessman Fred Veatch, who had formed a real estate firm with A.T. Spotswood in the late 1880s, started a successful orchard of

The Palouse was once dotted with fruit orchards. This display of Moscow apples was presented at an agricultural fair in Spokane, Washington in 1912. (Courtesy LCHS.)

cherries and apples 2 miles south of Moscow. Perhaps not surprising for an apple grower, Veatch also operated a cider and vinegar plant on Moscow's Main Street until 1930. Another Moscow businessman, Wylie Lauder, more commonly known for the brickyards he operated with partners Fred Clough and Thomas Taylor, also capitalized upon the area's fruit growing industry when he started the Moscow Fruit and Produce Company.

By 1910, however, fruit production was taking a backseat to grain production. Not only had large-scale fruit production developed in Central Washington, but Palouse farmers were increasingly reluctant to devote field space to anything but grain production. While wheat has been the predominate crop in the region, other crops have been and are successfully grown on the Palouse. In addition to flax, oats, barley, mustard, and rapeseed, two crops in particular—lentils and dry peas—are favorites among Palouse farmers. In fact, the industry's advocacy organization, the U.S.A. Dry Pea and Lentil Council, calls the Palouse the pea and lentil capital of the United States. Interestingly, while the council's mailing address is Moscow, the desk of the council's administrator straddles the state line between Idaho and Washington.

The climate and terrain of the Palouse produce large quantities of peas and lentils that are considered the best in the world. The identity of the farmer who grew the first crop of lentils on the Palouse is debated, but most agricultural historians credit J.J. Wagner of Farmington, Washington with the initial planting. Wagner may have been a follower of the Seventh-Day Adventist Church, and as such, may have been seeking a vegetarian source of protein. It is said a minister of the church suggested the cultivation of lentils as a substitute for meat, and in 1920, Wagner harvested a few test rows of the legume.

The early years of lentil production would give no indication that lentils would become a major Palouse crop. Markets were small; cultivation was complicated by the presence of weed and grain seeds that required pulling by hand (usually performed by teenage boys and girls); and harvesting was difficult because threshing machines were set up to handle wheat, not lentils. Yet, by the 1940s, these problems had been addressed with the development of specialized equipment and the identification of international markets. By the 1950s, Palouse farmers were producing between 1 million and 2 million pounds of lentils each year, and production in the nation's pea and lentil capital currently exceeds 135 million pounds each year.

Today, the impressive amount of wheat, peas, and lentils produced each year gives little indication of the major problem early Palouse farmers faced: getting their crops to market. Before 1885, when the first railroad line was extended into Moscow, transportation and communication throughout the entire Inland Northwest was difficult and expensive, and the Palouse was no exception. As early as 1875, stagecoaches ran between Paradise Valley and Lewiston, but the road was primitive. According to historian Janet LeCompte, a farmer driving a team pulling a wagon loaded to the brim with sacks of grain would find himself bounding over rocks, lurching through ruts, and swinging around curves on a road that qualified more as a trail. To top things off, this journey would be done with a descent of nearly 2,000 feet from the plateaus of Moscow to the sea-level valleys of the Snake and Clearwater Rivers in Lewiston.

For most Moscow area farmers, Walla Walla was the primary market. The Inland Northwest's primary trade center, Walla Walla also was a grain-growing area of long standing. In 1861, for example, between 4,000 and 5,000 acres of wheat and oats were harvested within a 15-mile radius of Walla Walla. Even though the town was over 100 miles away from Moscow and Lewiston only 27 miles, the trip to Walla Walla was less perilous because farmers could travel on a "highway," the Mullan Road. Completed in 1862, the 624-mile Mullan Road was constructed as a military road to link the Northern Rockies between Fort Benton, Montana and the Walla Walla area. The road had been completed under the supervision of army lieutenant and engineer John Mullan.

In the late 1870s, the veil of isolation surrounding Paradise Valley was lifted an inch or two when the Oregon Steam Navigation Company established shipping facilities at several ports along the Snake and Columbia Rivers. Although the steamboat landings were certainly closer to Moscow than Walla Walla, and about as far away as Lewiston, simply getting to the landings remained a problem. Agricultural historian Keith Williams describes the journey in his dissertation, "The Agricultural History of Latah County and the Palouse: An Overview and Three Case Studies":

> To get to the river, plateau farmers either had to brave sinuous, brake-burning grades with their teams and wagons, or use the tramways and gravity chutes constructed at several locations along the rim of the canyon. The grain chutes saved time and wear and tear on the farmers and their horses and wagons, and cut down on the danger, but the risk and expense still remained high because the grain had to await the uncertain arrival of an empty steamboat. In addition, sacked wheat arriving at a gravity chute had to undergo the time-wasting effort of de-bagging and then re-bagging at the bottom. The tramways did allow bags to be left intact throughout the journey, but they still required extra handling.

What farmers needed was the railroad and it was a native of Bavaria, Germany who gave it to them. Henry Villard came to the United States in 1853 and after careers in the law and journalism, he turned his talents to finance, investing in several western railroad and steamship companies. Villard was a cunning businessman and through a series of shrewd maneuvers, he gained control of transportation networks centered on the Columbia River: the Oregon & California Railroad and the Oregon Steamship Navigation Company. Villard then formed the Oregon Railway and Navigation Company by merging with the short-line railroad of Dr. Dorsey Syng Baker (who would later move to Moscow). To realize his two-fold plan of opening the Inland Northwest to colonization by European immigrants and exploiting the region's natural resources to establish a steel industry, Villard founded the Oregon Improvement Company in 1878.

In 1881, after another series of ruthless machinations, Villard gained control of the Northern Pacific Railroad, which had been chartered in 1864 to construct a transcontinental line across the northern plains and mountains of the United States. By November 1882, Villard not only controlled railroad service along the Columbia River—successfully connecting the Inland Empire to coastal Portland, Oregon—he had also managed to make the Oregon Railroad and Navigation Company a part of the Northern Pacific transcontinental line. With the charter of the Northern Pacific in his back pocket, the entire Inland Northwest lay open to Villard's princely dreams. During 1883 and 1884, his crew laid railroads throughout the region, reaching into remote areas formerly traversed only with pack animals.

While the Palouse could not be called remote, it was certainly isolated, and its residents anticipated the arrival of Villard's line with excitement and a sense of relief that, at long last, an affordable and practical means of transportation would soon arrive. The first railroad line into the Palouse came in July 1883 when the Oregon Railroad and Navigation Company reached the community of Palouse, Washington. By January 1, 1884, the railroad was inching closer to Moscow with the completion of an Oregon Railroad and Navigation line to Colfax, Washington, 25 miles west of Moscow.

Six months later, the line came ever closer as crews prepared the grade into Moscow and residents indulged their dreams of prosperity and mobility. But then work on the line stopped even though, as Charles Munson wrote in his autobiography, the crews had nearly completed the line, finishing even the bridges, and needing only "the ties and steel rails to carry the crops out and ship in the supplies."

Work stopped because Villard had lost control of the Northern Pacific; the line was in receivership, meaning that the Oregon Railroad and Navigation Company was now in competition with the Northern Pacific Railroad. As Charles Munson put it in his autobiography,

> This was a sad blow to Moscow [because the residents of Moscow] had expanded along all lines to be ready when the steam engine would be heard blowing the whistle as it entered Moscow no later than early spring of 1884. Two or more sawmills in the timber were working steadily. All the farms increased their acreage, and there was greater activity in town to take care of the increased business. This all produced a large surplus . . . but neither wheat nor flour could be sold. The wheat at the warehouse was retailed a sack or two at a time at 20 cents per bushel. Flour at the stores sold at 50 cents a sack or $1.90 per barrel.

The Oregon Railroad and Navigation Company was the first railroad in Moscow, arriving in 1885. This is a photograph of Engine No. 62 taken in 1907 with E.W. Baker (left) and Henry Carey. (Courtesy LCHS.)

Munson then goes on to describe more fully the woeful state of Moscow's young economy:

> There were no debt exemptions on property, and attachments were made on property that when sold brought very little on the payment of debts. There were a number of sawmills which had been doing a good business in 1883 that in 1884 had been attached, both mills and lumber—in fact, everything, as they could not find buyers for lumber or collect for lumber that had been sold. They were all standing idle, and there was no work in the timber, no logging of any kind. A number of small business houses in town closed their doors. Lieuallen and others with town lots who had expected to sell when the railroad was in sight in 1883 were hard pressed and broke up, some temporarily and some for good.

A year later, though, it was morning again in Moscow as the Oregon Railroad and Navigation Company began laying tracks from Colfax to Moscow. As the railroad approached, anticipation reemerged and a plan was hatched that changed Moscow forever. Back in 1884, the railroad grade had been built through the north end of Moscow, pleasing the businessmen on that end of Main Street. Charles Munson explains in his autobiography:

> This was very satisfactory to M.C. Moore & Company, for they were granted the privilege of the warehouse for their free right of way to the railroad. It was satisfactory to McConnell and to W.W. Baker of the First National Bank, for it was near their businesses, and it was satisfactory to A.A. Lieuallen, for his land joined that part of the town. All were satisfied as far south as Second and Main. From there on south, they were not pleased, but they were in the hopeless minority, for there were so few of them.

Munson goes on to explain that by chance Robert Barton, owner of the Barton House (on Main Street south of McConnell's and Lieuallen's businesses and near Third Street, which runs east-west), overheard the railroad's chief engineer comment at his supper table that "he did not like the entrance to the town. He said it would be a bad place from which to extend the road, if needed." Barton acted quickly, writes Munson in his autobiography, and "he at once told John Kanaly, who ran the saloon at the Barton House, that there would be a meeting at the bridge that crossed the Paradise [Creek] at eight o'clock, but cautioned him not to say anything about it." Barton then rounded up other south-end business operators, including Michael J. Shields, merchandisers Henry Dernham and William Kaufmann, and farmers and landowners Henry McGregor and James Deakin, and persuaded them to attend the "meeting" on the bridge.

Munson described why Barton, with a bottle of fine Kentucky bourbon in hand, had called the men together:

Mr. Barton now told them what he had overheard at the supper table and said now was the time to get the railroad moved to the south and build up their business. Mr. McGregor, who would have only a small amount of free right of way to give, saw the point at once, but Deakin, who had to give a right of way through all his place, plus a depot and ground for a lot of switches and warehouses, did not. Mr. Deakin was a very careful farmer who never went in debt on his homestead. He lived on the south side of Paradise Creek in a log cabin, and all his buildings were of logs; his 160 acres were fenced by a ten-rail fence. He did not farm it all but kept about half in pasture. He could not see why he should give all this right of way to a railroad company, but after taking freely of the bottle, he commenced to thaw out.

After Shields and Dernham agreed to compensate Deakin for any financial loss, Deakin agreed to donate his major portion of the right of way. Munson writes, "Mr. Barton had the papers for a free right of way in his pocket, and the meeting was adjourned. Next morning when the engineer came down for breakfast, he was told that if he would put the railroad on the south side, he would get all the free right of way that was wanted." After checking with his superiors in Portland, the engineer accepted the offer, and Third and Main Street, rather than First and Main where Lieuallen had located Moscow's first commercial business, became the center of town.

In preparation for the arrival of the train, crews quickly got to work building a depot and "a lot of warehouses," according to Charles Munson, as well as a "roundhouse, water tank, and turntable." These structures, which also included a grain elevator, were located at the southernmost end of Main Street, just east of Sixth Street, which runs east-west. Munson also explained that the roundhouse and turntable were a "long distance from the Barton House, and the wagon tracks went directly across to the depot without any attention to the streets, but in a year or two it was connected with some kind of buildings. The area was a veritable mud hole in the spring."

The depot building was 124 feet long by 31 feet wide and surrounded by a wide platform. It housed a passenger sitting room, freight office, and agent's office. The depot agent was F.W. Parker; he not only sold passenger tickets, dispatched trains, and handled freight, but also managed the Moscow office of the Western Union Telegraph Company. Several Moscow merchants, including Michael J. Shields, Henry Dernham, and William Kaufmann, built grain warehouses on railroad property along the tracks.

Wednesday, September 23, 1885 was no ordinary Wednesday—it was the day the railroad arrived in Moscow and its arrival was celebrated in grand style. When the locomotive entered town, the engineer blew its whistle with accompaniment by the Grand Army of the Republic cannons belonging to blacksmith Fred Zumhof. Before a large crowd (but probably not one composed of 10,000 people, as Charles Munson wrote in his autobiography), attorney and newspaperman

This photograph of farmers hauling their grain to the railroad depot north of Eighth Street was taken in 1907. (Courtesy LCHS.)

Willis Sweet spoke on behalf of the citizenry, as reported in the September 25, 1885 *Moscow Mirror*:

> We have waited long and patiently for the shrill whistle which today gladdens our ears; we have looked to the westward with strained and eager eyes for the appearance of yonder iron horse until it seemed as if its promised coming was only to provoke us to utter despair; we have built so many airy castles, only to see them ruthlessly destroyed, that what we see and hear today seems to us like the realization of the happiest dream of long ago. However, we are face to face, not with a dream, but with the most potent single fact yet presented in the history of our development. We are today a part and parcel of the world of commerce, politics, and social life, connected by rail and wire. We now have tied the three great factors, with which to fight the battle of progress and prosperity; viz: a fertile country; second, an energetic, ambitious, intelligent people; third, a line of railway over which to ship the products of our toil to market, and by which to receive the necessities and the comforts of life.

Charles Munson's account of the train's arrival paints a colorful, almost theatrical, picture of that special day in Moscow's history. In his autobiography, Munson writes:

> When at last the engine and coaches came in sight, a great cheer rent the air. As the train stopped, the great multitude packed around the engine

as tight as sardines. The engine was a very small affair compared to what you see today, but it had a tall smokestack, and it surely could blow a lot of smoke out of the tall chimney and a lot of steam from everywhere. As not more than 15% of the people had ever seen a train, it was great excitement to them.

Munson also remembers September 24 as the "day set for the excursion to Colfax." Riding in the car reserved for young adults, Munson recalls:

> [The] bridges on this road for some reason stood up high and reached the windows on the coaches, and they were painted red. The girls were sticking their heads out of the windows, and when we crossed the first bridge, there was a lot of screaming, for they thought they had had a narrow escape from death. [Once in Colfax, he] noticed there were two young girls from my own neighborhood east of Moscow, and they carried their lunch. I was not ugly, as I am now; in fact, some of the girls used to flatter me by saying I was not bad to look at, so it did not take long until I had one on each arm.

Like Charles Munson, the arrival of the railroad in Moscow was of great personal importance to Alma Lauder Keeling. Her father Wylie Andrew Lauder, more commonly called W.A., was a railroad man who, after being widowed in North Carolina, had accepted the offer of his brother William to join his railroad crew. Keeling writes in *The Un-Covered Wagon*:

> It was while he was helping lay tracks to the roundhouse near our South Main Street bridge over Paradise Creek that he noticed an attractive young lady passing every day uptown with her little tin lunch pail. On inquiring about her, he learned that she was Minnie Taylor, daughter of the owner of a large farm just south of town. . . . Young Wylie made a mental note that when he was through with this track-laying business he would drop in at the Taylor ranch and see if they might be able to use another hand!

After a year-long engagement, Wylie and Minnie were married in the front parlor of William and Priscilla Taylor's farmhouse on September 1, 1886. It is clear from Munson's and Keeling's recollections that that the railroad was the antidote to both social as well as geographic isolation.

The arrival of the Union Pacific Railroad in 1885 and the Northern Pacific in 1890 would secure Moscow's future as a transportation center in the Palouse. Moscow also would become a storage center for agricultural products, especially wheat. Technological improvements, such as the new Idaho Harvester, enabled farmers to put more acreage into cultivation, and in turn, they produced more. This led to surpluses, and with the move to transport grain in bulk rather than in sacks, farmers needed a means of storing the excess. Grain elevators were the solution.

In early times, grain elevators were no more than 12 miles apart so that farmers could deliver a wagonload of grain to the elevator, unload it, and return home in less than a full day's time. As wagons gave way to motor vehicles, the distances between elevators expanded. The first elevators were simply large wooden bins riveted together, but after the turn of the twentieth century, riveted bins were replaced by steel tanks that were either bolted or welded. Beginning in the 1920s, builders began using reinforced concrete for elevators and it is concrete grain elevators that distinguish the skyline of Moscow.

Clustered around Sixth Street are several skyscraper-tall, cylindrical grain elevators belonging to Latah County Grain Growers, Inc., which was formed in 1930 as a growers' co-operative. This grouping of elevators, most of which were constructed during the period between 1885 and 1942, has been called one of the most interesting collections in the state of Idaho. As Moscow's economy becomes increasingly global, for many townspeople these grain elevators or prairie castles, as they have been called, are a powerful visual reminder of Moscow's agricultural heritage.

Local photographer Charles Dimond took this photograph of Moscow's Sixth Street grain elevators in the 1940s. (Courtesy LCHS.)

4. Securing Moscow's Future

For Moscow area farmers, rail transportation had come none too soon. The harvest of 1885 was a humdinger. Even though roughly 6,000 tons of grain were shipped out of Moscow alone that year, tens of thousands of bushels of grain nonetheless overflowed the rudimentary storage facilities built by railroad crews. There was such bounty that additional trains were added to the Moscow run and the freight rates dropped from $8 per ton to $7.

With the completion of railroad lines, a spirit of exuberance permeated not just Moscow but the Inland Northwest as a whole. During the period 1885 to 1893, as the region and the nation became more urban, Moscow boomed. And Moscow's first newspaper, the *Moscow Mirror*, founded on July 4, 1882, certainly captured this spirit of optimism in a January 1, 1892 article entitled "The Builders of Moscow: Her Leading Businessmen and Business Houses: How Diligently They Have Labored to Achieve Success and Build a City of Which All Idaho May Be Justly Proud":

> The enterprising city of Moscow, the Venice of the north, is the county seat of Latah county, and is located in the center of a country which has as rich and fertile soil as the clouds of the morning and the evening have ever watered, and as productive as any the plow ever entered, or the foot of the agriculturalist ever trod—a country "flowing in milk and honey," a veritable paradise.
>
> Moscow is the principal town of northern Idaho, and we have good reason to think the best town in the Gem of the Mountains. True, Boise possesses the capital, but the capital alone will not make a great city, much as it may help. . . . One thing we do know to be a fact, learned from observation, that no city in Idaho is so well built as Moscow. . . . We will not say we are the largest town in Idaho, but we truthfully say we are the most enterprising.

By 1887, what had once been an isolated frontier village (a "few houses and sheds huddled together," as Charles Munson described Moscow the first time he laid eyes on it) was now a town with railroad connections and a second newspaper, the *North Idaho Star.* (The *Mirror* was for Republicans, and the *Star* for Democrats.) Despite the hyperbole of the description in the *Moscow Mirror*, there seems no better word than "enterprising" to describe Moscow following the arrival of the railroad.

Never before had there been a better time to exploit the natural resources of the area. Of course, farmers had already discovered the fertility of the Palouse hills, and now that they had a means of transporting their crop, commercial agriculture became even more important to Moscow as it served as a distribution and trade center. Around this time, gold was discovered near Moscow in the Hoodoo Mountains, and although the strikes were never as great as those of other western mining districts, Moscow served as a supply point for gold-crazed prospectors.

In 1890, a rare type of opal, the harlequin, was discovered north of Moscow near the Washington State line. Although much of the strike was centered in adjacent Whitman County, Washington, Moscow newspapers were quick to associate the mining activity with Moscow. In his history, *The Moscow Opal Mines, 1890–1893: The First Commercial Opal Mines in the United States*, Ron Brockett theorizes that Moscow became associated with the mines primarily because Moscow residents actively sought their development, especially Moscow jeweler James Allen, who vigorously sought to develop the opal district. One Moscow newspaper even boasted that Moscow would become the opal mining center of the United States.

The Moscow opal mines failed to be a mother lode of precious gems, but the newspaper's boast should not be ridiculed. It reflected the attitude of many Moscowans who believed that with a little effort and a little scheming, Moscow really could become the next Walla Walla. During the late 1880s and early 1890s, Moscow's boosters—most were both businessmen and civic leaders—took measures to secure the prosperity of Moscow and to position it as a community central to the affairs of the region and the state of Idaho.

Since 1883, Moscow's boosters had advocated for the incorporation of Moscow as a city and on July 12, 1887, they achieved their goal. Most likely, it was "merchant prince" William J. McConnell (as he was described in an early history of north Idaho) who spearheaded the movement to incorporate. At that time, Moscow was a part of Nez Perce County; therefore, the petition to incorporate was submitted to the board of Nez Perce County commissioners, whose membership included C.A. Leeper, H.J. Bundy, J.L. Naylor, J.C. Hattabaugh, and A. Quackenbush. Finding that the majority of Moscow's approximately 600 inhabitants had signed the petition, the commissioners approved it. They then selected a board of trustees to administer Moscow's first city government: William J. McConnell, W.W. Langdon, Michael J. Shields, William W. Baker, and Robert H. Barton.

Later that day at 7:30 p.m., the newly formed board of trustees, with McConnell as their chair, met in Moscow where they adopted 33 ordinances and designated standing committees to manage the new city's business. The standing committees were: accounts and current expenses, fire and water, health and police, and commerce. The trustees also passed an ordinance requiring that

A rare type of opal was discovered about 7 miles northwest of Moscow in 1890. Digging for the precious gem appears to have been a family affair. (Courtesy LCHS.)

businesses and trading establishments be licensed and that mandated a licensing fee; the ordinance specified that the fee could be paid in gold or silver coin.

In the years to come, many of the ordinances passed by Moscow's board of trustees regulated construction. For example, one ordinance required men over the age of 21 and under the age of 50 to donate two days of labor per year, between the months of April and October, to help construct streets and wooden sidewalks. This same ordinance specified construction techniques for building sidewalks, including the size and type of lumber. It further mandated that sidewalks on Main Street were to be 12 feet wide on the east side and 10 feet wide on the west; all other sidewalks need be only 5 feet in width. Another ordinance specified the size of nails to be used in building the sidewalks.

Other city ordinances determined street names. In a tradition that continues today, north-south streets (with the exception of Almon, Asbury, and Lieuallen Streets) were named after past United States presidents, and east-west streets (with the exception of Lilly, misspelled but nonetheless named in honor of Almon Lieuallen's daughter Lillie) were named with letters and numbers.

Like many American towns at the end of the nineteenth century, Moscow had a curfew. Moscow's was established with Ordinance 66, which specified that unless accompanied by an adult or with written permission from a parent or guardian, those 15 years and younger were not to be on city streets during the period from two hours after sunset to 4 a.m.

For the first four years of Moscow's city government, members of the board of trustees served as volunteers. Ordinance 17, however, provided remuneration of

These men were among Moscow's boosters. In the back row, left to right, are: Willis Sweet, Franklin Mix, and Arvid "Fatty" Hinman; front row, left to right, are George Weber, Robert Barton, Henry McGregor, and John Naylor. (Courtesy LCHS.)

a sort: "the distinguished honor of receiving the growls and curses of the citizens at large and no other compensation whatsoever. The city attorney shall receive the same salary as the trustees." By 1892, trustees had voted themselves a salary of $2.50 per meeting. That same year, Moscow's first chief of police, William J. Blacker, was appointed. He was paid $4 per day and if early maps of Moscow are any indication, there were enough lawbreakers around to justify a "calaboose," as the city jail was identified on these maps. The calaboose was located on the alley north of the city's waterworks near the north end of Main Street.

In the early years of city government, the mayor was elected by popular vote every two years and six city councilmen (they were all men because just as women, Native Americans, and other minorities were denied the right to vote, they were also prohibited from holding office) were elected for four-year terms. Later and until 1986, the mayor and five councilmen were elected at large by popular vote, the offices going to those who got the largest number of votes.

The incorporation of Moscow was but one wedge of the political pie of which Idaho's fledgling communities vied for control. The struggle to dominate decision-making had begun as early as 1863 when the Idaho Territory was separated from the Washington Territory. On March 4, 1863, President Abraham Lincoln signed the bill that created the Idaho Territory, an oversized territory that included the states that would become Idaho, Wyoming, and Montana. In 1864, after a series of boundary realignments that left the territory too large still, it was turned into what historians have called a "geographical monstrosity" in which its centrally situated mountains divided the territory into two nearly impassable parts.

Although Lewiston, located in the north, had been designated the capital of the Idaho Territory in 1863, members of the territorial legislature decided to move the capital to Boise City (now Boise) in the more-populated southern part of the territory in 1864. With this gesture, they also granted themselves an appropriation of $2,000 to remove the papers, books, documents, and other property belonging to the secretary's office, including the official territorial seal from Lewiston. In response to what they considered to be the theft of the capitol, the citizens of Lewiston requested and were granted an injunction to forbid the territorial governor, Caleb Lyon, and the secretary of state, S.D. Cochran, to leave Lewiston; however, in a covert mission worthy of a Tom Clancy novel, Governor Lyon escaped Lewiston by floating down the Snake River pretending to be hunting ducks.

Then, at the request of the territory's newly-appointed secretary of state, a detachment of federal troops stationed at Lapwai, south of Lewiston, sneaked into the city, stole the territorial seal, and delivered it to the legislators in Boise City. This action settled the matter and Boise City became the capital. That didn't mean, however, that Northern Idahoans were happy about it, and they were not reluctant to express their dissatisfaction.

In 1878, 96 percent of voters in northern Idaho ratified a constitution that would have aligned them with the territory of Washington, and in 1887, legislation that would have separated the northern part of Idaho, the panhandle, reached the United States Congress. Although the bill passed both houses of Congress, President Grover Cleveland refused to sign it, perhaps because Idaho's territorial governor Edward Stevenson and its territorial congressional delegate Fred Dubois opposed the bill. Cleveland's veto must have disappointed or angered many of Moscow's boosters because they had been ardent supporters of annexation.

One Moscow booster who did not support annexation, however, was Willis Sweet. Known for having a remarkable gift of persuasion, which helped him build a powerful political machine, Sweet was an attorney and newspaperman who significantly shaped the Moscow we know today. Shortly after Moscow was incorporated, Willis needed the full extent of his persuasive gifts to realize his dream of a new county for Moscow. Many shared Sweet's dream. The journey from Moscow to the Nez Perce County seat in Lewiston was inconvenient to say the least. Not only is there a nearly 2,000-foot difference in elevation between Moscow and Lewiston, but as early as 1878, more people lived in the northern part of the county than in the southern part, according to Nez Perce County census records.

Sweet had established a mutually beneficial relationship with Idaho's territorial representative to the United States Congress, Fred Dubois, and in 1887, the same year Moscow was incorporated, Sweet convinced Dubois to introduce a unique piece of legislation to Congress. The legislation called for the creation of a new county in the Idaho Territory to be called Latah. The word Latah is a combination of two Nez Perce words, La-Kah and Tah-ol. According to local historian Lillian Otness, the Nez Perce used the word La-Kah when referring to the area's pine trees; stone pestles used to grind camas roots into flour were called Tah-ol. A committee headed by William J. McConnell coined the word Latah by combining the first syllables of these two Nez Perce words, and gave the word the meaning of "place of the pestle and pine." With support from Moscow businessman and landowner Charles Moore, Dubois's legislation met little resistance in Congress, and on May 14, 1888, Latah County was created, the only county in the nation created by an act of Congress.

Thanks to Willis Sweet, Moscow now had its own county. In 1888, its revenues just exceeded $40,000; expenditures totaled $33,130, which included $20,000 for the construction of a county courthouse in Moscow, the seat of Latah County. But Sweet had even larger ambitions for his community. He wanted the state's land-grant institution to be located in Moscow. He knew a university would provide the town with a stable economic base, and in 1888, as a representative to the territorial legislature from the new Latah County, Sweet was positioned to get what he wanted. Sweet was not alone in this ambition for Moscow. Other influential Moscow residents, including William McConnell, William Taylor, William A. Watkins, and Dr. Henry Blake, also understood how significant the state's university would be to the community.

But it was not Sweet who introduced the bill to establish a university in Moscow. That job fell to another Latah County representative, John Brigham of Genesee, a farming community in the southern part of the county. With only one dissenting vote, the bill passed and the territorial governor signed the act into law on January 30, 1889. Moscow had gotten the university because representatives from the southern part of the territory were willing to do just about anything to keep the northern part of the territory—rich in timber, ore, and grain—from seceding. Thanks to William McConnell, a member of the territory's education committee, constitutional protections were put in place that would keep the legislature from relocating the university from Moscow. According to the state constitution, the legislature cannot remove any part of the university to another part of the state without first holding a constitutional convention.

In yet another significant matter, McConnell revealed his dedication to the public trust. In 1890, after the territory's congressional representative Fred Dubois became ill, McConnell traveled to Washington, D.C. to lobby for Idaho's statehood. On July 3, 1890, President Benjamin Harrison signed the bill that admitted Idaho, as well as Wyoming, into the union. Sweet was chosen Idaho's first representative to the United States Congress, and McConnell was elected as one of the state's United States senators. Although McConnell did not serve long, an article in the January 1, 1892 *Moscow Mirror* explains that his work in "the senate was characterized by the same masterly ability and aggressiveness as is shown in his mercantile business."

Moscow celebrated Idaho's statehood with a Main Street parade. Main Street, in fact, was decorated with evergreen boughs and red, white, and blue bunting.

Latah County is the only county in the United States to have been created by an act of Congress. (Courtesy LCHS.)

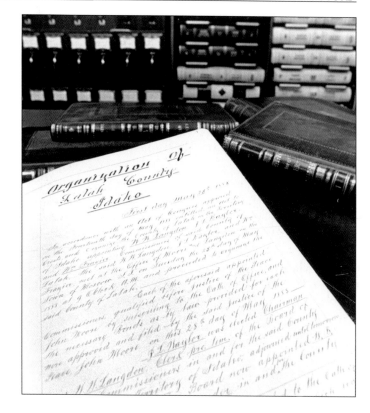

According to Idaho historian Rafe Gibbs in his history of the University of Idaho, *Beacon for Mountain and Plain*:

> The smallest float merited the most applause. It was a coaster wagon drawn by twelve boys. In the wagon sat a young daughter of W.J. McConnell, later to be elected a United States senator and governor of Idaho. The little girl in the wagon who was to become Mrs. William Edgar Borah, wife of the famed Idaho senator, held a banner inscribed, "Idaho, Gem of the Mountains." The float of the *North Idaho Star* newspaper had trouble. It consisted of a job printing press mounted on a flat wagon bed. Midway during the parade, the press fell off, and was demolished. D.P. Pride of Boise gave the speech of the day, concluding, "We are freed at last from the bondage of territorial servitude." The day was further rounded out with contests, including greased-pole climbing, greased-pig catching, and a baseball game.

Moscow's boosters had accomplished much in a brief period of time: the incorporation of Moscow in 1887; the creation of Latah County in 1888; and the selection of Moscow as home of the University of Idaho in 1889. Moscow's boosters had so aggressively lobbied for the university because they knew the state's land-grant institution would diversify Moscow's economy, thus securing its future. The importance of Moscow's selection as the site of the University of Idaho cannot be understated, for were it not for the university, Moscow might not have survived its glory days of the late nineteenth century.

There were other towns in Latah County that served as retail and trade centers for local farmers and ranchers during the late nineteenth century and early twentieth century, but only Moscow had the University of Idaho, and today Moscow is the most economically vital community in the county. A study commissioned by the university and completed in 2003 describes the university as Latah County's "economic powerhouse," contributing 49 percent of all sales in the county, 54 percent of the employment, and 55 percent of all earnings.

It is not surprising then that since its founding in 1889—a year before Idaho was granted statehood—the histories of Moscow and the University of Idaho have been intertwined, and the relationship between Moscow and the university has been strong and mutually beneficial. The establishment of the University of Idaho is the result of federal legislation passed when the nation was embroiled in the Civil War. On July 2, 1862, President Abraham Lincoln signed into law the Morrill Land-Grant Act, which granted each state 30,000 acres of land for each of

Physician Henry Blake, who married into the Lorettus Haskins family, was the first secretary of the Board of Regents for the University of Idaho. (Courtesy LCHS.)

its senators and representatives in Congress. The proceeds of the sale of the lands were to be used to endow colleges where students could receive scientific training, especially in agriculture. In 1887, another federal bill with significance to the University of Idaho passed. The Hatch Act established agricultural experiment stations in each of the universities begun under the Morrill Land-Grant Act. The agricultural experiment station at the University of Idaho actually went into operation before the university itself.

Moscow's boosters are due much credit for capturing the state's land-grant institution for their community, but despite all their effort and machinations, Moscow would not have been selected if legislation introduced in the 1887 territorial legislation had passed. That year, the legislature considered a bill that would have established a college in what would become Idaho Falls in the southern part of the territory. Territorial Governor Edward Stevenson vetoed the bill because he considered it to be "carelessly worded," according to historian Keith C. Petersen in his history of the University of Idaho, *This Crested Hill*. Petersen writes, "Had the legislation been carefully drafted, Idaho's university would not have located in Moscow."

One story that has prevailed as an explanation for why Moscow was chosen as the site of the university is simply untrue. Although Idahoans in the northern part of the state have been amused by the tale for many generations, it is not true that Boise, given the choice between the university and the state penitentiary, chose the penitentiary. The penitentiary had already been established in Boise when talk of placing the state's university began. The true story of how Moscow got the university is all about politics, and among the story's characters are many of Moscow's well-known boosters, including William McConnell and Willis Sweet. In 1888, when the last legislature of the Idaho Territory was convened, the primary issue of concern among its legislators was not the establishment of a university but the movement to disenfranchise the territory's Mormons. Nonetheless, Willis Sweet, representing the residents of Latah County and reinforced with a contribution of $100 each from Michael Shields, Henry Dernham, and William Kaufmann, traveled to Boise with the specific purpose of landing the university in Moscow.

Sweet had more than just money in his pocket. Like Fred T. Dubois, Idaho territorial representative to Congress, Sweet did not favor the annexation of the northern part of the territory to Washington. To support Dubois, Sweet put together a political machine that delivered votes from the northern part of the territory to Dubois in his reelection campaigns in both 1886 and 1888. Politics being politics, Sweet was banking on Dubois reciprocating the favor.

Once in Boise, however, Sweet got caught up in the disenfranchisement debate and failed to introduce legislation to establish a university in Moscow. Back in Moscow, William McConnell learned of Sweet's distraction and convinced another Latah County representative, John Brigham, to travel to Boise to redirect Sweet's attention. The day Brigham arrived in Boise he went directly to Sweet's quarters only to find him still in his bed. Figuring there was no time like the

Earl Sawyer drives a team of University of Idaho horses. As a land-grant institution, the university offered training in the sciences, particularly agriculture. (Courtesy LCHS.)

present, Brigham successfully argued the need for immediate action and convinced Sweet to finish writing the legislation so that it could be introduced before the legislature adjourned. A few days later, Brigham introduced the legislation, known as Council Bill 20. The bill passed easily, with only one dissenting vote in both houses, for two reasons. The legislators from the southern part of the territory were eager to appease those in the north who had been threatening to secede since the late 1870s. Second, the vote was an acknowledgement of Moscow's political loyalty to the territory's national representative, Fred Dubois.

On January 30, 1889, Governor Edward Stevenson passed Council Bill 20 into law. Surprisingly, the only legislator present to witness this significant event for the community of Moscow was John Brigham of Genesee. Willis Sweet's location remains an intriguing mystery. Despite the apparent nonchalance on behalf of the legislators, north and south, the newspaper of one southern community, the *Blackfoot News*, acknowledged Moscow's selection with the following words of support:

> You will remember, it is often told in southern Idaho that all roads in northern Idaho lead to Moscow, that Moscow has the loveliest ladies and the noblest men of any town in the Territory, that its surrounding country has the most fertile valleys and the most beautiful mountains and upon whose tops one can stand to tickle the feet of Democratic angels; well, in part this is true. Moscow has much to boast of, much to

be proud of. The legislature made no mistaking in locating the University at this point.

In the spring of 1889, Willis Sweet and Henry Blake, serving as members of the university's first board of regents, returned to Moscow with authorization to spend up to $15,000 to purchase land for the new University of Idaho. Dr. Blake was a Moscow physician who had been persuaded in 1877 to leave his practice in Colfax, Washington, to set up the town's first medical office. James Deakin, who had donated 30 acres to establish Moscow's commercial district 20 years earlier, sold Sweet a 20-acre tract of land on a hill roughly 2 miles northeast of Main Street; the purchase price was $4,000. In the fall of 1889, the site of the university's first building was excavated, but construction on the Administration Building did not begin until the summer of 1891. The company awarding the bid to lay the foundation of the west wing was that of Alma Lauder Keeling's father, Wylie Lauder, and her uncle Thomas Taylor. By the fall of 1892, Lauder and Taylor had laid the foundation and completed construction of the west wing.

According to Charles Munson, it was he who wore a path from Moscow to the site of the new university:

The university's first Administration Building was built in 1892 with brick from the brickyard of Wylie Lauder and Thomas Taylor. (Courtesy LCHS.)

> One day I came along Third Street with a load of wood. Dr. H.B. Blake, a local man who was a member of the first Board of Regents, came walking down the street. He was a short man but took long steps, for he was always busy. Says he, "I want 25 cords for the University of Idaho, and I will go along to show you where to pile it, so it will not be in the way." He got up on the load, and we started down Main Street.
>
> After passing the Barton House, we could see across the flat, for it was all commons. I thought the wood was wanted somewhere on the flat, but we kept driving across to the depot. When we got over the track, he directed me to drive west into the country. It was getting steeper and steeper, and at last we got to a summer fallow on a high hill, and he got off. He told me to drive up the hill and then on to where there were a lot of stakes, where one wing of the university was to be built. I had not figured on such a long haul into the country, but it was for a good cause, and I delivered the wood. Mine was the first track for a couple of days. Then others followed with all kinds of stuff—an engine, brick, lime, etc.

With Franklin Gault as its first president, the University of Idaho opened its door on October 3, 1892. Forty students were in attendance, and on the following day, Gault administered an entrance examination. No one passed. Because Gault considered no student qualified to perform college work, he essentially turned the university into a preparatory school with three separate levels of competence. Although the University of Idaho held its first classes on October 10, 1892, the classes were preparatory rather than collegiate in content.

For many years, the Administration Building was the only building on campus, but beginning in the mid-1890s, as the university gradually expanded its curriculum and the student population grew, small wooden buildings were constructed to house such disciplines as horticulture and military training. In 1896, the citizens of Moscow presented the university with a gift of 94 acres next to the campus for use as a farm. That same year, the governor of Idaho, William J. McConnell, returned to Moscow to inspect the university and to address its students.

It is difficult to know if McConnell was impressed with what he saw because the setting of the University of Idaho, with its yet-to-be-completed Administration Building and collection of wooden buildings, although scenically-located, was understandably primitive. A barbed wire fence encircled the campus, probably to keep "Idaho Violet" from roaming. Idaho Violet was the College of Agriculture's only cow, a purebred Jersey that some students described as wild-eyed, flighty, and given to chase at the slightest annoyance. Fortunately, stiles were put in place so that students could cross the fence, but they proved an unrelenting obstacle for female students with their long dresses.

In June 1896, amid this rustic environment, the University of Idaho held its first commencement. There were only four graduates: Charles Luther Kirtley of Salmon City, Idaho; Stella Maude Allen of Moscow; Florence May Corbett of Tacoma, Washington; and Arthur Prentiss Adair, also of Moscow. An indication that the pace of life was much different a century ago than it is now is the fact that commencement exercises for the Class of 1896 were held over a period of five days.

Only two years later, however, the mood for the commencement exercises for the University's Class of 1898 would be anything but celebratory. America was entangled in the Spanish-American War and two university students had already lost their lives. Paul Draper, a native of Mesa, Washington, had been killed while serving in the Philippines, and Ole Gabriel Hagberg, a native of Norway, had also died in the Philippines from typhoid fever. That only two students were lost is amazing because the university, with its two companies of volunteers, Company C and Company D, sent the highest ratio of volunteers-to-students of any college in the nation.

One member of Company D was Winslow Howland. In a letter dated July 31, 1898, Howland wrote his sister:

> [I] arrived today in Manila Bay after five weeks voyage from Frisco. We arrived and anchored just inside of the line of American warships under Admiral Dewey and in the water where the battle took place that has made Dewey's name immortal to history and to man especially if he be an American . . . Now the stars and stripes float from what was once the Spanish fortifications. It shows the difference in the skilled American gunner and the poor markmanship [*sic*] of the Spaniard with the big guns.

Students and townspeople celebrated the end of the Spanish-American War in 1898 with a parade in which the King of Spain was hanged in effigy, and in 1907,

The University of Idaho's first graduating class, the Class of 1896, poses for their group photo. (Courtesy LCHS.)

the university erected a statue of a soldier standing at ease as a memorial to the students lost in the war.

A year before, in 1906, the citizens of Moscow rallied around the university community to help it recover from a demoralizing blow. At 2:30 a.m. on the morning of March 30, 1906, the fire bells of Moscow announced that something was ablaze. As the members of the West Side Hose Company No. 4 and Neptune Hose Company No. 3 quickly learned, the university's Administration Building, a structure designed in a lofty architectural style meant to impress and inspire and topped by a tall, slender spire, was engulfed in flames. Efforts to stem the conflagration were in vain, as even the building's water lines burst from the heat of the fire.

The Lauder family house was only a few blocks away from the building, and she recalls her brother Ralph going to the west window of their house and looking in the direction of the university. Alma Lauder Keeling writes in her family history, *The Un-Covered Wagon*, that she was five years old when the Administration Building burned:

Captain Edward Taylor, the son of William and Priscilla Taylor, was killed in the Spanish-American War in 1899. (Courtesy LCHS.)

It was a rather strange thing to do, for ordinarily there would have been nothing to see but our orchard out of that window, but what he saw was almost unbelievable! Clouds of black smoke were rising from a burning building, covering the landscape. . . . The sight of that burned out, blackened shell of a building was almost incomprehensible! The smoke was rising in a great cloud from the interior and the tower had already fallen in.

A few items were salvaged from the fire that completely destroyed the building, including some academic records and the "Silver and Gold Book," which was actually a jewel box in the shape of a book. It had been a gift to the university from the women of Moscow and had been part of Idaho's exhibit at the Columbian Exposition in Chicago in 1893. The Silver and Gold Book had been formed of silver and gold and decorated with rubies and opals. On its cover, historical scenes, representations of the state's principal products, and a likeness of the university's Administration Building had been etched.

The fire was most likely the result of arson; early on, firefighters discovered that some of the fire hoses had been cut and that the nozzle of a hose, said to have been in place shortly before the fire, was missing. The actual cause of the fire, however, was never discovered. "Who would want to do a thing like that?" asked Keeling in *The Un-Covered Wagon*.

University President James A. MacLean and his faculty quickly mobilized to resume the operation of the university, and soon classes were meeting in buildings throughout Moscow. Until 4 p.m. each day, students met in Moscow's brand-new Carnegie Library. Classes were also held in the Methodist church and in the community's lodge halls. The university's library had been destroyed in the fire, but donations of books and cash went far toward rebuilding the collection. President MacLean took charge of the effort to build another Administration Building, and three years later, the central section of the new—and current—Administration Building was completed.

5. Economic and Municipal Growth

The founding of the University of Idaho in Moscow in 1889 reflected the spirit of the times. It was a time when Moscow's citizens were infused with an energetic, pragmatic, and confident spirit that produced results. It was clear that Moscow, like much of the rest of the nation, was enjoying an economic boom, and people were eager to reap its benefits. Across the Northwest, there was a phenomenal growth in population. In 1880, the population of Washington's Whitman County and Nez Perce County had totaled 11,179; Moscow's stood at 300. In 1890, the population of Whitman County and Latah County (which had been created only two years earlier) had more than doubled and stood at 28,282. Nearly 2,000 people called Moscow home.

After all, by 1890, when a branch of the Northern Pacific Railroad reached Moscow, the town could boast of three railroads and its own telephone service. Moscow's first telephone service, which connected Moscow only to Colfax, Washington, was established in 1885. In 1891, the city contracted with the Inland Telephone and Telegraph Company for phone service, and in 1903, additional lines would be added by the Interstate Cooperative Telephone Company. In 1910, the contract was awarded to T.A. Meeker and C.J. Langdon, who operated the Moscow Telephone Company. Between 1918 and 1925, the Moscow Telephone and Telegraph Company provided service; from 1925 to 1927, it was Interstate Utilities; and in 1927, General Telephone and Electric assumed responsibility for area telephone service.

With the twentieth century just a decade away, Moscow was not only a Palouse area transportation center, but also the home of the state's land-grant university. The citizens of Moscow had been granted the privilege of hosting the University of Idaho, and in turn, it was their job to build the university literally from the ground up. With the university serving as a role model, Moscow experienced a building boom during the period from the late 1880s through the early 1890s. Moscow's boosters became Moscow's builders, laying the foundation for the community we know today. It was during this period that many of the buildings that comprise Moscow's present downtown business district were built, and it was also during this period that important public services, such as electricity, first became available.

Prior to 1885, the downtown business district, which had expanded southward on Main Street from Almon Lieuallen's store, was a motley collection of log cabins and wooden buildings. Many of these early offices and shops had false fronts and were extremely vulnerable to fire. Builders used wood to construct commercial buildings because locally produced bricks were not available; however, between 1885 and 1888, Moscow's brick-making industry would flourish. As Charles Munson explains in his autobiography, "Lauder and Taylor got a large tract in the west part of town and started a large brickyard that would supply bricks on a large scale and fill orders for any amount."

The Taylor to whom Munson refers is not William Taylor but his son Thomas, who was not the first person with whom Wylie Lauder had owned a brickyard. An 1885 advertisement in a Moscow newspaper reads that Lauder & Clough had 200,000 bricks for sale, but a year later, the business partnership of Fred S. Clough and Wylie Lauder had been dissolved. Clough continued to manufacture brick, and in 1888, or possibly earlier, Clough built what is the oldest standing brick building in Moscow on the southeastern corner of Third and Washington Streets.

The Northern Pacific Railroad reached Moscow in 1890. This is a photograph of a Northern Pacific engine at Moscow's passenger depot in 1953. (Courtesy LCHS.)

Thomas Taylor, shown here with his wife Fanny, was a partner in one of Moscow's most successful businesses, Lauder & Taylor. (Courtesy LCHS.)

Before he became partners with Wylie Lauder, Thomas Taylor teamed with his father to manufacture bricks. According to Alma Lauder Keeling, Wylie's daughter, the first advertisement for the brickyard of her grandfather William and her uncle Thomas appeared in the weekly newspaper in September 1886. She goes on to explain that the first advertisement for the firm of Taylor and Lauder appeared in 1888. From their quarry located south of Sixth Street, between Elm and Ash, Taylor and Lauder provided the brick for many of the area's early buildings, including the original Administration Buildings for the University of Idaho and Washington State University in Pullman, Washington, and the first Latah County courthouse.

Taylor and Lauder did more than manufacture brick; they also were contractors and built many of the buildings on Moscow's Main Street. During the late 1880s and throughout the 1890s, the sound of construction must have been deafening in Moscow's downtown. One of the first brick constructions on Main Street was the Hotel Del Norte. Although there is no proof that Taylor and Lauder built Moscow's first brick hotel, it is known that the building was constructed of local brick in 1888 and was located on north Main Street. The Hotel Del Norte had a second-floor balcony that spanned the front of the building as well as an adjoining hall that was used by what historian Lillian Otness called secret societies.

Michael J. Shields built Moscow's first three-story brick building in 1889 after a fire destroyed the building housing his store, which had had an inventory of hardware, stoves, carriages, and wagon stock. According to an article in the January 1, 1892, edition of the *Moscow Mirror*, which promoted many of Moscow's leading businesses, Shields's business was so successful that he built a small addition to this building. The article goes on to describe what a shopper entering Shields's place of business would find:

> In the first building on the ground floor is hardware, knives, forks, cutlery, spades, shovels, tinware and all the other small articles, and variety of goods belonging to this branch of the business too numerous to mention, and the other. On the second floor is the door, sash, window glass, hardware, oils, paints, etc. The third story is exclusively devoted to stoves of every grade and quality. In the new building is an immense stock of implements, from hay rakes to threshing machines, buggies, carriages and phaetons, all from factories of the best reputation. An [*sic*] this building is also the harness shop and store, where they make and manufacture harness and saddles, in which there is an immense stock of goods of the finest grade. In the harness making department they give twelve men employment the year round. In this department, as in the other, they have required [*sic*] a great reputation for first-class goods at eastern prices.

Lauder and Taylor operated a brickyard, and a group of their employees pose for a photograph taken c. 1890. (Courtesy LCHS.)

> They also have a tin, plumming [*sic*] and galvanizing department which gives steady employment to about twenty men. The Shields Company did the work on the McConnell-Maguire Company's new building, and for workmanship and elegant finish it cannot be surpassed in any city in the Union. Their mechanics are all skilled artisans.

The same year Shields built his three-story brick building, 1889, he also built a planing mill on the corner of Sixth and Jackson Streets. According to the *Moscow Mirror* story on January 1, 1892, the planing mill gave "employment to 50 skilled mechanics. The wood work which they turn out cannot be surpassed anywhere, for they have all the latest improved machinery, and the most competent and skilled workmen they can procure. They do a very large lumber business, and have on hand about 3,000,000 feet of lumber."

Before the summer of 1889, the streets of Moscow were lit with kerosene lamps, but a change was in the works. In July, the City of Moscow contracted with Michael J. Shields to provide the town with electricity when they granted him the right to erect poles, lay underground conduits and wires, and install conductors in the streets, avenues, and alleys of Moscow for a period of 25 years. Initially, electric service was not available during the day, and during the night only Main Street was lit with carbon arcs that were replaced daily.

The City of Moscow paid $2,400 in 1894 to the Moscow Electric Light and Power Company, a corporation owned by Shields, for the maintenance and installation of a public lighting system. By 1899, the Moscow Electric Light and Power Company had become the Idaho-Washington Light and Power Company,

When built in 1889, the planing mill of M.J. Shields and Company was located on the southwest corner of Sixth and Jackson Streets. (Courtesy LCHS.)

with Shields as its president. At that time, Shields controlled the distribution of electricity to a half-dozen communities in Latah and Whitman Counties. In 1913, four years after Shields's death in 1909 at the age of 57, a regional utility company, Washington Water Power, was granted responsibility for providing electric service. Local historian Lillian Otness called Shields, who was worth over $300,000 at the peak of his career, the leading entrepreneur of Moscow from 1890 to 1910.

As a contractor, Shields also built Moscow's first public waterworks after the City of Moscow had drilled its first well and established a public water system around 1890. Shields managed the construction of some of the town's most prominent public and private buildings. It was Shields who built the McConnell-Maguire building, which Lillian Otness described as Moscow's "most elaborately decorated structure" when it was built in 1891. It remains one of downtown Moscow's most attractive buildings today.

The columns and other cast ironwork of the McConnell-Maguire building, located on Main Street, were provided by the Moscow Iron Works, owned and operated by George H. Goude and Charles D. Benson. "This is a business of which Moscow is proud, and one which is bringing her a splendid revenue," explained the *Moscow Mirror* in a January 1, 1892 story about Moscow's builders:

> No city the size of Moscow can well afford to be without a foundry. Besides doing general moulding [*sic*] and foundry business, the Moscow Iron Works repairs all kinds of machinery as well as make [*sic*] boilers. They are agents for and manufacturers of the Golden Gate Windmills. They are also agents for the Whitney Safety Fire Arms and take orders for loading ammunition as will be seen by their advertisement on another page. They [Goude and Benson] are both practical iron workers and understand the business thoroughly, as well as live, energetic business men. The success of their enterprise is no doubtful factor. They have done considerable repairing on our press and when we say they are first class mechanics we know they are from practical experience and we say to everyone who needs machinery repaired that they will find it to their interest to have their work done at the shops of the Moscow Iron Works.

The *Moscow Mirror*, in the same story, also had high praise for the McConnell-Maguire Company, which explained that the aim of the company "is to supply all the wants of the people, and at a small profit." The McConnell-Maguire building was completed in November 1891, and according to the *Moscow Mirror*, "The arrangement of the structure is superb." The first floor of the three-story building housed dry goods, hardware, groceries, clothing, and "a toilet room and a safety deposit vault in which to keep their books and valuable papers."

On the second floor were administrative offices, the millinery department, musical instruments, carpets, and reception rooms, which were "elegantly furnished with antique oak, beautifully polished and exquisitely carved." The article concluded with the observation, "The stock of goods in this new, elegantly furnished and palatial store is superb, and in keeping with a city of so much elegance and wealth. The shelves are groaning under the loads of the choicest silks and satins, and with the finest grades of every class of goods know [*sic*] to their business."

Another of Moscow's most successful general merchandise operations was the Dernham and Kaufmann Company. In 1881, William Kaufmann went into business with his brother-in-law Henry Dernham to form the U.S. Wholesale and Retail General Merchandise Store. In 1889, they built "their new, commodious brick building on the corner of Main and Third streets, which has an 80-foot front and running back to a depth of 125 feet," according to the January 1, 1892 *Moscow Mirror*. Dernham and Kaufmann's store accommodated four floors and was filled with an awesome variety of goods: trunks; clothing; caps; boots; shoes for gents, children, misses, and ladies; stationery paper, plain and fancy; carpets; linoleums; oilcloths; pianos; organs; sewing machines; crockery; glassware; china; lamps; window shades; and lace curtains. The store also contained a "millinery department in charge of a lady whose long experience eminently fits her for the position," according to same edition of the *Moscow Mirror*.

After 1891, on the other side of Main Street from the Dernham and Kaufmann Company was the Barton House, built by Robert H. Barton after fire destroyed the hotel he built in 1880, Moscow's first hotel. Originally referred to as "The Moscow," the Barton House was a three-story brick hotel, constructed at a cost of over $35,000. In addition to a candy and cigar shop, a barbershop, and a bar, there was a separate entrance for ladies, as was customary during this period. According to local historian Lillian Otness, the opening of the hotel on April 9, 1892 was a gala event at which the various orders connected with Masonry, Odd Fellows, Elks, and Knights of Pythias were represented. A special train ran from Spokane to transport visitors to Moscow's new grand hotel.

That same year, Joseph Niederstadt, who had managed the Moscow Brewery single-handedly after the dissolution of his partnership with Otto Fries, became partners with J. Schober and Franz L. Koehler to build another brewery, the Idaho Brewing Company. Located close to the Moscow Brewery, the Idaho Brewing Company (also known as Latah Brewing) would later fold, leaving Moscow without ice as well as beer. The brewery was the only business in Moscow that had had ice-making equipment. In 1895, Franz Koehler bought the Moscow Brewery, which had been in receivership with the First National Bank of Moscow, and according to W.G. Emery's 1897 history of Moscow:

> Mr. Koehler takes personal charge of every brew made. He uses only the best Palouse grown barley, and best Oregon and Washington hops. He makes his own malt, and makes only pure malt and hops lager beer. It is an interesting fact that the exceptionally pure water used is especially adapted to making a strictly pure lager beer, and that the product of the Moscow Brewery is the equal in flavor and keeping qualities of the best beer made in the east.

Robert Barton built the Barton House in 1880; it was Moscow's first hotel. The Red Front Livery Stable was operated in connection with Barton's hotel. (Courtesy LCHS.)

While Moscow's breweries were located on the northernmost end of Main Street, the heart of the business district was centrally located on Main Street between First and Sixth Streets. Most of Moscow's many "commodious" brick buildings were situated on this section of Main Street, and they were more than a reflection of the town's bustling prosperity. Because it was less vulnerable to fire than wood, brick made sense from a practical perspective, especially since before the ready availability of electric lights, highly flammable kerosene lamps and candles were the only lighting technology available. It also was common for interior floors to be oiled to keep down dust and dirt.

Before 1885, when most of Moscow's buildings were frame structures, the only firefighting equipment Moscow businessmen had on hand were barrels of water stored on the roofs of their wooden buildings. In 1888, three years after the first public meeting regarding fire protection was held, Moscow's first hook-and-ladder company was formed. A year later, in 1890, the Moscow Volunteer Fire Department was formed.

Blacksmiths Fred Zumhof and Marion M. Collins are credited with organizing Moscow's volunteer fire department, which was created with Ordinance 107. As of June 2, 1890, when it was officially formed and equipped, the department consisted of a chief engineer, first and second assistant engineers, a secretary, a treasurer, and the members of the Capitol Hose Company No. One and the Neptune Hose Company No. Two. The fire cart of the Capitol Hose Company

After fire destroyed the Barton House in 1890, Barton began construction of what would become the Hotel Moscow. Its four-chair barbershop included a shoeshine stand. (Courtesy LCHS.)

was located in a shed on First and Main Streets, while Zumhof and Collins kept the Neptune Company cart in their shop on Main Street near Sixth Street. The cart of the Summit Hose Company No. Three, which was formed in 1891, sat on Third Street between Polk and Howard Streets until well into the 1900s.

An additional fire prevention measure was taken in 1903 when the City of Moscow passed an ordinance prohibiting the building, moving, repair, improvement, or demolition of any building without first notifying the city clerk. The clerk would then notify fire officials who would, in turn, inspect the structure for accordance with the latest fire safety standards. That same year, Moscow's first house numbering system was instituted, and by 1911, Moscow had two more hose companies: West Side and Rescue.

On the roof of the shed that housed the cart of the Summit Hose Company was their fire bell. Before 1900, the firing of three pistol shots in rapid succession sounded the fire alarm. Between 1900 and 1927, the pealing of fire bells, located throughout the town, summoned firefighters to the scene. Lawrence Smith, who arrived in Moscow as a child in 1910 with his family, recalled the first time he heard the fire bell located near City Hall. It was, he wrote in a reminiscence in the archives of the Latah County Historical Society, no ordinary bell, "but one that could be heard for miles around. The sound was so loud and so penetrating that in the middle of the night it would wake you up and leave you hanging a foot above the sheets."

In 1927, five years after the Moscow Volunteer Fire Department had purchased their first fire truck, the department's first siren was installed on top of the bank building located on the southwest corner of Third and Main Streets. Other fire sirens were installed as the town grew, and although today's firefighters respond to fire and emergencies via pagers and radios, the Moscow Volunteer Fire Department still maintains two back-up sirens; one is located on a Sixth Street grain elevator and the other at the steam plant on the University of Idaho campus. The Sixth Street siren is still routinely tested at noon.

It would not be until 1927 that the fire department built its first station. Located on the southwest corner of Sixth and Main Streets, a brick building was built with proceeds from the annual Fireman's Ball, which is still held today. The brick building replaced a wooden structure that had been used as a "cream station" for many years by area dairy farmers who brought their product to Moscow for sale. In 1954, a second building was built, abutting the first building to the south.

In the early days of the department, before mechanization, horses drew the hose carts. In her history of Moscow's volunteer firefighters, Mrs. Kenneth O'Donnell includes an anecdote told by "pioneer drayman" George W. Carter

Fred Zumhof, holding the sign with the number "4," was a blacksmith and one of the organizers of the Moscow Volunteer Fire Department. (Courtesy LCHS.)

whose horses pulled the fire carts. One day, Carter's wagon and horses were standing on Main Street when the fire alarm was sounded. Immediately, the horses took off running southward on Main Street, "with Mr. Carter striving to catch them. Needless to say, they won the race as he wasn't able to reach them until they stopped in front of the blacksmith shop to pick up the horse cart."

With its volunteer fire department fully organized, the businessmen of Moscow need no longer store water in barrels on their roofs, but the City of Moscow decided it needed to store water as its population expanded. By 1892, the city had built a public water reservoir. Referred to as the "standpipe," the reservoir was an open cylinder 80 feet tall located in the city block bounded by Jefferson, Adams, A, and C Streets, north of Main Street.

During the early 1890s, Moscow's commercial district continued to grow. In 1891, George Albright established the Moscow Bicycle Works on south Main Street to sell, repair, and rent bicycles. By 1909, Albright switched gears and built Moscow's first automobile repair shop on the site of his bicycle shop. He advertised his business with the slogan, "We repair everything except a broken heart and the break of day."

In 1892, stonemason George Moody arrived in Moscow and opened the Northwestern Marble Works on the corner of Third and Jefferson Streets; Moody not only installed marble in Moscow's buildings, he also carved headstones. Many examples of his fine work can be found in the area's cemeteries. Moody also carved, with mallet and chisel, all the lettering on commemorative military monuments in the Moscow Cemetery, Moscow's East City Park, and the University of Idaho campus.

Like other towns throughout the nation before the era of bank regulation, there was no shortage of banks in Moscow. One of Moscow's first brick buildings housed the Baker-Clark Bank, established by Dr. Dorsey Syng Baker. Having made his fortune as a railroad man and banker in Walla Walla, Baker started a branch in Moscow and put Herbert Clark in charge. In 1889, Baker's bank became the First National Bank of Moscow. In 1890, Mason Cornwall founded the Bank of Moscow and built a three-story, vividly decorated building on Third Street to house it. In 1891, a former cashier of the First National Bank, Robert Browne, established the Moscow National Bank. Like Cornwall, Browne erected a building on south Main Street to house his bank.

Browne left Moscow in 1897 following the failure of his bank, which was not the only bank in Moscow to fail in the mid-1890s. Isaac Hattabaugh's Commercial Bank failed in 1894, as did the Farmers Bank in 1896. During the 1890s, bank failures were common as the nation went from boom to bust. There seems no better word than panic to describe what happened in 1893. That year, shortly after Grover Cleveland became president, the nation's reserve of gold bouillon dropped below the $100-million level, a number the public had long regarded as significant but was actually without meaning. In response to the drop, Americans panicked, and the economy went into a decline that culminated in what has been called the Panic of 1893.

Isaac C. Hattabaugh established the Commercial Bank in 1890. The building housing the bank also housed the newspaper known as the Star of Idaho. *(Courtesy LCHS.)*

That same year, to make matters worse, Mother Nature gave Palouse farmers the cold, rainy shoulder. In 1893, there was a disastrous crop failure, the result of an extremely wet spring and summer. As Charles Munson puts it in his autobiography, "When Palouse harvest time arrived, the gates of heaven were opened, and our crops could not be saved. Some tried to thresh between showers but were worse off, for the wheat spoiled in the sacks. All the crop was lost in this part of the Palouse."

In Moscow, the Panic of 1893 and the 1893 crop failure brought serious consequences for nearly everyone, including the man who had done more than anyone to secure Moscow's future. Civic leader William J. McConnell, who had been elected governor of Idaho in 1892, lost everything. Like most merchants, McConnell had extended credit to farmers who repaid their debts after harvest. When the farmers had nothing to harvest, they were unable to meet their obligations, and the merchants, in turn, were unable to pay their suppliers. McConnell was forced to declare bankruptcy and close his store on Main Street.

McConnell was not the only Moscowan who got caught up in the tide of the times. In his autobiography, Charles Munson includes an account of a Judge Piper who had foreclosed on a farm. Written 50 years after the event, Munson may have exaggerated the number of individuals participating in the event described in his memoir. While it is unlikely that "hundreds of men" were involved, the anecdote faithfully reveals the extreme measures desperate people will sometimes take:

> One night after dark hundreds of men on horseback rode into Moscow; they stopped at the judge's house at First and Washington and put up skulls and crossbones; then they rode down Main and tied their horses at the hitchracks, intending to get the judge. He saw the signs and ran across the street and crawled under the old McConnell warehouse, where he stayed all night. They went direct to his house and inquired where the judge was; Mrs. Piper said that she did not know. After a vain hunt all over town, they got on their horses and left after midnight.

Despite the recession brought on by the Panic of 1893, growth did not come to a standstill in Moscow. In 1894, Chris Anderson opened a wagon and carriage shop behind that of blacksmith Fred Zumhof, and within three years became the leading carriage maker, not just in Moscow, but also on the Palouse. In 1896, a business that is still in operation today expanded. Around 1891, George Creighton had opened a dry goods store in a Main Street building, which he advertised as "exclusive," called the Chicago Bargain Store. According to the article about Moscow's successful businessmen in the January 1, 1892 *Moscow Mirror*, "the motto of the Chicago Bargain Store was 'small profits and large sales.'" The article went on to explain that while Creighton "attends principally to the purchasing of the goods . . . Mr. Nelson looks after the store and sees that the customers are 'treated according to Hoyle.'" Eventually, Creighton changed the name of the store to Creighton's and bought the building into which the business had moved in 1896. Although Creighton's remains in operation, it is no longer located on Main Street.

Another business opened after the Panic of 1893 that still bears the name of its founder was the commercial laundry opened by Charles B. Green. Moscow's only commercial laundry, the Moscow Steam Laundry, was opened in 1896 on south Main Street. Green later added a dry cleaning service, which operates today under the name of Green's Cleaners. Also in 1896, Oscar McCartor, whose father Leonidas had erected a fine brick building on the east side of Main Street in 1891, established a mill on the southern end of Main Street to produce feed for animals. The Moscow Commission Company produced up to 15 tons of feed per day and was in business at the Main Street site until after 1930.

Near McCartor's feed plant on Main Street was the McGregor House, which would become the site of Moscow's first hospital. In 1891, one of Moscow's founders, Henry McGregor, had built a hotel called the McGregor House. In 1897, four years after their arrival in Moscow, physicians Charles L. Gritman and R.C. Coffey purchased the McGregor House and converted it into a private hospital. Although Dr. Coffey had left Moscow by 1900, Gritman continued the hospital until the time of his death in 1933. Now a not-for-profit organization called Gritman Medical Center, it offers medical services Dr. Gritman could only have imagined and is Moscow's only hospital today.

Prosperity began to return to Moscow starting around 1899, helped in large part by a generous appropriation from the state legislature in 1898 that provided

Owner-operator Charles B. Green replaced the wooden building shown behind the employees of the Moscow Steam Laundry in 1909. (Courtesy LCHS.)

enough funds to finish construction of the first Administration Building on the University of Idaho campus. As Charles Munson wrote the following:

> The university's first building was entirely finished in 1899. It was a most beautiful structure 183 feet from base to tower. Above the tower was a huge ball of Idaho gold and a flagpole where hung the United States flag. It could be seen and admired all over the surrounding country.

Another factor contributing to the economic recovery of Moscow was the commercialization of the timber industry in the northeastern part of Latah County. Led by Charles O. Brown in October 1900, a group of Moscow businessmen succeeded in capturing the attention of Frederick Weyerhauser, perhaps the most important of all American lumbermen. Brown pointed out to the Weyerhauser family that Latah County had the largest single stand of white pine in the nation, and the Weyerhauser interests took notice. In 1903, Weyerhauser formed the Potlatch Lumber Company. As Charles Munson put it in his autobiography, "This was of great importance, for it eventually got a lot of money to the country and added a new industry that employed many thousands of men, opened up the wilderness to railroads and towns and agriculture."

Moscowans, like the residents of several other Palouse communities, courted Weyerhauser's favor, hoping he would headquarter his mill in their town, but

87

In 1905, the Potlatch Lumber Company began construction on what was then the largest white pine sawmill in the world on a site roughly 25 miles north of Moscow.

their effort was in vain. In fact, according to historian Keith C. Petersen, an authority on the history of the Potlatch Lumber Company, Weyerhauser never seriously considered Moscow for the site of the mill. However, the courtship of Frederick Weyerhauser did provide the people of Moscow with one of its most repeated legends. According to Petersen:

> The account varies with the teller, but details remain basically the same. Potlatch Lumber Company directors were meeting in Moscow, discussing possible millsites, when Bill Deary [Potlatch's general manager] entered the room after an all-day trek through wet woods. Removing his shoes and socks by the stove, Deary heard someone asserting that Moscow offered the best mill location. Jumping up barefooted, he approached a large map spread on the directors' table and bellowed in his thick Irish brogue, "Gentilmen [*sic*], there isn't enough water in Moscow to baptize a bastard! The mill'll go here!" He then punched a hole in the map precisely where he was purchasing property along the Palouse River.

The place to which Deary pointed was located about 30 miles north of Moscow, and in 1906, Weyerhauser built the largest white pine sawmill in the world there. The site became the company town of Potlatch, Idaho. Even though the Potlatch sawmill was located some distance from Moscow, Moscow still benefited economically. Men from all over Latah County, including Moscow, worked in the mill, and a good portion of their paychecks found their way into the tills of Moscow's businesses.

One such business was Davids', a department store located on the southeast corner of Third and Main Streets that was a landmark of downtown Moscow for nearly a century. Since 1896, Frank A. David, with partner Wellington Ely, had operated the Badger Store in a building on south Main Street. In 1899, David and Ely moved into the building constructed in 1889 by Henry Dernham and William Kaufmann. The partners then changed the name of the business to the David and Ely Store. It became Davids' around 1919.

Besides the David and Ely Store, there was enough post-Panic prosperity in Moscow to support another department store. In 1904, Nathaniel Williamson moved his general merchandise store, the Greater Boston Store, to a portion of the building on south Main Street housing the business of Michael J. Shields. Soon,

This advertisement for groceries from the department store of David & Ely ran in Moscow's telephone directory. Moscow had phone service as early as 1885. (Courtesy LCHS.)

David & Ely's Phone No. is

——801——

PHONE in your Grocery order or call the clerks from any of the other complete departments. You are assured of satisfactory service.
Two delivery wagons going all the time, leaving at 9:00 and 11:00 o'clock, a. m., and 3:00 and 5:00 o'clock p. m.

High Grade Clothing Price and Quality Guaranteed

Women's Tailored Suits

Pingree Shoes

Walk-Over Shoes

FURNITURE at Lower Prices

THE SYSTEM CLOTHES

Prince

Williamson's business had grown to the extent that he needed his own building. In 1911, the same year the Moscow Chamber of Commerce was established, Williamson moved into the building that had once housed the McConnell-Maguire Store. An added attraction of Williamson's store, which now bore his name, was its restaurant. Never one to shy away from publicity, Williamson installed a huge electric sign bearing the store's name on the face of the building housing his store. Running almost the full length of the building, the sign included an ornament like a kaleidoscope that was visible for miles around Moscow.

In 1900, four years before Nat Williamson advertised his store as the Idaho's greatest, the City of Moscow had established its first City Hall. Municipal offices operated out of the McCartor building on south Main Street, and while the community was definitely becoming more sophisticated, signs of frontier life were still visible and would be for years to come. For the next quarter century, in fact, a wooden tower housing a fire bell, a large watering trough, and a long hitching rack used by farmers coming to Moscow from the surrounding area in horse-drawn wagons were located next to City Hall in its east alley.

Sophistication was also reflected by the members of what former Latah County Historical Society curator Joann C. Jones has described as a "social elite." This group of Moscow residents included successful businessmen, professionals, and those affiliated with the University of Idaho, including faculty, administrators, and their wives. Even after the loss of his business, William McConnell and wife

In 1911, Nathaniel Williamson moved his department store into the space that had formerly housed the McConnell-Maguire Company. (Courtesy LCHS.)

Louisa remained members of this circle of acquaintances that set the standard for fashion and behavior in Moscow's upper classes. Jones explains that fashion was important to the members of Moscow's elite, and they dressed in formal attire for parties and socials; men wore tails and white ties, and women came attired in evening gowns.

Just as personal fashion was important to the members of Moscow's elite so was the public expression of their standing in the community, and one of the most conspicuous symbols of their prosperity was their home. Beginning in 1885, especially after the arrival of the railroad, many members of Moscow's elite built large, elaborately decorated homes. Most were located in what was and remains one of Moscow's most prestigious neighborhoods, Fort Russell. The Fort Russell neighborhood was where Moscow's early social elite—judges, physicians, bankers, merchants, University of Idaho presidents and faculty, even a mining millionaire—built impressive new homes as a display of their economic and social status.

Among the several Moscow merchants who built new homes within what was designated the Fort Russell Historic District in 1980 was William J. McConnell. The McConnell family moved into their recently completed home on Adams Street, one block north of Third Street, on Christmas Eve, 1886. The reporters of the *Moscow Mirror* had kept Moscowans informed of the progress of the construction of the McConnell home on a nearly daily basis. On August 27,

William McConnell built this impressive home in 1886 only to lose it during the Panic of 1893. McConnell's wife Louisa and their daughters Mary and Olive pose in front of their home. (Courtesy LCHS.)

the newspaper reported that the McConnell family residence was nearly completed, adding, "Its appearance indicates comfort and elegance and we are of the opinion that when it is finished it will be a structure of which Moscow may be proud."

Mary Lind, whose Swedish parents arrived in Moscow via Minnesota in the late 1880s, worked as a "hired girl" for some of Moscow's prominent families. In her memoir *Today is Ours*, Mary's daughter Elsie Nelson recalled her mother sharing the story of her visit to the "elegant McConnell mansion" as a young woman. The "mansion" had just been completed when Mary and a girlfriend were invited to visit. According to Nelson, her mother recalled that the house was "interestingly and splendidly" furnished with lace curtains, imported rugs, oil paintings, hanging lamps, and a huge gold-framed mirror over the parlor fireplace.

Ironically, McConnell lost his home—which was placed in the National Register of Historic Places in 1974—in 1897 after suffering economic setbacks during the Panic of 1893. In 1901, physician W.A. Adair bought the house, owning it until 1935 when it was sold to Thomas Jackson. In 1940, Jackson sold the home to Frederic Church, a professor of history at the University of Idaho. Upon his death in 1966, Church bequeathed the house to Latah County for use by the Latah County Pioneer Association. In 1968, a volunteer group, the Latah County Pioneer Historical Museum, was formed to convert the house into a museum, now known as the McConnell Mansion Museum.

As Moscow entered the twentieth century, its population neared 2,500. It had an established residential district with a number of splendid homes, and its commercial community, recovering from the Panic of 1893, offered a wide range of goods and services. According to the *Illustrated History of North Idaho*, in 1901, the "business interests" of Moscow were:

> represented by five dry goods stores, three hardware stores, four drug stores, thirteen groceries, three banks, two railroads, two jewelers, three liveries, four hotels, four newspapers, two harness hops, two bakeries, three meat markets, four implement houses, one cigar factory, three millinery stores, five grain warehouses, one steam laundry, one foundry, one gents' furnishings store, one shoe store, one furniture store, two planing mills, one flour mill, one sawmill, one hospital, electric light works, and waterworks.

6. WORSHIP, ARTS, CULTURE, AND RECREATION

The *Illustrated History of North Idaho* reveals the heartiness of Moscow's "business interests" in 1901, but it does not provide a complete picture of life in Moscow during the last decades of the nineteenth century and first decades of the twentieth century. There is no ignoring the fact that people of this era worked long and hard simply to put food on the table and clothes on their backs, but it is also a fact that Moscowans somehow found the time to pursue artistic and cultural interests. They also made time for play and entertainment, and with the University of Idaho in their backyard, high on its crested hill, Moscowans established and refined institutions that have traditionally defined "civilized" society.

Before Moscow officially became Moscow, the residents of Paradise Valley had established a school. As early as 1871, teacher Noah Lieuallen held classes in a dirt-floor classroom housed in a log cabin. According to Alma Lauder Keeling:

> It is reported that [Lorettus] Haskins, [George] Tomer, and the Lieuallen brothers [Noah and Almon] hauled logs from the mountain [Moscow Mountain] and built the log schoolhouse. Since no lumber for the floor was available this side of Walla Walla, a week's journey, the men handpacked the dirt flour. Benches for the children were made of split logs with pegged legs.

Keeling notes that this school burned down in 1880. She also recalls that her mother attended school in this primitive building.

In 1897, W.G. Emery wrote *A History of Moscow, Idaho, With Sketches of Some of Its Prominent Citizens, Firms, and Corporations* as a supplement to the *Moscow Mirror*. In his history, Emery writes that Moscow's first officially designated schoolhouse was built in 1878 near the homestead of William Taylor, Alma Lauder Keeling's grandfather. The school was known as the Maguire School. Its location nearly a mile from Almon Lieuallen's Main Street Store, however, proved impractical for the majority of Moscow's inhabitants. Much to the dismay of those who lived outside of Moscow, the Moscowans submitted a petition to move the school

The students pictured here are members of what was probably Moscow High School's Class of 1899. (Courtesy LCHS.)

closer to Moscow. As the majority of Paradise Valley residents lived outside Moscow, it seemed a sure thing that the school would remain where it was.

"But," wrote Emery, "Asbury Lieuallen threw off his coat and rustled around among the floating population and by running a free bus all day between his store and the polls, carried the election." The building was not physically moved, but the people of Moscow eventually did get their own two-room, frame schoolhouse in 1884, constructed on land donated by John Russell. The site of Moscow's first schoolhouse, on the block between First and Adams and A and Jefferson Streets, two blocks northeast of Main Street, would serve as the location of the town's school as it underwent a series of changes, growing as the town's population grew. By 1888, the original school, named in honor of John Russell, became so overcrowded with energetic youngsters that a four-room addition was built.

In 1901, the Moscow Independent School District No. 5, formed in April 1888, built a new schoolhouse on the northeast corner of the block of land on which Russell School was located. Silas Imbler, described by W.G. Emery as "one of Moscow's beneficent citizens" in his historical supplement to the *Moscow Mirror*, donated the property for this school, which was named the Irving School in honor of author Washington Irving. Emery adds:

> No pains were spared to make this school second to none in the state. In this endeavor the trustees received the hearty endorsement of the citizens of Moscow. The school furniture was all of the most modern and improved manufacture. The interior of the building was so arranged that each department could be reached with the least possible confusion.

> . . . This is borne out by the fact that the entire school, numbering over
> 400 pupils has vacated the building in less than thirty seconds.

That the children could vacate the building in less than a minute must have comforted their parents in a time when fire was a constant, daily threat. Shortly, however, even this new building was overcrowded to the extent that a temporary building was secured: Emery's own photography studio on Main Street. In 1892, when this short-term measure had proven inadequate, the school board constructed a new building on Third Street, one of Moscow's major east-west arterials, to serve as a high school. Standing on the south side of Third Street between Jefferson and Adams, it was the second high school begun in Idaho at the time. Although the school was referred to as the Moscow High School, only one of the building's ten rooms was used for high school classes; the other nine served the lower grades.

More than a decade later, overcrowding in Moscow's school buildings was again a problem. In 1909, the school district built its first neighborhood elementary school. Located on Eighth Street on the eastern edge of Moscow, the Ward School, sometimes known as the Lincoln School, was a two-room wooden schoolhouse that served the school district for many years before it was sold and converted into an apartment house. Three years later, Russell School burned down. That same year, the school district built a new high school and changed the name of Moscow's first high school to the Whitworth School, in honor of a beloved teacher, Miss Isa Whitworth.

Old Clothes Day was a Moscow High School tradition for many years. Old seems to be a reference not to worn-out clothing, but to clothing representing past eras. (Courtesy LCHS.)

The 1912 Moscow High School, located almost directly across Third Street from the original high school, is an outstanding example of Progressive Era school architecture and is currently being used as Moscow's community center. In 1939, a new high school was built, again on Third Street, near the site of the original high school. In 1926, the Irving School was torn down, and on its site, a new Russell School, currently in use today, was completed in 1928.

It would take the post–World War II baby boom before Moscow would build its next school. In 1951, the Moscow School District built a new elementary school and named it in honor of teacher Lena Whitmore. As the boom reached its peak in the mid-1950s, West Park Elementary School, close to the university campus, was constructed in 1955. In 1958, on the northeastern perimeter of Moscow, the north end of the Moscow Junior High School was built. The south end was constructed in 1965. In 1968, another Moscow elementary school, McDonald, was built on Moscow's southeastern edge.

Forty years later, when it was time for the babies of the baby boomers to begin school, Moscow saw the founding of two public charter schools. The Moscow Charter School, the first charter school to be formed in the state of Idaho, was founded in 1997, and now has an enrollment of 74 in grades kindergarten through sixth. The Renaissance Public Charter School was founded in 1998 and serves nearly 60 students in grades kindergarten through 12th.

There is also a tradition of private education in Moscow, which started as early as 1908, when three Catholic nuns arrived in Moscow from Toledo, Ohio and

Teacher Lena Whitmore, shown here with her second grade at Russell School in the early 1940s, would be honored with the construction of Lena Whitmore Elementary School in 1951. (Courtesy LCHS.)

Members and coaches of the basketball squad of the Ursuline Academy pose for a team photo, c. early 1950s. (Courtesy LCHS.)

established the Ursuline Academy in the former farmhouse of Julia Moore on the northern edge of Moscow. The Ursuline Academy was both a primary school and a high school, and enrollment was inclusive, "open to all, irrespective of creed or nationality," according to the school's advertisements. In 1934, the Ursuline Academy expanded when a new high school and gymnasium were built, but due to declining enrollment, the high school closed in 1955. The next year, the parish of St. Mary's bought the academy and built a new school directly east of the original school; the school, named St. Mary's School, remains in operation today.

The Moscow area's first Seventh-Day Adventist academy was founded in 1917 in Viola, a small community north of Moscow. The church would later move that school to several other locations before settling on its present one in Spangle, Washington. In 1954, however, a new Seventh-Day Adventist school, the Palouse Hills Seventh-Day Adventist Academy, serving the elementary grades, opened its doors from its location near the camas fields of the Nez Perce. Roughly 30 years later, the private Christian school Logos School was established. From its original 18 students in 1981, the school now serves several 100 students in grades preschool through 12th.

Besides schools, the Lieuallen brothers were instrumental in establishing the first church in Paradise Valley. Noah Lieuallen, in fact, was an ordained Baptist minister, and Almon Lieuallen donated land on the southeast corner of First and Jackson Streets for the construction of Moscow's first church, the Zion Baptist Church. Before the construction of this church in 1878, the members of the community's various congregations met wherever they could, including Moscow's dirt-floor schoolhouse.

For Moscow, the decade of the 1880s was not so much a great awakening as a period in which the mainstream Christian denominations established their presence in a new community. The members of the First United Methodist Church completed their first church in 1886, and seven years later, built another. Built in 1903 of native basalt, the Methodist church is on the National Register of Historic Places and is one of Moscow's landmark buildings. Its spire, in fact, is a feature of the official logo of the City of Moscow. Sadly, William C. Lauder, the uncle of Alma Lauder Keeling, was killed in a dynamite blast at the quarry southeast of Moscow while supervising the extraction of the stone used in the church.

The first Presbyterian church building was constructed in Moscow in 1885 on Van Buren Street; it also served as an elementary and preparatory school. A member of the University of Idaho's first commencement class, Arthur Adair, graduated from this academy. The Episcopalians built their first church in 1899 on the corner of First and Jefferson Streets. William J. McConnell donated the land. This building was destroyed by fire in 1937 and replaced with the present building in 1938. Until 1975, when its present church on C Street was constructed, members of the Seventh-Day Adventist congregation met in a series of churches located on the corner of Third and Almon Streets.

Until 1961, there were two Lutheran churches serving the Moscow area. Thirteen Swedish immigrants organized the First Lutheran Church on October 12, 1884. The Swedish-speaking Lutherans built a church in 1889 on the corner of Second and Van Buren. In 1905, this building was relocated to Third and Howard for use by the Norwegian-speaking Lutherans who had organized Our Savior's Lutheran Church in 1902. In 1906, the Swedish Lutherans moved into a new church on the corner of Second and Van Buren that is now the home of Moscow's Unitarian Universalist Church. The two Lutheran communities merged in 1961 as the Emmanuel Lutheran Church. Their church is located on the western end of A Street.

Before 1882, the Roman Catholics of Paradise Valley held Mass in their homes, and the visit of Archbishop Charles Seghers on June 25, 1882 is, therefore, acknowledged as the origin of the Roman Catholic community in Moscow. The first Catholic church building in Moscow was built in 1886 on land purchased from William J. McConnell. In 1930, the new St. Mary's Church was dedicated; it is located on the corner of First and Polk Streets. A second Catholic church, St. Augustine's Catholic Center, was built in 1966 on the University of Idaho campus.

Also on the University of Idaho campus is the Institute of Religion built in 1928 by the Church of Jesus Christ of Latter-Day Saints. It was the only such institute in the world at that time. Currently, there are three LDS wards in Moscow, each part of the Pullman, Washington stake. In 1999, the church organized a new stake in Moscow: the Moscow, Idaho University stake, which includes six wards.

The Church of the Nazarene began in Moscow in 1917, holding services in several places, including Eggan Hall, until their own church building on the northeast corner of Third and Almon Streets was completed around 1920. Construction on the congregation's present church, an exceptional structure round in design, began in 1967, with remodeling completed in 1986 and 2000.

The roots of the Unitarian Universalist Church of the Palouse, which meets in Moscow in a church originally built by the members of the Swedish Lutheran congregation, go back to the 1940s when fellowships in Moscow and in Pullman, Washington were first organized. In 1953, the two groups merged informally, and in 1956, the Moscow-Pullman Unitarian Fellowship was legally incorporated. In 1985, after several years of meeting in a variety of places, the fellowship bought the Swedish Lutheran Church. Following its dedication on October 17, 1985, the fellowship officially became the Unitarian Universalist Church of the Palouse.

The members of Moscow's Unitarian Universalist Church meet in a building two blocks east of Moscow's current public library. The first building in Moscow to be used solely as a public library was constructed in 1906 with funds from the Carnegie Library Endowment. The Carnegie library was built directly south of Russell School on the site of Moscow's first Catholic church. In 1983, an annex was added to the original library building.

Moscow's first church was the Zion Baptist built on land donated by Almon Asbury Lieuallen in 1881. It was located on the southeast corner of First and Jackson. (Courtesy LCHS.)

The establishment of Moscow's public library dates back to 1885 when the Moscow Women's Reading Room Society was formed. The original location of this library is unknown, but it is known that in 1890, the library with its collection of around 1,500 volumes was moved to the law office of J.C. Elder. Elder served as librarian, and he must have spent more time on his law practice than on overseeing the library because the society's annual report shows that the number of volumes in the collection had dropped to 1,000.

In 1901, Moscow's reading women took it upon themselves to expand the community's library services. A subcommittee was formed with members from Moscow's two most prominent women's clubs, the Pleiades Club and the Moscow Historical Club. The wife of university president Franklin Gault and six other faculty wives formed the Pleiades Club in 1892 as a reading club. President Gault suggested the seven ladies name their club after the seven-starred Pleiades constellation, and in 1895, when the club joined the Idaho State Federation of Women's Club, it became one of the first federated women's clubs in the state.

The Moscow Historical Club, originally the Ladies Historical Club, was organized in 1895 to provide Moscow women with a more populist alternative to the Pleiades Club, composed as it was exclusively of the wives of university faculty and administrators. Formed by Mrs. C.W. McCurdy, herself the wife of a university of Idaho professor and member of the Pleiades Club, the Moscow Historical Club at first concerned itself with the study of history and literature, but went on to become a catalyst for cultural development in the community. While the Latah County Historical Society absorbed the Moscow Historical Club in 1983, the Pleiades Club is still active in the cultural life of Moscow.

Members of the library subcommittee literally went door to door soliciting funds to finance a better library for Moscow. Their initial attempts harvested

Thanks to the ladies of Moscow, the community received funding from the Carnegie Library Endowment to construct its public library building in 1906. (Courtesy LCHS.)

Members of the Pleiades Club in 1921 are as follows: Mmes. Truitt, Von Ende, Parsons, Barrows, Little, Hume, Upham, Lewis, Axtell, and Eldridge. (Courtesy LCHS.)

$340, and with it, the women established the Moscow Free Library and Reading Room and rented office space on the second floor of the Brown Building on Main Street. After paying the rent of $3 per month, the women purchased a stove for $15, 1,000 pounds of coal, a 15¢ coal shovel, a table, and 12 chairs. Initially, the library was open two afternoons and two evenings each week. Sometime later, the rent was increased to $8 per month, and in October 1902, approximately 100 books were added to the collection at a cost of $74. Magazines subscriptions were added that same year.

In 1903, Mrs. C.N. Little, Mrs. C.L. Butterfield, Mrs. Charles Shields, and Mrs. J.H. Forney, along with city council member Mr. Patton, formed Moscow's first library board. That same year, the library's first librarian, Etta B. McGuire, was hired; she served as librarian even after her marriage to Mr. McBride, sometimes full time and sometimes part time, until her death in 1950. By 1904, the women had become dissatisfied with the single-room library and contacted the Andrew Carnegie Library Endowment for assistance in financing the construction of a new building. In response to Carnegie's positive reply, the women selected a site and purchased the 85-foot by 90-foot lot from A. Dygert. In order to meet the endowment's requirement that the community fund the operation of the library, the citizens of Moscow approved a special tax in 1904, and construction of the building began after receiving the Carnegie award of $6,000.

Located on what is now the corner of Second and Jefferson Streets, the library was completed in 1906; it is one of the few examples of Spanish mission architecture in the Northwest and is still in use today by the Moscow branch of the Latah County Library District. After the library building was completed and opened to patrons, 64 pieces of furniture, including four dozen chairs and six white oak tables, were purchased for the amount of $564. However, before the library could be used as a library, it became a makeshift classroom for students enrolled in the university's preparatory school, following the Administration Building's destruction by fire in 1906. Until April 1907, the library was a shared-use building. The preparatory school classes met daily until 3:30 p.m., and beginning at 4 p.m., the building served as a library.

In addition to its library, Moscowans can also thank the Moscow Historical Club for developing the town's oldest park, East City Park. In 1882, Henry Baker, Robert Barton, E.D. Boyer, Herbert Clark, Charles Howard, Charles Moore, Frank Paine, John Paine, and William Simpson donated nearly 7 acres to the City of Moscow for a park on the community's eastern edge. In 1891, F.E. Mix and his son William donated and supervised the planting of the park's first trees; however, further development of the park was not taken until 1910 when the women of the Moscow Historical Club took up the cause, raising money for landscaping, benches, tables, and pathways.

Today, East City Park is one of Moscow's most used and beloved parks and is the site of both cultural and recreational activities. Just as Moscowans have historically valued their cultural institutions, so have they valued recreation. Making a living was hard, physical, grueling work for most people in Moscow's early days, and recreation was soon recognized as an important respite from the demands of daily existence.

Hunting and fishing, often necessary in order to put food on the table, were two commonplace outdoor recreational activities in Latah County during its early years. As historian Mary Reed explains, hunting was not restricted to men; in her oral history, Latah County resident Naomi Boll Parker recalled that while her mother never hunted elk or deer, as did Naomi and her brothers, she did hunt grouse and pheasants, finding it a pleasant break from the tedium of homestead life. Parker's mother also fished, as did many early residents of Latah County. Because many of the streams were located in remote areas of the county, sportspeople also had to know how to camp. And camping trips were often taken for their own sake as opportunities to enjoy and explore the wooded areas of Latah County. In the late summer, huckleberry-picking trips were especially popular.

Those not wishing to rough it could still enjoy the outdoors. Several picnic spots were developed close to Moscow on nearby Moscow Mountain. One of the best known was Idler's Rest, originally the site of summer homes owned by several Moscow residents. The names of these summerhouses were charming: Dingley Dell, Tarryawhile, Dewdrop Inn, Linger Longer, Camp Kenjockety.

During the 1890s, Americans discovered exercise for the sake of exercise, and being Americans, they threw themselves wholeheartedly into the pursuit of healthful living and physical culture. In Moscow, recreational activities such as skating, sledding, walking, camping, and bicycling were just as popular as they were in other parts of the nation. University of Idaho English professor William

Banks, in a letter to a friend dated January 11, 1952, attests to the enduring popularity of winter recreation in Moscow with the following wintertime description: "Many figures in snow suits walking home from sliding parties, walking in the street with the towering dikes of snow on the edges, wary of cars but gay."

During the summer, bicycling was as prevalent as were sledding and skating in the winter, and in Moscow's early days, bicycles became important status symbols. Individuals without bicycles were as hopelessly out-of-step with the times as are those who now remain "unconnected" to the internet. Floyd Cochrane was on the cutting edge of recreational technology when he ordered Moscow's first bicycle, and Jack Lieuallen, the son of Almon Lieuallen, purchased the second. Floyd and Jack's bicycles were the large front wheel type. Tom Reese and Roland Hodgins, partners in a drugstore business, purchased the first conventional bike.

The pleasure of devoting a Moscow summer day to cycling is well described by Professor Banks in an August 13, 1943 letter to his wife Mary. He writes that he and their son David took to their bikes one afternoon:

> and rode over to watch Bob Walls at work on his new addition. Left Bob's and rode over to Beecher's, remembered they were in Spokane. So we set out for the country in the bright fresh air. We followed the clouds north on the highway for a couple of miles then came home and got dinner. After that we set out for the Hoags, but they too were gone. We admired their view, really breathtaking, then went back through their big garden to the bikes on the lower road, visited with Greg Sohn and

Three Moscow ladies show off their beautiful bicycles at the turn of the twentieth century. Bikes were very popular at this time. (Courtesy LCHS.)

his Dalmatian pup, rode down to the U.P. tracks and followed the switch engine and a few box cars down the cinder siding among the warehouses. The engineer was willing to swap the engine for my bike if I would finish his evening's work.

Roller skating was another popular activity, and for many years, a public rink was located in the Main Street building owned by Michael J. Shields. During the winter, ice skating on the area's frozen creeks and ponds was a favorite pastime, a tradition that is continued today at the Palouse Rotary Ice Rink, located on the grounds of the Latah County Fair. In 1909, merchant Nathaniel Williamson opened Moscow's first swimming pool, the Natatorium, in a former fruit packing and cold storage building located on Asbury Street. Local folklore says that the ghost of a child who drowned in the pool haunts the present establishment at this location.

Moscowans also have been longtime participants in organized sports. As early as 1885, Moscow had community baseball teams. In addition, athletic competitions for the community's sprightly young people were routinely organized. One of the most successful contestants in these competitions was Alfred C. Gilbert. The son of Alfred T. Gilbert, president of Moscow's First

Members of the Lundquist, Ramstedt, and Johnson families enjoy a picnic on Moscow Mountain, c. 1900. (Courtesy LCHS.)

This is a photograph of the interior of Hodgins Drug Store, founded by Roland Hodgins and Tom Reese. The fellow was probably an employee of the store, which has been in continuous operation in the same location since 1892. (Courtesy LCHS.)

National Bank, Alfred C. Gilbert would go on to win a gold medal in the pole vault in the 1912 Olympics in London. Gilbert is perhaps better known as *The Man Who Changed How Boys and Toys Were Made*, the title of a new biography of Gilbert written by Bruce Watson. Gilbert was the founder of the A.C. Gilbert Toy Company, which manufactured a world-famous line of toys, including Erector sets, American Flyer electric trains, chemistry sets, microscopes, and other educational toys.

Gilbert has described his childhood in Moscow as one of the happiest ever. Known by the nickname of "Gillie," which he hated, Gilbert was a force to be reckoned with. As a ten-year-old, he and his buddies organized the Red Flag Fire Department to respond to actual fires in Moscow. The Red Flag Fire Department was quickly disbanded—what with one thing and another—such as the time one of the gang known as "Sugar Puss" for his fondness for sweets got stuck trying to slide his hefty-sized body down the makeshift fire pole in the Gilbert barn.

The Gilbert barn was also the home of the Moscow Athletic Club, which Gilbert formed when he was 12 years old. He installed a punching bag, climbing ropes, and a set of Indian clubs. Gilbert spent hours perfecting his boxing style,

Hardworking harvest hands pause to take in nourishment and to have their picture taken. Recreation was valued as much as hard work in Moscow. (Courtesy LCHS.)

and at one point ran away with a traveling minstrel show, calling himself "The Champion Boy Bag Puncher of the World." Gilbert's father retrieved his son in Lewiston. At the age of 14, Gilbert organized track meets, and it was his skill as an athlete that took him away from Moscow. In 1901, he left to attend preparatory school near Portland, Oregon.

Just as Americans threw themselves into participatory sports, they also became devout spectators of sports, and in Moscow, watching the Vandals (the athletic teams of the University of Idaho) has long been an important part of the recreational life of students and townspeople. The university held its first athletic event in 1893, hosting a competition with nearby Washington State College, later known as Washington State University. This competition was the start of a rivalry between the two schools that lasted for nearly 60 years. One of the most famous traditions of this rivalry was the "Loser's Walk," started in 1938. Washington State University is located in Pullman, Washington, only 8 miles west of Moscow. From 1938 to 1968, students of the school whose team lost the football game held annually between the two institutions would walk home from their respective stadiums.

Just as recreation has long been part of life in the Paradise Valley, so has entertainment. The valley's earliest inhabitants, the Nez Perce, combined business with pleasure when they conducted horse races during the camas harvest season. After the displacement of the Nez Perce, horse racing continued. During the 1890s, the Latah County Agricultural Fair Association staged horse races, including the Spring Speed, on their track on the northeastern edge of Moscow near what is now Mountain View Park. Today's Latah County Fair is a descendant of these events. Near the site of the present-day Latah County fairgrounds was the homestead of Frank White. Barnstorming planes would land in White's field, offering rides to anyone seeking adventure, at a cost of 1¢ per pound.

For the less adventurous, there was the vicarious thrill of vaudeville and cinema. One of Moscow's earliest entertainment halls was the GAR Hall on East Third Street. Built in the 1880s, the hall—with its stage, kerosene footlights, and 600 seats—hosted traveling theater troupes and minstrel shows. Fire destroyed the hall around 1905. Early in the 1900s, photographer Halvar Eggan operated a dance hall, roller-skating rink, and auditorium out of the ground floor of the building he owned on Third Street, directly west of the former GAR Hall. Eggan Hall was torn down in the 1940s. Those seeking highbrow entertainment could find it in the 500-seat Moscow Opera House, which was destroyed by fire in 1908.

In 1892, the Moscow Businessman's Club built the Moscow City Club. Located on the corner of First and Jackson Streets, in what has become one of Moscow's most notable structures, the Moscow City Club served as a place for the members of Moscow's first social club to gather. On the ground floor were a private bar, a card room and library, and a dining room and kitchen. The second floor was used exclusively as a ballroom, and a small tower was constructed on the second floor to serve as a bandstand. The building, however, was not a social center for long. In 1896, the Elks took over the building until vacating it in 1904; its main floor then served as the home of the Moscow Business College until 1908 when physician Warner H. Carithers converted it into the Inland Empire Hospital.

After the invention of moving pictures, Moscow also had several movie theaters, including the Orpheum, the Strand, and the Casino, which served every

In 1958, long after the Natatorium (Moscow's first swimming pool) closed, members of Moscow's swim team pose with their trophies. (Courtesy LCHS.)

107

child admitted a free ice cream cone. The first theater in Moscow to show movies was the Crystal Theater, located on Main Street. The site of the Crystal would become the location of the Kenworthy Theater built in 1926 by owner Milton Kenworthy. Now the home of the Kenworthy Performing Arts Centre, the structure was placed in the National Register of Historic Places in 2001.

Those seeking fraternity rather than entertainment could find it at one of several fraternal organizations established during Moscow's early years. The first lodge to be established in Moscow was Paradise Lodge No. 17 of the Ancient Free and Accepted Masons, organized in 1885. Moscow Lodge No. 31 of the Independent Order of Odd Fellows was organized in 1889, and the Moscow Idaho Elks Lodge No. 249 of the Benevolent and Protective Order of the Elks was charted in June 1893. This last lodge is the oldest in the state of Idaho.

Of course, a different type of men's organization also had its place in Moscow's history as it did in the history of other American frontier towns. Moscow's red-light district was located not quite on the "wrong side of the tracks," but close to it and just as close to the city jail. As many as four "female boarding houses," named the same as their street addresses, were situated near the intersection of A

Moscowans have long watched University of Idaho athletes compete. This 1908 athlete proudly wears his "I" sweater. (Courtesy LCHS.)

Mason A. Cornwall, a Moscow financier, founded the Latah County Agricultural Fair Association in 1888. (Courtesy LCHS.)

and Jackson Streets. According to local historian Lillian Otness, the "classiest" brothel in Moscow was located at 304 West A Street.

In Moscow, prostitution was prohibited by City Ordinance 19 and anyone convicted of establishing or maintaining a bawdy house was punishable with "a fine of not less than twenty dollars nor more than two hundred dollars with the costs of said action or in default of the judgment of such fine by imprisonment in the Town Jail not less than 10 days nor more than 90 days." If convicted, anyone "who shall frequent, reside in or become an inmate of any bawdy house" was subject to "a fine of not less than ten dollars nor more than one hundred dollars."

The prostitution ordinance was enforced in Moscow in the same ambivalent manner as were similar ordinances throughout the nation, but in 1891, Moscow's police judge resigned after a reporter for the *Spokesman-Review*, a Spokane, Washington newspaper, revealed "Moscow's Municipal Scandal." According to the reporter:

> Judge Griffin and Marshal Robbins had issued a license to each of the
> fourteen women here for the sum of $10, giving them the right to keep
> and be inmates of houses of ill fame. The receipts, which have both the
> judge's signature and that of the marshal, give the women the privilege
> of plying their business between September 1 and October 1. This act
> has brought down upon the heads of those officials the indignation of
> the respectable class of Moscow citizens.

In his defense, Judge Griffin claimed the $10 was a fine, not a license.

This is the Kenworthy Theater in 1949 before owner Milton Kenworthy remodeled it. The theater was placed in the National Register of Historic Places in 2001. (Courtesy LCHS.)

Prostitution was illegal in Moscow, but the world's oldest profession and law enforcement soon reached an understanding. Arrest records from 1892 to 1896 reveal that the same people were routinely arrested, but that their fines were smaller than the ordinance specified. Arrest records also reveal that prostitutes were rounded up in groups and arrested in six-month intervals. There are only two records, however, of the apprehension of women commonly known to be madams.

Prostitution, despite its illegality, was a part of Moscow's social life. At the other end of the social spectrum were public celebrations, such as parades and galas. As early as 1885, even before Moscow was officially incorporated, townspeople were hosting gala Fourth of July celebrations. Lawrence Smith, writing of his childhood in Moscow at the turn of the twentieth century, explained that Moscow's Fourth of July celebrations were not only extravagant but loud, too. On the morning of Independence Day, blacksmith Marion Collins "used two anvils, one on top of the other. He would place black powder between the two anvils and when this powder ignited—I swear that you could have hear the resulting bang as far away as Troy, Idaho."

Noise, according to historian Lillian Otness, was only one characteristic of Moscow's Fourth of July celebrations. Parades, music, oratory, picnic lunches, races, contests, baseball, dancing, fireworks, along with heat, fatigue, and patriotic fervor, were also "ingredients" on one of the biggest days of the year, equal only to Christmas for its celebratory mood. Moscow author Carol Ryrie Brink wrote in *A Chain of Hands* that the Fourth of July was the "biggest day of the year," adding, "Fourth of July was sunshine and noise and company; it was bliss and danger and sentiments that lifted and tossed the heart."

The *Moscow Mirror* claimed that 5,000 people attended the 1885 Fourth of July celebration. One of the fixtures of this parade, and other Fourth of July parades, was the Liberty Car. According to the July 10, 1885 edition of the paper, "The Liberty Car, so tastefully gotten up under the management of Mrs. W.W. Langdon and Mrs. R.H. Barton, was one of the grand features of the day, with its fifty richly attired girls surrounding the Goddess of Liberty, drawn by six spanking blooded horses and headed by the Moscow Silver Cornet Band, accompanied the games and sports and was the great feature of beauty all the Fourth."

In *A Chain of Hands*, Brink recorded the Fourth of July celebrations of her youth in Moscow in the early 1900s. She explained that Moscow prepared for the celebration weeks in advance, and townspeople began celebrating the holiday as dawn cracked forth. "Shivering in the summer dawn," she wrote, "we rushed out to explode our first firecrackers. Suddenly the town was crackling and popping from end to end."

Brink also wrote of the exhilaration of participating in Moscow's Fourth of July parade. She recalled that her aunt and the mothers of the girls with whom she was walking in the parade:

Since the days of the Eggan Hall, with its dance floor, Moscowans have enjoyed popular music. In the late 1950s, the famed Duke Ellington performed at the Moscow Elks Lodge. (Courtesy LCHS.)

put on their best hats and walked down to Main Street to see us ride by, in line with the five business floats, the high school band, the Civil War veterans, the decorated horseback riders and bicyclists, the buggies full of politicians and speakers of the day, the Latah County Pioneers, the Eagles and the Woodmen of the World, the Ladies' Auxiliary of the G.A.R. and the girls chorus.

The parade concluded at East City Park where speeches were made and lunch served. Brink explained:

> Here the mothers shone. Hampers and bags of food appeared; everything was set out on long tables made of planks laid across trestles. Cold fried chicken, deviled eggs and potato salad, lemonade and chocolate cake . . . tiny, cold baking-powder biscuits filled with devilled ham; the wonderful six-layer strawberry shortcakes, made the day before and chilled, that were cut into wedge-shaped slices, served up like ordinary cake. And the watermelons, oh, the watermelons!

Moscow continued to hold annual Fourth of July celebrations until 1917 when World War I put a stop to the festivities. Nor was a celebration held in 1918, but in 1919, with the end of the war, the custom returned. A Moscow

In its early days, Moscow held rambunctious Fourth of July celebrations that lasted for several days. The festivities include a horse show at which stockmen showed off their prize draft horses. (Courtesy LCHS.)

Townspeople have always participated in University of Idaho celebrations, such as the annual Homecoming Parade. The parade is held on Moscow's Main Street.

newspaper, the *Idaho Post*, reported on June 27, 1919 that a dancing pavilion with a 50-foot by 90-foot dance floor was being built on Main Street between Fourth and Fifth Streets for the 1919 celebration. But what really drew the crowds was the chance to see an airplane. Pilot Jay M. Fetters of Spokane made several flights over Moscow during its three-day celebration, and at one point, he dropped flowers over the university campus as a memorial to the students killed in World War I.

Moscowans also participated in university celebrations such as homecoming parades and, during the 1920s, pajama parties. In his history of the University of Idaho, *Beacon to Mountain and Plain*, Rafe Gibbs describes a pajama party:

> Wearing pajamas of wildly assorted colors (over other garments, because it was generally cold), the students serpentined through campus and town on the eve of the Homecoming football game and other major athletic events. Singing and shouting with Pep Band accompaniment, the students moved through dormitories and fraternity and sorority houses, picking up recruits as they progressed to Main Street. They twined in and out of theatres, up Third Street and eventually into the Faculty Club. . . . From the club, the pajama-paraders moved back to the corner of Third and Main streets, where a pep rally was held.

The corner of Third and Main hosted more than pep rallies. For many years, on the east side of the intersection stood a popcorn wagon operated by Fred D.

113

Gelwick; it was a popular fixture of downtown Moscow for many years. Fred's son Jerry would move his father's business indoors to a building on Third Street where it became a popular snack bar, newsstand, and hangout for high school and college students. It was popular too with an even younger set of Moscowans. In an August 20, 1943 letter to his wife Mary, then in Seattle, Professor William Banks recounts how their ten-year-old daughter Martha burst into his study with the following request: "Daddy, will you let us go to Jerry's for cones?"

After 1909, another popular place to hangout was the Pastime Pool Hall and Lunch Room on south Main Street; for Moscow men, it was both a social place and an employment office. Anybody seeking or needing temporary help at harvest or other times would check in at the Pastime Pool Hall. It was open 24 hours a day and was the only establishment in town that served food at all hours. When the pool hall was sold, the key to the front door could not be found; it hadn't been needed because the door had never been locked.

Fred Gelwick's popcorn wagon was a fixture of downtown Moscow for many years. (Courtesy LCHS.)

7. Moscow from 1900 to 1950

The suspension of the community Fourth of July celebration in 1917 and 1918 seems a clear signal that Moscow was no longer an isolated frontier village. During the early decades of the twentieth century, as the United States assumed the mantle of world leadership, Moscowans, like all Americans, would come to bear the responsibilities of citizenship in a nation seeking to shape its destiny on the world stage. But the unlocked door of the Pastime Pool Hall is also a sign that national events did not entirely eliminate Moscow's local culture.

Perhaps there are no better portraits of everyday life in Moscow during the last years of the nineteenth century and the first years of the twentieth century than those drawn by one of its own daughters. Carol Ryrie Brink, born in Moscow in 1895, would become the town's most acclaimed writer and the first Idaho author to receive national recognition. Ryrie, who married Raymond Brink, a professor of mathematics, shortly after her graduation from college, is perhaps best known for her children's classic *Caddie Woodlawn* for which she received the Newbery Award for excellence in children's literature in 1936 and the Lewis Carroll Shelf Award in 1959. In 1956, she received the Friends of American Writers Award, and ten years later, she earned both the McKnight Family Foundation Medal and the National League of American Pen Women award.

While Brink's contributions to children's literature are well known, she also wrote for adults. Among her most enduring novels is the Idaho trilogy—*Buffalo Coat, Strangers in the Forest*, and *Snow in the River*. Of the trilogy, *Buffalo Coat*, published in 1944, and *Snow in the River*, published 20 years later, examine the intertwined history of Brink's family and that of Moscow. Carol Ryrie was born in December 1895 in Moscow to Alexander and Henrietta Ryrie. She was delivered by her maternal grandfather, physician William A. Watkins, an influential member of the Moscow community whose strong personality either repulsed or charmed his fellow Moscowans.

Buffalo Coat is the story of a small western town, much like Moscow, during the period from 1885 through 1902. Many of the events in the novel are based upon actual events in Moscow's history, such as the suicide pact of a married doctor and the young daughter of the Methodist minister. But the novel also recounts the murder of Brink's grandfather William Watkins. In August 1901, while returning

Nationally recognized author Carol Ryrie Brink was born in Moscow in 1895. She was awarded the Newbery Medal in 1938 for the children's classic Caddie Woodlawn. *(Courtesy LCHS.)*

to his medical office on Second Street, Dr. Watkins was shot to death by a mentally ill young man named William Steffen.

Fleeing to his family's farm on the northwest corner of Mountain View Road and White Avenue, Steffen shot merchant George Creighton in the arm and fatally wounded Deputy Sheriff George Cool. Steffen would later die in a shoot-out with authorities on the family homestead. Although the official cause of death was a self-inflicted gunshot wound, it is disputed whether Steffen took his own life or was killed by police in the exchange of gunfire.

While the death of her grandfather was fictionalized in *Buffalo Coat*, *Snow in the River* was Brink's most autobiographical work. *Snow in the River* was a difficult book for Brink to write, for it was the retelling of the events surrounding the suicide of her mother in 1905. After Brink's father died of tuberculosis in 1900, her mother hastily married a local businessman, Nat Brown. Historian Mary Reed, now director of the Latah County Historical Society, is an authority on the life and works of Carol Ryrie Brink, and she describes Nat Brown as a complete scoundrel who drank and socialized to excess. With *Snow in the River*, Brink faced the tragedy of her mother's death while placing it within the context of the world in which she lived, a small town filled with ordinary people striving to balance selfishness and altruism.

116

Brink's portrayals of Moscow and its residents, when both she and the community were young, are depicted with sympathy and understanding, and they are valuable for the way they captured the spirit of a place at a particular point in time. In 1890, Moscow had a population of 2,000 people; in 1910, there were over twice that many people living with its boundaries, and during the period from 1900 to 1940, Moscow would move beyond its genesis as a frontier village to develop into a progressive community with contacts throughout the nation and the world.

As in communities throughout the nation, progress was not achieved without a few growing pains, as differing points of view vied for control of public policy and resources. During the first decade of the twentieth century, support for Progressive Era reforms and innovations grew as Americans acknowledged and sought remedy for the gross social, economic, and political inequities manifested in the extravagance of the Gilded Era. One of the social reforms associated with Progressivism was the temperance movement.

Representing the evils of intemperance was an institution that had been an essential part of frontier life: the saloon. In its early days, Moscow had plenty of saloons—as many saloons as churches, quipped the local residents—and one of its most famous saloon keepers was Fred Alfs, whose saloon bore his name. There were other saloons as well: the Wonder Bar, the Free Coinage Saloon, the Club Saloon, the Idaho Saloon, the Headlight Saloon, the Mammoth Saloon (with its back-alley bawdy house business), to name a few. In addition to its saloons, there was a brewery, of course. In 1902, Bavarian immigrant Ferdinand Francl had assumed ownership of the Moscow Brewery, which at that time had been operating only occasionally. Between 1904 and 1908, Francl put the brewery back on its feet, preparing high-quality products that he advertised as "pure, no chemicals used."

Moscowans would enjoy Francl's dark Bock beer for only four years because on August 5, 1908, the City of Moscow went "dry." Leading the temperance movement in Moscow were members of the Women Christian Temperance Union, including Clara Payne Grove, who served the organization at the local and state level for many years, and many of the town's clergymen, including Reverend Luce of the First Methodist Church and Reverend Orrich of the Christian church. One argument most frequently used in support of prohibition acknowledged the importance of the University of Idaho to Moscow. Reverend J.C. Abels pointed out, in the April 28, 1908 edition of the *Star-Mirror*, that "Moscow depends on the growth of the University and Moscow owes the University a dry town."

In the April 7, 1908 *Moscow Star-Mirror*, Jennie R. Headly is quoted as saying that the goal of the town's temperance activists was to "make Moscow as dry as Death Valley." To achieve this goal, temperance activists staged a series of public meetings. The first was held on April 12. Between 800 and 900 people gathered in the Methodist church to express their support of prohibition. From this meeting came a petition calling for the closing of saloons and a request to revoke

117

the licenses for the sale or manufacture of "intoxicating liquors." On April 26, another prohibition rally was held; those present voted 489 to 19 to present the prohibition petition to the city council.

In response, the city council called for a referendum, leaving it up to the people of Moscow to make the decision. According to brewing historian Herman W. Ronnenberg, on the day of the election, August 5, "dry forces marched little children down Main Street carrying banner printed with dry slogans." Of a total of 1,206 voters, 814 voted for prohibition; 392 were against. Having heard the voice of the people, the city council then passed an anti-liquor ordinance, prohibiting the sale or donation of malt liquor, but not its manufacture, surprisingly. The ordinance also made it unlawful to drink or be drunk except in one's own home.

Apparently believing that prohibition would be instituted, Francl had begun to retool his business and was producing a non-alcoholic grape beverage; however, his post-prohibition plans were for naught because the Moscow Brewery was destroyed by fire on July 29. In the weeks before and after the brewery fire, there had been a series of suspicious fires throughout Moscow that were believed to be the work of a young man by the name of Groff. Described by Ronnenberg as a "recluse who read the Bible and wrote poetry incessantly," Groff was arrested for starting the fires. However, he was not taken to trial, but was committed to the state mental hospital in Orofino.

For nearly 30 years, until December 1933 when the 18th Amendment to the United States Constitution was repealed, Moscow was a dry town, which is not to say liquor was nowhere to be found. Home possession of alcohol was not unlawful; advertisements for home delivery of beer by breweries from Colfax and Spokane were run in the *Moscow Star-Mirror*, and saloons sold near beer until that was later prohibited. Furthermore, the illegal distillation industry was not unknown despite Moscow's "sober, high class, law abiding citizenry," as attorney and future community leader Abe Goff described his fellow residents in an oral history conducted in the mid-1970s. In fact, Goff was a young lawyer in Moscow during the Prohibition era. He began his career defending bootleggers and moonshiners as a court-appointed lawyer.

Organized bootleggers who brought liquor in from Canada generally had their own lawyers; therefore, most of Goff's clients were poor moonshiners, operating small copper stills in the remote timbered areas of Latah County. These distillation "entrepreneurs" were occasionally picked up by Latah County sheriffs. Goff recalls that some of his clients tried to explain to sheriffs that the mash they had discovered was used to feed their pigs—how the sugar got into it was a mystery. One of Goff's favorite stories featured Pat Malone, who gained fame as the marshal of Bovill, a community in the timbered part of northeastern Latah County. According to Goff, Marshal Malone apprehended several lumberjacks with bottles of illegal liquor, and on the way to jail, the lumberjacks suggested they all have some of the seized whiskey. "Well, Pat was a good natured Irishman," said Goff, "by the time they got to the Justice of the Peace, they drank up all the liquor." With no "evidence," there was no case.

Longtime University of Idaho art professor Alf Dunn also encountered illegal liquor as a student at the University of Idaho in the early 1930s. Dunn worked his way through school by painting signs for sign painter Al Crisp, who Dunn describes as Moscow's only bootlegger. Dunn recalls one Sunday when Crisp revealed the secrets of illegal distillation. Into a big washtub in a room within a local cabinet shop, Crisp had emptied 5 gallons of grain alcohol. Into the alcohol, Crisp dumped well-fried cherry pits and oak shavings; the pits gave the liquid the right color, and the oak chips gave it an aged, oak barrel flavor.

"Over the top," said Dunn in an oral history conducted by the Latah County Historical Society, "like using a magic wand—he [Crisp] had a slat of clear white pine he was moving back and forth over the surface which was beaded with drops of oil." Crisp explained that the oil was fusel oil that would "give you the blind staggers if we don't get it off." After bottling the booze, Crisp hid the bottles around the bases of a number of outdoor posters located throughout Latah County. "That was his distribution system," said Dunn. Marketing was done word of mouth, and those purchasing the hooch for $2 a bottle included University of Idaho students.

The same year the sale of liquor was prohibited, there was electricity in the air, if not literally then metaphorically. In 1908, the Spokane and Inland Electric Railway arrived in Moscow, locating its depot on the corner of Almon and A Streets in northwestern Moscow. The Spokane and Inland Electric was indeed an

It is difficult to say if Moscow attorney Abe Goff (left) is presenting Dwight Eisenhower with an Idaho trout or if it's the other way around. (Courtesy LCHS.)

119

electric line, and it ran between Moscow and Spokane with branches to Colfax, Washington, and Coeur d'Alene, Idaho. Once one of the longest interurban lines in the nation, the Spokane and Inland Electric provided "soot-free service" between Moscow and Spokane, as well as electricity for Viola, a rural community north of Moscow, until 1943.

In 1910, Moscow still could not legally offer its population of nearly 4,000 a mug of beer, but it did provide its citizens a wide range of goods and services that, while not quite comparable to Walla Walla, was nonetheless impressive for a settlement not yet 50 years old. According to the *R.L. Polk Business Directory of Idaho, 1910–11*, Moscow had 23 retail stores, including one florist, five confectionaries, four drugstores, two jewelry stores, three dairies, one bookstore, and one automobile dealer. Among the 32 service providers listed in the directory were three banks, thirteen real estate agents, three insurance agencies, one collection agency, one mining broker, four dressmakers, two theaters, one billiard parlor, one undertaker, three plumbers, one horse dealer, one well driller, and four fruit growers. The professions were well represented too, with fourteen lawyers, twelve physicians, two osteopaths, three dentists, two veterinarians, and three music teachers.

A year later, in 1911, Moscow's first federal building was erected on the northeast corner of Third and Washington Streets. The building, which housed Moscow's post office, was Moscow's federal building for over six decades. (A new federal building was constructed between Fourth and Fifth Streets in 1974.) Perhaps it was this fine example of Federalist architecture, which now serves as City Hall, that served as inspiration to improve the avenues leading to its steps because the City of Moscow began paving its streets in 1912. Up until then, according to historian Lillian Otness in *A Great Good Country*, Moscow's streets were "deep in dust in summer and nearly impassable in wet weather." The sidewalks were "planks raised above the street level, with wooden crosswalks making foot traffic possible at intersections."

Not likely that he would have noticed, but it was too bad Moscow's streets were not yet paved when former president Theodore Roosevelt visited the town and the University of Idaho in 1911. Roosevelt arrived in Moscow on April 9, 1911 and, according to historian Keith C. Petersen, "made a bully time of it." Roosevelt's visit drew thousands of people from throughout the Palouse and beyond. From Moscow's train depot, Roosevelt was driven in an open car to the Hotel Moscow; his motorcade was four blocks long.

The next day, Roosevelt spoke from a platform in front of the University of Idaho Administration Building; the platform had been constructed of sacks of Palouse wheat that had been harvested, threshed, and sacked by a combine manufactured by the Idaho National Harvester Company. The platform was wrapped in red, white, and blue bunting, and behind it were two tall pedestals upon which were mounted a stuffed eagle. A large American flag flew in the background. In his speech, the former president addressed a variety of concerns, including the closing of the frontier, progressive reforms, the individual citizen's

This photograph captures the construction of Moscow's first federal building, which housed the post office, completed in 1911. (Courtesy LCHS.)

responsibility for government, and conservation. He also reminisced about his previous visits to Idaho. One reporter estimated there were 8,000 people in the crowd; another reporter claimed there were 10,000 present, but Roosevelt topped them both, claiming 20,000 had stood to hear him speak. After his speech, Roosevelt left Moscow to continue his tour through Idaho.

Six months later, President William Howard Taft visited Moscow, arriving on October 4, 1911. He arrived at 5:30 p.m. and left at 6:17 p.m. Rafe Gibbs explains that Taft's brief visit to Moscow lacked the "air of great excitement that had prevailed at Roosevelt's coming." During his visit, Roosevelt had planted a blue spruce tree near the Administration Building in an area that came to be called the Presidential Grove. Taft, too, made a contribution to the Grove, planting a Port Orford cedar tree.

The second decade of the twentieth century had begun illustriously with the visits of two national figures in Moscow, but it would end infamously with a world war and an epidemic of unprecedented proportions. With the nation's entry into World War I in 1917, Moscow and the University of Idaho would never be the same. Even in a community as isolated as Moscow, anti-German sentiment ran strong and patriotic fervor high. Merchant Nathaniel Williamson, whose department store was then the biggest in Moscow, organized a spectacular bonfire on Main Street and burned all the German-made materials in his store's inventory. One group of Moscow boosters had planned to erect 60-foot to 80-foot flagpoles from which the American flag would fly in front of every private home

Former president Theodore Roosevelt speaks from a platform made of sacks of wheat in front of the Administration Building of the University of Idaho in 1911. (Courtesy LCHS.)

in Moscow. Their plan did not come to fruition, but Moscowans, like Americans across the nation, found other ways to contribute to the war effort.

High school students formed cadet companies and grew "war gardens." Red Cross volunteers, generally women, organized fundraising events, such as dances, rummage sales, card games, and a community picnic to rally support for the war effort. Avery D. Cummings, a military science professor at the University of Idaho, formed a military auxiliary; its membership of 60 men included faculty members, students, and townsmen. Militia companies had existed in Moscow since the late 1880s. In 1885, hotelier Robert Barton created a Moscow unit of the Grand Army of the Republic, and in 1892, a Moscow militia unit was formed in response to the riots in the Coeur d'Alene mining district north of Moscow. Professor Cummings's auxiliary was a guard unit, prepared to defend the home front from sabotage. In 1917, A.W. Laird, general manager of Potlatch Lumber Company, headed the Latah County Council of Defense, a home defense unit.

Just as the townspeople of Moscow responded to the call to action, so did the members of the University of Idaho community. On March 21, 1917, the students of the university sent President Woodrow Wilson a telegram expressing their "vigorous support of your efforts for the protection and advancement of human welfare at home and abroad." Despite early rumors that the university would close, it did not, but conditions were far from normal on the campus. Sporting events and social functions were either discontinued or greatly cut back, and the College of Engineering instituted an accelerated program, enabling students to complete 70 percent of the normal four-year workload in two years.

And, of course, young men were expected to enlist in the armed forces. The university passed two resolutions, which made it easier for men wanting to sign up before the end of the school year. For the high school seniors of 1917 who wanted to join the armed forces, the university waived high school graduation requirements. It also allowed college seniors to join the armed forces instead of completing their spring semester classes. Thirty-two university students would lose their lives in the war; the first was Lieutenant Dudley Loomis, for whom the Moscow post of the American Legion is named.

As deadly as the war was the Spanish influenza epidemic that swept not just Moscow and the university but the world. The disease is believed to have been brought to the university campus by vocational training troops arriving from Wyoming. While Moscow remained nearly unscathed, ten members of the university Student Army Training Corps, a precursor to the ROTC, would die from the disease. While most were treated in Moscow's Inland Empire Hospital, during the height of the epidemic, temporary hospitals were established in the Elks Temple, the Episcopal church, and a fraternity house.

Esther Thomas, a University of Idaho student, may have spent some of her time in one of Moscow's temporary hospitals as a volunteer nursing those

Civilian military units in Moscow date back to its founding. Members of the local post of the Grand Army of the Republic pose for their photo, c. 1890. (Courtesy LCHS.)

stricken. In an October 20, 1918 diary entry, Esther wrote, "Churches and schools closed on account of the flu." Four days later, she wrote, "I take some flowers and apples to the 'flu' boys. They start me in as nurse. Needed!" On October 31, 1918, she wrote, "Private secretary I am. Write the boys letters." She wrote, "My last day of nursing," on November 5, 1918.

Less than a week later, on November 11, 1918, the Armistice was signed and Moscow celebrated. According to Rafe Gibbs in *Beacon for Mountain and Plain*:

> Moscow had early developed into one of the nation's best organized towns, and its Armistice celebration was a thoughtfully-planned affair. All businesses promptly closed, and "telephone trees" went into operation. At 1:30 p.m. sharp, the parade started, with flags flying and everybody marching with his proper unit—the SATC [Student Army Training Corps], Idaho National Guard, Boy Scouts, Red Cross, and all the various civic and fraternal groups. If it had been planned for months, it could not have been a better parade.

With the coming of peace and the demobilization of the military, the University of Idaho faced the problem of finding sufficient housing for its male student

This parade was held on Moscow's Main Street in October 1918 as part of a Liberty Bond drive. The women in white served as nurses and are carrying flags showing the members of their families in the service. (Courtesy LCHS.)

population. In 1919, Reverend William H. Bridge, pastor of Moscow's St. Mark's Episcopal Church, was appointed executive secretary to university President Ernest Lindley. Bridge, in cooperation with Moscow's Chamber of Commerce, developed an innovative plan to finance the construction of a new dormitory. He asked the citizens of Moscow to finance a bond of $83,000. Response to the plan was positive, and within a few days, Moscowans had raised the money. The three-story brick building designed to house 96 men was christened Lindley Hall upon its completion in 1920. In 1927, another Moscow-funded dormitory, Hays Hall for women, was completed.

That same year, the Idaho legislature passed a bill designating the Idaho Technical Institute in Pocatello, Idaho, the southern branch of the University of Idaho. The university maintained its junior college until 1947 when the legislature created a separate university in Pocatello: Idaho State University. In 1929, the university founded the William Edgar Borah Outlawry of War Foundation with a gift from Chicago attorney and peace advocate Salmon O. Levinson, who admired the Idaho senator's efforts to establish peace in the world. In the 1940s, the foundation would become the Borah Symposium, which continues to this day the tradition of bringing nationally acclaimed speakers to the University of Idaho.

Historian Keith C. Petersen has called the decade of the 1920s "a peculiar decade." It was the Jazz Age and a measure of restlessness permeated American culture like a thought that remains unremembered but settled on the tip of one's tongue. It was a time when national popular culture began to shoulder aside local culture, entering people's lives through movies, radio, and magazines. Perhaps all the time devoted to obtaining illegal liquor and occupying speakeasies was but a preconscious hoarding of pleasure in advance of the stock market crash in 1929.

Perhaps it was the times, then, that explains one of the most unusual and still controversial chapters in Moscow's history. In 1929, after Wall Street had laid its proverbial egg, Frank Bruce Robinson placed a small advertisement in a psychology magazine stating, "I talked with God—actually and literally." Robinson then went on to explain how it was possible to get on speaking terms with God by subscribing, for a fee, to a set of 20 Psychiana lessons. The lessons came, after all, with a money-back guarantee. That was the start of Psychiana, the "new psychological religion," that Robinson operated out of Moscow until his death in 1948.

Robinson arrived in Moscow with his wife and son sometime in the late 1920s to work as a pharmacist in the Corner Drug Store. While his days were spent filling prescriptions, during the evenings Robinson refined what he described as his "religious vision of the future." Shortly after arriving in town, Robinson began to hold public lectures at which he discussed this religious vision. His first lecture was held in the Moscow Hotel and was attended by about 60 people. Inspired by the success of these lectures, Robinson then launched the national distribution of his religion, with the financial help of several local businessmen and Geoffrey Birley, a wealthy British cotton exporter.

Among the $13,000 and 3,000 inquiries received in response to Robinson's initial Psychiana advertisement was that of Geoffrey Birley's. His response also included a photograph of himself. According to historian Keith C. Petersen, an authority on the history of Psychiana, Robinson later dreamed that he saw Birley making mystical motions over a corpse saying, "This is Psychiana, the power that will bring new life to a spiritually dead world." Robinson wrote Birley of the dream, and Birley then wired Robinson $40,000 to finance the dissemination of Robinson's religious message. With money in the bank, Robinson resigned his position as pharmacist in the Corner Drug Store to devote himself full-time to Psychiana.

Psychiana was Frank Robinson's way of reaching that part of nearly every person who loves success; his philosophy was a combination of positive thinking and religious rationalism, and it was directed toward the common person, unlike the other popular thinkers of his time. Here is an excerpt from one of Robinson's Psychiana lessons:

> Herein lies my discovery, which discovery I am now passing on to you. This discovery and the Power it teaches is a Spiritual Power, consequently whatever exercises I prescribe for you to do will be designed to enable you to recognize and become acquainted with this same Spiritual Power. It may be therefore, that some people may think that the simple little affirmations which I shall ask you to use have no value and cannot possibly be instrumental in changing your life from one of illness, poverty and unhappiness into one of overwhelming victory. . . . Don't forget this affirmation: "I BELIEVE IN THE POWER OF THE LIVING GOD," and if you will use it faithfully, it will not be long before you begin to realize that there is in existence, this dynamic LAW of which I am telling you, which LAW can operate for YOUR OWN Success, Health and abundant Happiness and Prosperity.

Reaching hundreds of thousands of people in over 60 countries, Robinson's message did not fall on deaf ears. And his students did not hesitate to share their success stories with him. N.B. Dalao of the Philippine Islands credited Psychiana for saving his life after the loss of his child. Mildred Gage recovered from breast cancer thanks to Psychiana. At first, Robinson personally answered the letters of his followers, but the volume of mail soon made that impossible. Instead, Robinson developed a system of form responses. Over 60,000 pieces of mail were sent out of the Psychiana office on any given day and thousands of checks were received daily. In the midst of this volume, Robinson still managed to advertise Psychiana in 180 magazines and 140 newspapers. He also broadcast his programs over 60 radio stations.

For a payment of $20, Robinson's students received 20 correspondence lessons, one every two weeks. The basic set of lessons was followed by an advanced set. If students forgot to make a payment, they received a short piece of string taped to a letter reminding them that their payment was past due. Most Psychiana followers purchased only the first set of lessons, which Robinson continued to rewrite and reissue throughout his life. Individual lessons were lengthy, about 10 pages of single-spaced typing, mass-produced, and without illustration.

But there were people in Moscow who disliked the flamboyant 6-foot, 4-inch Robinson, who had a fondness for fur coats and flashy cars. Some ministers condemned him from the pulpit. A Moscow newspaperwoman compared him to P.T. Barnum, and beginning in 1936, there appears to have been a conscious effort to discredit Robinson. That year, he was indicted for falsifying passport information, but was acquitted by a Moscow jury. Then Robinson, who was not a native American, having been born in England, was ordered deported by the United States government. However, Robinson had a friend in high places. Idaho Senator William Borah stepped in on his behalf, and through his help and a brief stay in Cuba, Robinson was granted a visa, and was able to return to the United States. In 1942, Robinson became a naturalized citizen. During the 1930s, Robinson was also investigated for mail fraud, but no charges were ever filed.

While some Moscowans condemned Robinson, one recalled him with affection for his lack of snobbishness. Lola Clyde, whose husband's family had come west to Moscow the late 1870s, had been born in Moscow in 1900. In an oral history, Clyde recalled this anecdote about Robinson:

Frank Bruce Robinson created Psychiana, the world's first mail-order religion in Moscow in 1929. (Courtesy LCHS.)

We had a woman here and they called her the Galloping Goose in Moscow. She was very retarded you know, and very odd and she walked on the road every place. And whenever she'd see a lovely free meal some place, she was hungry, she would go in and eat. So one day she was in the Moscow Hotel and the table was all set to entertain the state legislators, you know. They had lovely little red salads at all the places and she saw that beautiful food and went in and sat right down. And of course, the busboys and people came running and the heads of it came running to usher poor little Ida right out of there, you know, so she wouldn't disgrace the meeting. And Frank Robinson rose in his majesty of six feet four, two-hundred and twenty-five pounds and he just waved the busboys away. He said, "Ida is my guest today. She'll sit beside me and bring me her bill." And I love it. That put everybody in the proper perspective. People like that aren't all bad, are they?

Realizing he might be the cause of controversy in Moscow, Robinson had decided early on not to sell his lessons and books locally. Consequently, while many Moscow residents knew little or nothing about the controversies surrounding Robinson and Psychiana, many knew of Robinson from his generosity toward his adopted community. Besides being a considerate and progressive employer, Robinson built two new buildings in downtown Moscow, brought the town's post office to first-class status with the volume of his mailings,

Members of the Psychiana staff pose in front of their office in downtown Moscow, c. 1940. During its peak, Psychiana was Moscow's largest private employer. (Courtesy LCHS.)

operated three drugstores, provided the city with its first youth center, and donated land to the county for a park that bears his name and remains to this day one of Latah County's most popular recreation areas.

During the Great Depression, Psychiana was Moscow's largest private employer. Robinson employed typesetters, designers, printers, and bookbinders. In the Psychiana mailroom, staff were positioned around a table designed like an enormous lazy susan; they added pages to packets of lessons and then moved the wheel to the next assembly-line position. The Moscow post office hired extra employees to handle the volume of Psychiana mail, and as a result of the high volume, was granted status as a first-class post office. When Psychiana was flourishing, Robinson maintained a steady payroll for 40 to 50 workers, mostly women.

Robinson also gave Moscow a second daily newspaper. He started his own paper for two reasons. For one thing, he wanted his own press, believing he could print his writings more cheaply than paying someone else to do it, namely the *Moscow Star-Mirror*, Moscow's daily paper since the *Idaho Post* had been absorbed by the *Star-Mirror* in 1906. For another, Robinson was feuding with George Lamphere, the publisher of the *Moscow Star-Mirror*. The two powerful men were on opposite ends of the political spectrum; Robinson was a Republican and Lamphere was a Democrat, and there was no room for compromise in their beliefs. In addition, Robinson believed Lamphere was gouging him for printing his many Psychiana materials.

Therefore, in 1934, Robinson bought the *Elk River News*, a small paper in an even smaller town located in remote Latah County and moved it to Moscow, bringing with him its editor William T. Marineau. Robinson changed the name of the newspaper to the *Moscow News-Review*. In 1939, proving that journalism, like politics, makes strange bedfellows, the *Star-Mirror* and the *News-Review* would merge to form the *Idahonian*, which served as Moscow's daily newspaper for nearly three decades.

Less than ten years later, on October 19, 1948, Frank Robinson, who had suffered from heart disease for many years, died from a heart attack. Although Robinson's wife Pearl and their son Alfred continued Psychiana for a time, without Robinson, Psychiana had lost its driving spirit. Five years later, in January 1953, Psychiana closed its doors. Psychiana historian Keith Petersen concludes that Frank Robinson dealt honestly with people and that he caused none of his followers harm. In fact, he most likely enhanced their lives and he most certainly shared his financial success with the citizens of Moscow.

In 1938, as Frank Robinson urged his followers to put the God-Law to work in their lives, Moscow and the University of Idaho had a distinguished visitor. In March of that year, at the invitation of the Borah Outlawry of War Foundation, the nation's first lady, Eleanor Roosevelt, visited Moscow to address students and townspeople on the subject of peace. University president Harrison Dale was selected to retrieve Roosevelt, the first wife of a United States president to visit the University of Idaho, from the airport in Spokane.

129

President Dale made it as far as Spangle, Washington, a small farming community roughly halfway between Moscow and Spokane, before two flat tires disabled his car. He then made arrangements for a limousine to transport Roosevelt to Spangle, where Dale transferred the first lady to his repaired vehicle and resumed the journey to Moscow. A reception in her honor in President Dale's home at 514 East First Street was waiting.

Longtime Moscow resident Jean Cummings Rudolph remembers that reception vividly. She jokes, in fact, that she could have shot Eleanor Roosevelt. Jean was a teenager—and self-described tomboy—at the time of Roosevelt's visit, and she recalls that it was "fashionable among Republican families to make fun of the much traveled First Lady. She was an easy target, so visible, so into everything, not like former president's wives who stayed quietly in the background." Jean was well aware of the stir Roosevelt's visit was causing in Moscow, and being a typical teenager, she decided she would not be among the crowd straining to get a glimpse of the First Lady.

On the day of Roosevelt's visit, Jean stuffed her pockets with shells, grabbed her trusty .22 rifle, and headed out to shoot the squirrels that annoyed local farmers by burrowing in their fields. On the way, however, she reconsidered, changed course, and headed toward the home of President Gale. "As I pushed into the crowd of curious townspeople," she remembers, "a man tapped me on the shoulder and told me emphatically to take my rifle and leave. It was a simpler day. I suppose now the Secret Service would drag me off for investigation."

After the reception, Roosevelt was escorted to the campus. Before entering Memorial Gymnasium where she would make her speech, Roosevelt helped plant a tree in the university's Presidential Grove, as had another Roosevelt 20 years earlier. In her speech, she asked why we are so willing to pay for war but not for

Longtime resident and Moscow native Jean Cummings Rudolph poses with her family near the Ursuline convent, c. 1930. Jean is on the far right. (Courtesy LCHS.)

First Lady Eleanor Roosevelt visited Moscow and the University of Idaho in 1938. She is shown here planting a tree in the university's Presidential Grove. (Courtesy LCHS.)

peace, comparing the attitudes of nations to those of small boys who settle their difficulties with fist fights. She concluded her address by urging the powers to take action before events got out of hand.

But, unfortunately, a worldwide fist fight was not avoided, and Moscow, like small towns across the nation, changed profoundly following that infamous day, December 7, 1941. Samuel Butterfield, who was then student body president of Moscow High School, recalled hearing the news of the attack as he and his father were walking down Main Street after church. They both looked at each other and shook their heads. The next day, he and a group of students went around to the stores borrowing radios to put into every classroom so the students could hear President Roosevelt's address. By December 8, as people across the nation gathered around radios, Moscow and Latah County already had organized civil defense and Red Cross volunteers in case of attack or emergency. The local chapter of the Red Cross organized a first aid unit made up of Moscow High School students 17 years of age and older. A motor corps unit was also created, staffed by students at least 18 years old.

The mayor of Moscow, Bill Anderson, appointed a defense coordination committee to coordinate civil defense in Moscow. The *Daily Idahonian* published

131

civil defense instructions the week after the Pearl Harbor attack. In case of an air raid, Moscowans were to: "1. Keep Cool. 2. Stay Home. 3. Put Out Lights. 4. Lie Down. 5. Stay Away from Windows." Dr. Allan Lemon, chair of Moscow's Civil Defense Council, appointed captains for ten divisions: supply; social services; police and fire assistance; medical assistance; transportation; communications and collections; evacuation and demolition; air raid precaution; public relations; and clerical assistance. Women headed the last two divisions.

Gritman Memorial Hospital was designated the first casualty station, and first-aid stations were established throughout the city, including the infirmary at the University of Idaho. A nurse corps of professionals and volunteers was established, and they collected donated sheets and pillowcases for temporary beds and bandages. Coroner Howard Short volunteered to assist in ambulance work and the manual arts training classes at Moscow High School built stretchers. In addition, Moscow's Civil Defense Council developed a corps of airplane spotters. A small glass building was constructed on top of the 1912 Moscow High School.

Although Latah County was far from the Pacific Coast, block wardens enforced blackouts, patrolling their jurisdictions to make sure no light was visible. Residents were asked to have a shovel and bucket handy in case incendiary bombs should be dropped. Brown-outs were also common in Moscow so that the Kaiser Aluminum Company plant in Spokane could operate at full capacity. Fifty Moscow men responded to the call to staff Company H of the Home Guards, one of many Home Guard units established throughout the nation to deal with acts of sabotage, real or feared.

Civilian response to the war effort in Moscow was much like that of Americans across the nation. A collection center for rubber, aluminum, metal scrap, and paper was set up at the Latah County Fairgrounds on the southeastern edge of Moscow. The center was open every morning except Sunday. The local chapter of the Red Cross participated in the national campaign to raise funds for the war; Latah County's share of the national goal of $50 million was $5,250. In addition, the Red Cross established intensive first aid training classes, which were conducted by Dorothy Collard, Latah County's public health nurse. The Red Cross also distributed "Christmas comfort kits," containing writing materials, cards, knives, combs, shaving soap, and a packet of sewing supplies, prepared by local citizens.

But Moscow was also the home of Psychiana, the world's largest mail order religion, and in his own flamboyant manner, Frank Robinson also contributed to the war effort. Robinson mobilized a "spiritual Blitzkreig" against the Axis powers, urging people everywhere to repeat the following affirmation three times daily: "The unseen forces of God are bringing about the speedy defeat of the Axis." Robinson also submitted a proposal to Finnish Premier Risto Ryti that required each member of Psychiana, along with the entire Finnish cabinet and army, to spend 15 minutes daily in prayer to show that the power of God was superior to the powers of war, hate, and evil.

In her examination of the home front in Latah County, historian Mary Reed wrote that of all the effects the war had on American civilians, rationing is what they usually remember most clearly. Nancy I. Atkinson, who arrived in Moscow in 1943 to head the Catalog Department of the University of Idaho Library, recalled that she got "along pretty well" with rationing. She remembers that the she would give her monthly supply of meat stamps to the butcher who would deduct what was necessary as she bought each item. "I know that the Sanitary Meat Market gave me more meat than I had stamps. Ranchers in the vicinity who raised their own meat would bring in stamps for the benefit of those needing them."

She also recalled that butter was seldom available so she and her father would "split our ration of butter. I would hoard mine, doling it out each morning on my breakfast toast. He, however, would have nothing to do with my meagerly buttered toast and would put a generous amount on his slice of toast until his portion was gone and then do without." The rationing of rubber affected not only drivers but mothers, too. Jean Cummings Rudolph, a young mother during the war, recalled that even babies weren't exempt from the consequences of rubber rationing. "Rubber pants disappeared, and it was before there were plastic ones. Mother solved my problem by knitting 'soakers' to go over diapers. She ignored the traditional white/blue/pink baby color scheme and made them yellow 'because they'll get that color anyway.' "

Jean Cummings Rudolph recalls that, before local boards could be set up, schoolteachers were responsible for administering ration books. She adds that

During World War II, like Americans across the nation, Moscowans supported the war effort by sponsoring drives to collect rubber. The truck in this photo was parked in front of Frank Neely's Hudson dealership. (Courtesy LCHS.)

those serving on the ration boards and the draft boards "had to be willing to be unpopular." In addition to rationing, the war changed how people on the home front lived in other ways. With neither rubber nor much gasoline available and no public transportation system, Moscowans organized carpools or just walked. Like many of their fellow Americans, they planted victory gardens and learned to preserve the bounty of those gardens through home canning.

Nancy Atkinson recalls the time a fighter plane pilot, stationed in nearby Spokane, "buzzed" the university's Administration Building:

> One day, hearing the sound of a plane, I looked up to see the tilted wings of a plane fly by the window. That event seemed too close for comfort, and, indeed, the University did protest, and, I believe, the pilot was disciplined. Before I came to Moscow, one of those pilots became too daring and was killed when his plane crashed in a vacant lot on Third Street.

By 1942, sugar and coffee were added to the list of rationed commodities, and while there was a shortage of sugar in Moscow during the war, there was no shortage of entertainment and assistance to service personnel. There was a Latah County chapter of the United Services Organization (USO) chaired by Moscow insurance agent Laurence Huff. The American Legion Cabin, located on Howard Street between Third and Fifth Streets, became a home away from home for area servicemen. The cabin served as an informal nightclub, complete with dancing, music, and games. Winnie Robinson, then a high school student, recalls that young ladies were not allowed to leave the cabin in the company of any of the servicemen. "But you could go up the street on Third Street and meet them on the corner. And I remember the older ladies, probably all of 30, that were the chaperons."

Moscowans were also ardent buyers of war bonds. On one day in October 1942, Moscowans purchased over $125,000 worth of war bonds. "Buy a Bond for Bob" was the fundraising slogan that proved so effective, and Bob was Moscow's own Robert Ghormley, who was at that time commander of the Allied naval forces in the southwest Pacific. That day, Moscow's Recreation Park near the university campus was renamed Ghormley Park in his honor and a gala parade was held.

For the third national war bond drive in 1943, Latah County exceeded its quota of $725,000 in less than a month. For the fourth drive, Latah County sold $919,919 in bonds. Perhaps the town's Minute Maids were partially responsible for the successful drives. Local high school girls and University of Idaho women students organized as Minute Maids to express their patriotism and support for the war effort and to encourage their friends to buy war bonds and stamps.

In addition to the Minute Maids, other members of the University of Idaho community also responded to the call to action. On December 8, 1941, President Harrison Dale had addressed the students, urging them to devote themselves to the war effort and to practice tolerance. As Rafe Gibbs wrote in his history of the university, *Beacon for Mountain and Plain*, President Dale rallied the university community with the following words:

> At this stage we can best serve our country by doing our daily tasks plus 10 percent . . . Let us build up a reputation for American thoroughness, which manifestly is the sum total of all individual thoroughness. Finally, we want to make American democracy work. It will work only if we remember that all native American citizens whether of German or Italian or Japanese ancestry are American citizens by birth sharing with all of us their heritage of American democracy.

Unfortunately, in 1942, the university's president did not heed his own words. That year, University of Idaho sociology instructor Paul Hatt rescued six Japanese-American students who had fled the University of Washington in fear for their lives. His hope to enroll them in the University of Idaho were dashed when President Dale and Idaho Governor Chase Clark quickly passed a new policy prohibiting the admission of any out-of-state Japanese Americans. As in Seattle, the young men were chased from Moscow by a group of thugs who threatened the students with violence.

Of course, the biggest change the war brought to the University of Idaho campus was the absence of men, and male students wasted no time in leaving college; most left in the brief period between the bombing of Pearl Harbor and the end of the fall semester in December. Enrollment numbers reflect this: during the 1942–1943 school year, there were 2,155 students enrolled in the university; during the 1943–1944 school year, only 944. Yet college men were encouraged not to volunteer for service. The state of Idaho's selective service officer explained that college men were what he called "officer material" and would better serve the country by remaining in college to train as officers. It did not make sense, he added, to put them in the army to dig ditches.

Accordingly, the university's main role in the war effort was to train potential officers or skilled enlisted personnel; by doing so, the university continued to fulfill its original charge as a land-grant college to provide military training. After December 7, 1941, the university adopted a 12-month school year so that male students entering after high school could earn their bachelor's degree before reaching the draft age of 21. It also introduced an accelerated program to enable students to finish college in three and a half years instead of four.

One of the most successful military training programs held on the University of Idaho campus was the Naval Radio Training School. Between May 15, 1942, and January 15, 1945, nearly 4,500 sailors received instruction in the receiving and sending of code at one of the most celebrated radio training programs in the nation. The Idaho program used innovative teaching techniques that prepared its graduates for "real-life" combat situations.

Hal L. Roberts was one of the students at the university's radio training school in 1943. In his March 5, 1943 letter home, he writes:

Students of the Naval Radio Training School take a break from learning code to perform at the VFW Hall located on Howard Street. The hall was an informal USO Hall during World War II and remains in use today. (Courtesy LCHS.)

> Arrived at the U of I at 0200, the middle of the night. . . . Looks like this is going to be a very nice set up as for quarters and food are concerned. I will probably never be good at code and all that stuff about radio. . . . The University sits on top of a hill and the area is beautiful. Haven't seen the town yet. Am not going to take many liberties as it will take all my concentration to get this through my thick skull.

Seaman Roberts might have had a thick skull, but students in the economics classes of legendary University of Idaho professor Erwin Graue quickly developed thick skins. Professor Graue, a native of Germany, was a professor with a gruff, aristocratic bearing who simply demanded the best from his students, even after they had left his classes to serve their country. During the war, Graue maintained regular written correspondence with nearly 90 of his former students who were then enlisted in the military. Graue's letters were more than casual expressions of support; he continued to demand the best from his students, urging them to apply the principles he had taught them and to believe they would have a role in shaping the future.

Graue's letters were forward-looking, based on the premise that the Allies would win the war, and when V-E day—May 8, 1945—arrived at long last, Graue may have been among faculty, students, and townspeople who celebrated with a rally and parade that wound through campus and town. Following the surrender of the Japanese on August 14, 1945, Moscowans, like Americans everywhere, were eager to resume a normal life. As the millions of young men and women who had helped liberate the cities of Europe and the islands of the Pacific were demobilized, it soon became clear that getting back to normal would take a little time.

Most noticeably, there were still shortages to deal with, and one of the most difficult ones to overcome quickly was the shortage of housing. The home construction industry had ground to a standstill during the war, and there simply were not enough houses to shelter everyone. This was particularly true in a college town like Moscow. Upon their return to civilian life, former servicemen and women surprised the nation's experts by not entering the country's labor market. Instead, they took advantage of the education provisions of the G.I. Bill of Rights and enrolled in college. The University of Idaho was no exception to this trend. In 1945 and 1946, as World War II drew to a close, enrollment increased from 944 in 1943 and 1944 to 2,345. Enrollment peaked in 1948 and 1949 when 3,912 students were in residence at the University of Idaho.

University of Idaho Professor Alf Dunn recalled the "influx of male students like you wouldn't believe" after the war ended. "It was really interesting for us because in any one class you might have four or five Majors and Captains, and even a light Colonel or two . . . We had a lot of brass in our classes in those days, and they were wonderful students. Most of them were older than the average student and most were married."

University of Idaho Professor William Banks also recalled his "veteran" students. In a letter to a friend dated July 4, 1946, he writes:

> I have some 50-odd veterans (men) and two veteran Waves, who are a splendid group of persons. I cannot describe the maturity, courtesy, patience, good faith and natural courage of these veterans. They personally are the flower of our culture. In a horrific acreage of weeds and booby traps called American civilization today, these human beings are the clearest expression of what our society deserves to be and can yet be.

In 1946, as Professor Banks penned this missive, which included his hope that Americans could yet "salvage our society from its many vicious and corrupt presumptions upon itself," a severe housing shortage made life difficult for students and faculty alike. University student housing was so tight that Memorial Gymnasium was converted to temporary housing, with students sleeping on cots set up on the gymnasium floor. The university created three temporary housing villages in 1947, which housed both students and faculty. Referred to as "Veteran's Villages," these housing complexes consisted of war surplus trailers, prefabricated houses, and former military barracks.

While better than the alternative of homelessness, an apartment in one of the university's veteran's villages was anything but deluxe. Current Moscow residents Bill and McGee Parish lived in one of the veteran's villages after Bill was hired to teach electrical engineering in 1947. Their upstairs apartment in the

West Sixth Veteran's Village was 400 square feet with two bedrooms, a living room, kitchen, and bath, which they shared with their one-year-old son and three-month-old daughter.

In the fall of 1949, several university faculty and their wives, including Bill and McGee Parish, decided to take the problem of Moscow's housing shortage into their own hands. The group pooled their money, as well as their skills and talents, and built their own housing development within Moscow's city limits. After the engineers in the group had identified a suitable site, a former homestead on the southern edge of Moscow, Thomas R. Walenta, a professor of law, established the administrative framework for the endeavor. University Heights, Inc., a non-profit housing cooperative created for the purpose of designing and developing a new neighborhood of homes in Moscow, was officially incorporated by the State of Idaho in February 1950. During the next decade, the members of University Heights, Inc., who were not professional builders, built Moscow's first housing addition.

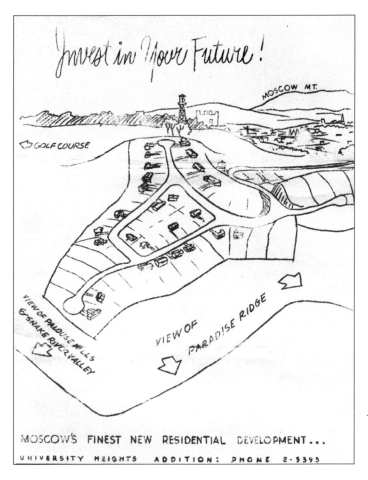

One response to Moscow's housing shortage was an endeavor called University Heights, Inc., in which a group of university faculty built their own—Moscow's first—housing addition. (Courtesy Bill and McGee Parish.)

8. Moscow from 1950 to the Present

The mission of University Heights, Inc. was based on the values of cooperation, mutual benefit, and self-sacrifice for the collective good, and the residents of the neighborhood that came to be called University Heights took these values seriously. It was commonplace for the residents to participate in work parties to help build each other's houses, clean up the neighborhood, and even install their own television cable system. A group effort that garnered something of a reputation (and a little notoriety) in Moscow was the annual barbecue for the "Heights Families," as board secretary Mabel Locke referred to her neighbors in the minutes of the November 8, 1954 annual meeting.

The event was no slipshod affair; the corporation even had a written procedure outlining the steps involved in preparing the barbecue pit and cooking the meat, which was placed in the pit for cooking about seven hours before the time of service. T.C. Thomas, who had penned the written procedures in a 1954 memorandum, advised the "Barbecue Master" (Thomas's term) to arrange for volunteers to stoke the fire during this period and that those gathered around the barbecue when the meat was put in the pit should be provided with a "little brown jug."

Four months after the incorporation of University Heights, Inc., the nation would be drawn into the Korean Conflict, and students at the University of Idaho gained a national reputation for the manner in which they expressed their support of the war effort. During the 1950–1951 school year, students organized what is believed to be the first campus-wide blood drive in the nation and donated more pints of blood than any college in the United States. The effort drew the attention of the national media, with pieces in *Life* magazine and on the radio programs of Drew Pearson and Walter Winchell.

In 1953, as the hot war in Korea cooled off and the Cold War with the Soviet Union heated up, residents of Moscow, with help from the university, the Red Cross, and the U.S. Department of the Treasury, celebrated May Day in a manner designed intentionally to compete with the famous May Day parade in Moscow, Russia. The day's events include a three-hour-long Main Street parade, complete with movie stars Touch Connors and Coleen Gray, speeches, and fireworks. At the end of the day, nearly $400,000 in savings bonds had been purchased and 1,672 pints of blood donated. The *Time* magazine reporter covering the event wrote that it was Moscow "destiny . . . to show the world the difference between there and here."

Three years after Moscow's widely covered May Day parade, the University of Idaho experienced a fire that would leave the community shaken and saddened. In 1956, fire swept through Gault Hall, a men's dormitory named in honor of the university's first president. Two students, John Knudsen and Paul Johnson, died as a result of the blaze, which was so intense that the wood inside the building's metal doors burned. Days later, 22-year-old Paul Matovich, a student from Kellogg, Idaho, confessed to the crime. The mentally ill young man had no explanation for his actions and was later institutionalized.

As the university recovered from what university historian Rafe Gibbs called the worst tragedy in its history, a group of Moscow women were rallying the community on behalf of its indigent and aged. In the late 1940s, Elena Goulder, the wife of the then-new pastor of the Methodist church, organized a women's group to assist those in the community who were disadvantaged financially. Among the members of this group was longtime resident, civic leader, and newspaper columnist Grace Wicks; she recalls the day in the mid-1950s when the group visited what was commonly known as the "poor farm."

Located on the northwestern edge of Moscow, the poor farm was officially the Latah County Farm; it was where the penniless, be they aged or ill, were housed in Latah County. At the time of Wicks's and Goulder's visit, the county farm was managed by one woman, Grace Dahl. With her husband and their five children, Dahl cared for an average of 47 boarders 24 hours a day, seven days a week. The boarders lived in an old farmhouse built around 1910, and it was a drafty, enormous house warmed by a single wood stove.

Dismayed at these conditions, the ladies determined that Moscow and Latah County needed a modern facility for the aged and indigent and began searching for ways to finance the project. With both federal and local funds, a new facility, the Latah Nursing Home, was constructed and officially incorporated on February 16, 1957. It was the first nursing home to be built and licensed in the state of Idaho. In 1987, the Latah Nursing Home, located on the southern edge of Moscow, became Latah Care Center; it continues to serve Moscow today as a nursing, rehabilitation, and physical therapy facility.

In organizing the movement to build a modern facility for the aged and indigent, Grace Wicks and Elena Goulder were following a long-standing tradition. For decades, women had assumed responsibility for providing social services for their community, but as Moscow and the nation entered the decades of the 1960s and 1970s, there would be a change. Moscowans, reflecting the attitudes of many Americans, would begin to demand that government, at all levels, become involved in the care of its citizens to a degree even greater than had been initiated by the New Deal legislation of Franklin D. Roosevelt.

At the same time, Moscowans and Americans would begin to question the federal government's involvement internationally. Just 14 short years after Moscowans (not Moscovites) had staged their widely-covered May Day parade in 1953, the political and social atmosphere of the nation would be dramatically different. While Moscow was not Berkeley or Selma and the University of Idaho was neither Wisconsin nor Columbia, as university historian Keith Petersen put it, townspeople and University of Idaho students were not shy about protesting the war in Vietnam and expressing their solidarity with such social movements as women's rights.

Moscow's first anti-war protest was held in 1967 with a small demonstration at the National Guard Armory located on the eastern edge of Moscow. Two years later, on October 15, 1969, students rallied to demand a moratorium on the Vietnam War, and in 1970, two firebombs gutted the university's Naval ROTC building. The day after the bombing, a crowd of over 500 people gathered on the Administration Building lawn to debate President Richard Nixon's decision to invade Cambodia.

During the period beginning in the late 1960s through the 1970s, the university and Moscow would experience much of the same social and political upheaval as did the rest of the nation. But from the turmoil rose an increased awareness of and appreciation for the diversity of American culture. No aspect of modern life was exempt from examination during this period when established

Moscowans show their support for the conflict in Korea by conducting a clothing drive. Even in times of war, they managed to find lighthearted moments. (Courtesy LCHS.)

perceptions and beliefs were challenged and, as a consequence, often redefined. Sometimes at the expense of their lives, members of ethnic minorities fought to elevate their status in society; sisters argued they could do it for themselves; senior citizens raised their voices in support of Gray Power; and there were those among us who cried the alarm that the food we ate, the air we breathed, and the water we drank were not safe.

Perhaps the greatest legacy of the late 1960s and early 1970s is the civil rights movement. While Moscow and Latah County have never had large minority populations, their histories include the contributions of individuals from a diversity of ethnic and religious heritages. The first wave of immigrants to the Palouse in the 1870s was primarily native-born Americans of European ancestry. Two individuals typical of this trend were William J. McConnell and Michael J. Shields. Both men were second-generation Americans born of parents who had immigrated to the United States from Ireland.

By 1880, native-born Americans would comprise 81 percent of the total population, and 90 percent by 1920. Immigration to the Palouse by non-Americans and non-Europeans was small but not nonexistent. One of the earliest ethnic communities in Moscow and the Palouse was the Chinese. On the Palouse, as throughout the West, Chinese immigrants initially settled in mining districts, working claims that had been abandoned by impatient or careless white miners. The Chinese were both ridiculed for working abandoned claims and

An unknown photographer snapped a picture of this railroad car, which was probably bound for Europe sometime during the Cold War. (Courtesy LCHS.)

resented if they did retrieve gold. Moreover, the Chinese were prohibited from filing claims in their own right and were thus forced to secure releases from the white miners who held the rights.

Historian Priscilla Wegars, who has documented the history of the Chinese in Moscow, writes that Chinese miners in Latah County were subject to harassment and violence by white residents. On more than one occasion, white miners murdered Chinese miners. The other industry in the American West that traditionally used Chinese immigrants was the railroad, and Chinese were among the laborers who laid the rails into Moscow. Even these transient workers were subject to harassment. Two members of what Wegars describes as an anti-Chinese society raided the house in which the workers were living. Fortunately, these men did nothing more than fire their guns into the air.

Following the arrival of the railroad in 1885, Chinese settled in Moscow to operate laundries and other businesses, especially restaurants and stores. It is likely that Moscow's first Chinese resident worked as a gardener. According to Wegars, the influence of the Chinese in Moscow reached its peak in the early 1890s when Chinese owned or operated at least ten separate Moscow businesses, including five laundries. Moscow also had a small "Chinatown," but there are recorded accounts of residents who remembered that the Chinese were driven forcefully from the community in the early 1900s. That might have been true, for by 1910, there were no Chinese residents in Moscow.

During the 1960s, students and faculty gathered on the lawn of the university's Administration Building to protest the war in Southeast Asia. (Courtesy LCHS.)

Besides Chinatown, Moscow also had a "Swedetown," a neighborhood in the southeastern part of Moscow with a high proportion of Swedish immigrants. Perhaps the only lasting reminder of the neighborhood's Swedish heritage is Lynn Street, an Americanization of the family name of Lind. The street was named after Swedish immigrant Andrew Lind who arrived in Moscow around 1886. Lind's first stop in the new world had been Waseca, Minnesota, and he came to Moscow not to homestead but to work as a gardener. His granddaughter, longtime Moscow resident Elsie Nelson, explained in her memoir *Today is Ours* that her grandfather was a "town man by nature" and had no interest in learning the business of farming.

As late as the 1920s, townspeople still used the term Swedetown in reference to that section of Moscow, according to Lucinda Tuttle Jenks. The Tuttle family arrived in Moscow on June 20, 1920 from Fairfield, Washington. Mr. and Mrs. Tuttle had decided their four daughters would have a university education, so they relocated the family to Moscow, buying a house, as they would learn, in Swedetown on the northwest corner of East Seventh and Lynn Streets. Jenks recalled in an article she wrote for the *Latah Legacy* that her new neighbors were friendly:

> Mr. Johnson told us that this part of town was called Swede Town. His son, Walter, worked in the office at Davids' store. On the other side of Johnsons were the Sampsons. Harry and Clarice Sampson also worked at Davids' store, in the grocery department . . . Across the street from us lived the John Ramstedts. John was bookkeeper at the creamery. Southeast of us, down on Lynn Avenue, were the Victor Ramstedts. Victor worked at Creightons. East of them were the Obergs. The Oberg Brothers Store was on Third Street across Washington from the post office.

Because many young Swedish women worked as domestic help or "hired girls," as they were commonly called, Swedish customs and traditions found their way into many non-Swedish homes. Elsie Nelson's mother Mary Josephine Lind is an example of one such young Swedish hired girl. Mary Lind worked in several Moscow homes, including the Willis Sweet family. Nelson wrote in her memoir that it was not a matter of financial necessity that her mother worked as a nursemaid or helper—her parents were "always good providers"—rather Mary had a "genuine interest in doing work in homes," even at the expense of her own education.

Besides the Swedes, other Scandinavians, particularly Norwegians, also settled in Moscow and Latah County in large numbers. In 1890, 44 percent of the total foreign-born Swedish population in Idaho and 23 percent of the Norwegian population lived in Latah County. Norwegians were among the area's first settlers, arriving as early as the 1870s. Danish and Finnish immigrants also settled in Latah County, but in much lesser numbers. Important to both Swedish and Norwegian cultures was the Lutheran faith, and in 1883, the Swedish Evangelical Lutheran

Congregation built Idaho's oldest Lutheran church building in Cordelia, 8 miles southeast of Moscow.

Other native-born European groups, especially the Irish and Germans, settled in Latah County, but their populations were small and scattered in comparison to the Scandinavians. Even fewer was the number of African Americans who permanently settled in Latah County; however, there were two African-American families that arrived early and stayed, leaving the county with an important legacy. Joe Wells and his wife Lou accompanied the Wells brothers, Grant and Crom Wells, west from North Carolina, arriving in Latah County in 1889. Joe, who worked as a blacksmith, loved to tell the joke that he was the only white man in the county and that the rest were Swedes.

Joe hired another African American, Eugene Settle, when he worked as a logger. Eugene's family had moved west from Arkansas, and on their journey to Bluestem, Washington, the train stopped briefly in Moscow where Eugene's father encountered Lewis Chrisemon, an African American who operated a restaurant in Moscow. Chrisemon urged Settle to stay, but he was determined to reach his Washington destination. Eventually, however, the Settle family returned to Moscow. Within a few years, Settle had saved enough money farming to buy land in the county.

In an oral history conducted with Eugene in 1975, he recalled little prejudice as a child and young man. "Well, of course, the first morning I went to school, all the

Eugene Settle's family was one of the few African-American families to settle in Latah County during its early days. (Courtesy LCHS.)

145

eyes were focused on me, naturally. That I expected. . . . And it seems like as soon as the kids found out that I walked and talked and breathed just the same as they did, then it wasn't long before I got to be a very popular student in the Moscow High School." However, after graduating from high school in 1914, he was unable to find a job in Moscow. " 'Course they didn't tell me it was on account of my color, but they just told me they didn't have anything for me. There was some people thought that I was so well-known around Moscow that I might have a pretty good chance of getting a job. But I didn't get anything."

Chrisemon, who had urged the Settle family to stay in Moscow, was the stepfather of the University of Idaho's first African-American graduate. Jennie Eva Hughes, Class of 1899, was the daughter of Louisa Chrisemon and Alexander Hughes. Little is known of Jennie's father, but after her mother married Lewis Chrisemon, the family moved west, arriving in Moscow in the early 1890s. They were Moscow's first black family. According to Jennie's University of Idaho registration card dated September 23, 1898, Louisa was a housekeeper. The family probably lived on Almon Street in the northwestern part of Moscow.

Jennie graduated from Moscow High School on April 26, 1895. As a student at the University of Idaho, Jennie was an excellent student. She won the prestigious Watkins Medal for Oratory in 1898, and graduated with a Bachelor of Science degree, one of seven students in her class. Later that year, she married George

Jennie Hughes was the first African-American graduate of the University of Idaho. She graduated in 1899, having won the prestigious Watkins medal for oratory in 1898. (#ID 2-110-1, Historical Photograph Collection, University of Idaho Library.)

Augustus Smith, and the couple lived in Wardner, Idaho in the Coeur d'Alene mining district, where George worked as a lead miner and owner. Jennie never returned to Moscow, but her first child Berthol did briefly attend the University of Idaho. Sadly, he died while attending the university.

As late as 2000, African Americans, as well as Native Americans, constitute less than 1 percent of the population of Latah County. Roughly 2 percent of Latah County's residents are members of Idaho's largest ethnic population, Hispanics and Latinos. The majority of Idaho's Hispanics and Latinos live in southern Idaho, as do members of one of Idaho's most distinct ethnic minorities, the Basques.

Another ethnic community not widely represented in Latah County is the Jewish community; although some of Latah County's most successful early businessmen—Henry Dernham, William and Emmanuel Kaufmann, and Moses Vandevantner—were Jewish. In 1949, local Jewish residents formed the Pullman-Moscow Jewish Community for the primary purpose of providing religious education for their children. Since then, the community has expanded its scope, offering High Holiday services; Sukkot, Hanukkah, and Purim celebrations; Friday and Saturday services; a Sunday evening discussion group; and a Sunday School program for children ages five to twelve.

One of the most recent religious groups to settle on the Palouse are Muslims. While most are from Pakistan and Kuwait and are students at either of the Palouse's two universities, the University of Idaho and Washington State University in Pullman, the number of Muslim families in the area is growing. In fact, the Palouse Muslim population is large enough that Pullman houses one of the few mosques in the Northwest and there is also an Islamic Center of Moscow.

With its small population of ethnic and religious minorities, Moscow and Latah County were not home to sizeable demonstrations for civil rights; however, that does not mean that members of other groups traditionally subjected to treatment based on factors other than merit did not organize and express themselves in Moscow. One of the few positions of authority open to women at the University of Idaho was the position of Dean of Women, and one of the university's most influential administrators, male or female, was Permeal Jane French.

French was the first Dean of Women. Prior to her appointment in 1908, the position had existed in a similar form with the title of "Preceptress," but with French's appointment, the position took on more significance, largely because she made it so. She built the university's first student union building, the Blue Bucket, using her personal funds and during her 28 years of service, touched the lives of many students with her thoughtful counsel. According to university historian Rafe Gibbs, Dean French treated each and every student with personal attention and courtesy, never letting them feel their concerns had not been seriously considered.

More than 60 years after French was appointed Dean of Women, for the first time the university would acknowledge the high amount of attrition among female students. With the passing of a student bill of rights in 1968, the university took the first step toward admitting that it treated female students differently from male students. The bill of rights prohibited regulations based on gender alone, such as the one that imposed a dress code only for women students. A few years after adopting the bill of rights, university President Ernest Hartung formed a committee to study the high attrition rate among female faculty. By 1973, that committee had become the Women's Caucus of the University of Idaho.

On May 18, 1973, the Women's Caucus filed a suit against the University of Idaho, charging it with sex discrimination in hiring, promotion, and salary. The Idaho Human Rights Commission ruled that the university had violated federal civil rights and equal opportunity acts and ordered it to hire a full-time Affirmative Action Officer, pay female employees retroactive salary adjustments, and undertake a study of staff salaries. The Women's Caucus was also responsible for the establishment of a women's center on campus and a women's studies program.

While the Women's Caucus is no longer an active organization on the University of Idaho campus, its advocacy did bring tangible improvements to conditions for women faculty, staff, and students. In Moscow, other advocacy groups have carried the banner for the rights of individuals with emotional, physical, and developmental disabilities. Two nonprofit organizations, Opportunities Unlimited, Inc., part of a larger organization serving north-central Idaho, and Stepping Stones, Inc. were created to help individuals with special needs learn the necessary skills to function and be accepted as equal members of mainstream society.

Thirty years after it was founded by the Women's Caucus, the women's center is an important tradition on the University of Idaho campus. It is a place where all students, female and male, are welcome, a place for "all the people, for everyone," to paraphrase pioneer Charles Munson's rationale for selecting Moscow as his home over a century ago. Among Moscow's citizens, Munson said, there was "no uppishness or snobs among them, for this was a true democracy."

Munson's comments are an indication of a spirit of populism and progressivism that has been a part of the Moscow tradition since its earliest days. Newcomers to Moscow will find no shortage of active grassroots organizations, each with a mission that reflects the diversity of thought and beliefs of its members. And as Rafe Gibbs wrote in his history of the University of Idaho, Moscow has always been a well-organized town. Combine the tradition of activism with effective organizational skills, and the result is a community that values and expects its citizens to be involved in all aspects of modern life.

As Moscowans work to shape their future, they are not forgetting their past. The Latah County Historical Society, a direct descendant of the Latah County Pioneer Association and the Moscow Historical Club, has led the effort to collect, preserve, interpret, disseminate, and celebrate the history of Latah County since 1968. The society maintains one of Moscow's landmark buildings, the Victorian-era McConnell Mansion, as a museum complete with restored period rooms and permanent and changing exhibits. The society, which has received both state and national awards, also maintains a research library, housing thousands of documents, photographs, and genealogical information.

The Latah County Historical Society also is actively engaged in the preservation of historic sites and buildings in Moscow and Latah County. Through its activism and that of the Moscow Historic Preservation Commission and the Latah County Historic Preservation Commission, nearly 30 buildings and two historic districts within Latah County and on the University of Idaho campus are in the National Register of Historic Places. Membership on both the city commission and the county commission is completely voluntary.

Because much of the architectural heritage of Moscow's Main Street remains intact, the Moscow Historic Preservation is exploring the possibility of designating the downtown area as a historic district. Several of the buildings that would be included in a downtown historic district are already listed in the National Register of Historic Places, including the McConnell-Maguire Building, built in 1891; the Skattaboe Block, also constructed in 1891 by Kenneth Skattaboe, a successful farmer and businessman; Davids' Center, constructed by Henry Dernham and William Kaufmann in 1889; and the Moscow Hotel, built in 1890 by Robert Barton.

Should the nomination to designate a historic downtown district be accepted, Moscow would then have two historic districts. In 1980, the Fort Russell

Bouquets of big, bright sunflowers are just a few of the beautiful items that are sold at Moscow's very popular Farmers' Market held on Saturday mornings April through October in downtown Moscow. (Courtesy Linda Pall.)

Historic District was placed in the National Register of Historic Places. The district consists of 116 structures similar in style and scale. Many of the structures in the historic district, located northeast of Main Street near Russell School, are homes within the Fort Russell neighborhood, one of Moscow's most prestigious neighborhoods.

It has been said that the great cities of the world have always taken art and architecture to heart, and with leadership from the University of Idaho, this has long been true of Moscow. Its citizens, in fact, often refer to Moscow as the "heart" of the arts in north-central Idaho due to the many talented artists that have called Moscow home, including painters Alf Dunn, George Roberts, Linda Wallace, and Mary Kirkwood and writers Ron McFarland, Mary Clearman Blew, and Carol Ryrie Brink. In addition to the summertime music festival, Rendezvous in the Park, Moscowans also support permanent arts organizations such as the Idaho Repertory Theater, the Idaho-Washington Chorale, the Washington-Idaho Symphony, the Palouse Folklore Society, and the Pritchard Art Gallery in downtown Moscow.

Moscow is also home to artists who use unusual media. The Palouse Patchers is a quilting guild with approximately 125 members that has received world attention for the originality and beauty of its quilts. Moscow resident Kathleen Warnick, one of the founders of the Appaloosa Lace Guild, is an expert on lacemaking. Her book *The Art of Lace* is one of the definitive works in the craft. Another Moscowan, Jeanne Leffingwell, is recognized as one of the nation's foremost bead artists.

In addition, the City of Moscow publicly supports the arts. The Moscow Arts Commission, with its mission of celebrating and cultivating the arts, offers several programs including a community band; youth choir; young people's arts festival; arts education; an art gallery on the third floor of City Hall, which is housed in a preserved federal building in the National Register; arts awards; a concert series; and last but by no means least, a farmers' market.

To say that Moscow's Farmers' Market is one of Moscow's most popular traditions is an understatement; the Farmers' Market is central to the social life of many Moscow residents. Established in 1977, the Farmers' Market is held each Saturday morning, April through October, in Friendship Square in the heart of downtown. Friendship Square was created when Fourth Street between the Moscow Hotel and the Skattaboe Building, two of Moscow's landmark buildings, was closed to traffic. The Farmers' Market is more than a place to find fresh, seasonal vegetables, fruit and flowers; it is a place to gather as a community in an environment of beauty, activity, and music.

Another tradition essential to the social life of Moscow is its annual Renaissance Fair. The roots of a springtime celebration in Moscow go back to 1910 when Dean of Women Permeal French organized the first Campus Day in May. After devoting the morning to cleaning up the campus, the afternoon was spent in relaxation and entertainment. A picnic was held, songs were sung, and the women students danced a Maypole dance.

During the next decades, this campus event would undergo a variety of permutations until the Maypole dance had become but a memory. In Moscow, meanwhile, the patriotic May Day celebration that had started in 1953 had continued intermittently. By 1965, it was no longer May Day but Loyalty Day, and as the era of peace and love gained momentum, this event became unfashionable. In contrast, in 1967, the first Peace Picnic was held on the university campus. Complete with jug music, anti-war speeches, and poetry, the Peace Picnic evolved into the Blue Mountain Rock Festival, which was held annually on campus until 1976.

In 1973, Moscow resident Jeannie Scott staged a Maypole dance in East City Park, and a year later, it was assimilated into the Renaissance Fair, which was organized that year as an arts and crafts fair by Bob Cameron. Ren Fair, as it is affectionately known, was organized, according to one of its early supporters, Jim Prall, "to provide a more wholesome alternative to the rock festival." Since then, Ren Fair, still held in East City Park, has become a true springtime celebration with food and entertainment as well as arts and crafts. Held during the first weekend of May, the celebration begins in downtown Moscow with a traditional Maypole dance.

The spirit of fellowship that characterizes the Renaissance Fair can be found on a weekly basis among the members of Moscow's "Friendly Neighbors." The late 1960s and early 1970s was a period of increased awareness, and among those groups receiving their due attention were senior citizens. Friendly Neighbors began in 1973 as the grassroots effort of a group of about 20 seniors who met weekly in Moscow's Moose Lodge to share a meal and each other's company. From this simple beginning, Friendly Neighbors has taken a leading role in serving Moscow's senior community.

The highlight of the day's activities, which tidied up the campus, was the Maypole Dance performed by the university's female students. (Courtesy LCHS.)

This postcard depicts a mural painted by K.J. Yuhasz on an old coal building on the south end of Moscow's Main Street to announce Moscow's annual Renaissance Fair, a celebration of arts, crafts, music, and food. (Courtesy LCHS.)

Working in partnership with the City of Moscow, Friendly Neighbors now provides lunchtime meals to over 100 seniors twice weekly. Had it not been for their efforts, two of Moscow's historic buildings—the 1911 federal building and the 1912 Moscow High School—might not have been preserved as community centers. In fact, Friendly Neighbors became one of the first organizations to use Moscow's latest community center, the 1912 Center, formerly the 1912 Moscow High School. The center's Great Room now serves as the organization's meal site.

Like Friendly Neighbors, the Moscow Food Co-op was started in 1973 by a group of friends with a shared purpose. Concerned about the high cost of food as well as the environmental impacts of corporate food production, Rod David, Jim Egan, and David and Katie Mosel formed a food-buying cooperative in 1973, and after receiving a small economic development grant, opened the first version of the Moscow Food Co-op. They called their enterprise the Good Food Store. While this would be Moscow's first food cooperative, local farmers had organized a farm cooperative in 1928, selling "fancy groceries and light hardware," according to historian Lillian Otness.

Located in a storefront on Second Street, the Moscow Food Co-op's initial inventory consisted of, not surprisingly, peas and lentils, as well as cheeses and spices. Its purpose, according to its founders, was to be a source of reasonably priced food for retail shoppers. Since then, the Moscow Food Co-op, a non-profit organization, has grown tremendously. From sales of $126.88 during its first month of operation, the Co-op now expects sales for 2002 to exceed $2.5 million.

From the storefront on Second Street, the Co-op kept outgrowing its space until it relocated to its present location on Third Street, just two blocks east of Main Street, in 2000.

From a completely volunteer staff, the Co-op now has a paid staff of 50 but remains committed to making a place for volunteers in the operation of the organization. Currently, over 100 people regularly volunteer at the Co-op, performing tasks as diverse as restocking spices to delivering the *Community News*, the Co-op's monthly newsletter, one of the few food cooperative newsletters in the nation still produced entirely by volunteers. Like the Friendly Neighbors, the Moscow Food Co-op serves the community as a warm and welcoming place where Moscowans of all ages, beliefs, and perspectives gather to share good food and fellowship.

On the shelves of the Moscow Food Co-op are many of the products made by Mary Jane Butters, a pioneer of organic farming in Idaho. Butters, a former forest ranger turned environmental activist, began producing organic products in 1989 and is now recognized as one of the leading organic producers in the nation. Her business Paradise Farms Organics, located near Moscow, produces and sells a diverse line of organic foods, from grain mixes to greens and flowers to backpacking foods. In 2001, Butters's sales reached nearly $400,000, and that same year, she introduced a nationally distributed magazine, *MaryJanesFarm*.

Before founding Paradise Farm Organics, Butters organized what would become the Palouse-Clearwater Environmental Institute (PCEI). Now in its 16th year, the Palouse-Clearwater Environmental Institute serves Latah and Whitman Counties as a grassroots organization with a mission to increase citizen involvement in decisions that affect the regional environment, through

Moscow designer Melissa Rockwood created this mural for the Moscow Food Co-op. (Courtesy Melissa Rockwell.)

community organizing and education. Like the Moscow Food Co-op, PCEI is powered by its volunteers, and among the many projects it has undertaken is the restoration and preservation of a 5-acre parcel of land as a nature park. Located along Paradise Creek near Moscow's first post office, the site was named in honor of Carol Ryrie Brink in the mid-1990s.

Another PCEI-powered project is the Latah Trail. In 1998, a group of citizens, sharing a common vision of a non-motorized transportation and recreation trail on the bed of the former railroad line running between Moscow and Troy, Idaho, in northeastern Latah County, organized to make their vision a reality. In partnership with Latah County, PCEI is working to develop this trail, which will connect with the Bill Chipman-Palouse Trail and Moscow's Paradise Path to the west and the Troy City Park to the east. The Bill Chipman-Palouse Trail, another rails-to-trails project, runs between Moscow and Pullman, Washington. The Paradise Path connects with the Chipman Trail on the west, runs through the university, and on through the eastern part of Moscow.

Located adjacent to the Bill Chipman-Palouse Trail, near the Idaho-Washington state line, is the Appaloosa Horse Club and Appaloosa Museum and Heritage Center. In 1946, George Hatley was a student of animal husbandry at the University of Idaho; he was also secretary of the Appaloosa Horse Club, formed in 1938 by historian Francis Haines. A year later, the Appaloosa Horse Club was moved to Moscow, and Hatley published the first Appaloosa Stud Book. In 1949, he produced the first national Appaloosa Horse Show. Since then, the Appaloosa has grown to be one of the most popular breeds in the nation.

In 1974, the horse club moved into a new building on the western edge of Moscow. In addition to housing the breed's international registry and the *Appaloosa News*, the club's magazine, the building is also the home of the Appaloosa Museum and Heritage Center. Founded in 1975, it is the first museum in the United States dedicated to a horse breed. The museum collects, preserves, and exhibits objects that illustrate the history of the Appaloosa horse and includes a library of approximately 500 books and 15,000 photos.

Besides the Appaloosa Museum and Heritage Center and the McConnell Mansion Museum, Moscow will soon be home to another distinctive cultural museum. The University of Idaho will build the International Jazz Collections, a $40-million museum and archive that will preserve the heritage of jazz. The museum is but one component of the University of Idaho's Lionel Hampton Center Initiative, which honors the jazz legend who fell in love with a small town in northern Idaho. In 1984, jazz great Lionel Hampton made his first appearance at the University of Idaho Jazz Festival, which had been founded by music professor David Seiler in 1968. In 1985, festival director and music professor Lynn Skinner asked Hampton to sponsor the annual festival, and the rest is history.

With the association of Skinner and Hampton, the jazz festival expanded its scope and was renamed the Lionel Hampton Jazz Festival. In little more than a decade, the festival has become a four-day event, held each February, that attracts some of the most famous names in international jazz, including Ella Fitzgerald, Doc Severinsen, Bobby McFerrin, Sarah Vaughn, Dizzy Gillespie, and Dianne Reeves. And as equally important as the performances are the clinics and competitions held for the over 12,000 students, from throughout the Northwest, who attend the festival each year.

In 2001, the university launched the Lionel Hampton Center Initiative. The multi-million-dollar project includes construction of a performance and education facility, an archive to house the International Jazz Collections, and the creation of an endowment to fund future festivals, scholarships, and professorships. Leading the fundraising component of the initiative is former President George Bush and Barbara Bush, and the education and performance facility will be designed by one of the nation's most illustrious architectural firms, Cesar Pelli and Associates.

The Lionel Hampton Center Initiative, as large as it is, is just one example of the University of Idaho's most recent building boom, which began in the late

This image of George Hatley, longtime champion of the Appaloosa horse, graces a poster promoting the Appaloosa Museum and Heritage Center. (Courtesy Marsha Anderson.)

1990s under the administration of university President Robert Hoover. Since 1996, new constructions and renovations have totaled more than $129 million, with a little less than 70 percent of the project costs coming from private donations. New buildings include the Ag Biotech Laboratory, Idaho Commons, J.A. Albertson Business and Economics Building (which was constructed entirely with private monies), the Student Recreation Center, and the Living and Learning Community, a new dormitory.

The scope of the university's facilities plan is comprehensive, just as the scope of the Lionel Hampton Center is international. The Lionel Hampton Jazz Festival brings musicians from all over the world to Moscow, and our community is graced with their presence each year. In turn, Moscow welcomes them, and the festival's many young students, with the warm hospitality of a small town.

In little more than a century, an isolated village founded in the most remote area of the American frontier has become an international community. From the halls and laboratories of the University of Idaho to the vast fields of grain that surround it, Moscow is a vital community that honors its history and traditions, as well as the diversity of its residents, to build a future that improves upon that which came before.

Jazz legend Lionel Hampton, at the podium, addresses the crowd gathered at the dedication of the university's School of Music as the Lionel Hampton School of Music. (Courtesy LCHS.)

BIBLIOGRAPHY

Extensive use was made of the resources of the Latah County Historical Society, including archival documents and articles from the *Latah Legacy*, the historical society's journal. The work of the following authors, as published in the *Latah Legacy*, was used in the writing of this history: Nancy I. Atkinson, Ron Brockett, Karen Broenneke, Ed Burke, Alfred Dunn, Homer Futter, Monica E. Hulubei, Rosemary Huskey, Lucinda Tuttle Jenks, Joann Jones, Alma Lauder Keeling, Marguerite Laughlin, Janet Lecompte, Lillian Otness, Keith C. Petersen, Mary E. Reed, Herman W. Ronnenberg, Jean Cummings Rudolph, Allen Slickpoo, Terry W. Soule, Lawrence Smith, Ann Stokes, Jeanette Talbott, University of Idaho Naval ROTC, Ted Van Arsdol, Grace Wicks, Keith Williams, and Carol Young.

Archival documents, on repository at the Latah County Historical Society and written by the following individuals, were also used: Mickey Aitken, E.T. Baker, Cornelius J. Brosnan, Alec Bull, and Mrs. Kenneth O'Donnell, as were those on repository at University of Idaho Special Collections and written by William E. Betts, Clara Ransom Davis, and Patrick McDonald.

ADDITIONAL SOURCES

Arnzen, Kenneth Joseph. *The First Hundred Years: A Centennial History of St. Mary's Church, Moscow, Idaho*. Moscow: Privately printed, 1982.

Banks, William Carr. *Kites in the Empyrean: Thoughts and Expressions from the Letters and Scattered Missives of William Carr Banks, 1903–1975*. Moscow: The University Press of Idaho, 1976.

Boone, Lalia Phipps. *From A to Z in Latah County, Idaho: A Place Name Dictionary*. Idaho Place Name Project, 1983.

Brink, Carol Ryrie. *A Chain of Hands*. Pullman, WA: Washington State University Press, in collaboration with the Latah County Historical Society, 1993.

Bunchgrass Historian. "Exploration of the Palouse Country: The Pacific Railroad Expedition of the 1850s." Colfax, WA: Whitman County Historical Society, 16.2 (1988).

Cook, David. "Just the Beginning." *Community News*. Moscow Food Co-op. September 1993.

Cox, Lloyd M. *In the Days when the Rivers Ran Backwards*. Self-published, 1994.

Daily Idahonian. 50th Anniversary Historic Edition, Supplement. 29 September 1961.

David, Homer. *Moscow at the Turn of the Century*. Local History Paper No. 6 of Latah County Historical Society, 1979.

Encyclopedia of Idaho Indians. St. Clair Shores, MI: Somerset, 2000.

Gibbs, Rafe. *Beacon for Mountain and Plain*. Caldwell, ID: The Caxton Printers, Ltd., 1962.

Hatley, George, "The Grass that Grew Appaloosas." *Palouse Journal*. 53. Spring/Summer 1992.

Idaho Geological Survey. *Geology of the Palouse*. GeoNote 9. Moscow, May 1986.

Idahonian. Moscow, Latah County, and University of Idaho Centennial Editions.

Johansen, Dorothy O. *Empire of the Columbia: A History of the Pacific Northwest*. New York: Harper and Row, 1967.

Keith, Thomas B. *The Horse Interlude: A Pictorial History of Horse and Man in the Inland Northwest*. Moscow: University Press of Idaho, 1976.

London, Bill. "Spring Fling." *Palouse Journal*. March 1986.

Moscow-Pullman Daily News. "Hamp's University of Idaho History." 2 September 2002.

Munson, Charles J. *Westward to Paradise*. Local History Paper No. 4 of the Latah County Historical Society. Moscow, 1978.

Nelson, Elsie Mary. *Today is Ours*. Available at Latah County Historical Society and through the Latah County Library District. Self published, 1972.

Otness, Lillian W. *A Great Good Country*. Local History Paper #8 of the Latah County Historical Society. Moscow, 1983.

Platt, Kenneth B. *Some Pioneer Glimpses of Latah County*. Local History Paper No. 1 of the Latah County Historical Society. Moscow, 1974.

Scheuerman, Richard. *Palouse Country: A Land and its People*. College Place, WA: Color Press, 1994.

Walker, Deward E. Jr. *Indians of Idaho*. Moscow: University Press of Idaho, 1978.

INDEX

TEACHER
UNIONS
AND SOCIAL
JUSTICE

Organizing for the Schools and Communities Our Students Deserve

EDITORS
Michael Charney
Jesse Hagopian
Bob Peterson

A RETHINKING SCHOOLS PUBLICATION

Teacher Unions and Social Justice:
Organizing for the Schools and Communities Our Students Deserve

Edited by Michael Charney, Jesse Hagopian, and Bob Peterson

A Rethinking Schools Publication

Rethinking Schools, Ltd., is a nonprofit publisher and advocacy
organization dedicated to sustaining and strengthening public
education through social justice teaching and education activism.
Our magazine, books, and other resources promote equity and
racial justice in the classroom.

To request additional copies of this book or a catalog of other
publications, or to subscribe to Rethinking Schools magazine, contact:

6737 W. Washington St.
Suite 3249
Milwaukee, WI 53214
800-669-4192
rethinkingschools.org

Follow @RethinkSchools

© 2021 Rethinking Schools, Ltd.

Book Production Editor: Leigh Dingerson
Cover and Book Design: Nancy Zucker
Cover Photo: Joe Brusky
Copy Editing: Tom Tolan
Proofreading: Lawrence Sanfilippo
Indexing: Carol Roberts

ISBN: 978-0-942961-09-6

Library of Congress Control Number: 2020946318

We dedicate this book to Karen Lewis (1953–2021), past president of the Chicago Teachers Union. Karen's life work demonstrated the power of social justice teacher unionism. She inspired countless educators to learn from and organize with colleagues, students, and communities to transform our schools and our world.

Acknowledgements

The idea of *Teacher Unions and Social Justice: Organizing for the Schools and Communities Our Students Deserve* started out as what we thought would be a relatively easy project: publishing a second edition of the 1999 Rethinking Schools' book *Transforming Teacher Unions: Fighting for Social Justice and Better Schools.* We quickly adjusted that plan. Given the changes in the educational landscape and the union movement we decided to create an entirely new book that was more comprehensive and reflective of the times we live in. The book would not have been possible without the hard work and advice of many people.

The editors relied heavily on the talent of two people: Nancy Zucker and Leigh Dingerson. Nancy, who oversees the design and layout of our magazine as well as many of our books, brought a crisp layout, color, and the many engaging photos and illustrations to *Teacher Unions and Social Justice.* As production editor, Leigh's insights as a community organizer and education activist and her many organizational and editing skills made this book possible.

Rethinking Schools editors Stan Karp and David Levine provided ongoing support and critical advice. Gina Palazzari, Missy Zombor, and Lindsay Stevens oversaw printing, marketing, and distribution efforts. Copy editor and fact checker Tom Tolan and meticulous proofreader Lawrence Sanfilippo added their expertise. The overall vision and many of the particulars of the book were guided by the suggestions and advice of 12 people from across the country who served on an advisory committee. Their names and brief bios are listed on the following page.

And finally, a special thanks to the many book contributors, photographers, illustrators, and union activists and leaders who are building social justice unions and organizing for the schools and communities our students deserve.

—Michael Charney, Jesse Hagopian, and Bob Peterson

Members of the advisory committee

Eric Blanc A labor activist and former high school teacher, currently a doctoral student in sociology at New York University. He is the author of *Red State Revolt: The Teachers' Strike Wave and Working-Class Politics* (Verso, 2019).

Michelle Strater Gunderson A 34-year teaching veteran who currently teaches first grade in the Chicago Public Schools. She serves as trustee for the Chicago Teachers Union and is the former co-chair of the Caucus of Rank and File Educators (CORE).

Arlene Inouye The UTLA secretary and co-chair of the UTLA bargaining team. She has been a speech and language specialist for 18 years in the Los Angeles Unified School District and involved in public education transformation for decades.

David Levine A retired education professor living in Columbus, Ohio. He is a founding editor of Rethinking Schools. His research interests include U.S. educational history and urban education.

Kelly McMahon A kindergarten teacher at Hoover Community School in Cedar Rapids, Iowa. She serves as treasurer for both her local and state associations.

Ikechukwu Onyema A chemistry teacher in New Jersey. He is co-founder of MAP-SO Freedom School, a local organization committed to racial justice in schools.

Turquoise LeJeune Parker A racial and social justice teacher in Durham Public Schools. She proudly represents as a Historically Black College graduate and is the NEA director for North Carolina.

Adam Sanchez A social studies teacher at Lincoln High School in Philadelphia. He is editor of T*eaching a People's History of Abolition and the Civil War,* a Zinn Education Project teacher leader and an editor of *Rethinking Schools*.

Eleni Schirmer A scholar, writer, and activist from Madison, Wisconsin. Her research explores the contradictory capacities of social movements—particularly teacher unions—to shape institutions, identities, and ideas.

Gabriel Tanglao A former social studies teacher in Bergen County, New Jersey. He currently works in the Professional Development and Instructional Issues division for the New Jersey Education Association.

Jessica Tang The president of the Boston Teachers Union. She was a co-founder of the Teacher Activist Group-Boston. She is the first person of color, first openly bisexual/LGBTQ leader, and first woman in more than thirty years to serve as president of the BTU.

Ingrid Walker-Henry A 20-year teacher in Milwaukee Public Schools. She is vice president of the Milwaukee Teachers' Education Association and works as a teaching and learning organizer.

CONTENTS

I walked the line in '89 Doing it again in 2019

INTRODUCTION

Teacher Unions and Social Justice
Organizing for the Schools and Communities Our Students Deserve

More than two decades ago in the first edition of this book, *Transforming Teacher Unions: Fighting for Better Schools and Social Justice*, we promoted a vision of social justice teacher unionism. We argued that such a vision was essential to improving our schools, transforming our unions, and building a more just society.

Since then much has happened. Public schools, the entire public sector, and the basic notion of the "common good" have come under severe attack. Wealth inequality has reached an unsustainable level. The scourge of white supremacy has been intensified by rampant xenophobia. COVID-19 has wreaked havoc and death around the world, illuminating the grave weaknesses of social and public institutions. And our planet is still on fire.

But within our schools and the larger society, seeds of struggle have sprouted and grown. In the past decade, militant strikes have revitalized the teacher union movement. We've witnessed the birth of the Black Lives Matter, Me Too, and Fight for $15 movements, along with struggles for immigrant rights, climate justice, gun control, and an end to mass incarceration.

By the end of May 2020 the horrific murders of George Floyd, Breonna Taylor, Ahmaud Arbery, and Tony McDade sparked a mass movement across the country and throughout the world demanding an end to police violence against Black people and other people of color. This unprecedented, multiracial Black Lives Matter (BLM) movement focused the nation's attention on white supremacy and institutional racism and fundamentally changed the national conversation on racial justice.

The BLM movement also pushed teachers and school staff to reexamine their teaching and school policies and to put social justice and anti-racism at the center of our classrooms, schools, and our unions.

Contemporary Roots of Social Justice Unionism

The massive uprising by teachers in Wisconsin in the spring of 2011 set the stage for the Occupy Movement, that followed a few months later, and for an exponential growth in social justice unionism across the country. In 2012, the Chicago Teachers Union (CTU) launched a historic and successful strike based on organizing members to move beyond a passive "service model" of unionism to embrace thoroughgoing rank-and-file engagement. As the CTU fostered internal democracy, it also built a strong alliance with the community by articulating and fighting for a comprehensive vision of how Chicago's schools and neighborhoods needed to change. Presented in a sweeping report titled "The Schools Chicago's Students Deserve," this vision called for a halt to racially biased school closings, the dismantling of segregation, the hiring of more teachers of color, restorative practices in place of punitive discipline, the removal of police from schools, and other fundamental changes within the city's schools. Just as important, the CTU championed a living wage, full employment, decent health care, affordable housing, and other measures to address structural class and racial inequality. This expansive commitment to transforming schools and communities moved the union to link its advocacy and organizing for educators' interests to a broader strategy of "bargaining for the common good."

The CTU was not alone. Teacher unions across the nation, including the Milwaukee Teachers' Education Association, the Saint Paul Federation of Educators, United Teachers Los Angeles, the Massachusetts Teachers Association, and the

Boston Teachers Union, moved toward social justice unionism. Inspired by the CTU, several of these unions worked with community groups to develop their own versions of "The Schools Chicago's Students Deserve" and, where possible, started "bargaining for the common good."

We changed the title and subtitle of this new edition to emphasize "The Schools Our Students Deserve" as a way to frame the key *strategy* of building broad union/community coalitions to demand real investment—at the local, state, and federal levels—in our public schools. This means "bargaining for the common good" in states that allow bargaining, and militant, collective action including statewide strikes like those in the winter and spring of 2018 in West Virginia, Kentucky, Oklahoma, and Arizona. These and subsequent strikes and walkouts in LA, Chicago, St. Paul, and elsewhere shifted the national conversation about education and led public opinion to more favorable attitudes toward public schools and educators.

Following the lead of the Schools and Communities United coalition in Milwaukee, we added "and Communities" to the "Schools Our Students Deserve" slogan in recognition of the inextricable connections between the well-being of the broader community and the health of our public schools. These connections include the need for family sustainable jobs, adequate housing, universal health care, criminal justice reform, paid sick days and family leave, and an end to institutional racism.

To create the schools and communities our students deserve, we must reclaim our profession and our classrooms from the corporate reform agenda of standardized testing, scripted curriculum, and top-down control. In its place, we need to make schools "greenhouses of democracy" in which teachers and other school staff collaborate deeply and hold each other accountable to provide all students with a rigorous and humane education. Such schools—sometimes called "transformative community schools"—welcome and support parents as respected partners. Such schools constantly work toward increasing equity and making classrooms places of deep learning and supportive, hopeful communities that foster civic engagement and concern for the common good among students.

To get such schools will be a struggle fought in the streets and in school boards, city councils, statehouses, and Congress. It will mean the hard work of one-on-one organizing and building popular power in schools and elected positions side by side with mobilizing campaigns, demonstrations, and elections. Teacher unions are strategically located to help lead these struggles in our communities and to be allies in the various social justice movements of today. More than 5 million members of the NEA and AFT throughout the country engage daily with students and

> To create the schools and communities our students deserve, we must reclaim our profession and our classrooms from the corporate reform agenda of standardized testing, scripted curriculum, and top-down control.

their families. They are well placed to understand and help meet the social and economic challenges the majority of people face. We believe that to successfully provide such leadership it's essential for teacher unions—from the smallest local to our national organizations—to embrace social justice unionism. To build the broad social movements we need, we must ensure democratic practices inside our unions, engage and organize—not just mobilize—our membership, and build lasting alliances with other labor, community, faith-based, civic, parent, and student groups.

To build a national trend toward social justice teacher unionism, it's essential that we inspire and learn from each other. We hope that this book contributes to such inspiration and learning. Below is a brief summary of the seven sections of the book that contain more than 60 articles, interviews, documents, contract language examples, and resource recommendations.

SECTION ONE Our Roots

In this section we consider the historical roots of teacher unionism through the lens of social justice. We start with an interview with the late historian Howard Zinn, who looks at the crucial yet imperfect role that labor unions have played in our nation's working-class struggles.

We then highlight Chicago teacher union leader Margaret Haley's famous 1904 speech "Why Teachers Should Organize" and CTU's long history of struggle against corporate attempts to control our schools and our students. We note the important and increasing role women have played in teacher unions in this highly gendered sector of the workforce. Historian Dan Perlstein describes the groundbreaking work of the early Teachers Union in New York City in promoting the teaching of African American history and uniting with the community on campaigns for justice. He also looks at the community control struggle and 1968 Ocean Hill-Brownsville strike that inflicted lasting damage on the union's relationship with the Black and Latino communities.

Labor activist Bill Fletcher Jr.'s interview emphasizes the importance of center- ing the issue of racism in our struggles and offers specific advice for new social justice-minded union leaders.

Our "Roots" section ends by examining key episodes of more recent teacher union history—a call for social justice teacher unionism in the 1990s by NEA and AFT union activists associated with the National Coalition of Education Activists, the historic 2011 Wisconsin teacher uprising, and the "RedForEd" wave of teacher strikes in 2018 that changed the landscape of current education politics.

SECTION TWO What Social Justice Unions Look Like

We start this section with our overview of the characteristics of three types of teacher unionism—industrial, professional, and social justice—recognizing that unions often consciously or unconsciously draw on or blend together different aspects of the three models, or call them by different names.

This section describes how teacher unions have worked for social justice through varied programs and organizing strategies—at times at odds with and at times in cooperation with district administrations. These initiatives include career ladders, home visits, restorative justice, peer assistance and review, and organizing for community schools. Many of these examples exemplify the "professional unionism" model. These articles emphasize that such programs are most effective when they incorporate key aspects of a social justice approach—heightening the involvement of union members and paying explicit attention to equity and the need to address white supremacy.

SECTION THREE Pushing from the Bottom Up

In many unions, sometimes the most dramatic changes stem from rank-and-file organizing that pushes leadership to take more militant, democratic, and radical action for social justice, and at times brings activists into leadership positions.

Noah Karvelis describes how the savvy use of social media helped widely scattered educators organize a 2018 statewide strike in Arizona. Michelle Strater Gunderson, an experienced leader of the Chicago Caucus of Rank and File Educators, reflects on her experience and the role of caucuses across the country. Former CTU president Karen Lewis describes in detail the Chicago caucus and her first years as president. This section concludes with reflections on rank-and-file organizing in Baltimore, Philadelphia, New Jersey, and North Carolina.

SECTION FOUR Reimagining Our Unions to Build Power

As union activists committed to social justice win elections and move into union leadership, they confront many challenges and opportunities. The first part of this section details the transformation of the Milwaukee Teachers' Education Association and United Teachers Los Angeles. Arlene Inouye shares how new leadership transformed UTLA and provides lessons from the 2019 strike. Lauren Quinn shares how the solidarity of that strike convinced her to get involved and become a leader in the union.

The rest of the section describes creative strategies for transforming unions and building power, including through school visits by union leadership, using traditional and social media, and hosting "Art Builds," where art activists and art teachers with union support hold mass events to create posters, banners, and parachutes for major campaigns.

SECTION FIVE Fighting the System

In this section we examine how austerity, white supremacy, privatization, school takeovers, and the corporate push for standardized testing continue to damage public schools and undermine the prospects for providing equitable, high-quality education to all students. We also look at how different state and local unions have responded to these attacks and draw lessons from their organizing. The responses range from a caucus-led boycott of the MAP testing in Seattle, to a Baton Rouge local challenging ExxonMobil, to a successful struggle for investment in public schools in Massachusetts, to a victorious effort to remove a pro-privatization governor in Puerto Rico.

In order to remind readers that our struggle is international, we've included an interview with Angelo Gavrielatos, president of Australia's New South Wales Teachers Union, who led a five-year anti-privatization campaign for Education International. We've also included an account of the teacher union movement in Colombia, where teacher activists and leaders have been assassinated and kidnapped by right-wing militias. These articles underscore the need for social justice unions to act in solidarity with educators and students around the world.

SECTION SIX Taking Social Justice into the Classroom

The imperative for teacher unions to work for social justice encompasses not only local, state, and national arenas, but also our classrooms. In a society that often fosters alienation, passivity, and disengagement, we need to foster among our students a sense of community, vibrant connection through shared learning, and optimism about changing the world. We need to help them think deeply about the forces that shape their lives: white supremacy, wealth inequality, gender injustice, and climate change. Just as importantly, we need to help them understand how people have joined together in social movements to work to make things better.

> In a society that often fosters alienation, passivity, and disengagement, we need to foster a sense of community, vibrant connection through shared learning, and optimism about changing the world.

Weaving social justice themes into the classroom enables educators to act in solidarity with the communities they serve, teaching critically about the issues that those communities care about. And when we engage union members about these issues, we educate them, and help them think more clearly about what unions can and should fight for. In this section we examine principles of social justice and anti-racist education, and provide several examples of how unions are increasingly promoting such teaching on issues ranging from climate justice to racial justice and economic justice.

SECTION SEVEN Resources

The final section is a compilation of resources that we think will be helpful for union activists and leaders. This includes excerpts from several different contracts that may inspire or provide helpful language for struggles elsewhere. We also list organizations, periodicals, websites, and books/pamphlets that provide more discussion on many of the subjects covered in this book.

Some of the articles from the first edition of this book that were not included in this volume are available at rethinkingschools.org, along with our quarterly magazine that regularly covers issues related to teacher unions and educational justice. Please stay in touch with us.

✳ ✳ ✳

As this book goes to press at the end of 2020, our world is in the midst of the COVID-19 pandemic with no clear end in sight. While much will be written about the pandemic in the months and years to come, one lesson is already clear: Well-funded, democratically run public institutions led by competent and visionary officials, accountable to public oversight and review, are essential to the overall welfare of our society and the survival of the entire planet. All justice-loving people have an important role to play.

Given the size and breadth of teacher unions, social justice unionism is an essential pillar of the activism needed to create a more sustainable and just future for the children who will inherit the earth.

> Michael Charney
> Jesse Hagopian
> Bob Peterson
> Editors of *Teacher Unions and Social Justice*

A note on the term "teacher unions"

While we use the word "teacher" in the title of our book we know that many current teacher unions include "non-teacher" educators and other school staff. We also know that relations between these different groups of workers have at times been divisive. We support democratic, wall-to-wall unionism in public schools and acknowledge just because all public school workers might be in one union, equity is not a given, and that it's essential that all union members are able to fully and equitably participate in union activities and decisions. We look forward to exploring efforts to unite all school workers into single public school worker unions and to publishing articles on this topic in future editions of *Rethinking Schools*.

Imagine if Your Union . . .

Worked in an ongoing alliance with community, parent, and labor groups to promote the schools and communities our students deserve.

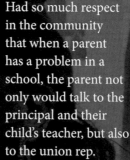

Had so much respect in the community that when a parent has a problem in a school, the parent not only would talk to the principal and their child's teacher, but also to the union rep.

Ran a mentoring program in cooperation with school administration to provide every new teacher with ongoing help from a mentor.

Had an outreach program in which union members regularly spoke at community and neighborhood groups, sororities and fraternities, and places of worship to garner support for public education and exchange ideas.

Operated a professional development center where teachers taught teachers and those being instructed earned university credit for participation.

Had a diverse leadership and membership that was more reflective of the district's student body.

Offered opportunities for members to engage and interact with members of other unions—nationally and internationally.

Started programs for high school youth to serve as union interns and learn about the labor movement.

Had a program to fight racism and prejudice, with a place where teachers could turn to for professional development, curricular resources, and support.

Maintained a resource center with working copiers, supplies, tech support, and a professional library of journals and books that served as a hub for common teacher planning.

Sponsored afternoon social justice curriculum-sharing sessions at the union's offices.

Held membership meetings that were lively exchanges on important educational and social issues, rather than top-down assemblies of leadership speeches and reports.

Invited members of community organizations and other labor unions to gatherings to discuss issues of mutual concern.

SECTION ONE

OUR ROOTS

People should: GO where they are not supposed to go, SAY what they are not supposed to say and STAY when they are told to leave."

—Howard Zin

Why Teachers Should Know History
An interview with historian Howard Zinn

Howard Zinn speaking at an antiwar rally at Harvard, 1970.

JEFF ALBERTSON PHOTOGRAPH COLLECTION (PH 57) SPECIAL COLLECTIONS, UNIVERSITY ARCHIVES, UNIVERSITY OF MASSACHUSETTS AMHERST LIBRARIES

The following is condensed from an interview with historian Howard Zinn, author of A People's History of the United States. *He was interviewed by Bob Peterson of* Rethinking Schools.

How has the labor movement contributed to the economic well-being of people in our society?

There is nothing in the U.S. Constitution that guarantees economic rights such as decent wages, or decent hours of work, or safe working conditions. As a result, working people have always been forced to act on their own. One way they have done this is through the labor movement.

Without the labor movement, for example, it's doubtful that working people would have won the eight-hour day. Not only did workers not have government on their side, the government was on the other side. All through the latter part of the 19th century and the early 20th century, the government was using the police and the Army and the National Guard and the courts to break strikes throughout the country.

In the 1930s, workers organized to extend the benefits of labor organization beyond the small percentage of workers covered by the AFL (American Federation of Labor) craft unions—that is, to extend the benefits to the women, people of color, unskilled workers, and immigrant workers who were excluded from the AFL. This led to the formation of the Congress of Industrial Organizations (CIO).

A more recent example is the farmworkers organizing on the West Coast in the 1960s to bring at least a modicum of decent conditions to people who had been left out of organized labor for a long time.

It's interesting that this country boasts so much about our standard of living compared to that of people in other countries. While that's generally true, this higher standard of living did not come as a result of governmental initiative—or some action by Congress, or the Supreme Court, or the president. It came as a result of working people organizing, going on strike, facing off with police, going to jail, getting beaten, getting killed. The history of labor struggles in this country is one of the most dramatic of any country in the world.

Why do you think that today less than 14 percent of the workforce in the United States is unionized?

For one thing, the history of working people and of the labor movement is not taught in this country. It's not in the schoolbooks and it's not in the mass media. So workers are unaware of past labor struggles, and this can have a debilitating effect.

It's also harder today to organize workers because of changes in the economy. Manufacturing has shrunk while the service industry has grown. But service and white-collar workers are much harder to organize than blue-collar workers in large factories. Now there is also the problem of organizing in an increasingly global economic structure.

One reason the American workforce has been so little unionized, even in its best years, has been the tensions between white and Black, men and women, played upon by the employers. But also, unions themselves have discriminated against people of color and women. Look, for instance, at the disproportionate number of men who hold official positions in trade unions. And often, unions have not fought hard on the issue of equal pay for equal work for women and minorities.

Then there is the intimidation factor. President Reagan broke the strike of the air traffic controllers almost as soon as he came into office in 1981, and that put a great fear into workers who might have been thinking about going on strike. Also, the National Labor Relations Board has, in recent decades, become more of a tool of corporations. Nor have the courts been quick to support workers' rights. All these factors are serious obstacles to workers trying to organize.

Have there been times when the U.S. labor movement has played a noticeably more progressive role, going beyond bread-and-butter issues for its members?
Here's one example. During the late 1930s, when fascism was rising in Europe, the progressive labor unions in the United States refused to work on ships from Germany. They also tried to establish boycotts of goods from Germany and Italy.

In the 1930s, the labor movement was farther to the left than it is today. The CIO, which later joined with the AFL, took a lot of important stands for peace and justice. There were CIO conventions where they talked about health care, job security, even basic changes that needed to take place in the social structure. This broader focus, however, changed almost immediately after World War II. The ferocious anti-communism of the Cold War led to demands that trade union leaders take loyalty oaths and swear they weren't involved with the communist movement. It was at this time that the labor movement dropped its concern with broader issues of peace and justice and international solidarity.

If you go back to the early 20th century, you have the Industrial Workers of the World (IWW), which was more than a labor movement and which fought for the total restructuring of society. The IWW went far beyond the focus of the AFL, which was to simply get higher wages and better working conditions for its narrow band of workers. Of course, the IWW was destroyed by the government during and after World War I.

In fact, one of the functions of war is to give the government an opportunity to get rid of troublesome, rebellious movements in society. The government in this country has been very good at taking the patriotic spirit that exists during war and using it to whip up hysteria and justify putting labor leaders into jail.

During World War I, for instance, the government put virtually all the IWW leaders on trial, for conspiracy to hinder the draft and encourage desertion, and gave them long prison sentences. And after World War II, during McCarthyism and the Cold War, progressive leaders of the labor movement were forced out of their positions. You have to remember that the Cold War and McCarthyism were not just phenomena of the Republican Party. They were part of a clearly bipartisan effort to get rid of the radical forces in the labor movement and get rid of the larger issues that the CIO was concerned with.

What role did the labor movement play in the Civil Rights Movement?
In my experience, the labor movement was not involved in the Civil Rights Movement in the South, one reason being that the labor movement has never been well organized in that part of the country. When the Civil Rights Movement began to act on the national level, there was a distinct difference in the way the unions

responded. The progressive ones such as District 65 of the Retail, Wholesale and Department Store Union and Local 1199 of the Drug, Hospital, and Health Care Employees Union reacted very positively and were helpful in fundraising and in giving support. There were also rank-and-file workers from across the country who supported the Civil Rights Movement.

But not all unions responded positively. For example, in 1964, the Civil Rights Movement fought for the rights of Blacks to be at the Democratic Convention and opposed [seating] an all-white delegation from Mississippi. That's when Fannie Lou Hamer, a courageous African American from the Mississippi Freedom Democratic Party—the name given to the disenfranchised Black people organizing their own political party in the summer of 1964—went on national television and appealed to the nation. But the top leadership of the AFL-CIO—then-head Walter Reuther, for example—wanted the Mississippi people to accept a very pitiful, token representation in the Mississippi delegation. They didn't want the Blacks to even have a vote, but to just sit there at the convention.

What has been the role of organized labor in other peace and justice movements you've participated in?

During the movement against the war in Vietnam, there also was a distinct difference between rank-and-file workers and some of the more progressive unions on the one hand, and the national leadership of the labor movement. The progressive forces were involved in the antiwar movement from the start. But the national leadership, which then as now was tied to the Democratic Party, was slow to join the forces against the war. It did so only when the country as a whole was disgusted with what we were doing in Vietnam.

Currently a debate rages about the role of government in society. What lessons can we draw from history?

This issue of the popular attitude toward government is very interesting. I believe this attitude is by and large created by politicians and the media. They have managed to take this very complicated question about the role of government and very cleverly make it seem like it's wrong when the government does something for poor and working people.

It's important to point out that big government in itself is neither good nor bad. It all depends on what class the government is favoring.

Remember the slogan that Clinton threw out during his last campaign? "The era of big government is over." That slogan shows how poorly people in this country have been taught our history. It is so misleading and hypocritical for Clinton to talk about the era of big government being over. For most of our history, government has been used to support the rich and the corporations. It is only relatively recently, in the 20th century—particularly in the 1930s with the New Deal and in the 1960s with programs such as Medicare and food stamps—that the government has responded to the demands and interests of ordinary people.

For most of our history, in fact from the very beginning with the establishment of the U.S. Constitution, the government has favored the upper classes. The Constitution was intended to create what we might call big government, a strong central government, for the purpose of aiding the bond holders, the slave holders, and the land speculators.

On the other hand, when government is affected by popular movements, citizen movements, or protest movements, it is possible that occasionally the government will do something that helps the people who are in need. We have examples of government doing very good and useful things. One thinks immediately of the G.I. Bill of Rights, right after World War II, when government funding enabled millions of WWII veterans to have a college education, and that democratized the educational system of the country almost overnight.

Today, interestingly enough, complaints about big government have been centered around welfare, Social Security, unemployment security, minimum wage. These are examples of where government is absolutely necessary, yet they are being attacked.

> Racism has historically been used in the United States to divide white and Black workers from one another. Sometimes people ask why is there no great socialist movement in the United States as has developed in other countries. One of the reasons is the division among workers.

On the other hand, we have big government today in the form of the Pentagon—government contracts to manufacturers of nuclear weapons and military hardware, jet planes and aircraft carriers. That's a very, very big government involved there.

I think it's important to point out the distinction between the historically pro-business actions of the government and the occasional pro-people actions of the government.

What role could teacher unions play in terms of promoting such an understanding?

If teacher unions want to be strong and well supported, it's essential that they not only be teacher unionists but teachers of unionism. We need to create a generation of students who support teachers and the movement of teachers for their rights.

In many cities, the teachers are mostly white and the students are mostly students of color. How has the labor movement hindered or helped in the struggle against racism?

This is an important issue. Racism has historically been used in the United States to divide white and Black workers from one another. Sometimes people ask why is there no great socialist movement in the United States as has developed in other countries. One of the reasons is the division among workers. And the biggest division is the racial division that employers have used again and again. Very often, the result has been that unions have been racist. The AFL consisted of white-only craft unions, and Blacks were excluded.

On the other hand, the IWW at the beginning of the century welcomed everybody, and the CIO organized in mass production industries such as auto, steel, and rubber, which had large numbers of Black workers who had come up from the South after World War I. The CIO had to organize both white and Black workers, and they struggled together during the strikes of the 1930s. That was a very positive movement in the history of race relations in the trade union movement.

But racism is a constant problem and remains a problem today. It raises the question of labor unions thinking beyond their most narrow interests and thinking in terms of larger social issues like racial equality and sexual equality. You would think that unions would be in the forefront in fighting against racism and sexism, but in fact unions have very often been obstacles.

I think progressive people who work in labor unions need to enlarge the social view of the labor movement, so that it understands that labor is most powerful when it can unite people across lines of sex and race, foreign born, native born, and so forth. This unity serves not only the immediate and practical purpose of strengthening the labor movement, but also speaks to the larger moral reason of doing it because it is the right thing to do.

Why do labor unions have a tendency to become bureaucratic and undemocratic?
It's for the same reasons that all organizations have a tendency to become bureaucratic: Success creates top-heavy leadership, and the accumulation of a treasury creates opportunity for corruption and high salaries. Also, union leaders negotiate with employers and begin to get closer to employers than to their own members.

Labor unions aren't the only ones who suffer from this problem; it's a constant struggle in all organizations to maintain the power of the active rank and file. What it means is that members of unions cannot be complacent. Every union has to have a constantly active rank and file, defending their rights every day. It's analogous to society at large, where citizens cannot just simply vote people into office and then relax.

What do you think about labor/management cooperation for teacher unions?
It's a delicate matter, because there is nothing wrong with cooperating on certain things with administrations or school boards, as long as you don't give up the independent strength of the teachers. It's also important that teacher unions become more inclusive and include part-time teachers, service workers, librarians, and secretarial staff—in other words, to become industrial unions rather than narrow craft teacher unions. That will strengthen the teacher unions, and then when they do things jointly with administration, it will help guarantee that they are not dominated by the administration in those joint activities. █

A Hard Lesson from History

BY BOB PETERSON

BENEDICT J. FERNANDEZ

Afriend who works for a teacher union recounted a discussion in which an anti-union teacher asked my friend why she supported unions. Her reply was simple. She said that without unions, particularly the one her dad had been in, she would have grown up in poverty.

For many that's reason enough to support unions.

It's an issue of survival and has been for 160 years, since the birth of the labor movement in the United States. But the labor movement's track record of promoting the general welfare of working people is uneven, as some people—particularly people of color and women—have been excluded or discriminated against by certain unions.

I saw this firsthand when I worked on the Milwaukee docks in the early 1970s. I witnessed the resistance of the International Longshoremen's Association to allowing women into the union. The ILA was continuing a long, nefarious tradition of some sections of organized labor. One of the first strikes in Milwaukee, for example, was in 1863 by typesetters at the *Milwaukee Sentinel* who struck to protest the hiring of women.

In these cases, the unions weren't just defending workers from greedy bosses; they were also "defending" unionized workers from other workers. Historian Robert Allen, in his book *Reluctant Reformers: Racism and Social Reform Movements in the United States*, documents how in many unions throughout much of the 19th and 20th centuries, white workers attempted to keep workers of color out of many jobs. As late as 1931, Allen notes, 14 national unions prohibited African Americans from membership.

This has been a historical weakness of unionism in the United States: fighting to improve conditions for certain poor and working people while undercutting the interests of other poor and working people. In other words, the dilemma of defending the interests of a sector of working people instead of the interests of all. Or to put more generally, developing a social pact for some versus social justice for all. Often this problem is racialized.

When unions have overcome this weakness and united workers regardless of race or gender, as did the Congress of Industrial Organizations during the 1930s, they became powerful social forces. Many workers in these unions had both an understanding of themselves as workers and a sense of social justice. The United Packinghouse Workers of America, for example, aggressively promoted both racial and gender equality among its diverse membership, making it a powerful union.

Teacher unions have faced similar issues. In the early 1960s, for example, there were still 11 segregated National Education Association (NEA) state associations; as late as 1974 the NEA still had a segregated Louisiana association. (Since that time the NEA has changed dramatically, as exemplified in its affirmative action staff hiring policies and in guaranteeing significant minority representation at its national conventions.)

But this historic dilemma for the labor movement—balancing the interests of its own members with broader issues of justice for all working and oppressed people—still persists.

For teacher unions, the challenge rests no longer in exclusion policies or segregated locals, but in more complex ways.

One such way is when teacher unions' defense of their members' rights and benefits conflict with the needs of students and the broader community. Perhaps the most prominent example of that was the 1968 Ocean Hill-Brownsville strike in New York City. The conflict centered on the extent to which local communities (in this case, mainly African American communities) could control their schools, particularly with respect to staffing. (See Perlstein, p. 42.)

Twenty-five years later, a similar conflict boiled over in Milwaukee regarding the staffing at two African American immersion schools. The schools were specifically set up to deal with high academic failure rates among African Americans. Because of the unique nature of the schools the community requested that one-third of the schools' teachers be African American. The union opposed the request because it violated contract provisions that set a maximum percentage of 23 to 28 percent African American teachers at district schools—even though no white teachers wanted to transfer into the two schools to fill existing vacancies.

In both these cases the unions won their battles, but at a daunting price, as members of African American communities summed up the actions of the unions as examples of racism on the part of white-dominated unions.

Another challenge that persists in many unions is an internal one—whose voices are listened to, who is hired as staff, and who is in leadership? While progress has been made, too often white males still dominate staff and leadership positions. Does leadership support caucuses that speak directly to racial and gender inequalities? Does leadership development target women and teachers of color? Does the union promote anti-racism and anti-bias among its members?

Addressing these and other challenges is particularly important given the crescendo of attacks on public schools and teacher unions and the need for unions to ally with communities to defend public education.

Teachers should recognize that their self-interests can no longer be defined using solely "narrow trade union" or even "professional" terms. Our interests and our future require teacher unions to balance those matters with a social justice perspective that places the education and welfare of our students in school and in society at the top of our agenda.

My friend who works for a teacher union and who argued about the value of unions did not talk only about her father's union. She talked of how early teacher union activists were mainly women, many of whom were involved in the suffragist movement. She explained the broader labor movement's influence on social policy legislation such as the minimum wage, unemployment compensation, and Social Security. She noted that the United Auto Workers were major backers of Dr. Martin Luther King Jr. and the Civil Rights Movement.

It is in the tradition of that sector of the labor movement—the one that promotes social justice for all—that we should situate our teacher unions. 📓

Bob Peterson, the former president of the Milwaukee Teachers' Education Association, is now a member of the Milwaukee School Board. He taught 5th grade more than 25 years at various Milwaukee public schools, and was a founding editor of Rethinking Schools.

Organizing in Defense of the Public Sector

An interview with labor union activist and writer Bill Fletcher Jr.

ARLENE HOLT-BAKER

Bill Fletcher Jr. has been active in workplace and community struggles as well as electoral campaigns. He has worked for several labor unions in addition to serving as a senior staff person in the national AFL-CIO. He's authored or co-authored several books on unions and is a syndicated columnist. This interview combines parts of an interview that appeared in the first edition of Transforming Teacher Unions *with one done in 2020. Both interviews were conducted by Bob Peterson.*

Public sector workers serve the public and are paid through tax dollars. They play a different role from autoworkers, steelworkers, or shipbuilders working for a private business. Given these differences, what special roles do public sector unions play in society?

Public sector unions play three roles. First, they defend the interests of their members. Second, and a lot of public sector unions talk about this so much that it's almost a cliché, they must look out for the interests of the community. A third role, which is not talked about a lot in the United States but is around the world, is that they must defend the public sector.

This third role is critical right now. Public sector unions need to articulate a coherent and credible defense of the public sector—to explain the role of the public sector and show why any kind of civilized society must have a public sector. I don't think public sector unions do that very well. As a result, they tend to come across as merely defending the interests of their members.

When I speak about the "public sector," I am not just talking about government jobs. I am referring to the larger question of public services and public space. For example, parks and recreational facilities are collective necessities that aim to improve people's quality of life and living standards. Many of these "spaces" and other public services were won through struggles over decades. I would argue that many, if not most, of these functions cannot and should not be operated with the profit motive in mind. Such services must be the concern of public sector unions. Thus, this defense of the public sector goes way beyond a matter of job protection; it speaks to a defense of society itself.

In recent years there has been increasing attention and fight back against school privatization. What's your take on the effort?
This fight back against various forms of school privatization is important, but we need to realize that there is no saving public education if the public sector as a whole goes down. It's not possible. There will be no public education sector island in the middle of a private sector ocean. To the extent that public school advocates are not engaged in the fight to defend the entire public sector, they will lose. That's the critical thing.

For 40 years we've witnessed a slow eating away of the public sector. In the U.S. the Clinton administration was one of the real problems on the progressive side of the aisle. That administration moved a neoliberal agenda with a velvet glove, and many progressive forces sat back and said nothing. Those forces lost significant credibility in their unwillingness or inability to fight the austerity budgets and privatization when articulated by political liberals.

We need to build a public sector reform movement that unions lead and that includes, but is not limited to, public education. Such a movement needs an alternative strategy and vision of the way that public sector should operate, who it should serve, and how it should be funded.

In 2009 when Congressman Jesse Jackson Jr. proposed a constitutional amendment creating the right of public education for every person, I supported that plan. I thought it was brilliant because it would have automatically changed the funding formula for education. I was dumbfounded and remain dumfounded that neither the NEA or AFT ever took that up. I have never been able to figure it out. Why not take that up? It's that type of thinking that we need to change.

One criticism of teacher unions is that they are part of a "government monopoly"—that public education is better served through privatization and other mechanisms to spur competition. What do you think?

The notion that the private sector is somehow more efficient is a complete fallacy. There are plenty of historical examples—the railroads, for instance. Why did railroads become part of the public sector? Because they were destroyed by private sector interests. Why did the subway system in New York City, which had been run by three private companies, become a quasi-public agency? Because it was being destroyed by the companies.

Public sector unions have to expose that kind of history. But we also need to talk about the fact that there are things necessary for a civilized society that cost money and may not always result in a profit.

In most school districts the public schools are governed by democratically elected school boards. Despite labor/management disagreements at times, it's in the interest of education workers to unite and cooperate with school boards to improve and defend public education. What's your take on this tension?

Terms such as labor/management collaboration have become very loaded, so I prefer to talk about issues such as "worker participation." It's important to look at the substance of the proposal, not simply the form and rhetoric.

For example, every time a union signs a collective bargaining agreement with an employer, it is agreeing to cooperate. That's a reality. It's actually part of the reason the Industrial Workers of the World (IWW) wouldn't sign collective bargaining agreements.

The labor movement has rejected the IWW approach, and recognizes that in a collective bargaining agreement we are agreeing to cooperate on certain things. To me, the question is not so much one of cooperation, but the terms of the discussions.

Unions also need to challenge what are seen as management rights—issues such as the future of the institution, the quality of the service or product, how best to serve the customer, and budget decisions. These are things that workers should have a say in, not necessarily as individuals but collectively through their union.

When you talk about public arenas such as public transportation or public schools, the unions should be a way for the rank-and-file workers to get involved in such discussions. If we want to be candid, we have to recognize that part of the problem is that many unions do not have ways for rank and filers to become involved, and then the workers become alienated from their union and, on an individual level, much more susceptible to management's view.

Historically, teachers have vacillated between viewing themselves as professionals—who want individual control over working conditions—and as workers who see the need for collective action. What would you say to those who think teachers should be treated as professionals and are hesitant about being associated with "blue-collar unionism"?

I think teachers should be treated and respected as professionals, because they are. But being professional shouldn't be seen as being superior. I come out of the industrial union mode of thinking on these questions, and tend to think that wall-to-wall is the best way to build power. It's not about whether teachers like janitors or janitors like teachers. The question is: How do you strengthen the power of the workers?

This issue is very much related to the question, which has come up in both the AFT and NEA, about who should be in the bargaining unit. I think that is a tactical matter that should be settled on the basis of an analysis of power. It's also a question of how you go about building a sense of identity.

Children and youth of color are large majorities in many school districts, and yet in many places teachers are majority white. What are the implications for teacher unions? What are ways that anti-racist union activists and leaders deal with white supremacy?

One of the things we should remember about the 1968 New York teacher strike is that the New York City school system was deeply segregated and there was an insufficient number of teachers of color. As far as I can tell there had been no systematic demand by the AFT—in that case it was the UFT—for the full desegregation of schools or significant hiring of teachers of color and other education staff. And that to me is representative of a major problem. And it's not just a problem that afflicts teacher unions; it's a problem that afflicts many unions where there is a transformation from a largely white workforce to a more diverse workforce. You see that in the skilled trades. What you may hear is "we are against discrimination," but what you don't get is any kind of active campaign on the part of the union to fight for fair hiring practices. Teacher unions need to argue for affirmative action and for the recruitment of teachers who look like and understand the issues of the student population. That's the minimum.

A second thing that teacher unions should do is change the nature of their internal member education and push for similar changes in districtwide professional development. To be blunt, there needs to be ongoing examination and understanding of the history of racism and the many ways racism manifests itself. The same is true for sexism and class issues. This understanding of history or race—both racist oppression and resistance—must be distinguished from so-called "diversity training." People need to critically examine U.S. history because the aim is not only about people getting along better, but also for teachers to really understand the system in which they are operating and to be able to relate to the issues that their constituencies—in this case their students—are grappling with.

Things that school districts do—Black History Month, Latino History Month, and all of that—are important, but not as important as integrating those histories of marginalized populations into the overall narrative of this country that is addressed in the curriculum.

I think about when I was in high school—and obviously this was a long time ago—and we actually talked about unions in my social studies classes, but the discussion never dealt with any issue of race. It was looking at a phenomenon very much from the outside and where the people who looked like me were erased. Unions should work with students and community allies to make sure the people who get elected or appointed to school boards have that kind of awareness and consciousness.

In 2011 we had the Wisconsin Uprising followed the next year by the CTU strike. Rank-and-file caucuses pushed social justice-minded activists into leadership roles across the country. In the spring of 2018 the red state strike wave surprised the nation. And then in 2019 we witnessed more strikes, including Los Angeles. What are some of the lessons from these uprisings?
I'll start with the positive example of Chicago and the Milwaukee Teachers' Education Association (MTEA). In both cases, the leaderships embraced a social justice unionist approach—whether they called it that or not—that included making the union in effect an instrument to advance and change education by aligning themselves with the interests of the students.

That model is very different from the Albert Shanker model. His method was in effect lifting the model of the steelworkers and the autoworkers and implanting it into the public sector. In the beginning it worked because the teachers were so poorly treated and badly paid that almost anything represented an improvement. But at a critical time, that model simply failed, because it wasn't intersecting with the real needs of the community.

I think what you folks did in Milwaukee and Chicago represented a very different approach. It necessitated that your unions, and the others that tried to follow a similar path, recognize that it wasn't just about rhetoric, but that the actual work of the union had to change and that there would be internal resistance to that and it would be difficult.

The upsurges of teacher unions and the strikes in conservative states have been really amazing. The challenges are twofold. One, to what extent can viable organization be built and rooted? And the second, to what extent can these upsurges be translated into the building of a progressive education movement that includes community-based organizations and parents?

Some people were surprised a state like West Virginia had such a powerful strike just two years after 68 percent of the people voted for Donald Trump. What do you make of that?
Terminology is very important. Some talk about "conservative workers" and say that "workers voted against their own interest." The problem with that formulation is that we are assuming these workers see their own interest in the same way that we do. The second problem is a direct result of racial capitalism—that we exist in a situation where class consciousness and class awareness are always affected by the prism of race. There are countless historical examples where you have militant trade unionists who are white supremacists.

So when you see the teacher militancy in West Virginia and say how is this possible given that many voted for Trump, I think that for many of these workers there is no inconsistency. They look at Trump as the guardian of white republic and the white republic's values—and they see him as someone who is speaking out against the so-called elites and bureaucrats. Teachers hate bureaucrats and elites. And the fact that these elites may be a code for Jews or a code for something else doesn't always rise to the surface. So many of the same people who are out fighting the good fight see no inconsistency between carrying out that fight and voting for Trump. We have to be very careful, and that's why the fight against right-wing populism needs to be central to the work of trade unionists in this era.

What suggestions do have for someone whose colleague in the classroom down the hall holds such views?

I would ask questions, not lecture. It's really important for class-conscious teachers to engage their colleagues in the dangers of right-wing populism and the dangers inherent in Trump and people like him by asking key questions. When people say Trump looks out for us, you have to have class-conscious teachers able to respond and say, "Let's look at the tax reform bill of 2017—how does that benefit working people? Who does it benefit?" That means people have to be on their toes, but members can learn how to do this.

In the past I've heard you say that having an education director in each union is essential. Why is that?

At different points in U.S. history, trade unionism member education was treated with significant value. However, in the context of the Cold War and the civil war that broke out in organized labor in 1948, internal education was reduced in importance by the more conservative forces that came to dominate many unions. They looked at member education as an unnecessary distraction, in some cases a base for the political left. So they reduced resources and education departments. To the extent they continued at all, the departments became holding pens for people the leaders didn't need or want around.

Part of the roots of this problem is that too often people in the U.S. dismiss the importance of education per se. The epitome is the saying "those who know, do; those who don't, teach." It's quintessential American. I can't imagine the saying being used in China or France. Not only do we put down education in general, but accurate history is dismissed and instead people hold on to myth. Simple myths like George Washington cutting down the cherry tree to the much more significant myths like that of the original Thanksgiving and treatment of the Native peoples at that time.

Honest member education is incredibly important because it is about vision. Our union education programs should help shape the consciousness of workers and provide a framework so that when workers read the news they can make sense out of it. That's a big part of a union leader's job, because if you are making sense of the world, then, to borrow from a famous writer, you are in a better position to change it. That's why the education role is so important.

Sounds good, but how does that work in smaller unions or union locals?
In smaller unions there is always a resource problem when it comes to such work. This is where central labor councils and regional or state union bodies can play important roles. Using webinars and online classes can help minimize expenses. A number of universities also have good labor education programs, and many have been under attack, as in Missouri and Nebraska. Unions should fight to defend such programs.

What advice do you have to new union leaders as they work to transform their unions into social justice unions?
First thing is to do an assessment of the union in terms of what's working and what's not. Then engage in some kind of planning process—a minimum of six to 12 months—to outline what the new leaders hope to accomplish. Fundamentally they need to come up with a basic and compelling vision about what it is they want to bring into existence.

There also needs to be a way of making the organization both fun and interesting. The organization needs to become an instrument for learning, including about the struggles going on in other parts of the country and world. That means everything from setting up informational programs, speakers, and webinars, to fun social events, cultural performances, or sponsoring a Little League team, so that their members feel like this is their family.

Create a community advisory committee where you get some key opinion makers from the community that you've worked with over time and meet with every month or two—to get their evaluation of how you are doing and what they think you should be doing and also so that the union can convey to them some of their concerns and where the union leaders might need help.

The top leaders are going to need coaching, and many will not think that they do or insist that they don't have time. The reality is that—particularly in a transformative moment—many leaders have no one to talk to confidentially.

Finally, there is one other thing that top leaders need. And that is a culture established from the very beginning, that the bubble that invariably develops around the leader is regularly burst. Too often such a bubble keeps out bad news with no one telling top leadership that certain things are not going fine.

What would you say to new leaders coming into a union local that has been staff-run and members are conditioned that when they have a problem they call the one or two staff people to solve their problem. You know, the union that is viewed as a third person singular—"they, it, the union"—versus first person plural—"We are the union"?
You have to seize on opportunities for members to win some struggles. That might be in the form of broader campaigns or specific demands at the school site.

This means educating shop stewards [building chairs/representatives] and field staff about their role. They are not glorified paralegals—they are fundamentally organizers. The leadership has to say from the very beginning that the members need to run this union. That we can't spend all our resources on a relatively small number of people who have problems. Because most members don't. Most members have collective problems as opposed to individual problems, so we want to spend most of our resources on the collective issues. And that point needs to be made time and again because we get hung up on that small number of people who have problems on a regular basis. And members know this, and that's one of the ways that the anti-union forces often operate and say to people, "Look, you never have a problem. Why are you paying dues?" as opposed to us saying, no, this is our collective thing.

This makes me think of a conversation I had with Jack O'Dell, a top advisor to Martin Luther King who was redbaited out of that position. He was in the National Maritime Union during WWII. I became good friends with him. I had seen a documentary on the Merchant Marine years ago, and one thing that the documentary said was that these ships were 100 percent union and every ship had a union committee that led union on the ship. There were no staff people. These were members.

When I talked to Jack, I said this is what I heard, is that true? And Jack said, "Yeah it's true, and we were expected to resolve issues while we were at sea. You weren't supposed to come back to New York and say there's a grievance and somebody's got to take care of it." They'd say, "No, resolve the damn thing on the ship." That's the model we need where the member organization is set up in such a way that [building] leaders and union committees are solving the problems at the site, and staff are training them to do that.

What role can teacher unions play in the future of the American labor movement?
Teachers help to shape the minds of the future generation. One important role is to help build awareness about unions and the labor movement. Some teachers don't want to talk to their students about unions; they see it as somehow unethical and misusing their position. That's ridiculous. Teachers need to help sow the seeds of the future of unionism.

Teacher unions also can play a pivotal role in fighting back against the attack on the public sector. Many years ago, I was talking with some teacher union officials about the attack on public education. I argued that they were absolutely right to raise this alarm, but that they needed to do so in the context of the overall attack on the public sector. They looked at me as if I were an alien from *Star Trek*. They stared and said, "Yeah, but we really have to defend public education."

I replied that if the public sector is destroyed, or the concept is so diminished that it's meaningless, then there will be no public education to defend. That's not to say we should ignore the specific importance of defending public education, but rather to emphasize that the attack is occurring in the context of an attack on the very premise of a public sector. ⬛

Visions of Justice:
Unions and the community in historical perspective

BY DAN PERLSTEIN

American teacher unionists have at times joined with working-class community activists in a common battle to win more equitable and democratic schooling for all children. At other moments, teacher unionists have defended the centralized administration of schools against activists demanding community involvement in educational affairs. Unions both have been active participants in efforts to promote racial and gender equality and have opposed such initiatives. In a society marked by profound social divisions, notions of social justice in education are inevitably as varied as those proposing them.

Two tensions have been especially pivotal for teacher unionists. Although advocates of social justice in education sometimes seem to expect teachers to foreswear any self-interest out of dedication to the children they teach, unionism sees teachers as agents and as beneficiaries of social justice. At issue is how teachers have understood the relationship of their self-interest (sometimes represented as business or bread-and-butter unionism) to broader political concerns (sometimes described as social justice or social movement unionism).

A second tension involves teachers simultaneously making demands upon the state while serving it. That teacher unions won the right to bargain with the state at a moment in the 1960s when the American welfare state was rapidly expanding its disciplinary power mirrors the ambiguous role that the American state has played in efforts to secure social justice more broadly. Questions involving the relationship of self-interest to social justice and the relationship of working people to the state have shaped the history of teacher unions and their participation in movements for social change.

In no city have the varied ideologies and alliances of American teacher unionism been more visible than in New York, and no city has played a more prominent role in the history of teacher organizing. New York's United Federation of Teachers (UFT) local continues to occupy a preeminent place in the American Federation of Teachers (AFT). Life in the epicenter of American teacher unionism has been in many ways atypical of conditions in the rest of the United States. Still, focusing on exceptional moments in American teachers' history can illuminate the obstacles to the pursuit of social justice teacher unionism as well as its richest potential.

Unionism, Professionalism, and Gender Equity

Teacher unions arose at the beginning of the 20th century, when elite schools responded to the social conflicts of America's burgeoning cities with new mechanisms of centralized governance and administration, new bureaucratic procedures to sort students and divide work, and new forms of technical and professional knowledge to guide and manage educators. As historian Marjorie Murphy demonstrates, elite reformers hoped to isolate teachers, most of them women, from the working-class communities in which they taught, to win teachers' allegiance to male central office professionals, and thus to have schools help maintain order in America's fractious cities.[1]

Teachers were torn between old neighborhood allegiances and the promise of a new professionalism. Unlike Chicago, where elementary school teacher Margaret Haley led a militant, community-based campaign that forced corporations to pay their school taxes and won a pay raise for teachers, leading New York teacher unionists shared the professional aspirations of elite reformers. Today's AFT flagship local, the UFT, traces its history to the Teachers Union (TU) and the Teachers Guild, inheriting from the two earlier organizations its commitment to professionalism. The TU was organized in 1916. Its founder Henry Linville possessed a Harvard PhD, and over the years, as the UFT brags, top teacher unionists included "PhD's, accountants, and even lawyers—men like Jules Kolodny, Dave Wittes, and Charles Cogen."[2]

The male-dominated TU showed little interest in gender equity. At the same time as the TU struggled to attract a handful of teachers to the labor movement,

New York's Interborough Association of Women Teachers, under the leadership of Deputy Superintendent Grace Strachan and with the support of Carrie Chapman Catt and other suffragists, organized 14,000 women teachers with demands for equal pay. Commitment to the social justice ideal of gender equity served the self-interest of most teachers, but also required participation in a movement of white women to transform their political status.[3]

Acceptance of male privilege and insensitivity to women's concerns, together with the intersection of gender and racial dynamics, have been ongoing issues in teacher union politics. Although women filled 50 percent of the TU Executive Board as early as 1925, and in the 1930s they outnumbered men at union meetings, when Linville's ideological descendants founded the UFT New York organizers once again dismissed women as potential unionists. "When teachers loudly and publicly bicker with each other, when tongue-clucking 'talk' and futile hand-wringing are substituted for vigorous action," UFT President Charles Cogen argued in urging teachers to abandon other organizations, "how can we expect anything but contempt?" Cogen labeled an "old woman" a teacher "of any sex or age who . . . accepts unquestioningly . . . [the] dictates of anyone in authority over him, and who refuses to protest—even mildly—any unwarranted transgressions into his professional domain." In the early 1960s, the UFT's founders focused their efforts on angry young men in the junior high schools—and were completely unaffected when thousands of female elementary school teachers participated in early UFT actions. When, in the late 1960s, the UFT was locked in bitter conflict with Black community activists rather than with central administrators, union leaders would again view inflexibility as a virtue rather than a failing.[4]

The Teachers Union

Today's UFT traces its ideological and organizational roots to New York's Teachers Union, formed by Linville and other social democrats. Through electoral campaigns and labor organization especially, social democrats sought to extend political democracy to economic life. They believed that the United States could evolve gradually toward socialism without a fundamental reordering of its political structure; that if distinctions of class could wither, other, more superficial social divisions would disappear even more easily; and that the U.S. might achieve a universally held culture, with universal standards of judgment, into which all would assimilate. Racial problems, in this view, were largely caused by and subservient to class conflicts. The social democratic response to American racism received its most famous expression from Eugene Debs, who proclaimed socialism a "slavery-destroying" movement capable of offering "inspiring music" to Black Americans "doubly enslaved" by the "unspeakable crimes" of the white race. Still, he claimed, "The Socialist Party is the party of the whole working class, regardless of color," and therefore it had "nothing special to offer the Negro."[5]

Aspiring to professional respectability while espousing a mildly reformist vision of socialism, New York's social democratic teacher unionists placed more faith in discrete lobbying campaigns than in mass demonstrations. Until the 1930s,

Linville and his followers retained firm command of the Teachers Union, but amid the growing activism and radicalism of the Depression years, teachers began to demand that the union take a more militant stand on school issues and broader political questions. When a communist-led rank-and-file coalition won control of the TU in 1935, the original socialist leadership bolted and formed the Teachers Guild, an organization that soon won the backing of the American Federation of Labor and in 1960 gave rise to the UFT.

Following the 1935 split, commitments to social justice animated both TU and Teachers Guild activities. But they were not always the same commitments. The communist-led TU, notes historian Clarence Taylor, attracted large numbers of teachers by simultaneously fighting to improve salaries and working conditions while also offering a compelling analysis of racism and class oppression and building a movement of civil rights, community, and labor activists to end poverty, racial discrimination, and other forms of social, economic, and political oppression. Despite the exodus of the social democratic faction and opposition from school officials, the TU grew from perhaps 1,500 members in 1935 to more than 6,000 in the late 1930s.[6]

One of the most significant differences between the TU's new leadership and Linville's more moderate group was its response to school racism, which the TU now made a major focus of its work. Although Blacks constituted only a small percentage of New York's students in the 1930s, school segregation and discrimination were already well established. "Old, poorly equipped, and overcrowded" schools were a primary source of Black discontent, a 1935 city investigation reported, and "many of the white teachers" assigned to Harlem schools "regard the appointment as a sort of punishment."[7] Even after he became disillusioned with communism and left the party, former communist leader George Charney fondly recalled TU's militant activism:

> Pressing their demands for better schools, more schools, textbook revisions, Negro teachers and principals, free lunches, and so forth . . . mothers came [to meetings] en masse to organize programs, assign delegations, and join in citywide activities. In every school, white teachers, with the active support of the Teachers Union, came forward to collaborate with the parents in this inspired effort to transform a community through education.[8]

Alice Citron, a leader in the overlapping communist and Teachers Union circles of the 1930s, epitomized Depression-era anti-racist school organizing. In her Harlem classroom, Citron replaced textbooks written by New York school administrators that portrayed happy, dancing slaves and defended the Ku Klux Klan with lessons inspired by Carter G. Woodson's *Negro History Bulletin*. After school, she compiled bibliographies on Black life for other teachers, organized campaigns to rectify derelict school facilities, and earned a reputation throughout the streets of Harlem for her role in battles against American racism.[9]

The theory on which the TU based its anti-racist campaigning originated in the American Communist Party. Extrapolating from the role played by national minorities in the Russian Revolution and influenced by demands for African American self-determination, communists reasoned that the union of the anti-capitalist working-class protest and Black community organizing could catalyze a movement to overturn class and race oppression in America. Even if the communist vision of self-determination for an "oppressed Negro nation" has rightly been dismissed as "a bit of 'fatuous romance,'" notes historian Mark Solomon, it led communists "to deal with racial issues and attitudes in ways that were totally beyond the awareness and comprehension of most white Americans," and gave rise to "the most determined efforts of a predominantly white organization to achieve equality since the abolitionists."[10]

TU members joined with parents and community activists to organize pickets against the brutal corporal punishment of Black students and to secure the construction of Harlem's first new schools in decades. For almost 20 years, TU-led coalitions remained New York's most militant and effective grassroots school reform effort. Although most teachers never joined the TU's radical campaigns, its principled efforts improved working conditions, enriched teachers' work and aligned teachers with efforts to democratize the wider society.

> Teachers Union members joined with parents and community activists to organize pickets against the brutal corporal punishment of Black students and to secure the construction of Harlem's first new schools in decades.

But the TU's ability to simultaneously promote the interests of white teachers and of Black communities provided it little protection from the anti-communist hysteria of the McCarthy era, when hundreds of activist teachers were forced out of the New York school system and parents were cowed into ending association with "subversives." In 1950, the Board of Education declared that school administrators were no longer permitted to "negotiate, confer, or deal with or recognize [the Teachers Union] in relation to any grievances or any personal or professional problems, nor grant to said Teachers Union any of the rights or privileges accorded to any teacher organization." The ban, which lasted until 1962, destroyed the TU and cleared the way for the rise of the UFT.[11]

The Teachers Guild and the UFT

Even in the heyday of the TU, Guild activists were promoting an alternative vision of teacher unionism, one that would lead directly to the establishment of the UFT and through it to the transformation of teacher organizing across the U.S.

Within the Guild, a younger generation of teachers combined the mild reformism of Linville's generation with the militancy of their communist competitors. The Guild, according to veteran socialist and future UFT leader Jeannette

DiLorenzo, "was a social movement as well as a trade union movement." Like many future UFT leaders, DiLorenzo had grown up in a home where "the religion" was "being part of an international movement." She studied socialism and Marxism at the Rand School and honed organizational and leadership skills in the Young People's Socialist League. Through countless meetings, debates, and bare-knuckle ideological and organizational battles, future UFT and AFT leaders mastered a vision of teacher unionism that they would maintain steadfastly through future decades. "I never stopped to analyze whether it was good people I was working for," DiLorenzo would remember. "It was the idea; it was working for a better world."[12]

When the Civil Right Movement arose in the South in the 1950s, the Guild's response was shaped by its continuing commitment to the Debsian ideal of equality for workers of all races. Prodded by the Guild, the AFT voted as early as 1951 to charter no new locals that practiced racial discrimination, and by 1956 the union ordered Southern affiliates to desegregate or be expelled. The AFT's efforts contrasted with those of the National Education Association (NEA), which did not fully desegregate until the 1970s.[13]

A vision of uniting all teachers and a strong commitment to unionism remained hallmarks of the New York AFT local when the Guild reconstituted itself as the UFT in 1960. "The goals of the embattled teachers," UFT founder Dave Selden claimed, "were the usual worker goals—higher wages, better benefits, and improved working conditions. Perhaps the ultimate goals were higher status and dignity."[14] AFT President Carl Megel argued in 1962 against equating teachers with such professionals as doctors and lawyers: "A doctor or a lawyer is a businessman. A teacher is a worker. You are a day laborer."[15]

When the UFT initiated its organizing campaign, it received tremendous support from the labor movement. Unions donated tens of thousands of dollars and lent field workers for the 1961 election in which the UFT won the right to represent New York's 43,000 teachers. Noting that white-collar employees had come to outnumber blue-collar workers in the U.S., Cogen acclaimed the election as labor's biggest collective bargaining victory since the United Auto Workers organized Ford's River Rouge Plant in 1941.[16]

While portraying teachers as workers, UFT leaders also sought to promote teacher professionalism. If a teacher were "considered a production worker," Selden conceded, issues such as class size would be non-negotiable questions of educational policy rather than issues of working conditions. "But a teacher is not merely a production worker. He is a professional," and like other professionals, Selden argued, teachers had a right to be "self-directed and use their judgment in their work." By this definition, he argued, teachers might rightly negotiate over class size not because large classes "sweated" teachers into undue hardship but because teachers rightly had a say in pedagogical issues.[17]

Unionists' understanding of teachers' work was not the only reason they invoked teacher professionalism as well as industrial unionism. The emergence of teacher unionism signaled important changes in American economic and political life. After World War II, automation and deindustrialization led to a decline in the number of factory jobs, and together with McCarthy-era repression and pro-management changes in labor law, to an even steeper drop in blue-collar unionism. Meanwhile, the number of state and local government jobs mushroomed. New York City alone lost 40 percent of its 1 million manufacturing jobs between 1950 and 1969, but increased its 375,000 government jobs by 40 percent.[18]

Union leaders were keenly aware of changes in the labor force, changes that made organizing groups such as teachers crucial to the future of the labor movement. When International Brotherhood of Electrical Workers President James Carey addressed the NEA's 1962 convention, he pointed to the UFT's New York campaign as a model for teachers across the U.S. The NEA's simple professionalism, Carey argued, "implies that your *craft* is somewhat above this world of ours; it implies a detachment, a remoteness from the daily battle of the streets, in the neighborhood, and in the cities." Without unions, he warned, teachers would lack decent wages and thus the ability to "afford integrity and honesty" in their work.[19] Another union official made the big picture plain. "How long will the file clerk go on thinking a union is below her dignity," he asked *Business Week*, "when the teacher next door belongs?"[20]

The synthesis of industrial unionism and professionalism proved immensely popular with teachers in New York and across the U.S. Still, teachers' self-directed activity involves the direction of other persons. Like the Progressive Era reorganization of urban schooling, the new professional unionism distanced city teachers from the urban communities in which they worked. Nowhere was the potential for conflict between urban teachers and the families they serve more clear than in New York.

By the late 1960s, the racial politics of education, together with wider changes in urban life, had undermined Black activists' faith in the goodwill of white teachers. The UFT never applied to local race relations problems the militant commitment to racial equality that informed its response to Southern struggles. Among the accomplishments of which the union boasted to teachers, for instance, was its having "killed the superintendent's plan to force teachers to transfer to difficult schools."[21] In 1964, when more than 400,000 of New York's 1 million students boycotted school in order to press for integration, the UFT declined to endorse the protest.[22]

Following the defeat of the campaign to integrate New York's schools, Black activists increasingly demanded that school curricula and jobs be controlled by Blacks themselves. In 1968, experimental local school boards in Harlem and Brooklyn's Ocean Hill-Brownsville neighborhood became the focal points of New York's political life. After the Ocean Hill-Brownsville board attempted to remove 13 teachers from the district's schools, the UFT went out on strike for much of the fall of 1968. By the end of the year, the UFT had won its strikes and effectively ended the movement for decentralized "community control" of schooling.

In defense of the union's position, UFT leaders argued that the same vision of professional autonomy, race-blind due process, and solidarity that had led them to support the Civil Rights Movement (and that would soon lead the AFT pioneer trade union advocacy of gay workers' right to be judged by their work alone and not their identity)[23] justified union opposition to community control. Nevertheless, in the context of the school conflict, invocations of professional autonomy increasingly dominated Debsian notions of working-class solidarity. Teachers, future AFT president Sandra Feldman claimed on the eve of the 1968 conflict, "in general support civil rights and equal educational opportunity, but their commitment to a fight for improved schools was . . . largely, and understandably, self-interest . . . a struggle to create a respected profession from a beleaguered, downgraded occupation."[24] "We don't deny their equality," a white teacher claimed while walking a UFT picket line, "but they shouldn't get it by pulling down others who have just come up. It's wrong and reactionary for them to pit their strength against a group that struggled for years to make teaching a profession."[25] "It has always been the intent of the UFT," Al Shanker claimed in the face of Black demands, "that community participation does not mean that those decisions under professional control should be surrendered." Union teachers, he declared, "will not continue to teach in any school or district where professional decisions are made by laymen."[26]

In addition to the heightened passions of the moment, the very conditions of urban school teaching contributed to teachers' willingness to distance themselves from the communities in which they worked. By the late 1960s, a majority of New York's students were Black or Latino; meanwhile, most teachers were white. An increasingly wide physical, cultural, and political gulf separated teachers, who could abandon cities for suburban retreats, from their students, who lived in decaying urban neighborhoods. The majority of teachers, New York teacher activist and future urban school reformer Deborah Meier has observed, brought prejudices against poor minority children to their work, and "rather than undermining these prejudices," the teaching experience "arouses them."[27] Amid the troubling and visible tragedy of widespread minority student failure, adherence to seemingly uniform, race-blind standards of instruction asserted teachers' professionalism while absolving them of responsibility for their ineffectiveness.

> By the late 1960s, the racial politics of education, together with wider changes in urban life, had undermined Black activists' faith in the goodwill of white teachers. The UFT never applied to local race relations problems the militant commitment to racial equality that informed its response to Southern struggles.

The same economic changes that led the labor movement to organize teachers and other white-collar workers also undermined the UFT's invocations of working-class interracial solidarity as a vehicle for advancing Black freedom. As factories disappeared, industrial democracy could no longer animate the imagination of New York's poor. Their grievances—welfare rules, police brutality, poor city services, urban renewal, and school policies—were the results of an oppressive state rather than an oppressive boss. Community activists in New York and across the U.S. increasingly abandoned residual faith in the promise of racial integration and embraced demands for Black Power. The people of Ocean Hill-Brownsville were a "community," as Black teacher activist Rhody McCoy argued, because "they were involved in struggles with poverty programs, with political machines. They've had common goals and interests."[28]

Despite the changes in urban life, UFT leaders insisted throughout the 1968 conflict that the social democratic politics of interracial solidarity remained the surest means of securing real power for Black Americans. Community control, Feldman argued, "strengthens segregation and places upon poor communities the burden of creating desperately needed, massive, substantive, programmatic changes in their schools." Only the federal government, Feldman insisted, "can provide the kind of resources needed" to substantially improve inner-city education "and only a massive coalition of forces can prod Congress into action."[29]

By 1968, however, the commitment of the U.S. to social welfare programs and racial equity had already begun to ebb. When AFL-CIO leaders endorsed the UFT's 1968 fight against community control, it was because of the union's importance "not only for the future of teacher unionism but for the growth and expansion of white-collar and public service employee unions as well." Labor leaders' endorsement of the UFT signaled both the rise of public employee unions and the declining power of labor in American life.[30]

The 1968 school crisis established the UFT's powerful role in school politics and urban life, a role that benefited teachers in later salary renegotiations. Victory in 1968 was, however, expensive for New York's teachers. In the years following the school conflict, racial tensions demoralized school work and undermined the very liberal coalition that the union claimed to seek. In an earlier time, the UFT's rhetoric of equal opportunity, due process, industrial unionism, and professionalism might have enabled members to transcend narrower views and individual bigotry. In 1968, the UFT's anachronistic invocation of interracial working-class solidarity distanced teachers from the poor communities in which their students lived and legitimized racial inequality in the contested world of the schools.

The Past and Future of Social Justice Unionism

Self-interest alone is inadequate as a guide to personal action or social analysis in part because self-interest is never really clear. "Conditions," philosopher and AFT founder John Dewey observed, are not "fixed or even reasonably stable. . . . Social conditions are running in different, often opposed directions. Because of this fact the educator . . . is constantly compelled to make a choice. With what phase and direction of social forces will he throw in his energies?"[31] Teachers' notions of their self-interest, the movements in which they participate, and the alliances they make inevitably reflect their interpretations of social reality.

Combating perceived threats from below left teacher unionists exposed to threats from above. With its 2018 *Janus* decision by requiring unions to offer services for which they are not paid, the Supreme Court joined the long-standing right-wing campaign to destroy the unions of teachers and other public employees. And even before *Janus*, teacher unions' lesser-of-two-evils fealty to the Democratic

Party and the state led them to give far more than they have received. In recent decades, Gates, Broad, the Waltons, and other billionaires have imposed their vision on the schools, while corporations have feasted at the schoolhouse trough. They and their advocates in government have promoted charter schools, vouchers, the outsourcing of teaching to the gig economy, and other neoliberal "reforms" that have undermined not only teacher unions but also the century-old system of school district governance and administration that constituted the conditions out of which the unions emerged.

In 2012, Chicago Teachers Union President Karen Lewis, who is Black, led teachers in a strike against the complicity of government and union officials with the privatization of the city's schools. Since then, soon after the election of Donald Trump gave rise to the notion that the white working class had fully embraced racist reaction, teachers in West Virginia, Oklahoma, Arizona, back in Chicago, and across the country have walked off their jobs to demand justice for themselves and their students. Some of these strikes were launched and directed by unions; others were wildcat actions in places that ban public sector strikes.[32]

Teacher unions have at times challenged the inequalities of American life, and fostered broader demands for the public good. At other moments, they have allied themselves with the state to place teachers' immediate interests and privileges above more expansive ideals. At times, teachers have been served reasonably well by such visions, even if their more disadvantaged students have not been. But teachers are also harmed by theories that lead them to ally themselves with class, gender, and racial privilege. In order to protect both material self-interest and the joy of their work, public school teachers must, in the long run, protect the public interest. Will today's attacks on schools and the political and economic conflicts they reflect lead teacher unionists to imagine ideologies responsive to today's realities? It is too early to know whether recent strikes herald a new form of teacher unionism and with it a new relationship to the groups and movements seeking social justice in America. The history of teacher unionism raises questions that only its future will answer. ⬛

Dan Perlstein is a historian whose work focuses on American education. He teaches in the University of California, Berkeley's Graduate School of Education.

ENDNOTES

[1] Murphy, Marjorie. 1990. *Blackboard Unions: The AFT & the NEA, 1900–1980*. Cornell University Press: p. 23.

[2] Schierenbeck, Jack. Feb. 19. 1996. "Class Struggles: The AFT Story, Part 1." *New York Teacher*. uft.org/your-union/about-uft/our-history/class-struggles-uft-story/class-struggles-uft-story-part-1

[3] Carter, Patricia. 2002. *"Everybody's Paid but the Teacher": The Teaching Profession and the Women's Movement*. Teachers College Press: p. 41–45; Santangelo, Lauren. 2019. *Suffrage and the City: New York Women Battle for the Ballot*. Oxford University Press: p. 71–73.

[4] Cogen, Charles. May 1960. "The President's Column." *United Teacher*: p. 2; Cogen, Charles. June 1963. "The Teacher's Public Image." *United Teacher*: p. 3.

[5] Debs, Eugene. November 1903. "The Negro and the Class Struggle." *International Socialist Review* 4(5): p. 259–60.

[6] Taylor, Clarence. 2011. *Reds at the Blackboard: Communism, Civil Rights, and the New York City Teachers Union.* Columbia University Press: p. 3, 60.

[7] Fogelson, Robert M. and Richard E. Rubenstein. 1969. "The Complete Report of Mayor LaGuardia's Commission on the Harlem Riot of March 19, 1935." Arno Press: p. 78, 81. Reprint from July 18, 1936 *Amsterdam News.*

[8] Charney, George. 1968. *A Long Journey.* Quadrangle Books: p. 99.

[9] Feffer, Andrew. 2019. *Bad Faith: Teachers, Liberalism, and the Origins of McCarthyism.* Fordham University Press: p. 112–115.

[10] Solomon, Mark. 1988. *Red and Black: Communism and Afro-Americans, 1929–1935.* Garland Publishing: p. 106, 163.

[11] Perlstein, Daniel. 2004. *Justice, Justice: School Politics and the Eclipse of Liberalism.* Peter Lang Publishing: p. 60.

[12] Ibid., 18.

[13] Ibid., 24.

[14] Selden, David. 1985. *The Teacher Rebellion.* Howard University Press: p. 109.

[15] Stinnett, Timothy M. 1968. T*urmoil in Teaching: A History of the Organizational Struggle for America's Teachers.* Macmillan: p. 159.

[16] Cogen, Charles. December 1963. "President's Column." *United Teacher*: p. 4.

[17] Selden, David. March 1964. "Class Size and the New York Contract." *Phi Delta Kappan* 45(6): p. 283–87; Selden. T*he Teacher Rebellion*, p. 82.

[18] Perlstein. *Justice, Justice*, p. 20.

[19] Carey, James. 1962. "Address," *Addresses and Proceedings of the National Education Association*: p. 48–49.

[20] "AFL-CIO Gets New York Teachers' Vote, May Lure in Other White Collarites." Dec. 30, 1961. *Business-Week*: p. 78.

[21] "UFT's Record of Gains for Teachers." June 1962. *United Teacher*: p. 4.

[22] "Executive Board Minutes." Jan. 24, 1964. *United Teacher*: p. 7; Montague, Richard and Alfred Hendricks. Feb. 2, 1964. "The Battle for the Schools." *New York Post*: p. 22.

[23] Frank, Miriam. 2014. *Out in the Union: A Labor History of Queer America.* Temple University Press: p. 18.

[24] Feldman, Sandra, 1969. "The Growth of Teacher Consciousness: 1967." *ISR Journal* 1: p. 41.

[25] Kovach, Bill. Oct. 23. 1968. "Racist and Anti-Semitic Charges Strain Old Negro-Jewish Ties." *The New York Times*: p. 1.

[26] Perlstein. *Justice, Justice*, p. 23.

[27] Deborah Meier interview, New York City, Sept. 11, 1990.

[28] Urofsky, Melvin. 1970. Interview with Rhody McCoy in *Why Teachers Strike: Teachers' Rights and Community Control.* Doubleday: p. 118.

[29] Feldman, Sandra. March 31, 1968. "N.Y. City Decentralization." *New America*: p. 5; Feldman, Sandra. April 15, 1968. "N.Y. City Decentralization" (Part II)." *New America*: p. 6.

[30] "AFL-CIO Leaders Back Teacher Union." Sept. 17, 1968. *The New York Times*: p. 41.

[31] Dewey, John. October 1934. "Can Education Share in Social Reconstruction?" *The Social Frontier* 1: p. 12.

[32] Blanc, Eric. 2019. *Red State Revolt: The Teachers' Strike Wave and Working-Class Politics.* Verso Books.

An Agonizing Decision—Crossing the UFT Picket Line

BY HERB KOHL

Brooklyn parents demonstrated for their children's right to a quality education.

As Dan Perlstein relates in "Visions of Justice" (p. 42), in 1968 a simmering conflict between teachers' self-interest and the demands of parents and community activists exploded in the Ocean Hill-Brownsville neighborhood of New York City. Herb Kohl was a teacher at the newly constructed Intermediate School #201. As the conflict between the union and the community ignited, Kohl made an agonizing decision. This is how he described it in his article "Facing Tough Decisions," which was included in Transforming Teacher Unions, *the first edition of this volume.*

This was 1968 during the height of the Civil Rights Movement. The Black Power movement was emerging and the Young Lords were organizing in the Puerto Rican community. With the refusal of officials to integrate the schools, parents and community activists abandoned the idea of desegregated schools and decided that the only way to create quality education was to have community control of schools—something that had always been the case in affluent white communities.

. . . By this time Albert Shanker was head of the United Federation of Teachers. As the controversy at Intermediate School 201 erupted, the community actually took control of the school and staffed it with a variety of educators, activists, artists, and other community members who had skills and cared about children. The community demanded an African American administrator, community accountability, and respect for the children and the parents.

The UFT . . . set up picket lines around the school to prevent students and parents from coming in.

To me this was one of the greatest ironies I have encountered in education: teachers striking a school, trying to prevent children from entering the building, and keeping parents at bay. I saw it as an expression of scorn for the community and disrespect for the children's ability, tinged with racism. I had to take a stand for or against the parents and the community. I decided to cross the teachers' picket line.

Crossing the picket line was difficult—I worried about what my grandfather would think, remembering his union pledge and the unquestioned loyalty every working person was supposed to feel for unions. But, weighing the lives of the children and the attempt by the union to protect incompetence, I chose the parents and the children. This was one of the most agonizing decisions I have ever had to make and, though I would do it again if faced with the choice, I still worry about it making the spirit of my grandfather restless and angry.

If I was clear about anything after my first six years of being a teacher and an educational activist, it was that the first priority had to be the children. Loyalty to any idea, institution, or organization was secondary. 🔧

Herb Kohl is an educator and writer whose most recent book is The Herb Kohl Reader: Awakening the Heart of Teaching.

Hundreds of Teachers Arrested in 1972 Strike

An interview with former Philadelphia Federation of Teachers president John Ryan

The Philadelphia teachers' strike of 1972 lasted nearly six weeks. A settlement was reached only when the city's labor movement called for a general strike. The following is an excerpt from an interview conducted in 2020 by Adam Sanchez with John Ryan, a former president of the Philadelphia Federation of Teachers. Ryan served as the union's chief negotiator during the 1972 strike. Ryan and the PFT president at the time were jailed during the strike for violating a back-to-work order.

Let's talk about that strike. That was one of the longest strikes in the union's history.

Right, we had two strikes in the one school year, a total of something like 11-and-a-half weeks. And by this time, we had increased to paraprofessionals, as well as Get Set, which was a pre-kindergarten program where they were paid miserably. They made a fraction of what the teachers in the regular schools were getting. So we had just gotten the right to negotiate for them. That was a big issue.

And during this strike, Frank Rizzo was mayor. He's been in the news a lot lately, because his statue still stands in front of City Hall and many want it removed. I think most people know him now as the anti-Black Power, anti-LGBT rights police chief and mayor, but he was also the mayor going up against the teacher union during these strikes.

I remember I think the morning we're going to go back out on strike in January and the lawyers and the judges all went into chambers to discuss things. And we're all sitting around outside and all the reporters are there. And a reporter with Channel 10 asks me, "John, what do you think about what the mayor said about you today?" I said, "I didn't hear what the mayor had to say about me today." And he says, "You didn't hear what he said? He said, 'Ryan don't run this city.'" And I snapped back "Ryan do too." And that became a chant on the picket lines and people had it on picket signs.

And Rizzo threw you in jail during that strike?

Right. They got a judge to call an injunction. Frank Sullivan, the union president, and I went to jail for 19 days. Rizzo had friends including the cardinal archbishop. My wife was a daily communicant and went to Mass every day. But because the archbishop was close to the mayor, he decreed that no priest or nun should visit me or my family.

During that strike there were hundreds arrested. They would pick a school. They would load the buses up and they all got arrested. But Rizzo came to regret doing that immediately. Because the labor leaders then went to him and said, "You're going to have trouble from us. We're going to close this city down."

Right. During this strike the AFL-CIO called a general strike. Was it because you had built relationships with other labor unions in the city, or the national organization helped organize it?

Both. Actually, the main reason for it was Johnny Morris, who was president of Teamsters Local 115. Johnny was tough as nails. And he got a lot of it done. There were a lot of other local labor leaders who supported us as well. The president of the (local labor) council wasn't very keen on it, but he went along with it mainly because so many of the powerful unions were on our side. But that was a big reason why we settled. I think we would've gone through June if they hadn't called that general strike.

We came to an agreement on the 27th and we had listed five things that we wanted. We got a lot more than that, but we got every one of those five, including big raises for the Get Set program. I think the minimum wage increase by the end of the contract was 20 percent, and for the Get Set program, some of the people went up 60 percent in three years. We got the class size down to 35. And then by the time I left in 1979 it was down to 33, which is pretty much where it's still at today. ⬛

A People's History of the Chicago Teachers Union

BY JESSE HAGOPIAN

*When America's great crisis is a story in the pages of history, there will be a signifi-
cant chapter devoted to the unfailing sacrifice of the Chicago teachers, who are now
carrying on under inconceivable difficulties, far beyond the point that might be fairly
considered the limit of human endurance.*
  —*National Education Association Journal,* 1933

*We've been fighting in Chicago for a long time, but our community and teachers have
realized that the turning point of survival has kind of been met. Public education in
Chicago is at stake, and if we don't take drastic measures, we're not going to have neighborhood schools that are available to all students.*
  —Jen Johnson, high school teacher, Chicago Teachers Union delegate, and
founding member of Caucus of Rank and File Educators, 2012

When Jen Johnson spoke of the extended struggle that Chicago
teachers have been engaged in, she may have been referencing
assaults by such corporate education reformers as Arne Duncan.
Yet the history of Chicago teachers putting down their pencils
and grabbing picket signs to defend public education dates back
to the late 19th century—and contains some of the great stories in labor's history.

Chicago emerged during the late 19th century as a major commercial, financial, and manufacturing center with the stockyards front and center. But in 1886,
Chicago also became known as the center of the struggle for the eight-hour workday, a struggle that culminated in a police massacre at Haymarket Square, the trial
and execution of four of the movement's leaders, and the establishment of May Day
as International Workers' Day. This same brawl between capital and labor would
soon break out in Chicago's schoolyards.

In 1898, William Harper, the first president of the University of Chicago, proposed a sweeping reorganization of Chicago's public schools. Modeled on New
York City schools, the plan was shaped by elites across the nation who sought to
reorganize public education to suit the needs of a newly emerging industrial society. Their main goals were to control children during the day while both parents
worked, provide basic education to the next generation of workers, and prepare

them for the rigid schedule of factory life. Harper sought to hire only teachers with college degrees, implement a new system of hiring and firing, and address the "feminization" of schools by establishing a sexist hierarchy—hiring more male teachers and raising their salaries above women's. He also proposed to lease schools, property tax-free, to Chicago businesses for 99-year terms.

Chicago Teachers Federation and the "Labor Slugger"

But Harper was unprepared to play hardball with schoolteacher Margaret Haley, dubbed Chicago's "Lady Labor Slugger." Haley was the seminal figure in a class struggle approach to teacher unionism and an early leader of the Chicago Teachers Federation (CTF), a precursor to the Chicago Teachers Union.

Haley's father had been a member of the Knights of Labor, the first national labor union. In Haley's first teaching job in Joliet, Illinois, she asked her superintendent for a raise from $35 to $40 per month. The superintendent at first agreed, but when he later stalled, Haley sent him an ultimatum: If he did not pay her a higher salary by noon of the first day of the fall term, she would resign. When he denied her raise, she took the next train to Chicago.[1]

Haley successfully organized teachers to resist Harper's 1898 school reorganization. Even though women lacked the vote, Haley reached out to women's clubs—suffragist-leaning social networks of "high society" women—sending speakers to win over the club members on the basis of feminism, as women made up much of the teaching force. Teachers organized their own afternoon teas at neighborhood schools, like the Hendricks School in one of Chicago's poorest neighborhoods, located next to the stockyards and meatpacking district immortalized in Upton Sinclair's *The Jungle*. This broad approach to struggle paid off, and the Harper bill to reorganize the schools failed in the Illinois state legislature.

> But [education reformer William] Harper was unprepared to play hardball with schoolteacher Margaret Haley, dubbed Chicago's "Lady Labor Slugger." Haley was the seminal figure in a class struggle approach to teacher unionism and an early leader of the Chicago Teachers Federation, a precursor to the Chicago Teachers Union.

This experience drew Haley to the CTF. Together with Catherine Goggin, Haley initiated the "Teachers' Tax Crusade" that examined the Cook County tax rolls and discovered some $2 million in unpaid taxes. Haley and the CTF forced the local tax boards to collect the money and provide it to the school system. After three years of legal wrangling by outraged businesses, a court reduced the amount to $600,000. This still provided a substantial raise to Chicago's teachers, and news of the campaign spread across the nation.

Yet Haley emphasized that the struggle was not for economic gains alone.

Haley was a powerful opponent of the increasing standardization of education that she saw developing in early 20th-century schools, calling it "factoryizing education." At the 1904 National Education Association (NEA) convention she spoke out against industrialists' efforts to turn the teacher into "an automaton, a mere factory hand."[2] (See Haley, p. 67.)

In 1902, Haley had inspired the CTF to formally join the Chicago Federation of Labor. Within a year, the teachers helped overthrow the corrupt labor leadership in Chicago. Under the reform president, John Fitzpatrick, the American Federation of Labor (AFL) began to organize women workers all over the city: milliners, packinghouse workers, chorus girls, laundry workers, domestic servants, department store workers, garment workers, and more. For Haley, organizing women workers was closely related to winning the right for women to vote. Her approach of fusing the social struggle for suffrage with the labor movement was instrumental in winning suffrage in the state in 1913.

Haley's radical reform approach, however, had a key blind spot: It never included African Americans. As Haley's biographer Kate

TWO CHICAGO GRADE TEACHERS INVESTIGATING TAX-DODGERS.

Miss Margaret Haley. Miss Catherine Goggin.

CHICAGO TRIBUNE, JANUARY 29, 1900

CHICAGO TRIBUNE, JANUARY 1929

Rousmaniere put it, "although an eloquent advocate of liberatory causes and human rights, she was profoundly ambivalent about African American political and economic rights, and she championed the cause of working-class whites—especially Irish Catholics—over any other group." During the Great Migration of African Americans from the South to Northern industrial centers during World War I, Blacks began the struggle for access to public education in Chicago. With few employment options open to African American women, teaching became the most popular occupation among young Black college-educated women—more than half of all Black college graduates became schoolteachers.[3] This development contradicted Haley's approach.[4] Nonetheless, her efforts helped the CTF achieve a groundbreaking, though modest, meeting of four local unions in 1916 that formed the American Federation of Teachers (AFT).

Chicago Teachers and the Great Depression: The CTU Is Born
By the eve of the Great Depression, although Chicago had the most unionized teaching force in the country, educators were still deeply divided and belonged to a

variety of different unions. The Men Teachers Union (MTU) organized male high school teachers and prompted the formation of the Federation of Women High School Teachers (FWHST). There were the Elementary Teachers Union (ETU) and the Playground Teachers Union (PTU) as well. These unions were often at odds, as the MTU and the FWHST attempted to maintain the pay differentials of high school teachers over elementary school teachers while Margaret Haley's CTF and the ETU fought for parity for elementary school teachers.

With the Great Depression in full swing, the *Nation* reported the impact on teachers in May 1933: "Homes have been lost. Families have suffered undernourishment, even actual hunger. Their life insurance slashed, their savings gone, some teachers have been driven to panhandling after school hours to get food."[5] Hundreds of teachers were laid off. Teachers went for weeks and months without paychecks. High school teachers went from six to seven classes a day. Class sizes swelled. One Chicago teacher succumbed to the financial stress and committed suicide.

Fueling teacher anger was the Citizen's Committee on Public Expenditures (CCPE), a corporate entity with the purpose of reducing the investment in public education. With the *Chicago Tribune* editorializing for cuts in "fads and frills" in education—things such as art, physical education, and music—the CCPE pressed the Chicago Board of Education to slash spending by declaring that the banks would not buy any more tax warrants from the board. Without the financial support of the banks, the school board was strong-armed into submitting to the CCPE.[6]

With the unions divided and the bureaucracies of the unions too often seeking to collaborate with, rather than confront, the school board and the business elite destroying public education, teacher John Fewkes organized a new group, the Volunteer Emergency Committee (VEC), which organized mass demonstrations to win regular pay for teachers. For four months in 1933 thousands of fed-up educators regularly stormed Board of Education and City Council meetings.

In his account of teacher unionism in Chicago, *Teachers and Reform: Chicago Public Education, 1929–1970*, John F. Lyons writes that as many as 50,000 pupils from West Side to South Side schools went on strike April 5 to protest the delay in the payment of teachers' salaries. During the day, police were called to stop the student disturbances and to control a student demonstration that descended on the home of acting Mayor Frank J. Corr. A number of teachers in various schools staged a one-day strike by reporting themselves sick. There was, according to a *Chicago Daily News* reporter, "an endemic series of strikes, demonstration, and disorder in protest to the delay in the payment of teachers' salaries." It was, according to *Time*, the "biggest and most exciting school strike Chicago had ever seen."[7]

The VEC also organized boycotts of stores, hotels, and other businesses that were tax delinquent.

The high point of the struggle erupted on April 24, the first day of spring vacation, when 5,000 teachers marched on five large banks—First National Bank, Harris Trust & Savings Bank, City National Bank, Northern Trust Bank, and the Continental Illinois Bank—whose refusal to pay their taxes was depleting funds desperately needed in the classroom. Lyons writes:

Teachers threw ink on the walls, tipped over desks, and broke windows. Surrounded by teachers shouting "Pay us! Pay us!" the bank executives had to call for the police to remove the teachers. On the following Wednesday more than 3,000 male teachers armed with schoolbooks again confronted the bankers, invading the Chicago Title and Trust Company, breaking windows and ransacking the building. Mounted police clubbed the teachers as they hurled books at the police and their horses.[8]

On June 9, the last day of the spring term, 5,000 teachers, parents, and students fought with police as they protested in downtown Chicago against the bankers, the CCPE, and the politicians.

The actions inspired eight teachers' organizations, including the CTF, the MTU, the ETU, and the FWHST, to merge and form the Teacher Welfare Organizations. As a result, the Chicago Public Schools rescinded many of the cuts to physical education, music, and the arts; most teachers went back to six classes per day, rather than the seven proposed; by September 1935, the board had reassigned all of the teachers dismissed in July 1933; and in August 1934 teachers finally received all of the back salary they had been denied. In October 1937, not coincidentally, the Chicago Teachers Union was born.

During and after World War II, the CTU worked alongside the Democratic Party and accommodated the anti-communism of McCarthyism. As CTU president Fewkes declared in 1949, "The increased heat in the Cold War now in progress makes it imperative that teachers in our public schools leave no doubt as to their fundamental Americanism." Consequently, the union did not defend communists generally, or their allies, from persecution.

Still, Fewkes and the CTU did mount some important struggles in this era and even opposed some of the most egregious aspects of the Red Scare witch hunts. For example, after a May 1945 NEA investigative report found that city politicians had used their power to influence which teachers were hired and promoted, the CTU used newfound public support to threaten a strike against the City Council's decision to block teacher pay raises. This proved enough to back the council down. The CTU also led important opposition to anti-communist attacks on teachers and their curriculum, writing in the union newspaper in 1941 against loyalty oaths that would prohibit communist teachers, "You cannot preserve freedom by taking it away! You cannot preserve democracy by totalitarian means!"[9] In an era when hundreds of teachers had been suspended or dismissed for noncooperation with the House Un-American Activities Committee, the harassment Chicago teachers faced was not as severe as teachers elsewhere, in part because of the CTU.[10]

> Teachers threw ink on the walls, tipped over desks, and broke windows. Surrounded by teachers shouting "Pay us! Pay us!" the bank executives had to call for the police to remove the teachers.

Labor Rights Are Civil Rights: Black Teacher Power

"The U.S. teacher used to be afraid to smoke, chew, cuss, or ask for a raise," *Time* magazine reported in 1963. "Now he denounces crowded classrooms, upbraids lawmakers, and goes on strike almost as readily as a dockworker. He even demands a say in things that school boards always considered their sole province. Teacher militancy is bursting out all over."[11]

One of the momentous yet often ignored achievements of the Civil Rights and Black Power movements was their decisive contribution to the winning of collective bargaining rights for public sector workers in the 1960s and 1970s. As Aaron Brenner points out, "Between the early 1960s and 1981, American workers engaged in an extraordinarily high level of workplace militancy, exhibiting a sustained rebelliousness not seen since the 1930s. . . . Drawing on the Civil Rights, Black Power, feminist, and antiwar movements, and on the labor movement's own traditions of militancy, rank-and-file self-organization, and workers control, they advocated a more aggressive, inclusive, democratic, and politicized union movement that they believed could win greater rights for workers both on and off the job."[12]

Teachers in Chicago were certainly beneficiaries of the mass social movements that swept aside the stifling politics of McCarthyism that had long stunted labor's growth. In 1967, this labor and civil rights upsurge contributed to the CTU's first officially negotiated contract with the Chicago Board of Education, where the CTU obtained Christmas vacation pay (the first AFT local to do so), a $500 per year salary increase, fully paid medical insurance, two personal days, a grievance procedure, class size caps, and a duty-free lunch period.

Yet while both Black and white teachers asked their union to negotiate higher wages and better benefits, Black teachers and Black community activists increasingly wanted the union to use its increased power to prompt school authorities to improve the quality of education in the inner-city schools—while too often their white colleagues wanted only a narrow focus on bread-and-butter issues. One simple fact highlighted the disparity within the union: Although about 60 percent of the students and more than a third of teachers were African Americans, the CTU negotiating team included no Black members.[13]

Another problem was that many Black teachers were categorized as Full-Time Basis (FTB) substitutes, which meant full-time work hours but not the benefits or job protection of certified teachers. They gave the FTB status to teachers who had met state certification requirements but not passed the Chicago Board of Education teacher certification examination required to teach in CPS. But many African Americans noted that they often failed the oral exam only because the racist board of examiners thought they had "unprofessional" Black Southern accents. One such teacher was Mamie Till Mobley, who campaigned on behalf of her son Emmett Till, the 14-year-old boy whose murder in Mississippi in 1955 was one of the catalysts for the Civil Rights Movement. She began teaching in CPS in the 1960s, but she failed the oral exam because the board of examiners thought she was on an "ego trip."[14]

As the Black Power movement grew in Chicago, Black students and parents began organizing for the introduction of Black studies into the curriculum and for the removal of white principals who would not embrace these changes. Unfortunately, the CTU leadership too often sided with the Board of Education and the white principals in these disputes.

The FTB subs, about 90 percent African American, began their own sickouts and strikes in 1968 to pressure Mayor Richard J. Daley to make them full-fledged classroom teachers and to stop the high teacher turnover rate in Black schools. When the CTU did not come to their aid, the FTB subs threatened to leave the union.

The CTU authorized its first official strike in May 1969, with around 75 percent support of teachers, who were able to convince most of their wavering colleagues to stay away from school.[15] Within a few days, Mayor Daley succumbed to the strike's pressure and negotiated a settlement that met all of the CTU's demands, including a $100 per month raise, and the recruitment of 750 new teachers to help alleviate overcrowded classrooms in segregated schools. Scared by the threat of large numbers of Black teachers leaving the union, the CTU finally took action to pressure the Board of Education and Mayor Daley to give in to the demands of the FTB subs—and the board lifted the exam requirement for FTB certification.[16]

Moreover, following the strike, the Chicago Board of Education bowed to the pressure of Black community activists and Black union militants and introduced new classes that focused on Black history and Black literary figures.[17]

The CORE of Education: A New "Slugger"

From 1969 until 1987, the CTU led seven strikes that won smaller class sizes, medical benefits, sick leave, and more preparation time.

But then for almost 25 years—in an era marked by neoliberal economic policies favoring privatization, deregulation, and the decline of unions—the union's combativeness waned, capped by its failure to lead a campaign against then-CEO of the Chicago Public Schools (and later U.S. Secretary of Education) Arne Duncan's disastrous Renaissance 2010 plan that slated around 100 schools for closure—predominately in Black neighborhoods—and converted many to privately run, nonunion charter schools or military academies. To make matters worse, the Great Recession hit in 2008, and the corporate education reform agenda kicked in to high gear as billionaires and their foundations, hedge fund managers, and their political sycophants in statehouses became determined to see teachers and public sector workers pay for a global financial crisis caused by rapacious Wall Street speculation.

When the Chicago Teachers Union refused to mount the struggle needed to defend teachers and public education, several teachers invited Jinny Sims, former president of the British Columbia Teachers' Federation, to teach them how the BCTF went on an illegal strike in 2005 and won a huge victory for their students and class size reduction. These teachers then put theory together with practice, formed the Caucus of Rank and File Educators (CORE), and began organizing colleagues and communities to resist the closures of some 16 schools, turning out hundreds of parents to picket Chicago Board of Education meetings and to testify in defense of their schools. As a result of this bold campaign and other organizing initiatives, teachers from the CORE slate were elected to leadership positions in the Chicago Teachers Union in the spring of 2010. Karen Lewis, the newly elected CORE president of the CTU, remarked at her acceptance speech:

> Today marks the beginning of the end of scapegoating educators for all the social ills that our children, families, and schools struggle against every day. Today marks the beginning of a fight for true transparency in our educational policy—how to accurately measure learning and teaching, how to truly improve our schools, and how to evaluate the wisdom behind our spending priorities. This election shows the unity of 30,000 educators standing strong to put business in its place—out of our schools. Corporate America sees K–12 public education as $380 billion that, up until the last 10 or 15 years, they didn't have a sizable piece of. . . . Our teachers and paraprofessionals are poised to reclaim the power of our 30,000 members and protect what we love: teaching and learning in publicly funded public schools.[18]

In the spring of 2012, Chicago Mayor Rahm "1%" Emanuel and his appointed Board of Education made up of millionaires and billionaires, including Hyatt Hotels heiress Penny Pritzker, began contract negotiations with the CTU with a plan to further impose the business model on the schools that has been shown throughout Chicago's history to not improve education. They proposed extending the school year without increasing pay for teachers; they suggested that class sizes could reach 55 students; and they sought to impose a merit pay scheme on teachers that would have narrowed the curriculum to drill-and-kill test prep.[19]

Shouting into a microphone outside of the Board of Education, CTU Vice President Jesse Sharkey described the response of the union: "We have met the attack with wide-scale vocal opposition, we have met the attack arm in arm with our partners in the community. We've occupied schools, we have marched, we have filled auditoriums, we have filled streets, and yes, we have voted to authorize a strike."[20] With more than 90 percent of educators voting in favor, the CTU began its first strike in a quarter of a century on Sept. 10, 2012, and held the line for more than a week in a strike that captured the imagination of workers around the country and headlines around the world.

Kirstin Roberts, a CTU preschool teacher, described the impact of the strike on the rank and file, writing: "The outpouring of solidarity was matched by an outpouring of creativity on the picket lines and at the mass protests every afternoon. Teachers and staff who had long been stifled and forced to deliver rote lessons designed solely for test preparation began to paint and dance and sing their struggle."[21]

While Chicago teachers were not able to defeat every last one of Mayor Emanuel's corporate reforms—for example, the contract stipulates that only half of new teachers hired must be displaced CTU members—the list of gains for students and teachers from the strike reveals a decisive win for labor:

- CPS must hire more than 600 additional teachers in art, music, physical education, and other subjects—helping to make the school day better, not just longer.

- The proportion that student test scores count toward teacher evaluations was lowered to the legal minimum.
- Language that promotes racial diversity in hiring at CPS to fight the loss of African American teachers in Chicago's schools.
- Anti-bullying language to help limit administration intimidation of teachers.
- A pool of funding for social workers, psychologists, special education teachers, classroom assistants, and counselors in schools with high caseloads.
- $250 annual reimbursement for teachers buying classroom supplies.
- A 7 percent rise in pay over three years, maintaining "steps and lanes," so experienced teachers and those with master's degrees earn more.

One of the primary reasons for the CTU's victory was this: It transcended a simple labor dispute and was transformed into a social movement, with the teachers fusing their struggle with that of the community they serve—organizing with parents for more than a year prior to the strike, making demands for increased resources for the students, advocating for racial equity in hiring, and joining in the Occupy Chicago movement that pointed out the root of societal problems—social and economic inequality. By striking not only for better wages, but also to defend and enrich public education for students of color and low-income families, the CTU's strike garnered 66 percent support from the students' parents[22] and earned the citywide solidarity teachers would need to give them enough courage to walk off the job. *Jacobin* magazine summed up the importance of the 2012 Chicago Teachers Union strike: "In 2012, Chicago hosted the most dynamic and successful strike to occur in the United States in at least 15 years, and the largest teachers' strike in nearly a quarter-century, all while fundamentally challenging a global movement to privatize and standardize public education."[23]

> "In 2012, Chicago hosted the most dynamic and successful strike to occur in the United States in at least 15 years, and the largest teachers' strike in nearly a quarter-century, all while fundamentally challenging a global movement to privatize and standardize public education."

Jesse Hagopian teaches at Garfield High School in Seattle and is an editor of Rethinking Schools *magazine. Jesse edited the book* More Than a Score: The New Uprising Against High-Stakes Testing *and co-edited the book* Teaching for Black Lives. *He blogs at IAmAnEducator.com.*

A longer version of this article originally appeared in the International Socialist Review *No. 86. To read about the history of the CTU since 2012, see the the next article by Jackson Potter (p. 70). For an in-depth article on Margaret Haley, see "Chicago Teachers Federation & Its Legacy" by Robert Lowe, rethinkingschools.org/TUSJ.*

ENDNOTES

[1] Haley, Margaret. 1982. *Battleground: The Autobiography of Margaret A. Haley.* University of Illinois Press: p. 20–21.

[2] Haley, Margaret.. 1904. "Why Teachers Should Organize." *Journal of Proceedings and Addresses.* National Education Association: p. 146.

[3] Lyons, John F. 2008. *Teachers and Reform: Chicago Public Education, 1929–1970.* University of Illinois Press: p. 15.

[4] Ibid., 27–28.

[5] Ibid., 32.

[6] Ibid., 30.

[7] Ibid., 39–40.

[8] Ibid., 40–41.

[9] Ibid., 128.

[10] Ibid., 132.

[11] Ibid., 133.

[12] Brenner, Aaron, Robert Brenner, and Cal Winslow. 2010. *Rebel Rank and File: Labor Militancy and Revolt from Below During the Long 1970s.* Verso: p. xi.

[13] Lyons, 175.

[14] Ibid., 200.

[15] Ibid., 203.

[16] Ibid., 204.

[17] Aarons, Dakarai I. April 4, 2012. "Chicago School Closings Found to Yield Few Gains," *Education Week.*

[18] Teachers for Social Justice video speech. vimeo.com/12642225

[19] Schmidt, George N. March 9, 2012. "Arne Duncan Gets an F." *Substance News.* substancenews.net/articles.php?page=3132&section=Article

[20] Labor Beat video. youtube.com/watch?v=UEx1DsJVNLQ

[21] Roberts, Kirstin. Oct. 9, 2012. "We Stood Up to the Bullies." *Socialist Worker.* socialistworker.org/2012/10/09/we-stood-up-to-the-bullies

[22] CTU blog. Sept. 13, 2012, ctulocal1.org/posts/as-chicago-teachers-strike-enters-fourth-day-a-new-poll-proves-majority-of-parents-and-taxpayers-approve-of-fair-contract-fight

[23] Cunningham-Cook, Matthew. Dec. 27, 2012. "One, Two, Many Chicago Teachers' Strikes." *Jacobin.* jacobinmag.com/2012/12/one-two-many-chicago-teachers-strikes-2

Why Teachers Should Organize

BY MARGARET HALEY

Teacher unions striking in Chicago in the early 20th century.

Editor's note: Haley, vice president of the Chicago Teachers Federation, gave this speech at the National Education Association convention in St. Louis on July 1, 1904.

Teachers organizations must be in harmony with the fundamental object of the public school in a democracy, namely to preserve and develop the democratic ideal. . . .

Nowhere in the United States today does the public school, as a branch of the public service, receive from the public either the moral or financial support needed to enable it properly to perform its important function in the social organism. The conditions that are militating most strongly against efficient teaching and that existing organizations of the kind under discussion here are directing their energies toward changing, briefly stated are the following:

1. Greatly increased cost of living, together with constant demands for higher standards of scholarship and professional attainments and culture to be met with practically stationary and wholly inadequate teachers' salaries.
2. Insecurity of tenure of office and lack of provision for old age.
3. Overwork in overcrowded schoolrooms, exhausting both mind and body.
4. And lastly, lack of recognition of the teacher as an educator in the school system, due to the increased tendency toward "factoryizing education," making the teacher an automaton, a mere factory hand, whose duty it is to carry out mechanically and unquestioningly the ideas and orders of those clothed with the authority of position and who may or may not know how to minister to them.

The individuality of the teacher and her power of initiative are thus destroyed and the result is courses of study, regulations, and equipment that the teachers have had no voice in selecting, that often have no relation to the children's needs, and that prove a hindrance instead of a help in teaching. . . .

There is no possible conflict between the good of society and the good of its members, of which the industrial workers are the vast majority. The organization of these workers for mutual aid has shortened the hours of labor, raised and equalized the wages of men and women, and taken the children from the factories and workshops. These humanitarian achievements of the labor unions—and many others that space forbids enumerating—in raising the standard of living of the poorest and weakest members of society are a service to society that for its own welfare it must recognize. . . .

> It will be well indeed if the teachers have the courage of their convictions and face all that the labor unions have faced with courage and perseverance.

If there is one institution on which the responsibility rests most heavily, it is the public school. If there is one body of public servants of whom the public has a right to expect the mental and moral equipment to face the labor question and other issues vitally affecting the welfare of society and urgently pressing for a rational and scientific solution, it is the public school teachers whose special contribution to society is their own power to think, the moral courage to follow their convictions, and the training of citizens to think and to express thought in free and intelligent action. . . .

How shall the public school and the industrial workers in their struggle to secure the rights of humanity through a more just and equitable distribution of the products of their labor, meet their mutual responsibility to each other and to society? . . .

Two ideals are struggling for supremacy in American life today: one is the industrial ideal dominating through the supremacy of commercialism, which subordinates the worker to the product and the machine; the other, the ideal of democracy, the ideal of the educators, which places humanity above all machines, and demands that all activity shall be the expression of life. If this ideal of the educators cannot be carried over into the industrial field then the ideal of industrialism will be carried over into the school. Those two ideals can no more continue to exist in American life than our nation could have continued half slave and half free. If the school cannot bring joy to the work of the world, the joy must go out of its own life, and work in the school, as in the industrial field, will become drudgery. . . .

It will be well indeed if the teachers have the courage of their convictions and face all that the labor unions have faced with the same courage and perseverance.

Today, teachers of America, we stand at the parting of the ways. Democracy is not on trial, but America is. ◗

Margaret Haley was the longtime leader of the Chicago Teachers Federation and a pioneer in organizing schoolteachers in America. According to PBS online, "Haley came to understand that it was up to teachers to fight for change, both in the schools and in society."

For background information on this speech, go to the Labor and Working-Class History Association, Document 7.2.: bit.ly/2J2hzfN.

Chicago Teachers Union Takes to the Streets Again

BY JACKSON POTTER

JOE BRUSKY | MTEA

Editors' note: In this article Jackson Potter, a longtime teacher activist and CTU leader, continues relating the CTU's history since 2012, the year the article by Jesse Hagopian ended.

Jesse Hagopian's article elucidates the arc of struggle from the robber baron era, when Chicago teachers fought to provide clean drinking water free of cholera to our students, through 2012, when we shook off a generation of austerity to jump-start a nationwide strike wave that has reinvigorated the labor movement.

The story does not end there. The action in 2012 was largely a struggle to stop the full-scale assault on our public school system and demonstrate that teachers and the broader public preferred investment over privatization and school closures. We won that fight, but it was not until our strike in 2019 that the tide turned definitively in our favor. That accomplishment is a testament to a sustained and protracted struggle that teachers waged to reverse decades of racist attacks on our students and their families. If there is one addition I would make to Hagopian's assessment of our fight, it's to emphasize our focus on racial justice as the centerpiece of CORE's efforts to transform schools in Chicago and beyond. When Karen Lewis lambasted the mayor and school board for creating a system of "educational apartheid," it galvanized Black and Latino parents across neighborhoods to support our strike. Ours is not simply a class struggle but a movement to establish economic and racial justice, and the 2019 strike belongs in the annals of history—in fact one of the Chicago Teachers Union's "greatest hits" in a century-long quest to win the "Schools Our Students Deserve."

For example, as a Chicago Public Schools (CPS) student from 1st grade through high school, and in my 17 years of teaching in the system, none of my schools ever had a full-time social worker or nurse every day of the week.

Ours is not simply a class struggle but a movement to establish economic and racial justice.

In the first contract the CTU secured in the era of legalized public sector bargaining, in 1967, the language states: "a plan shall be devised to make available to teacher nurses a list of vacancies to which they may indicate their desire to transfer." That language, providing no firm guarantee of staffing ratios, remained virtually unchanged for half a century. All subsequent contracts until 2019 include no references to bilingual education, dedicated staff and resources for our homeless students, case manager positions for our diverse learner population, sanctuary language to protect undocumented students from ICE, living wages for our lowest-paid paraprofessional members, or a dedicated article on early childhood education. Now, that's all changed.

After 52 years of struggle, and an 11-day citywide strike, in 2019 we were finally able to secure these critical demands—and more. We won 180 case manager positions, 20 English language program teachers, full-time staff for homeless students, up to $35 million to lower excessive class size, and even nap time for our little ones. This dedicated effort to win seminal staffing supports and educational justice for CPS students did not happen overnight—it's been a long and protracted fight for the schools they deserve.

During the lead-up to the 2019 strike, the editorial pages of the two major newspapers in town, the *Chicago Tribune* and the *Chicago Sun-Times*, took turns slamming us for intransigence, greed, and idealism, often in the same sentence. The *Sun-Times* ran an editorial in the days before the strike that demanded we "Take the deal" and stated we "should accept the latest contract offer from the Board of Education, a sweet deal that most Chicagoans would just love to get." Prior to the strike, Mayor Lori Lightfoot offered a 16 percent raise over a five-year agreement, a salary offer that the CTU eventually accepted. However, none of the central issues raised from when the strike began to when it ended had anything to do with that initial salary offer.

In the last months of 2018, the CTU collected hundreds of proposals from our 27,000 members. Of the hundreds of submissions, many described how to fix a broken and anxiety-ridden teacher evaluation system, how to ramp up preparation and collaboration time, adequate pay and benefits, and more. There were also a number of ideas that went well beyond a traditional collective bargaining agreement. One proposal demanded the school district provide housing for all 18,000 homeless students in the district by creating affordable housing through a real estate transfer tax, a corporate head tax, and utilizing the city's Tax Increment Financing (TIF) program. Despite Mayor Lightfoot's claims to support a progressive agenda that reflected the CTU's vision for schools, reality proved more complicated.

Lightfoot campaigned on a promise to prevent a strike by addressing our key concerns and demands. Yet, during negotiations, her team refused time and again to meet them.

Once CTU went out on strike on Oct. 17, Lightfoot claimed the contract was not the "appropriate place" to address the needs of homeless students. While she promised to add more social workers and nurses to the school budget, she refused to put it in writing and make those commitments explicit within the collective bargaining agreement. By the end of the strike, we made sure that both supports for homeless students and guarantees for more social workers and nurses were indeed put in writing. At the inception of the strike, Mayor Lightfoot was adamant that there was no more money for our contract. But by the end, we won tens of millions more dollars in the new contract.

This contract fight wasn't the first time the CTU raised "common good" proposals to elevate broader demands not typically associated with a union contract.

In 2010, we suggested that the Chicago Board of Education tap into the TIF program—a system where decades' worth of property taxes are frequently diverted from schools, parks, and libraries to support developments in the wealthiest parts of the city. At the time, Mayor Richard M. Daley's chief negotiator for the teachers' contract, Jim Franczek, told us that "TIF is too complicated" and that the funds were unavailable to schools due to a firewall between the city and school budgets.

By 2016, we cracked the purported TIF firewall and forced then-Mayor Rahm Emanuel to unleash a record $87.5 million to stave off a strike. In 2019, Mayor Lightfoot eventually followed suit and released another record TIF surplus of $163 million to the public schools.

On top of winning new funding streams, our broader social justice demands built upon victories in the earlier Los Angeles teacher strike, as well as Boston's teacher contract campaign that won language on class size restrictions. In no small way, the 2019 CTU strike was connected to a rising movement of teachers nationally that has fundamentally altered the political and labor landscape in the United States.

When we struck in 2012, the action was largely defensive in nature and came on the heels of Scott Walker's attack on collective bargaining rights in Wisconsin. Our 2019 strike represented a move into offense—beyond efforts to stop school closings, vouchers, bankruptcies, pension liquidation, or state takeovers. Instead, we've added about 750 new positions into our schools, staffing that will dramatically increase investments into our classrooms for the first time in decades. We've also added new language that establishes "sanctuary schools," requiring CPS to prohibit the entry of ICE agents into our buildings unless they have a warrant. The new agreement also provides critical immigration and legal services to our students and their families.

The labor movement will look back on the 2019 strikes in Chicago and LA as the time when #RedForEd began to supplant austerity and corporate reform with educational equity and investments into our Black and Latino school communities. Although we have a ways to go before public schools in Chicago match the school funding received by wealthy suburban districts, the 2019 agreement got us closer.

One of the keys to our victory was labor solidarity. Chicago teachers struck alongside the 7,000 school employees in SEIU Local 73, which did not occur in 2012. These school workers also won large-scale victories in their contract, and by standing with us on the picket lines, they showed the power of true collective action.

The victories in our strike built upon yearslong efforts to bring Chicago charter school teachers into the CTU, aligning 11 charter school contracts. This strategic choice led to the first charter school strikes in the nation's history and won provisions on class size and sanctuary schools that set the stage to win them throughout the district.

To win more, we teachers should consider partnering with private sector union struggles. Imagine if we had been able to join forces with the United Auto Workers in their labor struggle with GM, or coordinated with warehouse workers to shut down the region's supply chains. Such an approach could help build the social power necessary to advance a set of regional worker demands to significantly alter the political and economic landscape for all workers.

When I was a 1st grader in CPS in 1984, there weren't social workers or nurses in every school. There were no case managers, no coordinators for homeless students. Adherence to legal limits on special education, bilingual, and early childhood state laws was limited. On Nov. 16, 2019, more than 81 percent of CTU members ratified a contract that possesses all of those essential features. Although there are many demands we were unable to win, we made massive strides toward equity in the classroom.

Throughout history, social movement struggles have always been protracted. It's taken three contract cycles for the CTU to turn back nearly 40 years of attacks on our public schools. It's a shift made possible through strike action coupled with a burgeoning national teachers' movement—and taking risks to lift up working-class and racial justice demands that go far beyond traditional collective bargaining. 🔧

Jackson Potter is a Chicago Teachers Union trustee, member of the Big Bargaining Team, and a teacher at Back of the Yards College Prep.

The 1994 Call for Social Justice Teacher Unionism

I n August 1994, a group of 29 teacher union activists from a variety of AFT and NEA locals held a three-day institute in Portland, Oregon, sponsored by the National Coalition of Education Activists. They issued a statement, "Social Justice Unionism: A Working Draft," which was printed at the time in *Rethinking Schools* and subsequently in the first edition of this book. It guided and inspired unionists for years.

The statement was a call to action and advocated a new model of unionism, including this warning:

> . . . Without a broader conception of the interests of teachers and of teaching, our unions will find themselves on evermore shaky ground, defending fewer jobs and shrinking privileges against repeated attacks. Without a better partnership with the parents and communities that need public education most, we will find ourselves isolated from essential allies. Without a new vision of schooling that raises the expectations of our students and the standards of our own profession, we will continue to flounder. Without a new model of unionism that revives debate and democracy internally and projects an inspiring social vision and agenda externally, we will fall short of the challenges before us.

It went on to say:

> Social justice unionism cannot be implemented in a top-down fashion. Nor can it be just words on paper. It will require both enlightened leadership and rank-and-file mobilization. It will mean learning to teach in new ways; restructuring local union activities in new ways; reaching out to different communities in new ways; and building alliances at both local and state levels. It will require the national unions, perhaps one merged national teacher union, to provide leadership to build a national movement for social and economic justice.

The statement detailed seven components of social justice teacher unionism, which are listed in the flyer on p. 75. Activists distributed thousands of flyers and buttons at subsequent NEA and AFT conventions where a merger of the two unions was debated—and ultimately rejected in 1998. 🔲

The Real Question

is not whether one is for or against the merger. The question is how to build on the strengths of the NEA and AFT and create an even better organization.

A new organization needs to retain the best of traditional unionism and borrow from "professional unionism." Given the attacks on the social safety net and on public education, it must not only defend the legitimate interests of its members but embrace a vision of social justice for all those so often denied the full benefits of this society. If we want our members and save public educa-with the students, families and com-unionism is called "social justice to successfully defend the interests of tion, we must build an alliance munities we serve. This vision of unionism." Such a vision would:

SOCIAL JUSTICE UNIONISM

A NEW VISION FOR A UNITED NEA/AFT

1. Defend the rights of its members while fighting for the rights and needs of the broader community and students.

2. Recognize that the families and neighbors of our students are key allies, and build strategic alliances with parents, labor unions, and community groups.

3. Fully involve rank-and-file members in running the union and initiate widespread discussion on how education unions should respond to the crises in education and society.

4. Put teachers and others who work in classrooms at the center of school reform agendas, ensuring that they take ownership of reform initiatives.

5. Encourage those who work with children to use methods of instruction and curricula that will promote racial and gender equity, combat racism and prejudice, encourage critical thinking about our society's problems and nurture an active, reflective citizenry that is committed to real democracy and social and economic justice.

6. Forcefully advocate for a radical restructuring of American education.

7. Aggressively educate and mobilize members to fight for social justice in all areas of society.

Adapted from "Social Justice Unionism: A Working Draft: A Call to Education Unionists," July 1994. For a complete version send $1 to the National Coalition of Education Activists, PO Box 679, Rhinebeck, NY 12572. rfbs@aol.com.

❖ Social Justice Unionism ❖ A New Vision for a United NEA/AFT

This leaflet is published by *Rethinking Schools*, a grass-roots education reform journal. To follow ongoing discussions of social justice unionism subscribe to *Rethinking Schools*, 1001 E. Keefe Ave, Milwaukee, WI 53212. $12.50/year. 1-800-669-4192. www.rethinkingschools.org. For "Social Justice Unionism" buttons contact *Rethinking Schools*.

The Wisconsin Uprising—2011

BY ELENI SCHIRMER

Following the Great Recession of 2007–2009, managers of the country's public institutions imposed austerity measures on workers. Perhaps nowhere were these budget cutbacks more dramatically enacted than in Wisconsin. But then again, perhaps no other place witnessed a fightback so bold or inspiring. In February 2011, Wisconsin's newly elected Republican governor, Scott Walker, proposed surprise legislation curtailing public sector union bargaining rights. The legislation especially affected teachers, who in Wisconsin, as across the nation, represent the most unionized public employees. Immediately, teachers sprang into action. Within days of the bill's announcement, teachers coordinated massive sickouts, reporting to the halls of the state Capitol instead of their classrooms. Their bold leadership inspired others, including union leadership and Democratic Party officials. Soon workers and allies from across the state and country flocked to the Capitol in protest, drawing crowds of more than 100,000 people and occupying the Capitol for nearly two weeks. This massive popular resistance to attacks on public sector workers and institutions are today referred to as the Wisconsin Uprising. Both the Wisconsin attacks on union rights and the workers' resistance set precedents that would resonate across the country in years to come. This piece explores the origins of Wisconsin Act 10, its effects, and the historical uprising it inspired.

Where Did Wisconsin Act 10 Come From?

Wisconsin Act 10 took many by surprise. Removing public sector union collective bargaining rights had not been part of Walker's campaign. What's more, the state has a strong labor history. In the early 20th century, Wisconsin was home to the Progressive Party, and it boasted a legacy of socialist leadership in its largest city. In 1959, Wisconsin was the first state to grant public employees the right to unionize. How did the nation's first state to grant public sector workers' collective bargaining rights become the first to take them away?

While the long history of Wisconsin's weakened labor movement is beyond this article's scope, a key part starts with major political shifts that took place in 2010, when the midterm elections nationwide shifted political control to conservatives. In Wisconsin, Republicans gained majority control of the state Senate and Assembly, defeated longtime incumbent Democrat Russ Feingold in the U.S. Senate election, and won the gubernatorial office. Similar trends occurred across the country. Right-wing conservatism touted by the Tea Party movement gained influence in the wake of the 2008 economic collapse. Conservative leaders capitalized upon people's financial and racial anxieties by promoting an ideological program that held public social programs and their beneficiaries accountable for the economic crisis, and called for an end to "big government." In the U.S. House of Representatives, 39 of the 129 newly elected representatives were Tea Party members; in the Senate, five of the nine newly elected senators were.

In addition to the rise of conservative Tea Party-backed candidates such as Gov. Scott Walker, 2010 also saw deflated energy among Democrats. Especially compared with the 2008 elections, the previously energized young and progressive electorate had grown weary. Even Wisconsin's Democrats had unfurled a public sector austerity agenda. Walker's Democratic predecessor, Jim Doyle, had enacted his own budget cuts and imposed furloughs on state workers in the wake of the 2008 crisis. And Walker's 2010 Democratic opponent, Tom Barrett, also held the public sector responsible for the state's financial problems. As mayor of Milwaukee, Barrett had cut public employees' benefits and pensions and called for mayoral takeover of the city's public schools. Unable to significantly distinguish between the Democratic and Republican visions for Wisconsin, many voters chose to sit the election out. In November 2010, Walker won the gubernatorial election by nearly 6 percent.

> Conservative leaders capitalized upon people's financial and racial anxieties by promoting an ideological program that held public social programs and their beneficiaries accountable for the economic crisis

So, when Walker took office in January 2011, he not only faced anemic progressive opposition, but he also had the backing of a national conservative movement. He seized his advantage. As the financial crisis rolled into state coffers in 2011, Walker took the opportunity to impose "shock doctrine" policies. In the name of crisis management, Walker targeted a key pillar of the Democratic party: unions. Originally titled the "Budget Repair Bill," Act 10 was designed to give public administrators "the tools"—in Walker's words—to cut labor and healthcare expenses to cope with declining revenues.

What Was Act 10?

The language and inspiration for Act 10 came from the American Legislative Exchange Council (ALEC), an organization funded by the Koch brothers to draft conservative legislation. Along with laws to roll back environmental protections, increase gun access, and restrict immigration and voting access, ALEC drafted legislation to weaken labor unions. Act 10 was one of its bills and affected three key dimensions of union power. First, it changed *what* public sector unions could bargain over. The law restricted public sector collective bargaining to wages capped at inflation, roughly 2 percent annually. No longer could teachers bargain over class size. Nurses could not demand lower patient-nurse ratios or shorter shift lengths.

Power plant operators could not bargain over health and safety conditions in their workplaces. Health care and other benefits were no longer permissible bargaining topics. This was a particular sting for Wisconsin educators who, since revenue caps initiated in the 1990s, had exchanged wage gains for health insurance coverage.

Second, Act 10 changed *how* public sector unions were organized. In order to be legally recognized by the state and thus gain these meager bargaining privileges, Act 10 required public sector unions to conduct annual recertification elections. However, these were not simply "get the most votes and win" elections. The new law mandated that to win a recertification election, 51 percent of all eligible workers in a unit must vote yes; any non-vote counted as a vote against the union. Act 10 also removed automatic dues deduction, in which union fees are automatically taken from workers' paychecks. Now, each member would have to be organized to agree to pay their fees. No longer could unions assume either membership or dues without organizing for them.

The third dimension of Act 10 was *who* was included in the law. The law applied to all public sector employees, with the exception of police and firefighters—positions historically dominated by white males. Thus women and people of color who are disproportionately represented in public sector union membership suffered the most. As Walker himself admitted, his intention was to break unions by dividing and conquering—separating police and firefighters from other public workers, and public workers from private workers.

What Was the Wisconsin Uprising?

Immediately upon learning of Walker's proposed legislation, Wisconsin teachers jumped into action. Members of teacher unions in Madison and Milwaukee quickly initiated phone trees to organize teachers to call in sick and show up at the Capitol building in protest. Thanks to these local leaders' bold and decisive actions, union leadership across the state followed suit, calling on members to flood the Capitol in support. For nearly two weeks, protesters from around the state and country filled the Capitol building and grounds—refusing to leave until the bill had been killed. The 24/7 occupation of the Capitol lasted for two weeks, but large protests continued throughout the spring. During the uprising, solidarity was palpable. Protesters came from all sectors and backgrounds—public sector and private sector workers, the self-employed, the retired, students, community members, farmers.

The Wisconsin Uprising was the biggest labor protest in decades and offered key lessons in the coming years. First, it showed the power of direct action. Unions won public support by standing up and fighting for the public good, rather than waiting to play an inside game.

Second, the Wisconsin Uprising showcased the importance of rank-and-file leadership. Rather than waiting for the Democratic Party or union officials to announce their plans for resistance, workers themselves organized actions. (Just days before Walker proposed Act 10, the president of the state teacher union had offered serious concessions to Walker, to the surprise and chagrin of many teachers. Union leadership did not see its power as fighting against Walker's antagonism toward public institutions, but rather placating it.) Only when workers themselves took the lead to stand up and fight did Democratic Party leadership and top union officials follow suit.

Third, the Wisconsin Uprising demonstrated the potent energy of creative resistance. From the protest signs, to the chants, to the mutual aid networks that sprung into existence in the Capitol occupation, the Wisconsin Uprising offered a bold and energizing vision for the community and creativity demanded by resistance.

Fourth, the Wisconsin Uprising showcased the need for broad solidarity. Although the trigger for the uprising were attacks on public sector unions, the protesters came together from all walks of life and sectors. More than a particular group's rights, the Wisconsin Uprising was fighting for a broad public good—to defend workers' rights and to safeguard public institutions.

Why Does the Wisconsin Uprising Matter?

In the short term, the aims of the Wisconsin Uprising—to "kill the bill," as the protest chants went—were not successful. In June 2011, the Budget Repair Bill was signed into law, enabling draconian cuts to the state's public institutions. Schools faced massive budget shortfalls, educators fled the profession, and, in some cases, public schools even shuttered. Conservative governors in other states, such as Ohio, Indiana, and Michigan, quickly proposed their own copycat measures. In 2018, the United States Supreme Court's *Janus v. AFSCME* decision made Act 10-style labor law the rule of the land. The Wisconsin Uprising revealed the strength and organization of conservative, anti-union movements.

But the Wisconsin Uprising also inspired many progressive activists. Wisconsin's collective mobilization reminded workers and activists around the country of the power of standing up and fighting together. Within a year of the Wisconsin Uprising, other important movements emerged, such as Occupy Wall Street and the 2012 Chicago Teachers Union strike. Each of these were turning points in the fight against austerity; both took heavy inspiration from the Wisconsin Uprising. For example, Occupy Wall Street converted mathematical reality of income inequality into a collective identity—"We are the 99%." The Chicago teachers' strike reminded us that workers have the power to not just demand the public good, but also to strike for it with broad community support. Both of these movements grew from ground laid in Wisconsin. What started in Wisconsin continues forward. ◼

Eleni Schirmer reads, writes, and teaches about labor movements and education. She has a PhD in Educational Policy Studies from the University of Wisconsin–Madison.

The 2018 Wave of Teacher Strikes: A Turning Point for Our Schools?

BY STAN KARP AND ADAM SANCHEZ

JOE BRUSKY | MTEA

When 50,000 auto workers went on strike in September 2019 seeking pay raises, better health care, and the reopening of closed factories, filmmaker and labor activist Michael Moore said: "Let's give credit to the teachers. . . . In West Virginia, they started this. People watched those strikes in other states and thought, 'Yeah, why aren't we using the power that we have?'"[1] The teacher strikes that swept the country in the spring of 2018 continue to find echoes across the U.S.

The West Virginia strike began in late February 2018 when some 20,000 classroom teachers and thousands of other employees shut down schools across all 55 counties. Across the state, teachers and school workers demonstrated for higher pay and other gains. Protesters lined the streets with signs, and in Charleston, strikers swarmed outside the Capitol building and, at times, took over parts of it.

"This was a day that I will always remember!" wrote Tiffany Jones, a teacher at Bluefield High School in southern West Virginia, who was recalling one of the nine days of the strike. "The energy was palpable, and the enthusiasm could be felt across generations of educators."[2] This energy and enthusiasm, especially after the West Virginia strike won 5 percent raises for all public employees, inspired teachers in other states to take a stand, injected much-needed militancy into a waning labor movement, and fundamentally reshaped the struggle for public education.

By May 2018, walkouts in Colorado and North Carolina followed statewide actions in West Virginia, Oklahoma, Arizona, and Kentucky. Some of these protests won significant, if modest, gains in teachers' salaries and funding for schools. Others won political promises that have yet to be redeemed. But all contributed to the groundswell of teacher walkouts that captured the nation's attention and changed the landscape of education and labor politics.

What Drove the Teacher Rebellion?
The protests were more than red state revolts. They were rebellions against the austerity and privatization that has been driving federal and state economic policy for decades. The dynamics and political landscape are different in each state. Almost all of the places where statewide actions initially occurred, however, were right-to-work states, which have seen the steepest cuts in school funding and the sharpest erosion of teacher pay and benefits. The Center on Budget and Policy Priorities reported that "teachers struck or engaged in other protests in five of the 12 states that cut formula funding particularly deeply after the last recession—Arizona, Kentucky, North Carolina, Oklahoma, and West Virginia."[3]

Right-to-work states are less likely to have collective bargaining rights and local district contracts. This puts more focus on state budgets and state decisions about health care, school funding, and pensions, and encourages statewide action focused on the legislature. Moreover, while most school funding comes from a mix of state and local sources and both are subject to political pressure, it is ultimately the state that is responsible for education funding. Consequently, many of the walkouts were more akin to mass political protests, seeking broad changes in public policy, than to labor strikes against a single employer such as a school district.

But other common factors underlying these grassroots protests kept the rebellion spreading to "purple" states like Colorado (where there was a walkout in April) and North Carolina (May) and, beyond 2018, into blue states like California, where Los Angeles teachers won a landmark victory in January 2019, and Illinois, where teachers staged a bitter 11-day walkout in September 2019 that recalled their historic strike of 2012. Almost everywhere in recent years, in red states and blue states alike, budget and tax policy has been used to erode social services, shrink public space, undermine union power, and transfer wealth upward, all the while making the lives of working people harder.

Teachers have been both key targets and witnesses to this class warfare. As Katie Endicott, a high school language arts teacher in Mingo County, West Virginia, told a solidarity meeting in New York City, "I first started teaching 10 years ago and it was a different county. . . . Coal was booming and . . . a lot of our students came from coal-mining families. So, dad was making more than $100,000 a year as a coal miner. . . . Now some of these same families, 10 years later . . . we're having to hand out backpacks so they can eat over the weekend. . . . [Teaching] is now the best paying job that we have."[4] Yet teachers in West Virginia have seen their inflation-adjusted salaries fall by more than 11 percent since the 2009 recession.[5] Nationally, teacher pay is down nearly 5 percent.[6]

"Not surprisingly," noted an Economic Policy Institute report, "striking teachers live in states with some of the largest pay gaps. In Arizona, teachers earn just 63 cents on the dollar compared with other college graduates. That gap is 79 cents in Kentucky, 67 cents in Oklahoma, and 75 cents in West Virginia. These gaps amount to vast differences in earning over a career."[7] While the chronic underfunding of public education has always been a fundamental fact of school life in the United States, in many states it's been getting worse. As middle school science teacher Rebecca Garelli, one of the key organizers of the Arizona strike, told us, "Here you have to have two or three jobs, or you can't have a family." Whether teachers are forced to work a second or third job or sell plasma to make ends meet, it's clear that compensation in the states that have borne the brunt of federal and state austerity is at crisis levels.

Nationally, the number of public K–12 teachers and other school staff has fallen by 158,000, while the number of students rose more than 1.4 million.[8] The cuts to public education mean larger class sizes, old textbooks, and in Oklahoma and Colorado, a four-day week in many school districts. And in addition to lower salaries, teacher pensions and health benefits, where they exist at all, have been slashed. Often the reductions have been accompanied by high levels of disrespect. As the *New Republic* reported, "In West Virginia, Mingo County special education teacher Brandon Wolford said it was the insurance changes that started the wave of outrage: 'They were trying to make us wear Fitbits. If we didn't get so many steps per day, our premiums were going to increase $25 per month.'"[9]

These economic attacks paralleled more than a decade of bipartisan corporate "reform" that included test-based evaluation plans, reduced job security, the expansion of privatized charters, and the erosion of professional status—leaving teachers battered and demoralized. From No Child Left Behind, borne of a partnership between George W. Bush and Edward Kennedy, through the Obama administration's Race to the Top, national education reform politics has been a bipartisan exercise in creating a narrative of failure about public education and using it to justify repeated attempts to "fix" schools while blaming those who work in them.

But the struggle in West Virginia showed teachers around the country that a different path was possible. In Oklahoma, where organizing for a strike had begun before the West Virginia walkout, Larry Cagle, a Tulsa high school teacher and the creator of the Oklahoma Teachers United Facebook page, stated, "To have West Virginia teachers out there showing us what it was going to look like was important: the morale boosting that we weren't alone, that a whole state of teachers could stand together."[10] Likewise, Arizona middle school teacher Sarah Giddings wrote for the Rethinking Schools blog that before the West Virginia strike, "a growing number of teachers, including myself, began to feel overwhelmed, demoralized, and paralyzed in a system that worked to undermine our ability to be the effective and meaningful teachers that we could be." The West Virginia teachers' strike, Giddings wrote, "opened our eyes to an empowering alternative reality of what is possible if we collectively organize and come together in solidarity."[11]

Who's Afraid of the Teachers?

As the walkouts spread like wildfire, they came into conflict with some of the biggest corporate interests in the country, who on the one hand were increasingly desperate to contain the upsurge, and on the other were determined to press ahead with their plans for austerity and privatization. For example, as soon as the ink was dry on the West Virginia bill that gave public employees a 5 percent raise, Republicans began claiming they would fund the raise through cuts to services and Medicaid. But the final bill contained no such provision. According to West Virginia Spanish teacher Emily Comer, "Basically, they're kicking the can down the road. We're engaged in an ongoing fight to raise taxes on corporations and extractive industries; we don't want to see cuts to essential services, and we don't want to see regressive taxes like a soda tax or a cigarette tax. We don't want our raises funded on the backs of poor people."[12] High school student Cameron Olbert made a similar connection when speaking at a student rally during the Oklahoma walkout:

> The poor and working class . . . have already paid more than enough into the system. It's time to ask those who can best afford it to pay their fair share too. That means we stop starving public education just so we can feed Big Oil. That means we reform our income tax system. It means that we eliminate useless deductions that only benefit the rich and do nothing for people like us.[13]

Indeed, part of Oklahoma's funding crisis comes from the fact that legislators have consistently cut taxes on oil and gas companies and the wealthiest Oklahomans throughout the recession.

In Arizona, Gov. Doug Ducey and a Republican Legislature tried to quell the rebellion by belatedly promising pay increases and some modest restoration of school funding cuts. But at the same time, Ducey and the Koch brothers were pursuing the wholesale privatization of Arizona schools through voucher and charter schemes. Recent state budget proposals to "phase in" salary and school aid increases in response to the teacher walkouts also include millions for obscenely misnamed "Freedom Schools," which are actually right-wing think tanks housed at state universities designed to further the Kochs' privatization agenda. This is why the right-wing State Policy Network, funded by the billionaire Koch brothers and the Walton Family Foundation, put out a list of talking points to advise legislators on how to discredit teacher strikes. The talking points emphasize that "strikes hurt kids and low-income families," while ignoring the effects of chronic underfunding of schools, and they encourage legislators to contact the network if they "need assistance with messaging for your state's specific situation."[14]

But so far, the public's not buying it. An April 2018 Associated Press-NORC poll found that 78 percent of the U.S. population thinks teacher pay is too low and a majority supports the use of strikes to win better pay, with only 25 percent opposing. Even more encouraging is that among those polled who had heard of the teacher strikes, 80 percent say they approve of the tactic.[15] If this support continues to hold and teachers continue to win significant gains from striking, it's likely the walkouts will continue.

Beyond the Red States: How Far Will the Revolt Spread?

In a recent study, researcher Leigh Dingerson underscored how "The six-day strike by United Teachers Los Angeles (UTLA) in January 2019 took the 'Red for Ed' teacher protest movement to a new level. . . . The Los Angeles strike was the first to take place in a deeply 'blue' state. . . . [It] was an unambiguous public declaration that the 'red state rebellion' is happening in deeply blue states as well, challenging Democrats, as well as Republicans. The story is still unfolding."[16]

One reason the urge to fight back has crossed state lines at a rapid pace is that the attack on teachers and public education has been national and also thoroughly bipartisan. It was Arne Duncan, Obama's secretary of education, who declared austerity for school budgets "the new normal" and "an opportunity for innovation."[17] The expansion of privatized charters, erosion of teacher pay and job protections, and test-based teacher evaluation all had bipartisan support.

While the initial round of recent teacher revolts mostly hit Republican-controlled state legislatures, similar dynamics have been at work in blue states. As Jeff Bryant, editor of the *Education Opportunity Network*, reported in April 2018:

> In a startling sign that teacher uprisings may move to purple and blue states too, Colorado teachers recently left schools and stormed the state Capitol to protest their subpar wages—ranked 46th in the nation, reports the *New York Times*, and "rock bottom" when compared to other professionals in the state. "Colorado has a Democratic governor," notes the *Times*, "and a Legislature split between Democrats and Republicans."[18]

In fact, describing the teacher strikes as red state revolts tends to limit recognition of the national, bipartisan character of the attacks on public education rather than accurately explain what is happening. In West Virginia, for example, the state Legislature was controlled by the Democratic Party for 82 years, and only in 2014 turned Republican. It's impossible to understand the decades of attacks on public education and working-class living standards that produced the teacher revolt without including the role of the Democratic Party.

As Garelli, who worked as a teacher for more than a decade in Chicago before moving to Arizona, put it: "It's not only a red state thing. This is a nationwide crisis. That's because it comes down to the funding."[19] State-by-state funding comparisons regularly quoted in the media to pinpoint the causes of teachers' anger often obscure more than they illuminate. For example, while many red states are at the bottom in terms of teacher pay, when that pay is adjusted for cost of living, the results reveal an erosion of living standards that penetrates deep into Democratic-controlled territory. New York and California, typically ranked among the top in teacher pay, come out 17th and 19th when adjusted for cost of living—below Kentucky. Washington, with a Democratic governor and Legislature, ranks near the bottom, below West Virginia and Oklahoma. Democratic-controlled Hawaii is dead last.[20]

The state-by-state comparisons of education funding also can hide deep inequities within states. According to the Education Law Center (ELC), several Democratic-controlled states rank among the bottom in terms of the fairness of funding distribution. Illinois, for example, is ranked 50th because its regressive funding distribution means high-poverty school districts get only 73 cents for every dollar that low-poverty districts receive.

This is why the photographs of broken chairs and tattered textbooks Oklahoma teachers posted on social media during their strike eerily echoed the videos of Baltimore schools posted a few months earlier during a winter storm: Without money for heat, pipes in several Baltimore schools froze and burst, flooding classrooms and forcing students to wear winter coats. Though Maryland is ranked 12th by ELC in overall levels of school funding, it ranked 38th for funding distribution, with high-poverty districts in the state receiving 9 percent less funding than their wealthier neighbors.[21]

All this is not to ignore the fact that the attacks on teachers and schools have been particularly severe in many of the states where teachers walked out on strike. But it's worth underscoring that these states are just the weakest links in a national chain of austerity. Whether it's low teacher pay, a reduction in pensions or health benefits, large class sizes, aging textbooks, few supplies, crumbling buildings, or cuts to programs and services, no state has been immune.

Through headlines like "Rotten Apples" and "Why We Must Fire Bad Teachers," the corporate media has blamed educators for the failures of our schools while ignoring the cuts that make teachers' jobs increasingly difficult. Converting public schools to charters and using standardized test scores to close schools and fire teachers have been touted as "solutions" for our "broken" education system, ones that conveniently do not require increased or more equitable funding.

The fact that teacher protests and walkouts have changed the national focus on education from charters and testing to salaries and school funding is a remarkable shift. This shift has been strikingly visible in the 2020 presidential campaign, where Democratic primary candidates have emphasized plans to increase teacher pay and school funding and offered strong support for teacher unions. Rather than being on the defensive, fighting against school closures and increased tests, teachers have gone on the offensive, demanding that more money be pumped into the school system. In doing so, striking educators in West Virginia, Oklahoma, Kentucky, Arizona, Colorado, North Carolina, and elsewhere have been teaching us all. As high school student Ravi Patel pointed out at a rally during the Oklahoma strike, "Our teachers are setting an example of bravery by standing up to ignorance and inaction. Our teachers are setting an example of engagement in activism . . . our teachers are setting a better example than our legislators have for the past decade."[22]

The emergence of teachers as collective voices for their communities has been as impressive as their activism and bravery. As Cagle put it, "We made the argument early on to students that it was about them. Yes, I'd like a raise, but I'm mad because you're getting a crappy education, and you should be [mad] too."[23] The strikers in West Virginia and Arizona turned down raises that included only teachers and excluded support staff and other public workers. Many demanded increases in state spending beyond schools, for public services that had been starved of resources for years. While it will take broader, sustained efforts to win all the demands raised during the strikes, the walkouts were lessons in social mobilization, led largely by women and drawing inspiration and energy from #BlackLivesMatter, #MeToo, and the March for Our Lives.

One unanswered question is how this dynamic of grassroots uprising from below will play out in states with collective bargaining rights and union-negotiated local contracts. That landscape is shifting too, with unions battered by more than a decade of corporate reform, austerity budgets, accelerated privatization, and imminent legal attacks from the Supreme Court. As activist reformers and caucuses lead walkouts and protests in major cities like Chicago, Los Angeles, and Philadelphia, there is also the potential for a radical shift in the leadership and direction of the national teacher unions, one that could change the face and contours of the U.S. labor movement.

But the key question for teachers everywhere is whether they are organized enough to channel the energy sparked by West Virginia into fighting for greatly expanded support for public education and a broader political turn away from austerity and privatization. These rebellions have raised the expectations of teachers about what is possible. They channeled the years of pent-up anger into the largest strike wave in decades. Let's hope it continues to spread until every school has the resources needed to make high-quality education possible. 🔖

Stan Karp taught English and journalism to high school students in Paterson, New Jersey, for 30 years. He is a Rethinking Schools editor.

Adam Sanchez is a social studies teacher at Lincoln High School in Philadelphia, the editor of Teaching a People's History of Abolition and the Civil War, *a Zinn Education Project teacher leader, and an editor of* Rethinking Schools.

ENDNOTES

1 Michael Moore interview. Sept. 16, 2019. *All In with Chris Hayes*. MSNBC.

2 Jones, Tiffany. April 17, 2018. Email response to inquiry from Zinn Education Project.

3 Leachman, Michael, and Eric Figueroa. March 6, 2019. "K–12 School Funding Up in Most 2018 Teacher-Protest States, but Still Well Below Decade Ago." Center on Budget and Policy Priorities.

4 Endicott, Katie. April 2, 2018. "Solidarity with West Virginia Strikers!" WeAreManyMedia. youtube.com/watch?v=_cYpsDXXdHo

5 Chang, Alvin. May 8, 2018. "Your State's Teachers Are Underpaid. Find Out by How Much." Vox.

6 Picchi, Aimee. April 3, 2018. "The 9 States Where Teachers Have It Worst." CBS News.

7 Allegretto, Sylvia. April 4, 2018. "Teachers Across the Country Have Finally Had Enough of the Teacher Pay Penalty." Economic Policy Institute.

8 Leachman, Michael. Aug. 23, 2018. "Many Schools Still Facing Funding Challenges as New Year Starts." Center on Budget and Policy Priorities.

9 Jaffe, Sarah. April 18, 2018. "A True Labor of Love: Why Teachers Are Adopting a More Militant Politics." *The New Republic*.

10 Larry Cagle, in April 2018 discussion with the author.

11 Giddings, Sarah. April 30, 2018. "Making People's History in Arizona: Educators Rise Up." *Rethinking Schools Blog*.

12 Emily Comer, in May 2018 discussion with the author.

13 Olbert, Cameron. April 4, 2018. "Students Rally at the Capitol in Support of Teacher Walkout." NewsOK. facebook.com/NewsOK/videos/10155507366225794/UzpfSTYyMzQxMDQ3MjoxMDE2MDMzOTg1M-DcyNTQ3Mw

14 Bryant, Jeff. May 3, 2018. "The Right Lashes Out at Uprising Teachers." *Education Opportunity Network*.

15 Feldman, Carole, and Emily Swanson. April 23, 2018. "AP-NORC Poll: Amid Strikes, Americans Back Teacher Raises." Associated Press.

16 Dingerson, Leigh. July 2019. "Building the Power to Reclaim Our Schools." Reclaim Our Schools Los Angeles.

17 Duncan, Arne. Nov. 17, 2010. "The New Normal: Doing More with Less—Secretary Arne Duncan's Remarks at the American Enterprise Institute." U.S. Department of Education.

18 Bryant, Jeff. April 19, 2018. "Why Teacher Uprisings May Hit Blue States Too." *Education Opportunity Network*.

19 Rebecca Garelli, in May 2018 discussion with author.

20 Turner, Cory. March 16, 2018. "The Fight Over Teacher Salaries: A Look at the Numbers." NPR Ed.

21 Baker, Bruce D., Danielle Farrie, and David Sciarra. February 2018. "Is School Funding Fair? A National Report Card." Education Law Center.

22 Patel, Ravi. April 4, 2018. "Students Rally at the Capitol in Support of Teacher Walkout." NewsOK. facebook.com/NewsOK/videos/10155507366225794/UzpfSTYyMzQxMDQ3MjoxMDE2MDMzOTg1M-DcyNTQ3Mw

23 Larry Cagle, in April 2018 discussion with the author.

The West Virginia Educators Revolt

BY ERIC BLANC

CRAIG HUDSON | AP

T he West Virginia strike of 2018 was one of the most important labor victories in the United States since at least the early 1970s.

Though the 1997 UPS strike and the 2012 Chicago teachers' strike also captured the country's attention, there was something different about West Virginia. This strike was statewide, it was illegal, it went wildcat, and it sparked a sustained wave of teacher work stoppages across the country. To the surprise of pundits across the political spectrum, the first strike wave in decades erupted in Republican-dominated states where labor unions are weak, public sector strikes illegal, and collective bargaining almost nonexistent.

West Virginia's upsurge shares many similarities with the rank-and-file militancy of the late 1960s and early 1970s. But there are some critical differences. Whereas labor struggles four decades ago came in the wake of a postwar economic boom and the inspiring successes of the Civil Rights Movement, this labor upheaval erupted in a period of virtually uninterrupted working-class defeats and economic austerity.

No less importantly, West Virginia's strike—by shuttering schools from Feb. 22 through March 7, 2018—*won*. The bottom-up militancy and strike action of West Virginia's teachers and school employees wrested a whole series of important concessions, including stopping steep hikes to healthcare premiums, defeating pro-charter and anti-union bills, and winning a 5 percent raise for all public employees.

Charleston teacher and rank-and-file strike leader Emily Comer described the scene at the state Capitol in an interview a few hours after the strike won:

> We're overwhelmed with emotion. I have broken down sobbing more times than I can count today. There's probably video footage of me bawling while I'm surrounded by co-workers singing "Country Roads." There's almost a sense of disbelief, because for about a solid week there, we were really in unfamiliar territory. We didn't know what was going to happen.

How Educators Won

West Virginia has clarified the continued relevance of strategic insights that were long ago abandoned by much of the labor movement. How did they win? Four big factors stand out.

First, though it is against the law for public employees in West Virginia to strike, they struck anyway. To be sure, educators were initially very reluctant to consider engaging in an illegal work stoppage. On social media and in break rooms, teachers expressed their worries about getting fired, suspended, or fined.

A Jan. 13, 2018, debate on the West Virginia Public Employees United Facebook page gives a sense of the dynamic. One West Virginian skeptic argued: "I doubt you'll get enough public employees to participate in a protest, let alone a strike. Many public employees in this state have limted to no collective bargaining rights and there'll be repercussions, like job loss, for walking out. I'm afraid that you'll see a situation where it would be very easy to state that the person abandoned their job." To this, another replied: "that fear runs deep for most teachers :(It's really going to hurt our chances of ever getting anywhere."

There were various mechanisms through which union activists helped their co-workers overcome this fear. One was to point to past examples of successful illegal work stoppages, such as the 1990 teachers' strike in West Virginia. By starting threads about the lessons of 1990, Jay O'Neal—the Charleston educator who co-founded the Facebook group together with Comer—from early on sought to help public employees consider the feasibility of striking. As he put it in a Jan. 6 post to the group, "I think if we could educate more teachers about what the [1990] strike actually did for teachers here, we might get a lot of people on board." A skeptic replied that "WV teachers aren't allowed to strike," to which O'Neal responded "True, but they did anyway in 1990 and it made a big difference."

Breaking the law was not a decision easily undertaken. But once on strike, educators embraced their defiance. Highlighting the long tradition of taking illegal action to win a righteous cause, many strikers made homemade signs saying "Rosa Parks was not wrong." And on Feb. 25, a teacher posted the following to West Virginia's United page: "The way I look at it, Rosa Parks and Martin Luther King Jr. took a stand, I'd be in great company [if the state tries to throw us in jail]." The state initially threatened to file injunctions to end the strike, but it was forced to back down.

The second major factor explaining West Virginia's success was that its demands and participants were never limited to just teachers. It was a walkout of and for all school employees, including bus drivers, custodians, secretaries, cooks, and paraprofessionals.

> Breaking the law was not a decision easily undertaken. But once on strike, educators embraced their defiance.

At most schools across the country, support staff receive the least respect, the fewest benefits, and the lowest wages. Many people I spoke with in West Virginia felt that this was the single deepest divide among school employees. Seeing the need to build the widest possible unity, rank-and-file leaders in West Virginia consciously framed their movement as broader than just teachers. Stressing the contributions and dignity of the tens of thousands of service personnel was necessary to undercut the tendency of the media—as well as many rank-and-file teachers—to justify the protests by arguing that teacher pay was too low given their high educational levels and their specific professional responsibilities.

Those in power attempted to restrict this struggle as much as possible. And support staff marginalization within the schools and the movement did not disappear overnight. It frequently took sustained efforts by militant support staff in West Virginia to prevent their co-workers from standing aside from the general struggle. Mary Wykle—a bus driver in Wyoming County who played a key role in mobilizing other service personnel—explained:

> Many of us felt left out because everybody kept calling this a teachers' movement, a teachers' strike. I understood why personnel often got discouraged by this—but it was counterproductive. So I ended up giving pep talks to them, to explain why we all needed to be in this struggle together.

These efforts paid off. Unlike in the 1990 West Virginia teachers' strike—when schools stayed open through the labor of support staff and scabs—this time all employees went out together. Linda Vannus, a cafeteria cook in Ravenswood, recalled the ensuing transformation at her school: "We're usually ignored, but during the strike it was different—we were united. I felt like when teachers looked at me, they saw me more like an equal."

Without the efforts of service personnel, victory would have remained elusive. This dynamic became clear on Wednesday, Feb. 28, the pivotal "cooling off day" after West Virginia's governor and union leaders ordered workers to return to work the next day. As teachers across the state debated if and how to defy this edict, support staff took the initiative to make it clear to superintendents—and teachers—that they were staying out. By all accounts, the initiatives of drivers like Wykle to prepare for hard picket lines were central to the ultimate decision of superintendents across the state that evening to keep schools shut. "The service personnel were our saving grace," notes teacher Nicole McCormick. "In Mercer County, some schools would have gone back on Thursday, but they couldn't open without their bus drivers and cooks."

Third, the West Virginia strike consciously incorporated parents and students into the struggle. Teachers and service personnel took every opportunity to discuss with parents, explaining that educator working conditions were students' learning conditions. They waved signs in front of school, passed out informational flyers, and organized morning "walk-ins," during which they rallied together with parents and students.

Teachers and service personnel took every opportunity to discuss with parents, explaining that educator working conditions were students' learning conditions.

Because of this, educators could rely on the relationships of trust with parents and students generated by the very nature of education work. West Virginia's AFT union president Christine Campbell put it as follows: "Educators are embedded in our communities; people trust us to educate their kids. So when parents see the teachers of their children struggling to make ends meet, working at a second job on the weekend, this is a much more direct relationship with the community than in the private sector."

As the walkouts approached, educators began collecting food donations to give to those large numbers of children who were dependent on school lunches and free breakfasts. And once the strikes began, unions collected and distributed food to these same students, often hand-delivering care packages to their homes. A large number of teachers recounted experiences similar to that of Tanya Asleson in Ravenswood: "I went to the house of a parent who was really poor: his kids always desperately need food at school. The strike was a real hardship for his family—but instead of telling me to go back to work, he said: 'Ma'am, you stay strong now. You haven't won yet. Don't go back tomorrow.' It was so moving."

Fighting for students, and framing their struggles as a defense of essential services for the public, went a long way toward undercutting claims that striking teachers were hurting children. Educators made a case that they weren't walking from the students, but for them. As one West Virginia teacher explained in a March 1 letter to her students: "I love you, and that's why I'm doing this."

Finally, the strike succeeded because it relied on rank-and-file educators. Though West Virginia's three statewide educator unions eventually lent their support to the work stoppage, the initiative for the action came from below, as did the drive to continue the strike when union leaders attempted to prematurely stop it before a deal was reached with the state.

The movement was generally improvised from below, with all the strengths and limitations that this entailed. Without strong union organizations driving the strike forward, educators were obliged to step up in dozens of ways to make these walkouts a success. Many of these were unglamorous tasks like making signs, collecting food for students, reading up on legislation, speaking with confused parents, texting co-workers to remind them to participate in the strike vote, or driving a group of peers to the Capitol. Other actions required a bigger leap. For numerous strikers, this was the first time they had made a speech at a rally, convinced co-workers to participate in a political action, spoken to the press, chaired a mass meeting, or confronted a politician.

Many of those who were already union members only became active in the lead-up to the strike. Asleson's experience was illustrative: "I went from not wanting to be a [union] building rep, to being aggravated and involved, to now becoming president of the AFT [American Federation of Teachers] in our county. The strike forced me to find leadership skills within myself. We've all really grown in the last couple of months; it makes us proud."

These processes of empowerment went hand in hand with a rapid politicization of tens of thousands of workers, students, and parents. For weeks on end, politics became the 24-7 topic of conversation in lunchrooms, staff meetings, and even normally apolitical spaces like sporting events or church. The Facebook group witnessed a seemingly endless discussion over whether a work stoppage was possible, what to demand, and how to win. Over the course of the strike, the West Virginia Legislature website repeatedly crashed due to network overload.

This groundswell of collective action resulted in an unprecedented union membership surge. Thousands of members joined the unions in the course of the strike movement. Yet much of the upsurge also took place outside of union structures. Consider the following observation by Katie Endicott, a rank and file teacher leader from Mingo County, a southern coal-mining region that played a pivotal role in inspiring the rest of West Virginia to strike: "We learned that you don't have to have a union title, a position. You just have to have courage and a backbone to stand up for yourself, for your state, and your kids. And that's what we did."

Much of the communication and coordination took place over social media. As one veteran of West Virginia's 1990 union-sanctioned strike posted in late January, "This time around we have social media (this group right here) working for us!" Facebook made it much easier to communicate and mobilize large groups of people without, as in the past, having to undertake the arduous task of building up a well-resourced organizational infrastructure. It also changed the relationship and power dynamic between rank-and-file educators and their union leaderships;

without having to rely on official union channels, individual teachers from far-flung counties were easily able to share with each other their concerns, information, and ideas.

Social media proved to be especially important, since educators had to build a statewide movement to win their demands, unlike in blue states where there is mandatory collective bargaining within local school districts. "The United [Facebook] group became like one big faculty room where we could connect with other teachers and workers throughout the state," recalls Ashlea Bassham, a teacher in rural Logan County.

West Virginia's rank-and-file organizers, however, remained oriented on working within and pushing their unions forward. A Jan. 6, 2018, debate in the West Virginia Public Employees United group is illustrative of how the group moderators encouraged educators to participate in, and transform, their unions. One teacher expressed her frustration, widely shared across the state, that the unions were so continually ineffective. In response to this call upon members to stop paying dues, O'Neal responded:

> It's really become a cycle—people don't see the union doing much, so they don't join, which further weakens the union's clout, which makes more people think they aren't doing much, etc. One thing to remember though—unions are very democratic institutions—WE ARE THE UNION. . . . If we want to see real change in our unions, WE'VE got to make it happen.

The pressure generated by the Facebook group and its various escalating actions—combined with the galvanizing Feb. 2 walkouts initiated by unionized rank-and-file educators in southern West Virginia—was eventually sufficient to push statewide labor leaders to call a strike vote and to use their organizational as well as financial resources to ensure its success. In mid-February, educators at school sites across the state overwhelmingly voted to walk out. Union structures increasingly began to serve as a framework for educators and grassroots activists to coordinate the impending action with statewide officials and staff—and push back, when necessary, against the latter's hesitations. In the words of Katie Endicott, "We love our unions; we couldn't have accomplished what we did without them. But we did have to overstep them along the way at certain times."

By taking responsibility for the authorization votes and the strike itself, West Virginia's unions had finally placed themselves at the head of the upsurge. Rank-and-file organizers like O'Neal, Comer, and Endicott saw this as a positive development, as they never had any intentions of attempting to substitute for the unions.

At the same time, the school-site strike votes had also made it clear that the movement's legitimacy and authority fundamentally rested on the rank and file's democratic decisions. This set an important precedent when educators went wildcat on Wednesday, Feb. 28 by refusing to heed the call of union leaders to return to work before a deal with the Legislature had been signed into law.

Conclusion

West Virginia demonstrated the strategic centrality of strikes—and the need to challenge the law, unite with support staff, involve the community, and rely on the rank and file. But it would be a mistake to romanticize the strike, or treat it as a universal model. Different approaches are needed for contexts where unions are stronger and labor rights more robust.

The ease of mobilization and communication provided by social media has significant downsides. In the Internet Age, mass protests can scale up very quickly—sometimes too quickly for powerful organizations to develop. Yet without the political relationships and infrastructure forged through in-person organizing, strikes that rely on Facebook are relatively structurally fragile, ill-equipped to confront harsh, elite opposition, and prone to dissolution after the upsurge peaks.

> "We learned that you don't have to have a union title, a position. You just have to have courage and a backbone to stand up for yourself, for your state, and your kids. And that's what we did."

In the wake of the West Virginia strike, educators thus were not as well organized, or as politically powerful, as their counterparts in United Teachers Los Angeles, which had prepared for its January 2019 strike through four years of deep organizing. Although education unions in West Virginia are larger than before and various locals have been reinvigorated by new leaders, top union officials have generally pivoted back to their old lobbying efforts, and many teachers have returned to passivity. In response, many of those rank-and-file activists who initiated the 2018 strikes have now begun the arduous process of collectively organizing from below through the new West Virginia United caucus to transform their statewide unions.

To build lasting workplace power, there is no substitute for a militant and democratic trade union movement. Nevertheless, since labor unions remain so weak and legal restrictions so draconian in numerous states, it is likely that the years ahead will witness more volcanic, social media-inflected work stoppages like that in West Virginia. For educators and working people in all regions of this country, learning from its lessons can help effectively prepare for the battles to come. ◼

A labor activist and former high school teacher, Eric Blanc is the author of Red State Revolt: The Teachers' Strike Wave and Working-Class Politics *(Verso 2019). Blanc is currently a doctoral student in sociology at New York University.*

SECTION TWO

WHAT SOCIAL JUSTICE
UNIONS LOOK LIKE

Social Justice Teacher Unionism

What does it mean to fight for the schools and communities our students deserve?

BY BOB PETERSON

Less than a month into my third year of teaching I was laid off. My class of twenty-seven 4th graders had already created a strong sense of community as they shared their diverse family stories and pondered the resilience of Karana in *Island of the Blue Dolphins* during our daily read aloud. Sharing the unexpected news of my layoff at a class meeting was one of the hardest experiences in my three decades of teaching.

What made it even worse was the response from my union. Ironically, that response pushed me to question the very nature of teacher unionism.

Immediately after getting the layoff notice I called the union office and suggested they arrange a meeting of the 94 laid-off teachers. The staff person said no, asserting that union officials could individually handle any problems we had. I countered that a gathering could help us cope with this life-changing situation and organize against the layoffs. My suggestion was politely rejected.

Three days later, no longer working, I drove to the union office naively thinking I could convince them. This time the executive director came to the front foyer to repeat the union's line. We argued and I finally said, "I thought unions were supposed to organize their membership."

"We do, when necessary, but for the most part we provide services to our membership. If there is anything we can help you with in terms of unemployment or matters like that, let us know. Goodbye." He turned and walked backed to his office.

I was dumbfounded and furious.

Things got worse. At the time of my layoff a district official had told me that I had more seniority than some other teachers, but I had been laid off due to the district's super-seniority policy that protected teachers of color. I was fine with that—my involvement in the Civil Rights Movement as a high school student had taught me to be anti-racist.

Months later, however, I found out that the union—without ever consulting those of us who were laid off—had gone to court to challenge the policy. The union ultimately prevailed and straight seniority won out over super-seniority. By the time of the decision all of us who had been laid off had been offered our jobs back, so it didn't affect us. But during the following years I often argued in union meetings against the union's racist stand against affirmative action.

During my years as a young teacher, these and other experiences compelled me to organize rank-and-file caucuses, become a building representative, run for union leadership, and in 1986 co-found the quarterly *Rethinking Schools,* which published for its first 15 years as a newsprint tabloid. We promoted social justice teaching and social justice teacher unionism and built a cadre of supporters to distribute the paper free of charge to the nearly 10,000 teachers in the district. Union staff and the old guard elected leadership saw us as a serious threat.

These same experiences also helped shape my critique of what was wrong with my local union, a critique that was confirmed and deepened as I met and organized with other progressive teacher union activists from around the country through the National Coalition of Education Activists. In 1994 we issued a call for activist teachers to build social justice unions, contrasting them with what we called industrial and professional models of unionism. (See NCEA, p. 74.) We asserted, "Without a better partnership with the parents and communities that need public education most, we will find ourselves isolated from essential allies. Without a new vision of schooling that raises the expectations of our students and the standards of our own profession, we will continue to founder. Without a new model of unionism that revives debate and democracy internally and projects an inspiring social vision and agenda externally, we will fall short of the challenges before us."

> Sharing the unexpected news of my layoff at a class meeting was one of the hardest experiences in my three decades of teaching. What made it even worse was the response from my union. Ironically, that response pushed me to question the very nature of teacher unionism.

Over time I used a metaphor of a three-legged stool, arguing that teacher unions should incorporate traditional industrial unionism's focus on bread-and-butter issues, professional unionism's commitment to professional development and teacher voice in shaping educational policy and curriculum, and social justice unionism's commitment to racial equity and forging strong alliances with parents and the broader community.

The metaphor lacked nuance, however, and didn't capture some key features. A social justice lens should be omnipresent throughout *all* union work whether it's wages and working conditions, professional and pedagogical issues, internal union matters, or broader policy concerns. (See editors, p. 102.) This comprehensive approach should be animated by steadfast efforts to:

1. Be democratic, engage members in a variety of ways, promote internal dialogue and debate, and resist dictatorial control by cliques of staff or elected officials.

2. Listen to and build strong ties with students, families, civic and faith-based groups, and oppressed communities—at the school, district, and state levels—promoting educational justice and social justice movements.
3. Challenge union members to internalize anti-racist, anti-oppression values and to teach from a social justice, anti-racist viewpoint, free of deficit thinking.
4. Fight against school privatization and promote public community schools as an alternative, envisioning such schools as greenhouses of democracy, and centers of resistance and renaissance in our neighborhoods.
5. Be internationalist—promoting teaching and policies that are opposed to war and imperialism, in favor of climate justice and human rights, and in solidarity with the Global South.

Embracing and implementing this comprehensive vision of social justice unionism is a long-term project. Progressive caucuses and leadership slates can only bring it to fruition through convincing their fellow union members to actively participate in the effort. And this is work that needs to be nourished by constant reflection, a willingness to confront and remedy shortcomings, and the patience and stamina to build relationships and struggles over the span of several years.

In retrospect, yes, being laid off early in my teaching career was emotionally difficult and being subjected to a "service model" of unionism was disheartening. But both events helped propel me into a lifetime of fighting for educational justice and ultimately recognizing the power of social justice unionism. Now, more than ever, teacher unions need to embody social justice and organize for the schools and communities our students deserve. ✊

Bob Peterson, the former president of the Milwaukee Teachers' Education Association, is now a member of the Milwaukee School Board. He taught 5th grade more than 25 years at various Milwaukee public schools, and was a founding editor of Rethinking Schools.

Industrial, Professional, and Social Justice Unionism

OAKLAND EDUCATION ASSOCIATION BROOKE ANDERSON PHOTOGRAPHY

The following chart highlights differences between three models of teacher unionism that operate on different principles and priorities. Different union locals, state associations, and the two national unions at different times have drawn on characteristics of more than one model.

This chart is a useful discussion starter for leaders and members as they clarify their union's vision and purpose.

We recognize that any chart has limitations in drawing differences more sharply than may be warranted. We also know that other terms have been used to analyze unions, such as "business unions," "service unions," and "organizing unions." We attempted to weave those features into the chart.

This chart is an amalgamation of ideas and previous charts that draw on discussions and debates on the future of teacher unionism over the past 30 years. These debates have occurred in many forums and publications, including *Rethinking Schools*, the National Coalition of Education Activists, the Institute for Progressive Teacher Unionism, the Mooney Institute, the Teacher Union Reform Network (TURN), rank-and-file caucuses, and within teacher unions at all levels.

We believe that the future success of teacher unions in the United States depends on the degree to which they define themselves and act as social justice unions, while incorporating aspects of the industrial and professional models.

—the editors of *Teacher Unions and Social Justice:*
Organizing for the Schools and Communities Our Students Deserve

Key components in the three models of teacher unionism

INDUSTRIAL	PROFESSIONAL	SOCIAL JUSTICE
Orientation		
Emphasizes separation of labor and management. The role of the union is to limit what teachers can be asked to do and to increase the pay/benefits they get for doing it.	Emphasizes and defends teacher professionalism and promotes teacher leadership at school and district levels through union/district mentoring programs, etc.	Emphasizes alliances with parents and community to organize for social justice in schools, the community, and the curriculum. Challenges white supremacy and other forms of oppression.
View of Management		
Assumes labor/ management relations are hostile and adversarial.	Encourages management/ labor cooperation to promote quality programs and achievement.	Partners with management when they promote anti-racist social justice policies, and organizes with parents and communities against management when they don't.
Bargaining		
Win/lose bargaining with emphasis on bread-and-butter issues of salary, hours, and working conditions. Views the contract as way to institutionalize changes.	Interest-based bargaining that addresses teaching quality and programmatic initiatives, include MOUs outside of the contract. Views the contract as way to institutionalize changes.	Bargaining for the common good. Bargains bread-and-butter and professional issues, but balances those demands with the broader social justice issues in the schools and community. Views the contract as way to institutionalize changes, but rank-and-file and community organizing as key features in sustaining wins.

INDUSTRIAL	PROFESSIONAL	SOCIAL JUSTICE
District Decision-Making		
Management prerogatives respected at school and district levels. Union staff grieves management decisions.	Seeks to expand decision-making and instructional leadership at school and district levels. Joint labor/management committees address professional issues.	Democratic input by key stakeholders through democratically elected school boards, shared leadership at school level, and district councils and committees that include educators, administrators, parents, community, and students. Promotes creation of transformative community schools.
Internal Union Leadership		
Often a "business model" that is staff- and/or leader-dominated with limited member decision-making. Promotes member passivity except for occasional mobilizations. Members view "the union" as a third party—the staff and elected leaders.	Promotes moving significant leadership to the school level and works to infuse the district operations with teacher leaders.	Broad membership engagement and involvement in decision-making. Vision and direction provided by elected leadership; diversity and debate encouraged. Members view the union as "first person plural"—We are the union.
Service to Members		
Staff "solves" most individual problems through contract enforcement.	Emphasis on school-based problem-solving.	School-based leaders are trained to organize staff to solve most problems at the school level. Districtwide problems are solved through pressure and collective action.
Equity and Race		
At worst, defends white privilege; most commonly ignores such matters.	Main proponents of professional unionism are silent on race issues.	Strong emphasis on race and equity-supporting movements in the community on issues that don't directly affect teachers. Openly deals with racial issues internal to the union.

INDUSTRIAL	PROFESSIONAL	SOCIAL JUSTICE
Pedagogy and Curriculum		
Union cedes control of curriculum and professional development to management.	Union promotes additional responsibility for teacher leaders and brings teacher voice to design, implementation, and evaluation of curriculum, assessment, and instruction.	Union promotes more teaching and less testing, restorative practices over punitive discipline, and culturally relevant, anti-racist social justice curriculum that is participatory and connected to students' lives.
Student Rights/School Safety		
Focus is on teacher authority, classroom control. Teachers quick to refer students for discipline, without listening to students. Leads to zero-tolerance policies and enables school-to-prison pipeline.	Silent on the subject.	Promotes restorative practices and anti-bias training of staff, and fights for the "schools the students deserve," which includes full social and health services, counseling, and respect for students' personal rights.
Social Issues, Community, and Parents		
Limited involvement with social and community issues; parent outreach is emphasized only during bargaining or other contractual dispute with management.	Mainly silent on broader community issues. Works with parents to improve individual parent support for their child's learning.	Reaches out to community and parents to improve the quality of teaching and learning; supports social justice movements in the community even if not directly involved with schools and encourages members to participate in such movements.

INDUSTRIAL	PROFESSIONAL	SOCIAL JUSTICE
Relations with the Labor Movement		
Supports labor struggle when in the self-interest of teachers. (Historically NEA rank and file not encouraged to view themselves as part of the labor movement.)	Silent on the subject.	Views teacher unions as on the front lines to revitalize the labor movement. Stands in solidarity with labor struggles—both union-based and community-based, like $15 and a Union.

SOURCES

- Kerchner, Charles Taylor and Julia E. Koppich. 1993. *A Union of Professionals: Labor Relations and Educational Reform.* Teachers College Press.

- Rethinking Our Unions Institute of the National Coalition of Education Activists, Portland 1994.

- Charney, Michael and Bob Peterson (eds.). 1999. *Transforming Teacher Unions: Fighting for Better Schools and Social Justice* (first edition). Rethinking Schools.

- The Three Frames of Progressive Unionism, from the NEA's Center for Organizing.

Bargaining for the Common Good—
An Overview

BY SAQIB BHATTI AND MARILYN SNEIDERMAN

JOE BRUSKY | MTEA

It was September of 2017, and United Teachers Los Angeles (UTLA) had been in contract negotiations with the Los Angeles Unified School District (LAUSD) for months. Members of the union's bargaining team were preparing to host yet another session with the district's negotiators. But this session would be different.

UTLA had spent years transforming the union internally and carefully rebuilding what had been fractured relationships with community and progressive organizations around the city. The union had helped bring together a labor/community alliance—Reclaim Our Schools Los Angeles (ROSLA)—and was organizing to build a citywide movement for the schools LA students deserve.

The ROSLA partners knew that the union's contract negotiations with the district offered a significant opportunity for a citywide conversation about public education. Instead of confining their contract demands to the traditional issues of teacher wages and benefits, the union and its community partners wanted to force a head-on confrontation with the district, and with LA's extensive network of education "reformers" and millionaires. They wanted to talk about the decades-long neglect of the city's public schools and demand action on a wide range of issues that directly impacted students, staff, and communities. The strategy is called bargaining for the common good (BCG). It is taking hold in cities around the country, as community and labor organizations come together with a strong vision for what our communities should be and for whom.

Standing Up Against Privatization

For more than three decades, working Americans, public school students, and Black and Latino communities across the country have been the victims of a concerted campaign to dismantle the public sector and weaken democratic institutions.

A range of interests have merged to create this assault on the common good. These include Wall Street moguls who are attempting to pull more and more public funds—taxpayer dollars—into their own personal and corporate coffers. By driving public funds into private hands through strategies such as charter schools and voucher schemes, the public wealth can be controlled (and amassed) by private interests.

Conservative politicians are also in the game. They have an interest in neutralizing or splintering the political power of constituencies that typically support public and social services. That means working to limit access to the polls, especially for African American and Latino voters, and weakening labor unions—especially the powerful and Democratic-leaning teacher unions.

These interests have systematically built an extensive infrastructure of deep-pocketed philanthropy (the Walton Family Foundation, Broad Foundation, and others), policy development (American Legislative Exchange Council), so-called "Astroturf" advocacy groups like Stand for Children, think tanks (the Heritage Foundation, Thomas B. Fordham Institute), and message development in service of their agenda.

They have been undeniably successful: Voucher programs and charter schools continue to siphon billions of dollars away from public school districts each year. Voting rights are under assault in dozens of states. Communities of color—for generations the very foundation of support for public education—have splintered over the perceived "failure" of public education. Even the U.S. Supreme Court joined in the attack with their 2018 decision in *Janus v. AFSCME*, aimed squarely at weakening the role of public sector unions. And through it all, wealth inequality has soared to levels unseen in history. The rich are getting richer, labor is getting weaker, and somehow, public education has been branded as a "special interest." In 2014, just 25 hedge fund managers earned more income than *all* the nation's kindergarten teachers *combined*.

Something has been very, very wrong with this picture.

BCG is a rising strategy aimed at winning an economy and a public sector that serves the majority, not the wealthy few. In BCG, labor invites community allies to join with them to use the collective bargaining process to win reforms that strengthen communities and improve the lives of working people.

Working Together and Winning Big in Los Angeles

UTLA and its community partners in ROSLA built their BCG platform over months. Through that time, they systematically reached out to students, parents, and educators through community-based forums, one-on-one conversations, and broader surveys to identify the most important challenges in the sprawling LAUSD. What they heard, even from teachers, went well beyond wages and benefits. They heard frustration with the district's rapidly expanding charter sector, which required some public schools to share facilities. They heard students' frustration with the district's "random search" policy that disproportionately targeted Black and Brown students. They heard from teachers frustrated with classrooms jammed with 50 students. Together, the ROSLA partners built an expansive set of demands. And when the September 2017 bargaining session came around, UTLA invited representatives from a dozen partner groups—from Black Lives Matter to the Alliance of Californians for Community Empowerment (ACCE) to join them at the bargaining table.

The session was both tense and inspiring, remembers Ruby Gordillo, a parent member of ACCE. One after another, community representatives presented their demands to the bargaining teams. And over and over, the LAUSD negotiators made clear that the demands were "outside the scope of bargaining"—the state-mandated issues considered permissible for collective bargaining. "We cannot negotiate on these matters," repeated the district representatives again and again. But the union and its allies held firm for more than a year—even turning down a proposal from LAUSD that met their demands on salaries. "We knew that we had picked issues that resonated with parents across the city," recalls Gordillo. ROSLA knew that parents, students, and community members had the union's back.

And so, in January 2019, UTLA went out on strike, continuing to demand action on their common good platform for the Schools LA Students Deserve. And despite the pouring rains of that January, tens of thousands of parents and students hit the streets in support.

UTLA went on to win agreements on most of their platform issues. They won reductions in class sizes. They won commitments for additional green space at schools. They won a reduction in random searches, and support for greater teacher voice on charter co-locations. They won $12 million from LAUSD for the creation of community schools. They won new commitments to ensure that every school in the district had a full-time nurse. They won more librarians and counselors, and steps toward the reduction of time spent on standardized tests. They won supports for immigrant students and their families, and a path toward increased resources for ethnic studies. They won passage of a resolution by the LAUSD school board, calling on the governor to implement a moratorium on charter school expansion. And yes, they won their demanded increase in wages. (See Inouye, p. 252.)

Bargaining for the common good brought Los Angeles parents, community members, and students together with educators to make their voices heard against the billionaires who had been attacking their public schools for decades. The tide has turned in Los Angeles.

Key Principles of Bargaining for the Common Good

There are seven key principles that guide BCG as a strategy in preparing for and carrying out labor negotiations:

1. **Expand the scope of bargaining beyond wages and benefits.** Identify issues that resonate with members, partners, and allies, and that impact our communities. Put forth demands that address structural issues, not just symptoms of the problem.

2. **Go on *offense* by identifying, exposing, and challenging the real villains**, the financial and corporate actors who profit from and increasingly drive policies and actions.

3. **Engage community allies as partners in issue development and the bargaining campaign.** Bring in community partners *on the ground floor* and ask them what they need out of the bargaining campaign. In many BCG contract campaigns, labor unions bring community representatives with them to the bargaining table to engage in negotiations.

4. **Center racial justice in your demands.** Campaign demands should address the role that employers play in creating and exacerbating structural racism in our communities.

5. **Strengthen internal organizing, membership, and member engagement.** These campaigns must deeply engage the memberships of both unions and community organizations, and there must be opportunities for deep relationship-building and joint visioning between the members of the different organizations.

6. **Leverage capital in your campaigns.** We need to develop strategies that leverage the financial power of workers' pension funds and endowments in order to win common good demands.

7. **The campaign doesn't end once the union settles its contract. BCG is about building long-term community-labor power, not about giving unions some good publicity during a contract fight.** The boss doesn't automatically become a good actor once the contract is settled, and the community's demands don't become any less important.

Bargaining for the Common Good in Practice

BCG has been a key strategy in several successful labor actions over the past several years:

- In 2012 the **Chicago Teachers Union** (CTU) aligned their contract fight with the interests of community allies to call for smaller class sizes, improved school facilities, and more. Under the slogan "The Schools Chicago's Students Deserve," the 2012 CTU strike brought tens of thousands of parents into the streets to support their teachers and signaled a new relationship between teachers, parents, and community. Again in 2019, the CTU used contract negotiations to force agreements on a wide range of common good issues such as school closures, charter expansion, and school staffing. The teachers centered the issues of housing and homelessness and racial justice in their campaign.

- In 2013, teachers in **St. Paul** followed suit, working with community partners to draw up a list of 29 bargaining demands. Inspired by the work in Chicago, the demands were framed in a report called "The Schools St. Paul Children Deserve." The platform included a demand that the school district stop doing business with banks that foreclose on their student's families, which they won. The union invited community representatives to sit with them at the bargaining table to ensure that their voices and issues were being represented. In 2020 after their strike, the district agreed to spend an additional $5 million to hire more counselors, social workers, intervention specialists, nurses, psychologists, and bilingual educational assistants next school year to give students the mental health and multilingual support they need and expand their restorative justice work.

> In Bargaining for the common good, labor invites community allies to join with them to use the collective bargaining process to win reforms that strengthen communities and improve the lives of working people.

- In 2013, Service Employees International Union (SEIU) Local 721 in **Los Angeles** utilized a BCG framework in their contract negotiations with the city. Local 721 represents 95,000 public sector workers, including the city's street services and water treatment workers, librarians, sanitation workers, and others. SEIU's "Fix LA" campaign included other unions and community allies like ACCE and AFSCME. Together, they called out the austerity budget in Los Angeles, pointing out that more money was being spent on Wall Street fees than on street repair. Demands focused on the city's massive infrastructure needs. Targets included the Wall Street firms whose fees were overwhelming the city budget and forcing cuts to important city services.

The Bargaining for the Common Good Network

As BCG has emerged as a successful strategy to bring workers and community members together in common campaigns, practitioners have created a network to share challenges, tactics, and victories with each other.

In 2014, labor and community groups from around the country held the first Bargaining for Common Good Conference at Georgetown University in Washington, D.C., followed by gatherings focused on centering racial justice, housing, climate, and other issues in this work.

The BCG Network is coordinated by the Kalmanovitz Initiative at Georgetown University, the Center for Innovation in Worker Organization at Rutgers University, and the Action Center on Race & the Economy Institute (ACRE). Through training, connecting experiences and challenges, and hands-on support, the network has helped several BCG efforts win significant change. The national advisory committee includes a dozen labor and community organizers from across the country. Learn more at bargainingforthecommongood.org. ▨

Marilyn Sneiderman directs the Center for Innovation in Worker Organization at Rutgers School of Management and Labor Relations, bringing with her more than 30 years of experience in labor, community, faith-based, immigrant, and racial/gender justice organizing.

Saqib Bhatti is the co-executive director of the Action Center on Race and the Economy. He works on campaigns to win racial and economic justice by taking on the financial institutions that are responsible for extracting wealth and resources from communities of color and poor folks.

RESOURCES

Kalmanovitz Initiative at Georgetown University. lwp.georgetown.edu

The Center for Innovation in Worker Organization at Rutgers University. smlr.rutgers.edu/content/center-innovation-worker-organization-ciwo

The Action Center on Race & the Economy. acreinstitute.org

Fine, Michelle and Michael Fabricant. Sept. 24, 2014. "What It Takes to Unite Teachers Unions and Communities of Color." *The Nation.* thenation.com/article/what-it-takes-unite-teachers-unions-and-communities-color

McCartin, Joseph A., Marilyn Sneiderman, Stephen Lerner, and Maurice BP-Weeks. April 24, 2018. "Before the Chalk Dust Settles: Building on the 2018 Teachers' Mobilization." *The American Prospect.* prospect.org/article/chalk-dust-settles-building-on-2018-teachers%e2%80%99-mobilization

The Kalmanovitz Initiative at Georgetown University. March 11, 2019. "Bargaining for the Common Good Comes of Age." *Working-Class Perspectives.* workingclassstudies.wordpress.com/2019/03/11/bargaining-for-the-common-good-comes-of-age

ROSLA. July 2019. *Building the Power to Reclaim Our Schools: Reclaim Our Schools Los Angeles, United Teachers Los Angeles, and the Collaboration Behind the 2019 Teachers Strike.* utla.net/sites/default/files/reclaimourschools_case_study.pdf

Teacher-Community Unionism: A Lesson from St. Paul

How one teacher union brought parents and students into the bargaining process—and won

BY MARY CATHRYN RICKER

GLEN STUBBE | AP

When I was elected president of the Saint Paul Federation of Teachers (SPFT) in 2005, I thought my own story might help transform the relationship between teachers and administrators, as well as improve the image of teachers in the community. I was a veteran middle school English teacher, and I'd been honored for my work. And I had been active in the SPFT as a political and community volunteer, as well as the union's professional representative on local and state committees.

I had also spent enough time in my classroom and in the city to know—and be bothered by—the dominant story told about public school teachers and our union by the mass media, a number of Minnesota legislators, and in many local communities. On a local TV station's evening news show, a Republican state senator, Richard Day, had even declared, "We all know Minneapolis and St. Paul schools suck." In too many conversations, I got accused of failure unless I quickly told people about the awards I had won for creating a model English/language arts classroom and running a program for my colleagues on how to improve writing in middle schools. If local citizens, especially parents, could learn about our talent, our dedication, and our ideas, I was convinced their perceptions would change.

Students in urban public schools deserve teachers who are both creative and optimistic. In addition, spending many years of your career teaching in an urban setting can stimulate good ideas about how to improve that work.

In St. Paul, we knew we were doing wonderful things both inside and outside the schools. We applied for grants to teach middle school science to students alongside environmental and community activists while rebuilding the historic watershed on St. Paul's East Side, a largely working-class neighborhood. We held public sessions where students read their essays and stories. We designed geography and history lessons about the immigration patterns of our city and our students. We lobbied our school board to maintain funding for peer mediation programs. We were thrilled to wake up every morning and share our love of these subjects with our students.

We also knew the value—and the potential—of our union. We were committed to achieving a high-quality, universal public school experience for every child. The members of the SPFT could be on the front lines advocating that goal, and our contract could be the document that helped make it happen.

But first, we had to parry negative images about us. Administrators and politicians treated students and their families as the "consumers" of an educational system, whereas we saw them as partners in building better schools. That consumerist mentality framed us as nameless and faceless workers, instead of people who were forging relationships with children and their families. It's no wonder that the notion of teachers as greedy and lazy had taken hold.

To dispel that falsehood, we had to forge an active bond with the people we served. St. Paul is a city of about 300,000 people. More than three-quarters of children in public schools belong to communities of color, and more than a third speak English as a new language. More than 70 percent of students in St. Paul qualify for a free or reduced-priced lunch. Only by talking, listening, and working with our students and their families could we change the pernicious perception of teachers and become the union we aspired to be.

The first step was quite simple: to talk to one another. In union meetings, we deliberately discussed why we became educators in the first place, what public schools meant to us, what unions meant to us, and what a decent contract would look like. We crafted *A New Narrative for Teachers, Educators, and Public Education*, which became our guiding document. Our narrative was anchored by five key themes: We are committed to building a good society; we believe in honoring the value of each student and cultivating each student's potential; we believe that working in community is essential to student success; and we believe that educating students is a craft that requires talented and committed professionals. We are committed to working collectively as a powerful force for justice, change, and democracy.

We read from this document at the beginning of nearly every union meeting. We shared it with new teachers and asked them if this was the kind of union they wanted to join. We relied on it so much that the *Narrative* practically had a seat on our executive board. It was not unusual for a union leader to ask, in response to a question or during a debate, "What does the *Narrative* say we should do about this?"

Expanding Contract Negotiations

One practice that clearly needed to change was how we negotiated our contracts. By Minnesota law, public employee contract negotiations are open to the public; anyone can attend and observe the negotiations. Usually, a union team of five or six members sits across the table from administrators. But in 2009, we invited special education teachers to attend, and encouraged them to invite members of the families they served. In one session, we even had the traditional bargaining team get up and join the audience to allow special education teachers to advocate directly for themselves.

These actions were limited, but we learned a great deal from them. We learned not to assume that members were too busy to participate in negotiations. We also learned that families were interested in collaborating with their teachers and education assistants on issues that affected them all.

In 2011, we went into contract negotiations with a more developed plan to democratize the process. We encouraged *anyone* involved with the education of St. Paul children to attend. We managed to schedule negotiations on the same evening every week—Thursdays from 5 p.m. to 7 p.m.—to help fit it into busy lives. The first session attracted just eight people, but the audience grew steadily after that. By the end of the nine-month process, nearly 100 union members, parents, and others from the St. Paul community were showing up—and we had both parent and rank-and-file voices on our side of the table.

We focused on demands to improve the quality of our teaching. We want to expand a successful pilot program in which teachers helped one another. We wanted to require that any teacher who applied for a leadership position have a recent evaluation of their classroom performance on file. And we wanted to see that class sizes would not vary widely over time. We also wanted administrators to recognize Future Educators of St. Paul, our union's program to encourage local high school students to become teachers, as a valid extracurricular activity.

Over time, we built trust within our ranks and with the residents of St. Paul who cared about and had a stake in the health of the public schools. The more we engaged them, the more they believed in our cause and our motives. One union member stood up at a negotiation meeting and said: "I came to prove that you guys weren't doing your jobs at the table and that you were slacking off—selling us out—and what I learned was that you are fighting relentlessly for us."

"Us" had become the rank-and-file members who no longer felt the negotiations were being conducted behind their backs. Now, local shop stewards were being treated as leaders in the process instead of just following orders. "Us" had become a neighborhood group that had been organizing independently but was now our partner. "Us" became parents who attended negotiations and shared their hopes and dreams for their children in our public schools at the bargaining table. Dora Jones, executive director of Mentoring Young Adults, who came to work very closely with us through the last two contract campaigns, said, "We can talk to the school board all day and try to make changes there, but if we don't really start dealing with the issues inside of that classroom—where the teachers are every day—then we are not really going to change anything."

Of course, tensions within the union did not suddenly vanish. One group of members, hoping to gain higher wages and better fringe benefits, wanted to push further than others wanted to go. Some veteran negotiators on our side were anxious about bargaining in the presence of other members. We spent time talking this through and, at the end of our conversations, it came down to one question: "Do you ever recall saying anything at the bargaining table that you wouldn't have wanted our members to hear?" The answer was an emphatic "No!"

The Schools St. Paul Students Deserve

With our contract set to expire on June 30, 2013, I knew we had to prepare well before that and engage the community in the process along the way. So in the fall of 2012, eight months before our contract was set to expire, we began two study groups—or book clubs—made up of a cross section of members, parents, and community members, that met monthly until April 2013. One group read *The Schools Our Children Deserve* by Alfie Kohn; the other group studied *Teaching 2030* by Barnett Berry.

With the help of each book, the groups tackled three big questions: What are the schools St. Paul students deserve? Who are the teachers St. Paul students deserve? What is the profession those teachers deserve?

In April 2013, the study groups presented their contract ideas to our union's executive board. The priorities included educating the whole child, authentic family engagement, smaller and more predictable class sizes, more teaching and less testing, culturally relevant education, high-quality professional development for teachers and education assistants, and a significant increase in access to our preschool program. After a thoughtful discussion, we adopted their priorities and directed the union's bargaining teams to negotiate on that basis. We dubbed this plan "The Schools St. Paul Students Deserve." We were realizing the kind of partnership with the community we had begun to build four years earlier.

Unfortunately, negotiators for the school district did not share our vision. Together with some elected officials, they balked at negotiating with a union that didn't behave in the narrow way they expected a union to behave. For years we had been told that "unions would be respected more if you acted differently and showed that you cared about students." But now, school district officials and the lawyer they had hired to negotiate for them were essentially scolding us to get back in our box and "act like a union." It was apparently "not our job" to concern ourselves with these teaching and learning issues.

In Minnesota, matters not directly related to a teacher's wages, benefits, or working conditions are permissive, not mandatory subjects of bargaining. Of the 29 community-supported proposals we presented in May 2013, district representatives refused to negotiate on 20 of them. For the first time in history, they hired an attorney to be their lead negotiator. She correctly pointed out that state law did not compel them to negotiate about class size, the expansion of early childhood education, or hiring an adequate number of school nurses, librarians, and counselors.

But we would not drop these or other issues in our contract campaign that we thought were important, simply because the lawyer said so. We knew these were all permissible areas of negotiations. We would make the case that it was in everyone's interest to have agreements that made progress in each of these areas. So we arranged for representatives of the union, parents, and the larger community to present their views directly to the district negotiating team.

In September 2013 the board's team unilaterally closed negotiations to the public in the only way they could: by calling for mediation. We weren't deterred. We knew we had the community on our side, and frankly, they didn't appreciate having their ideas cast aside. At 5 p.m. on Sept. 19, 2013, the district bargaining team walked into a room filled

> The groups tackled three big questions: What are the schools St. Paul students deserve? Who are the teachers St. Paul students deserve? What is the profession those teachers deserve?

with more than 75 people and journalists from both local newspapers, read their letter, and immediately walked out—a series of smartphone photos, gasps, and scattered hissing following them. Because a small group of students, parents, and union members had been assembled to testify that evening on behalf of improved counselor- and social worker-to-student ratios and dependable access to physical education and librarians, we reassembled, listened to their prepared testimony, and then opened it up to hear what the audience had to say. The audience—made up of SPFT members, parents, and community members as well as our student presenters—brainstormed ways to continue the public dialogue about our priorities now that open negotiations were no longer possible for us.

We knew we had the upper hand if we could rally the community that had worked to create these solutions only to have them dismissed, so we went to work. We made phone calls, knocked on doors, put up "St. Paul kids deserve _____" yard signs (or, in our case, snowbank signs) and let people fill in what they liked. We held "walk-ins" inspired by the organizers of Moral Mondays in North Carolina.

Only we held our walk-ins at the main entrance of nearly every school in the district at the end of January 2014, in a blizzard.

Some 2,500 teachers, education assistants, parents, students, and community members started their day by rallying for the schools our children deserve. Photos of signs were posted on Twitter proclaiming "St. Paul Kids Deserve Preschool"; Facebook posts depicted dozens of educators and their students outside a school, covered in snow, rallying with parents for reasonable class sizes or "More Teaching, Less Testing." Some teachers played drums, others made up chants like "What do we want? Happy students!" or adapted the lyrics of popular songs to our cause.

Finally, SPFT members voted to authorize a strike. Our primary demands were better access to preschool, consistent class sizes, more teaching and less testing, and equitable access to nurses, librarians, counselors, social workers, art, music, and physical education. Two days before our last scheduled mediation, we held a rally in front of the district headquarters before the school board met. Parent after parent spoke to the crowd. They then filed into the school board meeting to make their views known.

When we emerged we had made progress in every priority area . . . and our cars had been shoveled out by a parent and community member.

When that final, mediated negotiation session before our authorized strike vote arrived, we spent almost 24 solid hours together with the district's bargaining team—now including three Board of Education members, just for this meeting—negotiating on every contract proposal that was put forward. When we emerged (in the aftermath of another blizzard) we had made progress in every priority area advanced by the study groups. And our cars had been shoveled out by a parent and community member, which almost brought us to tears.

In the end, we averted the strike and made progress on nearly every issue for which we had fought. We won a commitment to expand the preschool program and to hire additional nurses, counselors, librarians, and social workers. We won an agreement for reasonable and predictable class sizes and a reduction of standardized testing. We established School Climate Improvement Teams composed of educators and parents who would collaborate to make students of all ethnic and racial backgrounds feel welcome and reduce the number of suspensions and other measures used to discipline children. We also successfully negotiated a method of redesigning schools to replace the mandated school restructuring process, which had until then forced school closings, turned schools over to charter management organizations, or forced removal of half the teachers. Our process would be teacher-led, allow teachers and parents to design school programs together, and draw on the assets of the communities in which schools were based.

In a larger sense, we felt vindicated by the democratic process we had created. Members of all the groups who had worked together asked one another, "What comes next?" I had negotiated almost a dozen previous contracts for the SPFT.

But, for the first time, I felt that signing a contract was just one step in building a larger movement.

Later that year, in summer of 2014, I was elected executive vice president of the national American Federation of Teachers. And in 2019 I was appointed commissioner of education for the state of Minnesota.

The union-community partnership I helped build in St. Paul is a natural extension of the priority the AFT has given to community engagement, since we seek to improve our teaching and our schools, and not simply file grievances and try to protect our wages and benefits. Similar things are taking place in Chicago, Los Angeles, Toledo, New Haven, Albuquerque, and elsewhere. In local after local, teachers are rebutting those who view them as failures. Everyone is learning that teachers can be a powerful force to create the kind of schools their students deserve. ◼

Mary Catheryn Ricker is the Minnesota education commissioner. She has served as executive vice president of the American Federation of Teachers and as the president of the Saint Paul Federation of Educators, AFT Local 28. She has more than a decade of classroom experience as a middle school English teacher.

This article was originally published in the summer 2015 issue of Dissent *magazine. Reprinted with permission.*

A Cincinnati High School Forges Ahead as a Teacher-Led School

BY DAVID LEVINE

KEITH HENRY BROWN

As the bell rings for the last period of the day at Cincinnati's Hughes STEM High School, social studies teacher Allen Frecker is convening the 10th-grade team for its daily meeting. In addition to Frecker, the team includes the math, science, English, technology, Spanish, and special education teachers and two student teachers. As Frecker moves the team through several agenda items, the discussion is punctuated by humorous asides and laughter, reflecting the obvious camaraderie that animates them. The team efficiently reviews a range of topics: guiding students through a career exploration program, coordinating some required standardized testing, finding a volunteer to help a student with a capstone project.

When a teacher pledges to make a special effort to get up a student recognition display, Frecker says, "You are so kind. Thank you for volunteering all the time." He conducts the meeting with a crisp efficiency that safeguards consensus. As decisions are reached, he chimes in with an "Everybody good?" or a "Does that sound like a plan?" Frecker's work as chair of the 10th-grade team reflects his status as a "lead teacher." Like lead teachers throughout the district, he earns a $6,000 stipend by taking on extra work and responsibility in areas deemed critical to the success of his school.

Lead teachers are at the heart of a vigorous system of shared decision-making at Hughes. Their role within the Cincinnati Public Schools (CPS) grew out of an effort by the Cincinnati Federation of Teachers (CFT) during the 1980s and 1990s to move beyond industrial unionism to invent a new kind of professional unionism. This new approach held true to the traditional goal of fighting for better wages and benefits, but also sought to give teachers a meaningful voice in educational policies and school governance, and to build alliances with community members to make the school system more democratic and effective. Ginger Rhodes, a CFT leader who went on to become a school board member and later served as Hughes' principal, explains, "We wanted to use the union to build a powerful teaching staff to teach kids, but we also wanted to build a powerful citywide coalition of other organizations, and draw people in . . . to a mission of good schools in this city, and public schools that were run well and effectively for kids."

Careers in Teaching

Tom Mooney, the CFT president at that time, explained that this new brand of professional unionism builds "on teachers' desires for professional respect, status, and pay, but also appeals to their commitment to kids. It challenges and empowers teachers to adopt research-based best practices rather than clinging to tradition." In the late 1980s, a joint teacher/administrator committee fashioned a "career ladder" program. Implemented in 1990 and codified in the bargaining agreement, the initiative is designed to ensure that teachers are effective, to support professional growth, and to provide leadership opportunities. Teachers enter CPS as mentored "resident educators." If evaluated as competent, they advance to become "career teachers" as they gain further expertise. Career teachers assessed as "accomplished" gain the status of "advanced teacher." Advanced teachers with at least three years of teaching experience are eligible to apply to become lead teachers. According to Mooney, the union "wanted [teachers] to have an impact on how the school system was run. We wanted to give teachers a much greater voice in the professional decisions, leadership within the district." During the 1990s, the CFT also helped deepen democratic governance within the school system by collaborating with top CPS management to implement a systemwide move to site-based management and increasing reliance on grade-based teaching teams to coordinate instruction. As part of these initiatives, lead teachers served as team leaders, department chairs, curriculum developers, and program facilitators.

For the last 30 years, the CFT has fought to maintain and improve the Careers in Teaching Program, and especially to safeguard the role of lead teachers. Although some CPS administrators have been supportive of teacher leadership, the dominant administrative response has been resistance. Former CFT president Tim Kraus comments: "Every year and in every contract, the CFT had to fight to keep the program, because a lot of administrators saw it as a hindrance to their own power and authority at the building level and districtwide." This hostility, coupled with chronic underfunding of the school system, has often imperiled the lead teacher program. Yet the union has been able to preserve the strong role lead teachers play in the district. The present contract stipulates that lead teacher positions will amount to 10 percent of the district's total teaching force, although this percentage is subject to agreement between the union and management regarding available funding. The union created the position of professional issues representative to monitor and help administer professional development opportunities and to ensure that lead teachers are allowed to operate effectively. Kraus attributes the enduring viability of the program to the effectiveness of lead teachers in individual schools and the critical role they play on the district's Curriculum Councils, and Quality Improvement and First Level Grievance committees.

As an innovative school characterized by strong collaboration between staff and principal, Hughes was often a key arena where this struggle for democratic decision-making and teacher leadership played out. Despite often-contentious interactions with the central office, Hughes has been an exemplar of district efforts to promote innovative teaching and shared governance since the 1990s. In 2009, based on the work of a planning team composed of Rhodes and a small group of lead teachers, Hughes was reinvented in its present incarnation as a comprehensive grade 7 through 12 STEM (Science, Technology, Engineering, Math) school. Though many of Hughes' largely African American and low-income students arrive after years of instruction characterized by low expectations and watered-down curriculum, Hughes' teachers work to provide a nurturing, intellectually stimulating, and rigorous learning environment. As a STEM school, Hughes offers the traditional core subjects of math, English, social studies, and science, as well as "career pathway" courses in engineering, health sciences, plant and animal sciences, and programming and software development. Its signature features include project-based learning, daily advisory classes so teachers can provide academic and personal support, and twice yearly weeklong "intersessions" organized around career exploration and teacher-designed classes that often incorporate experiential learning and community engagement.

Every teacher I interviewed emphasized that to understand what made

> To understand what made Hughes tick, you had to understand that it functions as a "teacher-led" school.

Hughes tick, you had to understand that it functions as a "teacher-led" school. Teachers analyze and seek ways to strengthen classroom instruction through discussions in interdisciplinary grade-level teaching teams and academic departments. They plan schoolwide activities and address schoolwide issues through several committees: Positive School Climate, Curriculum, Data, Intersession, and Advisory (to guide the daily advisory meetings conducted by teachers). Like all CPS schools, oversight of the school's academic mission and budget is provided by a Local School Decision Making Committee, composed of administrators, teachers and other staff members, parents, and community members. An Instructional Leadership Team (ILT)—composed of the three administrators, grade-level team leaders, department chairs, two non-teaching staff members, and two parent representatives—guides the school through decisions regarding student conduct, resource allocation, and curricular/pedagogical issues.

Frecker and other teachers note that one critical ingredient to Hughes' success is Principal Kathy Wright's commitment to giving teachers a strong voice in school governance at all levels. In contrast to the stance of many traditional administrators, Wright has a strong commitment to collaborative deliberation. For example, in ILT meetings, she notes, "Everyone has an equal voice. It's a very democratic process. I try to be a full partner in sharing ideas around instructional pieces that are going to be impacting the qualitative learning of students." Although the range of topics at ILT meetings encompasses issues such as student conduct and operational matters germane to daily school life, Wright prioritizes discussion on how teachers can collaborate to deepen classroom instruction.

All staff members are encouraged to participate in the collaborative work of the school, with lead teachers playing decisive roles on staff committees. Hughes' lead teachers are effective because they are carefully chosen, are willing to put in extra hours and effort, and are adept at cultivating and relying on the strengths of their colleagues. Through considering the professional journeys and work of one prospective and two current lead teachers at Hughes, we can gain insight into the deep potential of teacher leadership at schools that are committed to democratic decision-making.

Angela's Story: The Rigorous Road to Becoming a Lead Teacher
As she completed her student teaching at Hughes six years ago, English teacher Angela Schnormeier felt she benefited tremendously from the strong team-based collaboration and mentoring the school provided. She then landed a job in a neighboring district where she taught for two years. When an English teaching job opened up at Hughes, her Hughes student teaching mentor urged her to apply. For Schnormeier, coming back to Hughes "was like a dream." She took on leadership roles during her first two years teaching at Hughes, and her potential was quickly recognized by her colleagues and Principal Wright. As a new teacher, she wondered if she was ready, but "with the support and encouragement and push of my [teaching] team" she applied to become a lead teacher and is currently in the middle of the application process.

As Schnormeier describes her current responsibilities as chair of the nine-member Intersession Committee, I can see why her team believes she will make a good lead teacher. As chair she has to make sure that every teacher in the school is committed to leading a weeklong educationally valuable intersession class of between 15 and 30 students. She also works out room assignments, monitors enrollment, collects data on student choices, disseminates sign-up choices to students and parents, and organizes the collection of permission slips and fees. She comments, "I've definitely strengthened my organizational skills: placing 1,000 students in 41 different intersessions is a huge task. And not only placing them, but also making sure they are not repeating the same intersession year after year."

To qualify as a lead teacher, Schnormeier is being assessed by a lead teacher candidate evaluator who herself went through a rigorous process to qualify for this role. To verify that Schnormeier is highly effective in the classroom, her teacher evaluator will make four unannounced visits to her classroom in a year and evaluate three interconnected lesson plans. Each lesson plan must be accompanied by any student assessments connected to the lesson, as well as a reflection document that explains how the instructional strategies used benefited students and how the lesson relates to district goals and curricular standards. Schnormeier notes, "It's a lot of being on your toes and really making sure that good teaching is happening every single day." In addition to demonstrating teaching excellence, lead teacher applicants must document strong leadership skills. They submit two recommendation letters from colleagues and complete a questionnaire that includes questions such as "Describe how you have demonstrated consistent leadership in your school community and the teaching profession." After completing her assessment, Schnormeier's teacher evaluator will make a recommendation to a Lead Teacher Panel composed of three lead teachers appointed by the CFT and three administrators appointed by the superintendent. The panel makes the final decision on her application.

Although Schnormeier is still in the application process, her thoughts are already racing ahead to what her focus might be as a lead teacher. A prime candidate in her mind is the district's Language Arts Curriculum Council, a committee of teachers and administrators that she believes falls shy of its potential. As district administrators press for higher test scores, she believes that they can be insufficiently empathetic and not "entirely aware of what our day-to-day is like. The demands they have put down on us are sometimes not reasonable." She believes that as a strong teacher and articulate advocate she would be adept at "bridging the gap" between administrators and teachers and fostering essential conversations on curriculum and assessment.

Halla's Story: Leadership for Equity

When Halla Shteiwi started teaching at Hughes, she felt bolstered by her own life experiences. From the age of 15 through her early 20s, she took on a varied range of responsibilities in her family's restaurant business. She notes, "As a teacher, you are focusing on 20 different things at one time and you need to make sure that everything is in its place. I think that [restaurant experience] was extremely helpful in helping me manage [as a teacher]. I think that going to college gets you the content material that you need, but I think that life experience gives you the management [skills] you need to run a classroom." She started college as a business major; but working as a college math tutor convinced her that she had an aptitude and passion for education. Even with the benefit of this life experience, and the seasoning of three long-term subbing positions, Shteiwi's first two years at Hughes were rough. Her students "had been through one teacher, and he left on the weekend and never came back. Then sub after sub after sub, and I came in." She stuck it out, determined to prevail over classroom challenges with the sentiment "If you think that I can't make it, watch me make it." As she developed her teaching skills during these first two difficult years, she was encouraged and guided by a supportive teaching team. Fortunately, during her second year, her team leader taught next door to her classroom and provided her with critical advice throughout the day. As a lead teacher and chair of the Math Department, Halla carries on this tradition of collegial support. She currently spends her lunch and planning period every Friday mentoring a struggling colleague.

Shteiwi's prime goal as department chair has been to boost the caliber of instruction. She believes this can happen as her department colleagues raise their expectations for students and implement policies and teaching practices that make higher expectations reachable. She is keen to challenge the belief among some teachers that "Because we are an inner-city school our kids can't do the work." This is an issue, she says, because "with our students we are trying to give them the same kind of education that you would find in a suburban school." To operationalize this commitment to racial equity in achievement, Shteiwi has implemented a policy that lets students retake tests on an unlimited basis. To retake a test, a student is required to correct test errors, complete skill-strengthening homework, and obtain a parent's signature. Shteiwi has gathered data that demonstrates that almost all the students electing to retake tests experienced growth in math achievement.

> She is keen to challenge the belief among some teachers that "Because we are an inner-city school our kids can't do the work."

The heart of Shteiwi's campaign to raise math achievement at Hughes is her effort to convince her Math Department colleagues to adopt standards-based instruction and assessment. To this end, she provides guidance on how to design lessons based on clearly defined and discrete objectives, effective teaching strategies, and careful assessments that lead to reteaching concepts as necessary. Moving toward effective standards-based instruction within the department has been difficult. She notes that "resistance was 100 percent at the beginning." Progress has come as Shteiwi has developed relationships with members of her department and moved her colleagues toward a culture of collegial support. She has initiated frequent departmental and team-based discussions on effective standards-based teaching and facilitated department members participating in professional development workshops. The department took a critical step by voting to adopt a system of peer observations designed to encourage collective and supportive reflection on classroom practice. Twice a month, each Math Department teacher has a 15-minute observational visit by a colleague, who records what they like and what the observed teacher might consider doing differently. These written observations are shared with the observed teacher and inform departmental discussions on how instruction can be improved. Although Shteiwi still gets frustrated when she believes a teacher is falling short, she is encouraged that now seven of the 12 members of the Hughes Math Department have integrated standards-based assessment into their classroom practice.

Randy's Story: Relationships Are Key

The last period of the day has ended, and I am sitting in on a meeting of 8th-grade lead teacher Randy Gibson's "Jedi Science Club." Reflecting Gibson's strong interest in helping his urban students engage with nature and ecological issues, this year the club is partnering with Cincinnati's Mill Creek Alliance, a local environmental group, to study the impact of trash on the creek. Gibson is guiding the students through a "photo voice journaling" activity, an approach that utilizes photos for creative narrative construction. The students collaboratively review dozens of pictures they took during a recent trip to Mill Creek—disparate images of foliage, a peaceful creek, liquor bottles and Styrofoam cups, an encampment of a homeless person—to select 10 photos that tell the story of their visit. They then move on to a guided activity through which they chronicle what they did, saw, and heard during the day, and pose a question they want to ask about the creek. Through subsequent visits to the creek and further reflective activities, the club members will create their own analyses on the sources and impact of trash on the creek, and collaboratively produce a video on their learning journey to be shared with the school. Throughout the club meeting, Gibson manifests qualities that make him an effective teacher: humor, affection for his students, respect for their analytical capabilities, and a penchant for creative pedagogy that builds upon student strengths and interests.

Gibson considers strong student-teacher relationships to be "the driving force" underlying academic success, a belief that grows out of both his 20 years of teaching experience and his own challenging journey to professional success. Growing up poor in a predominantly white Appalachian Cincinnati neighborhood, he went to CPS schools, attending a magnet science program at the integrated Woodward High School. He became a first-generation college student at the University of Cincinnati but dropped out with a 1.1 GPA. At 24, he enrolled in the small Mount St. Joseph College, where he felt sympathetic professors "took me by my hand" and enabled him to gain academic competence and a growing sense of direction. As a young teacher in CPS, growing success in the classroom and validation from colleagues he respected enhanced his self-confidence and led him to take on increasing professional responsibilities. He attended a powerful learning institute on an inquiry approach to science instruction in Colorado with a team of CPS teachers, and subsequently worked with district science coaches to teach district colleagues how to implement this way of teaching. He views this experience as "the beginning of seeing myself in a leadership role" and a few years later successfully completed the process of becoming a lead teacher. As a lead teacher, he has served as both a department chair and a team leader. He is currently taking a break from lead teacher responsibilities to complete a doctorate in action research through the University of Cincinnati.

As a team leader, Gibson found that more than half of team meetings needed to be devoted to effectively managing all sorts of day-to-day issues: emergent needs of particular students, scheduling and staff coverage of school events, parent liaison, and the ongoing work of agreeing on and implementing classroom routines and norms that "raise expectations and lower behavioral issues." While not neglecting these critical tasks, he was always keen to focus as much team meeting time as possible on discussions of how to deepen classroom instruction. He notes that teams were able to significantly shift the balance toward pedagogical discussions when team meeting times were expanded from a one-hour meeting weekly after school to their current schedule of meeting four periods a week during the school day.

Because of his intense interest in pedagogy, Gibson finds discussions of classroom teaching "an amazing place to be." He notes that for the past four or five years, there has been a helpful trend for teams and departments to examine data on student performance as an entry point for discussions on how to improve student learning. For Gibson, standardized tests are best considered one data point among many rather than the "be all and end all" assessment of student learning. Hughes' teaching teams also focus on significant data points that flow out of daily classroom instruction such as quizzes, science labs, and varied writing assignments. Gibson is enthusiastic about his current team's goal of using assessment data to promote writing across the curriculum. He thinks that this "cohesive way" of teaching across the curriculum has especially strong potential to help the many struggling readers within their classes.

I've Got Your Back, but Don't Dare Be Slack: When Solidarity Embraces Professionalism

Since the early 1980s, the CFT has sought to forge a new kind of teacher unionism in which militant defense of teacher rights and welfare is fused with teacher leadership to foster heightened professionalism, new paths of collaboration with administrators, democratic school governance, and deeper learning among CPS students. In large and meaningful measure, the staff at Hughes High School is enacting this vision. Their work to do so is beset by enduring difficulties. Principal Kathy Wright notes that the impact of the Common Core, shifting curriculum maps, and new textbook adoptions add up to pressure from the district for schools "to be very cookie-cutter." These challenges are exacerbated because it has often been hard to translate substantive learning within Hughes' classrooms into higher scores on state-mandated standardized tests, despite concerted efforts by the ILT to analyze weaknesses in student academic performance and coordinate teacher efforts to improve instruction. For Wright, the press on the school to standardize instruction often makes her feel that it's a struggle to stay true to what "makes us unique" as a school with a strong STEM identity manifested through a distinctive curriculum and pedagogy.

Hughes' staff is sustaining itself in the face of such challenges through a collegial culture that provides peer momentum toward both striving for excellent teaching and participating in collaborative decision-making. Wright notes that teachers "who just want to come to work, be told what to do, and leave . . . end up leaving after a year because they are wanting everything to be dictated to them." A key ingredient in nurturing this culture is the prime focus that lead teachers put into mentoring relationships. Such mentoring is evident when Schnormeier notes that Frecker "has kind of taken me under his wing" in teaching her how to take leadership, when Wright notes that Gibson is providing vital support to the new and inexperienced Science Department chair, and when Shteiwi prioritizes building relationships and providing one-on-one coaching to her Math Department colleagues. And, it is important to note, this is a kind of mentoring in which empathy is balanced by high expectations. Wright encourages department chairs and team leaders to find supportive ways to have difficult problem-solving conversations with colleagues regarding shortfalls in their teaching. She explains that when this happens, "the accountability just shoots way up because people don't want to disappoint the principal, but people [especially] don't want to disappoint someone who is in their department, who is their friend." In fashioning this blend of empathy, toughness, and collaboration, lead teachers at Hughes honor the pioneering work of the Cincinnati Federation of Teachers and provide an exemplar for teacher union activists throughout the United States. ▣

David Levine is a retired education professor living in Columbus, Ohio. He is a founding editor of Rethinking Schools. *His research interests include U.S. educational history and urban education.*

Peer Assistance and Review in Seattle

....

BY DREW DILLHUNT

SIMONE SHIN

Early on the morning of Tuesday, Sept. 15, 2015, following four months of contentious negotiations, a six-day strike, and hours of late-night deliberation, the Seattle Education Association (SEA) and Seattle Public Schools (SPS) reached a tentative contract agreement. The agreement, approved by the full membership the following Sunday, included a slate of bread-and-butter gains such as significant pay increases and lower student-teacher ratios. However, the contract also reflected an intentional shift by the union—guided by thousands of individual conversations with members—to expand the field of issues SEA would bargain well beyond the frame of traditional industrial unionism.

As a result, the new collective bargaining agreement also boasted an array of gains focused explicitly on social justice and racial equity. The agreement included 30 minutes of guaranteed, daily recess for all elementary students in the district (students of color continue to receive significantly less recess time on average than their white counterparts). It also guaranteed dedicated training and financial support for 30 racial equity teams in schools across the district. These teams support an ongoing analysis of how racism manifests itself at the building level; they work collaboratively to "interrupt the status quo by mitigating, disrupting, and dismantling the school system's initiatives that uphold racism."[1]

This shift toward social justice unionism helped to connect the bargaining process to the core values of the membership and communicated to the larger community that SEA was committed to prioritizing the needs of students and families,[2] even where that meant smaller traditional gains for members in terms of compensation and benefits.

On that final night of bargaining, the only issue left on the table was the indirect use of student test scores in teacher evaluations—a measure introduced in Seattle five years earlier to meet the requirements of the federal Race to the Top Program. The language in the 2010 collective bargaining agreement governing student growth measures had been developed collaboratively by SEA and SPS to ensure that while student growth scores could lead to a closer look at teacher practice, they would remain confidential and would not directly impact evaluations.[3] By the time the 2015 teacher strike arrived, however, the push from the SEA membership to have student test scores completely decoupled from teacher evaluation had swelled significantly.

The following morning at the bargaining table, the district bargaining team suggested Peer Assistance and Review (PAR) as a possible way forward that promised to satisfy the interests of both sides by separating student test scores from teacher evaluation while introducing a growth-oriented approach to accountability. It was from that suggestion that the two sides hammered out the remaining section of the tentative agreement:

> SPS and SEA agree to develop a Peer Assistance and Review (PAR) program using an interest-based bargaining process during the term of this collective bargaining agreement. The PAR . . . working group will . . . design authentic indicators of teacher performance and discuss the role of assessments in teacher evaluation. SPS and SEA agree to eliminate . . . District-Determined Growth Ratings for the term of this contract.[4]

These three sentences—the last lines to be added that early morning—were not the portion of the tentative agreement most talked about by the media, the community, or even by the membership of SEA. Nonetheless, this short piece of exploratory language not only helped to finalize the collective bargaining agreement, it also had a significant impact on the working relationships between the three constituent groups guiding the work of teacher evaluation: the Seattle Education Association, the central office of the Seattle Public Schools, and the Principals' Association of Seattle Schools. The interest-based bargaining process called for in this language would be the first of many steps in establishing the kinds of collaborative relationships needed to begin co-constructing systematic solutions to complex problems.

Professional Unionism

Driven throughout by the social justice unionism of the SEA membership, the 2015 collective bargaining process closed with an unexpected invitation from SPS to embark on a collaborative journey of professional unionism. Where traditional unionism understands accountability for the profession as an external responsibility and the exclusive arena of principals and managers, professional unionism strives to "look beyond the self-interest of individual teachers" by framing teachers as "professionals who uphold high teaching standards" while navigating "the interdependency of teachers with the local school authorities."[5] PAR systems, and the interest-based work required to develop and sustain them, sit squarely in the domain of professional unionism. (See p. 103.)

That October, the PAR working group, composed of 14 educators (seven SEA members, four district administrators, and three building principals), traveled to Montgomery County, Maryland, for a training at the Montgomery County Education Association titled "Leading to Organize: PAR & Teacher Evaluation."

During our first four days working with Montgomery County Public Schools, we expected our counterparts there to tell us about how PAR worked in their system. Instead, what they talked to us about was the larger Professional Growth System, of which PAR was just one part. Everyone we talked to in the system—be they teacher union members or district administrators—told us narratives unique to the role they played, and each story had a deeply shared sense of what it meant to be a professional in that district. These shared stories reflected a shared vision and mission around this work, which our system clearly did not yet have.

Most importantly, the entire Professional Growth System was framed through a model of distributed leadership, where those closest to the work drive the work—where educator voice is central to decision-making at all levels of the system. Distributed leadership empowers what Alma Harris has described as "collective influences" to positively impact organizational outcomes.[6] This immediately resonated as a key interest for the SEA members in the PAR working group.

We were pleased to discover that nearly all of the components of Montgomery County's Professional Growth System were already in place in Seattle. Unlike many of the other visiting districts, SPS already had a robust mentoring program for new-to-profession teachers and a parallel program for coaching experienced teachers who received below-proficient evaluation ratings, as well as a building-based teacher leadership program codified in the 2010 collective bargaining agreement. All three of these components already had dedicated financial and logistical support in our system. While there was plenty of work to do coordinating these components under a shared vision, we wouldn't need to build these components from the ground up.

What stood out to the working group most clearly was what our system was missing. A key component of the Professional Growth System in Montgomery County is their foundational coursework series. The series includes two courses on effective teaching practices (all teachers in the district take this course) and another on observing classroom practice and giving effective feedback (expected of all building evaluators and consulting teachers). These courses are designed and facilitated by teacher-leaders. We had nothing parallel to this in our system.

"Evaluation alone will not improve practice," writes Linda Darling Hammond; "productive feedback must be accompanied by opportunities to learn."[7] Any effective system of teacher evaluation and accountability must have at its core a system of growth-oriented supports. That system of supports must explicitly communicate and actively engage teachers in learning not just the standards of effective teaching, but also the *how* and *why* of effective teaching.[8] Ensuring an effective teacher in every classroom is impossible where we don't yet have a shared vision or language of effective teaching.

We left Montgomery County convinced that in order to develop an effective PAR system, we had to commit to undertaking the much broader and larger project of developing a truly coordinated system of professional growth by developing foundational coursework and fully integrating that coursework with our already existing components of support.

Identifying Shared Interests

Back in Seattle, the number of voices represented in the working group expanded, with each constituency identifying additional members to more fully represent the many perspectives in the system. The group of nearly 40 educators who agreed to be part of designing the new professional growth system included classroom teachers, mentor teachers, union leadership, union staff, building principals, and central office administrators. The next step was to develop a plan.

Given the fractured trust that still characterized the relationship of our three constituent groups as a result of the recent strike, Ellen Holmes, our NEA facilitator, encouraged us to take time to independently caucus as three separate constituent groups (SEA, central office, and the principals' association) both prior to and following our shared work together back in Seattle.

> Having the opportunity to name our differences in our constituent groups allowed us to better see our shared interests when we met as a full group. This process slowly fostered a sense of trust in our relationships with one another.

This intentional caucusing helped to normalize the reality that we would continue to have positional differences around some issues (e.g., compensation and class size) even as we identified significant overlaps in our shared interests.

Perhaps somewhat counterintuitively, having the opportunity to name our differences in our constituent groups allowed us to better see our shared interests when we met as a full group. This process slowly fostered a sense of trust in our relationships with one another. We were able to lean into productive conflict around our shared work. The process acknowledged that we didn't need to agree on everything, or even most things, in order to work productively together toward our shared interests.

From our list of shared interests—which, to the surprise of many of us, was not a short one—emerged five distinct working groups, each focused on a specific component of the coordinated professional growth system we were now designing. These components included Foundational Coursework, the Teacher Leadership Cadre, the Consulting Teacher Program, the PAR Panel, and the Professional Growth and Educator Support System (PGES) Steering Committee. The five proposals developed in these groups would eventually be formalized as the SPS Professional Growth and Educator Support System in the 2018–19 SEA collective bargaining agreement.

Unsurprisingly, the three-year path leading from the launch of the PAR working group to the adoption of those proposals was neither simple nor straightforward. Members left the working group; new members joined. We relaunched the interest-based bargaining process and we developed norms all over again. A new superintendent took the helm of the district just prior to the ratification of the one-year contract in which the proposals from the PAR working groups were codified in the collective bargaining agreement. Yet, as a result of the shared commitment to the work by all three constituent groups and because of the principled relationships that had been developed, the work continued to grow and our shared interests began to coalesce into a shared vision.

Peer Assistance and Review

Classroom teachers who are released from their building to provide individualized coaching and assessment of instructional practice, known as consulting teachers, are the core of any PAR program. In Seattle, these teachers serve for a term of no longer than five years and must return to a classroom assignment for at least three years before being eligible to reapply. Consulting teachers are chosen for their teaching and leadership skills and receive ongoing training around effective mentoring.

Because Seattle already had a well-established mentoring program, the biggest change that has resulted from the shift to PAR is the addition of the consulting teacher summative assessment of teacher practice. Assessment had not previously been part of the mentor role. The PAR program was piloted over the course of the 2017–18 school year with 10 participating classroom teachers, all of whom had already received a full year of mentoring (but had not yet reached a fully proficient overall evaluation rating).

The 10 teachers who agreed to participate in the pilot were offered the opportunity to receive a second year of consulting teacher support with the understanding that they would engage in and give feedback on the newly expanded consulting teacher role. The PAR pilot allowed the assessment processes outlined in the proposal to be launched on a small scale under low-stakes conditions with ongoing feedback from participating teachers. It also allowed the eight consulting teachers who took part in the pilot to share their perspectives on how a shift to PAR, and the inclusion of the summative assessment, might affect their practice as mentors and their learning-focused relationships with participating teachers.

In parallel, Seattle piloted the PAR Panel, a deliberative body composed of eight SEA members and eight members of the principals' association. The panel serves as the designee of the superintendent and makes consensus-based decisions about continuing contract offers, additional consulting teacher support, and non-renewal. All panel decisions are made in closed deliberations informed by anonymized principal evaluations and consulting teacher assessments. The identity of the classroom teacher, the building evaluator, and the consulting teacher are not known by the panel.

Over the course of the pilot year, the panel finalized its norms and engaged in practice cases. The PAR Panel also worked with SEA's Center for Racial Equity to begin the ongoing work of developing tools and protocols to explicitly name implicit bias as it shows up during the panel's consensus-based decision processes.

In the fall of 2018, following the ratification of the new collective bargaining agreement, Seattle's PAR program launched at full scale, serving both new-to-profession teachers and experienced teachers not currently meeting the performance schedule. Experienced teachers who were already working with a consulting teacher prior to the shift to PAR were given the opportunity to opt into PAR (which all of them did).

In order to truly cultivate distributed leadership, the design of a PAR program must be the result of an ongoing interest-based process at the local level. As a result, the mechanics of each PAR program, including how teachers enter into PAR, vary widely from district to district.[8] In Seattle, all new-to-profession teachers are automatically entered into PAR and receive a full year of consulting teacher support. That support can be extended to a second year—and in rare cases a third year—by the PAR Panel. Building evaluators may also refer experienced teachers with provisional contracts (three or less years of service in the district) for PAR support following two observations where significant performance concerns are identified and communicated explicitly to the classroom teacher.

Experienced teachers with continuing contracts are required to enter PAR only as the result of an overall below-proficient summative evaluation. However, experienced teachers with continuing contracts may also choose to request PAR in coordination with their evaluator, as soon as significant concerns are raised, in order to access early consulting teacher support. Teachers with continuing contracts generally receive consulting teacher support for one to two years.

Having the PAR program explicitly named in the collective bargaining agreement has guaranteed significant and consistent financial support from the central office for developing and sustaining the new PGES. In 2018, when all five components were added to the collective bargaining agreement, existing programs were consolidated, which streamlined the work and allowed us to hire three additional consulting teachers, bringing their total number to 21. This has allowed the consulting teacher program to ensure manageable consulting teacher caseloads (an average ratio of 1:17) as the assessment role of PAR is added to their work.

As a result, there are now 26 SEA members housed in the human resources department, coordinating and implementing the work of the PGES. This has been an essential step not only in ensuring that the PGES is a coordinated system but also in maintaining the connectivity between SEA and the central office needed for this interest-based work.

Foundational Coursework

During the final months of the working group's three-year design period, we finalized the overarching vision statement for the Seattle PGES, which would ultimately appear in the collective bargaining agreement.

> Seattle Public School Educators believe that education is a civil right. Our Professional Growth and Educator Support System . . . is designed and managed by those who work closest with students . . . and centered on quality student learning for all.[10]

While this language is deeply connected to our core values of educational equity and distributed leadership,[11] it does not in itself ensure any substantive change in our systems. What it does do is explicitly formalize those values as the foundation of our shared work in the PGES. This provides a dependable space from which to ask the question "Is the current design of our systems aligned with our professed values?" Where the answer to that question is "No," we must commit to change.

This vision statement has already had an impact on the development of the foundational coursework, which all new-to-profession teachers and all teacher leaders are expected to complete. While the design team's initial focus was almost exclusively on supporting educators in developing their practice as culturally responsive teachers,[12] we quickly realized that in order for the learning activities to align with the vision of "education [as] a civil right," participants would also need ongoing opportunities to develop and sustain their racial equity literacy—understanding that an examination of our own unconscious and dysconscious beliefs as teachers must be at the center of any culturally responsive practice.[13]

This realization led the design team to create an initial draft of what would eventually become Seattle's Foundational Beliefs for Supporting Student Learning.[14] These five foundational beliefs, intended to guide the work of all educators in our system, explicitly name the ongoing impact of racism in our system and the necessity of active countermeasures in all parts of that system. The adoption of these five beliefs by SPS has in turn supported both consulting teachers and building principals as they work to more explicitly communicate what effective culturally responsive practice looks and sounds like in the classroom.

The SPS foundational beliefs document continues to be an avenue for the work of the PGES to come alongside the already well-established anti-racist leadership within SEA and SPS. During the pilot of the foundational coursework, members of the SPS Department of Racial Equity Advancement engaged in the course as participants and provided actionable feedback on the coursework. This process helped not only to refine the content but also to make the facilitation of the coursework more culturally responsive. A key shift was beginning to intentionally disrupt the white supremacy norms (e.g., individualism, discomfort with feelings, and "product over process") that are consistently baked into the way we deliver learning to students and adults alike.[15]

Professional Unionism as Anti-Racist Work

School systems in the United States were never designed to serve all students. Peer Assistance and Review and the other professional structures will not inherently disrupt racist policies and practices. They must be explicitly designed to do so—otherwise they will simply reinforce and deepen existing patterns. In Seattle Public Schools, as in many districts across the country, teachers of color are disproportionally identified as having performance concerns. This pattern of disproportionality exists both in districts with PAR and in districts without it.

In a truly anti-racist professional growth system, we should expect that disproportionality to disappear over time. In order for this to happen, our PGES will need to come fully alongside the already established anti-racist leadership within SEA and SPS. We've been in partnership with the University of Washington from the very beginning of this work to collect baseline data to analyze the impact of the changes we've implemented. We will need to continue to ask hard questions to see if the systems we've created are doing the anti-racist work they were intended to do. If not, those systems will need to be redesigned.

Ultimately, the lessons we've learned as a system through this process are not about the importance of implementing a PAR program. Rather, our lessons as a system have been about the power of engaging in productive conflict using an interest-based approach, about implementing a model of distributed leadership where those closest to the work, in this case classroom teachers, drive the work.

It's too early to make any definitive claims about the impact the new PGES is having on teacher growth and student learning in Seattle Public Schools. However, what we do know is that, as a result of consulting teacher assessments, 59 new-to-profession teachers (roughly a quarter of those supported) have already been recommended for additional consulting teacher support, which they would not have otherwise received. This year, the consulting teacher program was also able to offer new-to-profession teachers of color the option of requesting a consulting teacher of color (an option that 23 teachers of color took advantage of).

Distributed leadership has already begun to create collaborative spaces within the PGES where collective influence is not only possible but also encouraged. The leadership of the PAR Panel and the PGES Steering Committee, for example—both composed of SEA, central office, and principals' association members—led to specific changes in how teacher evaluations are written to ensure they more clearly communicate a full picture of teacher practice. As long as Seattle's PGES continues to develop in alignment with the core values outlined in its vision statement, this collective influence will expand. However, only with members continuing to push from within—as well as from without—will we be able to fully interrupt and redesign our systems in ways that are explicitly anti-racist and which allow us to meet the needs of all educators and all students in our district. 🔦

Drew Dillhunt is PAR/PGES coordinator for Seattle Public Schools.

ENDNOTES

[1] Hawkins, Uti. April 20, 2019. Racial Equity Teams Institute. Training facilitated at Seattle Public Schools.

[2] Sheridan, David. 2017. "Seattle Educators Get Their Mojo Going by Embracing Equity in Collective Bargaining." *EdJustice*. neaedjustice.org/2017/05/11/seattle-educators-get-mojo-going-embracing-equity

[3] Collective Bargaining Agreement Between Seattle Public Schools and Seattle Education Association Certificated Non-Supervisory Employees (2010–2013, Article XI, Section E). Seattle Education Association. seattlewea.org/file_viewer.php?id=2227

[4] Collective Bargaining Agreement Between Seattle Public Schools and Seattle Education Association Certificated Non-Supervisory Employees (2015–2018, Article XI, Section F). Seattle Education Association. seattlewea.org/file_viewer.php?id=2198

[5] Peterson, Bob. 1999. "Survival and Justice: Rethinking Teacher Union Strategy." *Transforming Teacher Unions: Fighting for Better Schools and Social Justice* (Bob Peterson and Michael Charney, eds.): p. 11–19. Rethinking Schools.

[6] Harris, Alma. 2013. *Distributed Leadership Matters: Perspectives, Practicalities, and Potential.* Corwin: p. 116.

[7] Darling-Hammond, Linda. 2013. *Getting Teacher Evaluation Right: What Really Matters for Effectiveness and Improvement.* Teachers College Press: p .99.

[8] Danielson, Charlotte. 2013. *The Framework for Teaching Evaluation Instrument* (2nd edition).

[9] Johnson, Susan et al. *A User's Guide to Peer Assistance and Review.* Harvard Graduate School of Education. gse.harvard.edu/~ngt/par

[10] Collective Bargaining Agreement Between Seattle Public Schools and Seattle Education Association Certificated Non-Supervisory Employees (2018–2019, Article II, Section D). Seattle Education Association. seattlewea.org/file_viewer.php?id=20236

[11] See *Educational Equity: A Definition. National Equity Project.* nationalequityproject.org/resources/featured-resources/educational-equity-a-definition

[12] Using *Culturally Responsive Teaching & The Brain: Promoting Authentic Engagement and Rigor Among Culturally and Linguistically Diverse Students* (Hammond, 2014) and *The Skillful Teacher* 7th edition (Saphier, et al., 2017) as core texts.

[13] King, Joyce. 1991. "Dysconscious Racism: Ideology, Identity, and the Miseducation of Teachers." *Journal of Negro Education* 60(2): p. 133–146. doi.org/10.2307/2295605

[14] See *Foundational Beliefs for Supporting Student Learning* (2019, version 2.0). Seattle Public Schools. seattleschools.org/FoundationalBeliefs

[15] Okun, Tema. 2010. *The Emperor Has No Clothes: Teaching About Race and Racism to People Who Don't Want to Know.* Information Age.

[16] Smith, Allison. 2019. "The Counternarrative of Teacher Evaluation: The Kangaroo Court, the Salem Witch Trials, and the Scarlet Letter." *Education Sciences* 9(2): p. 147. doi.org/10.3390/educsci9020147; Drake, Steven, Amy Auletto, and Joshua Cowen. 2019. "Grading Teachers: Race and Gender Differences in Low Evaluation Ratings and Teacher Employment Outcomes." *American Educational Research Journal* 56(5): p. 1800–1833. doi.org/10.3102/0002831219835776

[17] "Driving Diversity with Data." 2019. University of Washington College of Education. education.uw.edu/research-that-matters/2019/diversity-data#cb01

Parent-Teacher Home Visits in St. Paul

BY NICK FABER

Two white middle school teachers walk up to a student's home in St. Paul, Minnesota. The community they are visiting is reflective of their school community: high poverty and primarily families of color. Though the teachers have taught here for years, this is their first time entering a home in this neighborhood.

There are two young men hanging out on the porch who nod as the teachers approach but say nothing as they walk up and knock on the door. The student answers and welcomes her teachers in with a smile and excitement. They sit with her mom in the living room and for the next 45 minutes, she talks with the teachers about her dreams for her child, their hopes for what the student is able to achieve this year, and about the mother's own middle school experience. Mostly, they just have heartfelt conversations around what they all have as a common interest—the student's success in school and life.

Outside, after the visit, the teachers are energized and excited. As white middle-class teachers, they were outside of their comfort zone, but they were surprised how quickly they became comfortable. They are used to talking to parents within the "safety" of their classroom. But here, they were somewhere new, somewhere the *parent* and *student* felt more comfortable. In the end, they walked away not only feeling they had a better understanding about this student and her family, but also about themselves.

And that's the point.

At the Saint Paul Federation of Educators (SPFE), the Parent Teacher Home Visits initiative has been a key for us as a union to help teachers break down the implicit bias they may have toward the students who are in their classroom and the communities where they live. And that's powerful and important union work.

A Welcoming School Isn't Enough

In 2000 I was working at a full-service community school in Saint Paul Public Schools—before full-service community schools were a "thing." Our district, along with a community partner, had a vision for schools with wraparound services that would serve as a hub on St. Paul's East Side—a community of poverty, immigrants, and a rich history.

My colleagues and I believed at the time that the school where we were teaching, John A. Johnson Elementary School, could also benefit from a stronger plan for parent engagement. Our school opened its doors at 8 a.m. and closed them at 8 p.m. All day long, parents and students came and went, taking advantage of the school's housing and job services and dental clinic. But we started to realize that, as teachers, we really weren't interacting with many parents. In fact, we pretty much just saw parents at parent-teacher conferences in the fall and spring. We would see a few parents—not necessarily the ones we most needed to reach—during parent nights at school to discuss curricular changes in math and reading or show them how they could help their students with core subjects at home.

We wondered why more parents didn't come to the school for these evening events and engage with their children's teachers. Among other things, we as educators began to realize that we were part of the problem: We were looking at parents from a deficit lens. We were essentially telling them, "You don't know something and we do, and we're going to ask you to come into school, a place where you don't feel comfortable, and we are going to tell you what you don't know." And then we (the staff) were going to stand around and wonder why they don't show up.

It was about this time that I heard about the Parent Teacher Home Visit Project (now Parent Teacher Home Visits, or PTHV) that had been operating in Sacramento, California, since 1996.

Parent Teacher Home Visits

PTHV was started by a Sacramento community organization that was seeking ways to strengthen the relationships between schools and communities. Through several years of careful organizing and assessment, it built a local home visits program and began to see strong results. As word spread about the success of the program, PTHV hired staff and began to provide training to districts outside Sacramento. It has since grown into a national organization.

The practice of teachers visiting students' homes is not new. But what PTHV brings to the process is an intentionality to ensure that real relationships are being built, and that both families and educators are deeply invested in the strategy.

PTHV's model is adapted in a wide variety of settings across the U.S., but follows five non-negotiable core practices:

- Visits are always voluntary for educators and families, and arranged in advance;
- Teachers are trained, and compensated for visits outside their school day;
- The focus of the first visit is relationship-building. We discuss hopes and dreams;
- No targeting—visit all or a cross-section of students so there is no stigma; and
- Educators go in pairs to all visits and reflect on them afterward together.

Interested in the model, we contacted the organization, and they were eager to come out and train some of our staff on their model of home visiting.

Learning How to Listen

I told our district's area assistant superintendent about the program and the training that they offered at a cost of $3,000. I got the typical response: "There's no money." So, I went to Mary Cathryn Ricker, at the time the union president (and as of this writing the commissioner of education in Minnesota), and asked if our local could fund the training. I explained to her that home visits could not only benefit our students, but also help our teachers become better acquainted with the community. She was intrigued and began looking for ways to fund the initiative.

Mary Cathryn eventually found grant funding for the PTHV trainers to come to St. Paul. They trained six teachers from our school (including myself), our community school coordinator, and our principal. Mary Cathryn participated as well.

During the three-hour training, we learned the nuts and bolts of this particular model, including how to set up the visit and questions to ask to get to know a parent quickly. Visiting teachers focus on asking about the parent's hopes and dreams for his or her child and what school was like for the parent when he or she was young. Such questions let teachers learn more about parents' interests in their children's education and enable parents and teachers to better relate to each other throughout the school year.

In the training, we also explored the barriers that might impede a strong visit: for instance, negative assumptions we may hold about our students' families, and fears we may have, such as making some sort of cultural faux pas when interacting with parents, especially those who are new to our country. And we discussed the importance of feeling comfortable around other cultures and languages—more than 70 are spoken in St. Paul public schools.

Those six teachers visited about 15 families that first year. After the visits, we met as a group to debrief. We realized we held so many different assumptions that proved to be wrong—for instance, that because a lot of our students lived in poverty, we were going to find parents who weren't passionate about their children's education and success, and houses that were falling apart and in disarray.

Instead, we found parents who really did care about their children's education and that the fundamentals to support their learning were available at Johnson Elementary. They shared their stories of where they were in life, how they got there, and how they wanted better for their children.

Many parents were resistant to our visits at first. They were suspicious of our interest in coming to their houses, and understandably so—teachers in St. Paul didn't typically do such a thing unless something was wrong (really wrong). But because we visited a cross section of our students, never targeting any subgroup, and offered to meet somewhere else in the community if the parents felt more comfortable doing that than meeting in their home, all the parents agreed to our visits and word got around that our efforts were sincere.

After these initial visits, we realized what a positive impact this program could make in the lives of our teachers and students. So we, as a union, decided to expand it. Again, we asked the district for financial support. And again, the answer was no. We were disappointed but not deterred.

Open Bargaining Helped Win Funding

A few months later, we brought the idea to our bargaining team during contract negotiations. The team loved the home visit concept and put it on the bargaining table. We conduct open bargaining here in St. Paul, meaning that the public can attend contract negotiations (and therefore parents are in the room). This proved to be to our advantage when presenting the program to the district negotiating team. It would have been hard for them to say, "No, we don't want our teachers going out and visiting parents." In the end, the district agreed to the program, and we won $50,000 that year in our teachers' contract to fund it. The amount, which has increased to $175,000 in our current contract, pays for stipends for teachers' home visits. Today, the district still primarily funds the stipends, while SPFE pays for conducting the trainings for teachers before the visits. That relationship is changing, however, as the district and union are working more cooperatively in this area and the district sees the value in the project. PTHV contract language is also in the other two paraprofessional bargaining units that SPFE represents as well. (See Resources, p. 418.)

Key Components of the Program

The Home Visit program in St. Paul is totally voluntary. Teachers in every public school in St. Paul can participate but are not required to do so. They are compensated $50 for each home visit they make—a stipend meant to cover their time setting up and making the visit as well as their transportation. Typically, home visits last 30 to 40 minutes.

To receive the $50, a teacher must complete our training, which we've extended from three hours to four. A training team made up of six teachers, a paraprofessional, and two parents—all of whom have been on (or, in the case of the parents, have received) home visits—runs the project, with occasional advice from two administrators. The team meets regularly to plan trainings and outreach and never holds a training without one of the two parents present. SPFE compensates parent trainers for their time at the same pay rate as our teachers.

The visits take place outside the regular school day, on the teacher's own time. We encourage teachers who participate in the program to conduct a home visit in the fall with each of their families. We also encourage a second visit in the spring. Teachers must go in pairs on the visits so that parents build relationships with two educators in the school building. And I say "educators" here, rather than "teachers," because our paraprofessionals do these visits as well. In addition to teachers, SPFE represents two groups of paraprofessionals: educational assistants, and school and community support professionals. These groups' contracts now also include the PTHV. They have the same language and compensation per visit as teachers have. Typically, these paraprofessionals go on home visits with a classroom teacher, but some paraprofessionals in our high schools visit together.

Because the emphasis of the first home visit is on establishing relationships, teachers and paraprofessionals don't bring anything with them. These visits are not for having a parent-teacher conference, getting an individualized education program (IEP) signed, or going over school rules—all of which can take place at another time and in a different setting. Home visit time is sacred and meant for establishing relationships, so we don't want to raise anything that might distract from that.

The educators also don't need to take notes during their visits, since visiting homes in pairs allows them to debrief together immediately after. They remind each other what was discussed and bounce ideas off one another. It's especially important for teachers to remember what they learn about students—their interests and any activities they participate in after school—so they can better connect with students and possibly work that knowledge into a lesson plan.

At the spring visit, the visiting educators might bring materials along based on the parent's expressed interests for the child from the fall meeting. Once you have established a relationship with the family and know about something the parent wants to work on with the child, you can follow up. For example, you might say something like "I know you've been talking about wanting to make sure your child is up to grade level in reading this year. I heard that at our first visit, and you mentioned it at parent-teacher conferences. So I brought you these books that you might want to read this summer to help your child's literacy skills improve. I know that's something that you really value and that we can partner on."

We want parents to know that we, as educators, see them as an asset. The philosophy of our home visit project can be summed up this way: No matter who you are, no matter what life has dealt you, you know something about your child you can share with me that can make me a better teacher.

Another key has been sharing experiences. We learned from other districts around the country that sharing home visit experiences and learnings during staff meetings or staff professional development was critical. Teachers must log their visits after they occur and submit records of those visits to the project coordinator. And they are required to attend a two-hour debriefing session after their visits in the fall and spring. To keep the program strong and growing, we felt that it was important to meet regularly as a group. Attendance at the debriefs, which take place at the union office, are required in order to be compensated. This has brought hundreds of members into our union hall each year who would not necessarily come otherwise. At the debriefs, we often take time for announcements about upcoming union events. And we spend time hearing from the home visitors what they are hearing from parents, so that we can advocate for those concerns in contract nego-

> The philosophy of our home visit project can be summed up this way: No matter who you are, no matter what life has dealt you, you know something about your child you can share with me that can make me a better teacher.

tiations or meet-and-confer meetings with the district.

SPFE continues to stay connected to the national PTHV project, whose roots are in community organizing. Although there are other models out there, other organizations, PTHV remains closest to its roots.

Challenges

Of course, there are challenges. Our biggest stumbling block right now is that most of our educators, like educators everywhere, are just short on time. In St. Paul, schools with teachers who are making the greatest number of home visits are the ones whose principals have unlocked the class list early in the summer so that teachers can visit families during their summer vacation, when they have greater flexibility in scheduling these visits. Our big push now is to convince the entire district to commit to sharing class lists with our teachers by Aug. 1. So even if teachers choose not to do home visits, they can still reach out to parents in some way, by phone or email, before school starts the day after Labor Day.

Their Favorite Part of the Job

Since it first began in 2010, our home visit program in St. Paul has grown significantly. We have gone from having a handful of teachers make 15 visits nearly 10 years ago to having close to 200 educators make more than 3,000 visits this past school year. And more than 50 of our schools, nearly all of them high-poverty, now have anywhere from two to 20 educators who have received training and have made, or are prepared to make, home visits.

Teachers and principals have been enthusiastic about this program and take pride in its success. At our debriefs, teachers report numerous benefits. They feel supported by their students' parents, and they talk about being able to communicate more freely with them. Greater communication allows teachers and parents to take care of academic and behavior problems quickly, before they get out of hand, enabling students to stay in class and therefore increase their learning time.

An evaluation of the program commissioned by the national Parent Teacher Home Visit Project and SPFE found that teachers do indeed value the home visit model. Of the educators who visited homes during the 2013–14 school year and who responded to a survey that was part of the evaluation, 76 percent said that home visits changed their assumptions about parents. And 93 percent said that making a home visit taught them something about their students they didn't already know. This echoes the results of a national evaluation recently conducted that showed this model of how visiting helps reduce implicit bias in educators and shift their mindset regarding their students and families.

According to the evaluation, which was also based on observations of debrief sessions, "teachers reported feeling energized by the process of home visiting," with some teachers calling it "their favorite part of the year or their job." It just makes sense that when teachers build relationships with parents and feel supported by them, they find their work more rewarding.

Home visits also helped teachers strengthen their connections with colleagues. As the evaluation makes clear, "In a profession that can often isolate teachers in their classrooms, the home visiting program gave them a shared experience and time to build relationships with their fellow teachers."

Students have been receptive to the visits. Some get very excited when they know their teacher is planning to see them in their home. It's not uncommon for students to eagerly ask their teachers, "When are you coming to my house?"

Parents have also welcomed the initiative. They respect the effort educators are making to come into their home. And just by teachers extending themselves outside the school day, they are showing parents that they actually care about their children.

Nationally, the PTHV project has been the subject of a series of evaluations and research studies (see Resources list below). All have found quantifiable results, including decreases in chronic absenteeism and improved assessment scores.

Just as important, the program in St. Paul, which is run entirely by educators and parents, has helped parents move away from seeing the teacher union as an obstacle. Now they are saying, "Wow. Our teachers' union wants its members to go out and visit us in our community and have a relationship with us." That's a pretty powerful message to send, and it's one that has helped us organize parents to advocate for the resources their children—our students—need.

Parents know things about their children that can make us better educators, but except for one or two parent-teacher conferences each year, we may not see them at school much or get an opportunity to talk with them about their child's interests. Many parents work long hours at multiple jobs to provide for their families. It's not the interest in their child's education they lack, but the time to devote to it.

This work can be uncomfortable at times. It can be scary at times. The same feelings are being felt by our parents, too. But we are at a unique moment. If there was ever a time where our need to understand each other was vitally important, it is now. If there was ever a time for members of our union to understand and feel comfortable in the community, it is now. 🎭

Nick Faber is an elementary science specialist in St. Paul Public Schools where he has taught for the last 35 years. He is currently on leave as the president of SPFE. Nick is also the former board chair of Parent Teacher Home Visits (pthv.org).

RESOURCES

Parent Teacher Home Visit Project. pthvp.org

RTI International. October 2017. *Mindset Shifts and Parent Teacher Home Visits.* pthvp.org/wp-content/uploads/2018/02/PTHV_Study1_Report.pdf

RTI International. September 2018. Parent Teacher Home Visits Implementation Study. pthvp.org/wp-content/uploads/2018/12/180904-PTHVImplementationStudyReportESFINAL.pdf

Sheldon, Steven B. and Sol Bee Jung. November 2018. *Student Outcomes and Parent Teacher Home Visits.* Johns Hopkins Center on School, Family, and Community Partnerships. pthvp.org/wp-content/uploads/2018/12/18-11-30-Student-Outcomes-and-PTHV-Report-FINAL.pdf

The Six Pillars of Community Schools
Public schools as greenhouses of democracy

JOE BRUSKY

n response to privatization and other damaging "school reform" initiatives, growing numbers of educators, community activists, and teacher unions have promoted a vision of "community schools" that incorporates key values and components that speak to what all children deserve. Such schools promote democratic practices and engagement in the broader community, the school, classrooms, and the curriculum.

Some schools label themselves as community schools because they provide some "wraparound" social, health, and recreational services. Although such services are important, they alone won't transform a school and are only one part of a successful community school. Such schools must also have engaging curriculum, high-quality teaching, inclusive leadership, positive discipline practices, and significant parent and community engagement.

These additional characteristics have been described in various ways. The National Education Association speaks of "the six pillars of community schools"—all of which promote equity and democratic practices. The components of community schools below are based on the NEA's six pillars.

1. **Strong and Culturally Relevant Curriculum.** Educators engage students with challenging, culturally relevant curriculum using teaching strategies that pro-

vide active, project-based learning with critical reading, writing, speaking, and thinking skills in all subject areas. Students learn to value all people and how to stand up and act to promote democracy and justice. Curriculum includes the students' lives and heritages as well as additional languages, fine arts, physical education, and before- and after-school programs.

2. **High-Quality Teaching.** Community schools are places of inspiration and freedom. Educators have adequate time to plan collaboratively and analyze student work to improve their teaching skills and pedagogical approaches. Creating student-centered classrooms, teaching problem-solving and critical thinking, and engaging students with rich, challenging curricula are a central schoolwide focus.

3. **Inclusive/Shared Leadership.** Leadership is a responsibility shared by the school principal with a community school coordinator and the community school committee that includes parents, community partners, school staff, youth, and other stakeholders.

4. **Community Support Services.** Community schools are hubs of their community. They provide a host of services, often in conjunction with community partners, including meals, health care, mental health counseling, and other services before, during, and after school.

5. **Positive Discipline Practices.** Community schools foster positive school climates and healthy relationships among students and between students and staff. Zero-tolerance policies that promote suspension and expulsion are replaced with restorative practices that build relationships and improve school climate. Discipline issues are dealt with in proactive ways. For example, restorative justice practices may be used to address conflict within a positive school climate that values and respects all members of the school community.

6. **Family and Community Engagement.** Parents and community members are full partners in community schools. They have substantive roles in school governance and setting school policies. Educators' expertise and experience are valued and respected, but all partners have a seat at the table and a voice in the learning community.

Past practice shows that in order to successfully implement these six pillars, schools need to hire a full-time community school coordinator, conduct regular needs and asset assessments, develop strategic plans, and create school-based problem-solving teams. Schools that do these things in collaboration with community stakeholders have become sustainable and show dramatic improvements.

When people hear of the six pillars, they often say, "That's what all schools should be like." That's true. But to achieve that goal requires resources, enlightened leadership, and the support of broad sections of a community.

It also requires intentional organizing and advocacy on many people's parts, particularly educators. Encourage your colleagues to ask your local union and parent and community organizations to help build the kinds of schools that all children deserve. ⬛

Reprinted with slight changes from The New Teacher Book.

Community Schools, Teacher Unions, and Black Lives Matter

An interview with Jennifer Johnson of the Chicago Teachers Union

Editors' note: This is an edited excerpt from a longer interview with Jennifer Johnson, CTU's chief of staff, from the book Black Lives Matter at School. *Jesse Hagopian interviewed Johnson about the racial justice victories of the CTU's 2019 strike.*

How does the CTU's contract with the Chicago Public Schools deal with social justice?

The fourth demand of our 2019 strike was around different social justice issues. Even though really all of our demands were around social justice, this is where we focused on the fight for affordable housing and community schools. We didn't win the affordable housing we had hoped to make the city agree to, but we did end up winning additional full-time positions in our schools where students have the highest rates of homelessness.

In our last contract in 2016 we won $10 million for 20 sustainable community schools. These schools follow principles like self-determination and racial justice, and then they work with the community to enact these principles.

Can you be more specific?

These schools focus on culturally relevant pedagogy, effective teaching instead of high-stakes testing, restorative justice, wraparound services, cooperative decision-making, parent engagement. We fought really hard to win expansion of that program. The district was threatening to cut it off but we won $10 million per year of the contract, so a total of $50 million to keep the program running.

What an amazing example of how to fight to change the school system to make Black lives matter. What do you think the role of unions should be in the struggle to make Black lives matter at school, and what is your vision for education that would truly make our Black students' lives valued?

Wow. Beautiful, big questions, Jesse. I think the role of teacher unions is critical. I am only a union leader because my rank-and-file colleagues in our caucus and our leadership believe that racial and social justice is inherently built into our work as educators. I would not be a part of our union if it was otherwise. The students who we serve are our partners. We need to be working with our students to design a future that we think is collectively best. We can only do that if we recognize the inherent value of our students' identities, our students' families, our students' communities, and their challenges. . . .

I am a Black woman myself, and so this is not something that I had to learn, but it's something that teachers, union leaders have an opportunity to teach those who might not see it this way. I think the unions have a very particular role to make all educators feel it is their responsibility to contribute to anti-racist work. That includes unions that are in mostly white districts. We have to actively push people to see their role whatever their location, and whoever their students are, as contributing to a more just society. Black Lives Matter at School Week, I think, is just such a powerful call to action because it gives educators everywhere the ability to join in this racial justice work. BLM at School gives educators concrete activities to make that work real. Otherwise teachers can sometimes just talk about it, or say that they believe it, but Black Lives Matter at School Week has concretized, and made space, and shared resources across the country for that work. It is a clarion call to hold educators accountable. This action asks educators, "What does it look like in your classroom?" "What does it look like in your school?" "What does it look like in your district and your union?"

Our goal must be to create a school district where students, parents, educators, administration, and community members are in partnership with a mission of racial and social justice. That requires educators, and administrators in particular, to relinquish some control and power, to see themselves as a part of a collective effort to educate one another. It's not just about educating our students in a one-way direction, but learning from our students and finding areas where we need to grow.

How is the goal of "collective power"—all stakeholders working together—being realized in community schools in Chicago?
Our sustainable community schools program is not perfect, but it's a contribution in the struggle for that kind of an education. We need to work at building more schools where decision-making is shared, because once decisions become shared, community voice and community wisdom can be respected. That's not easy; this is about breaking down power dynamics, and that's something that school districts inherently resist with their hierarchical organization. Sometimes is it something that teacher unions resist, because they can be hierarchical too. We have to struggle against those instincts and push for more democratic instincts that we have as educators to listen, to debate, but also to be able to listen to parents, students, and community wisdom. When we include everyone in the decision-making process—especially the Black and Brown voices that have been marginalized for too long—the vision of Black students' lives mattering to the school becomes attainable. ▮

Why Community Schools?

BY KYLE SERRETTE

It is common knowledge that there are neighborhoods and communities in the United States where children are supported so comprehensively that they can be whatever they want to be when they grow up. In these places, the children have strong public schools and affluent families, and they are lifted up no matter how many times they fall down.

In other places, it is rare for children to achieve their dreams. They attend under-resourced schools and live in beleaguered neighborhoods. Their family members often have low-paying jobs, if any, and face a variety of forms of discrimination.

This is societal inequity. Core questions for educators and teacher union

leaders include: What are the best strategies to address such inequality? What role can schools play? And how can school communities influence their surrounding neighborhoods and cities to address this inequity as well?

To date, there is one school-based strategy—community schools—that has demonstrated the ability to successfully challenge such inequities and foster an environment where *all* children have a solid chance at being able to achieve their dreams.

It may seem like a preposterous claim that there is only *one* school-based strategy out there that has worked to successfully challenge these inequities, but it is true. Consider that the average student spends 1,000 waking hours per year inside school and 4,500 waking hours outside of school. There is general consensus within the research community that academic success is dependent upon excellent enrichment during the 1,000 hours *and* the 4,500 hours. And the data also show higher-income families invest heavily to ensure their children have high-quality experiences outside of school (e.g., tutoring, soccer, piano, chess, coding classes, trips abroad, etc.).

In fact, the annual gap between what lower-income and higher-income families spend on out-of-school enrichment activities is $8,000, a figure that has tripled since 1972.[1] Meaning, low-income families generally do not have the resources to pay for high-quality activities outside of school time. If a student is in an out-of-school environment that is not only lacking in quality enrichment, but is perhaps harmful as well, then we know the chance of this student being able to achieve their dreams is slim, even if they have an excellent school experience.

The community school strategy, if implemented in a transformative way, has proved in a large number of research studies[2] to be very successful. This strategy mobilizes students, families, educators, and community members to develop a grassroots vision for their schools *and* their communities; together these stakeholders work to achieve their vision. In other words, the community school strategy targets the 1,000 hours spent in school, and the 4,500 hours spent outside of school, and works to improve *both*.

Yes, there are other school-based strategies that have resulted in students being able to achieve their dreams, but all those strategies rely upon some level of selectivity—a parent must apply, a student must test in or must keep up with the rigorous environment, etc.

What differentiates the community school strategy from other successful school strategies is that it is designed to work in any community, with any student body, and within any public school feeder pattern, while the other whole-school strategies rely upon selectivity to create the environment necessary to achieve those results. The problem with selectivity-based strategies is that they pick a small number of "winners" and leave inequity for everyone else. And of course, you can't scale up selectivity. This is why the community school strategy is special, and the only strategy that has proved to achieve transformational results on a small and large scale.

Demonstrated Success

In 2001, stakeholders in Cincinnati decided to turn all of their schools into community schools (called Community Learning Centers). At the time, Cincinnati was the lowest-performing district in Ohio and had an achievement gap between Black and white students of 14.5 percent. Today Cincinnati is the highest-performing urban school district in Ohio, and the achievement gap is only 4.5 percent. In 2010, two of the lowest-performing schools in Austin, Texas' highest-poverty neighborhood went from the brink of closure to becoming the highest-performing Title I schools in their city.

In the 1990s Kentucky converted almost all of its schools into community schools—called Family Resource and Youth Service Centers. Kentucky went from being consistently ranked one of the worst in the nation in education to outperforming half of all states and reducing their socioeconomic achievement gap to the smallest in the nation. Cincinnati, Austin, and Kentucky all accomplished these results without selectivity.

Some schools have implemented a community school model without explicitly naming it. In fact, this seems to be a characteristic of the community school strategy. As John Rogers, a community school historian at UCLA, stated: "Community schooling has achieved a peculiar form of longevity. Unlike other long-standing innovations such as standardized testing that have followed a direct pathway from the margins to the educational mainstream, community schooling seems to rise and fall in salience every generation. It is an idea that has been continually 'rediscovered'—by educators, community activists, policymakers, and presidents."

Take, for example, the great results[3] coming from Lebron James' I Promise School in Akron, Ohio, and the strategy[4] to which they attribute their success—STEM curriculum, wraparound supports, and trauma support systems (all hallmarks of the community schools strategy). You will not find one mention of the community school strategy on the I Promise website, and there is little evidence that they deliberately chose to use the community schools strategy. Instead, the I Promise School "rediscovered" the strategy, and it is working. The problem is that our students and communities can't wait for the community school strategy to be rediscovered. The strategy is urgently needed across the country.

Challenges and Opportunities

All this sounds good on paper and has proven quite successful, as discussed above. And yet this is a particularly challenging model to implement. Resource-strapped school districts often struggle to fund full-time coordinators at each school. Communities have different levels of wraparound services that are readily available, whether they're from the city or county governments or nonprofit social service agencies. And while before- and after-school programming can enrich non-school hours, that too costs money, to say nothing of the need for neighborhood improvements—housing, health care, violence reduction, and jobs. Thus in Cincinnati they've strategically targeted not only school improvement but neighborhood improvement as well.

Beyond the issue of money, some of the six pillars of community schools (see definition on p. 146) are particularly challenging. Inclusive/shared leadership is not a given in many school districts where hierarchal leadership styles are common. Similarly, discrimination and low expectations—by educators and the curricular offerings, and by the broader community itself, are not easily overcome.

And yet the power of this strategy is that it explicitly demands that such issues be addressed. Several school districts that have adopted this strategy insist that schools demonstrate their readiness through an application process and a favorable vote by students, staff, and parents. Building strong models from the very start is essential.

New York City

Many education justice coalitions and unions have worked together to take on the funding dilemma, at times winning millions to provide public schools with the resources to adopt the community school strategy, and new community schools are already starting to get great results. In New York City, for example, the Coalition for Educational Justice organized and won funding for 200+ schools to adopt the community school strategy. According to a 2020 RAND study,[5] the community school strategy is "having tangible impact on a variety of student outcomes."

Durham, North Carolina

The Durham Association of Educators (DAE) and a coalition of community allies set the goal of winning funding to start a small number of community schools. Given the history of top-down reforms in their district, the DAE wanted to approach their members from the bottom up. To do this, the DAE decided to hold a vote at four schools so that their members would determine whether or not their schools would adopt the community school strategy. Over the course of four months, a DAE organizer held information sessions, conducted one-on-ones, and mapped "yes" votes and "no" votes. The vote was approached just like a traditional National Labor Relations Board election campaign. While there wasn't the traditional union-busting counter campaign, there were hurdles due to member skepticism about "another school reform strategy." In the end, the four schools overwhelmingly voted to adopt the community school strategy, and their members and allies successfully pushed for funding from the county and the school board.

Los Angeles

Several years ago in Los Angeles, United Teachers Los Angeles (UTLA) and a number of powerful community organizations in LA started a coalition called Reclaim Our Schools LA (ROSLA). The platform the group developed was visionary and included a demand for community school funding. While ROSLA was still forming, the education landscape in Los Angeles shifted dramatically, with the loss of a pro-union school board majority. The shift was funded by a group of billionaires, led by Eli Broad. Before the new board was seated, ROSLA worked with the outgoing school board president and board to pass a resolution supportive of community schools. The resolution, which the board passed unanimously, called for the creation of a Community Schools Implementation Team (CSIT) composed of district leaders, community-based organizations and nonprofits, academics, and labor organizations. After a year of work that ROSLA led, CSIT submitted recommendations to the superintendent. At the same time, UTLA was engaged in a bargaining for the common good campaign that was aligned to the ROSLA platform. Years of deep member and community engagement preceded the negotiations, and eventually the 2019 strike. The district resisted ROSLA's bargaining proposals and eventually offered good pay and benefits, consistently leaving community school funding off the table. The bargaining team, which included ROSLA members, decided to stay on strike until their non-economic key priorities were agreed to, which included funding to start 30 community schools. UTLA and the district convened a labor-management community table to oversee the implementation of the community school strategy. There are many lessons from LA, but two important ones are: 1) build coalition power to win your priorities *and* make sure you maintain enough power to ensure your priorities are implemented with fidelity; and 2) build a community school implementation table that has real authority to make decisions, and make sure coalition partners are members.

Hillsborough, Florida

In Hillsborough, Florida, the Hillsborough Classroom Teachers Association worked with community organizations and the district to pass a community school resolution and policy. Today, Hillsborough is home to six community schools. The union is a lead partner in the implementation of Hillsborough's community schools. Borrowing a page from Los Angeles, Hillsborough created a labor-management community table to oversee the implementation of their community schools. Even though their program is only in its first year, they have already started to produce great outcomes.

Las Cruces, New Mexico

In 2015, Las Cruces, New Mexico, had an anti-union school board majority, a superintendent aligned with the worst aspects of education reform, and a new, determined education coalition that was eager to make big changes. (See Guisbond & Neill, p. 328.) In 2020, Las Cruces opened its fourth community school, there is now a friendly school board and superintendent, and nine new state-funded community schools recently opened after legislation passed last year appropriating more than $2 million to support community school efforts. All of this happened because the education coalition organized and organized some more. NEA-Las Cruces is a key member of the coalition.

Milwaukee

In Milwaukee, the Milwaukee Teachers' Education Association (MTEA) and the Schools & Communities United coalition convinced the school board to start three community schools as an alternative to draconian alternatives that were part of No Child Left Behind. Soon after, the local United Way got involved to help fund the community school coordinators, which in turn led to an agreement between the school district, the MTEA, and the United Way to be the three organizations to collaboratively lead implementation. As the community schools grew in number to 12, the United Way funded another position to supervise and assist the school-based community school coordinators. According to a recent study by the University of Wisconsin–Madison into the effectiveness of the strategy in Milwaukee, the high school completion rates of the two schools that have used the strategy the longest show more than double the growth of the rest of the district.

Conclusion

The community school strategy works because it is a strategy that grinds its way to equity under the power of the aspirations of students, families, educators, and community members. The concept is simple but its implementation can be challenging. Yet it works in rural, suburban, or urban communities throughout the country. Up until 2010, community schools did not have a powerful institutional force coordinating local, state, and national efforts to scale the strategy. Today, powerful institutions, the teacher unions, have dedicated significant resources to seeding and supporting the growth of community schools across the country. They have done this in collaboration with community school leaders, community organizations, student organizations, and parent organizations. The hope is to escape the pattern of rediscovery described by Dr. John Rogers. Let's hope for the United States' sake that they stick with it, so that one day a young person's dreams are not determined by their ZIP code. ⚑

Kyle Serrette is a senior policy analyst at the National Education Association.

ENDNOTES

[1] O'Day, Jennifer A., and Marshall S. Smith. 2019. *Opportunity for All: A Framework for Quality and Equality in Education.* Harvard Education Press. carnegiefoundation.org/wp-content/uploads/2016/02/ODay-Smith_Systemic_reform.pdf

[2] Maier, Anna, Julia Daniel, Jeannie Oakes, and Livia Lam. Dec. 14, 2017. "Community Schools as an Effective School Improvement Strategy: A Review of the Evidence." Learning Policy Institute. learningpolicyinstitute.org/product/community-schools-effective-school-improvement-report

[3] Poiner, Jessica. Oct. 23, 2019. "So Far, LeBron's I Promise School Is Keeping Its Promise." *Ohio Gadfly Daily.* fordhaminstitute.org/ohio/commentary/so-far-lebrons-i-promise-school-keeping-its-promise

[4] I Promise School website. ipromiseschool.akronschools.com/about/i_p_s_one_pager

[5] Johnston, William R., John Engberg, Isaac M. Opper, Lisa Sontag-Padilla, Lea Xenakis. 2020. "What Is the Impact of the New York City Community Schools Initiative?" RAND Corporation research brief. rand.org/pubs/research_briefs/RB10107.html?utm_campaign=&utm_content=1580746324&utm_medium=rand_social&utm_source=facebook

[6] Reclaim Our Schools LA. 2016. *A Vision to Support Every Student.* reclaimourschoolsla.org/wp-content/uploads/2013/08/Reclaim-Our-Schools-LA-A-Vision-to-Support-Every-Student-December-2016.pdf

Resources on Community Schools

American Federation of Teachers
aft.org/position/community-schools/resources

Coalition for Community Schools
Sponsors biennial national conferences and has many resources on its website, including *Community Schools Playbook: A Practical Guide to Advancing Community School Strategies* by the Partnership for the Future of Learning.
communityschools.org

Center for Popular Democracy
Community Schools: Transforming Struggling Schools into Thriving Schools, published by the Center for Popular Democracy, the Coalition for Community Schools, and the Southern Education Foundation.
populardemocracy.org

Journey for Justice Alliance
A network of more than two dozen community organizations that organize to improve public schools, stop school privatization, and promote transformative community schools.
j4jalliance.com

National Education Association
The Six Pillars of Community Schools Toolkit: NEA Resource Guide for Educators, Families & Communities
nea.org

Partnership for the Future of Learning
A helpful toolkit on the nuts and bolts of developing community schools.
Community Schools Playbook: A Practical Guide to Advancing Community Schools Strategies
futureforlearning.org/2019/04/19/community-schools-playbook/

"You Have to Stop. You Have to Create Space"

A union takes the lead in implementing restorative justice

BY LEIGH DINGERSON

G rowing inequality, poverty and homelessness, racism and the rise of open white supremacy, mass violence—the context of our daily lives and those of our students don't get left behind at the schoolhouse door. They impact our moods and our relationships with others in conscious and unconscious ways.

Too many schools have responded by hunkering down; adopting "no excuses" policies to control children and "hardening," reacting as if violence is inevitable; strengthening security systems; staffing schools with police officers; and even arming educators.

Taking a different direction, though, hundreds of schools across the country are turning away from rigid, compliance-based discipline and school management strategies and turning instead toward restorative justice, a school culture shift that views relationship building as a more effective way to strengthen school climate, make schools safer, and improve learning and teaching conditions.

One strong example can be seen in Howard County, Maryland, where the educators' union is leading an initiative to transform school climate by implementing restorative justice in a cohort that includes six of the district's 77 schools. And although the work is in its early stages and has yet to win the financial backing of the district, it appears to be making a difference for educators as well as students.

Howard County, Maryland: A Small District, Learning to Do the Right Thing

Howard County sits about midway between Baltimore and Washington, D.C. It is solidly suburban, and home to some of the most affluent communities in the state.

The Howard County Public School System (HCPSS) serves 58,000 students in 77 schools. The student body is diverse: 36 percent white, 24 percent Black/African American, 22 percent Asian, and 11 percent Latino. But that diversity is not as pronounced at the building level. Most of the schools are comparatively segregated. And most of the district's educators—86 percent of them—are white.

Though lauded as one of the most successful districts in the state when it comes to academic outcomes, the HCPSS has not escaped the impacts of racism. Black students in Howard County are between two and 18 times more likely to be suspended than the overall student population. Data show that nearly half of suspensions are for subjective offenses such as disrespect or disruption. And a recent effort by the district to redraw school boundary lines to adjust to population shifts in the county and attempt to diversify the schools by both race and economic status surfaced deep divisions between communities.

Restorative Justice Circles as an "Activity" . . . or Real Transformation?

For many years, the district has offered professional development in *restorative practices* as an "alternative to suspension." But, says Colleen Morris, president of the Howard County Education Association (HCEA), it has not equipped educators with the necessary foundation or knowledge to be effective practitioners. The

ERIK RUIN

trainings were shallow and inconsistent. And the use of circles focused primarily on students. While Maryland has articulated an option for schools to use restorative approaches, it has been marketed as something you do *to* students.

This approach to restorative justice does not shift school culture, Morris asserts. It should not be simplified as an alternative to suspension. Restorative justice, when implemented correctly, must begin with the *staff*, to ensure that they truly understand, believe in, and support the practices associated with the overall philosophy.

Three years ago, the HCEA decided to take a more active role in introducing a comprehensive approach to restorative justice in schools. Morris herself was frustrated with the professional development the district was offering, which, she said with thinly veiled sarcasm, "trained the entire district staff in about 20 minutes." Now, Morris cringes at the thought of that training. "It was just so wrong on so many levels," she says. Some schools were getting the 20-minute version of the training, others were getting slightly more. But the result of the trainings wasn't a transformation in school culture. It was increasing skepticism and cynicism among the district's educators, who began to believe that restorative justice didn't work, and certainly didn't meet their needs or the needs of their students.

When Morris stepped into the union presidency in 2017, she had a lot on her plate: building relationships with the superintendent, increasing the union membership, and impending work on policies and essential state funding. But she also wanted the union to play a role in figuring out how to implement restorative justice with fidelity. That year she also met Dwanna Nicole, a civil rights advocate who has been working to dismantle the school-to-prison pipeline and helping districts implement restorative justice for years.

> ## What is a circle?
>
> The most comprehensive restorative justice practice is a circle. A circle can be used proactively, to develop relationships and build community, or reactively, to respond to harm. Circles provide people an opportunity to speak and listen to one another in a safe atmosphere and allow educators and students to be heard and offer their own perspectives. Circles can also be used to celebrate students, begin and end the day, and discuss difficult issues.
>
> Source: Restorative Practices Guide. schottfoundation.org/sites/default/files/restorative-practices-guide.pdf

Identifying Committed School Leaders First

Morris collaborated with Nicole, who works with practitioners nationwide through the Restorative Justice Partnership, to provide a series of professional development offerings. In the first year, 11 targeted schools were invited to participate. The schools were invited based on their suspension and referral data, and level of high-needs students. The HCEA also invited schools based on union surveys of overall morale at the buildings.

Participants were required to come in teams, including the school's principal, interested educators, and at least one community member. These initial opportunities included both four-day peace circle trainings and one-day workshops on the school-to-prison pipeline and restorative justice.

Out of these initial trainings, four cohort schools were originally chosen. What they were looking for and found, says Nicole, was school leadership that was interested and committed to the work. "In the end, the principals chose us," she says.

Research on restorative justice implementation has found that one of the strongest indicators of success in transforming school culture through restorative justice is strong leadership. "You have to have someone at the top who really believes in it," says Nicole. "You can have staff that want to do it, but if you don't have the building leader on board, it won't happen schoolwide. And to do it right, it has to be a whole-school effort."

The current six-school cohort in Howard County includes two high schools, two middle schools, and two elementary schools. One of the high schools—Long Reach High School—won the agreement of the district to create a 9th-grade academy called the Reach Academy as an initiative immersed in restorative justice. The academy draws about 100 entering 9th graders each year. The students are selected through conversations between middle and high school educators looking for students who are performing fine in middle school, but who could excel if provided with intentional supports and motivation. The academy centralizes relationships as the key to learning. Students play a role in building school community, participate in an accelerated course progression, and experience an infusion of co-curricular activities with the intention to increase engagement in school.

"You Have to Breathe"

The work of implementing restorative justice well is time-consuming and requires a lot from educators, including a real shift in mindset.

Plenty of educators have been resistant, Morris notes. For the most part, that's because they've been frustrated by professional development in positive behavior practices that are inadequately taught and poorly implemented. "We have to demonstrate that this is different," she says.

Josh Wasilewski, principal at Long Reach High School, agrees. "The restorative practices professional development originally offered by the school system placed an emphasis on how to facilitate community circles as a means to develop a sense of community and trust in an instructional setting. It wasn't until I experienced the four-day restorative justice training that I realized the philosophy extended way beyond meeting in a circle. The training provided a space for participants to explore and understand the philosophy behind restorative justice as well as learn the important essential elements of facilitating a peace circle. It was by far the most powerful professional learning I have ever experienced."

The power of these trainings notwithstanding, one of the biggest challenges for educators is the lack of time. They are under so much pressure to get everything done, and it feels impossible to take the time to fully engage in the training and practices necessary to fully embrace restorative justice. In response, the union has arranged substitute days so that they are able to pull educators into these intensive trainings in small groups, so that only a few of them are away from the building at a time.

This time-consuming process is critical to the culture shift, though. "One of the biggest takeaways from the process and the trainings is exactly this: You have to stop. You have to create space and time for your students if you want to build the relationships that are at the heart of this school culture shift. If something has to give, you have to change your mindset that the rewards—what you're going to get back and how you're going to change the culture of the school—are fundamental to investing this time in your students," says Morris. "You have to breathe."

Finding the Right Resources

A key partner in the Howard County effort has been Dr. Kevin F. Gilbert, director of the HCPSS Office of Diversity, Equity, and Inclusion. He has been supportive and willing to advocate for restorative justice within the administration, as well as assist with hands-on training and implementation. The district is viewed almost as a cohort in and of itself, Gilbert notes. The union's strong relationship with his office, as well as with the superintendent, have been invaluable.

The role of the union and the union's president has been critical. "Colleen has really showed up as union president. She's in the schools, at the meetings, at the trainings," says Nicole. Her presence neutralizes some of the educators' fears and concerns.

But the district has so far not been able to designate funding for this work, other than allowing some of the professional development funds to be utilized. To date, most of the funding has come directly from the union. Morris estimates that the union has invested about $200,000 toward this work in the last 18 months. In 2019, the union won a new grant from the NEA to help with implementation. But more and ongoing funding is needed.

At the core of the work are the four-day peace circle trainings, which take place regularly and with different groups of people. To ensure that the needs of those trained continue to be met, the HCEA offers a monthly space for them to build community and reflect on their practice and experiences. Principals and their restorative justice teams receive an implementation training every summer before the school year begins. And now, students are being trained to keep circles, even at the elementary school level. "This work is about sharing power, and what better way to do that than to have students keep circles on topics that are of interest to them and their peers," says Nicole.

So far, the union has been able to cobble together the resources needed to continue. But at some point, they know the district will have to step up and embrace the work.

Challenges and Next Steps

Challenges to the work of transforming school climate through restorative justice can come from outside. In 2019, Howard County Superintendent Dr. Michael J. Martirano announced an effort to redraw attendance zones to better balance the schools, not just for race, but also for economic diversity. The system is a high-performing one overall, but segregation inside individual schools needed to be addressed.

The proposal ignited an ugly episode. Communities were angry that some children would be moved to other schools. During the public comment period there was racist language used to describe a number of schools within the county, including some of the cohort schools. It was a painful moment. The cohort schools were able to host healing circles to address and acknowledge the harm and think through ways they could support each other moving forward.

One challenge continues to be engaging impacted families, particularly to help drive political will inside the district to fund the work. Too many impacted families feel that they've never been listened to at their child's school. And issues of race and class play out between families, educators, and administrators. But including families in this work is vital, Nicole says. The Restorative Justice Partnership has been able to assist with this effort. By partnering with the union and school district, they recently held a public panel discussion about restorative justice and the ongoing work within the cohort schools. The panel included students, families, staff, and administrators from within Howard County; Paterson, New Jersey; and Denver.

> Issues of race and class play out between families, educators, and administrators.

"We are moving the needle," says Morris, albeit slowly.

More educators are coming to the union, asking for the training. Nicole says that the focus for 2020 was to get more people engaged. "We need to work with the folks who really want to do this. Sure, some educators are waiting to see if this is just the shiny new thing that eventually goes away. For now, we are focused on investing in those who are committed, while continuing to provide education and resources to those who need and want it."

Beyond the Reach Academy, the union doesn't have much quantitative data on the results of their work yet. But experiential indicators are beginning to be reported. "To see the changes that have occurred since implementing restorative justice proves to me that all of the work that our staff and students have done to build community and relationships has positively impacted the day-to-day life at Swansfield," says Allison Birmingham, a pre-kindergarten teacher at Swansfield Elementary.

Laurel Porter, her school principal, agrees. "Staff are truly learning and growing together! The relationships being built among our staff are ultimately having a positive impact on our students. Those relationships are important when working and supporting students and creating a network of people to support each other and the students we work with," says Porter. "One of the most telling signs is that we have staff members who are asking for more professional learning. While at first they thought they should see immediate change, they have learned and recognize that it takes time to do this right, and they have a real desire to do just that. People believe in the power of us taking this journey together and believe we owe it to every student who walks through our doors each morning."

For Colleen Morris, the academic outcomes will happen. But in these initial years, the cultural change has been gratifying. "We have been able to breathe. When we can create space for our educators to breathe, they'll be able to create space for their students to breathe." ▪

Leigh Dingerson is a former community organizer, and currently a freelance writer and researcher on community and labor struggles for education justice. She is the author, most recently, of Building the Power to Reclaim Our Schools, *a case study on the 2019 Los Angeles teachers' strike.*

RESOURCES

- Boyes-Watson, Carolyn, and Kay Pranis. 2014. *Circle Forward: Building a Restorative School Community.* Living Justice Press.

- Costello, Bob, Joshua Wachtel, and Ted Wachtel. 2009. *The Restorative Practices Handbook for Teachers, Disciplinarians, and Administrators.* International Institute for Restorative Practices.

- Editors of *Rethinking Schools*. Fall 2014. "Restorative Justice: What It Is and Is Not." *Rethinking Schools* 29(1). rethinkingschools.org/articles/restorative-justice

- Restorative Justice Partnership. rjpartnership.org

- Schott Foundation Restorative Practices Working Group. 2014. *Restorative Practices: Fostering Healthy Relationships & Promoting Positive Discipline in Schools: A Guide for Educators.* Schott Foundation. schottfoundation.org/sites/default/files/restorative-practices-guide.pdf

- Stutzman Amstutz, Lorraine, and Judy H. Mullet. 2005. *The Little Book of Restorative Discipline for Schools: Teaching Responsibility; Creating Caring Climates.* Good Books.

Teacher Strikes Boost Fight for Racial Justice in Schools

BY SAMANTHA WINSLOW

During their 2019 strike, Los Angeles teachers demanded an end to random searches where students were yanked out of class to be frisked. By the time they walked back into work, they had won a partial victory.

As of 2020, these searches were coming to an end districtwide—landing a blow against racism in the schools.

LA teacher union activists, like their counterparts in Chicago, Seattle, St. Paul, and other cities, are making contract demands to confront segregation, underfunding, and the criminalization of the students they teach—problems that hit Black and Latino students hardest.

The LA strike elevated a wide range of demands, including smaller class sizes and more nurses and social workers. After listening to students about their top concerns, strikers also highlighted the issue of random searches.

The district started this practice more than 25 years ago after school shootings, with the stated goal of keeping weapons out. But as of 2019, LA was one of very few districts using random searches—only 4 percent do nationwide.

Students are pulled out of class while administrators and security officers search their bags and scan them with a metal detector. When these staff are short-handed, teachers and counselors are sometimes asked to do the wanding.

Not So Random

A UCLA report on two years of searches (2013–15) found that overwhelmingly, ordinary items were confiscated, not guns and weapons. Contraband included markers, highlighters, white-out, lighters, and body spray.

And the "random" searches weren't so random. The student-led group Students Deserve, which also includes parents and teachers, reported that students in magnet schools and advanced classes were rarely searched. Black students got searched most often.

Students said it made them feel like suspects at their own schools. Marshé Doss, a senior at Dorsey High School during the strike, had been searched and had her hand sanitizer confiscated; a school official accused her of bringing it to school to get high.

"As Black and Brown students, we have all of these things piled up against us," said Doss. "I had so many questions after that experience."

Teacher Sharonne Hapuarachy sponsors the Students Deserve chapter at Dorsey High. When the random search happened in her classroom, she was shocked. "It was really disturbing and scary for me, even as the teacher," she said. She was taken aback by the way the students were spoken to. "It felt very serious; it creates a sense of anxiety."

Made Them Bargain

Ending random searches was one on a long list of union demands that the district did not legally have to bargain over. The district ignored these—until the walkout.

"Because the strike brought out public opinion in support of our issues," said Arlene Inouye, secretary of United Teachers Los Angeles (UTLA), "we were able to leverage that at the end to get things we would never get before."

In the deal that ended the strike, the district committed to a pilot program, letting 14 schools apply to opt out of the searches for the 2019–20 school year; 14 more would become eligible the following year.

Other union wins were class size caps, more staff, legal support for undocumented students, and green space on school campuses.

But the strike momentum led to a bigger win on the issue. In May, a school board seat opened up. With UTLA's help, a union ally won the seat. And in June, the board voted to sunset the random searches with the end of the 2019–20 school year.

Joined Student Activists

Four years before the strike, teachers came to union leaders complaining about the searches, Inouye said.

She recalled one teacher in particular who brought the issue to her attention. "He never thought that the union would be interested in the issue," Inouye said. "Of course we would," was the leaders' response, she said, "but we have to build and organize around it."

Teachers and counselors said when they were asked to conduct the searches, it broke the trust they were trying to build with students. They also argued the searches were a waste of time that could be spent learning.

So UTLA teamed up with Students Deserve and the American Civil Liberties Union to launch the Students Not Suspects campaign. They organized forums and protested at school board meetings. High school students designed and handed out 18,000 #studentsnotsuspects buttons. Students and parents spoke up about why searches weren't making schools safe.

"We fear it [being stopped and searched] outside of school," said Amee Monroy, a Students Deserve activist who is a Dorsey senior this year. "We shouldn't have to fear it in school."

Students had been organizing on this issue since 2016. But "having UTLA on our side added way more people to the movement," Monroy said. And the strike added big leverage.

Counselors Not Cops

LA teachers aren't alone. The Chicago Teachers Union (CTU) has been outspoken about the racism of that city's school system.

Schools with many students of color are disproportionately deprived of funding and staffing. And before their 2012 strike, Chicago teachers battled a wave of school closings in parts of the city where the district should have been adding resources, not subtracting them.

When Seattle teachers struck in 2015, they demanded funds and training for every school to form an equity team, which would identify and change racist discipline policies. They won these teams in 30 schools.

A central demand in St. Paul teachers' near-strike in 2016 was alternatives to harsh discipline practices that disproportionately affected students of color. They won that push.

In 2017, teacher activists in Philadelphia and Seattle first organized a week of action on the theme Black Lives Matter at School. Since then, a growing number of unions and grassroots education activists around the country have participated every February. One united demand is to end "zero-tolerance" discipline policies that impose mandatory suspensions or push students into the criminal system for certain infractions.

Many school districts have moved to limit suspensions. But unions assert in bargaining that it's not enough just to change the rules. What students need instead is more time and attention from trained adults; districts have to put money into staffing.

In fall 2019, teachers in Chicago made racial justice demands again when they walked out for 11 days. On top of guaranteed nurses, counselors, and librarians in every school, they proposed that the district allow high schools to reduce the number of police officers stationed inside and redirect that funding to hire staffers trained to counsel students.

They also demanded that the district stop cooperating with Immigration and Customs Enforcement and with the city's police database of gang members.

A Learning Process

The CTU has protested the decline of Black teachers in the district—from 40 to 20 percent in two decades. It calls for the district to create pipelines to train and recruit teachers of color.

The union works in coalition with police accountability groups. When the city says there's no more money for schools, teachers point to its creation of a $95 million cop academy.

Students on Strike

Dorsey High School students who were active in the Students Not Suspects campaign supported UTLA's six-day strike in 2019.

The district was trying to keep schools open during the strike, but student activists encouraged their peers to increase the pressure by not attending school.

Instead, 150 students attended a block party nearby. They made art and played music, then headed over to the school board for a protest and sit-in to show their support for striking UTLA members.

Students from different schools joined candlelight vigils and protests at the superintendent's Malibu mansion and at school board members' houses, demanding that the board meet the teachers' demands and end the strike.

For Amee Monroy, an 11th grader at the time, a standout moment was joining 40,000 UTLA members and supporters in an enormous march through downtown LA despite pouring rain.

"I will always think about holding my umbrella and being in a sea of red," she said. "It was so fun, and we were making change at the same time."

All this action for racial justice didn't crystallize overnight. It has taken discussion for members to build a consensus that school climate is a union issue. And those discussions aren't over.

"There's a lot more work to do to help people think about this differently, how racism presents itself economically [in terms of allocation of resources]," said CTU's chief of staff, former social studies teacher Jennifer Johnson. "Our students don't need punitive systems, but support systems."

In Chicago and LA last year, district negotiators spent months dismissing demands that went beyond legally sanctioned topics like wages and benefits.

"Of course the district said no at first," Inouye said. "They weren't going to hear any 'common good' demands." It took strikes to make the districts move.

The CTU did not win its demand to swap out school police for support staff. But it did win increased staffing for nurses, social workers, and therapists, and new contract language about restorative justice, an alternative approach to student discipline that emphasizes solving problems and making amends rather than punishing infractions.

Next, Pepper Spray

In LA, the Students Deserve coalition as of 2020 had set its sights on ending the use of pepper spray against students. In one incident at Dorsey High, school police used pepper spray on students who were fighting—but also ended up spraying other students who were trying to break up the fight or just walking by.

Since the random searches were coming to an end, Students Deserve presented the school board with its list of proposed school safety alternatives. The students recommended adding more staff to offer help and guidance. They also recommended that the district involve the community, rather than the police, in a "safe passage" program to provide adult supervision on routes where kids and teens walk home from school.

Student activists were to organize this campaign the same way they'd organized the last one, Doss said: "talking to students, doing direct action, doing things bigger."

For the union, taking on the issue of random searches has uncovered new leaders like Hapuarachy. She said campaigns like this one have gotten her more active in the union. For her, UTLA's mission includes "fighting for racial justice in schools, making sure there aren't pockets of schools where students are being treated differently [than students are] in other parts of the city." ⬚

Samantha Winslow writes about K-12 education and organizes with teachers and teachers unions. She is the former co-director of Labor Notes. She was previously an organizer for SEIU-United Healthcare Workers West in California and later for the breakaway National Union of Healthcare Workers .

A version of this article appeared in *Labor Notes* #491, and in the Labor Notes blog on Feb. 7, 2020. Reprinted with permission.

SECTION THREE

PUSHING FROM THE BOTTOM UP

I teach my Students to STAND UP for themselves and here's my TURN

The Power and Challenges of Social Justice Caucuses

BY MICHELLE STRATER GUNDERSON

n a media interview during the 2012 teachers' strike in Chicago, a reporter asked me, "Do you speak for the union?" I thought about this for a minute, then replied, "No. Because we have a democratic process at the Chicago Teachers Union, my union speaks for me."

I have not always felt this way. For many years during my three decades as a Chicago teacher, our union was run in what is called a "business" or "industrial" union model. It focused almost exclusively on the contractual needs of membership, such as pay and benefits. It was not until 2010 when the Caucus of Rank and File Educators (CORE) gained leadership in the Chicago Teachers Union (CTU) that I felt I had a voice in my union and that my union was ready to fight for the schools our children deserve.

Since 2012 I have been in leadership of CORE. I have also been an active leader in the United Caucuses of Rank and File Educators (UCORE), a national network of social justice caucuses.

Individuals can't transform their unions alone. But working together in rank-and-file caucuses can be vehicles of such change. In the last decade caucuses have had a meteoric rise and will likely play a significant role in the labor movement in coming years. In this article I give an insider view into the workings and purposes of union caucuses. To find additional details on caucus work, read *How to Jump-Start Your Union: Lessons from the Chicago Teachers*, published by Labor Notes.

What Is a Union Caucus, and How Do They Work?

A union caucus is a group of members who share a social and political analysis of their union and come together to try to change it. It may be a particular issue—such as the imposition of an odious district policy that the union has ignored. It might be general concerns about the lack of member input or lack of union leadership in the time of crisis. At times caucuses focus on winning union elections.

In the process of forming, caucuses often see the need to develop a shared set of principles. The mission statement of UCORE consolidated the principles of more than 25 caucuses that are members. This is the preamble:

We are social justice educators and unionists committed to creating schools and workplaces that advance economic justice, racial justice, and democracy. We call for equitable public education as a human right. We assert that the workplace rights of educators are an essential element of public education and that the well-being of communities in which our children live is as much a part of our mission as the work we do in our schools.

Most caucuses also agree to a set of rules or bylaws in order to keep work focused and productive. An important aspect of a caucus is that it's member-driven and members are able to have deep discussions to build unity around goals and strategies. In CORE, the members elect a steering committee that is in charge of general organizing. It gets input from members during monthly meetings. There are also informal ways for members to meet with one another through regional meetings, book clubs, and Listserv discussions.

Emergence of Caucuses

Over the past 10 years we have seen an emergence of teacher union caucuses across the country—in urban centers such as Los Angeles, Philadelphia, and New York—and in entire states as in Massachusetts, North Carolina, and New Jersey. In most instances, the concerns of these caucuses have roots in the negative impact of corporate education reform and the failure of entrenched union leadership to react appropriately.

In my case, I saw the increased amount of standardized testing completely change the culture and curriculum in my school. I joined CORE as a place to put my energy fighting what I saw as a war on the work teachers do. I also saw austerity budget measures in Chicago being used as an excuse to attack our union. Schools were being starved of resources, and teachers were being blamed for our "failing schools."

Each caucus member has individual reasons for joining and yet what we are experiencing in schools is also universal. There are no safe places in the United States where teachers are not affected by what Diane Ravitch calls "vulture philanthropists" like the Koch brothers, who use their wealth to promote an anti-union agenda, or the Gates or Walton foundations that have negatively influenced education policy for more than two decades. When Barbara Madeloni, former president of the Massachusetts Teachers Association and a leader in the Educators for a Democratic Union caucus, talks about neoliberalism, she puts it in a broad perspective: "We're not just fighting the Koch brothers. We're fighting every Koch brother that's ever been."

Social Justice Unionism

The term social justice unionism can mean different things, depending on the context and priorities of activists and caucuses. One way of defining the concept is to compare it to other union models. (See Editors, p. 102.) The main union model historically has been "business" or "industrial" unionism, which describes a framework of unionism that is transactional—concerned mostly with the "bread-and-butter" issues such as pay, conditions, and benefits. That model is often accompanied by a top-down leadership style. A second model is "professional unionism" that focuses on promoting teacher leadership in educational matters. Social justice unionism builds on the strengths of these two models but goes well beyond them. It is interactional, with members working with each other and the community to address broad social issues as well as bread-and-butter issues and pedagogical concerns. A key element of social justice unionism is that it involves bottom-up grassroots organizing, and that it promotes democratic practices throughout the union instead of a hierarchal leadership style where union members only look to elected officers and staff to take care of member concerns.

> We cannot compartmentalize our teaching lives when so many outside factors influence our work and the lives of the students we teach.

During a CORE steering meeting, Karen Lewis, former president of the Chicago Teachers Union, said, "Love doesn't end when we walk out of school." This is one of the foundational tenets of social justice unionism. We cannot compartmentalize our teaching lives when so many outside factors influence our work and the lives of the students we teach.

The terms "social justice" and "social justice unionism" can be watered down or co-opted. Some activists and leaders believe that passing resolutions in solidarity with different struggles (often a positive thing) makes a union a "social justice union." Others label programs "social justice," but because of top-down leadership and a lack of membership involvement, such programs are less effective than they might be. A new leader or leadership team can't just declare that by virtue of their politics they are now a social justice union. It's hard work. Real transformation of a union encompasses change in many areas: internal decision-making processes, vision, campaigns, addressing race and gender issues, relationships with parents and communities, and much more.

Caucuses Transforming Unions

A key way a caucus can push their unions to be more democratic is to analyze how power is structured inside the union. Madeloni describes it clearly, "The power is not in the leadership. It is in us." In other words, we—all members—are the union.

To make that a reality often requires both structural changes as well as a change in the mindset of members. This might include organizing for changes in union election rules, the composition of bargaining committees, or who gets released to do union work. In some cases this leads to struggles over amending the union's constitution or challenging age-old practices.

Caucus work can also seed union democracy by providing space outside the normal union structures to have deep discussions about the direction of the union.

An example of a structural change in Chicago was the expansion of the bargaining team in the 2019 contract negotiations. Our team had more than 40 members, chosen for their leadership in CORE and committee work throughout the union. A small team of elected union officers wasn't in a position to know the working conditions of such a large district with the various job descriptions and types of schools. Broadening the leadership can be clumsy, but it does increase the likelihood that contract demands reflect a wider range of members and concerns.

"When we fight, we win" is a common phrase used in organizing. A large part of caucus work is deciding which issues to address and building the capacity in members to organize around these issues while simultaneously modeling how the entire union should organize. There are clear differences between just mobilizing people to come to an event or rally and doing the hard work of deep organizing that builds real union power. (See Schirmer, p. 248.)

> Broadening the leadership can be clumsy, but it does increase the likelihood that contract demands reflect a wider range of members and concerns.

Amy Roat, a leader in the Caucus of Working Educators in Philadelphia, summed it up this way: "You can't just do one thing and expect movement."

Lewis built a three-pronged test for us to measure whether or not to move forward on an idea. She would say, "Does it build our power? Does it build our strength? Does it unite us?"

Caucuses aren't always oppositional. They can help union leadership make strategic decisions. We know our working conditions and can better gauge whether our fellow workers will embrace proposed strategies or campaigns. For example, when the CTU decided to have informational pickets at our work sites caucus members helped our union develop the literature and cover schools in the district that did not yet have strong school site organization. This normalizes the importance of organizing union power at the work site so that the leadership or union staff doesn't swoop in to solve a problem. And when members learn to fight collectively at the building level the entire union is stronger for larger struggles.

Challenges of Caucus Work

The agenda of social justice caucuses can be incredibly ambitious. We seek to change the social and racial inequities driven by government and corporate entities that have vast resources and power. We are the Davids in the current struggle with corporate Goliaths. We are trying to transform and help lead teacher unions that have many strengths and in some cases much baggage. Because of the enormity of the tasks, the dialogue, decision-making, and resulting tensions inside caucuses can be difficult.

The purpose of caucus work is to bring people together who share a common understanding of how to grow this work, but this does not mean that there is agreement on all issues. There is often discord at CORE meetings, and the debate can take lots of time. None of the decisions are easy. We have to constantly reflect as to whether or not we are living our values as a caucus.

Another dilemma that caucuses face is to not replicate the power and privilege that is omnipresent in broader society. Many union locals have long-established leadership that is removed from the workers in the schools and oftentimes women and people of color have historically been marginalized. That can happen in caucuses as well.

And finally, the day-to-day life of teaching under increasingly demanding working conditions is hard enough, to say nothing of working in a union caucus at the same time. "We need to talk about the truth of how exhausting this work is," says Roat. This speaks to the importance of building large enough caucuses so that the load can be shared among many people. Someone has to order the pizzas, print the agendas, book the meeting spaces, make the phone calls, and monitor social media. The inner workings of a caucus require lots of unglamorous but essential work. A few people can't do it alone.

Conclusion

If you are currently working in a school, ask yourself, "What is our union doing to promote education justice?" Think of your role as an educator and the world you wish for your students and yourself. If your union is stagnant and reluctant to fight for students, teachers, and communities, it is time for deep and structural change. This is the purpose of a caucus. Consider joining one or creating one with your colleagues.

In the end, we want to put ourselves in a place that protects children and the integrity of our work as educators. As a parent at my school said to me recently, "A Chicago without CORE becomes an uglier place." ◙

Michelle Strater Gunderson is a teacher and union activist from Chicago. She is a 34-year teaching veteran and currently teaches 1st grade in the Chicago Public Schools. She serves as trustee for the Chicago Teachers Union and is the former co-chair of the Caucus of Rank and File Educators (CORE).

Lessons in Social Justice Unionism

An interview with former Chicago Teachers Union president Karen Lewis

In 2008 Karen Lewis was a chemistry teacher, one of eight Chicago teachers who formed the Caucus of Rank and File Educators (CORE) to fight school closings. Lewis was elected president of CTU in 2010 along with a slate of CORE members. In 2012, as president of a transformed, democratic Chicago Teachers Union (CTU), she led the 30,000-member union in a successful strike in the city that has been a launchpad for opposition to neoliberal education strategies. This interview with Lewis was conducted in 2012 by Jody Sokolower, Rethinking Schools' *managing editor at that time. Lewis retired in 2018.*

Set the scene for us: What were the issues that led to the Chicago teachers' strike this fall?

The strike was a result of 15 to 25 years of anger about being blamed for conditions that are beyond our control. That's part of it. The other part was a clear rebuke to the mayor and his friends about the top-down "reform" agenda and how it absolutely does not address the needs in the schools.

As soon as Rahm Emanuel [President Obama's former chief of staff] came to town to run for mayor, he had as his education advisor the head of a charter school network, Juan Rangel. We knew from the very beginning this was going to be an ugly, bitter fight. Once Emanuel won the primary, before the general election, he was already heavily dabbling in Springfield and insisting that we not have the right to strike. Working hand in hand with Jonah Edelman from what I call "Stand on Children" [Stand for Children], he tried to raise the bar so high that we would have our right to strike theoretically, but wouldn't have it in reality. They got legislation passed that meant we need 75 percent of our entire membership—not our voting membership—to authorize a strike.

Our membership was incensed; this was a law carved out just for Chicago. My response was: "Brothers and sisters, if we don't have 75 percent of our members in favor of a strike, we shouldn't strike. A strike is not something you do lightly." Then we spent more than a year talking to members about the contract, getting them involved in the contract fight, getting their wishes and desires as part of the proposal that we presented to the board.

The parents understood that the mayor was bullying us. Parents also understood that we were being blamed and attacked for stuff that had nothing to do with how we managed our schools. They were clear about that. But we were adamant: We have a contract; we expect you to follow that contract.

Because you wanted the extra time to organize?
Absolutely. Had to have it. We were not mobilized, we were not organized, we were not ready. We needed the extra time to organize, but also to plan for the better day.

In the past, union leadership always said, "Save your money, we might go on strike." But that's not how you get people ready to strike.

We did not want to strike. I assumed that Emanuel would do everything he could to settle it before we had a strike. I was very wrong about that. We had a lot of pressure not to strike from politicians and advocacy organizations. But all along, we were very open about what we were going to do and how we were going to achieve it.

Building for the Strike

When did you realize that you might need to strike?

About when we announced it.

You thought they would settle?

I knew they would settle because they said they wanted to. Finally I said, "Well, I guess you don't want to enough."

How did you prepare for the strike?

We had a timeline based on the new law and we backwards-mapped based on what we would need to do if we were going to strike in September. We wanted to be prepared for it. Most unions aren't prepared for a strike. It's more a threat than a reality.

We created contract action committees in every school. We created an organizing department; our union never had an organizing department. We created a research department that we never had before. Between organizing, research, and political action, we had the ability to go to schools and talk to people about what meant the most to them. One thing we did was get and use data. We asked people, "What do you think? What do you want?" We went on listening tours for a year before.

We started talking to our members, building by building, pointing out that the board had given us a list of proposals that basically gutted our contract. Then we started with simple things like showing solidarity—wearing red on Friday. That became a big campaign and, as we got close to the end of the school year, people were wearing red everywhere. So a principal would say, "You can't wear red on Friday." We told our members, "Look, if you all wear red on Friday, the principal can't write you all up. So here is a way to address your principal and show that you are in solidarity with one another."

There are things that happen in a building that are out of the contract and there's nothing you can do: "The principal's being mean to me," for instance. There's no grievance you can write. But what you can do is figure out how to solve the problem. A lot of times if you talk to other members about a teacher who is being targeted by the administration, they'll say, "Oh, that's one of the crazies." We tried to have our members embrace disaffected teachers rather than isolate them. "If the problem is over there now," we said, "it's going to happen to you next." Because one of the things that has been happening in Chicago is we have a very high turnover in principals, not just in teachers. They recruit very young people as principals, people who don't see principalship as a culminating event of their career, but as a steppingstone. One of the problems with having young principals is, by and large, they don't have the wisdom of experience. They tend to be more into control, more into data, as opposed to establishing good relationships with teachers and staff. Older veteran teachers are frequently targets of new principals.

We discussed how to have relationships with people in the building you don't necessarily like or agree with, how to conquer differences by doing things as a building, doing things in solidarity.

We also talked about having conversations with parents. I tell our members, "The first conversation you have with a parent cannot start with 'Your child is driving me crazy.' The first conversation should be about how glad you are to have their child in your class, what your plans are for the year, and saying, 'If there is any help I can give you, please call me. I'm sure if we work together, we can make it be a great year for your child.'"

"We Won Some Respect"

What are the most important things you won?
You might be surprised. One of the things our members wanted was the ability to do their own lesson plans and not have lesson plans imposed on them.

We got textbooks and materials on the first day of school.

For clinicians, we got a room with privacy, access to locked doors.

We got a paperwork reduction. If you add something you want us to do in terms of paperwork, you have to subtract something else.

We have an anti-bullying clause because we have some principals who are out of control; they stand up in front of the entire faculty and staff, and belittle and humiliate people.

But the most important thing we won is some respect we didn't have before. The clear understanding that this union moves together. That was a very important win.

What are the most important issues on which you had to compromise or put off a fight until later?
One would be money. Also, we couldn't bargain class size without the board's agreement to put it on the table, because it's a permissive rather than mandatory subject of bargaining, and that means we couldn't strike over it. It's problematic that we could not lower class sizes.

Moving Past "Color Blindness"

When we talked shortly after your election as CTU president in 2010, you explained that one of the results of privatization and layoffs in Chicago (like elsewhere) has been the disproportionate firing of teachers of color, particularly African American teachers. Did the strike address that as an issue?
I had to fight to get language in our contract that says that the district will actively recruit racially diverse staff. I had to fight to get the word racial put in our contract. The essence of the problem is so-called "color blindness." This man who has a lot of power on the other side of the table said, "I don't care what a teacher's color is, I just want good teachers."

I said: "But you are recruiting nothing but young white teachers. There's a problem with that. There's something wrong with your measurement of 'good' if the only people you're hiring to work in Chicago are young white teachers who don't stay here."

I promised him, "I'm going to have a conversation with you about white privilege." There's a whole field of academia on white studies.

But now we have language in our contract that includes the board being obligated to consult with us on a "systematic plan designed to search for and recruit a racially diverse pool of candidates to fill positions," specific training for principals and head administrators on how to implement the plan, and union access to data and periodic meetings to assess progress. And we're going to enforce that.

Changing the Conversation About Education

How do you think the 2012 strike changed the situation in Chicago?

It has awakened a lot of labor unions to what solidarity looks like, what it means. We had so much support from police, from fire, from laborers, from all kinds of different places you wouldn't necessarily expect. It says a lot about working people in Chicago, what kind of pressure we've been under.

The strike has changed the conversation about education in Chicago. It made clear that we are the experts on education, not these consulting firms, not these millionaire dilettantes. They have a lot of money to throw around, but they're not educators. We have taken them to task for that.

It also brought to light that people actually like teachers. You do the polling and it turns out that people like teachers. They don't like the union, but they like teachers. What we tried to show is that the union and teachers are one, we're not separate entities.

What about the union's relationships with community organizations?

We have had school closings and all kinds of dysfunctional stuff happening in Chicago since 2004. So we have built relationships with communities since then. This didn't happen to us overnight. This CTU leadership has had experience working with community organizations for a very long time. We have a community advisory board. Unions never had that before. We're trying to build a coalition of people and organizations to explore policy and have a voice, for goodness' sakes—unlike other organizations that just tell you what you should be doing to support them. We really believe in the democratic process.

Women's Oppression, Women's Leadership

There was such a strong presence of women at every level in the strike. Obviously part of that is because most teachers are women, but do you think there were specific ways that women's leadership and women's strength played a role in the Chicago events?

I do. I think it's part of the clash between myself and the mayor. I don't think he's used to anyone like me who can tell him no. I said, "Look, I want to work with you, but we have to have some modicum of respect here."

I am a woman, so I don't know what's it's like to be a man. I'm Black. I don't know what it's like to be white, and being Black is infinitely more problematic than being female; that's my experience. But I'm looking at an assault on social services. Who provides those? This mayor closed down mental health clinics, curtailed library hours. How are you picking out social workers, librarians, and teachers? By and large, these are occupations that are done by women.

In the CTU today, all of our area vice presidents are women; we have a preponderance of women on our executive board and a preponderance of women in our house of delegates—because that's the nature of teaching.

Fighting with Our Tools, Not the Bosses' Tools

Every city is different, but are there things you have learned that could be helpful to teacher activists in other districts?

I think a democratic, rank and file-driven union doesn't hurt anywhere—a union leadership that is not only responsive but actively seeks input and advice from a variety of members, including people who you don't necessarily share the same politics with.

Some people think you elect a president and the president makes all the decisions for the union. No, that's not it, that's not how it works. In the past, what we saw in Chicago was leadership that tried to stifle opposition. I think that opposition deserves to be heard and deserves to be part of the process. We had a very large rank-and-file bargaining team, 35 people. And they included people from all the different caucuses. Because we're a large local, we have a lot of different factions. We felt that going into the negotiations, we needed to be on the same page with one another because this affects everybody. We went across the political divides and reached out to make that happen.

In a lot of locals, leadership is a little wary of trusting rank-and-file membership with the responsibility of negotiations, but I think it helps so much and informs the process.

We're fighting a corporate strategy that's trying to destroy public education. Union leadership needs to be really honest with its membership about whatever is happening in that community because I can guarantee you, wherever you are, you're going to have a "Stand on Children" or a StudentsFirst, or a Democrats for Education Reform, or something similar. There is nothing like the disinfectant quality of sunshine. You need to point out who these people are, what organizations they belong to, what boards they sit on, how they intertwine with other people who are making decisions about public schools who are not public school parents, teachers, or kids.

> Some people think you elect a president and the president makes all the decisions for the union. No, that's not it, that's not how it works.

It all comes down to how you teach people to fight with the tools they have. We have been fighting with the bosses' tools. We can spend a lot of time doing legislation. I think that's fine—have a legislative approach. But understand that you don't control that process. We can talk about electing the right people, but ultimately, unless we have a statehouse full of teachers and paraprofessionals and clinicians, I don't think we'll get what we want coming out of state legislatures. You need to have good relationships with legislators; you need to have members get in touch and let them know what's important to you. That's one tool. But it's not the only tool.

Our best tool is our ability to put 20,000 people in the street. I don't care if one rich guy buys up all the ad space. The tool that we have is a mass movement. We have the pressure of mass mobilization and organizing.

And we have the first line of defense, which is the parents! We can see parents every day if we want to. Once parents believe that what you're fighting for is something that's good for their children, they're on your side. If you're just fighting for money, you're never going to win the parents over. The parents don't care, except in a situation like ours where we had a longer day—parents do understand about that—but you have to do the work to find out what it is their children really need.

> And we have the first
> line of defense, which
> is the parents!

Another tool is knowing what is on your members' minds. A lot of union leaders tend to think for their members without asking them, "What do you think?" And you need to be honest. You need to say, "This is what we did get, this is what we're going to try to get next time." Because a contract is not the solution to all your problems. A contract will, by necessity, be a compromise. The key is to keep people engaged in the process of movement building. ◼

A longer version of this interview is available in the Winter 2012 Rethinking Schools *(Vol. 27, No. 2).*

The Seattle Educators' Strike

BY JESSE HAGOPIAN

TED S. WARREN | AP

O n Sept. 20, 2015, thousands of Seattle Education Association (SEA) members voted to approve a new contract with the Seattle Public Schools. The vote officially ended a strike that had delayed the first five days of school. The new contract contained many hard-fought social justice wins:

- An end to the use of standardized test scores in teacher evaluations—a huge blow to the testocracy in Seattle and across the country. This victory built on the yearslong struggle of educators, students, and parents in Seattle in opposition to high-stakes tests, including the boycott of the MAP test that began at Garfield High School in 2013 and spread to several other schools in Seattle.
- A guaranteed minimum of 30 minutes recess in every elementary school. Recess had been vanishing in Seattle's schools, particularly those that serve low-income students and students of color. The campaign for recess was launched by a citywide organization months earlier called Lunch and Recess Matter, which was made up of parents, students, and teacher members of Social Equity Educators (SEE), a rank-and-file caucus of social justice educators in Seattle.
- Enforceable caseload caps for educational support associates, such as school psychologists and speech language pathologists, who provide vital support to some of our most vulnerable students.
- Racial Equity Teams. Black Lives Matter activists and racial justice organizers, including Seattle NAACP members who issued a statement supporting the strike, got behind the demand for Racial Equity Teams in every building. The school district originally agreed to teams in only six schools, but the power of the strike pushed the district to agree to anti-racism committees in 30 schools. Given that Seattle schools suspend African American students at four times the rate of white students for the same infractions, it is clear that every school in the city needs to organize actively against inequality and racism.

These were groundbreaking victories. And yet with the overwhelming support of the Seattle public, SEA could have won so many more of the most basic necessities for students and teachers.

It's hard to overstate the outpouring of support for the strike. Marching band students used their pep band anthems to root on striking educators at picket lines around the city, and local businesses donated to the picket lines. Thousands of parents supported the strike actively—from signing petitions, to joining Facebook groups in support, to delivering food to the picket line. One of the greatest developments from the strike was the group Soup for Teachers that formed to bring sustenance and solidarity to picket lines at every school in the district. Liza Rankin, who went on to run for school board in 2019 and win, formed the organization and had many parent volunteers join her. Even the mainstream media reported that parents were in support of the strike and that the educators were winning. In fact, the enthusiasm for educators was so great, Seattle City Council, led by socialist councilmember Kshama Sawant, passed a unanimous resolution in support of the strike.

With this unprecedented outpouring of support, SEE members helped launch the Coalition for the Schools Seattle Deserves (CSSD), to unite parents, students, and community organizations around the city to support the strike. SEE had truly hoped that SEA would organize this kind of coalition with parents and social justice groups, as had been done in cities like Chicago, where there was a strong commitment to a social justice approach to unionism since the Caucus of Rank and File Educators (CORE) won leadership and led a strike in 2012. Leaders in SEE argued that if the union could galvanize the widespread public support into a visible showing of solidarity, they would be able to win so much more at the bargaining table.

The strategy of mass mobilization of membership and community is prerequisite to a social justice union approach, as has been shown in cities around the country. In Los Angeles during their 2019 strike, for example, UTLA organized multiple rallies of the membership that were joined by parents, students, and community—mobilizing some 60,000 people at a time in the streets. Those mobilizations helped give all educators—and especially the bargaining team—the confidence to demand more in their contract. In the end, UTLA reached one of the most impressive union victories in recent history that included a full-time nurse in every school, a full-time librarian in every middle and high school, enforceable class size caps, reduction of standardized testing by 50 percent, and more. Unfortunately, despite the widespread call from the members, including from SEE, SEA refused to organize a single rally of all of its members during the strike. Worse, union officials chastised association representatives who decided to lead their picket line in a march to the school district headquarters to help show solidarity with the bargaining team and show that there was pervasive support for a rally.

While SEA refused to organize a mass rally, SEE and the CSSD joined Grammy-winning singer-songwriter Kimya Dawson to host a benefit concert for the striking teachers that drew many hundreds to Seattle's historic Neptune Theatre. The crowd filled the venue, and this became the only large-scale gathering during the strike. The success of the event was undeniable. Thousands of dollars were raised for those most impacted by missed paychecks. It allowed educators to speak publicly to the issues that mattered most in the strike. Much of the local media attended and captured images of kids getting their faces painted and students learning lessons of collective struggle from their parents and educators. The SEA bargaining team attended briefly, before they had to return to the bargaining table, and it helped to show them the support from the community that existed.

With a visionary set of demands and the overwhelming support of the parents, students, community, and even the Seattle City Council, it was disappointing that the union ended the strike before we achieved all we could at the bargaining table. Seattle is among the nation's top 10 cities for highest cost of living. Educators at that point had not had a cost of living increase in six years, and they are increasingly unable to live in the city where they teach. It was a mistake to agree to raises

> These were groundbreaking victories. And yet with the overwhelming support of the Seattle public, the SEA could have won so many more of the most basic necessities for students and teachers.

ranging from 3 percent the first year to 4.5 percent the third, which couldn't even offset rising healthcare costs.

With the new contract, school nurses were still forced to split their time among several schools and thus unable to provide the care that students deserve. Unfortunately, kids don't get sick only on Mondays, Wednesdays, and Fridays, and we can't have nurses only available at schools on specific days. It is truly outrageous that in the city of Seattle—a municipal area that is home to the two richest people the world has ever known and some of the wealthiest corporations in history—that there are kids who go to a school where their basic health is not cared for. We also know that nursing services are especially important for low-income students—disproportionately Black, Latino, and immigrant—who likely have no health insurance or are underinsured. It is simply stunning to me that the union didn't build a massive publicity campaign and rally, with parents by their side, to demand a full-time nurse in every school, every day. With all the overwhelming support for our strike, we truly missed an opportunity to fight for equity and the well-being of our youth.

The strike achieved lower student-to-teacher ratios in some preschool and special education programs, but the union actually agreed to a 30 percent caseload increase for the special education Access Program. We also acceded to the district's demand to lengthen the school day by 20 minutes. With more of a focus on mass rallies to unite teachers and parents, it is clear that we could have won important victories for students and educators in these areas.

Nonetheless, the strike was an important part of showing educators the purpose and power of unions. The union's demand to end the use of high-stakes testing in teacher evaluation helped educate the public about the misuses of standardized testing and helped support the growing opt-out movement at the time. The strike helped illuminate the issue of disproportionate discipline as a component of the school-to-prison-pipeline. In addition, the strike went a long way toward educating the public about the need to fully fund our schools at the state level. But the most important outcome of the strike won't be found in the fine print of the agreement. The true triumph of this contract battle was the solidarity—between teachers, office professionals, nurses, school librarians, instructional assistants, parents, and community organizations—in the struggle for public schools. When the union decides to fully embrace the power of that solidarity, well, then we can win the schools our children deserve. 🎗

Jesse Hagopian teaches at Garfield High School and is an editor of Rethinking Schools *magazine. Jesse edited the book* More than a Score: The New Uprising Against High Stakes Testing *and co-edited the book* Teaching for Black Lives. *He blogs at IAmAnEducator.com.*

You Need Rank and File to Win

How Arizona teachers built a movement

BY NOAH KARVELIS

Across the nation, a powerful teachers' movement has been growing. The potential of this movement first became apparent when West Virginia's teachers went on strike in February 2018, and ultimately won a 5 percent raise for all public school employees. Following this, Oklahoma's educators mobilized and won raises and additional funding. Then teachers in my own state of Arizona went on a six-day strike in April and May 2018, and won $406 million in new funding. In the following two years, educators in Los Angeles, Oakland, and Chicago also waged successful strikes.

The successes of these movements, as well as the persistent and rampant attacks on public education, have inspired many educators across the nation to build teachers' movements in their own states. While every movement has been different, I want to share my experience as one of the teacher-organizers who helped with the Arizona movement. I hope that by breaking down what happened in Arizona, I can help others as they begin to build or grow their own teachers' movements to fight for the schools that they and their students deserve.

The Spark

The seeds of a teacher rebellion in Arizona were sown more than a decade ago when a steady barrage of cuts to education funding first began. Years later, and despite a growing economy, this funding was never restored. By the time teachers mobilized in the 2018 #RedForEd movement, Arizona's schools were suffering from a budget deficit of $1.1 billion, per-pupil spending was 48th in the nation, and Arizona's teachers were among the lowest paid in the country. For years, we taught in crumbling schools, lived paycheck to paycheck, and struggled for even the most essential resources for our students.

When West Virginia teachers went on strike—and won—Arizona teachers saw a glimmer of hope. Following the strike, our union president, Joe Thomas, put out a tweet asking Arizona's teachers if they had been watching what happened in West Virginia and if and how they wanted to mobilize in Arizona. I responded and said that yes, we had been watching and I believed Arizona's teachers were supportive of going on strike. After a quick back and forth on Twitter, Thomas sent out two additional tweets: "Talking is good. The first step toward any statewide action is local actions. What can you do locally—at your site—to reveal the level of readiness for a statewide action?" And, "Having everyone wear Red for Ed (a red shirt) on the same day would be a fine indicator."

I never imagined anything would come of this exchange. Teachers, far too often, view teaching as a passion and an act of martyrdom, and Arizona was no exception. But in the wake of West Virginia, the atmosphere was different. There was hope for change. As I started sharing a simple Facebook event and a call to action, word of the first #RedForEd day spread quickly. A few days later, the Facebook page had more than 7,000 people who said that they were interested, or planning to participate. And on March 7, 2018, Arizona's schools were a sea of red as thousands of teachers showed that they were ready to fight back.

The Structures

The first #RedForEd event quickly ballooned into a massive form of protest. As interest grew, it was clear that there were both a need and a desire for something beyond a single day of action.

In the days leading up to the T-shirt action, I had connected with Rebecca Garelli, Derek Harris, and Dylan Wegela. We quickly decided to create a Facebook group, Arizona Educators United (AEU), as a space to plan further action and get organized. Much like the #RedForEd Facebook event, this group quickly swelled to several thousand members. The page functioned, and continues to function, as the central hub of the Arizona teachers' movement. The five teachers who serve as the group's "administrators" post events, share information, organize mobilizations, discuss our actions, and agree on demands with 52,000 other educators and supporters. Another team of about 12 teachers reviews content, screens requests to join the group, and moderates the Facebook page.

While several other teachers' movements such as those in Oklahoma and West Virginia utilized Facebook to organize, we embraced the platform in a different way. Instead of having one group page where educators executed essentially all elements of the movement, we created a network of Facebook pages. Our main page existed solely for movement leaders to disperse information and organize the rank-and-file educators. Other pages, such as the AEU Discussion Hub and local #RedForEd Facebook groups, were organized by district or town. Teachers and supporters were encouraged to discuss the movement and plan actions in their communities.

In addition, we collected data and contact information from the very beginning so that we could reach teachers outside of Facebook through email blasts, calls, and texts. Without any funding or resources, this was done primarily through the work of Vanessa Arredondo, a teacher and AEU organizer in Yuma, Arizona, who dedicated herself to developing the infrastructure through countless email lists and Google Forms. In doing so, Arizona's movement circumvented one of the primary drawbacks to organizing through Facebook—the fact that (especially in a group of 40,000–60,000 people) the amount of content and information on the page can be overwhelming, and vital information is consequently quickly buried or lost.

Engaging the State Affiliate

Arizona's movement was also unique in the way the grassroots activists in AEU were able to work with the state's union (Arizona Education Association) leadership. Our union leaders realized that we had ignited a spark that they'd been unable to cultivate and told AEU that they wanted the teachers to remain at the helm of the movement. We worked hand in hand with the union as we built a movement that was designed to engage all educators, regardless of union membership. Through this relationship, our grassroots energy was matched with the institutional power and experience of the union to create a mass movement in a "right-to-work" state. This relationship between rank-and-file activists and union leaders was vital to the successes in Arizona.

Site Liaisons

Along with the Facebook pages and the close relationship between the union and grassroots leaders, we also built a "site liaison" network. This is a network of more than 2,000 individual teachers who are volunteer organizers for their campuses. These teachers communicate with movement leaders primarily through the AEU Site Liaisons Facebook group and email as they direct the day-to-day activism of the teachers at their schools. Most of these teachers were also union site representatives, but for many this was their first experience in organizing. By developing the liaison network, we were able to create a bottom-up infrastructure that allowed teachers and advocates to engage in meaningful local actions as well as to lead the larger statewide fight.

Site liaisons are in charge of dispersing information to all of their colleagues at their campuses. They also perform essential tasks such as organizing and hosting the strike vote, which was facilitated by both AEU and AEA. Through this structure, local leaders become empowered to not only perform these tasks and help sustain the movement, but are also encouraged to organize their own local actions. Many site liaisons began organizing actions such as "bridge takeovers" where dozens of teachers stand on overpasses with signs bearing education facts and phrases while wearing red shirts, individual sick-outs that shut down entire districts, local marches, car painting events, and dozens of other tactics to help increase momentum and grow power. As movement leader and teacher Dylan Wegela put it, "The site liaisons are essential to the movement. They organize at the ground level to build power of #RedForEd." Without their involvement, #RedForEd would never have built the power that we have now.

The Tactics

We knew that the grounds for a teacher strike had to be developed through a series of deliberate tactics focused on increasing our power and support. And one strategy we borrowed from West Virginia was a slow escalation of tactics.

Our first tactic in this gradual process was the #RedForEd T-shirt action in early March 2018, when thousands of teachers wore red on the same day to signal that they were ready to take action. We encouraged teachers to not only wear red, but also to post images of themselves in red shirts on social media and use the hashtag #RedForEd. Then we engaged teachers in another simple yet more personal ask. We asked teachers to wear red again, but this time to post a picture with a piece of paper and the three reasons why they were #RedForEd. Through this tactic, we showed the faces of the teachers and began to tell the stories of why we were fighting back. For example, 8th-grade English language arts teacher Chad Schafer held up a sign with these three reasons:

- I live with three other teachers just so we can afford rent.
- Schools and students are losing amazing teachers because they cannot survive on their salaries for educators.
- We elementary teachers are more than 20 percent below the national average for teacher salary.

About two weeks later, the union had its annual "Day at the Capitol" where educators on spring break lobby legislators and learn about the bills being heard. The union invited both members and non-members to the event, bringing together more than 100 teachers. A week later, around 350 teachers arrived for a second lobby day. By opening this event up to all teachers, the union showed that it was willing to work with the rank-and-file members of AEU. This event proved that the #RedForEd movement was not simply a social media phenomenon but was prepared to mobilize in person and hold legislators accountable.

As both energy and participation grew, we continued to mobilize largely in person. After building the confidence and power of teachers through social media actions and the Day at the Capitol events, we knew that we could then move away from online organizing and begin to ask teachers to show up at events and protests in person. The actions that followed included protesting Gov. Doug Ducey's appearances on a local radio station, testifying in legislative committee hearings, and the near-constant efforts of site liaisons in local protests. While these actions were taking place, it became clear that a full-fledged teachers' movement was truly developing.

Five Demands

We hosted a series of polls in the main AEU Facebook page that allowed teachers to offer suggestions for demands and vote on what was most important to them. Ultimately, these polls developed what became the five demands of the movement. These demands included a 20 percent raise for teachers, competitive wages for all classified staff, no new tax cuts until Arizona's per-pupil spending reaches the national average, a return to 2008 funding levels, and yearly raises until Arizona's average teacher salary reaches the national average. Middle school science teacher and AEU organizer Rebecca Garelli summarized the demands as intended to "secure the future of public education in Arizona and fight for the schools our students and educators deserve."

We officially announced these demands at a rally on the Capitol grounds that was attended by several thousand teachers and education advocates. It was clear educators were prepared to take radical action, and talk of a strike began to spread quickly.

Securing Community Support

All this had taken place in roughly four weeks. Beyond our network of educators and advocates, our communities were largely unaware of the desperate state of our schools, as well as the goals of the Arizona #RedForEd movement. We knew that we must engage with our communities. We're in a conservative "right-to-work" state, and without community support, we were destined to fail. So we utilized the walk-in tactic that was used in West Virginia. We created Facebook events and encouraged site liaisons to communicate with parents to tell them that we would be holding walk-ins and what could be expected. And for two consecutive Wednesdays, teachers wore red as they met with parents and students outside of school before classes began to discuss the issues that we all faced in Arizona schools, as well as the #RedForEd movement's goals. Then, teachers and community members walked into their schools together in a show of solidarity.

These walk-ins proved to be essential in securing the support of parents and community members. On one walk-in day, more than 110,000 community members and educators entered schools together in bold solidarity and sent a resounding message throughout the state. Just days before, after an interview at the local radio station KTAR, the governor had brushed the movement off and claimed that it was "political theater" and that he has a "day job" and no time to concern himself with our demands. Yet, one day after the massive walk-in mobilization, the governor announced that he had a plan for 20 percent raises for all teachers.

The tactic of the walk-in was, and is, the defining moment of the Arizona #RedForEd movement. By engaging with our community and winning their support, the entire playing field shifted. Suddenly, the movement was no longer just angry teachers in red shirts. Now, the entire community was behind us. The governor simply had to act or be crushed by the sheer force of the movement.

> Suddenly, the movement was no longer just angry teachers in red shirts. Now, the entire community was behind us. The governor simply had to act or be crushed by the sheer force of the movement.

However, the governor's proposal was riddled with holes. It ignored four of our five demands, left out pay raises for our colleagues such as bus drivers and paraprofessionals, stole funding from other public services, and had no sustained revenue source. It was a sham, so we continued to escalate our actions and soon called for a strike vote.

Before the vote, there was a sense among movement leaders that many educators were willing to accept the governor's pay proposal. We wondered if educators would stand with their students and colleagues and continue to fight or if they would take off their red shirts and take the governor's 20 percent pay raise. But when the results of the vote came in, the answer was clear as 78 percent of all school staff across Arizona—union and non-union, AEU member and non-member—voted to authorize a walkout.

The Strike

While the strike eventually secured a $406 million investment in public education, resulting in significant raises for many teachers and school employees, it also became clear that the governor and the Legislature were not willing to replace the remaining $700 million still missing from our schools.

We were left with a difficult decision. With the legislative session closed and the legislators leaving the building, should we stay out of our classrooms and continue the strike, or turn to a new tactic? Could we force a special session? We had to act quickly, as the budget passed and another school day slowly crept nearer and nearer.

We quickly sent teams of leaders and union staff to talk to teachers on the ground at the Capitol and see what they wanted to do. We asked the teachers, "If the budget passes, do we stay out on strike or change tactics?" While we were not able to conduct a full, democratic vote (one of my personal regrets from the entire movement), the teachers at the Capitol told us overwhelmingly that if the budget passed, they wished to return to their classrooms.

In response, we called for an end to the strike. However, the movement's leaders understood that teachers could not go back to our classrooms and accept pay raises without winning anything for our students and our colleagues who went on strike with us. We needed to change our tactics. AEU's leadership endorsed the InvestInEd initiative—a tax increase on the top 1 percent of income earners to generate $700 million for education. In roughly five weeks, teachers and advocates gathered more than 227,000 signatures to put the InvestInEd initiative on the November 2018 ballot. However, in August the Arizona Supreme Court, overturning three prior rulings, controversially pulled the InvestInEd initiative from the ballot.

While this was a devastating development in the movement, Arizona's teachers remain dedicated to the fight for public education. We simply changed our focus to the November elections and asked candidates to sign a pledge of support to the movement and its demands. By Election Day, we had 78 candidates who had signed pledges. Teachers then knocked on more than 80,000 doors to help secure seats for these pro-public education legislators. We saw the results of these efforts as several teachers and public education advocates—including Kathy Hoffman, a public school speech therapist, first-time candidate, and now Arizona superintendent of public instruction—won major electoral victories.

The Lessons

The first lesson I hope people take away from Arizona #RedForEd is that a grassroots, rank-and-file movement is absolutely necessary—particularly in "right-to-work" states. Whether the rank and file assume leadership through Facebook pages, forming local collectives, or by getting elected to official union leadership positions, it is clear that the energy and leadership of teachers themselves is what is needed to lead these battles. And while the rank and file must lead, they should also be deliberate in securing the support of their union leadership in order to create a powerful partnership. Simultaneously, union leadership must be willing to not only work with rank-and-file teachers, but also to allow them to assume authentic, meaningful leadership roles.

It is important to recognize that teachers need to be allowed the space to grow as leaders. As Jay Barbuto, a middle school English teacher and now established movement leader and union organizer, said: "I'm passionate about teaching. I'm the teacher that goes above and beyond for his students. They're family. So, when #RedForEd became a thing in Arizona, it just seemed like an opportunity for me to show these leadership skills and enthusiasm in a different light." Leaders in both union and grassroots organizations must constantly recognize that teachers like Jay are waiting for their opportunity.

The second lesson is the need to have a community-centric orientation to teachers' movements. In Arizona, the turning point occurred when we went into our communities and spoke with our neighbors and friends about what was happening. In response to walk-ins, town halls, and car window painting events for parents, the community threw their support behind the teachers and the entire tide shifted. Suddenly, #RedForEd signs were in the windows of homes on every block, car windows were painted with education facts, and the force of the movement was felt far beyond the walls of the school. This community-based approach to a labor movement was what made transformative change possible in Arizona.

The third lesson is that democratic organizing, whether through union reforms or establishing new structures such as Arizona Educators United, must be embraced. Through the site liaison network, thousands of teachers became powerful local leaders. And by using online platforms such as Facebook to vote on tactics and demands, the voices of the teachers were not only heard, but also acted on. This authentic engagement of the rank and file created spaces for teachers—regardless of political affiliation or union membership—to participate. As elementary school substitute teacher and #RedForEd supporter Allison Ryal-Bagley told the *New York Times* as she voiced her support for new taxes to fund public education, "I'm a die-hard Republican, and I'm dying inside. Republicans aren't taking care of our kids." By engaging in democratic organizing that both respected and welcomed people like Allison, we were able to create a movement that cut across partisan lines and mobilized thousands of public education supporters.

Another lesson is that the gradual escalation of tactics that was embraced in Arizona and elsewhere is a vital strategy that can be duplicated in nearly any setting. We realized that we could not simply dive headfirst into a statewide strike. We needed to bring more teachers into the movement, develop our message, and provide time to engage with our community, gain their support, and recognize their values and ideas. By gradually escalating our actions, we were able to accomplish this while we simultaneously built structures such as the liaison network, which allowed us to begin building toward lasting power and not simply a strike.

Finally, the most important lesson to be learned is that teachers have tremendous power. It is simply undeniable. Across the nation, we have seen the power of teachers when they unite and fight for what they believe in. And as conservative and neoliberal attacks on our schools continue, it only becomes clearer that there is no hero waiting in the wings to save us. Teachers themselves must become the very leaders who will save our schools. And there isn't a second to lose. It is time to fight back. ⬛

Noah Karvelis is a PhD student at the University of Wisconsin–Madison. Previously, he has worked as a K–8 music teacher, union president, and co-founder of the organization Arizona Educators United that, along with the Arizona Education Association, led the 2018 walkout in Arizona.

New Teachers Energize Their Union!

BY GABRIEL TANGLAO

BRIAN STAUFFER

As a child, I looked forward to visiting my mother's workplace. Like many Filipinos, her pathway to U.S. citizenship was as a professional nurse. One winter day at the hospital, we pulled up to a spectacle that left me in awe: A large group of people marching in circles along the sidewalk. We were greeted by my mother's co-workers with warm hugs, and the sounds from the crowd were rhythmic and uplifting, as everyone raised their voices in unison. "What are they saying?" I asked. Mom replied, "Our chant lets people know that we are powerful together." This experience marching with my mother at this union rally planted the seeds of collective joy in action that later grew into a deep passion.

Years later when I started teaching in Bergenfield, New Jersey, my first impressions of the local union were less inspiring. The hurricane of paperwork, meetings, lesson plans, and dozens of new colleagues converged into an overwhelming stream of information. It felt like drinking water from a fire hose. I remembered sitting uncomfortably in the dense August air of the auditorium for orientation. A captive audience of new and returning teachers was enduring a long lineup of white, male, suit-wearing authority figures. "What a waste of time! These are the same PowerPoints they used last year," complained a veteran teacher loudly from the back row.

The local Bergenfield Education Association (BEA) president was the final speaker for that day. He made a mostly dry presentation about legal rights, contract language, grievance procedures, and evaluation processes. In retrospect, the union president's placement at the end of a long, boring program left him with an impatient audience anxious to be set free. "Ugh! We could have just read through the PowerPoints ourselves. Don't they know how much work we have to do to prepare our classrooms?" proclaimed a fearless young lady in the hallway. Her honesty felt like a breath of fresh air cutting through the humidity. We became instant friends.

Jasmin had a quick wit and a wealth of knowledge that made her an engaging person and a great teacher. It must have been fate that we shared a classroom, and taught different sections of the same financial literacy course. I remember being motivated by her relentless commitment. Jasmin spent countless hours planning, preparing, and modifying lessons for her modern world history class. She also served as advisor to the Genders & Sexualities Alliance and Academic Decathlon, and she rarely missed an after-school game. As we grew close, I learned about how influential Jasmin's family was in shaping her character. Her mother, like mine, was also a proud union member.

> "Our chant lets people know that we are powerful together."

Jay, a close colleague of ours, taught honors U.S. history two doors down from our classroom. He was highly respected by students, despite his reputation as the "hardest history teacher." Ironically, we had grown up in the same hometown, but only later became friends through teaching. One day during lunch, Jay pitched a game-changing question: "What are your thoughts on our contract?" I admitted, "I haven't carefully read the contract." Then I asked, "How do contract negotiations even work?" This moment eating lunch in the workroom sparked a conversation that lit a flame.

For the next few weeks, we started exploring the contours of our district that led to the current contract. Since we are in a state that recognizes collective bargaining rights, our local union reps negotiate on behalf of all teachers, including teachers at every grade level and all education support professionals. The salary guide is a complex grid that allocated pay scales based on years of experience and level of education. This often leads to thorny decisions that sometimes encourage union leaders to prioritize increased pay for senior teachers over new teachers or vice versa. We also looked into how our pension payments and healthcare costs added nuance to the calculations. It took time to understand the complex process of contract negotiations, but the trail of bread crumbs made us hungry to learn more.

We checked in with each other regularly to share our discoveries. Jay had a methodical nature that gave us important context for the bread-and-butter issues that impacted our take-home pay. Jasmin had great instincts and people skills that helped uncover personal accounts of how contentious elements of the contract played out. I started to identify key players and assess power dynamics through a social justice lens. Bergenfield was one of the most diverse communities in New Jersey with a 40 percent Latinx, 30 percent white, 20 percent Asian, and 10 percent Black student population. But the administrative staff and school board were dominated mostly by white men.

We reached out to the local union officers and asked how we could get involved. After some time, we received no response, and I followed up in person. "Hello," I said to our union president during a break at an inservice. "I'm Gabriel. I just wanted to follow up on an email we sent last week asking about how Jasmin, Jay, and I could get involved with the union, and help out." His confused face confirmed that he did not read the email or take us seriously. "Help out?" he repeated. His implication was clear. I was viewed with suspicion as an eager young educator of color—a rarity in this longtime union officer's circle, I imagined. Our exchange felt a long way from the warm hug that I remember the day of my mother's union rally. Still, we persisted.

Jasmin encountered a more patronizing, but equally dismissive attitude. Jay was up next. It may have been his powers of persuasion, or his position as a white, heterosexual, cisgender man, but he was our most effective messenger—evident by the result. Soon we were all nominated to serve as "building reps" and asked to attend "just one monthly meeting." Each meeting started with an opening monologue by the local president who spent an exhaustive amount of time disseminating information. The central message was clear: He speaks, we listen. The occasional daydream would cross my mind of those rally chants: "We are powerful together."

We began to exercise our voices to ask questions. "Should we use Robert's Rules of Order during meetings?" I asked. "Where can we find copies of our constitution and bylaws?" Jasmin followed up. "Will we receive an agenda in advance of the next meeting?" Jay asked. This volley of questions was not meant to be disruptive, but rather to help us move business forward and make our union processes more transparent. I was soon nominated by a veteran building rep to serve as sergeant at arms and help enforce the rules of parliamentary procedure. These rules can be bureaucratic and confusing, but it was also an opportunity to open up discussion and include more voices. I did my job, perhaps too well.

One of my responsibilities was to keep time during meetings. This sometimes meant calling "time" on people who spoke too long, including officers. "Sorry, that was three minutes," I would say respectfully. The president bristled at any attempt to check his control of discussions. Having been in power for more than a decade, the local president seemed used to unquestioned authority. This tension grew into hostility at my first winter leadership conference, a regional union event that offered leadership training for members.

As I made my way through the hotel lobby, I walked over toward familiar faces expecting to be welcomed with some friendly greeting. My local president took a swig of his drink and slammed his glass on the countertop. He turned to me and said, "You're not going to tell me I have three minutes to speak in my meeting!" He then launched into a verbal barrage. At first I tried to de-escalate the situation, but I eventually raised my voice to demand some respect. Flanked by the vice president to my side, the president was able to slip away without a clear resolution. His message could be summed up as "know your place, and stay in it." In that moment, I realized changing that dynamic would require more than an individual confrontation; it would take collective action. It was time to squad up.

> In that moment, I realized that changing that dynamic would require more than an individual confrontation . . . it was time to squad up.

I texted Jasmin to ask if we could meet up after our first training session. We found a quiet table near the lobby to speak privately. She listened intently as I told her about the encounter. Rather than react, we decided to take time to think about our next steps. The following week, Jasmin invited a few trusted co-workers to her house for an informal meeting. I shared my experience with the group, uncertain of how it would be received. I felt affirmed when people shared similar experiences. "This leaves us no choice. How can we continue to work with these people?" one person said. The purpose of the meeting quickly shifted into a strategy session, and thus started "A New Day for the BEA."

The confrontation with the local president was a turning point in our union journey. It prompted us to organize a slate of candidates and challenge the incumbent officers in the upcoming elections. Our team of five candidates for union office was majority women, and one person of color. Jay ran for president, Jasmin ran for vice president, and I ran for treasurer. We asked Phyllis, the person who nominated me for sergeant at arms, to run for corresponding secretary. She was a veteran middle school teacher with union experience. Fortunately, a friendly elementary school teacher also decided to run for recording secretary. The attitudes of the incumbent officers grew increasingly hostile, but there was no turning back.

In an effort to learn about issues that impacted our members, we organized a districtwide listening tour. Within three weeks, we visited seven out of eight schools, and connected with nearly a quarter of our 450 members. Representatives who were loyal to the old regime attempted to put up roadblocks, but rank-and-file members showed up. Almost every teacher, librarian, secretary, counselor, custodian, and paraprofessional shared stories of their struggles, frustrations, and hopes. "This is the first time I can remember candidates running for union office having ever visited our school," one woman said with gratitude. The common theme was a desire for greater communication.

It became clear that democratic process had not been exercised regularly in the local for many years. Most people were hard-pressed to remember the last time there were any challengers, let alone a slate of candidates. In fact, it took weeks to even receive a copy of the constitution and bylaws that outlined the election rules, procedures, and timeline. One event that we were encouraged to attend was a meet-the-candidates debate. "They are going to frame us as weak and inexperienced. That will be our advantage," Jay said with a cool resolve. As coach of the debate team, he was ready to go toe to toe with anyone. The outcome of that event was as clear as the outcome on the ballots.

We won a resounding victory for all five union officer positions. Having successfully campaigned for office, we hoped to transform the culture of our union to be more inclusive and transparent. Our team shared a sense of urgency about the need to engage members from our generation. We were acutely aware from our recent experiences that fresh blood in the ranks of active membership meant a healthier union. It was also visibly apparent that we did not reflect the rich diversity of the Bergenfield student body or local community. "I should not be the only person of color at the leadership table," I affirmed. But we were moving in the right direction.

We kept the concerns of members from our listening tour at the forefront of our minds. We centered organization, communication, and engagement as our main priorities. Internally, we focused on the empowerment of building reps with opportunities for training, support, and resources that we wished we would have had. That summer, about one-third of our building reps attended the statewide summer leadership conference to participate in trainings on a variety of issues. As I walked into the crowded dining room on the first night, I had a flashback to the previous winter's confrontation. I heard my name, and started walking over toward the familiar faces waving me over.

In an effort to strengthen face-to-face relationships, we mapped the buildings to connect building reps with clusters of members located in their respective hallways.

One of our new building reps had thoughtfully saved us all seats at a table in the conference dining room. We sat together and shared our excitement about the weekend. This was a new experience for most of our team, and it felt good to have other people to share in the journey. We checked in with each other at each meal to share discoveries. "Do we use any funding from the PRIDE Community Organizing grant?" one person inquired. "Is there an Evaluation Committee?" added the new building rep. "Who serves on our Legislative Action Team?" another person asked. This was a very different experience from the last conference. It felt like that collective joy in action.

This wave of momentum carried our growing team into the following school year. Starting with small teams of people, we revived the committee structures including the Legislative Action Team, "PRIDE" Community Organizing Committee, Evaluation Committee, and others. In an effort to strengthen face-to-face relationships, we mapped the buildings to connect building reps with clusters of members located in their respective hallways. This effort paid dividends when we invited people to the social events that Jasmin would plan. From happy hours for new members to retirement celebrations, we tried to attract educators to take collective ownership of our union.

We grew into each leadership role with every experience. Jay was our contract guru who mastered the grievance procedures, organized the negotiations team, and was the lead defender of members' rights. Jasmin's dynamic personality and thoughtful nature was an incredible asset as she led, planned, and launched a series of membership engagement events throughout the year. I discovered the radical possibilities of this union work in and beyond the district. I represented our local to the Parents Association, community groups, political organizations, and our state and national affiliates. We each discovered our own leadership style, and added to the collective vision in different ways.

I admit that the work was fun and challenging, but also frustrating at times. As chair of our Legislative Action Team, I wanted our union to have a real impact in our larger community. As we acknowledged the lack of diverse representation in our administrative staff and faculty, we set our sights on the local school board elections. It took months to identify worthy candidates and navigate the complexities of local politics. We spread the word throughout our membership. We partnered with the Parents Association, who hosted a meet-the-candidates night. We even organized a community door-knocking to turn out the vote with Bergenfield residents who were also union members.

We reshaped our local to be more intergenerational and inclusive for educators, students, and families of color.

Despite all of the time and effort, we were able to help elect only one candidate of color. This did not shift the balance of power, or change the racial dynamic in a substantive way. This "L" was not a loss, but a lesson: The strategic vision of transformational change takes time, and could take years of sustained collective action. We were also reminded that the power is in the people, not in the position. Organizing to support the campaigns of school board candidates of color led to deeper connections with the community.

At the swearing-in ceremony of the newly elected school board members, I was greeted by Andres, a board candidate who had lost the election. Andres, who had migrated from the Dominican Republic to earn his doctorate and planted his family roots in Bergenfield, was a parent of a former student of mine and board president of the Bergenfield Public Library. "Welcome, my friend," he said. "We would like to invite the Bergenfield Education Association to partner with us on our annual Multicultural Celebration." That was the beginning of a partnership between our organizations that has allowed us to collaborate for more sustainable change in the community.

From our core team to our rep council, from local membership to community spaces, we used our union as a vehicle to drive change forward. It took time and effort, but we reshaped our local to be more intergenerational and inclusive for educators, students, and families of color. In three years, we reached a contract agreement in record time, established community partnerships, and started to shift the political landscape of our district. None of this was easy, and it could not be done alone. It was a collective effort and truly a labor of love. We learned some simple, yet important lessons: 1) show up; 2) step up; 3) squad up; 4) build community; and 5) enjoy the journey. ▣

Gabriel A. Tanglao is a former social studies teacher in Bergen County, New Jersey. He currently works in the Professional Development and Instructional Issues division for the New Jersey Education Association. This article first appeared in the third edition of The New Teacher Book.

Social Justice Unionism Comes to Baltimore

BY RACHEL M. COHEN

Three co-founders of the BMORE caucus, Natalia Bacchus, Corey Gaber, and Cristina Duncan Evans

JOCELYN PROVIDENCE, BMORE

n the middle of May 2019, 37-year-old Diamonté Brown won her bid to lead the Baltimore Teachers Union, defeating Marietta English, who had led the nearly 7,000-member union for most of the past two decades. The shakeup in Charm City school politics marked a victory not just for Brown, a middle school English teacher, but also for the Baltimore Movement of Rank-and-File Educators (BMORE), a social justice caucus that has been organizing since 2015.

The change in leadership was not without debate. English, who had been seeking her ninth term in office, said she could not "in good faith concede" and demanded a revote—alleging Brown and the slate of candidates she ran with committed a series of election violations, such as illegally campaigning on school grounds. Critics said the incumbents had their own campaign missteps to account for, including writing rules that discouraged challengers and trying to suppress the vote.

The American Federation of Teachers, the national parent union for the BTU, had to step in and hold a formal hearing to adjudicate the complaints. The election drama reflected a stark departure from what are typically sleepy Baltimore affairs.

Still, with roughly 500 more ballots cast during this election compared with the previous one, observers said the increased interest in voting marked a significant shift in Baltimore's union culture.

BMORE caucus members say they're here to stay, joining a national movement dedicated to using teacher unions as a vehicle for broad social change. This movement first caught fire with the Chicago teachers' strike in 2012, an eight-day protest of educators, parents, students, and community members who called for increased funding for public services. Similar radical caucuses have since emerged in cities like Philadelphia, Los Angeles, Seattle, and St. Paul and now they're banding together to support each other.

Building a Caucus

BMORE's story began with Natalia Bacchus, an ESL teacher who moved to Baltimore in 2013 after teaching in suburban Maryland for nine years. Bacchus was bewildered by the bureaucratic hurdles she encountered at nearly every turn.

"When I worked in Montgomery County, I didn't know anything about our union. I was just like, I'm a public school teacher, I'm a public servant, I have a unionized job, that's cool," she said. "Then I came to Baltimore, and I was like, wow—everything is a hassle every step of the way. And what do you mean kids can't drink from the water fountain? And kids have to go to bathroom in groups? All these restrictions that would never fly in Montgomery County."

> "I was like this could be big, and Chicago's social justice caucus was called CORE and New York's was MORE—we should call ours BMORE!"

Bacchus didn't know many other Baltimore educators, and didn't know if she was alone in feeling this way. Eventually she met Helen Atkinson, executive director of the Teachers' Democracy Project, a local education advocacy group. In 2014 Atkinson invited Bacchus to become a TDP fellow, where she would research progressive teacher unions around the country.

The next year Bacchus and Atkinson started traveling to different cities to learn from activist teachers. In August 2015, they went to Newark, New Jersey, for the annual United Caucuses of Rank and File Educators conference, and began asking more practical questions about what launching a union caucus might look like.

"I was like this could be big, and Chicago's social justice caucus was called CORE and New York's was MORE—we should call ours BMORE!" Bacchus said.

That fall, Atkinson introduced Bacchus to two other radical educators she knew in Baltimore—Cristina Duncan Evans and Corey Gaber. Bacchus was then working at a traditional public elementary school, Gaber was a charter middle school teacher, and Duncan Evans was teaching at a specialized high school for the arts. Their diverse experiences struck them as a powerful opportunity.

Together they started a book club, reading texts like *How to Jump-Start Your Union*, about the Chicago Teachers Union, and *The Future of Our Schools*, by education scholar Lois Weiner. They traveled to Chicago later that year to meet the CORE educators in person. That summer, Samantha Winslow from Labor Notes, a union activist media organization, came out to Baltimore to lead an organizing workshop, and five Baltimore educators went to Raleigh, North Carolina, in August for UCORE's next conference. Leaders describe BMORE's beginnings as "a lot of slow, but really deep" organizing.

In the fall of 2016 the newly formed BMORE steering committee decided to launch their first campaign—a petition drive to allow absentee voting in BTU elections. That winter, they organized the official BMORE launch party at a local barbecue restaurant, wondering if anyone would even show up. Nearly 70 people did. "We knew then that this type of connection and work was resonating with people," said Gaber.

Amplifying Black leadership and centering racial equity, they stressed, would be at the core of their efforts. They created a closed Facebook group for members, and began holding regular meetings at different schools. By April 2017, they had formally met with their union's leadership, receiving guidance from Philly's social justice caucus on how to approach that conversation. The BTU, they said, was surprisingly receptive to their group.

"Marietta even offered to come to our meetings, but we said no, that's not how we operate," explained Bacchus. "We're from the rank and file."

BMORE's organizing got an unexpected jolt the following winter, with local and national media reports on Baltimore students trapped in freezing classrooms with broken heaters. Some schools never even opened because of malfunctioning boilers, while others sent children home early. BMORE quickly organized and sent a list of demands to the school board and the school district CEO, signed by more than 1,500 supporters. The school CEO, Sonja Santelises, wrote BMORE back with gratitude for "fiercely advocating for solutions," and the school district largely adopted their recommendations. The next month BMORE joined educators in 20 other cities in hosting a Black Lives Matter at School Week of Action, demanding things like more culturally competent curriculum and the hiring of more Black educators.

In the summer of 2018 BMORE leaders started discussing running their own candidates in the next union election—something that happens every three years. They decided to team up with another young social justice group, the Caucus of Educators for Democracy and Equity (CEDE), and run jointly under the banner of the Union We Deserve. Diamonté Brown would run for president, and they'd run additional candidates—including Gaber and Duncan Evans—for the executive board. The Union We Deserve slate would compete against the Progressive Caucus, a slate that included English and had held power in the union for years.

The insurgent candidates admitted there were some things the BTU already did well. Baltimore teachers have some of the highest salaries in both Maryland and the nation, and their healthcare benefits are notably strong. "At a time when people are going on strike over low wages and poor health care, the Progressive Caucus has pushed for even more salary increases and our good health care to get even better," said Corey Debnam, the Progressive Caucus chair and a Baltimore educator for the last 19 years.

Still, the teachers with the Union We Deserve said they wanted more than an effective service union, and to prioritize more than just good pay, benefits, and professional development. They wanted to mobilize teachers into a political force for students and communities—through the ballot box, at the bargaining table, and through direct action.

"I taught American government for nine years, and 6,000 organized voters can really have a big impact on electoral politics when you look at the turnout in some of our races," said Duncan Evans. Baltimore is a deep-blue city, and in the last Democratic primary for mayor, the winner emerged with less than 2,500 votes.

A Contested Election

English did not respond to a request for an interview, but Sandra Davis, chair of the union's chapter for paraprofessionals and school-related personnel (PSRPs), and a member of the Progressive Caucus, told the *Nation* that their disputed election was extremely unusual, and that in her 30 years as a Baltimore educator, she's "never seen anything like [it]." Upholding Brown's presidency would mean Brown would serve over a joint executive board—with the teacher chapter chaired by Duncan Evans, and the PSRP chaired by Davis.

> They wanted to mobilize teachers into a political force for students and communities—through the ballot box, at the bargaining table, and through direct action.

Davis and Debnam said union members contacted them to object to BMORE/CEDE supporters' canvassing at their homes in the weeks before the election. The union's guidelines prohibit the BTU from sharing members' personal contact information, leading some to view the canvassing as a violation of their privacy, even if BMORE/CEDE didn't get the home addresses from the union itself.

"We had people who were really offended that someone late at night—at 6 or 7 p.m.—is coming to their home to campaign about an internal election," Debnam said. "That's just something we would never do."

The Progressive Caucus had not just accused BMORE/CEDE of wrongly canvassing at people's homes. They also accused them of illegally campaigning on school grounds. With additional election rules like prohibitions against teachers' leaving campaign literature in educators' mailboxes and sending campaign literature on work email accounts, candidates are left with few ways to actually reach prospective voters. Critics say that's by design, to protect those already in power. Bacchus, who resigned in 2018 and now works with the Teachers' Democracy Project full time, said the Union We Deserve's main goal throughout the campaign was to spread awareness about the upcoming election. "Most teachers don't even know that every three years there's an election for BTU leadership," she said.

BMORE/CEDE, for their part, said the BTU leadership tried to suppress the vote before and during the election, in part by limiting voting hours, removing a voting location, and denying a block of absentee ballots. On Election Day, local media also covered complaints from educators who said the ballots on their voting machines were designed in a confusing way, formatted as if to encourage reelecting the incumbents.

Duncan Evans said she wasn't entirely surprised her caucus's victory was contested. "The BTU has challenged elections in the past," she said. "So I certainly knew this was in the realm of possibility."

On July 11, almost two months after the election was held, the AFT released the results of its investigation, confirming that Brown was indeed the winner. BMORE leaders said their next steps would be to meet with individual members, revamp their union website, and bring full-time organizers on staff.

"I'm looking forward to people understanding more about how a union works, but I think a large part of transparency means us listening," said Duncan Evans, the newly seated executive board member and teacher chapter chair. "This is all long overdue." ✊

Rachel M. Cohen is a contributing writer for the Intercept *and a freelance journalist based in Washington, D.C. An earlier version of this article was first published by the* Nation *on June 7, 2019. Printed with permission.*

For more information on the BMORE caucus, see their website at bmorecaucus.org.

How One Elementary School Sparked a Citywide Movement to Make Black Students' Lives Matter

BY WAYNE AU AND JESSE HAGOPIAN

SHARON CHANG

I t was the morning of Sept. 16, 2016, and a conscious party of resistance, courage, and community uplift was happening on the sidewalk in front of John Muir Elementary in Seattle. Dozens of Black men were lined up from the street to the school doorway, giving high fives and praise to all the students who entered as part of a locally organized event called Black

Men Uniting to Change the Narrative. African American drummers pounded defiant rhythms. Students smiled and laughed as they made their way to the entrance. And teachers and parents milled about in #BlackLivesMatter T-shirts, developed and worn in solidarity with the movement to make Black lives matter at John Muir Elementary.

You never would have known that, just hours before, the school was closed and emptied as bomb-sniffing dogs scoured the building looking for explosives.

That September morning was the culmination of a combination of purposeful conversations among John Muir administration and staff, activism, and media attention. John Muir Elementary sits in Seattle's Rainier Valley, and its student population reflects the community: 68 percent of Muir's roughly 400 students qualify for free or reduced lunch, 33 percent are officially designated transition bilingual, 10 percent are Hispanic, 11 percent are Asian American, 11 percent identify as multiracial, and almost 50 percent are African American—mostly a mix of East African immigrants and families from this historically Black neighborhood.

By that autumn, John Muir Elementary had been actively working for months on issues of race equity, with special attention to Black students. The previous year, Muir's staff began a deliberate process of examining privilege and the politics of race. With the support of both the school and the PTA, Ruby Bridges—who as a child famously desegregated the all-white William Frantz Elementary School in New Orleans in 1960—had also visited Muir as part of a longer discussion of racism in education among staff and students. During end-of-the-summer professional development, with the support of administration and in the aftermath of the police killings of Philando Castile and Alton Sterling, school staff read and discussed an article on #BlackLivesMatter and renewed their commitment to working for racial justice at Muir.

As part of these efforts, DeShawn Jackson, an African American male student support worker, organized the Black Men Uniting to Change the Narrative event for that September morning. In solidarity, school staff decided to wear Black Lives Matter/We Stand Together/John Muir Elementary T-shirts designed by the school's art teacher.

A local TV station reported on the teachers wearing #BlackLivesMatter T-shirts, and as the story went public, political tensions exploded. Soon the white supremacist, hate group-fueled news source *Breitbart* picked up the story, and the right-wing police support group Blue Lives Matter publicly denounced the effort. Hateful emails and phone calls began to flood the John Muir administration and the Seattle School Board, and then the horrifying happened: Someone made a bomb threat against the school. Even though the threat was deemed not very credible by authorities, Seattle Public Schools officially canceled the Black Men Uniting to Change the Narrative event at Muir out of extreme caution.

All of this is what made that September morning all the more powerful. The bomb-sniffing dogs found nothing and school was kept open that day. The drummers drummed and the crowd cheered every child coming through the doors of John Muir Elementary. Everyone was there in celebration, loudly proclaiming that, yes, despite the racist and right-wing attacks, despite the official cancellation, and despite the bomb threat, the community of John Muir Elementary would not be cowed by hate and fear. Black men showed up to change the narrative around education and race. School staff wore their #BlackLivesMatter T-shirts and devoted the day's teaching to issues of racial justice, all bravely and proudly celebrating their power. In the process, this single south Seattle elementary school galvanized a growing citywide movement to make Black lives matter in Seattle schools.

Organizing Across the District

Inspired by that bold action, members of Social Equity Educators (SEE), a rank-and-file organization of union educators, invited a few John Muir staff to a meeting to offer support and learn more about their efforts. The Muir educators' story explaining how and why they organized for Black lives moved everyone in attendance, and SEE members began discussing taking the action citywide.

Everyone agreed that there were potential pitfalls of doing a citywide Black students' lives matter event. The John Muir teachers had a race and equity team and dedicated professional development time the previous year to discuss institutional racism, and they had collectively come to the decision as an entire school to support the action and wear the shirts. What would it mean at a different school if some teachers wore the shirts and taught anti-racist lessons, and others didn't? What if only a few dozen teachers across Seattle wore the shirts—would that send the wrong message? What if other schools received threats? What if those threats materialized?

These and other considerations fueled an important discussion and debate among SEE members, and highlighted the need to educate our communities about why this action was urgently needed. However, with the videos of police killing Philando Castile and Alton Sterling fresh in the minds of SEE members, the group decided that to not publicly declare that Black lives matter would be a message in and of itself.

And it wasn't just about the police murder of Black people that motivated SEE to organize an action across the school system. It was also because of the institutional racism infecting Seattle's public schools. Seattle has an alarming pattern of segregation both between and within schools, with intensely tracked advanced classes overwhelmingly populated with white students. Moreover, the Department of Education's 2013 investigation found that Seattle Public Schools suspended Black students at about four times the rate of white students for the same infractions.

SEE members decided that on Oct. 19, 2016, they would all wear Black Lives Matter shirts to school and voted to create a second T-shirt design that included "#SayHerName." The African American Policy Forum created this hashtag in the wake of Sandra Bland's death while in the custody of Waller County (Texas) police, to raise awareness about police violence against women, to raise awareness about police violence against Black women, and to raise awareness about police violence particularly against Black queer women and Black transgender women.

As part of this action, SEE also developed a three-point policy proposal that would serve as an ongoing campaign to support Black Lives Matter in schools and aid in the struggle against institutional racism:

- Support ethnic studies in all schools.
- Replace zero-tolerance discipline with restorative justice practices.
- De-track classes within the schools to undo the racial segregation that is reinforced by tracking.

In addition, SEE voted to bring a resolution to the Seattle Education Association (SEA), the union representing Seattle's educators, to publicly declare support for the action of the John Muir teachers and community, and to call on all teachers across the district to actively support the Oct. 19 action.

At the September SEA Representative Assembly, SEE member Sarah Arvey, a white special education teacher, brought forward the following resolution:

> Whereas the SEA promotes equity and supports anti-racist work in our schools; and,
>
> Whereas we want to act in solidarity with our members and the community at John Muir who received threats based on their decision to wear Black Lives Matter T-shirts as part of an event with "Black Men United to Change the Narrative"; and,
>
> Whereas the SEA and SPS promote Race and Equity teams to address institutionalized racism in our schools and offer a space for dialogue among school staff; and,
>
> Therefore be it resolved that the SEA Representative Assembly endorse and participate in an action wearing Black Lives Matter T-shirts on Wednesday, October 19, 2016, with the intent of showing solidarity, promoting anti-racist practices in our schools, and creating dialogue in our schools and communities.

SEE members expected a difficult debate at the SEA Representative Assembly, and many didn't think the resolution would pass. But they underestimated the impact of the ongoing protests against police brutality and racism that were sweeping school campuses. Inspired by San Francisco 49ers quarterback Colin Kaepernick, the Garfield High School football team captured headlines around the city and nation when every single player and coach took a knee during the national anthem—and maintained that action for the entire season. The protest spread to the girls' volleyball team, the marching band, the cheerleaders, and many other high school sports teams across Seattle. When it came time for the SEA vote, the resolution to support Black Lives Matter at School Day passed unanimously.

As word got out about the SEA Representative Assembly vote, and in reaction to the threats against John Muir Elementary earlier in the month, allies also began to step forward in support of making Black Students' Lives Matter. The Seattle NAACP quickly endorsed the event and lent its support. Soup for Teachers, a local parent organizing group formed to support the 2015 SEA strike, as well as the executive board of the Seattle Council Parent Teacher Student Association, also endorsed the action and joined in solidarity.

SEE helped gather representatives from these organizations for an Oct. 12 press conference to explain why parents, educators, and racial justice advocates united to declare Black lives matter at school. Predictably, news outlets repeatedly asked teachers if they thought they were politicizing the classroom by wearing BLM shirts to school. Rita Green, education chair of the Seattle NAACP, responded directly: "We're here to support families. We're here to support students. When Black lives matter, all lives matter."

Arvey told reporters, "It's important for us to know the history of racial justice and racial injustice in our country and in our world . . . in order for us to address it. When we're silent, we close off dialogue and we close the opportunity to learn and grow from each other." Other teachers pointed out that students were having discussions all the time in the halls, during sports practice, and outside of school about racism, police violence, and the Black Lives Matter movement. A better question to ask, teachers asserted, would be "Is school going to be relevant to the issues that our students are discussing every day?"

In an effort to build greater solidarity for Seattle educators taking part in the Black Lives Matter at School Day, one of us—Wayne—organized a national letter for professors to sign in an effort to build support for the action. After only a few days, close to 250 professors, many of them well-recognized scholars in educational research locally and nationally, had signed on. Another letter of support was signed by luminaries such as dissident scholar Noam Chomsky, former MSNBC anchor Melissa Harris-Perry, 1968 Olympic bronze medalist and activist John Carlos, Black Lives Matter co-founder Opal Tometi, noted education author Jonathan Kozol, and Pulitzer Prize-winning journalist Jose Antonio Vargas.

Inspired by San Francisco 49ers quarterback Colin Kaepernick, the Garfield High School football team captured headlines around the city and nation when every single player and coach took a knee during the national anthem—and maintained that action for the entire season.

As support for Seattle's Black Lives Matter at School action swelled, in a move that surprised many, the Seattle Public Schools administration, with no formal urging from activists or the school board, officially endorsed the event. An Oct. 8 memo read:

> During our #CloseTheGaps kickoff week, Seattle Education Association is promoting October 19 as a day of solidarity to bring focus to racial equity and affirming the lives of our students—specifically our students of color.

In support of this focus, members are choosing to wear Black Lives Matter T-shirts, stickers, or other symbols of their commitment to students in a coordinated effort. SEA is leading this effort and working to promote transformational conversations with staff, families, and students on this issue.

We invite you to join us in our commitment to eliminate opportunity gaps and accelerate learning for each and every student.

At that point, we in Seattle felt that we had accomplished something historic, because for perhaps the first time in Seattle's history, the teachers and the teacher union, the parents and the PTSA, students and the Seattle Public Schools administration had all reached a consensus support for a very politicized action for racial justice in education.

As the Oct. 19 Black Lives Matter at School Day approached, orders for the various Black Lives Matter T-shirts soared. John Muir set up a site where T-shirt purchases would directly benefit the school's racial justice work. SEE's online T-shirt site received some 2,000 orders for the BLM shirts, with proceeds going to support racial justice campaigns and a portion going to John Muir. Other schools created their own T-shirt designs specific to their schools. Seattle's schools were now poised for unprecedented mass action for racial justice.

Black Lives Matter at School Day

As Oct. 19 arrived, Garfield High School senior Bailey Adams was in disbelief. She told Seattle's KING 5 News, "There was a moment of like, is this really going to happen? Are teachers actually going to wear these shirts? All of my years I've been in school, this has never been talked about. Teachers have never said anything where they're going to back their students of color."

But sure enough, every school across the city had educators come to school wearing the shirts. Hundreds of teachers took advantage of the day to teach lessons and lead discussions about institutional racism. SEE and Soup for Teachers partnered to make a handout called "Teaching and Mentoring for Racial Justice" that suggested BLM resources for both teachers and parents. SEA also emailed suggested resources to teachers.

Some schools changed their reader boards to declare "Black Lives Matter." Parents at some elementary schools set up tables by the front entrance with books and resources to help other parents talk to their kids about racism. Many schools coordinated plans for teaching about Black lives, including lessons about movements for racial justice and lessons about the way racism impacts the school system today. Several teachers across the district showed the film *Stay Woke* about the origins of the Black Lives Matter movement, and held class discussions afterward. Some educators used the opportunity to discuss intersectional identities and highlighted how Black and queer women had first launched the #BlackLivesMatter hashtag.

Schools such as Chief Sealth International High School and Garfield High School put up Black Lives Matter posters/graffiti walls, which quickly filled up with anti-racist commentary from students and educators. A teacher at Dearborn Park International Elementary built a lesson plan from a photo of Colin Kaepernick kneeling. To capture the power of the day, educators from most of the schools around the district took group photos wearing the BLM shirts and sent them to the union for publication.

During lunchtime, the Garfield faculty, staff, and students rallied on the front steps of the school. In one of the most moving and powerful moments of the day,

Black special education teacher Janet DuBois decided she finally had to tell everyone a secret she had been quietly suffering with. In front of all the assembled school community and media she revealed that the police had killed her son several years ago—and this had happened after he had been failed by the education system and pushed out of school. Fighting through tears, DuBois said, "When our kids are failed, they have to go to alternative places and end up with their lives hanging in the balance because someone does not care."

To cap off the extraordinary and powerful day, SEE organized a community celebration, forum, and talent showcase that evening that drew hundreds of people. The event was emceed by educator, organizer, poet, attorney, and soon-to-be Seattle mayoral candidate Nikkita Oliver. Spoken word poets, musicians, and the

Northwest Tap Connection (made up of predominantly Black youth performers) delighted and inspired the audience. Black youth activists from middle and high schools engaged in an onstage discussion about their experience of racism in school and what changes they wanted to see to make the education system truly value their lives. Seahawks Pro Bowl defensive end Michael Bennett came to the event and pledged his support of the movement, saying, "Some people believe the change has to come from the government, but I believe it has to be organic and come from the bottom."

By the end of the day, thousands of educators had reached tens of thousands of Seattle students and parents with a message of support for Black students and opposition to anti-Black racism—with local and national media projecting the message much farther. While the educators who launched this movement were quite aware that the institutions of racism remained intact, they also knew those same institutions had been shaken.

Lessons Learned

In many ways we had a successful campaign around making Black lives matter in Seattle schools, and, from an organizing perspective, we learned several important lessons. To begin, we learned that one school can make a big difference: A single elementary school bravely took a stand that provided a spark for an already simmering citywide movement, and influenced national discussions as educators in Philadelphia, Rochester (New York), and elsewhere followed suit with similar educationally based #BlackLivesMatter actions.

We also learned that acting in the context of a broader social movement was critical. The police killings of Castile and Sterling in the summer of 2016, as part of the long-standing pattern of Black death at the hands of police, ensured that there were ongoing protests and conversations associated with #BlackLivesMatter. This broader movement created the political space and helped garner support for the actions of both John Muir Elementary specifically, and Seattle Public Schools more generally.

In addition, we learned that sometimes when the white supremacists, "alt-right," and right-wing conservatives attack, it can make our organizing stronger and more powerful. In the case of Seattle, it was the avalanche of hateful emails and calls, the right-wing media stories, and the bomb threat against John Muir Elementary that ultimately galvanized teachers and parents across the city.

We also learned that developing a broad base of support was essential to the success of the campaign to make Black student lives matter in Seattle schools. Garnering the official support of the teacher union, the executive board of the Seattle Council PTSA, and even Seattle Public Schools, as well as gathering acts of solidarity from scholars and others nationally, helped build a protective web of political support to shield Seattle educators as they moved forward with their action.

In the end, we also learned that, with more time and resources, we could have done better organizing. For instance, we had to grapple with the fact that when the John Muir Elementary staff made the decision to wear their #BlackLivesMatter T-shirts, it was after being a part of sustained discussion and professional development that took place over multiple years. Ideally, all schools should have had the opportunity to have similar discussions as part of their typical professional development so that when a moment like this happens, all school staff have stronger basic understandings of racial justice to guide their decision-making.

Another improvement would have been to be able to offer a clearer vision of curriculum across the district for the Black Lives Matter at School Day. Despite the strength of the handout developed by SEE and Soup for Teachers, the quality and depth of what children at different schools learned on the day of the districtwide event varied wildly from school to school. With just a little more time and resources, we could have provided teachers with a cluster of grade level-appropriate teaching activities that they could have used on that day if they wanted. In particular, this is something that might have helped teachers around the district who wanted to support the action but struggled with ways to explicitly make Black lives matter in their own classroom curriculum.

It wasn't until the end of the school year that we learned two more lessons. The first was that, despite widespread community support for the Black Lives Matter at School Day, the passive-aggressive racism of some of Seattle's notoriously liberal, white parents had been lurking all along. In a June 2017 story, local news radio station KUOW reported on a series of emails from white parents who live in the more affluent north end of Seattle. According to the story, white parents complained not just about the perceived militancy and politics of the Black Lives Matter at School Day in Seattle, but that children couldn't handle talking about racism, and that we should be color-blind because "all lives matter." Importantly, many of these parents openly questioned the existence of racial inequality in Seattle's schools.

The second lesson we learned well after the Black Lives Matter at School Day was that our action helped strengthen the political groundwork for a continued focus on racial justice in Seattle Public Schools. On July 5, 2017, the Seattle School Board unanimously passed a resolution in support of ethnic studies in Seattle Public Schools in response to a yearlong campaign from the NAACP, SEE, and other social justice groups, including formal endorsement from SEA. While this policy shift happened on the strength of the community organizing for ethnic studies specifically, Seattle's movement to make Black Lives Matter in School demonstrated to the district that there was significant public support for racial justice initiatives in Seattle schools, effectively increasing the official space for other initiatives like ethnic studies to take hold.

Putting the Shirts Back On

The school year ended with a horrific reminder of why we must continue to declare the value of Black lives when on Sunday, June 18, 2017, Seattle police shot and killed Charleena Lyles, a pregnant mother of four, in her own apartment after she called them in fear her home was being burglarized. She was shot down in a hail of bullets in front of three of her kids, two of whom attended public elementary schools in Seattle. The immediate media narrative of her death dehumanized her by focusing on the fact that the police alleged Lyles was wielding a kitchen knife, that she had a history of mental illness, and a criminal background. This was the usual strategy of killing the person and then assassinating their character in an attempt to turn public opinion in support of the police.

But in Seattle, there were the countervailing forces of Lyles' organized family, community activists, and Seattle educators who forced a different public discussion about the value of Black lives and the callous disregard of them by unaccountable police. SEE and the SEA immediately put out a call for teachers to put their Black Lives Matter shirts back on—many of which also featured #SayHerName—for a districtwide action in solidarity with Lyles and her family on June 20. Within three days of Lyles' death, hundreds of teachers came to school wearing heartbreak, rage, and solidarity in the form of their Black Lives Matter T-shirts—with shirt sales this time going to Lyles' family.

A couple hundred educators swelled the ranks of the after-school rally that day with Lyles' family and hundreds of other supporters at the apartment complex where she had been killed. With educators from her sons' schools and all across the district rallying to Lyles' side, the press was compelled to run stories talking about her as a woman, as a parent of Seattle schoolchildren, and as a person with talents and struggles like everyone else.

Seattle's Black Lives Matter at School Day is only a beginning. Having nearly 3,000 teachers wear T-shirts to school one day doesn't magically end anti-Black racism or white supremacy. If that were the case, then perhaps Charleena Lyles would still be alive today to drop her kids off at school, chat with other parents on the playground, and watch the children play.

But something powerful and important did happen in Seattle. At John Muir Elementary, the school staff and community stood strong against white suprema-cist hate, and across Seattle schools, teachers and parents found a way to stand in solidarity with Black students and their families. In the process, the public dialogue about institutionalized racism in Seattle schools was pushed forward in concrete ways. And while we have so much more work to do, in the end, what happened in Seattle showed that educators have an important role to play in the movement for Black lives. When they rise up across the country to join this movement—both inside the school and outside on the streets—institutions of racism can be challenged in the search for solidarity, healing, and justice. ☷

Wayne Au and Jesse Hagopian are editors of Rethinking Schools. *Au, a former public high school teacher, is a professor in the School of Educational Studies at the University of Washington Bothell. Hagopian teaches ethnic studies at Seattle's Garfield High School and is a member of Social Equity Educators (SEE). You can follow him @JesseHagopian.*

Organizing a Caucus in Philadelphia, Step by Step

BY LARISSA PAHOMOV

CHRISTIANE GRAUERT

O n Nov. 7, 2019, I walked into a meeting of hundreds of people I had never met before. The event was at the Church of the Advocate, a historic landmark in North Philadelphia with a deep progressive history, from hosting Black Panther conventions to ordaining the city's first female Episcopal priests. That evening, the cavernous sanctuary bustled with energy, framed by soaring stained glass windows and murals depicting scenes of faith and justice. More than 300 educators from around the city were gathered, sharing food and stories from the school year. Children ran around the clusters of high-backed wooden chairs, and many attendees sported T-shirts with an image of the Liberty Bell and the slogan "Working Educators for a Stronger Union!"

I bumped into an old friend, and we took in the scene together. We were witnessing the culmination of a dream: a campaign launch to win leadership of our union. After six months of active planning, we were just three months away from the election where the Caucus of Working Educators would hopefully take control of our union, the Philadelphia Federation of Teachers (PFT).

"I just can't believe how far we've come in the last few years," said my friend. "And to think, this all started with a handful of people meeting in a room."

I laughed. "I can't believe how far we've come in the last six weeks." After devoting my summer to campaign planning, I had given birth to a baby boy at the end of September. This was my first event back, and the parade of new faces overwhelmed me, in the best way. In each circle, new recruits talked animatedly with organizers who'd been caucus members for months or years. We had successfully activated rank-and-file union members by reaching out, educator to educator.

Curriculum and Classroom Roots

The Caucus of Working Educators (WE) has several origins, but one of the most significant is the Teacher Action Group of Philadelphia (TAG), a grassroots organization founded in 2008. With a small core of dedicated educators from both public and charter schools, TAG quickly became a force in the city, providing political education for teachers, both to transform their curriculum and classroom practices and to push back on neoliberal education policies, from No Child Left Behind to local charter school expansion. From the beginning, TAG organized events such as an annual curriculum fair and Inquiry-to-Action Groups, mini-courses that explored topics from mindfulness to social justice unionism. Over the years, TAG took on political projects of increasing size and scope, including organizing rallies outside the school district office in response to school closure plans in 2012, and coordinating a "Faces of the Layoffs" website when 3,000 district employees lost their jobs in 2013 to budget cuts. These projects helped raise political awareness but reached only a small fraction of Philadelphia's thousands of educators. TAG was, by definition, a network of activists, seeking to share a message but not build a base of members.

TAG's approach could not have been more different from the PFT's, whose leadership believed in a top-down business model of unionism, where members have minimal input and paid staffers refuse to give out direct phone numbers or

> We had successfully activated rank-and-file members of our union by reaching out the best way we knew how: educator to educator.

email addresses. Predictably, the union leadership did not embrace the activism of TAG, ignoring or rejecting requests to promote or collaborate on projects, and refusing volunteer help in organizing efforts. In the midst of this frustration, the Chicago Teachers Union strike in 2012 showed us how an urban teacher union—led by their new progressive caucus, CORE—could engage an entire city in the fight for better schools. CORE showed us that transformation of our union was possible. However, Philadelphia was still far away from what Chicago had achieved.

Most PFT members had never voted in a union election or even knew it was possible to form a caucus. After a few of us attended the first UCORE conference in Chicago, we pulled together a group of like-minded educators from around Philadelphia and officially founded WE in March 2014. Like TAG—which continued to operate—we had a mission statement and a website. But like union caucuses in other cities, we identified ourselves specifically as being "of the Philadelphia Federation of Teachers" and created an official membership status, where members select the monthly donation they can afford.

From the Classroom to the (School) Board Room

TAG's formative influence on the caucus meant that our early projects focused more on classroom practice than union matters. One of the first caucus committees was the Racial Justice Committee ("RJ"), which seeks to advance an anti-racist agenda to transform both individual educators and school policy. Inspired by the Black Lives Matter at School Day organized by Social Equity Educators in Seattle in 2016 (see Au and Hagopian, p. 209), RJ members began to think big about how the spirit of this day could be brought directly into classrooms. We decided to organize an entire Week of Action in January 2017, complete with lesson plans across subject areas, resources, readings, and daily events for educators, students, and community members. The first year's program helped educators make huge inroads for racial justice in their school environments, where sometimes even saying the phrase "Black Lives Matter" had been taboo. School staff around the city incorporated the guiding principles of the movement into their lessons, whether it was reading a children's book that celebrated Black women and girls or adopting restorative justice practices in their classrooms.

After that year's success, RJ reflected on what had been achieved and weighed where to go next. It would have been easy to simply replicate the previous year's program, but instead, committee members asked some hard questions: What would it look like to push for racial justice beyond just individual educators? How could the week advocate for more systemic change?

The answer came out of BLM week's nationwide explosion in popularity. Sister groups around the country established their own Weeks of Action, and this network established a set of national demands, including mandating Black history and ethnic studies, ending zero tolerance, and hiring Black educators. As public school parent and organizer Tamara Anderson put it, the demands were intended to "become ongoing actions in individual school districts." In Philadelphia, that meant constantly pushing the administration to release demographic data based on race and provide proof it was following through on its claims of commitment to diversity. Eventually the school district released data on teachers alongside a new initiative to recruit and retain Black educators.

This success demonstrated that transforming classroom practices could jump-start larger systemic organizing. But we had questions about how we could expand our influence.

To help guide this growth, our caucus invited two special guests to facilitate our 2018 Summer Organizing Institute: veteran organizers Jane McAlevey and Bill Fletcher. McAlevey led us in conversation about our own strengths and challenges as a caucus, especially when it came to the question of how to connect with the entire membership of the PFT. She shared examples of her approach to whole-worker organizing, including preventing the closure of a public housing complex in Stamford, Connecticut. Fletcher pushed us to reflect on our commitment to racial justice and how to bring our values to the larger union membership. He emphasized that, for majority-white organizations, fighting racism was not simply a moral imperative, but one that serves members' self-interest, since racist practices affect all workers. McAlevey and Fletcher helped us zero in on a campaign that would meet all of these criteria: the abysmal physical condition of our schools.

A Campaign for School Facilities Renovation

With a critical mass of buildings built before 1970, and many more than a century old, our school buildings are in perpetual crisis. A 2018 report by the *Philadelphia Inquirer* revealed cases of severe lead poisoning and botched asbestos cleanup that increased student and teacher exposure. For years the district would make some effort at cleanup but defer major renovations due to lack of funds, especially since the "most urgent repairs" alone were estimated to cost $3 billion.

> Fletcher emphasized that, for majority-white organizations, fighting racism was not simply a moral imperative, but one that serves members' material self-interest, since racist practices affect all workers.

As educators we knew exactly what effect this neglect was having, both on ourselves and our students. The call to action was clear: Fix our toxic schools! We drafted a petition that demanded all buildings receive proper remediation for lead, asbestos, and pest control—and named viable funding sources that could help make it happen, including corporations and universities in Philadelphia that have benefited from large tax exemptions.

This petition marked the continued evolution of our organization from an activist model to an organizing one. Unlike projects like BLM Week, which involved extensive outreach but were fundamentally opt-in programs, the building conditions petition was designed to move quickly and comprehensively, collecting as many signatures of PFT members as possible during the first part of the school year. We knew that the issue was urgent, but we grappled with whether this campaign would distract from programs like the Black Lives Matter Week of Acton. Could the core beliefs of WE be preserved as we shifted into a campaign with even broader reach?

The answer lay in the framing of our work. As educators began circulating the petition in fall 2018, WE's organizing core discussed how to approach the "average" PFT member—one who may not be familiar with structural critiques of our schools. In the activist model, the general expectation was that participants already had the same political analysis as the organization. Programs like Black Lives Matter Week of Action advertised our politics in the title, so the vast majority of participants were already on board with the message.

Of course, we knew that we were fighting to fix our schools for the same reasons we printed thousands of T-shirts that proclaimed "Black Lives Matter"—that it was structural racism, which valued the education of Black and Brown children less than their white counterparts, that had caused chronic underfunding of our school district. We wanted to make sure our colleagues understood this analysis as we asked them to sign on. As a majority-white union, we have many members—including more conservative Black members—who are skeptical of engagement with so-called "social justice issues." We knew this type of organizing would require us to evolve our tactics. How would we bring all our diverse membership on board effectively?

The answer was one that also came out of our classroom expertise—just ask questions. Instead of leading with statements about generational inequality and structural racism—common terminology in the caucus, but less so citywide—we developed a campaign script that asked our colleagues to describe the difficult conditions of their school buildings first, and then point out that nearby suburbs had quickly dealt with mold, asbestos, and other issues as soon as they appeared. And then, the simple question: "Why do you think that is?"

In response, we were able to see what level of political analysis our colleagues held. Some immediately demonstrated the same conclusion we had: "Well, it's racist." But even those who took the answers one step at a time would move toward a more systemic analysis:

"Well, they have more money than us."

"And why is that?"

"Their property values are higher, and they can collect more taxes."

"Yes, and how did that happen?"

"Wealthier people live there because the schools are better."

"And why do we rely so heavily on local taxes for funding our schools?"

". . . Because politicians in our state don't care. Nobody's looking out for the city."

"And what's the racial makeup of these suburban districts like?"

"Overwhelmingly white."

"And do these students deserve more than the Black and Brown students in our schools? Do we not deserve buildings free of mold, or asbestos, or mice?"

We never found anyone who felt that this inequity was just—which means that, even if they did not have the exact vocabulary to express it, our citywide colleagues knew quite clearly what impact systemic racism was having on our schools. This approach produced more than 3,000 signatures, which we presented to our school board and City Council the following spring. Just a few weeks later, $15.6 million in additional funding was announced for building repairs, and more than 20 schools got physical improvements over the summer.

Seeking Power

The conclusion of our building conditions petition rolled us directly into our campaign for leadership of the PFT. Caucus members took on the formidable task of campaigning in other schools and having the organizing conversations that form the building blocks of a high-participation union. Again, we found the best practice for organizing was the one we used in the classroom—ask questions and build common ground from the answers we received:

- If you could change one thing about this school to improve learning conditions for your students, and working conditions for you, what would it be?
- Now, what do you think it would take for our union to win those terms in our next contract?
- Does this sound like something you want to be a part of?

As we built relationships in schools across the city, the answer to that last question was almost always a resounding "Yes!" Few of our citywide colleagues had ever been asked to do anything meaningful by our union leadership, so this conversation was their first taste of what an activated union *could* be like. Our building conditions petition spoke to our own track record of wins, especially in the schools where the funding had resulted in repairs.

Broadening Our Base

When asking people to pledge their vote for us in the upcoming election, I would often finish by saying, "If all you do is vote for us and nothing else, nothing will change. This conversation is the start of a fundamentally different way of running our union." What's more, those conversations led to new movements within the campaign. As more paraprofessionals connected with the campaign, it was clear they had not been adequately supported by our union leadership. While paras are the second-largest bargaining unit in the district, the vast majority of them start at a full-time salary of less than $15,000—and they are consistently treated as interchangeable and expendable. Out of frustration with these enduring conditions, the ParaPower movement was born. Spearheaded by a handful of classroom assistants from different schools, ParaPower quickly developed its own list of contract demands, gained traction on social media, and hosted a summit in the months leading up to the vote.

Moving Forward

On election day, we won 2,700 votes for our complete slate of candidates—twice as many votes as we'd won four years before, and close to 40 percent of the total vote. We had successfully brought many members into our vision of a high-participation union, but fear of change—and an entrenched incumbency who encouraged that fear in their campaign literature—still kept many members from voting for WE. As a result, we did not win any seats on the executive board. This was an intense disappointment, but not a failure, as our campaign had been built to do much more than just claim an office and a title. By engaging with members one-on-one, we activated thousands of new supporters and developed leaders in almost every district school in the city. Those contacts became more active union members over the course of our work, whether it was organizing staff walkouts over elevated asbestos levels or reaching out across bargaining units to ensure that all PFT members earn a living wage in our next contract. And all of it was done with an analysis centered on workers: We are the educators on the ground, and we know what's best for our own students and buildings. Our organizing model has changed the landscape of our union, expanding mindsets and raising the expectations of our fellow members. As the next round of contract negotiations have already opened, we hope that our fellow members will see that a stronger union is within our reach—and that we will build it one conversation at a time. 🕊

> "If you could change one thing about this school to improve learning conditions for your students, and working conditions for you, what would it be?"

Larissa Pahomov is a veteran teacher in the School District of Philadelphia and a founding member of the Caucus of Working Educators. A National Board Certified Teacher, she is the author of the teaching handbook Authentic Learning in the Digital Age *and writes about both the practice and politics of working in schools.*

NATE KITH

"It's Not Magic. It's Organizing!"
The powerful journey of North Carolina teachers

BY ELENI SCHIRMER

I n March 2013, just months after Republicans gained a supermajority in the North Carolina legislature and won the governor's office, state NAACP president Rev. William Barber II stood before educators at the annual convention of the North Carolina Association of Educators (NCAE) and delivered an electrifying keynote speech.

Barber, a civil rights leader who led the state's "Moral Monday" movement and, later, the national Poor People's Campaign, called on teachers to confront the conservative agenda taking apart their states through direct actions, protests, and organizing. If educators saw public education as a cornerstone of democracy, they would need to stand up and fight for it. His exhortations struck a new tone in the NCAE, an organization better known for lobbying elected officials than leading mass movements against them.

"He lit the room on fire," remembered Durham high school teacher Bryan Proffitt. Inspired but new to the NCAE scene, Proffitt texted a veteran NCAE friend: "Bring everyone you know who wants to do *that* to the back of the room."

The assembled teachers quickly realized they wanted—indeed, needed—to get to work. Three weeks later, they met to talk more. Shortly thereafter, they put together a workshop about organizing skills for their colleagues—how to have one-on-one conversations, map workplaces to gauge membership, assess power structures. They began study groups about the neoliberalization of education, structural racism in education, and the role of teacher unions.

In April 2020, that scrappy group of teachers from the back of the state convention won the NCAE's statewide leadership elections.

These teachers' successful organizing marks an important landmark in today's teacher union movement. Although often overlooked in popular accounts of teachers' recent "red state revolts," North Carolina's progressive caucus, Organize 2020 for Racial and Social Justice, offers crucial lessons for building social justice teacher unions. Their name defined their goals and their method: to organize a fighting union that prioritized racial and social justice by 2020.

> In April 2020, that scrappy group of teachers from the back of the state convention won the NCAE's statewide leadership elections.

Tamika Walker Kelly

Turquoise LeJeune Parker

Bryan Proffitt

Caucus members Tamika Walker Kelly and Bryan Proffitt will serve as the NCAE's president and vice president, respectively; Turquoise LeJeune Parker will become North Carolina's National Education Association director. To date, they are one of the few progressive teacher union caucuses to win state-level leadership elections. In one sense, Organize 2020 has achieved its namesake: to organize a progressive, racial justice-focused teacher union by 2020. But perhaps more accurately, their success reflects the work of years of careful organizing, a patient buildup of strength, and a movement still hitting its stride.

In the past decade, North Carolina has become the extreme right's frontier. In 2010, Republicans won the state's General Assembly, as the legislature is formally known, for the first time since Reconstruction. In 2012, they took the governor's mansion and achieved a three-fifths majority in both houses of the legislature. With Tea Party and Koch brothers backing, the Republican supermajority pushed through a series of American Legislative Exchange Council (ALEC)-sponsored legislation. ALEC is a right-wing corporate-backed association that drafts and advances conservative legislation. In North Carolina, ALEC legislation starved the public sector, cut social spending to the bone, and deregulated corporations and private entities. The General Assembly slashed the earned income tax credit for working families, cut Medicaid coverage, and ended federal unemployment benefits for 170,000 in a state with one the nation's highest unemployment rates.

Meanwhile, legislators rolled back corporate taxes, estate taxes, and personal income taxes to the lowest in the country. The ensuing budget shortfalls devastated public schools. Per-pupil spending plummeted. Schools lacked basic supplies. Those who stayed saw their wages decline 9.4 percent since 2009, dropping to among the lowest teacher salaries in the country. At the same time, North Carolina legislators reallocated funds to private and charter schools. In 2011, Republican legislators removed a cap on charter schools. In 2013, they created private school vouchers, drawing even more money from public school budgets. North Carolina's Republicans were turning the lights out on public education.

Building a Base, Step by Step

While public education's enemies assembled new power and strategies, the teacher union seemed frozen in place. Throughout much of the preceding decades, North Carolina had been governed by moderate Democrats, such as Jim Hunt and Mike Easley. Thanks to a strong alliance with the NCAE, these "education governors" passed reforms that made North Carolina's public education system shine across the South, from class size reductions to teacher salary increases to prized principal training institutes. It was a stable compact: the NCAE secured teachers' bread-and-butter protections in exchange for teachers' votes and political contributions. But by the 2010s, as the right gained power, Tea Party and Koch brother-backed Republicans seized the legislature and governorship, and the NCAE's lobbying strategy crumbled—along with its influence.

Across the state, teachers increasingly saw the union as an irrelevant, even impotent, force of change. Membership dropped precipitously. But when the Chicago Teachers Union won a historic strike in 2012 against one of the country's most powerful Democrats with unprecedented levels of community support, educators around the country began to reimagine possibilities for their own unions. The Chicago strike helped many, including Proffitt, realize a "union isn't like a mythical creature. It's just a set of humans." A union could change. But how?

Weeks after the NCAE's 2013 convention, Rev. Barber began North Carolina's Moral Monday movement. Thousands gathered each week in Raleigh to demand voting rights, immigrant rights, racial justice, tax reform, and public funding for public schools. Although NCAE leadership did not participate, Proffitt and fellow educators Raquel Robinson, Jessica Benton, and Kristin Beller jumped in. They spent the summer of 2013 walking through the crowds holding up a clipboard that read "Public School Worker?" By the end of summer, they had connected with hundreds of fired-up teachers. When they ran an all-day organizing training the Saturday before school started in the fall, more than 75 people showed up. "It was really wild to do an organizing thing the Saturday before school started," explained Durham teacher and Organize 2020 leader Turquoise LeJeune Parker. "Like really wild. And I liked that." Casting aside the notion of teachers as docile rule-followers, these educators got to work. After all, the rules were dismantling their schools.

> "A union isn't like a mythical creature. It's just a set of humans."

In 2013, the North Carolina legislature made additional funding cuts to public education, raised class size limits, and for the fifth year in a row denied a salary increase for teachers. This group of educators decided to organize actions to draw attention to their students' pressing needs and their poor teaching conditions. That fall, educators in 90 schools across the state led a "walk-in" campaign, in which rank-and-file teachers invited families and community members to gather before the bell and then simultaneously walk into schools en masse. The following year, the Alliance to Reclaim Our Schools lifted up the tactic, and began a series of nationwide "walk-ins" by teachers and parents that galvanized labor and community coalitions across the country. The teachers weren't walking *out* on students—they were walking *in* for them.

Meanwhile, the General Assembly was doing everything possible to divide and conquer teachers. That summer, it proposed a measure offering 25 percent of teachers $500 if they surrendered their due process and appeals rights; everyone else would face short-term contracts and lose their career status. The NCAE immediately brought a lawsuit challenging the bill. But Proffitt and his fellow educators had a different strategy. The union's lawsuit might win, but it would do little to engage anybody, nor would it build teachers' power. Quickly, they developed a "Decline to Sign" campaign. They gathered signatures of teachers who would not accept the new contract terms, and then helped others develop local campaigns to pressure their school boards to oppose the bill. Within a few months nearly half all of the school boards in the state passed resolutions opposing the law. When the law was finally rejected, teachers got to understand it as their victory, too—not just something that lawyers or lobbyists had won *for* them. This success encouraged the educators who participated in this campaign to officially become a caucus: Organize 2020.

In 2014, a leadership change in the NCAE altered Organize 2020's relationship with the state union. The NCAE's new executive director was decidedly less friendly toward Organize 2020 and thwarted many of their efforts to utilize the union's official channels. Rather than fighting against obstinate would-be allies, the group decided to prioritize internal political education. The caucus, which at this point in time was predominantly white, organized a series of workshops around race and racism. "One of the things we say in Organize 2020," Walker Kelly explained, "is that we believe the job of the union is to defend and to transform education. If we're really going to do that, we have to talk about the institutional barriers racism creates." Prior to Organize 2020, issues of race and racism had seldom been addressed within the union. "We spent a lot of time talking about bread-and-butter issues like pay and working conditions and things like that, but we didn't really spend a lot of time talking about what does it really mean when we say want every child to have a high-quality public education?" said Walker Kelly. Approximately 51 percent of North Carolina's public school students are students of color; less than 20 percent of the teaching workforce is people of color. Organize 2020's trainings drew in many leaders of color, establishing Organize 2020 as a multiracial caucus.

These trainings empowered educators to understand the structural dimensions of racism and educational inequality. They also aimed to build educators' organizing skills, and leadership development especially, to address these problems. Leadership, Organize 2020 believed, like organizing, was a skill; it could be learned and taught. The caucus was deeply reverent of Ella Baker's organizing philosophy and legacy, especially her emphasis on building relationships and the bottom-up development of power. The caucus especially heeds the leadership definition of scholar Marshall Ganz, whose scholarship offers academic codification of much of Baker's work. Leadership, Ganz defines, is "accepting responsibility for creating the conditions that enable others to achieve shared purpose in the face of uncertainty." (Proffitt quipped that Organize 2020 leaders hold that definition so dear, all will eventually tattoo some portion of it on their bodies.) As LeJeune Parker explained, "So much of the work of teaching is about teaching young people about the world that we live in and we want to live in and helping them understand how they fit in there and how necessary their voices are. You have a huge role to play in this, and I need you." For Organize 2020 teachers, developing a sense of personal and collective agency was critical to their work as educators and unionists.

Durham Association of Education Takes the Lead

But Organize 2020 wasn't content with political education alone; they wanted to win power to advance their vision. They decided on a strategy of building up locals; the union was, after all, "an assemblage of locals." In 2015, Proffitt began organizing and successfully ran for president of the Durham Association of Educators (DAE). He quickly built up relationships with teachers and administration at every school, making hand and face contact with as many educators as possible. Mass meetings, which previously had eight or nine in attendance, became boisterous events of 50 or 60 people, in which key decisions and campaigns were plotted out. "People don't hate meetings," Proffitt explained, "they hate *bad* meetings." DAE meetings bustled with clear structures, agendas, goals, celebrations, opportunities for discussion, organizing work plans. Rather than time to aimlessly grumble and complain, DAE meetings became key spaces for advancing the union's campaigns. Walk into a DAE meeting and call out, "It's not magic" and the whole room will respond, "It's ORGANIZING!"

The local also developed a sophisticated system of building organizers and district organizers to keep tight communication between school-based organizing and union leadership. Campaign actions all became "structure tests" to gauge the strength of the organization, checkups to assess the depth and breadth of workers' participation. (See McAlevey, p. 423.) These actions gave information about the strength of organizing at each school—where participation was high or low, leadership strongholds and gaps. This informed where they needed to build strength in the next round of organizing.

Running constant campaigns not only built the union's internal organizing strength, it also developed their external power. Between 2015 and 2018, DAE won a series of bold campaigns to protect and defend their students, communities, and fellow workers, who were under increasing attack from conservative legislators. In 2015, they won a wage raise for classified staff, the first time in years. In 2016, when a high school student was kidnapped on his way to school by Immigration and Customs Enforcement, DAE took the lead in advocating for the student's return. This campaign not only successfully brought the student home, it also shifted how the union related to questions of immigration reform, putting it at the center of the union's purview. After all, teachers' primary responsibility is to protect students.

The next year, when the Republican governor threatened more school budget cuts, Proffitt, LeJeune Parker, and fellow Organize 2020 members marched from Durham to Raleigh, demanding a meeting with Gov. Pat McCrory about the cuts. When the governor did not show up to the meeting, despite the fact that this group of teachers walked 20-plus miles in two days to meet with him, they refused to leave. Fourteen teachers were arrested. Their action not only brought attention to schools' budget crisis, it also weakened McCrory's credibility. That fall, he was voted out of office. Organize 2020 successfully backed candidates for Durham school board, installing one of the most progressive school boards in the South. In 2017, when a controversial school takeover bill targeted a Durham public school to be converted to a charter, teachers organized a campaign to keep it open. A year later, they had not only defeated the bill, they had also built the school into a flourishing community school.

In 2018, when West Virginia teachers led a historic statewide strike, North Carolina teachers wondered if they could do something similar. But a successful statewide strike requires more than an email blast from a few teachers. Organize 2020 teachers knew they would need incredible unity and strong organizing, especially in a right-to-work state with minimal union protections. The teachers understood two factors behind West Virginia and the other states' successes: One school district led the way for the rest, and enough teachers requested personal days that superintendents had no choice but to close schools. "Durham was our Mingo County," Proffitt explained, referring to the pivotal West Virginia county in coal miners' 1920 bitter struggle to unionize. The well-organized Durham local sprang into action. Within weeks, enough teachers requested personal days that the school board closed the schools. Soon, 42 school districts across the state followed suit.

On May 16, 2018, 30,000 North Carolina teachers participated in the statewide day of action.

In previous years, the NCAE held an annual lobbying day in Raleigh. A few hundred teachers would show up and politely request meetings with legislators to plea for their issues. This year was different. Organize 2020 sought to build teachers' power, not to bow down to the legislators. Instead of sending teachers into the statehouse to meet with legislators, teachers invited legislators out to the mall to speak with them. Rather than milling around for speakers and a photo op, Organize 2020 facilitated mass meetings for each county to further discuss how to push their legislators. While Organize 2020 leaders knew the conservative legislature was unlikely to actually move on their demands, they knew a win was still possible. The victory? Defeating the fear and hopelessness that prevents us from standing together to address shared conditions.

Feeling Powerful

On that May 16, Walker Kelly woke up early. She hadn't slept much the night before. Although the whole day had been carefully planned, she still was nervous—who would actually show up? But within hours, buses poured into Raleigh, 30,000 teachers streaming forth, all wearing red, in the new fashion of "RedForEd" movements. The teachers had never seen anything like it. As Proffitt described, "It was multiracial, multigenerational. It was the entire state. And everybody's in red." Proffitt, Walker Kelly, and another Organize 2020 teacher, Kristin Beller, stood at the back of the downtown mall, watching educators join the march. They wanted to get the size of the thing. When the streets had totally filled, the three of them linked hands and began walking very slowly through the center of the crowds, greeting their thousands of colleagues. At one point, Proffitt, carrying a microphone, jumped on to a ledge. "Do y'all feel powerful?" he yelled to the crowd.

"YES," they roared back. "Do y'all feel scared?" "NO," they repeated. "Do y'all feel powerful?" he yelled again. "YES," they bellowed once more. In the face of uncertainty, they were finding shared purpose.

As much as anything the May 16, 2018, day of action proved the strength of the Organize 2020 caucus and sharpened their ambitions. Conditions had hardly improved over the past year, and Organize 2020 knew there was more work to do. During the 2019 NCAE state convention that spring, Organize 2020 began pushing for another day of action. They polled teachers to assess what issues they should tackle this year, and by the end of the convention, the NCAE approved a list of five demands: to increase school librarians, psychologists, social workers, counselors, and nurses in schools; to provide a $15 minimum wage for all school personnel and a 5 percent raise for all educators, including a 5 percent cost-of-living adjustment for retirees; to reinstate retiree health benefits that had been eliminated by the 2017 legislature; to restore advanced degree compensation that been stripped by the General Assembly; and, most controversially, to expand Medicaid. Although the teachers knew they were unlikely to convince the Republican legislators of their demands, demanding them was nonetheless important. It helped people articulate connections between education and broader social policies. Those connections, Walker Kelly explained, were the point. "Educators were leading the conversations about what our state needs," their political education deepening. "It was a beautiful thing," she said.

May 1, 2019, furthered Organize 2020's organizing capacity. In 2018, the caucus recruited 50 volunteers for their day of action; in 2019, they had 180. After years of building up structure tests, Organize 2020 believed it had the organizational power to win a statewide union election. In April 2020, the "TB for L" campaign—Tamika and Bryan for Leadership—won. They nearly tripled the number of voters, taking nearly two-thirds of all votes. Their victory opens the doors for new possibilities, new leadership development. Their movement is advancing.

Organize 2020's success is one of reimagined proportions. North Carolina's billionaire-backed conservative movement fighting to dismantle public education is one of the strongest in the nation. A victory in a right-to-work state, in which racism, segregation, poverty, and urban-rural divisions have been enabled to fester, is a triumph for progressive movements everywhere. But Organize 2020's triumph isn't magic—it's organizing. ⬛

Eleni Schirmer is a scholar, writer, and activist from Madison, Wisconsin. She is currently a PhD candidate at University of Wisconsin–Madison studying Educational Policy and Curriculum & Instruction. Her research explores the contradictory capacities of social movements—particularly teacher unions—to shape institutions, identities, and ideas.

STOP STARVING OUR SCHOOLS

Mayor Lightfoot Come Back to the Light !! Keep Your Promise Put it in Writing

SPEED LIMIT 35 NOT CLASS SIZE

WE SUPPORT CHICAGO TEACHERS AND STAFF

School on Strike

EN HUELGA

SOL TE ST

deserve class

JOE BRUSKY | MTEA

SECTION FOUR

REIMAGINING OUR UNIONS
TO BUILD POWER

A Revitalized Teacher Union Movement
Reflections from the field

BY BOB PETERSON

BARBARA MINER

When I was elected president of the Milwaukee Teachers' Education Association (MTEA) in April of 2011, people didn't know whether to congratulate me or give me condolences. The election took place in the midst of one of the largest worker uprisings in recent U.S. history.

Unfortunately, that spring uprising, although massive and inspirational, was not strong enough to stop Wisconsin Gov. Scott Walker from enacting the most draconian anti-public sector labor law in the nation.

That law, known as Act 10, coming just a year after the U.S. Supreme Court's *Citizens United* decision, received support from the Koch brothers and a cabal of national right-wing funders and organizations. It was imposed on all public sector workers except the police and firefighter unions that endorsed Walker, and whose members are predominantly white and male.

Act 10 took away virtually all collective bargaining rights, including the right to arbitration. It left intact only the right to bargain base wage increases up to the cost of living. The new law prohibited "agency fees," in which all employees of a bargaining unit pay their "fair share." It also prohibited payroll deduction of dues. It imposed an unprecedented annual recertification requirement on public sector unions, requiring a 51 percent (not 50 percent plus one) vote of all eligible employees, counting anyone who does not vote as a "no." Using those criteria, Walker would never have been elected.

Immediately following Act 10, Walker and the Republican-dominated state Legislature made the largest cuts to public education of any state in the nation and gerrymandered state legislative districts to privilege conservative, white-populated areas of the state.

Having decimated labor law and defunded public education, Walker proceeded to expand statewide the private school voucher program that has wreaked havoc on Milwaukee, and enacted one of the nation's most generous income tax deductions for private school tuition.

Under these conditions, public sector union membership plummeted, staff has been reduced, and resources to lobby, organize, and influence elections have shrunk.

People familiar with Wisconsin's progressive history—in 1959, for example, we were the first state to legalize collective bargaining for public sector workers—find these events startling. And they should. If it can happen in Wisconsin, it could happen anywhere.

And it did. Following Wisconsin's lead, Tennessee abolished the right for teachers to bargain collectively, and state legislatures in Ohio, Michigan, and Iowa passed laws restricting public sector collective bargaining. In city after city, privately run charter schools started to dominate the education landscape. And in 2018 the U.S. Supreme Court in *Janus v. AFSCME* prohibited the collection of "agency fees" for all public sector unions in the nation.

Fortunately, teacher union activists across the country are revitalizing their unions and standing up to these relentless attacks. An unprecedented rise in rank-and-file militancy—from the 2012 Chicago teachers' strike through the 2018 strike wave sparked by West Virginia teachers up to strikes in Los Angeles, Oakland, Chicago, and St. Paul—demonstrate that educators are learning to fight back.

This growing militancy and push to transform the very nature of the teacher union movement may well be the most important force in our nation to defend and improve public schools and, in so doing, defend and improve our communities and what's left of our democratic institutions.

This revitalization builds on the strengths of traditional "bread-and-butter" unionism. But it recognizes that our future depends on redefining unionism from a narrow trade union model, focused almost exclusively on protecting union members, to a broader vision that sees the future of unionized workers tied directly to the interests of the entire working class and the communities, particularly communities of color, in which we live and work.

This is a sea change for teacher unions (and other unions, too). But it's not an easy one to make. It requires confronting racist attitudes and past practices that have marginalized people of color both inside and outside unions. It also means overcoming old habits and stagnant organizational structures that weigh down efforts to expand internal democracy and member engagement.

From Bread and Butter to Social Justice

The MTEA is a member of the National Education Association (NEA), which has a long history of being staff-dominated. In some locals, elected presidents were (and still are) just figureheads. Allan West, a national NEA staff member, memorialized this staff-run union approach in a widely distributed 1965 speech. According to West, the executive director was the one who should be the public spokesperson, develop agendas for elected executive boards, and direct most of the union's affairs. This power structure was written into our local's constitution, and it had profound consequences. When a member of a progressive rank-and-file caucus in Milwaukee was elected president in 1991, for example, it took him six months just to get a key to the office. For nearly a decade we pushed for a full-time release president, a proposal resisted by most professional staff.

Meanwhile, by the late 1980s and into the '90s, teacher activists in Milwaukee were connecting with other rank-and-file teacher union activists through Rethinking Schools and the newly formed National Coalition of Education Activists (NCEA). In 1994, 29 teacher union activists from both the NEA and the American Federation of Teachers (AFT) met at the NCEA conference in Portland, Oregon, and issued a statement: "Social Justice Unionism: A Working Draft." (See p. 74.)

Social justice unionism is an organizing model that calls for a radical boost in internal union democracy and increased member participation. This contrasts to a business model that is so dependent on staff providing services that it disempowers members and concentrates power in the hands of a small group of elected leaders and/or paid staff. An organizing model, while still providing services to members, focuses on building union power at the school level in alliance with parents, community groups, and other social movements.

Three components of social justice unionism are like the legs of a stool. Unions need all three to be balanced and strong:

- We organize around bread-and-butter issues.
- We organize around teaching and learning issues to reclaim our profession and our classrooms.

- We organize for social justice in our community and in our curriculum.

Unfortunately, before Act 10 few public sector unions in Wisconsin adopted this model of unionism. As long as unions collected agency fees from everyone and could protect members' compensation and benefits, most members were happy.

Public sector unions paid the price for defining our unions narrowly as contract bargainers and enforcers. After Act 10, when we'd try to sign up members, many were aware that our collective bargaining rights had been severely limited. Often they responded, "Why should I join?" Others thought we didn't even exist, as our identity had been so tightly woven to the contract. Membership in public sector unions in Wisconsin plunged from 50.3 percent in 2010 to under 18.9 in 2017.

Transforming Our Local

Our challenge in Milwaukee was to transform a staff-dominated, business/service-style teacher union into something quite different. The local had focused narrowly on contract bargaining and enforcement, with the staff primarily playing the role of insurance agents who would intervene on members' behalf to solve their problems—instead of helping members organize to solve their own problems. It was a codependent relationship—members didn't have to do much more than make a call to have their problems taken care of, and staff didn't have to go out to do the hard work of organizing members, except for occasional mobilizations at contract time. The importance of parent/community alliances was downplayed, and the union usually took the attitude that it was not their responsibility—but rather the administration's—to ensure quality education.

Our challenge in Milwaukee was to transform a staff-dominated, business/service-style teacher union into something quite different.

A few years before I was elected MTEA president, our local's elected leadership agreed that the three legs of social justice unionism should guide our work. But it's easier to agree to a principle than to change old habits and put new ideas into practice.

So when I stepped in as president of our local, the professional staff was hostile to the organizing, member-driven approach on which I was elected. I was excluded from most staff meetings and only saw the union newsletter after the staff had sent it to the printer. The 22-member elected executive board was split. There was a slim progressive majority, including several people who were elected at the same time as I was. A few people were allied with the old staff through friendship; others were scared of any change because of the uncertainties fomented by Act 10.

Within four months, other leaders and I initiated a campaign to "reimagine" our union to make it more democratic and participatory, based on a vision of social justice unionism. Key elements of our local's "reimagine" campaign and our subsequent work included:

- Building strong ties and coalitions with parent, community, and civic organizations, not only on educational issues, but also on broader issues of community concern.
- Replacing the now-banned collective bargaining with collective action. With collective bargaining limited to only base wages, we put more emphasis on organizing members to appear en masse at school board meetings, to lobby individual school board members, and to enlist parents and community members to do the same. One of our earliest victories was securing an extra $5/hour (after the first hour) for educational assistants when they "cover" a teacher's classroom.
- Building our union's capacity to reclaim our profession by becoming the leading education organization in the city and consistently promoting culturally responsive, social justice teaching.
- Transforming the internal dynamics within our organization to increase member and leader participation, change the role of professional staff, overhaul our communications with and among members, and encourage members to lead our work. This included providing child care at all our monthly representative assemblies and major events and also greatly enhancing our social media presence and organizing.

To help make this work possible, within six months the elected leadership decided to release two teachers to be organizers; three months later we added two additional released teachers to head up a new teaching and learning department. Eventually we also released an educational assistant organizer and a social media organizer. (See Dingerson, p. 289.) A year after my election, we amended the constitution to shift certain powers from the staff to the elected leadership. A few months later, we bargained a staff contract that encouraged the professional staff who didn't want to adapt to a new organizing vision to leave. All but one left. The new professional staff committed themselves to a broader vision of unionism with an emphasis on organizing.

We did this all in an increasingly hostile, anti-labor, and anti-public school environment. State budget cuts caused substantial layoffs. Our massive mobilization of members and allies to recall Walker failed because Walker outspent his Democratic opponent seven to one, and convinced vast swaths of the white working class to vote their prejudice, not their class interests. "We don't want Wisconsin to become another Milwaukee," Walker said.

Social Justice—Rooted in Alliances

The strength of the 2012 Chicago Teachers Union (CTU) strike, under the leadership of Karen Lewis, rested in large part on their members' connections to parent and community groups. That year in two other cities—Portland, Oregon, and St. Paul, Minnesota—the unions put forth a vision of "the schools our children deserve" patterned after a groundbreaking document by the CTU. Their joint educator-community mobilizations were key factors in forcing the local school districts to settle on contracts before a strike.

In Milwaukee, our main coalition work was building Schools & Communities United, a broad coalition of nearly two dozen education and non-education groups that fights against school privatization and for concrete educational improvements within the public schools.

The coalition grew out of an earlier group, the Coalition to Stop the MPS Takeover, that—with allies on the school board and state Legislature—successfully fought a Democrats for Education Reform attempt to get rid of the democratically elected Milwaukee school board. Three years after that fight, the MTEA helped revive the coalition in order to fight the Metropolitan Milwaukee Association of Commerce's legislative plan to turn Milwaukee into a New Orleans-style recovery zone.

As we organized press conferences, picket lines, and lobby days, we realized we needed a more formal organizational structure and a broader purpose. We wanted to move past reacting, being on the defensive, and appearing to be only against things. After some intense planning sessions, we renamed ourselves, created short- and long-term plans, and formalized organizational membership.

Key to the coalition's renewal was the development of a 32-page booklet, *Fulfill the Promise: The Schools and Communities Our Children Deserve*. Building on the work of the CTU, our document addressed school issues and added concerns of the broader community beyond the schoolhouse door. Specifically, we critiqued the return of the "New Jim Crow" to Milwaukee. The 19 groups issuing *Fulfill the Promise included* the NAACP, Voces de la Frontera, Centro Hispano, ACLU, Milwaukee Inner-City Congregations Allied for Hope, Parents for Public Schools, Institute for Wisconsin's Future, Wisconsin Jobs Now, 9to5, Youth Empowered in the Struggle, and AFT and NEA locals.

We released the document and eight-page summaries in English and Spanish on May 17, 2014, the 60th anniversary of the *Brown v. Board of Education* decision. A march, program, and networking session attracted more than 500 people and put our coalition on the map.

The coalition has focused on fighting school privatization, promoting transformative community schools, and supporting progressive legislation. We are part of a national community schools movement that sees schools as hubs for social and health support, not only for the students of the school but also for their families and the surrounding community. The transformative model seeks to build strong community-school ties and help empower parents and community activists. It also requires shared leadership and a commitment to engaging, culturally relevant teaching and restorative practices instead of punitive discipline.

The coalition work is difficult. All participants have other organizational priorities, making meetings and communication a challenge. As we broaden the coalition, differences in strategies and priorities emerge. This work reminds me of the words of activist/musician Bernice Johnson Reagon, of Sweet Honey in the Rock: "If you are in a coalition and you are comfortable, that coalition is not broad enough."

Differences emerge in various ways. For example, as we've discussed how schools need to improve, some community members believe that a strong phonics emphasis will solve reading problems. Others see forced adherence to a rigid basal reading program that downplays literature as a key problem. One way we have sought to bring such divergent perspectives together is by focusing on proven practices that we can all agree on—such as developmentally appropriate practices at the early childhood level.

In line with our reimagine campaign, we've worked hard to build coalitions beyond those focused on education. Unfortunately, for years the MTEA's main coalition work was with the police and firefighter unions to get rid of a city residency requirement. This did not sit well with the communities of color we serve. In contrast, after our reimagine campaign, the MTEA has been a strong supporter of Voces de la Frontera and their youth group, Youth Empowered in the Struggle, standing with them for immigrant rights, for in-state university tuition for undocumented high school graduates, and in solidarity with a long strike by immigrant workers at Palermo's Pizza. We have supported a variety of other community issues, including raising the minimum wage, paid sick days, expanding healthcare coverage, voter rights, incarceration reform, stopping unfair hiring practices at a major federal housing project, and the Black Lives Matter movement. Our support ranges from financial aid to street protests, press conferences, lobbying, picket lines, and electoral work.

> Organizing our members to be leaders on all K–12 educational issues is an essential pathway to a revitalized teacher union movement.

Although coalition work is essential for building mutual trust and creating sustainable social movements, its success will ultimately depend on our capacity to move beyond having a coalition of leaders of community, civic, and religious groups at the city level to building power at each school site—involving union members and parent leaders in coalition activities that directly affect their lives at the school and neighborhood levels.

Reclaiming Our Profession

Another essential pathway to a revitalized teacher union movement is organizing our members to be leaders on all K–12 educational issues. Although some locals have taken on the hard issues of teacher evaluation through peer assistance and review programs, that is only the beginning.

For us, this has meant making sure new teacher orientation and mentoring are available and of high quality. It also has meant working to sustain the quality teacher evaluation and mentoring program that was in our contract before it ended under Act 10. I told my members that if there is a classroom down the hall or a school down the street that you would not send your own child to, then we have work to do.

In the past, too often union activists ignored curricular issues, dismissing them as the administration's responsibilities. We failed to make sure practicing classroom teachers were intimately involved in educational innovations and initiatives. We need to become the "go-to" organizations in our communities on issues ranging from teacher development to anti-racist education to quality assessments.

At the MTEA, this has required a change in some of our priorities and rearrangement of resources. Our two full-time release directors of teaching and learning play a key role in this work. Soon after becoming president, I proposed that we set up a nonprofit organization, the Milwaukee Center for Teaching, Learning, and Public Education. The center focuses most of its attention on teaching and learning issues, but also promotes public education among parents and the community. For several years it had a pro-public school canvassing program, funded by the school district, that goes door to door, encouraging parents to send their children to the Milwaukee Public Schools (MPS).

Our teaching and learning work has focused on reclaiming our profession in three primary ways:

- We provide professional development and services to our members.
- We advocate/organize around specific demands to reclaim our classrooms and our profession.
- We partner with the MPS administration through labor/management committees to ensure maximum success of district initiatives and practices.

For years, many members viewed our union office (if they knew where it was) as a place to go if you were "in trouble" or had a question about insurance or retirement. A scattering of members attended committee meetings. Now our offices are bustling with multiple committee meetings, inservice trainings, book circles (for college credit), and individual help sessions on professional development plans or licensure issues. When the district failed to provide quality inservice training on student learning objectives that are a mandated part of the new state teacher evaluation system, we offered workshops that drew 150 teachers at a time. We had to schedule additional workshops once word spread. More teachers were convinced to join our union, too, because our teaching and learning services are open only to members.

Another example of our success in reclaiming our profession is in the area of early childhood education, where our teachers have been very active. Working with allies on the school board and in the community, we used collective action at board meetings and hearings, and our connections to parent and university partners, to convince the MPS administration and entire school board to mandate 45 minutes of uninterrupted play in 4- and 5-year-old kindergarten classes. We also won a staggered start to the school year for all kindergartens: one-third of each class attends on three separate days at the beginning of the year so that teachers, students, and parents can build better connections from day one.

Our bilingual/English language learner committee held its meetings in the heart of the Latino community, including educators, community activists, and parents. We have taken up a broad range of issues and mobilizations, including convincing the school board to systematically expand bilingual education programs throughout the district. At the school level, union activists have worked closely with parents in two key areas: school-based canvassing around issues and pro-education candidates, and organizing to remove ineffective principals.

But we have a long way to go; at times it feels like a losing battle. Each year more teaching and planning time is stolen from teachers by new initiatives and mandates, most of which are linked to technology, tests, and standards. New teachers are learning to define teaching as data collection and more data collection. The heavy workload imposed on all teachers shrinks the time and energy they can dedicate to being union activists.

With the plethora of federal and state mandates and the data-ization of our culture, even the best-intentioned school boards and principals balk at promoting policies that support the craft of teaching.

It's clear to me that what is necessary is a national movement led by activists at the local, state, and national levels within the AFT and NEA—in alliance with parents, students, and community groups—to take back our classrooms and our profession.

Promoting Social Justice Teaching

A key, but less talked about, aspect of social justice unionism is promoting social justice content in our curriculum. We need to fight for curriculum that is anti-racist, pro-justice, and that prepares our students for the civic and ecological challenges ahead.

It's important for teacher unions to promote social justice in the classroom for two main reasons: First, it educates students—the future members of society—in how to be active, critical participants in that society. Second, it educates teachers. Too many teachers don't know the real people's history of our nation. And that includes labor history. Many years ago, I interviewed the late historian Howard Zinn, who said that teachers not only need to be strong unionists, but they have to be "teachers of unionism." (See Zinn, p. 25.) The more successful we are in promoting social justice teaching among our members, the greater will be their capacity and willingness to be active in our broader political campaigns.

To that end, we have hosted workshops and other activities. For example, our book circles have read Lisa Delpit's *Multiplication Is for White People*. Teacher advisers to Youth Empowered in the Struggle participated in a role play workshop about the U.S.-Mexican border.

Promoting social justice teaching also includes organizing against its opposite—reactionary curriculum policies and standards promoted by school boards, state textbook adoption committees, or publicly funded voucher or privately run charter schools.

A Final Challenge

With the Wisconsin state Legislature dominated by right-wing Republicans waiting to use any perceived or real weakness in public schools as an excuse to accelerate their school privatization schemes, we must proceed with caution in our public criticism of and organizing around school district policies.

On the one hand, we must fight to improve our public schools by organizing our members and allies to speak out against a host of problems, including poorly rolled-out initiatives; large class sizes; the school-to-prison pipeline; lack of music, art, physical education, counselors, and librarians; restrictive curriculum mandates; and rogue principals. On the other hand, such criticism can play into the hands of the privatizers as they seek to expand privately run charters in Milwaukee, which is home to the first and one of the nation's largest publicly funded private school voucher programs.

This dilemma forces us to carefully consider our approach at the district level. We use a variety of tactics, including participation on labor/management committees, lobbying school board members, and balancing mass mobilizations with the threat of mass mobilizations. In the end, we recognize a key element in fighting privatization is to improve our public schools.

A Social Movement for Educational Justice

And that's a hard thing to do in the face of the corporate shitstorm that has engulfed much of public education over the past few decades. But, just as I have been amazed at the resilience of some of my most beleaguered students, so too am I heartened by the increasing number of teacher, student, and community activists organizing for educational justice. Rank-and-file union members and growing numbers of union leaders recognize the need for new approaches to fight attacks on public schools and our profession. In addition to the work in Milwaukee, Chicago, Portland, and St. Paul, rank-and-file caucuses and local leaders in many areas of the country are having increased success moving their unions toward a social justice, member-based stance.

In Los Angeles, an activist caucus, Union Power, won leadership of United Teachers Los Angeles, the second largest teacher local in the country. The Union Power slate, led by Alex Caputo-Pearl, had an organizing vision for their union. They have worked with parents fighting school cuts and recognize the importance of teacher-community alliances. In Massachusetts, Barbara Madeloni, a leader of the University of Massachusetts edTPA boycott, was elected president of the Massachusetts Teachers Association in 2014. She ran with the Educators for a Democratic Union caucus and helped organize teachers in the struggle against high-stakes standardized testing.

On the national level, the sentiments and actions of members attending recent AFT and NEA conventions are more militant and focused on building organizing capacity internally and in alliance with other groups to fight the corporate reformers, obsessive testing, and privatization. The national "days of action" of the recently formed Alliance to Reclaim Our Schools have encouraged locals to build community coalitions and take an activist approach to fighting privatization and promoting public school-based improvements.

Will it be enough, soon enough? Will unions be able to transform themselves to go beyond their past limitations, reclaim our profession, and participate in the broader social justice movements? Will progressive union leadership and caucuses be able to convince recalcitrant members and staff stuck in an untenable past? Those are the questions activists will answer in the next few years as we organize for social justice in our classrooms, our schools, our unions, and our communities. ▪

Bob Peterson, the former president of the Milwaukee Teachers' Education Association, is now a member of the Milwaukee School Board. He taught 5th grade more than 25 years at various Milwaukee public schools, and was a founding editor of Rethinking Schools.

This is an edited and updated version of the article that appeared in the Winter 2014–15 issue of *Rethinking Schools.*

Three Theories of Change
Organizing, Mobilizing, and Advocacy

BY ELENI SCHIRMER

Why have unions gotten so weak, and how can they strengthen? In her book *No Shortcuts: Organizing for Power in the New Gilded Age* (Oxford, 2016), labor organizer and strategist Jane McAlevey argues that a major factor in labor's decline has been that unions have abandoned the work of organizing, relying instead on the more superficial methods of building power, namely mobilizing and advocacy. What are these three different methods of union strength, and what path toward power does each build?

To organize is to build mass support and strength among ordinary people. Organizing draws its power from working people's biggest strength: our numbers. Working people may or may not see themselves as activists or politically active or even in political agreement, but through organizing, they come together to act in common cause. The work of organizing is systematic and rigorous: It requires connecting with every single worker in a shop, every educator in a building, every building in a district. At its core, it asks people to understand their own agency and to make choices about how they will exercise it. The work of organizing is difficult; ordinary people are seldom confronted by their own agency nor asked to make choices that recognize their own power. As McAlevey notes in her first book, *Raising Expectations (and Raising Hell): My Decade Fighting for the Labor Movement* (Verso, 2012), a memoir of her organizing work: "In the normal course of human events, workers don't expect much from their jobs, government, or unions, because the reality is they don't get much. The job of the organizer is to fundamentally change this." The work of organizing is difficult, but as McAlevey argues, it is essential: There are no shortcuts.

Mobilizing, by contrast, activates an already-convinced membership. Mobilizing encourages those who already support a cause or a mission to take action to defend their belief—for example, by attending a protest, wearing a button, or signing a petition. Mobilizing is a very important step for building movements, but it is not the same thing as organizing. The crucial difference between mobilizing and organizing is that mobilizing relies on the actions of people who have already been brought on board; organizing is the work bringing ever more people on board, having a stake in the direction and outcomes of the actions (mobilizing can be an important component of organizing). McAlevey distinguishes mobilizing as

BRIAN STAUFFER

relying on the participation of a "self-selecting" group—people who have chosen to participate in something due to personal preferences or beliefs, such as environmental protection groups, the ACLU, or Planned Parenthood. Organizing, by contrast, relies on "structure-based" groups, groups determined by a predefined, often structural, relationship, such as working for the same employer, living in the same housing complex, or attending the same place of worship. Membership in a structure-based group, unlike a self-selecting group, is not a result of personal affinity. In a structure-based group, the number of possible members—and therefore people to organize—is finite and knowable: the number of workers in a firm, residents in a housing building, or members in a church, for example. Whereas mobilizing relies on participation from a self-selecting group, organizing builds high participation among all eligible individuals.

Advocacy is the work of creating change through the actions of professionals or technical experts—lobbyists, pollsters, lawyers, communication specialists, researchers. Advocacy relies on the expertise, status, and know-how of these groups of people to make change. Advocacy usually happens in a closed-door room; ordinary people play a small to nonexistent role in its efficacy. Advocacy has become a dominant strategy for unions and liberals. But its efficiency comes at a cost; it disables the masses of ordinary people who have a stake in the issues under scrutiny by advocates.

These three forms of making change do not exist in isolation; a successful campaign may very well rely on all three strategies. Yet organizing, McAlevey argues, is the most fundamental: The base of any campaign should come from its organizational capacity above all. Yet in reality, according to McAlevey, it's often the strategy most avoided or shortchanged. After all, it is often hard, slow work that requires building connections with mass numbers of people. As a result, it's often sidestepped for quicker grabs for power—mobilizing or advocating support, rather than organizing for it.

McAlevey's framework rests on a more fundamental argument about power. In an age of massive inequality, many see power as the province of the elite—the small, powerful minority who run the courts, the banks, and the media in the U.S. and around the world. From this perspective, forging change is the process of altering who occupies those powerful institutions: voting in new leaders, appointing new judges, securing better regulators who can safeguard the system with an eye toward fairness. In McAlevey's words, this belief is little more than replacing one set of elites with another, better set of elites. It relies on advocacy and, to a certain extent, mobilizing to get the job done.

Yet exclusively focusing on the undemocratic hyper-concentration of elites obscures the power of ordinary people. Ordinary people have two major forms of power: our numbers—there are more of us than them—and our ability to withhold our participation in a system that denies us fairness, dignity, and health: They need us to keep working. Organizing, especially organizing with an eye toward building strikes, activates both forms of power. Successful labor movements and social movements often use a combination of advocacy, mobilizing, and organizing. But as McAlevey argues, organizing is the most important of those tasks—yet often the most overlooked. Her work aims to bring the movement back into labor, and winning back into the movement. 🎵

Eleni Schirmer reads, writes, and teaches about labor movements and education. She has a PhD in Educational Policy Studies from the University of Wisconsin–Madison.

	ADVOCACY	MOBILIZING	ORGANIZING
Theory of Power	Elite. Advocacy groups tend to seek one-time wins or narrow policy changes, often though courts or backroom negotiations that do not permanently alter the relations of power.	Primarily elites. Staff or activists set goals with low to medium concession costs or, more typically, set an ambitious goal and declare a win, even when the "win" has no, or only weak, enforcement provisions. Backroom, secret deal making by paid professionals is common.	Mass, inclusive, and collective. Organizing groups transform the power structure to favor constituents and diminish the power of their opposition. Specific campaigns fit into a larger power-building strategy. They prioritize power analysis, involve ordinary people in it, and decipher the often hidden relationship between economic, social, and political power. Settlement typically comes from mass negotiations with large numbers involved.
Strategy	Litigation; heavy spending on polling, advertising, and other paid media.	Campaigns, run by professional staff, or volunteer activists with no base of actual, measurable supporters, that prioritize frames and messaging over base power. Staff-selected "authentic messengers" represent the constituency to the media and policymakers, but they have little or no real say in strategy or running the campaign.	Recruitment and involvement of specific, large numbers of people whose power is derived from their ability to withdraw labor or other cooperation from those who rely on them. Majority strikes, sustained and strategic nonviolent direct action, electoral majorities. Frames matter, but the numbers involved are sufficiently compelling to create a significant earned media strategy. Mobilizing is seen as a tactic, not a strategy.
People Focus	None	Grassroots activists. People already committed to the cause, who show up over and over. When they burn out, new, also previously committed activists are recruited. And so on. Social media are over-relied on.	Organic leaders. The base is expanded through developing the skills of organic leaders who are key influencers of the constituency, and who can then, independent of staff, recruit new people never before involved. Individual, face-to-face interactions are key.

Reprinted with permission of Jane McAlevey from her book No Shortcuts: Organizing for Power in the New Gilded Age *(Oxford University Press, reprint edition: April 1, 2018).*

Lessons from the Los Angeles Strike

BY ARLENE INOUYE

From Jan. 14 to 22, 2019, United Teachers Los Angles (UTLA) had its first strike in 30 years, the third in our union's history. The vast majority of members, myself included, had never been on strike. I'm certain we'll remember the many sights and sounds: The 60,000 people standing in the rain, in a city where it never rains, covered by a sea of red umbrellas and ponchos; the sound of cheering students singing heartfelt songs to their teachers, as the smell of freshly baked goods, tacos, and coffee filled the air.

Even a year later, the buzz of solidarity continues throughout LA. It seemed like everyone was on the side of the 34,000 UTLA members: parents, hundreds of community organizations, the 300 unions in the Los Angeles County Federation of Labor–AFL-CIO, our state and national affiliates, all supporting our diverse membership of K–12 teachers, early and adult educators, substitutes, and dozens of health professionals. Polls showed that 80 percent of the public in LA supported the strike.

This strike was about our students: exploding class sizes, lack of nurses, librarians, counselors. Our students deserved this strike, and we decided not to be silent any longer. It was about supporting public education and taking a stand against unregulated charter schools and the disinvestment in public education. Work stoppages are risky, but our strike brought relief and joy. Members told me of feeling overwhelmed as parents and community members joined the picket line bringing gifts of food and thanking them for being teachers—a new experience for many. There was dancing and singing in the rain, as members got to know their colleagues: the teacher from across the hall, the psychiatric social worker, or substitute who joined the strike. The UTLA strike unleashed the power of the collective.

From the outside, our strike seemed to be magically synchronized. In reality it took years of work—building an infrastructure, forming crucial parent and community alliances, and engaging our rank-and-file members. Our employer, the Los Angeles Unified School District (LAUSD) attempted to create fear, uncertainty, and doubt (we called it "FUD") about striking. We had to frequently inoculate our members against FUD as we talked through their financial concerns and the exaggerated consequences threatened by the LAUSD.

Our strike was part of the "Red for Ed" movement sweeping the nation. We were preceded by the red state revolts in West Virginia, Kentucky, Oklahoma, and

Arizona, and followed by the strikes in Oakland, Denver, Chicago, and Little Rock. This time the educators in our schools, with student and community support, were drawing a line in the sand and making history. We were calling out the billionaires who were profiting from tax loopholes and privatization schemes that were bankrupting our schools. And it is notable that as a predominantly female-of-color workforce in Los Angeles, we had risen up to take our place as leaders in the teacher strikes and labor movement.

As a UTLA officer, I was the first in my extended family to be active in a union. But my Japanese American roots were shaped by the alien land law, the incarceration of my family during World War II, and the model minority myth thrust upon us. While I worked as a speech therapist for a number of years, what drew me to the union was my organizing a coalition to fight militarism in the schools. And once active in the union, I was encouraged to run for UTLA office by a group of women who wanted to change our union to be more responsive. I was open to new challenges and willing to do what the union needed. I learned by stepping up and taking on new experiences, from co-leading the UTLA bargaining team, to building the infrastructure of UTLA, to organizing school chapters, itinerants, and more. But I've learned that because of structural barriers, lifting up women into union leadership needs to be intentional and include trainings, mentoring, and support. This is foundational for a member-driven union and growing the teacher union movement.

What We Won

UTLA's strike shifted the narrative locally, statewide, nationally, and even internationally. We boldly fought for the schools our students deserve and the respect and recognition that public educators have been longing for. What did we win? In addition to a 6 percent salary increase, we got enforceable class size caps for the first time and a class size reduction program. We won more nurses, librarians, counselors, funding for community schools, a reduction in standardized testing, and resources for ethnic studies. We won improvements in special education loads and itinerant workspace. We won a greater voice for educators in schools targeted for charter co-location. We won an LAUSD resolution calling on the state for a charter moratorium, improvements in adult and early education, the elimination of random student searches, expansion of green space and the removal of unused bungalows (portable classrooms) on our campuses, legal support for immigrant families, and the will to fight for more state and county funding.

It has been said that a union is strong because its members are strong. And members do not become strong overnight. Because of the sheer numbers and diversity in UTLA, we methodically and strategically built up the infrastructure and confidence of our members for five years prior to striking. The answers to how we did it are described in eight lessons of the LA strike.

Lesson 1: Build a Rank-and-File Movement with a Progressive Vision

UTLA had long been known as a union without a clear vision . . . a union that shifted depending on the personality and politics of the president. That changed in 2014 when members of the Progressive Educators for Action Caucus (PEAC) joined forces with other progressive caucuses within UTLA, and ran a team of seven officers and dozens of rank-and-file Board of Director candidates from across the city. Our campaign was focused and clear: We would take on privatizers such as Eli Broad and the Waltons of Walmart. We would do what's right, challenging racism and other oppressions and reaching out to parents and community members. We believed in transforming UTLA into a powerful organizing union. At a time when strikes were not taking place, we recognized that strike power is essential to build our power.

At first, our members had difficulty comprehending this mindset because it was truly a shift in the culture of UTLA. But once they heard us, hundreds of chapter chair leaders endorsed the "Union Power" slate. It was the first time that an entire team won every contested seat on the first round (seven full-time officer positions and a majority of the 48 board seats). This alone meant that we were united around a common vision and committed to working together.

Lesson 2: Retool the Union from the Inside Out

As the newly elected team of officers, we recognized the need to restructure UTLA at the same time that we worked to build the confidence and trust of our members. As we moved from a service model to an organizing one, we explained what we needed: more political, communications, and data capacity; a parent organizing team; and a research department.

As word of our new mission spread, we attracted top-notch staff with organizing and campaign experience to work at UTLA. At the same time, we undertook the very difficult process of letting go of staff members who could not buy in to our new union vision. While this process was sometimes painful, we learned from allies around the country willing to share their experiences, that it would be a mistake to not clean house from the start. The talent and skills of our new staff have been a tremendous asset in building our union's capacity and power.

Together, we built an organizing culture where we engaged members in various capacities. Officers and staff made hundreds of school site visits to listen to members and to share our program and goals. It was important for us to hear directly from members and to know their concerns. In turn we invited them personally to engage in the work: to help with a petition drive or to plan a picketing action with parents. We also worked with members to understand the multiple roles they played in their communities—teacher, parent, member of a religious or civic group. We needed members to understand the web of relationships and perspectives they could bring to the union.

Initially we needed to build the confidence of our members. In our first year, we won a new contract that included our first pay raise in eight years. Then, we asked members to support a dues increase—a difficult but necessary request, to build a union that could fight and win on big issues. We negotiated transitional funding with the AFT and NEA (UTLA is a merged local). We never would have been able to build up to a strike if we did not have the infrastructure and funds to make it possible.

Lesson 3: Build a Strategic Plan, Together

Since the 1970s, power, influence, and membership of unions in the United States have declined dramatically. To counter that trend we acknowledged and embraced our powerful, self-sustaining base of members.

We reached out to every sector of our membership. For example, we encouraged our itinerant members to meet with leadership both together and in subgroups (art teachers, music teachers, etc.). We asked them what their needs and priorities were. We wanted to know what the most important issues were for them, but also what they saw as the most important issues for the union to address for its members as a whole. (We wanted all of our members to not only see their own interests reflected in our contract demands, but to recognize our common interests as well.) These conversations led us to realize that in some cases we needed additional chapter chairs to provide a greater voice for itinerants. The key priorities we took from these and other conversations became part of our contract proposals. And through this process, we gained the buy-in of members across the union by inviting them to forward their ideas and step into their democratic leadership roles.

Strategic planning has been central to keeping us focused and united. It has become part of the culture of UTLA. Every year the officers and directors take a couple of days to thoroughly discuss and chart out strengths, weaknesses, opportunities, and threats—then goals, objectives, strategies, and tactics.

We also take significant time to discuss, brainstorm, and review the strategic plan with the UTLA Board of Directors. While people may have different opinions about priorities, at the end of the day, we all agree and get behind what we have decided together.

The strategic plan operationalized our goal of moving from a predominantly service-oriented union to an organizing one. For example, we totally reorganized how the union deals with grievances. We designated a staff leader as grievance coordinator, and worked through all of the pending grievances to settle them. Then we developed a new process that centers problem-solving inside individual school buildings. Our Chapter Action Teams (CATs, see below) now work to organize around problems and find collective solutions. As a result of this work, the backlog of grievances has dropped from around 3,000 to about 300.

Lesson 4: Engage Your Members. Develop New Leaders

Building school site structures was absolutely key to having power on the picket lines at every school during the strike. It was these structures that resulted in 98 percent of educators participating in the strike at 900 district schools.

First we focused on ensuring that we had a leader at every school (what we call "chapter chairs"). While in the past this role was not heavily promoted or strongly encouraged, we made it a priority. Because our union is large and geographically spread out, we established point officers and union staff for each of our eight regions, for relationship building, assistance on representation, and ongoing organizing at each school site.

Some schools hadn't had a chapter chair in years. In those cases, two of us, usually an officer and staff member, would go on a "school site blitz," knocking on classroom doors during the lunch or recess break. Many members opened their doors to us, and our conversations convinced some teachers to take on leadership roles at their school. We learned that we needed more than one person at the larger school sites, so we set up CATs to identify one leader for every 10 members. The CATs provided the structure for one-on-one conversations, and allowed communication to flow in both directions, between schools and the union.

The results of this one-to-one member engagement were visible when the strike began when an incredible number of members stepped up. "This was the first time I really wanted to get involved in the union. I felt like the union needed me," said one 18-year veteran teacher. There were also many new organic leaders who emerged, some of them new teachers with only a year or two in the school. "I thought you could either teach—be in the classroom—or organize and be a union leader," one young teacher told me. "But in the lead-up to the strike, I learned that I could be both."

5. Commit to Parent/Youth/Community Organizing

Another important piece of our work was building parent/community relationships and alliances. After two years of meetings with existing educational and community-based organizations, we launched Reclaim Our Schools Los Angeles (ROSLA) in 2016. ROSLA began with four anchor organizations: the Los Angeles Alliance for a New Economy, the Alliance of Californians for Community Empowerment (ACCE), Students Deserve, and UTLA. Other community organizations joined us throughout the campaign.

We shared a common political understanding of the potential power of both an education justice and a labor justice alliance. We also acknowledged that in the past UTLA had not been an honest partner. "UTLA's practices had pretty profoundly alienated organizations it should have been allied with," said one local advocate. Cesar Castrejon, an organizer with ACCE, agreed: "Historic relationships with the union have been hard. UTLA used to parachute in when they needed something from the community. And then they'd leave. It was hard to get over that history. We needed to learn how to communicate with one another, and sometimes to push back." Clearly, the union needed to rebuild trust by listening to these issues and concerns and taking them on as our own.

At the same time, we trained our members to organize parents at their school sites. While this may seem obvious and basic, many teachers are uncertain about how to do this, having been conditioned over the years to believe that their conversations with parents had to be narrowly focused on curriculum and student behavior. We used a survey to have members identify community organizations that they were involved in.

Corporate reformers and privatizers have carried out a well-financed campaign to discredit public educators and to pit us against our students, parents, and communities. But we know that nationally, parents trust their teachers and educators. An important strategy to solidify that trust was our commitment to bargain for the common good. This meant that in addition to the mandatory subjects of bargaining (salary and working conditions), we also included permissive subjects such as reducing testing and insisting on class size caps. Then we took it further by systematically asking members of our ROSLA partners to prioritize their issues. The issues they identified included having more green space on campuses, removing bungalows, creating an immigrant defense fund, and ending the racially discriminatory practice of wanding students to search for weapons.

UTLA then demanded and received an agreement with the LAUSD, to allow our parent/community members to present our common good demands at a bargaining session in 2017.

This experience was memorable for the community presenters. Ruby Gordillo is a former student at Trinity Elementary School in South LA. Her son now attends the school. When Trinity was targeted for a charter co-location, Ruby was one of the parents who joined in a protest against the co-location. From there, she attended a meeting of the local school council. Gradually, she realized that she had a role to play as a parent leader. So when UTLA invited members of ROSLA groups to present to the bargaining teams on the common good demands, Ruby stepped up to talk about co-location. Since then, she has become one of ROSLA's most active parent leaders, and even attended a national NEA conference with me to tell the story of the strike.

For the next year, we systematically brought these interests together, educating our members through meetings, chapter materials, and union communications, and holding dozens of trainings, planning meetings, and actions that engaged both union members and our grassroots and student allies. As our contract negotiations continued, leading up to the strike, it was clear that the common good demands were fundamental—that we would not compromise and sell out our allies. This allegiance to the relationships we had built together meant that, when we went on strike in January 2019, the community was on strike with us.

Lesson 6: Escalate Your Actions

Throughout our yearslong restructuring of the union and building toward the strike, we knew that we had to test the effectiveness of our organizing, and the level of engagement of our members. On a regular basis we consciously planned events or actions that measured our members' commitment and willingness to take action under increasing levels of militancy and risk.

Each step was important and built on the previous one. At UTLA we had 11 so-called "structure tests"—from wearing red on Tuesday, to signing petitions, to participating in a parent flyering activity, to picketing, etc. One big test for us was a community rally one Saturday in December before our January strike. Whereas most of our rallies had been during the school day, which made parent/community attendance difficult, we used the Saturday rally as a structure test to know if our allies were really with us. That day, more than 15,000 people came out to our rally. We knew that we had the support we needed for our strike. (See McAlevey, p. 423.)

These escalating actions were also important in building leadership responsibilities. And they helped emotionally, to prepare members to go further than they might have thought possible.

Sandra Soto, an elementary school teacher, was a great example. Soto had been laid off a couple of times, so when the union called on members to wear red T-shirts to school (an early structure test), Sandra was afraid. She didn't want to do anything to draw attention to herself. But she was willing to attend a book discussion where she and others read and analyzed some of the issues facing the district. Suddenly, she told me, it made sense to her why she'd been laid off! She began to recognize the role of austerity, and the complicity of billionaires like Eli Broad and Superintendent Austin Beutner in the ongoing attacks on her school. She was determined to fight back. She became a chapter chair at her school, and helped lead some of the most creative activities during the strike. Soon she was speaking to all 800 of UTLA's chapter chairs, leading them to the streets.

Lesson 7: Go on Offense, Control the Narrative

During the red state revolt, we learned the roles that social media play, both in providing information to members about our common situation, and in mobilizing people to action. We used every means of communication to get our message across: social media and our website, email blasts, phone messages, traditional media, and a paid media campaign that included billboards, benches, and an insert in the *Los Angeles Times*. Before and during the strike, we put out daily Facebook Live news to prepare our members for the strike, to answer common questions, and inoculate members against the misinformation that the district kept putting out. This work generated an exponential growth in followers, both among educators and among parents and community members. We built a massive database of people, and coded it by school site, region, interest area, and more. This allowed us to target communications directly to our constituency.

Our communications and research staff took control of the narrative on public education in significant ways.

In 2016, we commissioned a study on the fiscal impact of charter school growth on UTLA and found that $600 million per year is drained out of district schools by charters. Our communications staff focused on circulating information from this study showing the concrete cost to neighborhood schools: how many counselors, nurses, librarians, after-school programs were lost from schools with every stage of growth in the charter sector. This was the first time the impact to public schools from charter growth was quantified.

We called out the California Charter School Association (CCSA) for what it is—a billionaire-funded industry lobbying firm, not an educational advocate. We used CCSA's own stated plans against them, including their call for every student in California to be in a charter-like school by 2030, and their primary stated goal of attacking UTLA.

In 2018, a report commissioned by Beutner painted a picture of a school district on the brink of financial collapse. The culprits? The report—called "Hard Choices"—found LAUSD teachers were "overpaid," that the district was spending too much on supplies, that the teacher workday was too short, and that class sizes were too low. UTLA quickly produced a rebuttal ("False Choices, Hidden Agendas") that identified the misrepresentation of data and facts used in the LAUSD report. The union also created a two-page flyer comparing the "Hard Choices" claims to the actual facts. Teachers were incensed. The flyer became a standard educational tool.

Our communications also showed what systemic underfunding looks like, and we shared this information at every school site visit. We used an infographic illustrating that California, as the fifth richest economy in the world, was 44th nationally in per-pupil spending. We showed that LAUSD was putting 24 percent of its budget, or $2 billion, into a reserve fund, while claiming there wasn't money to meet our demands. We showed how California compared to other states in our lack of access to nurses, on class size (we are the highest), and more.

Our organizing, research, and communications changed the debate in Los Angeles, showing that educators were working under impossible conditions, yet still giving of their time and resources for their students because they believed in them, and in public education. And we exposed the forces aligned against us—naming them and publicly shaming them.

Lesson 8: Build the State and National Movement. Never Forget Where Our Power Lies.

From day one, we had the support of our state and national affiliates—the California Teachers Association (CTA) and California Federation of Teachers (CFT), the National Education Association (NEA) and the American Federation of Teachers (AFT). Their commitments, of both money and people power, showed that none of us are isolated, and our successes are interconnected. When one of us wins, we all win.

As the proportion of low-income students and students of color has risen in LA schools, funding has decreased and public educators who are predominantly female have experienced a drop in our wages and attacks to our health care and benefits. The 2018–19 Red for Ed strike wave, whether in the Republican Southern states or in the deep blue state of California, has made clear that this is a national issue of priorities and political will.

We are facing an important historical moment with opportunities and possibilities ahead. We followed up the strike with "Our New Deal for Public Schools," a set of five principles that continue to drive our work: Nurture the Whole Child; Respect Educators; Respect Students and Parents; Fully Fund Public Schools; and Stop Privatization.

As we continue to flex our political muscle, the NEA and AFT need to continue to allocate resources to organizing and building the movement in locals across the nation, with less reliance on the typical political relationships. Strikes work, and we continue to feel widespread support—our "strike bump"—at all levels of the city, county, and state governments. We have seen increased funding, movement on housing issues, and the first statewide initiative to address property tax inequities in 40 years.

We must never forget where our power is from. It was not the politicians or the LAUSD superintendent who came from Wall Street, but the collective action of more than 60,000 educators, parents, community, and labor that forced change and won public opinion. We are building on this social movement that merges racial, social, and educational justice for our students with labor and economic justice for our members. ⬕

Arlene Inouye is UTLA secretary and co-chair of its bargaining team. She has been a speech and language specialist for 18 years in the Los Angeles Unified School District and involved in public education transformation for decades.

RESOURCES

Bradbury, Alexandra et al. 2014. *How to Jump-Start Your Union: Lessons from the Chicago Teachers*. Labor Notes.

Bradbury, Alexandra et al. 2019. *How to Strike and Win*. Labor Notes.

Brooks, Chris et al. 2018. *Secrets of a Successful Organizer*. Labor Notes.

Building the Power to Reclaim Our Schools: Reclaim Our Schools Los Angeles, United Teachers Los Angeles, and the Collaboration Behind the 2019 Teachers Strike. reclaimourschoolsla.org/wp-content/uploads/2019/07/0719-Reclaim-our-Schools-Case-Study.Report-pg_p-002.pdf

McAlevey, Jane. 2016. *No Shortcuts: Organizing for Power in the New Gilded Age*. Oxford University Press.

Walk the Line

On the ground during the historic Los Angeles teachers' strike

BY LAUREN QUINN

There comes this moment when you're standing in the piss-pouring rain, huddled under the 4 inches of overhang you can fit beneath without your feet edging onto school property, when you feel yourself failing.

The morning light is gray and asthmatic through the thick rain clouds. The spokes on your drugstore umbrella have bent. Your jeans are wet and clinging to the long johns underneath. Your sneakers are soaked through for the fourth day in a row, because you live in Los Angeles and have never owned a pair of rain boots.

You've been up since 5:30 a.m., marching and chanting and trying to rally everyone. But this morning, your heart's not in it.

That's when one of your co-workers turns to you, face peeking out from her parka, and says, "We need a pep talk."

All the other heads nod.

And you see that it's not just you who's struggling this morning—everyone is tired, aching, beaten down. As union chapter chair of your school, it's your job to pep them up, remind them why they're out here, say something that will reinvigorate and inspire them.

But when you open your mouth, nothing comes out.

It's then, on the fourth day of the Los Angeles teacher strike that's being billed as historic, monumental, game-changing, that you feel wholly inadequate to the task at hand.

* * *

It started eight months ago.

Really, it started 41 years ago, before you were born—when California passed Proposition 13 and slowly started to bleed its public schools of funding, stripping support staff like nurses, counselors, librarians; slashing arts and enrichment programs; and raising class sizes to some of the largest in the country.

But for you, it started in May. Your union, United Teachers Los Angeles, had been in contract negotiations with the Los Angeles Unified School District for a year. Your school didn't have a union representative, so you heard about the UTLA rally through an email blast. You grew up in a union family, your mom a teacher, your dad a firefighter. Stopping downtown for an hour after school seemed the least you could do.

When you arrived at Grand Park, a sea of red-clad teachers swarmed in the shadow of City Hall. They were holding handmade signs, chanting, playing drums, dancing. A palpable energy radiated off the crowd of 12,000. It was strength and unity, yes, but also a collective power bigger than the sum of its parts.

You wanted in.

*   *   *

After the presidential election, I was despondent. I wanted to do something, but I didn't know what or how. I kept hearing that people had to find their place, their cause, their group—and act.

So I tried. I went to local political and community organization meetings that ran the gamut, but nothing quite jibed.

When I became my school's chapter chair and attended the UTLA leadership conference that July, I felt like I'd finally found my tribe. People of all stripes filled the conference rooms, a rarity in a city as diverse but deeply segregated as Los Angeles (and a quality distinct to the LAUSD, where teaching staff more closely resemble their students than most cities). You had old Brown Berets sitting next to wide-eyed 20-somethings fresh out of their credentialing program. You had white ladies translating the Spanish-language presentations to dudes with dreads in "Danger: Educated Black Man" shirts. The diversity wasn't labored or self-congratulatory; it was fluid, unpretentious, and united by the stone-hard conviction that our public schools were worth fighting for.

This unity of vision didn't mean we always agreed, or that subsequent meetings were always enjoyable. When the school year began, I attended area meetings in the cold cafeteria of Roosevelt High School, and the reality of union work sank in. People argued, hogged the mic, asked endless rounds of repetitive questions. After a full day of teaching, the meetings could feel downright tedious. Sometimes I'd zone out while I nibbled on Costco pizza and counted the minutes until I could go home.

Through the course of these meetings, I learned the context for the current negotiations. The fight was about more than a raise, more than even class sizes and support staff and overtesting and charter co-location. It was about saving the soul of public education.

Perhaps that sounds grandiose, but the stakes were that high. Our pro-charter school board had appointed as our new superintendent Austin Beutner, an investment banker with no prior education experience (think DeVos 2.0) who ran with a pro-privatization LA billionaire crew, fronted by Eli Broad. Beutner had brought on as his chief of staff Rebecca Kockler, the woman responsible for dismantling public schools in New Orleans—a city where, as of this school year, there are no remaining public schools. (Kockler has since resigned.) Beutner was toying with restructuring the LAUSD using the portfolio model that has decimated other public school districts. In short, Beutner wanted to break the LAUSD and break the union.

The plan was ambitious, UTLA leadership told us, but not impossible. School districts in smaller cities—Detroit, New Orleans, and Newark, New Jersey—had been driven to near extinction by the same contingent of pro-charter reformers. Now they wanted to try their hand in the nation's second-largest school district.

We couldn't just be on the defensive, UTLA officers told us. We had to have a plan that was equally ambitious and visionary.

You want to get a room full of teachers fired up? Ask them to imagine schools with full-time nurses and librarians; where counselors and psychologist social workers have time to actually meet with students; where teachers don't have to waste days of instruction showing movies while they administer one-on-one standardized tests in the back of the classroom; where instead of random stop-and-frisk searches, restorative justice practices guide school discipline. Ask them to imagine fully funded schools where teachers can actually meet their students' needs.

A strange feeling rises when asked to imagine something so far from reality. As teachers, we spend so much time in the trenches that we sometimes forget just how bad things are. Class sizes of 40 start to seem normal. Taking home six hours of grading over the weekend does, too. We stock our own supplies of granola bars for the kids we know are always hungry. A student starts coming to class high and stops engaging with the work. We try home calls and one-on-ones and restorative conversations, but the student needs more than that. We can hear the cry for help, but there's no help to be given.

When one stops and really thinks about it all, the feeling that comes isn't one of sadness or hopelessness or even rage. It's the feeling that comes after that, the feeling of we've had enough.

Some folks might just throw up their hands and go home, or else change careers. And a lot of teachers do that. The ones who stay, though, are a special breed, possessed of a mix of dedication and grit. You can say a lot of things about schoolteachers—we're unpolished, unsophisticated, exhausted—but one thing you can't do is mess with us. If the system doesn't break us—if the years of crushing workloads and the heartbreaking inability to meet our students' needs don't turn us cynical and hard—nothing will.

Certainly not the threat of weeks of no pay.

Certainly not hand-wringing over inflated budget deficits.

Certainly not an investment banker and his billionaire cronies.

Certainly not, it would turn out, the biggest rainstorm of the season.

In every area meeting, there'd be at least one moment when that feeling of fight was palpable. Some salty old teacher would go on a tirade about students sitting on stools in classrooms crammed past capacity, and people would nod and mm-hmm.

"Strike," someone would start chanting. "Strike, strike." People would stand, pound tables, clap their hands, stomp their feet. "Strike, strike, strike."

The room would be electric. Our voices would vibrate off the walls. We'd sound bigger than a room of educators, bigger than all the bullshit and billionaires. We'd sound like a force, like thunder.

This superintendent doesn't know who he's messing with, I'd think.

*　　*　　*

The lead-up to the strike lasted months. There were lunch meetings, after-school meetings, student meetings, before-school leafleting, strike authorization voting, phone banking, email writing, question fielding, planning and organizing and logisticizing. All of this was unpaid, in addition to a regular workday. It was good work, important work, but it was definitely work. Just as I had come to learn that most of teaching isn't revelatory moments of enlightenment but rather the mundanity of unjamming copy machines and confiscating cell phones, I came to realize that a lot of striking isn't rallying hearts and souls, but staple-gunning signs to picket sticks, and trying to secure a reliable restroom.

In a lot of ways, I'm a strange choice for a chapter chair, but no one else at my school wanted to step up. Located in East LA, we're a small pilot school, an LAUSD model in which schools receive additional funding and autonomy in exchange for added work hours and responsibilities for teachers. The additional work meant folks were already stretched past capacity; no one was jumping at the chance to go to more after-school meetings.

So we were stuck with me. I'm good at the parts of union work that involve organization. I can write one hell of a bulleted and subheaded email, but I'm not a rile-you-up kind of person. I feel uncomfortable being the center of attention. I don't possess natural leadership abilities, like anticipating people's needs and giving inspirational speeches. I'm the same way in the classroom: I can write a good curriculum and blaze through a stack of essays, but I'm not the teacher you go talk about your problems with. As in teaching, as in union work, as in life, it's the people part I struggle with.

As far as being a chapter chair, I was lucky—my school's administration was supportive, and all the teachers and counselors were committed to striking. Because we receive extra funding, our school already has the resources other LAUSD schools lack, resources that were key demands of the contract—a full-time nurse and librarian, English language arts class sizes as low as 24, and two full-time counselors and a psychologist social worker for a student body of 400. (In contrast, 80 percent of LAUSD schools lack a full-time nurse; class sizes are as large as 48 on some secondary campuses; and the counselor-to-student ratio is 1-to-945.) Because our school has those extra resources, our teachers understand firsthand their importance. "We're fighting so that all LAUSD students can have what you guys have here," I told students in our pre-strike lunch meetings.

The school year crept on, the strike looming like a rainstorm on the horizon.

The backseat of my car overflowed with flyers and signs as the district pulled one tricky maneuver after another, stalling the fact-finding process and filing last-minute court injunctions.

"They're trying to break our momentum," UTLA leadership told us.

At times, it seemed like it was working. "Can we just get this over with?" my co-workers would ask. We had to follow every step of the bargaining process in order for the strike to be legal, but we were all frustrated.

Originally scheduled for early October, the strike was pushed back to Jan. 10, then at the last minute, Jan. 14.

That rainstorm on the horizon—it was finally here. Figuratively and literally.

*　*　*

The night before the first strike day, I slept four hours. I kept waking up from nightmares in which no one showed up, or I lost all our supplies, or my phone died.

My stomach crunched and my mind raced as I drove to school in the pre-dawn dark, rain coming down in sheets. Amidst all the preparation, I'd forgotten that I was actually in charge of the picket line. I wasn't just taking notes and sending emails anymore.

Puddles pooled on sidewalks and gutters overflowed as my co-workers started arriving. I ran through my checklist: Take attendance, distribute signs, make sure all the gates and entrances were covered. I kept trying to text the chapter chairs from the other schools on our shared campus, but no one was replying.

We must have been a sorry sight, marching in a slow circle in the pouring rain. We should start chanting, I knew, but I was too awkward and stressed to get a word out. The first few cars honked as they passed, almost pityingly.

Finally F raised his voice: "When our schools are under attack, what do we do?"

And we answered, "Stand up, fight back!"

He kept us chanting, even as our signs soaked through and turned to mush in our hands. Students and teaching assistants (who aren't part of our union) joined us. The more rain came down, the more cars honked, a little blast of validation each time. We cheered, jumped, raised our fists.

After morning picketing, we headed downtown for the first-day march, where teachers from across the 700-square-mile district gathered in front of City Hall. A sea of red umbrellas and ponchos filled the four-block length of the park—red for UTLA, but also #RedForEd, the official color of educator resistance since the wave of wildcat strikes in 2018. The color was a symbol—we were now part of that bigger fight.

I'd never seen so many Angelenos in the rain. "We don't do this here," I kept saying, wondering if people in other parts of the country would grasp the significance. Teachers beat drums, banged tambourines, blew whistles and horns. Helicopters pulsed in the air above us; news vans surrounded us. We were on the national stage, and we knew it.

In every pocket of people, a chant bellowed. A voice would start: "Everywhere we go, people want to know." And other voices would answer "Who we are, so we tell them." Every face you saw looked familiar, even if you didn't know the person. "We are the teachers, the mighty, mighty teachers." It was a face that was lit up with conviction and ready to fight. "Fighting for justice, and for education." It was a face you knew, it was your face, and you were part of that fight.

I had no sense of how large the crowd was. I just knew I felt like an ant in a huge swarming line. Umbrellas bumped and snagged as we moved painstakingly slow, so crowded we had to stop every couple of steps.

"Wow, seeing the pictures on the news, impressive!" a friend texted. But all I could see were the shoulders in front of me.

When we came to the Second Street tunnel, we put our umbrellas down for the first time that day. I craned my neck around, finally able to see the crowd. We were massive. We filled the tunnel from side to side and as far forward and back as I could see.

Our voices boomed and echoed against the concrete walls. One person shouted into a megaphone "UT," and we all answered "LA!" We chanted it again and again, the name of our union, but also something else, something bigger and more powerful. Our voices grew stronger with every chant.

Suddenly I didn't feel like an ant anymore. I didn't even really feel like me. I felt like a part of a movement.

When the rally ended, we had a couple hours to rest before afternoon picketing. I stopped at my apartment, changed my wet socks, put on a dry sweater. I lay on my bed and felt the pangs in my legs from walking, and rested just enough to be able to return to school for another round of picketing.

By the end of the day, I'd walked 10 miles. My shoes were soaked and my feet ached. My voice was hoarse from chanting. I was more tired than I could remember being.

But I'd done it. We'd done it. We had held a picket line for a day.

*   *   *

No one warns you how a strike will take over your life.

Seven a.m. picketing, mid-morning rallies, a short rest, then more picketing until 4 p.m. By the time you're done, your body's toast. Your brain is fried. Your voice is shot. It's all you can do to crawl home, peel off your wet layers, and scroll through the union emails and texts that need replies.

The scenes that remain from those first days are a blur of drudgery and exaltation: a fellow teacher blasting salsa from a massive speaker and barking into a microphone like a street hawker, "Viva la huelga! We are East LA! We are fighting for our schools, we are fighting for our community!"; doing the have-to-pee dance while waiting to use the Jack in the Box bathroom; eating pan dulce that had gone soggy from the rain; line dancing in the crosswalks during red lights, while the marching band played under a tarp, instruments wrapped in trash bags; the blast of horns from garbage trucks and public buses and delivery vans and sheriff patrols and damn near every sedan that passed; the thick deep sleep I'd fall into during my afternoon power naps; the throb in my lower back the day my period came; the tide of red flowing from the Little Tokyo metro stop and into the street like a blood trail, all the cars honking around us; the East Area rally turning into a block party where people danced under their umbrellas to "Jump Around" and "Killing in the Name Of" and every other song on the soundtrack of 1990s middle school dances.

As chapter chair, I kept my head down and focused on what needed to get done. I organized donations and bought supplies. I sent texts and emails to keep people updated. I picked up supplies at 6 a.m. and delivered them to nearby campuses. The only thing keeping me together was the afternoon break, in which I could go home and dry off for an hour.

Luckily, other folks stepped up. F stood in the rain with no umbrella and led chants until his voice went hoarse. Then M would take over. P danced in the crosswalks until all the cars honked. R showed up even though he'd had surgery the week before. On the picket line, you got to see a different side of your co-workers, who for most of the workday stay hidden behind their classroom doors. You got to see who rolled hard, who the ride-or-dies were, and you got to do it together.

As the rain hammered on, the community rose up around us. A restaurant brought hot soup one morning. Local unions brought coffee and doughnuts. Parents brought tamales and pupusas, and the teaching assistants who weren't striking brought breakfast burritos. The neighbors carried over an outdoor heater. The raspados shop across the street gave us free coffee and let us use their bathroom. A neighborhood dude unloaded a truck bed full of bottled water. Even our students brought us food, of the endearingly teenage variety: boxes of Jack in the Box french fries.

You always hear about how people love teachers, but when you actually see them show up and demonstrate that love, especially when you're soaking wet and bone tired, it's enough to make you cry.

*　　*　　*

At the end of every day, I'd lay my wet clothes on my furnace to dry, crawl into my bed, and scroll through the news coverage. Before the strike, even progressive outlets like the *Los Angeles Times* and KCRW focused their coverage on pay. Now their reporters were on the line, talking to teachers. Stories led with interviews and personal anecdotes from classrooms, followed by descriptions of lively picket lines and powerful rallies. Finally, news coverage focused on the reality of our teaching conditions, which were our students' learning conditions, which is what we were fighting to improve.

They said we were making history, but I was too close and too tired to have much perspective on the impact of what we were doing. I'd scroll through images of teachers in red ponchos and aerial shots of huge crowds, and hardly believe that I was a part of it all. It felt like being a dot in an impressionist painting.

"Do you think this is what it was like in the Civil Rights Movement?" some-one asked while we were Lyfting back to campus. I wondered the same thing—whether the people making history ever know they're making history, or if they're just a bunch of tired, fist-raising bodies in a crowd, with a vague sense of society's gears changing around them?

Other people reflected back to me the immensity of what we were doing. Friends from all over the country messaged and texted. Teachers across the United States posted solidarity photos. A public school from New York City "adopted" my school and donated funds for food and transportation. "We're fighting similar forces out here," they wrote.

Restaurants all over LA were providing free or discounted meals to striking teachers, but I was too tired to take advantage of any of them. After a day on the picket line, I was too shot to do much of anything. All I could do was ladle out some soup, answer emails, and then turn off the light by 9 p.m.

*　　*　　*

When the alarm went off at 5:30 a.m. Thursday morning, I didn't want to get out of bed. The night was black outside, and I could hear rain thundering down. But I couldn't bail—I was in charge. I sighed, tugged on my still-damp layers and laced up my still-soggy sneakers. I didn't bother to put on makeup or fix my bed head—there was no point.

It was the fourth day of the strike and the worst rain yet. All of our signs were beaten and wrinkled. No one chanted. No one marched. Hardly anyone spoke. We wanted to be back in our classrooms, warm and dry and with our kids—fist bumps at the door, learning objectives on the projector, pair-shares and turn-and-talks and stacks of do-nows and exit slips piled in trays near the classroom entrance.

"We're tired," G said. "We need a pep talk."

I opened my mouth, but nothing came out. I was beaten too.

"Some of us live too far to go home in the middle of the day," S added. "We've been out here all week, without any place to rest up and get dry."

I looked at their wet, exhausted faces, and realized I'd been so wrapped up in organizing the logistics of the picket line that I'd forgotten about the most im-portant part: the people. I'd been going home every day to nap, and it was the only thing keeping me together. How could I have overlooked the fact that not everyone had that?

I hadn't felt so inadequate since my first year teaching, another high-stakes, high-emotion situation when you struggle to keep your head above water. You do your best, but you feel yourself screwing up all the time, and feel the weight of all the people you're letting down in the process.

What could I do in that moment? Stutter a "Shit, sorry" and kick myself for my lack of care and thought. But the right words still wouldn't come. They needed inspiration, and I couldn't give it to them.

Just then, a station wagon plastered in the logo for local radio station 97.9 La

Raza pulled up, music blasting from inside. A mustachioed DJ in a windbreaker jumped out. "You guys hungry?" he asked, his arms outstretched.

Before we could answer, he opened the hatchback. The entire back of the car was filled with taco fixings. "We support you! 97.9 La Raza supports you!" he exclaimed as we gathered around. The tacos were still warm and the bowls of guacamole plentiful. The DJ took pictures with us. It was the edible pep talk we needed.

When the rain let up later that afternoon, I gathered all of us together.

What did you say, you want to know. I wish I could tell you, but I was too tired and nervous to have any idea, let alone remember. I might have acknowledged how rough the day had been and how whipped we all were. I might have said that the district was waiting for this moment, to see if we'd break—if we'd roll hard for three days, then get tired and give up. Whether we'd give up on our kids.

I like to think I said that this moment was when it counted, when we had to show the district, the community, the country, and our kids that we really meant it. "We've come this far," I like to think I said. "We've showed up every single day, like fucking soldiers, and we can't stop now. Everyone is looking to us. We've become something bigger than a single school or strike, bigger than an 'I' and 'you.' We've truly become a 'we,' and I've never felt more a part of something important than right now, right here, with you guys."

Maybe I said that. But probably I stood there red-faced and mumbled something about sticking together and staying strong, then left us all to go home.

*　　*　　*

The next week, on the sixth day of the strike, we sat in a nearby park eating chile relleno burritos. We'd had so many donations from our adopted school and from individuals that our lunch was paid for. The rain had finally broken, and it was back to a typical 65-degree LA winter day.

We were relieved but anxious. UTLA had just announced victory—a tentative agreement with the district. It seemed the fight was almost over. "Let's wait until we see the agreement," R said.

So we did. We hunched over our phones while we ate, reading aloud the summary and trying to make sense of the 47-page document we were to vote on in a couple of hours.

The summary sounded good. The LAUSD had finally agreed to drop a contentious article in our contract that allowed for unequivocal raising of class sizes. Within two years' time, every school would have a full-time nurse and librarian. The counselor-to-student ratio would be reduced to 1-to-500.

"One-to-500?!" M asked. "That's still too high."

"It's the state average," I answered. "The district probably wouldn't offer better than that."

"We're the biggest school district in the state," M replied. "We should be leading the way. I mean, what have we been striking for?"

The more we dug through the contract, the more thorns appeared. Class size reductions in most content areas would occur at a rate of one student per year for three years, leaving most teachers with only slightly less painful class sizes. Meanwhile, special education and K–3rd grade didn't see any reductions. While we'd gained counselors, there was no additional funding for mental health services, such as psychologist social workers. "They're the single most important thing in keeping students from dropping out," F said.

I looked around at people's faces. They were disappointed. "We can do better than this," some said. "This is crumbs," others said.

I tried to remind them who we were dealing with—a pro-charter board and a billionaire superintendent who had been hired to decimate our school district. Previous contract offers included raises contingent on additional work hours and healthcare cuts to new employees, and no offers on our other demands. The fact that we'd gotten this much was huge.

"This isn't what we stood out in the rain for," F said.

The more we talked, the more I understood their perspective. We'd come out more unified and forceful than even the union predicted. We were a movement. UTLA had been stoking the flames of a smoldering fire, the burn for something better that existed in all of us. Now that it had been unleashed, people didn't want to concede. They didn't want to settle for the status quo. They wanted that vision of fully funded schools. Or at least class sizes below 30.

"I'm voting no," M said, her face set in stone.

"It's gonna look so bad if we vote it down," I said. The agreement had already been announced to the media as a victory. Would parents stand behind us if we voted it down? Would teachers start crossing the line? If that happened, the district would likely come back with a worse offer.

We felt like our hands were tied. We had to vote in four hours. I wrote down people's questions as I headed to a last-minute meeting, but when I returned to campus to administer the vote, I only had an answer to one. People were pissed, and as the chapter chair, I was the one receiving the piss.

"We're being forced to vote on a document we've barely read," F said.

"This isn't good enough," M said as she filled in the bubble for "no."

I wished I could disagree.

* * *

The agreement did pass. UTLA announced it that night on Facebook Live. I watched the storm of angry-face reactions float up the screen and felt my heart sink. We'd been so united, and now we were breaking apart.

I was relieved the agreement passed, but only because I thought the scenario of it not passing was worse. I wasn't excited about the agreement, and in all my messaging that evening, I hadn't talked to a single person who was.

But I couldn't dwell on it for too long. After all, I had to lesson plan. I had to be back in my classroom in less than 12 hours.

*   *   *

I wish I could say our staff rode back into school the next day in red shirts, on a wave of victory chants, high-fiving students in the hallways and basking in pride over what we'd achieved.

As it was, we mostly kept our doors closed. We nodded at each other in the halls, greeted our students, said hello to the office staff. But the disappointment was thick.

"What happens when the revolution fails you?" someone asked in a Facebook post.

But had we been a revolution? We were a union in contract negotiations. We were going to have to compromise. We weren't going to change public education in six days.

But, watching the footage and reading the coverage, I began to zoom out of my individual perspective. In a single week, we'd shifted the narrative around education. We'd opened the public's eyes to the real conditions of our schools. We'd taken the focus off teacher pay and onto school resources; we'd connected the issue to funding and taxes at the state level; we'd demonstrated the power of organized labor; we'd inspired teachers in other cities who were experiencing the same conditions. We'd stood in the rain, danced on the picket lines, and filled the streets. Maybe we were something close to a revolution.

I think the real victory of the LA teacher strike will be the shift it has inspired. Already, coverage of the Denver, Oakland, and Virginia strikes is different. There's less talk about "greedy teachers," and more explicitly connecting school conditions to corporate tax breaks and charter growth. Even in Denver, where the main dispute is over pay, coverage is contextualized and includes teacher interviews. LA teachers created momentum for a broader movement to reinvestment in public education.

I wish that were enough for my co-workers, and I wish it were enough for our kids. The fact is, most of our students returned on Jan. 23 to the same conditions they'd left on Jan. 11.

So what do you do when you've envisioned something transformative, then been asked to settle? When you've felt a movement growing, only to have it yanked from your fingers? When you've marched 49 miles in a week and messed up and let people down and kept showing up anyway?

You do what you always do.

You get up, keep teaching, and keep fighting. ♀

Lauren Quinn is a writer and teacher based in Los Angeles. She is currently at work on a young adult novel.

This article was originally published on Hazlitt and in the Fall 2019 *Rethinking Schools* (Vol. 34, No. 1).

Trusted and Respected
Seattle's site-based organizing

BY JOHN DONAGHY

KATHERINE STREETER

"Shannon—but she doesn't like the union," said a 3rd-grade teacher, then a 4th-grade teacher, and then eight more teachers over the course of the day we spent at an elementary school in North Seattle in spring 2014. My partner, a board member of the Seattle Education Association (SEA), and I were on a union listening tour. The question we'd posed to each teacher, after first asking how their year was going and about our upcoming bargaining, was "Who's trusted and respected here in the building?"

SEA was then two years into an effort to reorganize. We'd visited at least 80 of the District's 100 schools and spoken with more than half of SEA's 6,000 teachers and certificated staff, para-educators, and office administrators.

The reorganization would culminate in a seven-day strike in September 2015, led by a 40-member bargaining team of largely first-time bargainers and activists. The action won guaranteed recess time for students, removed any connection between test scores and teacher evaluations, won significant raises, and launched Racial Equity Teams in dozens of schools.

The cornerstone of the reorganization was an effort to identify natural school leaders—educators trusted and respected by their co-workers, regardless of their disposition toward the union—and invite them to engage with and shape the union's direction.

New Leaders Elected

Recognizing their union was not nearly as powerful as it could be, a new slate of SEA officers and the union's executive director, Glenn Bafia, looked for a new approach in spring 2012. Membership participation and educator morale were low following the bruising regime of an education reformer as superintendent. The union had eaten a high-profile, though somewhat symbolic concession on teacher evaluations and student testing without much of a fight. The regular monthly meetings of building representatives were contentious and caustic, often focusing on "taking positions" on issues but with little action to back them up. Member engagement lagged well behind other locals in the state. SEA staff were buried in disciplinary hearings, grievance meetings, and evaluation conferences, without a strategy or much time to organize.

SEA's new president, Jonathan Knapp, was a high school auto-shop teacher who'd just finished a term as vice president. Phyllis Campano, an elementary special education teacher, was the new vice president. They were both on full-time release from their teaching jobs. When I first met them, after I was assigned by the Washington Education Association (WEA) to support local organizing, the two indicated they wanted to meet one-on-one with every SEA member. Across WEA and other NEA state affiliates, local leaders were being asked to sit down with each member for a half hour or so to get to know them. I looked at my watch, pressed a button, and said, "Go!" With only four-year terms, they would need to start right away.

In Aesop's fable, the strength of a single stick is contrasted with that of a bundle of sticks. A single stick can easily be broken, but wrap together enough of even the flimsiest sticks, and they can't be broken. This is of course the very premise of unionism. But while Aesop's fable holds much truth, we know as organizers that rather than members being simply scattered individuals, they have instead already grouped themselves informally around natural leaders. The work of the union, then, is to unite as many of the natural leaders as possible, who then bring along those in their circles of influence.

In unions that regularly and successfully organize unorganized workers, the identification and recruitment of natural leaders is the basis for developing effective campaigns. When the employer fights back hard against the union, either the natural leaders can assure their co-workers that the struggle is worth it, or the campaign is defeated.

The opposite approach, which is more common, puts a premium on activism and affinity for the union over actual leadership. The ticket to getting union roles is simply willingness to do something—lobby, make phone calls, come to a school board meeting—rather than any ability to bring others along. Some who get involved are in fact leaders, but many are not. When activists complain about co-worker apathy, a common refrain, it can be an indicator they simply do not have leadership. I was on a building visit in another local, and my partner there began recruiting someone we'd just met to be a building rep after she told us how big a union supporter she was—even though she also told us that she was new in the building and isolated from everyone else! We had no reason to think this person would influence any of her co-workers; if she did become rep, it was likely to be a frustrating experience for everyone.

SEA's leaders instead decided to apply a natural leaders approach. Early in the reorganization we were running phone banks for an upcoming school levy vote. Our usual turnout methods—email blasts, announcements at union meetings, etc.—were getting the usual poor turnout. One afternoon we received a call from an elementary teacher, Michael Tamayo, asking for the phone-banking details. A half-dozen or so of Michael's co-workers had named him among the most trusted and respected educators in his school. A few hours later, he showed up with eight co-workers in tow. Although the union was a bit of a vague idea to him, he cared a lot about the school levy, since it provided more resources to his low-income school and to a program that provided a path for people of color to become teachers. Jonathan and Phyllis continued to seek him out, and he became progressively more involved in SEA, especially around teacher quality and racial equity, and eventually he became SEA's president in late 2019.

With the understanding that natural leaders exist in every school, our plan was to identify and engage such leaders across Seattle's 100 schools. That seemed more doable than sitting down individually with 6,000 members! Our theory of change went something like this: "We can reboot the Seattle Education Association by relentlessly identifying natural school leaders, building relationships with them, and inviting them to lend their leadership to a new shared purpose."

The First Listening Tour

Eager to help the state's largest local reinvent itself, WEA's state president and executive director joined the SEA team of staff and local officers in June 2012 for the first listening tours. We broke into teams of two to go from room to room and office to office in our target schools to seek out staff for brief one-on-one conversations. We didn't announce our visits ahead of time, lest various gatekeepers—principals, office managers, human resources—try to herd us into break rooms or otherwise restrict access.

The teams spoke individually with more than 700 educators in 20 schools over four days. While some union staff feared members would close their doors to us or even be hostile, the opposite occurred. Members were eager to talk with us. If they couldn't speak when we visited, they'd insist we come find them later in the day. While some shared criticisms, most were curious about our visits and hopeful that the union could make a difference.

The individual visits were intended to last about 10 minutes. These were not classic one-on-ones, but a survey with an eye toward mapping important relationships in the building. We mostly asked how their year was, what the school was like, and what they thought their union should be focusing on. And then we asked, who would you say is trusted and respected here in the building?

Trust and respect are the main currency in cultivating a following. You can trust someone without respecting them, or vice versa. You might have a colleague you trust enough to share complaints about the principal, but whose teaching doesn't meet your standards. Likewise, you might admire someone's excellent lessons, but you wouldn't share a complaint with them for fear it would get back to the principal. Without a measure of both trust and respect, it's unlikely someone will have much influence with you.

When the Seattle teams returned to the union office, they wrote visit reports, and then, on large posters of each school's roster, placed a colored adhesive dot next to a person's name for each time they were named by someone as trusted and respected. Dozens of educators had five or 10 dots next to their names, and in larger schools some had more than 20! While some of those members (and with union shop in place, nearly all were members) were known to union staff and leaders, others were not. Many were wholly uninvolved in SEA.

As the team looked at the posters, it was inspiring to think of the power educators could wield if these natural leaders were united. In subsequent presentations we've done with other locals, showing leaders and staff one of these charts is enough to set them salivating.

Based on my experience in Seattle and then in other locals around the country, not all team members are immediately successful at asking the "trusted and respected" question. Sometimes they aren't fully committed to the reason for asking (which can result from a less than timely orientation). They may think that the real value of the tour is in showing members their union is active and cares about them. That's a common viewpoint, but unfortunately one that reinforces the idea that the union is a third party. Others may struggle because the question can feel like a non sequitur. It takes a bit of skill to have a 10-minute conversation with someone where you establish enough trust and credibility that you can get up from the table and say, "Great talking with you today. Before we go, who would you say are some of the folks who are really trusted and respected among the staff here at Longwood Elementary?"

In the experience of most tour leaders, members are actually happy to answer that question and recognize some esteemed co-workers. It does tend to be better not to ask them directly who they *themselves* trust and respect; that can feel too personal. But asking them who is generally trusted and respected seems to create the needed personal distance (and in fact often results in the member sharing who they personally trust and respect, saying for example, "She's such a great teacher.") The No. 1 mistake we make is not to give enough time to answer the question. Instead of letting the question hang out there while the person mentally goes down the building's roster (or looks at the roster we have), we rephrase the question, most typically into something like "you know, who do people go to?" That's actually a different question, one that tends to result in a skew toward naming people with more access to knowledge or resources, such as department chairs, team leaders, office secretaries, union building reps, or even the principal.

Combating Racism and Implicit Bias

Evidence-based leadership identification and recruiting is an important check on implicit bias. Without it, we are likely to pick people who tend to be like us. At future decision points, SEA leaders would check the name of every potential recruit to a committee, lobbying team, or other union body against what their co-workers indicated. We weren't shy about calling each other out for seeking to elevate someone we personally liked in the absence of evidence of leadership. If none of your co-workers placed you among their most trusted and respected colleagues, it wouldn't make sense for the union to ignore their views and elevate you into a representative role. This created some delicate situations when eager volunteers or longtime activists were turned away. While this could be awkward, officers believed the benefit to the union made it worthwhile.

Officers and staff were keen to discern the leadership of educators of color. On one hand, we had a fairly objective measure, but on the other, it was an overwhelmingly white certificated workforce (parapros and office staff were much more racially mixed) naming whom they trusted and respected. Although there were in fact many educators of color who were named by their white co-workers as trusted and respected, we chose to bake an assumption of bias into our future recruitment efforts. If you ask a white educator to name colleagues they trust and respect, we assumed that they would be at least somewhat more likely to think of other white people first. So when we were recruiting elementary teachers to a committee, for example, we might build a starting list from all the educators of color who received at least three dots and all white educators who received at least five dots.

While this method supported robust recruitment of educators of color into union roles—membership of color on SEA's 40-member bargaining teams has been at least 40 percent over the last three bargains, far higher than the share of educators of color in the workforce—some wondered whether the chosen educators of color were those who were named more by their white peers than their peers of color and how that might be skewing representation. (No one argued that the leadership of an educator of color who was frequently named by white peers should be discounted, only that we needed to be sure that educators of color were represented by leaders of their choosing as well.) To some degree this concern was met by over-recruiting from schools with higher proportions of educators of color, virtually guaranteeing that the leaders were named by educators of color. SEA has also begun in recent years to enter more data into NEA's new membership database, called NEA 360. This allows the union to note exactly who each member names as those they trust and respect, and thus reports can be generated that provide some insight into that question. In the meantime, SEA did generate one useful data point on that question: a survey about new graduation requirements asked 1,000 high school staff to name staff they trusted and respected to serve on a bargaining committee with the district. SEA was able to disaggregate responses by race and compare who educators of color and white educators each chose and fine-tune recruitment (although in that survey, at any rate, largely the same educators were chosen by both groups).

Intentional Leadership Recruitment

The issue that led us to Shannon's North Seattle school in 2014 was that we'd gotten almost no signatures from there on a petition to place a class size initiative on the Washington state ballot. The union's building rep told us people were apathetic. We were puzzled, as members at other buildings were collecting signatures like cra-zy—the first fruits of our efforts to involve more natural leaders over the previous two years. For the first time anyone could remember, SEA was among the state's leaders in participating in a coordinated WEA action.

Members at the school told us that Shannon (not her real name) didn't like the union and had spoken against the initiative at a meeting. It would have been easy to take a pass on initiating contact with Shannon—there were 100 other schools to get signatures from. But not every school has a Shannon, trusted and respected to the virtual exclusion of anyone else. We often find three or four staff taking top billing. If we were going to get any signatures from her school, or probably much support for anything union, we needed to meet Shannon.

Vice President Phyllis Campano stopped by a few days later. As it turned out, Shannon was not anti-union, but rather simply believed the union's priority needed to be compensation, not class size. Phyllis couldn't persuade her our ballot initiative was the right priority, and we never did get many signatures from her school. But a relationship was begun that eventually led to Shannon being a member of the 2015 bargaining team, and then of SEA's executive board. In the years that followed, I can't recall a union event that Shannon attended, and there were many, where she didn't bring along a sizable group of colleagues.

After the initial round of visits in June 2012, SEA visited another 50 schools the following school year. But the follow-up with leaders was slow and not terribly successful. The officers invited identified school leaders to lobby days and other events, but had few takers. SEA's leadership team knew the union wasn't seen as very powerful, and these natural leaders were clearly reluctant to invest time and energy in an uncertain proposition. Also, many of them were already highly en-gaged both at school and in their personal lives.

One leader at a North Seattle high school was on our radar for several years. Although she always seemed on the edge of getting involved, she never made the leap. She led a vibrant after-school horticulture program, was science department chair, and was in training to be a principal. A few weeks *after* the strike in 2015, however, she walked into the union office and told us she'd stepped down as de-partment chair and wanted to prioritize union activism. It took the success of the strike for her to believe collective action by educators, and her union, held more potential to make the change she wanted to see. While we were fortunate that not all natural school leaders needed this level of proof, there is a positive feedback loop between organizational success and leadership commitment: More of one spurs more of the other.

The leadership team pivoted in the winter of 2013–14. Instead of recruiting leaders to join the union's work, which hadn't borne fruit, we set up a series of meetings that simply brought these leaders together to meet and talk about what was important to them. We approached about 75 of the newly identified leaders, most of whom had little or no union involvement, and more than 60 participated, an astonishing turnout. After a brief welcome from Jonathan and Phyllis, they rotated World Café-style in groups of four for the next hour or so, responding to some open-ended questions. The leaders were excited to have met and to have had rich conversations, and were intrigued by what this convening said about their union.

The meeting did not include an ask, which is something of a sin in organizer circles, but making an ask is what they expected us to do, and we knew we needed these new leaders to join us in figuring out what was worth asking and doing as a union. We never did get around to reconvening these groups, but they provided an important entrée to establish new relationships and signal to these leaders that there was untapped possibility in their union.

Time to Fight Back

SEA's leaders correctly assessed that there was a significant lack of trust in the union and its leadership. SEA had accepted a concession on testing and evaluation in 2010 and failed to remove it in bargaining in 2013. While the practical impacts of the provision were limited, and the contract settlement was otherwise pretty typical, the contract passed by only a thin margin. Educators at Seattle's Garfield High School had organized a high-profile and successful boycott of the district's use of the standardized MAP tests that spring, but the union had failed to leverage that into a robust or successful contract fight over testing and evaluations. Members were understandably reluctant to express approval for a deal that reflected that failure. While the union had tried to organize some pushback in the summer of 2013, it was too little, too late.

In truth, the natural leaders of the workforce were largely on the sidelines as far as the union was concerned and were not responsive to calls to action, such as there were. Most immersed themselves in the work of their individual schools. Some joined Social Equity Educators (SEE), a member caucus, to push the union and Seattle Public Schools toward a more progressive agenda. When natural leaders did choose to become reps, many quickly quit or confined themselves to their buildings. As many confessed to us, they found the monthly Rep Assembly absurdly contentious, and seemingly irrelevant. Indeed, the first Rep Assembly I witnessed featured a lengthy debate over a letter to an elected official of another state. Meanwhile the union's bargaining team had just begun bargaining and virtually no time was devoted to any meaningful discussion of what was at stake.

Following the 2013 bargain, SEA's leadership team and staff conducted more school visits but also focused on following up with the hundreds of members identified as natural leaders. They found that almost to a person they were angry about education reform, cynical about the district's leadership, and, although wary of SEA, appreciative that union leaders had recognized their leadership and were reaching out to them. Finally feeling some sense that they could turn things around, union leaders were challenged in early 2014 by an announcement from the district that it was going to cut 50 positions due to an unexpected budget shortfall.

> With many schools at a loss on how to cope with the coming cuts, they began recommending that schools vote down their budgets.

Union leaders believed the district had enough in reserves to cover the shortfall, but complaining publicly about that in board meetings hadn't stopped such cuts before. So rather than focus on getting a few dozen or even a few hundred people to a school board meeting to protest, leaders devised a strategy to create chaos in the school-by-school budgeting process then underway. It would require schools to vote down their budgets, which by contract would trigger a mediation process facilitated by a central office administrator. Even though the superintendent held final say over each school's budget, such a strategy would have the potential to involve thousands of educators right where they worked.

Successful execution of the strategy would require influential educators in each school to endorse it and validate the union's recommendation to vote no on their school budget, *even if their school was untouched by the cuts.* The SEA Rep Assembly endorsed the strategy somewhat lukewarmly, expressing doubts about the union's analysis and strategy. But SEA's leaders then began reaching out to the school leaders they had been cultivating relationships with to get their thoughts on the strategy. With many schools at a loss on how to cope with the coming cuts, they took a leap of faith and, along with many of the building reps, began recommending that schools vote down their budgets to force central office administrators to come explain themselves.

Within three weeks, nearly 50 schools voted to reject their budgets, with more reporting in each day. After the first school's mediation, and faced with the prospects of dozens more, the district called the union to say they were re-analyzing their budget for ways to avoid the cuts. In a school board meeting shortly thereafter, the district's budget director publicly thanked SEA for pointing out that there was a "fudge factor" that could cover the cuts. District administrators then privately appealed to the union for help in getting new school budgets passed, without the cuts, expressing particular bewilderment about "all these solidarity votes" where even schools without cuts had rejected their schools' budgets.

Following the budget action, SEA began recruiting its team for the upcoming bargaining. While the budget fight had garnered SEA's leadership some credibility, they still barely won re-election later that spring. The following school year, SEA's leadership team proposed quadrupling the size of its bargaining team. We wanted as many members as possible to know someone on that team who held their trust and respect. The countless hours of relationship-building, the success of the budget fight, and the commitment to open the process to many more people led to a tremendous amount of interest from heretofore inactive leaders in joining the new team.

2015 Bargain and Strike

The 2015 bargaining kicked off a year later as locals up and down the I-5 corridor had been going on one-day strikes against the Washington Legislature. Seattle chose May 19 for its one-day strike, the day *before* bargaining was to start. The march through downtown Seattle was a blocks-long warning shot to the school district; this was not the SEA they had been dealing with in recent years. While everyone from SEA's building reps to district officials expressed doubt that a 40-member team could functionally bargain, as team members walked into bargaining in their red T-shirts, still jubilant from the previous day's action, our power was evident.

Most team members were new to bargaining, and many to being active in the union. Others were seasoned bargainers, and at least five were members of the SEE caucus. SEA's leaders had made a particular effort to recruit natural leaders who were in SEE, including their candidate for vice president in the recent election. SEE members, for their part, made it clear they weren't going to drop their critique of union leadership nor back off from their own progressive advocacy, including guaranteed recess for all students, not a typical union demand (and which was immediately dismissed by the district as outside legal bargaining parameters).

The union officers knew that all on the team, even their critics, were highly credible to their co-workers, and that would lead to a cohesive and effective bargaining team. The team debated and hashed out proposals from recess to teacher quality, from racial equity for students to the pay gap between ESPs and certificated staff, and won on virtually all of them (including recess). When the district brought a late-game takeaway to the table, a raucous meeting of thousands of SEA members gave the team unanimous authority to call a strike. When talks broke down the night before school was to start, our team let the district know that we were now on strike.

Any large strike of any length is a story in itself, and Seattle's seven-day strike is no exception. Almost to a person, the WEA and NEA staff who joined in to support our strike noted how incredibly well organized each school's strike operation was, and how little was needed of them. The natural school leaders were in charge. ▪

John Donaghy is a former middle school math teacher and president of the Highline Education Association, as well as a former organizer for SEIU. He served as executive director of the Seattle Education Association from 2013 to 2019 and now works for the NEA Center for Organizing.

Media Advice for Social Justice Union Leaders

BY SCOTT STEPHENS

SALLY DENG

Tom Mooney throws back his last swallow of scotch and signals the bartender for another drink. It is a Sunday evening in the quiet lobby bar of the Hyatt Regency Hotel in downtown Los Angeles. Through a window, a hazy sun descends into the Pacific Ocean. Mooney, a vice president of the American Federation of Teachers, has to be in Boston the next day. But instead of taking the red-eye out this evening, he lingers with the unlikeliest of companions: a group of skeptical newspaper reporters who have spent the weekend talking about charter schools and education policy in a forum sponsored and attended by Eli Broad.

"This was great," Mooney declares happily about his confab with the Fourth Estate. "We need to do this more often."

Mooney, who would die unexpectedly within a year, grasped the notion that if you do not tell your story, someone else will tell it for you. In his role as president of the Ohio Federation of Teachers, Mooney talked with hundreds of reporters about the dangerous path the state was pursuing with for-profit charter schools and vouchers. He connected the union's role in empowering not only his members, but also the students those members taught and their families, and improving the communities in which they lived. He was passionate and prepared. He armed himself with reams of data and he conducted his own research. On some level, Mooney shamed and challenged the media into taking a critical look at these issues. Here are the facts. Here is the research. Why aren't you reporting on this?

Even union leaders with Mooney's energy, charm, and intellectual capacity can encounter difficulty when navigating the media landscape. There are a variety of reasons for this. Fewer and fewer Americans have a parent, aunt, or uncle who was a union member. The NewsGuild-CWA, the largest media union in North America, still represents a fraction of working media workers. These factors mean that the average reporter has little if any experience with signing a union card or negotiating a contract. To some of them, a union is as foreign as an oddball religious sect. More important, privateers—eyeing a huge pot of public dollars—hijacked the word "reform." As a result, anti-union leaders like Michelle Rhee became "reformers" and teacher unions became barriers to "reform." Just think about the words reporters use when they write about labor. Unions "demand." Management "offers." Unions "walk out." Management "replaces." At best, reporters have a vague notion that teacher unions represent educators in the workplace, negotiating contracts and filing grievances. At worst, reporters carry around the bias that teacher unions are greedy, protect dead wood, and don't care about kids.

It barely matters that the most famous quotation attributed to former American Federation of Teachers president Albert Shanker is probably apocryphal. "When schoolchildren start paying union dues, that's when I'll start representing the interests of schoolchildren," Shanker is widely quoted as saying, although multiple attempts to verify the quote have turned up dead ends. The point is it really doesn't matter. The alleged "quotation" is an article of faith for many reporters and members of the public, a concise summation of their worst fears about teacher unions.

My perspective on these issues is unique. I worked for 30 years as a newspaper reporter, spending a significant portion of that time at the *Plain Dealer* in Cleve-

> The average reporter has little if any experience with signing a union card or negotiating a contract. To some of them, a union is as foreign as an oddball religious sect.

land covering education at a local, state, and national level. As a reporter, I headed the union local at my newspaper, negotiating contracts and filing grievances for reporters, copy editors, photographers, and support staff. I served six years on the Newspaper Guild-CWA's International Executive Council and worked on contract campaigns and other issues for locals in the United States, Canada, and Puerto Rico. Later in my career, I joined the communications staff of the American Federation of Teachers, traveling and writing for AFT President Randi Weingarten and working on contract and organizing campaigns for teachers, school support workers, and hospital nurses across the country. For the past seven years I have been a public school administrator, first in Chicago and now in Ohio. I have dealt with issues ranging from curriculum to communications. I am one of the few people who has been on both sides of the bargaining table.

That unique set of experiences has convinced me that nobody is right all the time. That said, the role of teacher unions in social justice and true education reform tends to be covered poorly when it is covered at all. A 2011 study by FrameWorks Institute, a nonprofit think tank based in Washington, D.C., presents a stark and troubling view of where teacher unions stand in the eyes of the news media and, by extension, the general public. "Teachers' unions are overwhelmingly cast as the enemy, seeking to perpetuate the dysfunctional aspects of the system at the expense of the innocent student casualties," wrote researchers Moira O'Neil and Nathaniel Kendall-Taylor. "Media materials rarely covered reforms proposed by teachers' unions themselves and rarely explored reasons why teachers' unions would oppose specific reforms."

What can be done? Is the narrative that teacher unions are obstructionist impediments to reform so entrenched that it will never go away? I don't think so. In fact, I believe there are a handful of no-cost, common-sense guidelines that, if followed by union leaders, could drastically change the way teacher unions are portrayed:

1. Build relationships. Don't wait for a reporter to call you. Encourage casual, off-the-record engagements over lunch, a cup of coffee, or a beer. Pitch a story you'd like published with data. Provide names and contact information the reporter can use. Ask the reporter what they need and how you can help. Give them your personal cell phone number.

2. Acknowledge problems and detail how you plan to fix them. The *New Yorker*'s exposé on the so-called New York City rubber rooms played into the worst stereotypes about teacher unions. Weingarten, who was connected to the story via her previous job as president of the United Federation of Teachers, acknowledged the problem, took steps to correct it, and switched the conversation to issues such as providing adequate professional development and supports for teachers who needed help.

3. Be a source of information rather than a purveyor of propaganda. Clichés and sloganeering turn reporters off. Sound arguments backed by data have a lot more traction. Teacher unions can and should be a valuable information source for reporters. Collective bargaining rights give them unusual access to data, documents, and other inside information. It's often easier and quicker for a reporter to obtain information from the union rather than from a large bureaucratic school system.

4. Think like a reporter. Read serious coverage in newspapers and understand what a story is. A teacher putting on a talent show in his or her class is nice, but it's not news. A teacher taking his or her students to a state capitol to grill legislators about public education funding is news and will likely attract media interest.

5. Humanize the union movement. If people think about unions at all, it's usually in the context of contracts, salaries, and benefits. The Teamsters for years have suffered from the image of a group of burly tough guys of shadowy repute. Only recently have people noticed that in reality, Teamsters are also young mothers who drive delivery trucks or senior citizens collecting tolls on a turnpike. Like nurses, teachers are generally respected and well-liked members of the community. They, rather than elected union officials, should be the face of a teacher union. Have a kindergarten teacher at your news conference to talk about the impact of class size on our youngest learners, or a paraprofessional to discuss the challenges of administering a feeding tube to a student. Sometimes, it's even better to have a supporter from the community, such as a parent or clergy member, do the talking. Doing so lends your message third-party validation and undercuts the argument that you are motivated only by self-interest. And don't forget to offer media training to your spokespeople. Union leaders are used to speaking in front of television cameras, but most folks are not. A one-day training session, including role-playing, can build confidence and make your message that much stronger.

Obstructionists? Barriers to change? Yes, there are still plenty of those stories out there. But there is also evidence that teacher unions can be portrayed as progressive agents of change when their efforts are properly marketed.

The AFT's "Reconnecting McDowell" initiative comes to mind. Recognizing that educational opportunity and economic prospects are inextricably linked, Weingarten and the AFT have been catalysts for a major initiative in McDowell County, West Virginia, among the most disadvantaged areas in the United States. Poverty and unemployment are widespread, schools are struggling, and health problems are pervasive. In an unprecedented display of collaboration and cooperation, the AFT put together close to 40 local, state, and national groups to transform the region. The initiative touches on education, health care, housing, and other fundamental issues.

The Pittsburgh Federation of Teachers and their president at the time, John Tarka, received national acclaim for helping negotiate a five-year contract in 2010 that included performance-based pay and a teacher evaluation system that incorporated student achievement. The pact won praise in a report from the nonprofit Aspen Institute and helped the district secure a $40 million grant from the Bill & Melinda Gates Foundation to improve teacher effectiveness. While controversial in some labor circles, the effort was generally applauded as an unprecedented collaboration between labor and management for the good of children.

Finally, a series of statewide strikes by education workers beginning in 2018 have been widely praised in the media as bringing economic inequity issues to the forefront. Motivations for the strikes included desire for increased wages for teachers and support staff, larger school budgets, smaller classrooms, and other issues. Coverage of the first of that series in West Virginia was lauded and largely successful, and media accounts were uniformly positive. The strike— which ended when teachers returned to their classrooms a month later—inspired similar, statewide strikes in Oklahoma and Arizona. It also inspired protests by school workers in Kentucky, North Carolina, and Colorado, and led to a school bus driver strike in Georgia and a protest by adjuncts in Virginia over pay. In January of 2019, United Teachers Los Angeles went on a six-day strike. Teacher walkouts in Virginia, a longtime right-to-work state, as well as in Denver and Oakland, followed. These collective actions, often known as "Red for Ed" because striking workers wore red shirts to show solidarity and that public school budgets were in the red, captured public attention and media coverage because they featured rank-and-file educators. They were actions that seemed to rise from the bottom up rather than coming from the top down. In West Virginia, for example, it was widely reported that top AFT and National Education Association officials agreed to the strike only after pressure from local union leaders.

> Teachers are generally respected and well-liked members of the community. They, rather than elected union officials, should be the face of a teacher union.

In Los Angeles and Chicago, striking teachers and school workers were successful in rallying community and media support by framing their action under the banner of the "Schools Our Children Deserve." Rather than highlighting pay and benefits, these campaigns were successfully identified as fights for students and the resources they needed to be successful. More often than not, parents and students—rather than teachers and union heads—were featured in media reports. In both cases, the strategy to win was based on bargaining for the common good, which brings demands in collective bargaining that benefit the entire community, not just union members.

"This is a historic victory for public education educators, students, and parents. Class size reduction, limits on testing, and access to nurses, counselors, and librarians will change our students' lives forever. We won this victory through our unity, our action, and our shared sacrifice," said Alex Caputo-Pearl, president of UTLA, after reaching a tentative agreement in January 2019. "Educators and parents reached a boiling point . . . about conditions in classrooms."

Using the same tactics, the Chicago Teachers Union won broad support from parents, families, and community members when the union called a strike in October 2019. According to a *Chicago Sun-Times/ABC7* Chicago poll, 49 percent of voters in the city either strongly supported or somewhat supported a walkout. Even influential politicians were supportive of the CTU's fight: At the time, five of the nation's Democratic presidential candidates—Joe Biden, Julián Castro, Kamala Harris, Bernie Sanders, and Elizabeth Warren—expressed solidarity with the CTU.

> Tom Mooney understood the importance of building relationships with the news media to clarify and define the role of teacher unions in social justice and education reform. All of us should understand it as well as he.

These examples provide hope that teacher unions are turning a corner in the court of public opinion. In her latest book, *Slaying Goliath*, education historian Diane Ravitch argues that the so-called education reform movement has been defeated by parents, teachers, and other public school advocates, including teacher unions. While it's too early to dance on that grave, it at least should put a bounce in the step of teacher unions.

Tom Mooney, as president of the Cincinnati Federation of Teachers and later vice president of the AFT, understood the importance of building relationships with the news media to clarify and define the role of teacher unions in social justice and education reform. All of us should understand it as well as he. 🖉

Scott Stephens is executive director of communications and engagement for the Shaker Heights City School District in Ohio. Previously, he worked at the Chicago Public Schools as executive director for strategic communications, served at the American Federation of Teachers, and worked for 30 years as a journalist, most of that time for the Cleveland Plain Dealer.

Using Social Media as an Organizing Tool

BY LEIGH DINGERSON

From left to right: Union members ride a bus for a citywide enrollment canvass; Black Lives Matter social justice printmaking; students paint a mural for the school's restorative practices room; students plant garden beds in front of the school.

PHOTOS: JOE BRUSKY | MTEA

Most organizers would agree that there are no shortcuts in organizing. Nothing can replace face-to-face contact and relationship-building with individuals. That's true. But union locals are getting increasingly sophisticated about their use of social media to maintain connections with members, to educate and mobilize them, and yes, even to bring new members into the fold. Smart social media can help build your power.

The Milwaukee Teachers' Education Association (MTEA) has been a leader in their use of social media. And increasingly, they are sharing their strategies with progressive organizations across the state and country. This article explores some of their work.

Increasing Member Engagement with the Union

The MTEA created a full-time release position for a social media organizer in 2014 as part of their larger project of reimagining their union. Fourth-grade teacher and photographer Joe Brusky was tapped for the job. He was released from his teaching duties, and the union paid his salary.

Brusky had been helping his union with social media as a volunteer, but joining the union's communications director in a full-time capacity allowed the local to quickly amplify its presence with its members.

The first effort was Facebook. The union has both a closed group and a public Facebook page. They use the members-only group as an easy way to organize around different campaigns. It allows for dialogue and discussion, and also helps the union keep its finger on the pulse of what's happening with its more than 5,000 members. The closed group also enables the union to share news with members who might not otherwise see posts in their Facebook newsfeed from the union's public page.

The public Facebook page touts the good things happening within the district and positions the union as a community partner. In an effort to counter the ubiquitous negative press about the "failing" Milwaukee Public Schools, Brusky created a "media request" form that members can fill out online, letting the local know about good work, events, or presentations happening at their schools. Teachers were quick to respond. Brusky got permission from the district administration to take pictures inside school buildings (as long as students had signed standard release forms) and began attending events across the district, photographing them, and posting his pictures on the union's public page with short descriptions of the activity. He would then share them on the members-only Facebook page. Before long, there were multiple albums of teachers and students, in their classrooms, "doing what they do," says Brusky.

As these pictures started appearing on Facebook, traffic to the site skyrocketed. Participating teachers received praise from colleagues while sharing creative projects and activities with hundreds of members. The union tracked the growth on the Facebook administrator page and was able to analyze when members were signing on, what they were "liking," what kinds of posts were effective and ineffective. It was clear that teachers loved seeing themselves and their students in action, and they loved seeing what other educators were doing. The union's public page grew from around 1,000 page likes to nearly 18,000 likes.

Memes as Organizing Tool

The union started creating memes to highlight the words of leaders or members, provide commentary on public education and the education profession, and to respond to proposed legislation or privatization attacks. Memes are popular on social media because they convey a ton of digestible information in one graphic (photo with text over it). The MTEA uses memes to highlight member testimony at school board meetings by putting short quotes from testimony over a photo of the person testifying.

Memes are often shared widely by members and spur members to act. For example, in response to Wisconsin state Sen. Alberta Darling (R-River Hills) co-authoring a bill to hand Milwaukee Public Schools' lowest-performing schools over to private charter operators in 2015, the MTEA posted a photo of Darling with text at the top saying "Senator Darling Says Please 'Stop Calling'" and in big bold text at the bottom, the phone number to Darling's legislative office. Darling's office was flooded with phone calls and emails. Other memes created by Brusky help explain complicated concepts like school privatization or the differences between a public school and a private charter school to voters.

Seizing a Moment

One teacher realized that the union's Facebook page was the go-to place when she found a disturbing flyer on her doorstep one morning.

The flyer was from a local city charter school, announcing the opening of its enrollment window. The flyer announced that the school was offering a $200 signing bonus for new students. Outraged, the teacher posted the flyer on the MTEA Facebook page. How could a charter school be allowed to *pay* families—presumably with their public dollars—to enroll in the school? The next day another member posted a *different* flyer from *her* neighborhood, this one from a different charter school offering an even higher cash bonus for registering.

Facebook hummed with responses. The union recognized the opportunity. Brusky suggested then-President Bob Peterson write and post a blog about the "enrollment bribes" from charter schools desperate to build their student bodies. A reporter from the *Milwaukee Journal Sentinel* picked up the story from Facebook and wrote it up for the front page of the newspaper. Outrage ensued.

The following month, the Milwaukee City Council passed an ordinance outlawing enrollment incentives at city charter schools. Just like that, the union's quick thinking and social media presence inspired the mainstream media to respond and led to concrete policy change.

Connecting Through Twitter and Instagram

The MTEA uses Twitter to share content easily, not just with its members, but more widely. Its Twitter account has nearly 3,000 followers, including local journalists and national education advocates. Well-written tweets—as we've learned in the age of Donald Trump—can spread like wildfire and direct readers' eyes to news stories, photographs, or ideas. Author Diane Ravitch often retweets posts from the MTEA, and occasionally writes a blog piece about the information she has gathered from the feed. When the union used Twitter to ask members to respond to a *Milwaukee Journal Sentinel* editorial, the response was robust enough that the newspaper subsequently published a news story that included many of the points that union members made in their tweets.

The MTEA's Instagram posts mostly mirror its Facebook page, but they add lots of relevant hashtags to posts to increase visibility and reach new audiences.

"It's important to know which audiences are using which platforms," Brusky notes. "A lot of our younger union members and supporters have moved to Instagram, so we keep that platform pretty active."

Since Brusky posts many photos of students and teachers on Instagram, many younger Instagram users see the content and often follow the account. A video Brusky made in 2020 of Rufus King High School students responding to a racist image out of West Virginia went viral nationally, and the students from the high school played a big role in making that happen.

Both Instagram and Facebook can also sync advertisements, a feature the MTEA has used during campaigns, including electoral campaigns. During the 2019 school board races, the union ran ads supporting a slate of five candidates in different targeted ZIP codes using photos of the candidates acquired over the years. The photos of candidates testifying at public hearings or participating in a march or rally were more dynamic and informative for members than a candidate's official photo. The entire slate won.

Mobilizing and Building a Database

When the Alliance to Reclaim Our Schools organized a series of national "Walk-Ins" in 2016 and 2017, the MTEA used its members-only Facebook group to track building-by-building organizing for the events. The walk-ins were nationally coordinated days of action when teachers and parents rallied outside their school before the first bell rang. Each local union planned a set of relevant messages, reflecting the education issues current in their cities at the time—whether it was opposition to charter co-locations, fighting budget cuts, or simply supporting public schools. A short rally would be held, and then teachers and students would enter the school together to begin the day. Parents would be invited in as well, for coffee and snacks, and to talk about next steps in organizing campaigns. Union members participating in the walk-ins were given a list of social media instructions for their walk-in. This included relevant hashtags, talking points, and directions on how to take and post a good group photo on social media (in front of the name of the school, with the photo cropped tightly around members).

In Milwaukee, the walk-ins targeted the state Legislature's attempt to take over several "low-performing" schools. As teachers at a school agreed to host a walk-in, they would call that information in to the union offices. Each day, the union would post a graphic listing the schools signed up to participate on the union's Facebook page and the "Stop the Takeover of MPS" campaign Facebook page. "It didn't take too long before members were calling and asking why *their* school wasn't on the list," Brusky remembers. "You have to decide as a building to participate," he would tell them. Within a day or two, the school would call back and ask to be added. Every day a new graphic would be posted with the new schools added to the list of participating schools. The growing list on the Facebook page created buzz and a sense of momentum for the upcoming actions and spurred school-based organizing that might have otherwise not happened.

Building a Database

The MTEA, like most unions, has begun to build an extensive database of both members and community supporters. The database helps the union keep track of individual member interests, as well as what types of actions they are likely to engage in—whether phone banks or demonstrations or others. The union uses the platform Action Network to build these lists.

In the summer of 2014, Republican state legislators passed a plan to begin to dismantle the Milwaukee Public Schools. The union's communications team immediately branded the legislation called the Opportunity Schools Partnership Program as a "takeover." Before long even the local media called it the "takeover bill." The legislation empowered the county executive to appoint a "takeover commissioner" who would choose schools to hand over to charter school companies. The law required these takeovers to begin in the 2016–17 school year.

The union fought back, creating School Defense Committees" and mobilizing their members and parents to sign online or paper petitions. (See Mizialko, p. 320.) Brusky visited schools every week, coordinating his visits with the school's union building representative. The petition was a tear-off card in which the petition collector kept the signer's name and contact info while giving the signer the remainder of the card, which had relevant information and key dates to keep them involved with the campaign. The online petition was through the Action Network, which collected nearly 7,000 signatures. Brusky took photos of the parents with their children during these one-on-one petition signings and shared them on social media. Parents would tag themselves in the photos and share on their Facebook timelines, widening the reach and increasing the personal connection to the campaign. In other words, social media enhanced the one-on-one organizing—it didn't replace it. The MTEA held walk-ins around the district, and every attendee was entered into the Action Network database. The names gathered from the petition and walk-ins were later used to alert the community to future events, and also to help organize to defeat a military voucher school from locating in Milwaukee's Riverwest neighborhood.

Keeping an Eye on Decision Makers

Shortly after Joe Brusky began as the MTEA's full-time social media coordinator, he began attending Milwaukee Board of School Directors meetings and livestreaming them with his cellphone to the union's Facebook page.

Predictably, the school board and MPS administration were wary of the union's effort (Milwaukee board meetings were not regularly televised live). They started throwing obstacles in the way, telling Brusky he couldn't sit in the first row (which was for media only), or that he couldn't set his phone on a tripod. One incident, later covered by National Public Radio, caught then-Superintendent Darienne Driver's chief of staff giving Brusky the finger during a heated night of public testimony from teachers. His actions were caught on the union's social media and posted online. The official was immediately removed from his position following the incident. One by one, the union asserted its right to set up at the meetings and to record the proceedings. One by one, the barriers fell. Within a few months Brusky was offered a dedicated spot to set up his tripod.

With some regular publicity about the livestream, teachers around the city began tuning in. Hundreds of them. Real-time responses and comments began to flow on the Facebook livestream, and communications directly between educators and board members let the board know that teachers were paying attention.

> "The [Facebook] livestream of [Milwaukee school] board meetings has really helped hold the board accountable. The board is hearing from our members on a regular basis, and our members are in a much better position to weigh in on policy debates and actions, whether they're in the room or not."

"The livestream of board meetings has really helped hold the board accountable," says Brusky. "The board is hearing from our members on a regular basis, and our members are in a much better position to weigh in on policy debates and actions, whether they're in the room or not."

Building Solidarity Across Districts

When teachers in Los Angeles and Oakland went on strike in early 2019, the MTEA "lent" Joe Brusky to the union locals in those cities to document the strikes with his camera, and to help with social media. It also helped spearhead and formalize the concept of "art builds" for progressive events, both in Milwaukee for March for Our Lives and other progressive causes, and nationally. (See Brusky/Cosier, p. 296.)

When teachers in Little Rock, Arkansas, went on strike in October 2019, Brusky didn't travel to Little Rock, but he organized a photo shoot with MTEA leaders at their monthly assembly holding an Overpass Light Brigade message of support for the strikers. Brusky is a core member of the OLB and has often incorporated their lighted messages into campaigns or actions. The Little Rock photo was posted on the MTEA's Facebook page. It ended up being shared 1,200 times on Facebook and was viewed by more people in Little Rock than in Milwaukee! The site's metrics showed that it had a reach of 128,000 hits and hundreds of comments offering solidarity and encouragement to the Little Rock teachers.

Cost-Benefit? It's Been Worth It

Brusky's full-time release position costs money, of course. The decision to create the position was not an easy one for the union, particularly after they'd lost bargaining rights and were threatened with losing members.

Many locals will not have the budgetary resources to include a full-time released social media organizer. Before Brusky was hired at the MTEA, the union had created a committee of social media-savvy members to help compile articles, memes, and links to later post on the public Facebook page. This helped spread the work among many shoulders. But the full-time release position has paid off. "Most of the time, I'm out in buildings, taking pictures, helping members see themselves as part of something larger," says Brusky. He is also signing up new members.

Brusky puts together a report each year for the union's executive board, providing an overview of all the social media initiatives and some of the metrics gleaned from them. He's able to show how frequently teachers are visiting the Facebook page and which posts are garnering the most response. The report demonstrates the effectiveness with cold, hard numbers and new member sign-ups.

The smart utilization of social media has helped union locals all across the country expand the engagement of individual teachers, mobilize educators and community members, and speak truth to power. Who knows where the next decade will take us when it comes to digital communications? ⬛

Leigh Dingerson is a former community organizer, and currently a freelance writer and researcher on community and labor struggles for education justice. She is the author, most recently, of "Building the Power to Reclaim Our Schools," a case study on the 2019 Los Angeles teachers' strike.

Joe Brusky's photos often appear in Rethinking Schools *and other newspapers and magazines around the country. He has facilitated union social media workshops at numerous conferences around the country, including sessions for Labor Notes and the National Education Association.*

Before the March, Before the Strike: The Art Build

BY JOE BRUSKY AND KIM COSIER

"**N**ow I get it," said Keisha, a 5th-grade teacher from Oakland, California. "It's an art party with a mission!" Several high school students laughed and nodded in agreement as we all worked together to paint a design that had been traced onto a 24-foot parachute banner. In Oakland, as in other places that have employed artistic activism as an organizing tool, hundreds of teachers, staff, students, and family members happily pitched in—and made friends in the process—in the run-up to the February 2019 Oakland teacher strike. Together, we created "600 picket signs, 1,000 patches, five parachute banners (24 feet wide), 40 to 50 smaller banners, numerous T-shirts, and 500-plus posters" in three days in Oakland, according to our collaborator Nicolas Lampert.

Art builds are about visualizing a political message, but they are also community-embracing events that provide spaces for movement building for social justice. Artists and non-artists alike are able to take part because there are lots of activities that can be done without art experience.

A Space for Art and Justice

In Oakland the union hall and its parking garage were humming with energy during the three-day build in January 2019. To get started, everything was first covered in tarps, and then workstations were set up throughout the spaces. The main office on the second floor was transformed into a print shop, with artists at screen-printing stations churning out thousands of prints. Volunteer "runners" grabbed the fresh prints and hung them to dry on clotheslines that zigzagged across the conference room. When the prints were dry, other runners rushed them downstairs, where volunteers hand-colored them. The copy room/workspace was filled with the sounds of friendly chatter and tearing fabric as another team worked on prepping muslin for screen prints. Another room was set aside for a team of volunteers to project and trace banner designs on fabric to be painted by others. A wide hallway was designated as a kind of food court. Local vendors occupied spaces between tables filled with snacks and drinks people were sharing.

Downstairs, the party continued as volunteers and organizers worked in a parking garage that had been cleared for the build. Rows and rows of folding tables held multiple 4-foot by 10- to 20-foot banners that were being painted by a host of volunteers, including young children and retirees. A dad with a baby strapped to his chest chatted with a neighbor, who happened by and couldn't resist joining the fun. Dried screen prints brought down from above were hand-colored by more people on other tables and, when complete, were run to another set of clotheslines to dry.

On the other side of the cavernous space, another crew was painting and assembling the wooden frames for picket signs. Two large children's play parachutes were laid out in opposite corners of the garage, and groups of volunteers were hunched over or sitting on the ground happily painting together, sharing stories about their schools and how they came to learn about the art build. A local journalist arrived and scribbled notes as a teacher explained why she was planning to strike, as she helped paint the parachute.

As they were completed, signs, patches, and hand-painted banners were hung inside and outside the building. Surrounded by artwork, Keith Brown, president of the Oakland Education Association, held a livestreamed press conference to announce that a strike vote would take place within days. There were also chant building, drumming, and movement workshops, live music from a high school jazz band, food from local vendors, and lots and lots of momentum built for the cause. It truly was an art party with a mission.

Joe Brusky (this article's co-author) and other photographers and social media-savvy members documented and shared work as it happened, which served to recruit more help as people began to see the party online. This documentation and sharing continued once the work hit the streets. Such still and moving images of teacher uprisings have helped make union activism recognizable, memorable, and successful. They are impactful not only because of a sea of teachers dressed in Red for Ed, but also through the banners, picket signs, painted parachutes, and other artwork that get featured on social media posts and in broadcast and print news sources.

Art Build Workers Collective

We are part of a collective called the Art Build Workers. We have been traveling around the country helping to organize multiday art builds that help unions build movements and amplify their messages through visual art, media, and archiving. From Los Angeles to Little Rock, Arkansas, art builds have changed the way demonstrations look, amplified the movement's social media presence, and helped create spaces for movements to build community and generate a powerful sense of solidarity and shared purpose.

Back home in Milwaukee we collaborate with groups working on issues including gun violence, climate, sexual assault, and immigration. One of our early and regular collaborating partners is the Milwaukee Teachers' Education Association (MTEA). The MTEA was at our very first build in 2016, which was sparked by a visit from

Meet Our Collective

The Art Build Workers collective includes Joe Brusky, who focuses on photography, video, and social media; Jeanette Arellano, Kim Cosier, and Josie Osborne, who specialize in banners, design, and art education; Nicolas Lampert and Paul Kjelland, who work on design, printmaking, and archives; and Claudio Martinez, who does graphic design and banners. We work locally with a variety of partners including Voces de la Frontera, an immigrant rights powerhouse in Milwaukee; the People's Climate Coalition, which includes Extinction Rebellion Milwaukee, Youth Climate Action Team, Sunrise Milwaukee, and 350 Milwaukee; and Peace Action Center. We've also partnered with gun violence organizers from Moms Demand Action and March for Our Lives, as well as organizers on the campus of the University of Wisconsin–Milwaukee who focus on ending rape culture. Youth from our local ACLU chapter have partnered with us as well.

activist David Solnit, a veteran artist/activist and art build coordinator. Success with early MTEA campaigns caught the attention of Nate Gunderson, a visionary organizer who works at the National Education Association (NEA). Nate saw the power of the work created at MTEA art builds and was excited about the ways it was deployed in demonstrations in Milwaukee. He invited us to do a build with union members in Minneapolis/St. Paul, and we have been partnering with the NEA and union locals across the country ever since.

Art builds create visual tools that are used to amplify intersectional messages, which link various social issues to more traditional concerns of education activists. The role of the image in this movement is more important than ever before, because news is increasingly shared through platforms that limit word count and rely on photographs, images, and videos. Art builds create opportunities for activists and artists to work together to imagine a more just world.

Advanced Planning Vital

A good art party with a mission requires planning. Ahead of a build, union leadership and artists/designers work together to prepare. Among the preparations:

- Slogans are developed and refined collaboratively.
- A call for images using the slogans is shared widely, with a date for submission that allows time for prepping designs.
- Local artists as well as ones from around the country are invited to participate.
- Supplies must be ordered (or donations accepted) ahead of time, including bolts of muslin fabric (we have also painted on sheets that were found at thrift stores), paint, ink, silk screen printing tools, brushes and rollers, buckets, clothesline and clothespins, plastic tarps, tape, rags (lots of rags), and more. A clean-out sink (such as a janitor's slop sink) is very helpful, but a hose and a drain can do in a pinch.
- An invitation to join the build should be designed with a clear indication that no art experience is required and that all ages are welcome. (Depending on how you want children to participate, it can be helpful to plan a children's area and activities.)
- A plan for how to feed and hydrate the volunteers should be made.
- A plan should be in place for inviting the press and coordinating social media shares to generate a buzz for the build and for the action you are working toward.

For big builds, it is a good idea to form a planning committee that can coordinate tasks before, during, and after the build. Such planning has ensured successful events that have resulted in building movement momentum, visualizing and amplify messaging, and creating solidarity and excitement among members and their supporters. (For more tips, see artbuildworkers.com.) Some builds have been huge, such as in Los Angeles, Oakland, and Chicago, while others have been smaller, but no less impactful. Smaller builds can even be organized by energetic and hardworking individuals.

In Little Rock, for example, art teacher Amanda Mamula organized multiple art builds after learning our organizing techniques at the NEA's conferences on racial and social justice and representative assemblies in Minneapolis (in 2018) and Houston (in 2019). Amanda said: "I knew Arkansas was having a big 'Red for Ed Rally' in October 2018. . . . I wanted Little Rock's presence to be noted at the rally, since it was in our backyard, and I wanted to look professional and organized like your group." Amanda has gone on to organize many more art builds as the fight continues in Arkansas. In an email, she wrote: "Art builds are the perfect mix of my organizing skills and . . . my art and political science degrees. My time painting with your group is my favorite memory of Minneapolis that summer. You reinvigorated my social justice warrior and showed me a new way through art."

From Los Angeles to Little Rock, art builds have changed the way demonstrations look, amplified the movement's social media presence, and helped create spaces for movements to build community and generate a powerful sense of solidarity and shared purpose. Increasingly, teacher unions are using art and art builds as tools for social justice. ▨

Kim Cosier is a teacher educator, activist, and artist who lives in Milwaukee with her wife and collaborator, Josie Osborne.

Joe Brusky is a 4th-grade teacher in Milwaukee Public Schools on a full-time release from his classroom to do organizing and social media for his union, the Milwaukee Teachers' Education Association. He's also a photographer and activist as a core member of the Overpass Light Brigade and the Art Build Workers. His photos documenting movements for justice, including teacher strikes in LA, Oakland, and Chicago, as well as two trips to the Standing Rock resistance camp in 2016, have gone far and wide.

If you would like to reach out to us, please email Kim at kcosier@uwm.edu and/or Joe at BruskyJ@mtea.org.

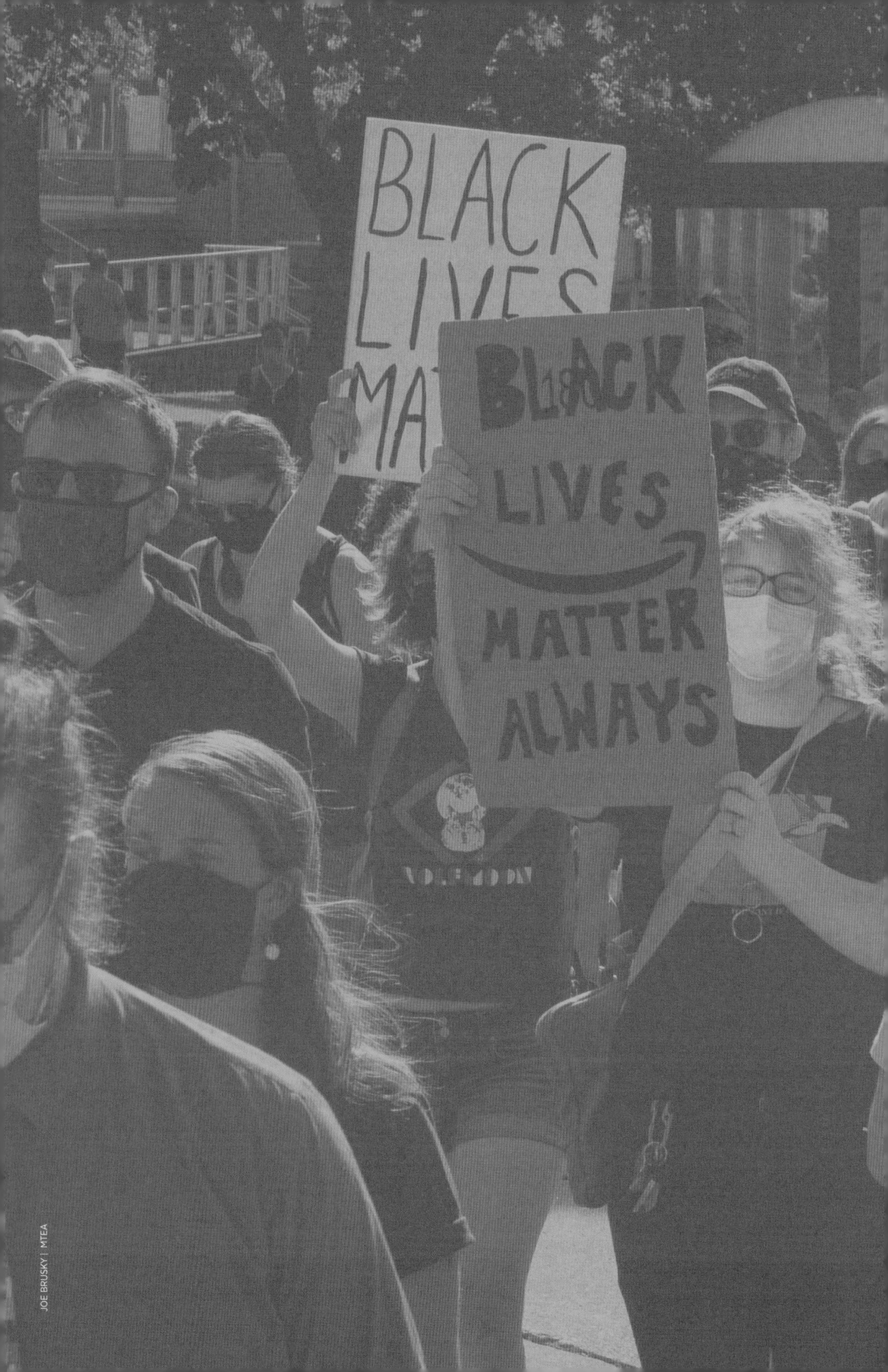

JOE BRUSKY | MTEA

SECTION FIVE

FIGHTING THE SYSTEM

Confronting the Education Debt

BY THE ALLIANCE TO RECLAIM OUR SCHOOLS

During winter and spring of 2018, teachers in West Virginia, Kentucky, Oklahoma, Arizona, Colorado, North Carolina, and Puerto Rico took to the streets demanding greater investment in their public schools. Their protests emerged, in part, out of frustration that so much school funding, slashed during the Great Recession of 2008, has yet to be restored.

But for African American and Latino communities, the underfunding of public schools goes back generations. Over the past 50 years we have shortchanged students and their schools by hundreds of billions of dollars in federal education funding alone.

Policymakers argue that there is no more money for education—*especially* in districts serving low-income and Black and Brown children. Yet there is a direct correlation between dwindling resources for public schools and the ongoing political proclivity for transferring public dollars to the nation's wealthiest individuals and corporations. The rich are getting richer. Our schools are broke on purpose.

In a 2006 address, Gloria Ladson-Billings, then president of the American Educational Research Association (AERA), introduced the concept of the "education debt." Focusing solely on the "achievement gap," she argued, failed to acknowledge the historic, economic, sociopolitical, and moral foundations of the disparate educational outcomes between white students and students of color.

Confronting the Education Debt, by the Alliance to Reclaim Our Schools (AROS), embraces Ladson-Billings' theory and argues that still today, the relative disenfranchisement of communities of color has allowed elected policymakers to pursue priorities that deny millions of children the educational opportunities they deserve.

Instead of funding our schools, policy decisions are made that increase personal and corporate wealth, drawing down public revenues in the process. Instead of funding our schools, we have seen an explosion of policies that criminalize Black and Brown communities, including staffing their schools with police officers instead of guidance counselors. Instead of funding public schools, privatization—through charters and vouchers—soaks up education dollars and strips the budgets of traditional public districts. All of these trends continue to compound the education debt.

While acknowledging the historic nature of the education debt, the AROS report takes a snapshot of time—the years between 2005 and 2017. A student who entered 1st grade in 2005 would have graduated from high school in May 2017. AROS uses that time frame to explore the decisions and trends that have continued to deny Black, Brown, and low-income students access to the schools they deserve, while enhancing the bank accounts of the richest Americans.

Based on data compiled for this report, between 2005 and 2017, public schools serving majorities of low-income students in the U.S. were underfunded by $580 billion in federal dollars alone—for programs specifically targeted at our most vulnerable children. Over that same period, the personal wealth of the nation's 400 richest people grew by a combined $1.57 trillion. Priorities chosen and decisions made by U.S. elected officials are implicated in both of these facts.

As our elected officials have stripped funding from schools, they have also presided over the systematic transfer of wealth from public to private hands, a massive investment in the criminalization of people of color and waged a methodical campaign to privatize public education through the proliferation of charter schools and voucher programs. Taken together, these policy priorities add up to a devastating assault on public schools in Black, Brown, and low-income communities and the students they serve. The debt we owe these students, schools, and communities is vast and growing.

Public education itself is not the problem. Thousands of public schools across the nation have functional technology in every classroom, well-stocked libraries, and state-of-the-art science labs. Their young people are expected to be future leaders. There are public schools with classes small enough that teachers can individualize their instruction according to student needs. Public schools work, but only where they are fully resourced to do so. And that tends to be in white, middle-class, and affluent communities.

In contrast, without comparable resources, Black and Brown students are more likely to:

- Sit in crowded classrooms.
- Be taught by first-year teachers and/or by teachers who have not met basic certification requirements.
- Attend schools with higher teacher turnover rates.
- Have less access to high-level math and science courses (often a prerequisite for college).
- Have less access to guidance counselors, librarians, nurses, technology, and other critical resources.
- Be removed from the classroom altogether and placed in some form of detention.

Schools that fail to serve these children are not accidental, nor are they the fault of students, educators, unions, communities, or parents—all of whom seem too often to take the blame. They are the logical outcome of the systematic exclusion of Black and Brown communities from the halls of political power where priorities are set and budgets determined.

The Historic Underpinnings of Exclusion

The history of public education in the United States is a chronicle of great promise and of systematic exclusion. Until the 1960s, the nation did not even *profess* to serve all children equitably. Thomas Jefferson proposed a two-track education system, with schools serving "the learned" separate from those designed to serve "the laboring." Southern states enacted laws making it a crime to teach enslaved people to read. Industrialists in the early 1800s created schools that emphasized discipline and obedience in order to turn out compliant factory workers. Children of the privileged class attended schools designed to turn out thinkers and leaders. Racial and class divides were strictly enforced.

In 1954 the U.S. Supreme Court declared the doctrine of "separate but equal" unconstitutional, ordering public schools to be integrated to better serve children of color and our collective good. Resistance to the Court's ruling, from white people who sought to maintain the advantage of superior schools for their own children, was immediate and fierce. In most places, racial and class segregation persisted.

In the 1960s and 1970s Congress sought to address systemic funding and resource disparities in public schools across the country. Since then, many state courts and legislatures have acknowledged the stark chasm between the resources provided to majority-white schools and those offered to Black and Brown children. The laws have bent haltingly toward justice, but action has lagged. The excuse is often the same: There is no money, or money doesn't matter.

Money Matters

Although critics of public education have argued for years that money doesn't matter for quality education, research has proven time and again that in fact, it matters a lot.

Districts serving white and more affluent students spend thousands to tens of thousands of dollars more, per pupil, than high-poverty school districts and those serving majorities of Black and Brown students. The challenges faced by these schools—larger class sizes, fewer experienced teachers, the lack of libraries, science equipment, technology, and counselors—all reflect a lack of resources. By failing to provide adequate funding, we deny these children the chance to fulfill their potential.

The fact that these funding disparities exist is not news. Since 2003, researchers in 25 states and the District of Columbia have conducted 41 "adequacy" studies that quantify the resources and conditions that students need to succeed in school. All but one of those studies recommended increased funding for public schools. Yet only eight states and D.C. have even partially adjusted state funding based on the findings. And the other 25 states have failed to even take on the task of determining what students need and how much it would cost to provide it.

Educational racism is continuing and growing worse. Beginning in 2014, more than half of public school students are students of color. And despite decades of promises of equal justice under law, Black children are more segregated in their schools today than they were 30 years ago.

Congress Has Failed to Fully Fund Targeted Federal Education Programs

Though the federal government contributes only about 8 percent of all spending on K–12 public schools, it is critical funding, because the majority of that funding is directly targeted at students with the greatest needs—low-income children and students with disabilities. Five decades of congressional failure to fully invest in the two largest K–2 funding streams has denied these children—and, we argue, all children—the additional supports they need.

Title I: A War on Poverty Without the Investment to Win

President Lyndon B. Johnson, in launching his War on Poverty, recognized that a key front in the battle against poverty was the nation's public schools. With the 1965 passage of the Elementary and Secondary Education Act (ESEA), the federal government acknowledged that public schools in low-income communities need additional educational resources. Title I of the ESEA directs federal dollars to schools with high concentrations of students living in poverty.

Not only did lawmakers recognize the need for additional resources—they attempted to quantify it. Embedded in the law is the authorization—established by Congress in 1965—to provide school districts an additional 40 percent for each Title I-eligible child so that their schools could offer supplemental supports such as reading specialists and smaller class sizes.

Having established that additional 40 percent target in the law, Congress immediately failed to fully fund it, not only in 1965 but *in every year since*. Over the past dozen years, congressional appropriations for Title I have averaged less than half the promised funding. That means that the more than 56,000 Title I schools across the country lack the money they need to fully provide the supplemental supports viewed as critical by Congress in enacting the bill.

The impact of those annual underfunded appropriations is wrenchingly clear: If

Title 1 Full Funding (40% estimate) vs. Actual Appropriation

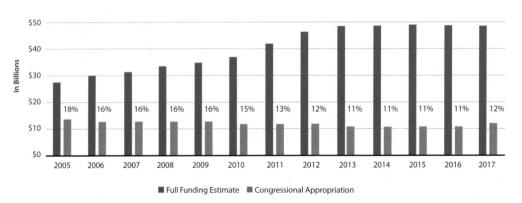

Source: Original research conducted by the Education Policy and Practice Department, Center for Great Public Schools, National Education Association. February 2018. For more information, see educationdebt.reclaimourschools.org.

Title I was fully funded by Congress, the nation's high-poverty schools could provide:

- Health and mental health services for every student, including dental and vision services; *and*
- A full-time nurse in every Title I school; *and*
- A full-time librarian for every Title I school; *and*
- A full-time additional counselor for every Title I school, *or*
- A full-time teaching assistant in every Title I classroom across the country.

If Congress funded Title I to the full amount authorized, schools serving concentrations of low-income students would have more resources that could make a real difference in student outcomes. But appropriation levels have never once met the congressionally established goal. The same holds true for federal dollars authorized to support students with disabilities.

Individuals with Disabilities Education Act (IDEA): A Promise Denied

In 1975, a decade after passing the ESEA, Congress sought to address the educational needs of students with disabilities. The Education for All Handicapped Children Act (now known as the Individuals with Disabilities Education Act, or IDEA) signaled a recognition by members of Congress that students with disabilities need additional services to allow them to achieve academically and sit side by side with their peers, and that the federal government had an obligation to help fund at least some of these services. IDEA is the second largest federal education program after Title I.

IDEA *requires* schools to identify and evaluate students thought to have disabilities and then to provide them with the supports they need in school. The financial assumption underlying IDEA is that on average, the cost of educating a child with disabilities is *twice* the cost of educating a non-disabled student. IDEA made providing these additional services mandatory and Congress pledged that the federal government would pay up to 40 percent of the cost. Under the law, local and state funds must cover the remaining costs.

Once again, having established the formula, Congress failed to invest in it. Federal funding of IDEA has never approached the promised 40 percent mark. And because IDEA *guarantees* the necessary services for all students with disabilities, state and local governments must not only contribute their share, but also cover the unfunded federal contribution. With an estimated 6.5 million students currently being served by IDEA, even the best resourced school districts are finding it difficult to meet the needs. But in districts already struggling for resources, the mandate of IDEA has shattered school budgets, affecting educational quality for *all* students—those with and those without disabilities.

Since 2005, the aggregated federal underpayment to states to help provide services to students with disabilities has reached $233 billion. This amounts to an average of $2,637 in additional funding each year for every special needs student in the country, 53 percent of whom are students of color.

Fully funded, this federal contribution would have been more than enough to assign an additional teacher's assistant for every 12 students with disabilities in a school.

The drain on local school district budgets has been so substantial that some states or districts have conspired to deny services to students who need—and have a right to—them, and/or to slash programming and staffing across the board in order to meet the legal mandates of IDEA.

State and Local School Funding Shortchanges Black, Brown, and Low-Income Schools

Federal shortchanging of public schools, just through the two formula programs mentioned above, approached $55 billion in 2017 alone. But federal funding provides only a small portion of total spending on public education. Most education spending comes from local and state funds. Here too, schools serving Black and Brown students are systematically sabotaged.

Local sources—primarily property tax revenues—contribute about 45 percent of funding for public schools (this percentage varies from state to state)—a foundation of education funding that inherently discriminates against low-income communities.

With land and houses valued less on the market, low-income communities raise less revenue from property taxes than wealthy communities, and therefore have less to spend on their schools. This entrenched inequity has been recognized for decades. The Ohio Supreme Court has found that state's system of funding public schools through property tax revenues unconstitutional—four times. But change has proven difficult. Low-income communities have less political power. Wealthy districts are happy with the status quo.

State governments, which provide an average of 47 percent of school funding, can choose to use state money to offset local disparities in school resources. Only 11 states do so. Twenty states have flat funding formulas that do not distinguish between high- and low-poverty districts, and 17 states actually channel *more* resources to *wealthier* districts than to high-poverty ones.

The recession in 2008 put the squeeze on overdrive. Property values—particularly in low-income communities—rapidly lost value. Faced with emptying coffers, and with tax hikes either barred by law or perceived as politically suicidal, state and district leaders responded with budget cuts and, incredibly in some cases, with further tax cuts to wealthy corporations. Public schools, typically the largest line item in local budgets, bore the brunt. The impact was devastating in Black and Brown communities:

> In 2011, in the midst of the recession, the School District of Philadelphia laid off 150 school nurses. Two years later, 12-year-old Laporshia Massey suffered an asthma attack at her school. Without a nurse on hand to evaluate her, school staff encouraged Laporshia to finish out the day. By the time she got home, her condition had deteriorated, and she died as

her father rushed her to the hospital. A few months later, a 7-year-old at Philadelphia's Andrew Jackson Elementary School collapsed. Again, no nurse was on hand. The child died.

Elected policymakers' responses to the recession impacted schools across the country, regardless of race or income. But because inequities in resources were already entrenched before 2008, and because schools in low-income communities were already on shoestring budgets when the recession hit, the impacts for them were much more dramatic. And even as the recovery began to take hold, the resource chasm between schools serving white and more affluent children and those serving children of color deepened.

The Education Trust found that in 2015 on average, districts with large majorities of students of color provided about $1,800 (13 percent) less *per student* than districts in the same state serving the fewest students of color.

The same study found that *low-wealth* school districts on average receive about $1,000 less per student in state funding than wealthy districts.

State legislatures have the power, but perhaps not the will, to ensure even a modicum of fairness in the funding of public schools. The "moral debt" identified by Gloria Ladson-Billings reflects, as she notes, "the disparity between what we know is right and what we actually do."

In the face of clear and convincing evidence that schools serving Black, Brown, and low-income students are being systematically underfunded, policymakers typically argue that there simply is no more money. But that is not entirely honest. We live in the wealthiest nation in the world. Funding public education—or not—is a matter of priorities.

*   *   *

The Alliance to Reclaim Our Schools put forward a three-point road map for confronting the education debt. It includes full funding for Title I and IDEA, a federal commitment to create 25,000 sustainable community schools, and the rededication of the U.S. Department of Education to its stated role of ensuring equity in the nation's public schools. To get there, AROS identifies ways to increase the tax burden on the wealthiest Americans—revenues that can be clawed back at the local, state, and federal levels and provide billions of dollars to public budgets. Indeed, a number of labor/community alliances around the country are working actively to win some of these new revenues for schools. One such campaign is profiled on p. 353. 🔲

Excerpted from *Confronting the Education Debt: We Owe Billions to Black, Brown, and Low-Income Students and Their Schools*, 2019 by the Alliance to Reclaim Our Schools. The full report is available at educationdebt.reclaimourschools.org.

The Dangerous Narrative That Lurks Under the "Achievement Gap"

And the counternarrative about Black student potential

BY ERIC HIGGINS

EBIN LEE

When we hear the words "achievement gap," many of us think about Black students underperforming academically compared with their white peers. Federal, state, and local governmental agencies have been called on to study the gap. Presidents, governors, mayors, and school personnel all speak about the need to close it. If you heard the words "achievement gap" and directly associated it with failing Black students, teachers, and schools, you have been directly influenced by a dangerous narrative.

This narrative, which has taken root in our news and politics, insinuates that Black students are academically inferior to their white counterparts. It tells the story of a miserable Black existence filled with poverty, dysfunctional families, and absentee fathers. According to this narrative, Black students are not only ill-equipped to handle the rigors of academia, but also innately prone to violence, drug use, and hypersexuality.

For many people, a good school is synonymous with a white school. Indeed, one 2016 study by researchers Chase M. Billingham and Matthew O. Hunt found that for every 1 percentage point increase in the Black enrollment at a hypothetical school, white parents were 1.7 percent less likely to enroll their children in that school.

And this anti-Black narrative not only affects parents' perceptions of school quality, but also teachers' perceptions of their students and their abilities.

This narrative is false.

The concept of the Black/white achievement gap as it is widely understood is a tool of oppression—and a total fabrication. Indeed, this "gap" is no more a true reflection of the potential of Black students than the achievement gap between Asian American and white students reflects the academic potential of white students. It is true that many Black students and schools are not performing well on a variety of measures of academic success, but these outcomes go beyond school achievement; they are directly linked to systemic racism, unequal treatment, and the denial of opportunities for Black families subjugated to second-class citizenship.

> "For many people, a good school is synonymous with a white school."

I contend that there is a counternarrative that tells a much different story of achievement and oppression. The counternarrative speaks of systemic racism, segregated and unequal schools, redlining, undervalued property in Black neighborhoods, blight, white privilege, and white wealth built on the back of Black oppression.

White supremacy—a system of dominance in which white people overwhelmingly control political, economic, and cultural power—makes people believe that majority-white schools are successful because white students are smarter and more disciplined. To believe this, you must turn a blind eye to how centuries of racism have denied opportunities to Black people and to government policies that have ravished Black neighborhoods.

Take for instance the G.I. Bill, which helped propel white families out of poverty and helped them accumulate wealth through homeownership. This great opportunity was denied to Black veterans for whom the dream of homeownership often became an illusion. The major racial disparities in this program can directly be tied to white wealth accumulation and educational opportunity disparities for Blacks. However, when Black student achievement is discussed we too often forget the economic and political conditions that contribute to the plight of these students. The history of ruthlessness is dismissed and forgotten.

Nearly 25 years ago, scholars Gloria Ladson-Billings and William F. Tate IV made the case for this counternarrative in their influential article "Toward a Critical Race Theory of Education." They rooted their analysis of school equity on three central propositions: "Race is a significant factor in determining inequity in the United States," "United States society is based on property rights," and "the intersection of race and property creates an analytic tool through which we understand social (and, consequently, school) inequity."

It is only because of disenfranchisement and systemic racism that we still ignore this counternarrative and blame Black students for their own lack of educational opportunities.

When I hear words like "the achievement gap," I understand that certain schools are designated "failing" because it fits the narrative of white supremacy. If we truly cared about the education of Black students, we would dismantle the institutions of white supremacy that help keep Black families in a cycle of poverty—the judicial system that forces many Blacks to live in a police state through unfair sentencing, the healthcare system that fails to equitably treat Black patients with preventative services and care, the private job sector that discriminates against Black job seekers.

We need more white voices bringing attention to the racist institutions and more people actively working to dismantle them. Imagine how quickly conditions would change if we shuttered the doors of white neighborhood schools or underfunded predominately white schools to the extent we routinely do to majority-Black schools. Black students deserve educators who are willing to challenge the conditions that help create school failure, not punish students and schools who are underperforming. ◆

Eric Higgins has worked in education for more than 13 years, first as a science and English/language arts teacher and now as an assistant principal of a K–6 elementary school in Missouri's St. Louis County.

This essay first appeared in the Dec. 6, 2019, *Education Week*. Reprinted with permission of the author.

The Many Faces of Privatization

JOE JOE BRUSKY | MTEA

Privatization threatens the very existence of public education and its role as a foundation of our democracy.

Every state constitution guarantees the right to a free public education for all children, regardless of their abilities, special needs, home languages, or immigration status. Historically, public schools have been locally controlled within a broad policy framework set at the state level. In most districts, public schools are overseen by an elected school board.

Privatization of public education upends this right, by providing public funds to non-public entities, without the guarantees and transparency offered by public schools. Privatization takes several forms and evolves in various ways.

Charter Schools—Publicly Funded, Largely Unregulated

Charters are often described as "public" schools because they are authorized and funded by state law, but they are overwhelmingly privately run. They may not charge tuition and cannot teach religion. Typically, charter schools are granted a "charter" that exempts them from many regulations governing traditional public schools. In exchange, they are supposed to "experiment," improve academic achievement, and share the lessons learned. Charters first appeared, often with community and teacher union support, in urban districts in the late 1980s and early 1990s.

Over time, however, charters have become part of a charter "movement"—a national and well-funded campaign organized by investors, foundations, and educational management companies to create a parallel, more privatized school system with less public accountability and less democratic oversight. The Walton Foundation, perhaps the most aggressive funder of this movement, has given money to a quarter of all charter schools.

Oversight of charters is based on state law and can vary significantly. Some states allow for-profit charter schools and/or cyberschools. Unlike traditional public schools, most charter schools are governed by appointed boards not subject to public oversight or approval. Board members of privately run charters are not required to live in the community the school serves. They can limit their enrollment and may not have to admit students after the school year begins. Students usually must apply.

> From 2006 to 2016, charter school enrollment nearly tripled . . . while more than 4,000 traditional public schools were closed.

Charter schools are in virtually all states. From 2006 to 2016, charter school enrollment nearly tripled—from 1.2 million students to an estimated 3.1 million—while more than 4,000 traditional public schools were closed. Charters and public school closings are mainly concentrated in urban areas with high numbers of Black and Latina/o students.

Some major cities like Washington, D.C.; Detroit; San Diego; Cleveland; Milwaukee; Gary, Indiana; Newark, New Jersey; and many others have a third to more than half of their students going to privately run charter schools.

Most charter schools emerge one by one as individual operators apply for licenses from state-designated "authorizers." But sometimes, efforts to wrest control of public schools from the public happens suddenly.

In some states, legislatures have facilitated privatization by creating state-run "recovery districts" or "achievement districts." Under these initiatives, the state assumes control of a subset of "failing" schools, and begins the process of turning management of the schools over to private operators. These takeover districts have been created in Louisiana, Tennessee, and elsewhere.

After Hurricane Katrina devastated New Orleans in 2005, pro-privatization forces moved in and quickly assumed control of virtually all of the schools in the city. Both state and federal law facilitated the transfer. Today, there are no truly public schools left in the city. Writer Naomi Klein calls this rapid process of privatization the "Shock Doctrine." A similar attempt began in Puerto Rico in the wake of Hurricane Maria. (See St. John, p. 334.) Many fear that the pandemic of 2020 will similarly lead to efforts to vastly increase privatized learning, particularly by corporations like K12 that promote online "virtual" schools.

Vouchers—Still Publicly Funded, Even Less Regulated!

Voucher programs allow students to attend private schools by providing public dollars to cover some or all of tuition payments. Some programs allow parents to establish personal bank accounts to use for a range of educational expenses.

The longest-running and largest voucher program is in Milwaukee, and siphons off more than $250 million each year from the city's public schools. Other programs exist in Cleveland, New Orleans, and Washington, D.C.

In 2020, 29 different voucher programs are operational in 16 states plus Washington, D.C., and Puerto Rico. They take three main forms:

- Traditional private school vouchers provide direct public money to pay for all or part of a student's tuition in a private school. Most vouchers are used for religious schools, including Catholic, Lutheran, evangelical, Jewish, and Muslim institutions.
- Tax credit vouchers provide individuals or corporations with a 100 percent, dollar-for-dollar credit to send what they would otherwise owe in taxes to private nonprofit organizations. These organizations then offer vouchers to students to cover private school tuition.
- "Education Savings Accounts" offer public funds that can be deposited into personal accounts that are then used to pay for private school tuition or other educational expenses such as tutoring, online courses, or homeschooling.

In general, private schools that accept vouchers may impose student eligibility requirements and/or conditions on student performance. Private schools do not have the same legal responsibilities as public schools and operate with minimal oversight or transparency. Private schools, for instance, do not have to provide the same level of special education services as public schools. They can sidestep basic constitutional protections such as freedom of speech or due process when students are expelled. They generally do not have to follow requirements for open meetings and records. Religious voucher schools can teach church doctrine that is at odds with public policy, for instance basing their science classes on creationism or teaching that homosexuality is a sin or women should be obedient to men.

What Can Teacher Unions Do to Stop School Privatization?

All children deserve good schools and no one questions the desire of parents to find the best options they can for their children. But the central question for public policy is whether expanding charters is an effective strategy for improving public education as a whole. Experience shows it is not. Nowhere have charters produced a model for equitable districtwide reform, and in many places charters have weakened support and funding for public education while increasing new forms of inequality. It's time to stop charter expansion and refocus public policy on providing excellent public schools for all.

To accomplish this, we educators and our unions, working in alliance with parents, community groups, and students, need to build broad alliances, coalitions, and social movements that are politically strong enough to shift policy. We must work with parents and communities to ensure that public schools are adequately and fairly funded. Affordable housing, health care for all, and living wage jobs are necessary so that our students and their families have the quality of life they deserve. As educators we should insist that our unions, the single largest organized voice for working people in this nation, take up social justice issues and make them a reality. It's up to us the take the next steps. 🔧

A version of this article was published in *The New Teacher Book* (Rethinking Schools, 2018).

DEFEND PUBLIC EDUCATION

JOHN FLEISSNER

Resources on School Privatization

Books

Nancy MacLean
Democracy in Chains: The Deep History of the Radical Right's Stealth Plan for America
(Viking, 2017)
An in-depth and highly readable examination of the systematic assault on public schools and other public institutions.

Barbara Miner
Lessons from the Heartland: A Turbulent Half-Century of Public Education in an Iconic American City
(New Press, 2013)
An engaging narrative nonfiction account of the ongoing struggles against school privatization and segregation in the city with the largest private school voucher program in the nation.

Diane Ravitch
Slaying Goliath: The Passionate Resistance to Privatization and the Fight to Save America's Public Schools
(Knopf, 2020)
An overview of many of the efforts throughout the country to fight school privatization.

Noliwe Rooks
Cutting School: Privatization, Segregation, and the End of Public Education
(New Press, 2017)
A comprehensive look at the historic underfunding of public schools that serve students of color and the impact of voucher, charter, and other privatization schemes through a lens of race and class.

Organizations

Public Funds, Public Schools is a national campaign against voucher programs. Their website has many useful resources. pfps.org

In the Public Interest is a national organization that opposes privatization in all forms, including in public education. inthepublicinterest.org

Unite! Resist! And Win!

Organizing against public school takeovers in Milwaukee

BY AMY MIZIALKO

I n the spring of 2009, just months after he was appointed secretary of education by newly elected President Barack Obama, Arne Duncan told the Associated Press that he "will have failed" if, when his tenure was up, more urban districts weren't in "mayors' hands."

Milwaukee was a low-hanging fruit. Duncan, along with Wisconsin's Democratic Gov. Jim Doyle and Milwaukee Mayor Tom Barrett, tried to pick it.

They failed. As did the next two attempts by Republican Gov. Scott Walker, the Metropolitan Milwaukee Association of Commerce (MMAC), and the gerry-mandered Republican Legislature.

Some details and lessons follow.

Milwaukee as a Privatization Petri Dish

Milwaukee is considered the birthplace of public school privatization. In 1990 the state Legislature started a city-based private school voucher program. Once the conservative Wisconsin Supreme Court ruled the program could include religious schools, it grew to be the largest such program in the country. It now includes more than 120 schools, almost all of which are religious, and annually funnels more than a quarter of a billion tax dollars into these non-accountable private schools. This was nothing short of a long-term project to break up and privatize the Milwaukee Public Schools (MPS), which are governed by a democratically elected school board.

In 1993 the state government enacted its first charter school law, allowing school boards the authority to charter schools. Four years later, another law was enacted permitting the Milwaukee city government to authorize privately run charter schools. (It was the first city in the nation to gain that authority.) The law also gave similar authority to the University of Wisconsin–Milwaukee and the Milwaukee Area Technical College. Dozens of new charter schools opened up. My union, the Milwaukee Teachers' Education Association (MTEA), did not draw a hard line when the number of privately run charter schools (called "non-instrumentality" charter schools) authorized by the Milwaukee School Board also increased significantly.

As the combined total of voucher and charter schools rose above 160, the popularity of an open enrollment law added to MPS' problems. That law allows families (most of whom are white) to send their children to predominantly white suburban schools. As a result, 2020 enrollment declined to the point where only 56 percent of children living in the city attend MPS.

The Takeover Attempts

In the midst of the voucher and charter laws that propelled this unprecedented growth in school privatization, the MMAC, right-wing ideologues, and both Democrats and Republicans promoted a new tactic to privatize additional Milwaukee schools: the "takeover."

Attempt #1

In the fall of 2009 the Democratic governor of Wisconsin and the mayor of Milwaukee promoted state legislation that would replace Milwaukee's elected school board with one appointed by the mayor. Arne Duncan supported it, as did Democrats for Education Reform—who sent paid organizers into the state to lobby legislators. In response the NAACP and Educators' Network for Social Justice issued a call to community and labor groups to build a coalition to fight back. Within weeks, the Coalition to Stop the MPS Takeover included the MTEA and AFT Local 212, and soon grew to include nearly two dozen other community and student groups.

The coalition picketed homes of Democratic legislators and challenged the mayor at public events, arguing that, given that Milwaukee was home to the largest population of African Americans and Latinos in the state, this was nothing short of disenfranchisement of people's right to vote. Ultimately, the coalition and its supporters put enough pressure on the legislators to narrowly defeat the legislation.

Just a year after the defeat of the first takeover attempt, in February 2011, newly elected Gov. Walker unleashed the most anti-worker legislation in Wisconsin's history, stripping collective bargaining from most public sector unions, ending fair share and payroll deduction, and forcing union locals to hold annual recertification elections. (See Schirmer, p. 76.)

A short time later Walker expanded the private school voucher program statewide and made the largest cuts to public education funding since the Great Depression.

Attempt #2

By 2013, based on the guidelines of the federal Race to the Top program, 50 MPS schools were labeled "failing" by state officials. The bottom 5 percent were slated for major "innovation." The MMAC saw this as an opportunity to take over a large number of MPS schools and privatize them. The MMAC invited the leaders of the state-run Recovery School District in Louisiana and of Tennessee's state-run Achievement School District in Memphis to a private briefing for the business community.

When news of the private meeting leaked to the press, the MTEA contacted the NAACP, and jointly they called back together groups that had successfully defeated the previous mayoral takeover attempt. New groups like Wisconsin Jobs Now that led the Fight for $15 campaign in the city joined the revived coalition. We held a massive "Public Education Is a Civil Right" march through Black and Latino neighborhoods, with high school drum lines and representatives of many organizations. We also picketed the offices of the MMAC and lobbied local and state officials to reject any permutation of the plan. Thanks to the vehement resistance, the idea was eventually shelved.

We knew that such a defeat was only temporary. The key groups of the Coalition to Stop the MPS Takeover met and decided to change the coalition's name to indicate not what we were against, but what we were for. After many meetings we decided to rename ourselves Schools & Communities United. We also decided to do surveys and hold meetings to develop a document similar to "The Schools Chicago's Students Deserve" created by the Chicago Teachers Union. We released our 32-page document, "Fulfill the Promise: The Schools and Communities Our Children Deserve," on May 17, 2014, the 60th anniversary of the *Brown v. Board* decision, after a large march and rally. In the aftermath of that campaign and with strong encouragement by the MTEA, the school district created its first three community schools in schools that had been labeled as "needing improvement."

Attempt #3

In June 2015 Walker inserted MPS takeover legislation into the state budget. It gave Milwaukee County Executive Chris Abele authority to appoint a "takeover czar" who would have the power to identify several MPS schools over a series of five years beginning in fall 2016 and turn them into privately run charters. With so many voucher and privately run charter schools already operating in the city, this legislation had the potential to rapidly dismantle the Milwaukee Public Schools. The county executive appointed a suburban school superintendent, Demond Means, as the takeover czar to lead this new takeover effort.

The MTEA, along with Schools and Communities United, immediately began organizing at the school level across the city. We encouraged our building leaders to establish school defense committees to inform staff and parents and to prepare to take action. In the beginning, union members were fearful, asking over and over, "Which schools are they going to take over first?" and "Can we see the list?" The MTEA's response was clear from the beginning—we will not allow one school to be taken over by privatizers. We will fight, organize, and rally any targeted school and vow to fight the way we would fight for our own school, because these are all our schools.

We mapped the schools and neighborhoods identified as "failing." We declared that none of the schools had "failed"; rather, the schools had been failed by the state of Wisconsin, the entity constitutionally responsible for adequately funding public schools. MTEA and SCU members bird-dogged the Milwaukee County executive and his takeover czar at nearly all of their public appearances. We confronted them at town hall meetings, the county courthouse, community presentations, and even in Mequon, the suburb where Means was superintendent, at one of his school board meetings. We distributed hundreds of "No Takeover/Say Yes to MPS!" lawn signs throughout the city. We held coordinated walk-ins where staff and parents met before school, held anti-takeover rallies, and then walked into school together. After a year of unrelenting resistance by MTEA and SCU members, the takeover czar resigned in fall 2016, and exactly zero MPS schools were taken over.

A Few Lessons

The lessons from our experiences were several. For one, teacher unions can't stand alone as insular organizations. Rather, these unions must work in multiracial coalitions with community organizations, united in our demand for fully funded public schools.

Moreover, in order to sustain a fighting union and engaged membership, our union needs to work toward three goals:

1. Improve the economic standing of public education workers, who are overwhelmingly women.
2. Fight for social justice inside our classrooms and in our communities.
3. Organize and lead our profession toward culturally responsive pedagogy, anti-racist teaching, developmentally appropriate instruction, and restorative discipline practices. ▣

Amy Mizialko is president of the Milwaukee Teachers' Education Association and former special education teacher in MPS.

The Fight Against Standardized Testing

How a rank-and-file caucus ignited a national movement

BY JESSE HAGOPIAN

NOAM GUNDLE

The origin of the Social Equity Educators (SEE) caucus in Seattle mirrored that of the Caucus of Rank and File Educators (CORE) in Chicago. In 2008 a number of progressive teachers got involved in the struggle against closing several schools, all of which had a majority of students of color. Despite our efforts, the Seattle Education Association did not oppose the closings.

The struggle over school closures convinced several of us that we needed to form a rank-and-file caucus within our union that could help the union stand up to the onslaught of corporate education "reforms" and demand racial and social justice. As a result, when the battle over closures was over in 2009, we transformed the group that had opposed the closings into a new organization of union educators called Social Equity Educators (SEE). We were inspired by the Caucus of Rank and File Educators (CORE) in Chicago, which had started as a small study group but ultimately organized a successful win in the union election in 2010, took over the top officer positions, and reoriented the union's stance on social justice issues.

Over the next few years, SEE organized forums on a range of issues. One included Diane Ravitch, who had newly flipped from supporting to opposing the corporate reforms of the No Child Left Behind Act, and another was titled Achievement Gap or Opportunity Gap? Fighting Racism in the Public Schools. We organized contract struggles during contract negotiations against using standardized test scores as a basis for teacher evaluation, and we helped pass a resolution in the union against the use of the Measures of Academic Progress (MAP) test being used to evaluate educators.

In 2013, the growing network of SEE organizers was put to the test in an eruption of activism against high-stakes standardized testing. My colleagues and I at Seattle's Garfield High School started the rebellion by calling a press conference to announce our unanimous vote to refuse to administer the MAP test. That announcement led to what became known as the "MAP test boycott." The boycott quickly spread to several other schools in Seattle (including Orca K–8, Chief Sealth International High School, Ballard High School, Center School, and Thornton Creek Elementary), while solidarity with the boycott spread around the nation and then around the world. Most of the schools that took up the boycott had members of SEE helping to lead and coordinate the effort. One focus of our boycott was on the way that standardized tests perpetuate racial inequities; we emphasized academic research showing that standardized testing much more accurately measures wealth and proximity to a dominant white culture than it does aptitude or skills. The racial justice focus of the boycott helped us win the support of our local NAACP chapter and helped broaden the discussion to a larger one about the purpose and power of education.

When we at Garfield High School took that first step, we had no idea where our actions would lead. Would we be ignored? Would we be vilified as bad teachers? Would the math and language arts teachers in the tested subject areas be reprimanded, suspended, or fired? In fact, throughout the school year, our struggle against the MAP test reached such a magnitude that Seattle Public Schools not only retracted its threat to suspend the boycotting teachers for 10 days without pay, but also ultimately dropped its requirement that the MAP test be used at the high school level. The success of the MAP test boycott in Seattle contributed to the formation of a sizable civil rights movement, composed of parents, teachers, educational support staff, students, administrators, and community members around the country who increasingly began organizing against high-stakes standardized testing and for reclaiming public education from corporate reformers.

The MAP boycott had taken SEE from the fringe of the union and put the group squarely in the center of the most critical education struggles in the country. It proved to educators that we had a vision and a strategy for direct action and organizing that could win real gains in public education. SEE ran an electoral campaign in 2014 that came within 50 votes of taking over the leadership of the union and won several seats on the union's executive board. This, in a vote that had one of the largest turnouts in our union's history. As a result of these electoral wins and increased support from members, SEE proposals gained new weight in the union, and demands for racial justice and opposition to corporate education reform gained much more traction. With a newly mobilized membership committed to the issues SEE had been raising for years and new leaders in the union who were more sympathetic to the goals of SEE, the Seattle Education Association went on strike in 2015, raising important social and racial justice demands.

In 2015, Seattle Public Schools had only recently come under federal investigation by the Department of Education when it was found that Black students were being suspended at approximately four times the rate of white students for the same infractions. SEE began a campaign to raise awareness about this blatant practice of institutional racism, and the Seattle Education Association took up the cause in its contract negotiation. Leaders of the union made an important democratic reform when they expanded their very small bargaining team into a group of several dozen—including members of SEE. This new, much more robust bargaining team advanced some of the most important bargaining issues around racial justice anywhere in the country. The union's demand for Race and Equity Teams in the schools, for example, was groundbreaking. The Seattle Education Association advocated that every one of the public schools have such a team to tackle issues of disproportionate discipline and institutional racism. At first, Seattle Public Schools said they would agree to these teams in only six schools. The power of the strike, however, was such that in the tentative agreement reached between the union and the district, 30 schools were allowed to establish these anti-racist committees. This was an important victory in the struggle to uproot institutional racism and a powerful example of what's possible when you organize a social justice, class struggle approach to unionism.

The fundamental problems of our education system are really the same fundamental problems shared by all the institutions in this country, for they are all the product of a highly unequal economic and political structure. Capitalism treats our schools as potential sources of profit, as a crucial mechanism for disciplining youth, and as a training ground to teach students to accept our deeply unequal society—not as places to help students unlock their potential and learn how to meet the greatest societal challenges. You see this in the disproportionate suspension rates that punish students of color at dramatically higher rates than their white peers; the increasing numbers of police officers patrolling hallways; the privatizers and philanthropists who promote charter schools; and the testocracy that finds ways to make millions of dollars by testing our kids over and over and over again, so that now students on average take 112 standardized tests in their K–12 careers—creating a multibillion-dollar industry for Pearson and other testing corporations. And you can see this view clearly in the corporate education reform movement, summed up by billionaire media mogul Rupert Murdoch, when he says, "When it comes to K through 12 education, we see a $500 billion sector in the U.S. alone that is waiting desperately to be transformed by big breakthroughs that extend the reach of great teaching."

Today, the eight richest people in the world control the same amount of wealth as the bottom half of humanity. You can't have that kind of obscene concentration of wealth without dire problems in education, health care, housing, public transportation, the environment, and all other basic social needs. The resources needed to provide for those social needs are hoarded by those who already have too much. Our task, then, is to weave together our racial justice analysis with our understanding of a highly unequal economic system that requires racism in order to function—and to build a union movement that uses the labor power of striking educators to dismantle institutional racism and bring equitable education.

Martin Luther King Jr. explained the necessity of building a racial justice movement on the basis of opposing capitalism—but, of course, this isn't the King you learn about in school. In school, you usually hear, at best, excerpts from King's most cited speeches, but if you dig a little deeper you might find these words:

> You can't talk about solving the economic problem of Black people without talking about billions of dollars. You can't talk about ending the slums without first saying profit must be taken out of the slums. You're really tampering and getting on dangerous ground because you're messing with folks then. You're messing with the captains of industry. Now this means we are treading in difficult water, because it really means we are saying that something is wrong with capitalism, that there must be a better distribution of wealth and maybe America must move toward democratic socialism.

The strike wave of educators—from red states to blue—over the last couple of years has demonstrated that it isn't only the "captains of industry" who have power. The great abolitionist Frederick Douglass once said, "The limits of tyrants are prescribed by the endurance of those whom they oppress." We educators have endured all we are willing to endure. Now it's time to truly make Black lives matter in our education system—a precondition to making the lives of every student matter—and take the wealth from the rich to make that happen. 🔹

Jesse Hagopian teaches at Garfield High School in Seattle and is an editor of Rethinking Schools *magazine. Jesse edited the book* More Than a Score: The New Uprising Against High-Stakes Testing *and co-edited the book* Teaching for Black Lives. *He blogs at IAmAnEducator.com.*

A version of this article appears in *Strike for the Common Good* (University of Michigan Press, 2021).

Fighting the Tests in the Land of Enchantment

BY LISA GUISBOND AND MONTY NEILL

When Congress passed the No Child Left Behind Act (NCLB) in 2001, it triggered what the national anti-testing organization FairTest calls a "testing arms race." Influenced by a neoliberal agenda, the law instituted sweeping mandates for standardized tests and imposed brutal sanctions on schools that failed to make "adequate yearly progress." Schools were turned into test prep factories and teachers were subject to warnings—and even firing—if their students didn't produce "adequate" scores on the tests.

But the testing arms race is gradually ebbing, through the hard work of teachers, parents, students, and unions that refuse to buy in to the idea that you can improve schools through constant measurement and punishment. Here is one example that is worth learning from.

Las Cruces, New Mexico, sits about 45 miles north of El Paso, Texas, and the Mexican border. While New Mexico doesn't often come to mind when we think about deep and persistent poverty, the state was ranked 50th out of the 50 states for child well-being by the Annie E. Casey Foundation's *2019 Kids Count Data Book.* The state was also listed 50th in the education domain with some of the lowest test scores and graduation rates in the country. And Las Cruces hasn't escaped those rankings.

Never particularly strong, the state's public schools have been under siege since the Great Recession that began in 2008. Republican Gov. Susana Martinez, who took office in 2011, slashed education spending, expanded privately operated charter schools, and imposed a punitive regime of teacher evaluation based, in large part, on high-stakes testing.

After a series of school-based conversations with teachers, parents, and students exposed widespread frustration with the test/test prep agenda, NEA-Las Cruces (NEA-LC) launched a campaign in 2013 to reduce testing in the district.

The union helped pull together a group called People Against the Standardization of Students (PASS), which included university and high school students, parents, and rank-and-file union members. Using social media and flyers to mobilize, the group held a rally outside the school district's central office in Las Cruces. More than 800 people attended to show their opposition to excessive testing. Speakers included state legislators, students, parents, union leaders, and school

board members. The superintendent's response was to criticize the protesters for "emoting" in the parking lot. The union responded by gathering 1,000 signatures on a petition calling for a reduction in testing. The petitions were sent to the superintendent, governor, and secretary of education in Santa Fe. NEA-LC filed a grievance against the school district, charging it with violating a professionalism clause in its contract that mandated that administration collaborate with teachers "in the selection of student assessment methods." Eventually, NEA-NM filed a lawsuit against the state Public Education Department on the issue of local control.

It seemed that neither state nor district policymakers had a clear sense of the problem. So, in February 2014, the union surveyed its own members to lift up the reality of over-testing. The survey asked the names of each of the assessments teachers were giving, how often they were used, and how much time they took to administer. It asked how effective (or ineffective) the tests were in informing their own instruction, what kinds of teacher-created assessments they used, and their effects on students and staff. Compiling the data from more than 500 responses, the union developed a PowerPoint and presented it to the school board the following summer. The school board, which had a 4-1 conservative majority, took no action. But the information and personal voices collected through the survey were key to the union's effort to educate the public about the extent and effect of endless assessments on the district's educators and students.

"You Can't Be Passive"

In response to the lack of action on the part of the school board, the union and its allies sprang into action, involving themselves in the election for two open school board seats in 2015.

"You can't be passive. Otherwise, you don't accomplish things," retired teacher Becky King told *NEAToday*. King held a "meet and greet" at her home with the two union-endorsed candidates, attended campaign events, and was among the many educators who collectively knocked on more than 2,000 doors.

"This was about getting out there and doing something," King says. "Had we not gone door to door, it probably would have been status quo."

The union worked to make testing a front-burner issue at forums throughout the school board campaign. Members wore T-shirts with the slogan "Take Back Our Schools" on the front and "Teaching over Testing Crew" on the back. By election day in the spring of 2015, testing was, in fact, a key issue, and the union and its allies succeeded in getting their endorsed candidates elected.

Mary Parr-Sanchez, then vice president of NEA-NM, and married to the president of NEA-LC, reflected back on her leadership when union members and allies at times disagreed on how far to push the testing issue. For example, the union leadership was uncomfortable with holding the initial large anti-testing rally. "We were scared no one would show up, and we were scared everyone would show up," Parr-Sanchez remembers. The concern revolved around some members of the PASS coalition, who held more radical views on this and other issues. Would the message at the rally be consistent, and in line with the union's position on the issues? In addition, they knew that they had agreed to work together with the superintendent and the governor on the testing issue, and they were worried that a large rally would create tensions with these critical partners.

"In the end," said Parr-Sanchez, "we realized that union leadership shouldn't be comfortable. If you are, you probably aren't doing your job." They worked with the other stakeholders to plan the best rally that they could, working through the uncertainty. They knew the over-testing was the main issue that would resonate with the public. They knew that the union's members were lit up about using the tests in teacher evaluations. So they led with that issue. And it worked.

Building Momentum

That same spring (2015), students increased the pressure by organizing "Students Against Testing," working with both state and national opt-out organizations. That May, hundreds of students walked out of the city's middle and high schools. The protests spread to Santa Fe and Albuquerque.

Changing the makeup of the school board changed everything. The new board, with strong encouragement from the union, hired a new superintendent the following year. Dr. Greg Ewing was skeptical of testing and issued a moratorium on district-mandated assessments. He encouraged all school principals to eliminate any school-based tests and to administer only state- or federally mandated tests. He encouraged teachers to "close the door and teach."

Not stopping with the district moratorium, NEA-LC joined with allies across the state, including AFT New Mexico, to reduce state-mandated tests as well. In 2017 the LC school board passed a resolution against excessive state testing, which was sent to the New Mexico School Boards Association, and from there to the New Mexico Legislature. The Legislature took action by reducing the amount of time spent on PARCC exams and eliminating the use of interim tests in high schools.

The 2018 gubernatorial race opened new opportunities. Progressives and unions across the state worked hard to elect Democrat Michelle Lujan Grisham governor in 2018. Within the first 48 hours of taking office she began reversing education reform initiatives that had been put in place by Gov. Martinez over eight years. Just days after taking office, Grisham signed executive orders ending PARCC, along with a test-based teacher evaluation system, and the A–F school grading system.

Turning from Testing to Supporting Children

As the testing pressure was subsiding, NEA-LC took a leadership role in promoting community schools for New Mexico. One result of NEA-LC's strong "teaching over testing" work in 2013 was their linking up with Ngage New Mexico, a nonprofit coalition that serves as a catalyst to advance the well-being of all people of Southern New Mexico. They had launched a cradle-to-career initiative in 2013. The state NEA, in partnership with NEA-LC and coalition partners in Ngage, spearheaded a successful effort to establish the district's first community school in 2017. Statewide, other groups, including AFT-NM, have also been strong advocates for community schools. The new governor ran with community schools as part of her education platform in 2018.

Buoyed by the governor's focus, the community schools work took hold across the state. The Albuquerque-Bernalillo County partnership in the state's largest city lent help and expertise to Las Cruces. These efforts have continued to grow, with Las Cruces opening its fourth community school in 2020, and the Legislature that year appropriating more than $2 million to support an additional nine community schools elsewhere in the state.

Working with the national NEA, NEA-NM has stepped up as a statewide leader in transforming schools to community schools. In 2018, NEA pulled together experts from New Mexico and across the nation to write a training module for community schools on-site coordinators. (See Serrette, p. 150.) NEA-NM has become a hub across the nation for school personnel, including school board members, superintendents, principals, on-site coordinators, teachers, ed assistants, and others for training in community school methodology, and holding national virtual forums to bring people together to problem-solve issues.

The movement for creating community schools received increased attention in the spring of 2020 as the COVID-19 pandemic caused massive school closings and exposed the widening inequities on key social conditions—housing, health care, food security—that impact the lives of students.

NEA-NM President Mary Parr-Sanchez told Jeff Bryant, a writer for *Our Schools*, a project of the Independent Media Institute, that "In our state's response to the pandemic, we've had to be very sensitive to issues of poverty, and the state has challenged districts to reach all children, including special education students and homeless students." She explained that the community school model enables schools to do just that. "What happens during the school day is not enough to improve the trajectory of children until you deal with what is really going on in children's lives. Are they hungry? Are they homeless? The testing agenda took us away from addressing this. Community schools can bring us back."

When asked by *Rethinking Schools* editor Bob Peterson how she'd sum up the impact of the union's long history of work around testing, Parr-Sanchez admitted that although the union has made progress in reducing testing, it still plays "too prominent a role in our schools and continues as part of our school culture. Because of it, teachers are leaving the profession." She concluded: "We need to continue to organize to put learning and children first. The future of testing? It's yet to be determined." ◆

Monty Neill, EdD, now retired, was executive director of FairTest.

Lisa Guisbond is the executive director of Citizens for Public Schools and a former assessment reform analyst for FairTest.

Resources on Standardized Testing

Books

Pencils Down: Rethinking High-Stakes Testing and Accountability in Public Schools
Edited by Wayne Au and Melissa Bollow Tempel
(Rethinking Schools, 2012)
Through articles that provide thoughtful and emotional critiques from the front lines of education, *Pencils Down* deconstructs the damage that standardized tests wreak on our education system and the human beings who populate it. Better yet, it offers visionary forms of assessment that are not only more authentic, but also more democratic, fair, and accurate.

More Than a Score: The New Uprising Against High-Stakes Testing
Edited by Jesse Hagopian
(Haymarket Books, 2014)
Many inspiring stories of educators, parents, and students fighting to end the scourge of high-stakes testing.

Organizations

Defending the Early Years
dey.org
An organization of early childhood educators and advocates who rally educators to take action on policies that impact the education of young children, especially around testing and standards.

FairTest—The National Center for Fair and Open Testing
FairTest.org
Excellent materials in English and Spanish on alternative forms of assessment and problems with standardized testing.

New York Performance Standards Consortium
performanceassessment.org
A network of schools using high-quality assessment alternatives to standardized testing.

Massachusetts Consortium for Innovative Education Assessment (MCIEA)
mciea.org
MCIEA is a partnership of Massachusetts public school districts and their local teacher unions, joined together to create a fair and effective accountability system that is guided by a set of principles and offers a more dynamic picture of student learning and school quality than a single standardized test. MCIEA seeks to increase achievement for all students, close prevailing achievement gaps among subgroups, and prepare a diversity of students for college, career, and life.

(Also see additional organizations listed on p. 425)

Building Community-Labor Solidarity Against Privatization in Puerto Rico

BY PATRICK ST. JOHN

Like flowers blossoming after a storm, deep and widespread social movements in Puerto Rico have emerged to confront the brutal austerity regime imposed by Wall Street and Washington, D.C., and enforced by the island's own political and economic elites. The summer of 2019 saw more than 1 million Puerto Ricans take to the streets and go on strike against Gov. Ricardo Rosselló and all that he represented, culminating in his resignation in August. Teacher union members played a large role in this powerful movement.

Puerto Rico's Colonial Past and Present

Puerto Rico's colonial status with the United States dates back to 1898, when the U.S. won its war against Spain and ignored Puerto Ricans' demands for independence. Like all colonies, Puerto Rico has been politically and economically exploited by this arrangement. Most recently, in 2016 the U.S. Congress passed the Puerto Rico Oversight, Management, and Economic Stability Act (PROMESA), handing virtually total control of the island to an unelected Financial Oversight and Management Board. While the role of the board was defined as helping to restructure the island's debt, the overriding purpose has always been the maintenance of profits for Wall Street investors and other large holders of Puerto Rican debt on the backs of Puerto Ricans. In the same vein as the infamous structural adjustment programs the World Bank and International Monetary Fund have imposed on nations in the Global South, the board has promoted massive cuts to public sector institutions, including K–12 schools, the University of Puerto Rico, and pension programs. The board has also pressed privatizing public services, including the island's electric utility.

The aggressive reforms by the Financial Oversight and Management Board sparked public outrage, even before Hurricane Maria smashed into the island in September 2017. The hurricane devastated the island, killing thousands, damaging countless homes and schools, and taking out the power grid.

ADOLFO VALLE

In addition to inspiring examples of mutual aid within and across Puerto Rican communities, dozens of U.S. unions and aid groups organized support after the storm. The American Federation of Teachers, its affiliate on the island—Asociación de Maestros de Puerto Rico—and several other organizations distributed tens of thousands of water filters to families across the island. Others provided meals, medical care, and other supports.

But while these efforts to provide immediate support to island residents were underway, those in power began plotting and setting the stage for the privatization of Puerto Rico's public schools. Just four months after the hurricane, the island's Secretary of Education Julia Keleher proposed closing more than 300 schools (nearly a quarter of the island's total). Two months later, the Legislative Assembly passed a new law permitting both charter schools and vouchers.

> Just four months after the hurricane, the island's Secretary of Education Julia Keleher proposed closing more than 300 schools (nearly a quarter of the island's total). Two months later, the Legislative Assembly passed a new law permitting both charter schools and vouchers.

By the summer of 2019, with little real progress in rebuilding essential infrastructure, and the filing of corruption charges against Keleher and another administration official, massive demonstrations began to sweep the island.

One target of those demonstrations was the proposed privatization of Puerto Rico's public schools. The demonstrators charged that the privatization agenda took a page from post-Katrina New Orleans: backroom deals that would have gutted educator benefits and shuttered hundreds of public schools all across the island, many to be replaced by charter schools.

In the fall of 2019, members of the Journey for Justice Alliance (J4J) visited the island to support and learn from these demonstrations and share what they could from fights against privatization on the mainland. J4J is a nationwide education and racial justice network spanning more than 30 cities. Their visit and movement exchange culminated in a joint conference on the island.

Later that fall, the Schott Foundation for Public Education hosted an opportunity for conference participants to reflect on what they learned. Three primary lessons emerged from the discussions.

1. Struggles for Education Justice Are Linked. Advocates Should Be, Too.

"The fight against school privatization is not new in the United States, and it's not new on the island," noted Jitu Brown, director of J4J. "Brave parents and community members and educators have been fighting school privatization in Puerto Rico."

The playbook of privatization—mass school closures, attacks on employee pensions, and the imposition of charter schools—is the same one used both in Puerto Rico and on the mainland, pushed by the same constellation of powerful forces. "Since Hurricane Maria, there's been an effort to do similar to what's happened in New Orleans: to take advantage of human disaster . . . to privatize," Brown said.

Zakiyah Ansari, organizing director for the New York-based Alliance for Quality Education, described the post-disaster exploitation as "vultures that come in and try to tear up our communities. That's something that's very relatable" to cities across the country.

Members of J4J and organizers in Puerto Rico found cooperation natural. "When we started talking to each other, we realized we were going through the same thing. Often, policy initiatives that may have started somewhere else are just repackaged. . . . When we talked about what our children need we were on the same page. We knew we needed community schools, we knew we needed to end zero-tolerance policies. Building unity wasn't hard," said Brown.

Organizers came together, lifting up and sharing each other's stories and experiences. "The stories we share and offer as a way to unify but also to fight back," Ansari added. "We can learn from each other." One of the things Ansari found powerful at their conference "was the centering of women of color: how our power, that of Black and Brown women, is so centered in what we do."

Another organization that participated in the conference was AgitArte, an organization of working-class artists based in both the U.S. mainland and Puerto Rico who create projects and practices of cultural solidarity with grassroots struggles against oppression, and propose alternatives. Jorge Díaz Ortiz, AgitArte's executive and artistic director, talked about the ways that popular education and art were integrated into the struggle for education justice in Puerto Rico. "When we're talking about cultural organizing," he said, "we're talking about organizing, just with culture as an entry point."

2. Attacks on Public Goods and Attacks on Democracy Go Hand in Hand.

The abolition of democracy in public education, through attacks like state takeovers, mayoral control, and other emergency measures, is often the first stepping-stone in bypassing the community and forcing drastic policy changes upon them. From Chicago to New Orleans to Puerto Rico, it's a tried-and-true tactic.

While attacks on the public sector have been ongoing for decades, noted Diaz, "really, the big thrust to shut down schools starts with the imposition of the fiscal control board, which was a measure that the White House under President Obama did with bipartisan support. It established a dictatorial board that is over the Puerto Rican government."

This is an important lesson for communities: If elites go after democratic institutions, privatizations and sell-offs will not be far behind. But it also means that the positive projects of public reinvestment and re-democratization must go together as well: If we win the former without winning the latter, it's easy for those victories to be rolled back.

Resisting these attacks takes the grassroots coordination and integration of people across varied groups and locales, including students, parents, educators, and community members who are willing to invest their resources and take the needed risks to pressure policymakers and economic elites.

The Federación de Maestros de Puerto Rico (FMPR) has been leading grass-roots mobilization efforts in Puerto Rico, connecting with grassroots groups and hitting the streets against the corporate control of the island's schools. Mercedes Martinez, FMPR's president, wrote in *Labor Notes* in August 2019:

> This has been a glorious summer, where hundreds of thousands of Puer-to Ricans participated in the biggest general strike ever on the island. The strikes and demonstrations that brought down the Rosselló regime were largely spontaneous and broadly democratic, but the seeds of the insurrection were planted by decades of struggle.
>
> These struggles have been led by feminists who fought against gen-der violence and homophobia, muckraking journalists who uncovered the depths of government corruption, activists organizing for the debt to be dropped, community members building autonomous centers of self-organization, environmentalists who stopped a pipeline, students who went on strike to keep their universities public, artists who pre-served and created culture, and unionists who refused to compromise away working people's futures.
>
> No one party, organization, or union called for the strike and demonstrations. Many groups contributed to their outbreak and politi-cal character.
>
> If we can learn something from this victorious moment, it is that the road ahead lies in fighting back for the future and refusing to com-promise.

3. People-Powered Organizing Can Halt the Advance of Privatization and Build Momentum Toward Positive Reforms.

History shows that isolated struggles can grow exponentially and win when they spread outside of their sector, embracing and lifting up the collective interests of a wide swath of society. As Audre Lorde put it, "There is no such thing as a single-is-sue struggle, because we do not live single-issue lives." Breaking down barriers between movements is difficult but important, and when it comes to education justice, no barrier more urgently needs to be dismantled than that between com-munity groups and labor unions.

The FMPR is a good example of a social justice/social movement union: an organization that's based in communities and works alongside other organizing groups. It is one of the key groups that spearheaded the recent protests against Gov. Rosselló that expanded into a larger, more comprehensive struggle. "FMPR as a union has deep roots in many communities," Brown said, "so there's a strong relationship with parents, with students, and with other organizers and activists."

Despite the 2018 charter school law, which would have allowed the conversion of 10 percent of the island's schools to charters, only two schools out of 856 have been privatized. "That is because of the battles that teachers, students, and parents have given in defense of public education," noted Martinez.

Grassroots organizations like J4J have also offered tried-and-tested solutions to the crisis—ones that can work across many contexts, like sustainable community schools and the replacement of harmful and racially biased school discipline policies with restorative justice; as well as ones that are specific to Puerto Rico, like the abolition of PROMESA and the reinvestment of public funds into pensions, schools, and public services.

Moments of resistance are also moments of imagination.

Moments of resistance are also moments of imagination: a break in the logic of state and capital opens up possibilities that may have been previously unthinkable. When social movements explode against privatization and reactionary measures, what moves many people isn't just a yearning for a return to the previous status quo, but for a more liberated, just, and democratic future.

Brown emphasized that it is within struggles against the worst that we can begin to imagine the best. "It provides a moment to dream about what education might look like on the island."

Labor-Community Alliances Need Support

As we saw in Los Angeles and Chicago in 2019, building ongoing relationships with community-based allies is key to winning the schools our students and neighborhoods deserve. While the gold standard for community organizations is a membership-based dues structure to ensure not only consistent funding but also independence, in its absence these groups have to rely on individual donors, philanthropic funders, and unions (ideally with as few strings attached as possible). Unions in particular, as dues-based organizations themselves, should provide financial support to help expand and sustain local grassroots work. This support should be not just in the run-up to a contract fight but on an ongoing basis, with a healthy acknowledgement that there will be points of disagreement that should be seen as a chance for patience, growth, and mutual understanding—not a prompt for one partner to take their ball and go home. As a recent series of case studies on community-labor partnerships pointed out:

> The alliances that were successful over time were not restricted to traditional school issues: They took an expansive view of what affects the community and thus, its students, engaging on policy issues including immigration, home foreclosures, police violence, local wages, and child care and early childhood resources outside of the school day.

All empires fall, and all oppressed people eventually stand up. Horizontal links of solidarity between working people across jobs, neighborhoods, borders, and oceans—like those formed in the education justice struggle today—are the tinder upon which the flame of justice and liberation will be kindled. It's up to all of us to encourage every spark we see to catch. ▣

Patrick St. John is an organizer, writer, and graphic designer based in Vermont. He is currently the creative & online communications director at the Schott Foundation for Public Education.

Founded in 1991, the Schott Foundation is a national public fund serving as a bridge between philanthropic partners and advocates to build education justice movements to provide all students an opportunity to learn.

RESOURCES

Martinez, Mercedes and Monique Dols. Aug. 15, 2019. "Teachers Fighting for Public Schools Were Key to the Uprising in Puerto Rico." *Labor Notes*. labornotes.org/2019/08/teachers-fighting-public-schools-were-key-uprising-puerto-rico

"Keeping Students First: Building Community Labor Partnerships for Strong Schools." April 2018. The Schott Foundation and Building Movement Project. schottfoundation.org/report/keeping-students-first-building-community-labor-partnerships-strong-schools

Throwing Books at Bullets

Despite violence and intimidation, Colombia's teachers have been a bulwark for workers' rights

BY BOB PETERSON

BARBARA MINER

Tuesday, Aug. 25, 1987, began like any other day for Luis Felipe Vélez, president of the teacher union of Antioquia, Colombia's second-most populous state. Shortly after 7 a.m., Vélez said goodbye to his wife and three young children and headed to the union's office in downtown Medellín.

But as the 33-year-old was about to enter the modest adobe brick building, two assassins leapt out of a green Mazda 626 and opened fire, riddling his body with bullets. Vélez died two hours later.

Word spread quickly among human rights activists, teachers, and Vélez's colleagues in the Association of School Teachers of Antioquia, and by 5 p.m. a large crowd had gathered at the union office for a vigil.

Among the throng were Héctor Abad Gómez and Leonardo Betancur, two well-known human rights leaders. As Abad Gómez and Betancur entered the union office, two men jumped off a motorcycle and walked toward the crowd. One shot Gómez six times; the other chased Betancur into the office and killed him.

It was a bloody day in a bloody period. During the 1980s and '90s, assassinations were an everyday reality for union and human rights activists in Colombia. And violence, while on the wane, continues to this day.

According to Colombia's National Labor School (ENS), more than 1,000 teacher union leaders were killed between 1977 and 2014—the equivalent of 7,000 teacher union leaders being murdered in the U.S. The ENS has also documented more than 14,000 incidents of violence against labor activists, ranging from assassinations to beatings, kidnappings, and torture. The perpetrators have been brought to justice in only 1 percent of the cases.

This campaign of intimidation and murder (in combination with neoliberal restructuring) has taken a toll on Colombia's labor movement. Union membership is 4.4 percent of the national workforce today, down from 17 percent three decades ago.

As the movement has shrunk, public educators have become increasingly important. Teachers in Colombia now make up about half of the membership of the Central Union of Workers, Colombia's main federation of unions.

And they have one more thing in common with teacher unionists in the U.S.: They're fighting neoliberal reforms tooth and nail.

Global Front Lines

In December 2015, during a long visit to Colombia to study Spanish and learn about the situation in the country, I walked into the same teacher union office where Vélez was assassinated. On the wall hung portraits of Vélez and the 66 other teacher union leaders in Antioquia murdered since 1977. Above the pictures, a wooden sign read (in Spanish): "Here we are and here we will be forever in the heat of the struggle in defense of human rights."

Seeing the dozens of portraits of slain teachers was chilling, a stark contrast to the congratulatory plaques lining the office walls at my own union, the Milwaukee Teachers' Education Association.

I had been aware of the danger facing private sector union activists in Colombia—especially those organizing against multinational sugarcane, banana, and mining companies—but the pictures drove home the importance of public sector workers to the struggle for justice and human rights in Colombia. Elites in the country literally had them gunned down to try to weaken popular resistance.

While the situation outside Colombia is less dangerous, public sector unionists across the world have emerged as a bulwark against efforts to eviscerate public services. From Chicago to Colombia, teachers have leveraged their position in society to fight the privatization and disinvestment national governments and international institutions are pushing.

Teachers and schools are in nearly every town and city in the world. Urban and rural teachers are in daily contact with impoverished and disenfranchised communities. And despite anti-union attacks and growing privatization, teacher unions remain among the largest in the world. (In the United States, the National Education Association and the American Federation of Teachers have some 4.7 million members, making K–12 public education one of the country's most unionized sectors.)

Educational International, the global federation of teacher unions, has launched an international campaign against the commodification of education. But much more is needed.

To be successful, teacher unions must take our struggle beyond the schoolhouse door and fight for more than just the rights of our members. We must struggle for a more genuine democracy, a more expansive social justice.

Colombian teachers, many of whom have given their lives, are on the front lines of this struggle.

Culture of Fear

Though separated by thousands of miles, my conversations with teachers and union activists in Colombia underlined the commonality of our struggles.

Teachers from Colombia and the U.S. alike decry the growing emphasis on standardized testing, the tendency to blame teachers for not solving problems created by pervasive poverty, the top-down commands that devalue teaching as a profession, and the narrowing of the curriculum, which edges out all-important issues such as social justice and critical thinking. They object to corporate reforms that privilege private schools and defund public education—reforms that, at their heart, represent an attack on democratic rights.

"We are fighting privatization of our public schools," said John Avila, a former social studies teacher and later head of research for Colombia's Federation of Educators (FECODE) in Bogotá. "The neoliberal agenda . . . is strong in Colombia."

In the spring of 2015, the federation led a 15-day national strike that focused on two issues—meager pay and a new teacher evaluation system that consisted of a single written test. The union made gains on both, winning a 12 percent pay increase over three years and a more sophisticated evaluation system that does not include a written test.

Indeed, despite right-wing violence and a culture of fear, despite limits on organizing, despite the prohibition of agency fees, Colombian educators have persevered—roughly 70 percent of the country's teachers are union members.

The Longest Civil War in Modern History

To fully understand the challenges and potentials facing Colombia's teacher unions, a bit of history is necessary.

Colombia's civil/guerrilla war dates back to the 1960s and is considered the longest contemporary struggle in the world. A central issue was land tenure—

wealthy landowners and multinational corporations seizing land for mining and banana and palm oil plantations. Another issue was the country's closed political system—the ruling oligarchy and their two political parties had formed a national front in the 1950s that effectively prevented legal means of politically challenging their rule.

In the 1980s, Colombia's narco-trafficking escalated, further complicating the country's politics and unleashing an increased level of violence. This situation became more problematic when both paramilitaries and left guerrillas began to use the drug trade to help fund their operations.

The U.S., meanwhile, linked its War on Drugs with its crusade against left movements in Latin America. The high point was in 1999, when President Bill Clinton and Colombian President Andrés Pastrana signed "Plan Colombia" to fight drugs and terrorism in Colombia. From 2000 to 2008, the U.S. Congress provided more than $6 billion to Colombia, making it the largest non-Middle Eastern recipient of U.S. military assistance. How much went to fighting drugs and how much to fighting left guerrillas has never been clear. As the MIT Center for International Studies noted in 2008, Plan Colombia is "a counter-narcotics strategy that has turned into a counter-insurgency one."

But both the War on Drugs and the counter-insurgency failed. Colombia remains the world's leading producer of cocaine, and the government was unable to defeat the leftist guerrillas. When I visited, after decades of violence in the country, there was a yearning for peace in Colombia.

The 2016 peace accord between Colombia's government and leftist guerrillas raised hopes that teacher unions would be able to bring even more people into their ranks. As Carlos Diaz Lotero—longtime labor leader and now the director general of the ENS—put it: "It's a lot easier to organize for worker rights if leaders are not routinely murdered."

Two decades ago, peace talks between the government and the guerillas led to the formation of the Patriotic Union, a left political party. But both the Patriotic Union and the peace process collapsed when the ruling oligarchy and paramilitaries launched a campaign against the nascent party. According to the House of Memory Museum in Medellín, nearly 5,000 members of the new party were "assassinated, disappeared, or massacred" between 1984 and 1997.

In 2012, peace negotiations were restarted again in Havana, Cuba, between the Colombian government and the Revolutionary Armed Forces of Colombia (FARC). The process gained public support and attracted international scrutiny and assistance. A final agreement was reached in August 2016. However, a referendum in October to ratify the agreement lost after 50.2 percent of the voters voted against the deal, while 49.8 percent voted in favor. Six weeks later FARC and the Colombian government signed a revised deal and it was ratified by both houses of Congress.

Every educator and teacher union leader I spoke with supported the peace process, in the hopes that it will rein in paramilitary death squads and provide space for organizing and social transformation.

Unfortunately, implementing the agreement has been difficult, complicated by the continuing assassinations of dozens of labor, community, Indigenous, and environmental leaders.

Perseverance

As the peace process in Colombia struggles forward, the unions have developed a broad agenda to fight for worker rights. And because of Washington's continued involvement in the country, Colombian union activists say the solidarity of U.S. progressives and unions is essential.

Diaz Lotero spoke in particular about provisions in the U.S.-Colombia free trade agreement, which was signed in 2011. Because of pressure from the U.S. and Colombian labor movements, the pact included a Labor Action Plan intended to safeguard worker rights. Now Colombian unions are fighting to make sure that language is put into practice.

Provisions of the Labor Action Plan include establishing a ministry of labor, ending subcontracting designed to prevent unionization, opening an office of the International Labor Organization in Colombia, and changing legal codes to expand and enforce basic labor laws.

The plan also calls for measures to prosecute perpetrators of anti-labor violence and increase protection for activists, including government funding for bodyguards and armored cars. Intimidation is an ongoing concern. According to the U.S. Department of Labor, "threats against labor leaders and activists have increased significantly, in the form of text messages, phone calls, letters, emails, and other forms."

But as I spoke with teachers and union leaders in Colombia, I was struck by their matter-of-fact perseverance—a persistence examined in a book that all union activists in Medellín seem to have read: *Tirándole libros a las balas* (*Throwing Books at Bullets*). The book chronicles the history of violence against teachers in Antioquia from 1978 to 2008.

Fernando Ospina, president of the Antioquia teacher union, explained the title's significance: "Teacher unions have been targeted by violence and bullets," Ospina said. "Our response has been with education, social research, and social justice. They shoot bullets. We throw books." 🏫

Bob Peterson, the former president of the Milwaukee Teachers' Education Association, is now a member of the Milwaukee School Board. He taught 5th grade more than 25 years at various Milwaukee public schools, and was a founding editor of Rethinking Schools.

Earlier versions of this article were published in *Jacobin* (April 6, 2016) and in FECODE's magazine *Educación y Cultura* (Edición 115, Julio 2016).

Education and Social Justice: A Global View
An interview with Angelo Gavrielatos

Angelo Gavrielatos addresses members of the National Education Union (NEU) demonstrating outside the AGM of multinational assessment service Pearson in London in protest against investment by the corporation in 'low-fee' private schools provider Bridge. Bridge, one of the world's largest education-for-profit companies, aims to extend its influence throughout Africa and Asia.

MARK KERRISON/ALAMY LIVE NEWS

Angelo Gavrielatos is the president of the New South Wales Teachers Union. Previously he was the federal president of the national Australian Education Union, and he worked five years for Education International, leading EI's response to privatization and commercialization of public schools. He was interviewed on Feb. 8, 2020, by Bob Peterson.

How did you originally become a teacher union leader?
The answer goes back to why I became a teacher. Like many others, I was inspired by my own teachers. I grew up politicized because of my family background and was active politically at the university. Early on I recognized that public education is a great social enterprise that has the transformative power to create a better society. It led me to joining my union on my very first day of teaching.

Once a teacher, I realized that if you want to make change in your classroom alone, that's great, but if you want to make change beyond your classroom or school, the only way to do that is through the collective strength of our unions.

What pushed you to believe teacher unions should go beyond narrow trade union demands and take up social justice issues?

I was never attracted by narrow economistic unionism. We are privileged in the teacher union space to be able to go easily beyond the narrow unionism. In some other unions and industries, making that connection with social justice issues is more difficult. I was always drawn to an appreciation of the broader role of education and unionism in building community and movements. I realized the power of the collective in transforming schools and society. My perspective was further influenced by writings about social justice unionism in *Rethinking Schools* many years ago. I am referring to the taxonomy that distinguishes between economistic unionism and social justice unionism. There was one other publication of yours, *Rethinking Globalization*, that sticks with me. In that, a high school student was . . . quoted saying something like "once you've tasted the thrill of solidarity, there is no way of going back to individualism." I use that statement in mass rallies with young teachers all the time.

What is Education International?

Education International (EI) is a global federation of teacher unions and other education employees. Together it represents more than 32 million members from 179 countries and territories. Among other things, EI promotes the "principle that quality education, funded publicly, should be available to every student in every country."

What was your role in EI?

Previous to me working for EI I was connected with its leadership while serving as president of the Australian Education Union. In 2012–2013 we realized that we had become very good at describing the problem of privatization and commercialization of our schools and that we gave great speeches, but what we hadn't done was figure out what we were going to do about it. In 2015 I stepped down from being AEU president, moved to Brussels, and became responsible for leading EI's global campaign against the growing threat of commercialization and privatization of education.

At that time, large global corporate actors had already started using their huge reach, depth, and strength to target public schools with no regard for national borders. These forces are capable of exerting incredible influence across the globe. They are stronger than most governments in the countries in which they are operating. EI decided enough with describing the problem—if we are going to confront it, we needed to start building a genuine global response to deal with the global dimension of privatization.

Who are some of the key players that you are referring to?

Pearson is the biggest global actor, and it has changed dramatically as a company. What started off as a publisher some decades ago has now made a conscious decision to move almost entirely into the digital space and is seeking to expand its reach over public education. It's pretty much a tech company now, and it [and] a few other tech groups are driving this privatization agenda.

It's not only the corporate world. We also have this agenda being driven by the World Bank and other related international financing institutions and intergovernmental organizations They are doing it all for ideological and financial reasons. Education is valued around $6.3 trillion (U.S.) a year. It's a "very lucrative market" as they would describe it, but to get to that market, education has to be removed from the public sector. Some five or six years ago there was a meeting of venture capitalists in the U.S., and they declared they were satisfied with the extent to which they had privatized health care, and their new frontier was education. Education is not only a lucrative market for these groups, but it is the most sustainable market in the world.

How many countries did you visit in your five years as leader of the anti-privatization campaign at EI?
I don't know. I've lost count—many countries, maybe 40 or 50, but I actively worked with a smaller number. In each country there are various manifestations of privatization—depending on historical and political factors. But every country was somewhere on a continuum of levels and types of privatization.

What's an example of a privatization attempt?
Liberia. In 2016 the Liberian government announced its intention to outsource all of its primary and pre-primary schools to one global actor called Bridge International Academies supported by the likes of Pearson, the World Bank, Zuckerberg, Gates, and others.

That is the endgame. The moment when a government hands over all of its education system to a corporate entity. People have said to me, "Liberia is an outlier. Is that the best example you got?" Interestingly, at same time in February 2016 that the Liberian government was announcing its intention to outsource all of its schools to private actors, David Cameron, England's prime minister, announced an almost identical policy stating his intention that all schools that remained in control by local government authorities become academies operated by private actors. Academies are analogous to privately operated charter schools in the U.S. So it's not just Liberia but countries like England. I dare say that's the intention of the Trump administration—to see all schools in the hands of private actors, destroying that social enterprise of free, quality, secular, universally accessible public education for all.

What's the status of the anti-privatization fight-backs?
There are lots of fight-backs underway. It's important for teacher union leaders to recognize that the biggest and maybe the last barrier capable of stopping these privatizers' dreams is the teacher union movement—domestically and internationally. There are other organizations defending public education, but unions are the strongest and most capable of mounting a sustained, organized defense. That's why we've become targets of the privatizers and governments as well.

When we launched our anti-privatization campaign in the Philippines, a union leader said to me, "Angelo, you realize that you are asking us to do something that could get us killed." Taking on these corporate actors like Pearson and their partner in the Philippines, Ayala Corporation, led this union leader to say that to me.

Our colleagues in Colombia, who are very familiar with targeted killing of their leaders, also said taking up this anti-privatization struggle could get more of their people killed. "We are taking on vested interests," one leader told me.

In Uganda supporters of privatization fabricated allegations against our researcher in 2016, and he was arrested and detained.

We never used to hear about this in the education sector. We heard about it in other sectors of the labor movement when vested interests were being exposed in mining, fishing, and logging. Welcome to the modern world of education that is worth $6.3 trillion.

We are having some success. Is it at the magnitude we'd like? No, but ours is a long struggle.

Give me an example of a success.
I mentioned Liberia, where the government initially sought to outsource all the schools to one actor, Bridge International Academies. We forced them to retreat. We attacked their strategy, and they were forced to come up with a pilot plan involving a number of actors. We weren't fooled; we knew what they're all about. In education policy, whenever a reformer uses the word "pilot," one should read it as "We will do you slowly." It's the politics of gradualism and attrition. We continue to fight in Liberia. In Uganda because of our efforts the high court deemed Bridge International an "illegal operator" that "set out to operate illegally" and the court called on them to be shut down.

There was a similar case in Kenya. So our efforts using a variety of political and legal and other organizing strategies have resulted in some wins. But it is a long struggle. We will persevere, we must persevere at all levels—whether at the local, regional, national, or the global level. It is one struggle.

What are key lessons you've learned?
We started the global campaign in 2015 and refined it periodically based on our ongoing evaluations. We quickly realized that strategic research was crucial for us to understand the dynamic in each country, which varied greatly. There are a large number of activist researchers, academics around the world who want to help unions. Our researchers examined the various manifestations of privatization. Based on those findings we built national campaigns to confront privatization. A national campaign with a powerful inside-outside communication strategy is necessary. The inside communication was necessary to organize and mobilize our own members. The outside strategy was to inform and build the necessary alliances with other unions and like-minded organizations.

Building unity was also critical. Regrettably, in many countries around the world there are three, four, five, seven, or more teacher unions. In those countries unity is just a word. EI tries as much as possible to build solidarity—local, national, and global through action. Some of the solidarity actions were very powerful.

Give an example of one such action.
On a couple of occasions we linked the U.S. and U.K. unions with African teacher unions in actions against Pearson and the World Bank. We had leaders from a number of countries descend on Pearson's annual shareholder meeting. We got inside and it was pretty powerful for a leader of the Kenyan teacher union and a Ugandan teacher union leader to ask them, "Can you explain to me why you think it's a good idea what you are doing to my country? When did you ask us?" These were powerful moments, and the media and social media coverage in different countries helped spread our message.

Let's change the conversation and bring it to the United States. What are your thoughts on the red state revolts of 2018 and subsequent strikes by UTLA, the CTU, and others?
Teacher unionists from a distance are looking very closely and have been following these developments in the U.S. It's inspiring and motivating to see teacher unionists in these "right to work" states say "enough is enough," and it's inspiring to see them rise up articulating the needs and aspirations not only of themselves but more broadly the needs of their students and public education. Those struggles in the U.S. in the last few years have been well located within the frame of social justice unionism.

U.S. historian Howard Zinn once told me, "If teacher unions want to be strong and well supported, it's essential that they not only be teacher unionists but teachers of unionism." How important do you think it is for unions to encourage their members to teach about the working-class struggles and social justice movements?
People have asked me why these large corporate actors—the Mark Zuckerbergs, Bill Gateses, and the Rupert Murdochs of the world are so determined to privatize schools. Do they really need to become richer? That question relates to Zinn's statement, because there is something more fundamental that the privatizers want to control—the curriculum. Everyone recognizes the power of curriculum, because any curriculum taught today will shape the society of tomorrow. Given that . . . it's key that both teachers and students understand the struggles and value of unionism and other social movements.

This raises the related issue of the importance of member education. As union leaders we must always ask, "How can we better educate ourselves and our members?" One of my colleagues in Canada talks about the need for leaders to "reach within, reach out, and reach beyond." We need to reach within to ensure the heart of the union operation is operating in a democratic and effective manner and that we are getting the best out of all union leaders, officials, and employees. We need to reach out to all the members to make sure that they are fully appreciative of the struggle ahead and to enlist the support and the expertise in our broader membership. We have large memberships of very smart people. Are we working hard enough to enlist their engagement, their activism, their expertise? And then are we reaching beyond to the broader community of unions and union members and others to strengthen our movement? We need to do all three things.

Howard Zinn is absolutely right. We not only need to be students of unionism but we must be teachers of unionism.

You are returning to Australia to work in New South Wales, where massive fires have consumed millions of acres and killed an estimated billion animals. What advice do have for teacher unions on the matter of climate justice?
We have the responsibility as teacher unionists to do four things, and I list them in no particular order: To look after our members, our schools and students, our communities, and our planet.

We are living in a climate emergency. What has occurred in Australia in the last couple of months [December 2019 and January 2020] has provided ample evidence for all those deniers. People ask, "Do you believe in the science?" What a ridiculous question. People might as well ask me if I believe there is a solar system or if the world is round.

The science tells us what's happening. But like many other countries, in Australia the fossil fuel industry is corrupting the political process. There's lots of work to be done. We need to fight that industry and their supporters. We need to ensure that we have the best curriculum available for teachers. We teach the science, we embrace science, we don't teach dogma. The more we and our students understand the science, the better we can build the movement to confront the deniers.

In the U.S. and internationally, white supremacy and xenophobia are growing. How has the Australian teacher union responded to those issues?
The rise of xenophobia, the politics of fear, the politics of division—we are seeing that grow globally aided and abetted by the Trump administration; in Latin America with Bolsonaro and now in Bolivia after the coup; in Europe with Orbán in Hungary—it's all around the world. In Australia we are not immune from these politics. Let's not forget that modern Australia hasn't reconciled its past with our First Nations people. For example, we still celebrate "Australia Day," similar to your Columbus Day. Australia Day celebrates the Jan. 26, 1788, arrival of the Europeans to this continent, which was populated by more than 500 Indigenous groups. How can we seriously celebrate Australia Day when our First Nations brothers and sisters consider it to be invasion day? How is that a day of national unity? It's a big debate. Conservative commentators attack anyone who dares question that holiday. A satirist said, "You'd think it'd be easy to get a consensus that committing genocide is a weird excuse for a barbecue."

Of course, the politics of fear and xenophobia is not restricted to our Indigenous brothers and sisters; it also plays out through Islamophobia. Australia is not in a good place in terms of racism and xenophobia, and we will do everything, whatever we can, to develop the necessary racism awareness for our members and our students in order to confront and deal with racism. One of the things we say: "Racism stops with me."

How has international solidarity between teacher unions been in recent times?
The leadership of the NEA and AFT is active on the international stage and we know that we can rely on the NEA and AFT to extend support to struggles involving sister unions around the world. That needs to be acknowledged. Regrettably, that is not apparent to everyone, but from my experience, I know the broader movement is grateful. And similarly, the broader union movement has lent support to our brothers and sisters in the U.S.

During the height of the Red for Ed strikes in the spring of 2018, a lot of unions from around the world extended messages of solidarity to the U.S. At the height of detention of families and children at the U.S.-Mexican border when the U.S. government were putting children in cages, a lot of the unions around the world that had in the past been recipients of solidarity messages from the U.S. reciprocated, not as an act of reciprocity, but because it was an important statement to make. The challenge for all of us is to grow international solidarity at all levels of our unions. We need to reach within, reach out, and beyond on this issue as well.

How do we enhance notions of international solidarity among our members?
First, we acknowledge that our members are busy and stretched. Their work is ever increasing with the top-down compliance measures. I understand when our members say, "I haven't got time to do more." It's through no lack of desire on the part of teachers to be informed and get involved. Teachers know that when it comes to the well-being of children, our concern goes beyond our classroom, our school, our borders—it's global.

We should encourage the notion of solidarity that the well-being of any child anywhere in the world is teachers' business.

How do notions of building solidarity intersect with the ongoing wars and massive refugee crises that exist in several places around the world? It's easy to have divergent views on unions taking up those issues.
Promoting peace is teacher union work. Not long after WWII, dozens of countries formed the United Nations Educational, Scientific and Cultural Organization (UNESCO). Australian teacher union leaders came back from one of UNESCO's early conferences with a message that has remained part of the DNA of our union ever since. That message was: Every war that is fought, is fought against children—it denies their hopes and dreams. That's why peace and the antiwar movement is teacher union business. How many times have we in the teacher union movement been told, "It's not teacher union business"? We've been asked, "Why are you involved in the peace movement and antiwar movement?"

It's because every war is fought against children. I think of war memorials that have stone panels engraved with names of those who died in war. Often such panels have blank spaces waiting for future names. Well, those panels will be engraved with the names of our future students, to say nothing of the thousands of civilians, many of them children who will forever remain nameless. If anyone says it's not our business, then whose business is it? ◙

"We Won! Now We Keep Fighting"

Winning investment in the schools Massachusetts students deserve

BY LEIGH DINGERSON

Boston Public Schools students and parents hold a May 2018 Talent Show

ARI BRANZ

For more than a quarter-century, advocates for public education have been fighting for resources for public schools in the commonwealth of Massachusetts. It has been a campaign saga marked by wins, draws, and defeats. In 2019, advocates celebrated when Gov. Charlie Baker signed new legislation that promises to send nearly $1.5 billion to public schools over the next seven years. This victory was won through a multifaceted campaign that brought together litigators and organizers, lobbyists, parents, students, and teachers united in a demand to "Fund Our Future."

Yet, on the day the new law was signed, the only realistic message was "We won! Now we keep fighting." Ensuring the investment that our students deserve is an ongoing struggle. This is the story of the campaign in Massachusetts.

History and Context

While Massachusetts is often lauded as the birthplace of public education in the United States, and while the state boasts some of the top student outcomes in the nation, Massachusetts struggles, like other states, to ensure that all students have access to the resources they need and deserve in their schools.

In 1990, a lawsuit challenged the state's school funding formula—or, more accurately, *lack* of a formula—for offering state dollars to supplement district spending and help equalize access to resources across the state. In 1993 the Supreme Judicial Court (SJC) ruled that the state was in violation of its constitution, and ordered the legislature to come up with a way to ensure adequate funding, particularly for districts without enough local resources to fully fund their schools.[1]

Even before the court ruling, the Massachusetts General Court, as the legislature is formally known, had seen the writing on the wall, and passed a new law to address disparities in educational resources. The 1993 Education Reform Act, signed by the governor just three days after the SJC issued its ruling in the legal case, established one of the first "foundation formulas" for education funding in the nation.

The act[2] established the estimated cost of a minimum set of resources, materials, and learning conditions that each child deserved access to, according to the court. The cost of those resources was calculated by district, based on enrollment. On top of that, the new formula added additional monies on a per-pupil basis, for students with special needs, English language learners, and very low-income children. Combined, the formula created a "foundation budget"—the amount each district should spend on its public schools.

Next, the new law assessed the amount of money that each district could afford to contribute toward that budget through local revenues. This amount was set as the district's "minimum required contribution." The new formula then committed the state to making up the difference between each district's minimum required contribution and its foundation budget.

The legislature set a target of ensuring full funding within seven years, and mandated incremental annual increases to keep up with inflation.

Two Steps Forward, Two Steps Back

In its initial years, the Education Reform Act pumped significant new resources into school districts across the state, particularly disadvantaged ones. In FY 1993, for example, the state's lowest-income districts spent about $1,400 less per pupil than the highest-income districts. By FY 2000, this gap had narrowed to $370 per student.[3] But after about 10 years, the progress stagnated while costs climbed and budgets tightened. At the local level, districts were unable to keep up with the growing costs because of anti-tax legislation passed in the 1980s, which limited property tax increases. And at the state level, a series of tax *cuts* enacted between 1998 and 2002 made additional spending on education difficult.

The rising costs of education did not affect only low-income districts. Sky-rocketing healthcare costs were a large part of the problem. In addition, the costs of providing services to students with special needs were also rising. Neither of these expenditure areas was subject to belt-tightening. Health care was a contractual right for all employees. The bills just had to be paid. And the provision of services for students with disabilities is mandated by federal law. In order to meet these costs, most districts were forced to pull funds from other areas of their budgets, leading to larger class sizes, declining facilities, and reductions in programming and staff. In schools across the state, the promise of adequate school funding was becoming a promise denied, year after year. And the state legislature did not have the political will to act.

> In schools across the state, the promise of adequate school funding was becoming a promise denied, year after year.

By early 2015, as conditions worsened, legislators began to feel growing pressure to address the inadequacy of the foundation budget. Finally, the General Court called for a Foundation Budget Review Commission (FBRC) to reassess the calculations the budget was based on. The commission held six public hearings around the state, hearing from teachers, parents, students, and administrators.

The FBRC's report, released on Oct. 30, 2015, was blunt.[4] The body found that "dramatic growth" in healthcare costs was breaking district budgets and that the foundation formula had underestimated the number of students with special needs, as well as the costs of providing the services they were entitled to. The commission found "a sharp rise" in the numbers of new immigrants, many of them refugees from war-torn regions who often arrived with serious social and emotional needs and limited formal education for schools to build on. Additional support was needed, noted the FBRC.

Finally, the commission found that the weights written into the foundation formula were insufficient to provide needed support for low-income students. Overall, the commission found that the way the state calculated the foundation budgets understated the cost of educating students to the tune of at least $1 billion per year.[5]

The commission report served as a wake-up call for the general public. But already, community groups, teacher unions, and student-led organizations were beginning to build a campaign to reclaim public education in Massachusetts. For them, the commission report was validation of their message: We need more for our public schools, and we need it now.

The Massachusetts Education Justice Alliance

In late 2015, the Massachusetts Education Justice Alliance (MEJA) brought together a wide range of labor and advocacy groups, including the Massachusetts Teachers Association, the Boston Teachers Union, Citizens for Public Schools, FairTest, Jobs with Justice, AFT Massachusetts, PHENOM (the Public Higher Education Network of Massachusetts), the New England Area Conference of the NAACP, and Youth on Board, a Boston-based youth-led organizing group. The statewide alliance emerged from the successful work of the pre-existing Boston Education Justice Alliance, built by the Boston Teachers Union, which was already having an impact in reducing cuts to the Boston Public Schools budget.

MEJA began networking across the state to encourage and support local labor/community coalitions, eventually helping to create chapters in more than a dozen cities. Members of each of these local alliances met regularly, cross-pollinated with other MEJA chapters, attended trainings and information sessions, and planned initiatives to educate and persuade their representatives to the General Court and the general public about the challenges, threats to, and needs of the state's treasured public schools.

MEJA's trial by fire arrived the following year, when the state's charter school lobby, frustrated by the legislature's refusal to lift the cap on the number of charters permitted in the state, filed petitions to place the issue on the ballot in the November 2016 elections.

"NO on 2"—MEJA Beats the Charter Industry

Question 2 on the ballot in Massachusetts in November 2016 asked voters to approve lifting the cap on charter schools. The lavishly funded "Yes on 2" campaign was run through the Massachusetts Charter Public School Association and relied on its messages of a parent's right to choose and the supposedly long lists of parents waiting for a charter seat for their child. The governor, and even the state's secretary of education, were vocal (and, it turned out, financial) supporters of the initiative.

MEJA led the opposition, focusing on the financial impacts of charter schools on local districts, and the role of billionaires in the state who supported charters, while failing to pay their fair share of taxes to support public schools. MEJA and its partners mounted a formidable grassroots campaign, including coordinating resolutions in opposition to the initiative from 215 of the state's 318 school committees.

MEJA's message, which has been successfully used in other states as well to highlight both the corporate backing of the charter industry and the false narrative of austerity, resonated in Massachusetts. On Nov. 8—the same day that Donald J. Trump won the presidency—Question 2 was defeated by a wide margin (62 percent opposed). The outpouring of opposition signaled a resurgent commitment to public schools by the state's voters, and it stunned the charter industry.

A Plan for New Revenue: Raise Up Massachusetts

Adding to the winds of change, a separate coalition, called Raise Up Massachusetts had also formed, and was advocating for a $15 minimum wage as well as guaranteed family medical leave. They had also proposed a "Fair Share Amendment" that would increase taxes on incomes over $1 million and dedicate the anticipated $2 billion in annual revenues from that tax increase to education and transportation projects across the state. Here was a way to insist that the state's millionaires and billionaires contribute to the general welfare.

As an amendment to the state constitution, the Fair Share Amendment required signatures from across the state, and then votes in two consecutive years, by the General Court, convened in a constitutional convention. Raise Up had jumped these hurdles, and the amendment was cleared for the November ballot in 2018 and widely expected to pass. MEJA joined the coalition to support the millionaire's tax.

Fund Our Future!

The General Court took up the FBRC report in their 2018 session. Several bills aimed at recalculating the foundation formula and pumping new money into education were filed and debated. Legislators, who had twice signaled their support for the Fair Share Amendment, assumed that the millionaire's tax, scheduled for the November ballot, would provide the revenues needed to fund an education formula overhaul.

They also passed a new minimum wage law, and family medical leave. It seemed that progressive breezes were blowing.

But in the middle of the legislative session, the Supreme Judicial Court struck the Fair Share Amendment off the ballot for technical reasons. And despite determined organizing work, the school funding bill failed in the very final hours of the very last day of the legislative session. Senators and representatives—while agreeing that a new formula was necessary—could not agree on the numbers.

As the session was gaveled to a close, MEJA issued a scathing press release, vowing to be back in 2019. The failure of the legislature to act allowed MEJA to increase the militancy of its organizing and approaches to lawmakers. It also offered time for some MEJA partners—those with the ability to engage electorally—to crystalize their work for candidates in the November 2018 election cycle, by demanding new faces on Beacon Hill—legislators who would fight even harder for the investment that Massachusetts students deserve. Indeed, the chair of the state's House Ways and Means Committee, who had been a staunch opponent of new funding for schools, was toppled in November, signaling that there would be political implications if the legislature failed to act on school funding in the next session.

In December 2018, MEJA and other allies launched Fund Our Future—a campaign specifically directed at winning passage of a new foundation formula.

Organizing to Fund Our Future

By 2019, the Fund Our Future campaign was mobilizing across the state as parents, educators, and students demanded action on Beacon Hill. The campaign wanted to be certain that any bill that passed would include full funding, based on the FBRC's $1 billion price tag, and that it didn't include any steps backward on charter schools, state takeovers, or other conservative education proposals.

Local Organizing Was Key to #FundOurFuture

Key to the success of #FundOurFuture was the organizing that happened outside of the state Capitol.

Malden, Massachusetts, is one of the most diverse, and the most chronically underfunded districts in the commonwealth. An influx of immigrants has had a dramatic impact over the past decade. There are now 70 different languages spoken in the Malden schools.

Students in Malden have spent their entire elementary and secondary years in underfunded schools. The city has put in "every spare dime" that it could, but this hasn't been enough. "The school funding formula hasn't been changed since I was 12 years old!" says Deb Gesualdo, president of the Malden Education Association (MEA). "How is that OK?"

The district has an early learning center, five K–8 schools, and one high school. Most students don't have access to world languages until they get to high school. Access to music and art at the elementary level is limited. The district has only a single charter school, but district financial transfers to that school suck $11 million annually from the district budget. Down the road in wealthier communities, it's a totally different landscape.

The teacher union hosted a community forum in the spring of 2018. More than 200 residents, students, parents, and educators turned out to hear their state senator, along with an officer of the national NEA and the president of the Massachusetts Teachers Association, talk about the need for new school funding legislation.

As the #FundOurFuture campaign moved forward, the MEA hosted school walk-throughs with the mayor, and their state senator. They had the senator sit down with students, who explained what underfunding looked like to them every day. They held focus groups with teachers and organized smaller events as well.

They also organized resolutions supporting the school finance report. These resolutions were passed by the local school committee and the City Council.

"When the Student Opportunity Act passed, we had this feeling of elation . . . but also disbelief," said Gesualdo. "It's hard to wrap your mind around what this could actually mean for our schools."

But soon the union was back at it, scheduling new forums to start planning their platform for the next round—the development of a plan for spending the new money, which was required by the law. "We're going to bring educators, students, parents, and guardians together to provide input," Gesualdo noted.

"It's going to be life-changing. This will literally change lives of our students."

New England Patriots players Devin McCourty, Jason McCourty, and Duron Harmon wear T-shirts in support of the Massachusetts "Fund Our Future" campaign.

MEJA began to hold "boot camps" to educate parents and teachers across the state about the legislation. A series of Days of Action mobilized parents, students, and educators to call their representatives in the General Court. While thousands were mobilized for a rally on the Statehouse grounds in May 2019, local MEJA chapters and unions took resolutions in support of a new funding formula to their school committees and other elected bodies. More than 100 school committees, city councils, and other governmental bodies passed resolutions calling for full funding—most of those by unanimous vote.[6]

Countless in-district meetings with legislators took place, with teachers, parents, and students making their case. In many cities, legislators were taken on tours of schools to witness firsthand the conditions that students and their teachers were working under.

Even some members of the New England Patriots spoke out. Three members of the Players Coalition—a national advocacy group of NFL players focused on racial justice and equity issues—went to the Statehouse to testify in favor of new investment in education. They took legislators on a tour of a local school and kept the issue alive on their social media platforms. The players gained national attention when the Patriots twitter feed featured a photo of the three players on the practice field, sporting Fund Our Future T-shirts.

Actual negotiations around the bills took place behind closed doors. But the bill that emerged from conference in October 2019 stunned advocates. Instead of the $1 billion recommended by the FBRC, the bill called for even more funding.

It was passed unanimously by both the Senate and the House and signed by Gov. Baker just days before Thanksgiving 2019.

The Student Opportunity Act

The Student Opportunity Act (SOA) committed the state to inject nearly $1.5 billion into the commonwealth's schools—exceeding FBRC recommendations. There were virtually no poison pills—no charter expansion, no new testing requirements.
In specific, the act:

- Lifts the definition of low-income to 185 percent of poverty, up from 133 percent, allowing more schools and districts to qualify for additional aid;
- Increases per-pupil funding by as much as 100 percent for low-income students in districts with high concentrations of poverty;
- Increases special education and English language learner allocations;
- Adjusts/considers additional costs for guidance and psychological services for students;
- Adjusts for the actual costs of health insurance to employees and retirees;
- Expands additional reimbursements to include transportation costs, and more.

The law also included an embedded organizing handle. Although advocates were not in favor of an increased oversight role for the state Department of Elementary and Secondary Education, the law required superintendents and school committees—with input from parents and other community stakeholders—to submit three-year improvement plans, specifying how the new money will be spent.

MEJA summed up the campaign in a victory statement the day the governor signed the bill: "We Won! Now We Keep Fighting."

Looking Forward

There was little time to savor the victory. For the grassroots advocates, all eyes were now on the development of local district plans, due in April 2020. "Money doesn't solve problems unless there's a real vision," says Charlotte Kelly, the director of MEJA. "Suppose a district stands to get $100 million in new funding through this bill, and they decide to spend it on increasing the police presence in schools. There's still a fight to be had. If we don't center our work around anti-racism and dismantling white supremacy in our schools, we're avoiding the core of the problem that brought us here in the first place," she noted.

In late winter 2020, MEJA was holding a series of "boot camps" around the state to help local labor/community coalitions develop platforms of resources and supports they can take to the table as district plans were being developed.

Groups knew they would also have to monitor the governor and legislature to make sure they held to their commitments. And Raise Up Massachusetts renewed its efforts to win a millionaire's tax on the 2022 ballot. There was much to be done. But spirits were bolstered in January 2020 when Baker released his FY 2021 budget proposal. It included $355 million toward the new law—just *over* the amount needed to meet the scale-up of the funding commitment. "We will keep a close watch on Beacon Hill over the next seven years to make sure lawmakers fulfill their pledge to provide every student with a high-quality education no matter where they live, their family income, the color of their skin, the language they speak at home, or the services they need to succeed," said Denise DaPonte Mussotte, of Fall River, whose son had been a lead plaintiff on a pending lawsuit, again challenging the state's funding formula, when the legislature passed the SOA.[7]

A huge swath of Massachusetts residents has been mobilized and educated to understand the school funding debate. Through grassroots organizing, sophisticated lobbying, communications, and strategically mounted litigation, the commonwealth is now full of people who will monitor the implementation of the Student Opportunity Act, and quickly stand up to the next—no doubt inevitable—effort to circumvent the law or cheat students out of the resources they are entitled to.

The fight doesn't end, and won't. But the 2019 victory has every appearance of being historic. 👤

Leigh Dingerson is a former community organizer, and currently a freelance writer and researcher on community and labor struggles for education justice. She is the author, most recently, of "Building the Power to Reclaim Our Schools," a case study on the 2019 Los Angeles teachers' strike.

ENDNOTES

[1] *Jami McDuffy & others vs Secretary of the Executive Office of Education & others*. June 15, 1993. Supreme Judicial Court. masscases.com/cases/sjc/415/415mass545.html

[2] Massachusetts General Laws: Chapter 70: School Funds and State Aid for Public Schools. malegislature. gov/Laws/GeneralLaws/PartI/TitleXII/Chapter70

[3] Report on the Status of the Public Education Financing System in Massachusetts. July 2013. Massachusetts Department of Elementary and Secondary Education. old.mma.org/images/stories/Advocacy/foundation_budget/dese_report_status_of_public_ed_financing_system.pdf

[4] Foundation Budget Review Commission. Oct. 30, 2015. doe.mass.edu/finance/chapter70/FBRC-Report. docx.

[5] "Bipartisan Commission Issues Report Calling for Improvements to School Funding Formula." Nov. 2, 2015. Massachusetts General Court. Press release.

[6] Fund Our Future. fundourfuturema.org/about/#resolutionmap

[7] State House News Service. Jan. 27, 2019. "Lawsuit alleging unconstitutional disparities in public school funding in Massachusetts dropped." MassLIVE. masslive.com/news/2020/01/lawsuit-alleging-unconstitutional-disparities-in-public-school-funding-in-massachusetts-dropped.html

Teacher Strike Threat Backs Off ExxonMobil

BY BARBARA MADELONI

Sometimes the boss offers us a fight that directly exposes the destructive effects of corporate power.

In Baton Rouge, Louisiana, that moment came when ExxonMobil asked for yet another handout from taxpayers—property tax exemptions totaling $6 million.

For the 9th-largest corporation in the world, it was a routine request. ExxonMobil is accustomed to receiving such perks from obedient state officials. But teachers saw it differently: as a $6 million theft from the local school budget.

Educators and other school employees voted 445-6 on Oct. 23, 2018, to stage a one-day walkout the following week. Teachers planned to pack a hearing on ExxonMobil's requests.

Within hours of the union vote, the company's exemption bids were off the Board of Commerce and Industry's agenda.

Government + Business = ♥

The backstory here is how members of two teacher unions and an SEIU local in East Baton Rouge got educated about the connection between corporate giveaways and the deteriorating conditions in their schools.

These unions participate in a faith, labor, and community coalition called Together Baton Rouge, which holds its Civic Academy Series to educate about community issues, including education. It was there that union members learned more about the state's Industrial Tax Exemption Program (ITEP).

ITEP, enacted 44 years ago, makes corporations eligible for tax exemptions if they can show—or claim—that their expenses for projects will contribute to a community's economic growth.

In this round of requests, ExxonMobil was asking for tax exemptions for work completed in 2017. The company didn't even bother to argue that the new exemptions would bring jobs or more revenue.

In the Civic Academies, union members learned to find ExxonMobil's submissions and read them for themselves. "They see the date of submission and the

date of project completion and they see it doesn't make sense," said Shanize Byrd, an organizer with the National Education Association. "The projects were already completed."

"We started educating our employees and showing how these exemptions affect everyone," said Angela Reams-Brown, president of the East Baton Rouge Federation of Teachers. "The children of our district suffer when we don't have qualified teachers, when bus drivers are driving old and dilapidated buses—this lack of money has far-reaching consequences."

Teachers haven't received an across-the-board raise since 2008.

"It hurts to see my colleagues working part time at a fast-food restaurant because their full-time job is not enough to sustain them," said Tia Mills, then-president of the East Baton Rouge Parish Association of Educators. "Teachers put a lot of their money into classrooms just to make them conducive to learning."

Corporate Handouts

Together Baton Rouge did the research that the unions used to educate their members and the community. That education was not just about who's stealing from the district—it also exposed the distortions of corporate philanthropy.

"Exxon comes back and says, 'Look at all the time and money we are putting back into the city,'" said Reams-Brown. "We say, 'If you are paying your fair share of taxes we will not need your handouts.'"

Louisiana ranks fourth in the country in income inequality. Between 2007 and 2017, the ITEP exemption had already cut ExxonMobil's property tax in East Baton Rouge Parish (Louisiana's equivalent of a county) in half. Over the last 20 years, exemptions for the oil giant have cost the parish $700 million, even while 1,900 ExxonMobil jobs have been lost.

Teachers and other workers' input into the ITEP process is new, brought in under current Gov. John Bel Edwards. Edwards ordered that requests for tax exemptions include resolutions from parish councils and any relevant school, municipal, police, and sheriff boards supporting the request.

Exemptions are reviewed by the state Board of Commerce and Industry. If approved, municipal councils have 30 days to put the issue on their own meeting agenda and 60 days to approve or reject. Prior to Edwards' order, municipalities had never had a chance to weigh in.

Leading up to Election Day, teachers were focused on the nine open seats in the school board elections, where out-of-state money from corporate-backed Democrats for Education Reform helped two charter school proponents outspend the other 13 candidates by almost double. Both pro-charter candidates were elected. Baton Rouge public schools lose more than $10 million a year to charter schools, which capture state funding on a per-pupil basis.

Strike Wave Fired Them Up

There were rumblings of a walkout in Louisiana last spring as educators watched teachers strike from West Virginia to Arizona. "Most definitely the red state rebellion influenced the teachers," Reams-Brown said. "We said it is always possible but it requires great planning. We want the community and the parents on our side."

Members were still fired up at her union follow-up meeting, the week after ExxonMobil removed its requests and the walkout was canceled. Some were disappointed not to walk out. Byrd said she had never before seen members not wait for staff or leadership to tell them what the next steps would be: "They said, 'Let's do this.' They have learned the mechanics of organizing. They are ready to go back into their schools, talk to people, and take action."

While school employees are continuing to organize—including making plans for a walk-in to celebrate public education—the unions have also filed a lawsuit against the tax assessor, who they claim has improperly left ExxonMobil and other corporate properties off the tax rolls, costing the district millions of dollars.

Meanwhile, Mills said, the superintendent just indicated he's going to recommend deep cuts in next year's budget. "We are going to be experiencing deep cuts but we are giving money to a big corporation," said Mills. "How is giving money to business good for our children?" ✊

Barbara Madeloni is the education coordinator for Labor Notes. Prior to working for Labor Notes, she was the president of the Massachusetts Teachers Association.

A version of this article appeared in *Labor Notes* #477. Reprinted with permission.

SECTION SIX

TAKING SOCIAL JUSTICE INTO
THE CLASSROOM

STOP WHITE-WASHING EDUCATION

#EthnicStudiesNow

Teacher Unions and Anti-Racist, Social Justice Teaching

BY BOB PETERSON

Two decades ago, when I interviewed historian Howard Zinn for the first edition of *Transforming Teacher Unions*, I asked him what role teacher unions should play in promoting the teaching of social movements and unions.

Zinn responded, "If teacher unions want to be strong and well-supported, it's essential that they not only be teacher unionists but teachers of unionism." As a historian and activist, Zinn promoted a radical vision of unionism from the Industrial Workers of the World to the Congress of Industrial Organizations. This vision of unionism crossed racial divides and fought to empower the entire working class. To be a teacher of unionism in Zinn's vision means to be a teacher of anti-racism and social justice.

Right-wing claims notwithstanding, teacher unions in the United States have rarely heeded Zinn's advice.

But that is starting to change.

In recent years, for example, progressive teacher unions have encouraged members to participate in the annual Black Lives Matter at School Week of Action. Around the country local and state teacher unions have supported social justice conferences and curriculum fairs organized by social justice teacher groups. And on the national level both the NEA and AFT have expanded their outreach and encouragement of social justice teaching.

But what does it actually look like? How does it compare to curricular approaches of industrial and professional teacher unions of the past? Why and how should teacher unions promote such teaching?

What Is Anti-Racist, Social Justice Teaching?

When Rethinking Schools started in 1986, a key purpose of the founders was to promote anti-racist, social justice curriculum and teaching. We envisioned classrooms as places where students and teachers gain glimpses of the kind of society we could live in and where students learn the academic and critical skills needed to make it a reality.

Our early books—*Rethinking Columbus* and *Rethinking Our Classrooms*—outlined the integrated components that we believe comprise a social justice classroom: grounded in the lives of our students; critical; multicultural, anti-racist, pro-justice; participatory, experiential; hopeful, joyful, kind, visionary; activist; academically rigorous; culturally and linguistically inclusive; and empowering. (See *Rethinking Schools* editors, p. 380.)

We were inspired by Brazilian educator Paulo Freire, who wrote that teachers should attempt to "live part of their dreams within their educational space." We agreed with his criticism of teacher-centered "banking models" of education. And we welcomed his "problem-posing" pedagogy that connected to the lives of students and encouraged students to not only "read the world" but to change it as well.

A Mixed History of Curriculum Advocacy

Prior to the late 1800s most teachers were men. A major argument for hiring women as teachers was they were cheaper to employ—so teachers' fight for better wages, hours, and working conditions from the early 1890s to the 1960s was integrally tied to the struggle for women's equality.

> We envisioned classrooms as places of hope, where students and teachers gain glimpses of the kind of society we could live in and where students learn the academic and critical skills needed to make it a reality.

Occasionally some unions such as the Chicago Teachers' Federation led by Margaret Haley (1861–1939) also fought against "'factoryizing education,' making the teacher an automaton." She and her members opposed vocational tracking of students in junior high schools and the use of racist "intelligence" tests. Such efforts were important struggles, but they did not include the kind of critical teaching described above. (See Haley, p. 67.)

The women-led Milwaukee Education Association did address pedagogical issues. In the 1920s it promoted progressive child-centered teaching such as the interdisciplinary project method inspired by the democratic perspectives of John Dewey and William Kilpatrick. An example was described by Meta Berger, a friend of the union and a socialist member of the school board. She observed a 5th-grade class where the students were

> . . . getting the history, English, arithmetic, art, and all kindred subjects while studying Daniel Boone. The boys were measuring and making log cabins; the girls were measuring and making dresses for the early Americans. Discipline did not enter the classroom for each child was so absorbed and interested that there was the most perfect of all discipline—i.e., perfect freedom and interest.

While such teaching was a significant improvement over the teacher-centered, rote learning that dominated U.S. schools in the early 1900s, it was far cry from social justice education. In fact, often it was labor groups outside of the schools that pushed for better representation of unions and workers' issues within the school curriculum—concerns that were not raised or even supported by teacher unions. For example, in 1919 the Milwaukee Federated Trade Council found a school play that negatively portrayed unions, and they demanded that the school board conduct an investigation and forbid "this and all similar . . . plays to be . . . acted in any of our public schools."

Undoubtedly one of the most active and explicitly social justice teacher unions in the United States was the New York City Teachers Union (TU). In 1935 a left-led rank-and-file caucus took over union leadership and for the next two-and-a-half decades promoted anti-racist, social justice teaching. They fought for the teaching of Black history and intercultural education and to rid the schools of racist textbooks.

In their textbook campaigns the TU built community alliances with the NAACP and other groups, drawing on the writings of W. E. B. Du Bois and Carter G. Woodson. In his 1935 work, *Black Reconstruction in America 1860–1880*, Du Bois critiqued high school textbooks for their white supremacist account of Reconstruction and their racist portrayal of African Americans.

In 1948 the TU created a pamphlet, *The Children's Textbooks*, that argued that the New York City textbooks made children susceptible to "anti-Semitism, Jim Crow, and racism." The union also opposed the school district's ban of Howard Fast's *Citizen Tom Paine* and the *Nation* magazine.

According to historian Clarence Taylor, writing in his book *Reds at the Blackboard*, the TU "used a number of methods to promote Black history, ranging from the creation and distribution of pamphlets for teachers to use in the classroom to sponsoring events featuring scholars of American History."

In 1951 the TU promoted "Negro History Week," which had been established in 1926 by Woodson. The TU's anti-discrimination committee produced a special supplement to their *New York Teacher News*. The committee, according to Taylor, "believed that Black history was being neglected in the classroom because teachers just did not have enough material."

The TU met its demise during the anti-communist hysteria of the McCarthy era. (See Perlstein, p. 42.)

The Turn Toward Professional Unionism

In the late 1980s and early 1990s some AFT and then NEA locals started addressing professional issues more directly. Teacher unions until that time had mostly concerned themselves with the material demands of teachers' work, especially wages and benefits. However, in the aftermath of the 1983 release of "A Nation at Risk: The Imperative for Educational Reform," a report commissioned by President Ronald Reagan's education secretary, the stage was set for subsequent corporate attacks on public education, ranging from private school vouchers to national standards enforced by a growing number of mass standardized tests.

In 1996 Adam Urbanski of the Rochester Teachers Association and Helen Bernstein of United Teachers Los Angeles started the Teacher Union Reform Network (TURN), which sought to "expand collective bargaining to include instructional and professional issues" such as career ladders, peer review, and professional development. In a few years, more than two dozen major AFT and NEA locals joined the network to share ideas and influence their national unions.

But despite TURN's commitment to prioritizing the needs of their students and teacher professionalism, the idea of unions promoting anti-racist, social justice teaching and curriculum was rarely addressed at their national meetings or in their publications.

It's worth noting that while it is essential that unions take up these professional issues, and "reclaim our classrooms" in the face of burdensome scripted curriculum, data collection, and out-of-control testing, unions should do so by aligning their interests with the communities they serve. The ideology of professionalism can distance teachers on the basis of race and class from the students and families they serve, at times ending up in serious union-community disagreements. The most poignant example was when in 1968 the New York City United Federation of Teachers sought professional control over the curriculum and teacher assignments in the midst of demands for community control.

Why Promote Anti-Racist, Social Justice Teaching?

There are four powerful reasons why union leadership should encourage their members to teach anti-racist social justice.

The first, as Zinn says, is to mentor the next generation to become active, critical participants in our society, promoting justice and democracy. I've always viewed encouraging this disposition—and the critical skills necessary to accomplish it—as a moral and civic responsibility of a teacher.

Second, such encouragement politically educates teachers and changes their attitudes. This is based on a premise that I recognized early in my teacher career—if I was going to teach something well, I had to really know the subject.

Unfortunately, many teachers don't know the "people's history" of our nation well—they didn't learn it in high school or in teacher education courses—whether it's the heroic resistance of Native peoples, labor union struggles, the fight for women's suffrage and rights, the Civil Rights Movement, or the struggle against U.S. imperialism and war. By promoting such teaching, unions simultaneously help their members learn this history and draw connections to current problems that affect their students and themselves. Such knowledge links past labor struggles and social movements to current struggles for justice.

Let me give a tiny example. Several years ago, my local union asked me to do a workshop on the teaching ideas from a book I edited with Bill Bigelow, *Rethinking Globalization: Teaching for Justice in an Unjust World*. The union bought a copy of the book for each participant and more than two dozen people came. Several of them, including a couple of young African American teachers, stayed afterward and said that it was the first time they had been to the union office, and that they were interested in coming to similar events. Another said the workshop helped him understand why the union must fight against school privatization.

The third reason why it's beneficial for unions to promote anti-racist, social justice teaching is that it improves student learning by increasing motivation and student ownership. It has the potential to build credibility with the broader community, particularly parents and communities of color.

And the fourth reason is that it attracts progressive, anti-racist teachers who might not otherwise be interested in joining or getting involved in the union. When teachers encourage the union to take action on these shared values, it establishes a pole within the union that in turn can attract even more members who can develop organizing programs around those values.

Yes, at times there might be opposition within the membership.

This was the case when I was president of the Milwaukee Teachers' Education Association. Our executive board decided to co-sponsor a Black Lives Matter protest after a Milwaukee police officer killed Dontre Hamilton, a 31-year-old Black man, shooting him 14 times during an altercation that followed the officer waking him up for sleeping on a park bench. We sent an email notice out to members encouraging participation. The next day three members called me and said they were quitting the union and disagreed with the union's position on this issue. Each one was married to a police officer.

> Anti-racist, social justice teaching improves student learning by increasing motivation and student ownership.

When unions take positions or encourage teaching about what some view as a controversial issue—such as promoting teaching activities during the Black Lives Matter at School Week of Action or Indigenous Peoples Day—there may be opposition, even strong opposition. That's why making sure there is a democratic process in place for making such decisions is important, and that leaders and members see the importance of having difficult discussions like those about race and white supremacy. These are not easy conversations, but they are the kind of discussions that are essential as we build multiracial unity in our schools, in our unions, and in coalitions with families and community members.

Promoting Anti-Racist, Social Justice Teaching

In 1987 the California Federation of Teachers, at the behest of several progressive teachers, established the CFT Labor in the Schools Committee. According to Fred Glass, one of the committee's founders, it had four original purposes: an information clearinghouse, curriculum development, teacher training, and building cooperation between labor and educational institutions.

The committee's initial project was the development of a video, *Golden Lands, Working Hands*, a history of the California labor movement, looking at it from the bottom up, not the "Great Man" approach to history. Started in the mid-1990s and finished in 1999, it became a three-hour, 10-part series. The project was funded by teacher unions and other labor organizations. The video and accompanying teaching guides were popular among high school history teachers as well as local unions that used the videos for member education.

Drawing on experience and expertise from the School for Workers at the University of Wisconsin, and drawing on lessons in *The Power in Our Hands: A Curriculum on the History of Work and Workers in the United States*, the committee developed role plays on collective bargaining and produced supplementary materials for the videos. With funding from a federal grant and the school district, two high school teachers were released for several years to do full-time professional development on labor history in the Los Angeles Unified School District. Using a unique approach, the trainers would stay in a high school class an entire week, modeling the collective bargaining role play and role plays of important conflicts in California's labor history, such as the 1934 Longshore Strike.

The modeling by veteran teachers demonstrated to other teachers: "This is what your students can do," and simultaneously shared content usually left out of the dominant narrative, and participatory pedagogy techniques. This deep professional development was provided to hundreds of teachers and ultimately affected tens of thousands of students.

Glass reflected on the committee's work over the years, saying unless unions "devote time and resources to bringing a picture of labor's accomplishments on behalf of working people to teachers and kids, they will grow up in a culture that has increasingly forgotten what labor's accomplishments were and are."

Support of Social Justice Teaching Conferences

Since the early 2000s teachers in different areas in the country have come together to form social justice groups. Teachers for Social Justice (TSJ) in Chicago was one of the first such groups. They have spoken out and organized on Chicago school issues—against school closings, for a democratically elected school board, and in support of the Chicago Teachers Union (CTU). They also hold an annual Social Justice Curriculum Fair for educators. Many of their members were active in or supported the Caucus of Rank and File Educators, elected to office in 2010. Since that time the CTU has supported and publicized TSJ activities.

Similarly activist teachers in Portland, Oregon, and Seattle, Tacoma, and Olympia, Washington, organize the Northwest Teaching for Social Justice Conference (NWTSJ), an annual one-day conference that in recent years has drawn more than 1,000 people and offered more than 80 different workshops led by classroom teachers. The NWTSJ receives financial support from the Washington Education Association, the Oregon Education Association, the Portland Association of Teachers, the Seattle Education Association, and the Social Equity Educators caucus in Seattle. The unions have also paid for printing of the programs, sponsored attendance of members, and promoted the events to members. Conferences have increased in recent years, with similar events and groups in the Bay Area, St. Louis, the Twin Cities, New York City, and Philadelphia.

Directly Providing Social Justice Professional Development

Increasingly, unions are taking on anti-racist, social justice education themselves. It can be as simple as setting up book circles, or getting a local authority on an important subject to come in for an evening discussion. In some cases unions develop their own materials, such as when the Cleveland Teachers Union developed and issued a teaching booklet on African American history (see p. 378).

In Milwaukee the teacher union released two teachers to lead teaching and learning activities of the union. Among their duties was coordinating teacher-to-teacher staff development. Three times a year, the union organizes a dozen or so workshops/book groups and invites all members to participate. The union also set up a nonprofit 501(c)(3) to get additional grants to fund the professional development. Workshops have included topics such as rethinking Columbus, climate justice, teaching for Black lives, National Board Certification, surviving as a new teacher, and restorative practices.

> Increasingly, unions are taking on anti-racist, social justice education themselves.

Some state organizations offer the professional development at annual conferences or through online classes. In New Jersey, early career teachers and others have pushed for more social justice, anti-racist professional development. Activists within the New Jersey Education Association (NJEA) have worked hard, with some success in recent years, to lift up social justice themes and resources in union work and events and to connect the union to community and progressive groups.

NJEA Executive Director Steve Swetsky reflected on his conversations with members. "Members of color will speak highly of NJEA in the abstract, but when you ask about their personal experiences either in their locals or in looking at the *NJEA Review* or in so much else that NJEA does, they're looking and not seeing themselves," he said. "We are getting better, but we have a long way to go."

That's true in many places and for many unions. And even if the union successfully brings quality professional development to its members, there are many more educators who remain untouched. In other words, unions can't do that job by themselves.

Pushing for District Support for Social Justice Teaching

Unions have worked to overcome this challenge in two main ways.

One is to work directly with district officials and school board members to push/lead them to see the importance of promoting professional development on anti-racist, social justice teaching. Such teaching sparks student motivation, connects students to the curriculum, and engages them in critical thinking and action, with a result of better academic achievement in writing, speaking, critiquing, reading, and mathematics.

The second strategy is to work with already existing community efforts such as the Black Lives Matter, Indigenous Peoples Day, immigrant rights, and climate justice campaigns, and to encourage those groups and movements to work jointly with the union to push the district to educate students about these topics. This might mean having the district share lesson plans to coincide with different historic days or create specific classes like ethnic studies or environmental sustainability courses or whole programs like bilingual education. Campaigns against racist or biased textbooks or racist or stereotypical mascots or logos are also fertile grounds to do extensive education among students and entire communities. Regardless of where such campaigns start, when the union and its members join together with students, families, and the broader community, the likelihood of success increases.

Campaigns against racist or biased textbooks or racist or stereotypical mascots or logos are also fertile grounds to do extensive education among students and entire communities.

A historic example of this was when activists, students, and union members in Portland pushed their school board to pass a resolution mandating the creation of a K–12 climate justice curriculum, developed by teachers, students, and community activists. (See Bigelow, p 392.)

Another example is when the CTU embraced and helped implement the court-ordered Reparations Won curriculum dealing with police brutality and reparations. (See Johnson, p. 383.)

Other strategies include writing and speech contests. On the national level the writing contest of the National Association for Bilingual Education is a powerful model. The Wisconsin Labor History Society conducts a contest asking students to write about the importance of unions in their family and community. In Milwaukee, a local contest started decades ago by a rank-and-file caucus has grown over the years to a large annual Martin Luther King Jr. writing and speech contest celebrated on his birthday.

Changing State Law

Demanding new state laws or educational requirements on social justice issues is another means by which unions can discuss important topics among members and, if successful, force the state to provide resources and professional development for curriculum or courses on important subjects. For example, the Washington Education Association supported passage of a state law requiring ethnic studies classes in high schools. After a major conflict around Native fishing rights in the 1980s in northern Wisconsin, the Legislature passed a law that requires "that all public school districts and preservice education programs provide instruction on the history, culture, and tribal sovereignty of Wisconsin's 11 federally recognized American Indian nations and tribal communities." The state teacher union lobbied in favor of the law. Similarly, after many years of lobbying, the Wisconsin Labor History Society got a law passed to require the teaching of collective bargaining in high schools. Ironically, that law passed just months before Gov. Scott Walker banned collective bargaining for most public employees.

Conclusion

Howard Zinn's words from decades ago still ring true: "... it's essential that they not only be teacher unionists but teachers of unionism." He added, "We need to create a generation of students who support teachers and the movement of teachers for their rights."

For teachers and teacher unions, Zinn's advice should be taken to heart. Our students deserve not only social justice in their schools and communities, but in what they study. Anything less would be a disservice to the next generation that will need to confront enormous challenges of racism, inequality, and climate chaos. ⬚

Bob Peterson, the former president of the Milwaukee Teachers' Education Association, is now a member of the Milwaukee School Board. He taught 5th grade more than 25 years at various Milwaukee public schools, and was a founding editor of Rethinking Schools.

SOURCES

Bigelow, Bill, and Bob Peterson, eds. 1998. *Rethinking Columbus: The Next 500 Years*. Rethinking Schools.

Bigelow, Bill et al., eds. 2007. *Rethinking Our Classrooms: Teaching for Equity and Justice, Volume 1*. Rethinking Schools.

Du Bois, W. E. B. 1935. *Black Reconstruction in America 1860–1880*. Harcourt Brace.

Taylor, Clarence. 2011. *Reds at the Blackboard: Communism, Civil Rights, and the New York City Teachers Union*. Columbia University Press.

A Union Promotes African-Centered Teaching

BY MICHAEL CHARNEY

I n the early 1990s African American activists pushed Cleveland Public Schools to institute an African-centered curriculum. I was a member of the executive board of the Cleveland Teachers Union (CTU) at the time, and convinced union leadership of the importance of supporting this effort. Across the country similar proposals generated controversy, so we decided the CTU should provide lesson plans to help teachers move away from the Eurocentric focus in their classrooms. We worked with the district's Afrocentric Studies teacher specialist and assembled a group of teachers from across curriculum areas to produce a booklet of lessons to support teachers in this transition.

We called the 82-page booklet *First Steps Towards an African Centered/Multicultural Curriculum*. We added "multicultural" to the title to encourage inclusiveness and called it "a booklet for teachers and by teachers." The CTU leadership supported this effort and gave substantial funding. The pamphlet's introduction used the metaphor of curriculum being both a mirror and a window—students could see themselves while also looking at the outside world. The lessons varied across the curriculum and were practical without an explicit ideology. I contributed an article highlighting part of *The Autobiography of Malcolm X* where Malcolm Little's 8th-grade shop teacher dismissed Malcolm's desire to become a lawyer, saying he wanted him to use his hands, not his mind—a classic example of lowering expectations for a bright African American student. Yet as I pointed out, Malcolm X did in a sense become a lawyer, spending his adult life putting white society on trial.

Cleveland has never been much of a place for curriculum conflict, as teachers are more interested in materials that can assist them directly in the classroom. The booklet did that, and was well received and used in workshops across the district. In fact, the school district provided funds for a second printing after seeing the positive response.

When Molefi Asante, a scholar of Afrocentrism then at Temple University, came to Cleveland, he was flabbergasted that the teacher union was behind this initiative. His experience had been quite different with other teacher unions.

Unfortunately, as the district started focusing teachers' attention on mind-numbing high-stakes testing—effectively sidelining most curriculum innovation—we never produced a sequel. Still, teacher unionists should never underestimate how much influence they can have creating and promoting anti-racist, social justice curriculum. ✊

Michael Charney served on the CTU Executive Board for almost 20 years. At the time of First Steps *he was the professional issues director and a social studies classroom teacher.*

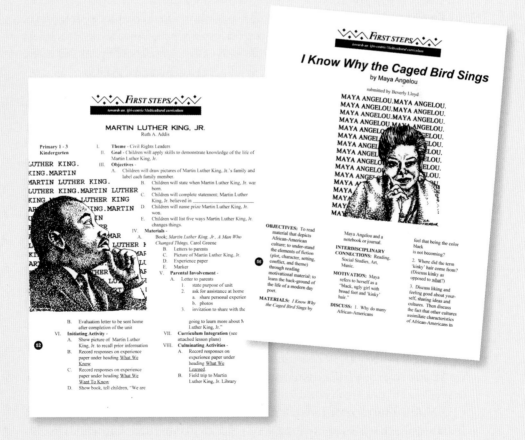

Key Principles of Equitable and Social Justice Classrooms

BY THE EDITORS OF RETHINKING SCHOOLS

A s educators, we begin from the premise that schools and classrooms should be laboratories for a more just society than the one we now live in. Unfortunately, too many schools are training grounds for boredom, alienation, and pessimism. Too many schools fail to confront the racial, class, and gender inequities woven into our social fabric. Teachers are often simultaneously perpetrators and victims, with little control over planning time, class size, or broader school policies—and much less over the unemployment, hopelessness, and other "savage inequalities" that help shape our children's lives.

But *The New Teacher Book* is not about what we cannot do; it's about what we can do. Brazilian educator Paulo Freire wrote that teachers should attempt to "live part of their dreams within their educational space." Classrooms can be places of hope, where students and teachers gain glimpses of the kind of society we could live in and where students learn the academic and critical skills needed to make it a reality.

No matter what the grade level or content area, we believe that several interlocking components comprise what we call a social justice classroom. Curriculum and classroom practice must be:

Grounded in the lives of our students. All good teaching begins with respect for children, their innate curiosity, passions, and their capacity to learn. Curriculum should be rooted in children's needs and experiences. Whether we're teaching science, mathematics, English, or social studies, ultimately the class has to be about our students' lives as well as about a particular subject. Students should probe the ways their lives connect to the broader society, and are often limited by that society.

Critical. The curriculum should equip students to "talk back" to the world. Students must learn to pose essential critical questions: Who makes decisions and who is left out? Who benefits and who suffers? Why is a given practice fair or unfair? What are its origins? What alternatives can we imagine? What is required to create change? Through critiques of advertising, cartoons, literature, legislative decisions, military interventions, job structures, newspapers, movies, agricultural practices, or school life, students should have opportunities to question social reality. Finally, student work must move outside the classroom walls, so that scholastic learning is linked to real-world problems.

Multicultural, anti-racist, pro-justice. In the book *Rethinking Columbus*, Rethinking Schools used the discovery myth to demonstrate how children's literature and textbooks tend to value the lives of Great White Men over all others. Traditional materials invite children into Columbus' thoughts and dreams; he gets to speak, claim land, and rename the homelands of Native Americans, who appear to have no rights. Implicit in many traditional accounts of history is the notion that children should disregard the lives of women, working people, and especially people of color—they're led to view history and current events from the standpoint of the dominant groups. By contrast, a social justice curriculum must strive to include the lives of all those in our society, especially the marginalized and dominated. As anti-racist educator Enid Lee points out in an interview in *Rethinking Our Classrooms*, a rigorous multiculturalism should engage children in a critique of the roots of inequality in curriculum, school structure, and the larger society, always asking: How are we involved? What can we do?

> All good teaching begins with respect for children, their innate curiosity, passions, and their capacity to learn. Curriculum should be rooted in children's needs and experiences.

Participatory, experiential. Traditional classrooms often leave little room for student involvement and initiative. In a "rethought" classroom, concepts need to be experienced firsthand, not just read about or heard about. Whether through projects, role plays, simulations, mock trials, or experiments, students need to be mentally, and often physically, active. Our classrooms also must provoke students to develop their democratic capacities: to question, to challenge, to make real decisions, to collectively solve problems.

Hopeful, joyful, kind, visionary. The ways we organize classroom life should seek to make children feel significant and cared about—by the teacher and by each other. Unless students feel emotionally and physically safe, they won't share real thoughts and feelings. Discussions will be tinny and dishonest. We need to design activities where students learn to trust and care for each other. Classroom life should, to the greatest extent possible, prefigure the kind of democratic and just society we envision and thus contribute to building that society. Together students and teachers can create a "community of conscience," as educators Asa Hilliard and Gerald Pine call it.

Activist. We want students to come to see themselves as truth-tellers and change-makers. If we ask children to critique the world but then fail to encourage them to act, our classrooms can degenerate into factories for cynicism. Although it's not a teacher's role to direct students to particular organizations, it is a teacher's role to suggest that ideas should be acted upon and to offer students opportunities to do just that. Children can also draw inspiration from historical and contemporary efforts of people who struggled for justice. A critical curriculum should be a rainbow of resistance, reflecting the diversity of people who acted to make a difference, many of whom did so at great sacrifice. Students should be allowed to learn about and feel connected to this legacy of defiance.

Academically rigorous. A social justice classroom equips children not only to change the world, but also to maneuver in the one that exists. Far from devaluing the vital academic skills young people need, a critical and activist curriculum speaks directly to the deeply rooted alienation that currently discourages millions of students from acquiring those skills. A social justice classroom offers more to students than traditional classrooms do, and expects more from them. Critical teaching aims to inspire levels of academic performance far greater than those motivated or measured by grades and test scores. When children write for real audiences, read books and articles about issues that really matter, and discuss big ideas with compassion and intensity, "academics" starts to breathe. Yes, we must help students "pass the tests" (even as we help them analyze and critique those tests and the harmful impact of test-driven education). But only by systematically reconstructing classroom life do we have any hope of cracking the cynicism that lies so close to the heart of massive school failure, and of raising academic expectations and performance for all our children.

Culturally and linguistically inclusive and empowering. Critical teaching requires that we admit we don't know it all. Each class presents new challenges to learn from our students and demands that we be good researchers, and good listeners. This is especially true when our racial or social class identity, or our nationality or linguistic heritage is different from those of our students. As African American educator Lisa Delpit writes in her review of the book *White Teacher* in *Rethinking Our Classrooms*, "When teachers are teaching children who are different from themselves, they must call upon parents in a collaborative fashion if they are to learn who their students really are." Teachers need to challenge all forms of privilege, especially white supremacy, in ways that respect and empower the communities and students they serve. And we must embrace students' home languages, helping them preserve their linguistic heritages while also helping them navigate in English-dominant settings.

We're skeptical of the "inspirational speakers" whom administrators bring to faculty meetings, who exhort us to become superteachers and classroom magicians. Critical teaching requires vision, support, and resources, not magic. ◆

This essay was published in its original form as the introduction to Rethinking Our Classrooms: Teaching for Equity and Justice, Volume 1 *and revised for* The New Teacher Book, *3rd edition—both published by Rethinking Schools.*

Reparations Can Be Won— And Must Be Taught: Lessons from the Chicago Public Schools' Reparations Won Curriculum

BY JENNIFER JOHNSON

Darrell Cannon at an event honoring survivors of Chicago police torture in February 2016.

SARAH-JI

'll admit it. I was nervous. Usually, addressing the Chicago Teachers Union's (CTU) 600-plus elected delegates gives me jitters, even after five years working as a CTU staff member. But at the Jan. 11, 2017, monthly meeting, my heart was racing because Darrell Cannon was going to talk about his experience as a survivor of police torture and why educators should teach the new

Chicago Public Schools (CPS) Reparations Won curriculum. I was nervous because our membership includes members whose political orientations vary in their thoughts about police and policing. While our CTU leadership is committed to a racial justice platform, including protecting people of color from being victimized by systems of policing and incarceration, not all educators see taking a position on this as a priority for our union.

But I should have felt confident before Cannon spoke: The CTU leaders and members *had* amassed a record of rejecting the violence of policing in Chicago. In November 2015, we participated in the large Black Friday protests generated by the police shooting of 17-year-old Laquan McDonald.[1] In December 2015, our House of Delegates endorsed a resolution to support the creation of a Civilian Police Accountability Council in Chicago.[2] In January 2016, the same body endorsed a resolution calling for the resignation of Cook County State's Attorney Anita Alvarez,[3] who ultimately lost her reelection bid because of her failure to swiftly prosecute McDonald's killer.[4]

While I believe teachers and our union should fight alongside our communities for social, economic, and racial justice, not all educators share that view. Some argue for neutrality. Yet "neutrality" is invoked unevenly. For example, some CTU members argue against taking a position on whether the city should have democratic accountability mechanisms for police, despite agreeing that CPS should have an elected rather than mayor-appointed school board.

As Chicago educators, we *should* feel an imperative to fight for racial justice. Our jobs are about the Black and Brown young people who attend CPS. Between 2002 and 2019 CPS enrollment declined from nearly 440,000 to just over 355,000, as a result of systemic neighborhood disinvestment.[5] The decline was used to justify the closing of roughly 50 mostly Black schools in 2013. Black teachers were disproportionately laid off. The percentage of Black teachers in CPS declined from 40 percent in 2000, to 21 percent in 2018 when 36 percent of the student population was Black.[6]

By 2018, 52 percent of CPS teachers were white, though only 10 percent of students were.

For some, the Reparations Won curriculum tells a particularly challenging history. However, educators can and must teach this story about how Black survivors of police torture in Chicago won an unprecedented and historic reparations package.

The Long Fight to Win Reparations
Plainly stated and sparing the awful details, Chicago Police Commander Jon Burge and officers beneath him tortured more than 100 Black men between 1972 and 1991.[7] The physical and psychological abuse was varied and extensive and was used to elicit mostly false confessions that led to convictions and long prison sentences.[8] Even though survivors recanted their confessions and attested to the torture they experienced, they were not immediately believed.

In 1983, days after Cannon's abuse occurred, he drew a stick figure for his lawyer and described the torture he experienced: a cattle prod to his testicles, shotgun in his mouth, berated with the N-word, all while handcuffed.[9] He was only exonerated and released from prison 21 years later.[10]

A group of survivors, calling themselves "The Death Row 10," demanded new court hearings in the 1990s and brought needed attention to their torture. Their efforts led to some pardons and commutations, and contributed to the moratorium on the death penalty that passed in Illinois in 2011. Another group, Black People Against Torture, called for reparations and successfully lobbied for official condemnation from the United Nations' Committee Against Torture.[11] Though Burge was fired from the Chicago Police Department in 1993, he was not prosecuted and convicted until 2010. Even then, Burge was sentenced to serve only four-and-a-half years for perjury and obstruction of justice. He never was convicted for his role in the torture itself and received a police pension even after his prison term. He died in 2018.

While there were victories, there was no reckoning or acknowledgement of the full breadth of the torture until 2015. The grassroots organization Chicago Torture Justice Memorials (CTJM) formed in 2011 and developed a pivotal campaign for an alternative version of justice including reparations. CTJM hosted an art exhibit in 2012 called "Opening the Black Box," where an early version of a city ordinance, penned by Joey Mogul, CTJM co-founder and longtime People's Law Office attorney, was on display along with more than 70 designs for speculative memorials about the torture.[12] Events in and outside of Chicago helped advance demands for reparations: The demonstrations led by Black Youth Project 100 (BYP100) in response to the 2013 acquittal of George Zimmerman, Trayvon Martin's killer; Ta-Nehisi Coates' 2014 article, "The Case for Reparations";[13] the uprising in Ferguson, Missouri, after Michael Brown was killed by police; and the national Movement for Black Lives galvanized public pressure and attention. Just three months after Michael Brown was killed in 2014, young Black and Brown Chicago activists in We Charge Genocide (WCG) traveled to the United Nations and named the violence of the Chicago Police Department.[14] Protests after the killing of Laquan McDonald that same year, and the exposure of the cover-up after Rahm Emanuel's re-election as Chicago mayor in 2015 heightened the cries for redress.

Educators can and must teach this story about how Black survivors of police torture in Chicago won an unprecedented and historic reparations package.

Years of protest and political pressure finally led to the passage on May 6, 2015, of an unprecedented city ordinance[15] that included:

- An acknowledgement and condemnation of the torture.
- A formal apology to those affected by the torture.
- The formation of a commission to disseminate monetary reparations to the survivors.

- The formation of a fund of $5.5 million to provide up to $100,000 to each torture survivor with a credible claim.
- The creation of a counseling and training center on the South Side for survivors, family, and anyone impacted by police abuse.*
- Free city college tuition for the survivors and their family members.
- Job placement assistance to formerly incarcerated survivors.
- That CPS teach a curriculum in 8th and 10th grades about the history of the torture and the fight for justice.
- Hearings for torture survivors still in prison.
- The creation of a public memorial honoring the survivors and their fight.
- A minimum of $20 million for the reparations, counseling center, curriculum, and memorial.
- Legally pursuing the ending of Jon Burge's police pension.

Chicago is the only municipality that has offered reparations to victims of police abuse. The comprehensive reparations package is a model for "reimagining what justice looks like" according to CTJM co-founder and longtime activist Alice Kim, and what can be won when we dream audaciously and strategize out of the legal box.

Making Reparations Teachable

Darrell Cannon had a toothache when I met him for the first time in November 2016. It was at an orientation session for a small group of teachers about to pilot a near-final draft of the curriculum. He gritted through his pain that day and explained why teaching the curriculum was vital. He joked about never using profanity and afterward he gave me a warm hug and called me "sister." Funny and kind, he reminded me of my father. It could have happened to my father.

My CTU involvement provided an avenue to connect to the reparations victory. Because I was a native Michigander, the Burge torture was new to me. I taught high school history in CPS for 10 years, but I left my classroom in 2013 to work full time at the CTU. When the ordinance passed, despite being eager to teach this material, I no longer had a classroom. Winning a commitment to teach the reparations fight was just the beginning. Actual curriculum had to be created. A couple of colleagues and I participated periodically in meetings convened by the CPS social studies office to work with teachers and other experts to write, pilot, and implement what became the Reparations Won curriculum units for both middle and high school. To their credit, the district staff worked diligently to manage the differing expectations for the curriculum, and it went through many revisions. It could not possibly be perfect, but there was real effort to make it as accurate, powerful, and teachable as such a complex history could be. (To see the full curriculum, go to websites listed at the end of this article.)

---

* The Chicago Torture Justice Center opened in May 2017 and, among myriad other programs, is running a speakers bureau. Schools and organizations can request that a torture survivor or family member come tell their story.

During the pilot implementation phase, I accompanied CPS officials on visits to three schools. I saw middle school students at a predominantly Black elementary school on the South Side engaged in an energetic debate about how people should be treated when stopped by police. Middle school students at a largely Latinx elementary school read primary and secondary source documents about the torture itself. Lightbulbs and chatter broke out in the room when they realized that Burge served only three-and-a-half years in prison. High school students at an all-Black South Side school grappled with the time and range of people it took to win the ordinance.

In their final forms, the middle and high school curriculum units use primary and secondary sources to allow students to uncover the history of the Burge torture and the decades-long fight that led to the city ordinance, and the development of the curricula itself. Since both the 8th- and 10th-grade curricula are required to be taught, they are not identical. Students are presented with a foundational understanding in middle school and then are asked to go into more historical depth in high school. Both curricula units incorporate social-emotional components such as restorative circles and journaling, to let students reflect and process their reactions to this tough history. Both units profile the causes of the torture, testimonials of torture, and the broad array of people who sought justice for years.

The comprehensive reparations package is a model for reimagining what justice looks like.

Each unit has unique and, I believe, radical features. The middle school unit focuses on the roles and responsibilities of police. Early on, students are asked to imagine that they are creating a new city and they must decide if they want their new city to have a police force. If they do, they must write a rationale and describe what the mission of police should be. It is a huge victory that the unit boldly allows students to question the assumption of the need for police in the first place. Without forcing students to take a certain position, this exercise allows the abolition of police to be a rational vision for the future. In the closing activity, students stage a classroom town hall aimed at developing strategies to improve community-police relationships. The students' final assessment is to write their own individual op-ed pieces based on what they've learned.

Building on the middle school unit, the high school one is framed around four main factors that allowed the torture to occur, and how major failures related to each of the factors enabled survivors to be victimized, incarcerated, and dismissed for years. At the end of the unit, students evaluate whether the reparations package was sufficient to provide justice for the survivors. For the high school final assessment, students design their own proposal for an appropriate memorial connecting them directly to the outstanding work of fulfilling the ordinance's promise of an actual city memorial. The recent opening of the National Memorial for Peace and Justice in Montgomery, Alabama, dedicated to remembering America's obsession with lynching Black people, is a timely reminder of how significant physical places that allow us to contemplate racism can be.

Responding to Pushback

Pushback has emerged from predictable communities: predominantly white neighborhoods with a high concentration of police officer residents. We have tried to meet this challenge.

In January 2017, while the curriculum was being piloted, CTU colleagues and I received about 40 responses to a survey of social studies teachers. How much did educators know and what did they feel about this curriculum? What excited and worried them about teaching the curriculum?

A sample of comments demonstrates their range of thinking:

- "I believe this is an inappropriate intrusion into the classroom. I would expect the CTU to stand up for the expertise and autonomy of social science teachers and refuse to support a court-ordered curriculum."
- "Most importantly, won't this further divide Chicago youth and Chicago police officers? Have you considered the conflict of interest regarding CPS teachers being asked to teach such a curriculum? Many of us are children, spouses, and parents of Chicago police officers."
- "It will allow individuals who suffered injustice [to] have their voices and experiences heard and lessons passed on to future generations."
- "We've been discussing the role of the police at great length since Ferguson. Even children of cops have strong opinions about what should and should not happen, including alternatives to policing."

We expected this varied reaction. Winning a broad understanding of the value of teaching the Reparations Won units requires time and ongoing education. After the pilot phase, CPS invited all schools to send social studies teachers and counselors to a three-and-a-half-hour mandatory professional development (PD) session in April 2017. I attended one session on the far north side in Uptown. Most of the educators were white. The teachers were quiet, especially when torture survivors Anthony Holmes and Darrell Cannon told their stories. The reactions of teachers at many of the South Side PD sessions, I was told, were different. Majority-Black educators emoted vocally about the imperative to do right by the curriculum.

While the district PD was well done, we at the CTU thought that we could and should provide teachers an optional, more in-depth experience. I convinced a racially mixed group of six rock star CTU teachers to develop and facilitate our own PD. We created three modules: one that focused on what teachers should do before teaching the curriculum, one on the best practices for teaching it, and the final one on how to engage students in reflection and action after learning the curriculum. The teachers and I designed a six-and-a-half-hour PD with several goals in mind. We wanted to:

1. Provide teachers tools to create a **classroom climate of support and inquiry** needed in order to responsibly teach the curriculum.

2. Emphasize the importance of teaching **institutional racism**. The torture happened to Black men. It occurred due to the endemic racism in our society that is a part of what scholar Saidiya Hartman calls "the afterlife of slavery."[16] Only in naming racism and how it operates can students lead us in undoing it.

3. Give teachers time to **examine the middle and high school curricula** so they themselves are familiar with it and the facts.

4. Emphasize the need to teach the curriculum in **historical and current context**. The Burge torture and the long fight for justice did not occur in a vacuum. Considering how the Burge torture is related to the War on Drugs, the Vietnam War, and the rise of "tough on crime" policies and mass incarceration cannot be understated. Teachers must help students connect the history in the curriculum to recent and present struggles.

5. Ask teachers to **partner with their students in reflecting** on what they learn from the curriculum and to provide them a framework for doing so. Students are capable learning partners who can assess what worked and what did not. While the assessments in the curriculum elevate student voice and creativity, students may want to take concrete action and teachers must be prepared to provide opportunities to do so.

Some educators are taking responsibility for addressing concerns on their own. I learned, after the fact, that a teacher at a (predominantly white) school in Jefferson Park, on the far northwest side of Chicago, ran a meeting in September 2017, with the support of her principal, where she took parents through the curriculum page by page to allay their fears.

Why the Unimaginable Must Be Taught

To my relief and elation, Cannon received a standing ovation at that January 2017 House of Delegates meeting. He had told his story probably hundreds of times to police, lawyers, reporters, and more. To our members, he stressed the profound significance of teaching the curriculum:

> It is imperative that the teachers teach this curriculum, because if the children are not familiar with the past and the present, they are doomed in the future. It is imperative that you, the teachers, understand what happened to us for far too long and take a stance and teach our children about this ugly chapter of the past. We will teach our children about the Laquan McDonald case [too, because] Laquan McDonald would not have happened if we, the torture survivors, hadn't been tortured by Jon Burge and company . . .

Dustin Voss, one of the original pilot teachers and a CTU delegate, taught the curriculum again in the 2017–2018 school year and had Cannon come to speak to his class for the second year in a row. Of this visit, a student wrote: "You could tell that he wasn't here just to tell his story. Darrell Cannon came to inspire us to make change where we see it needs to be made. . . . He was motivating us to want to fight to fix the problems that might affect us deeply by telling us how he changed his own life and the lives of many other people."

As a burgeoning Freirean educator, I believe teaching is political. Our role as educators is to help students become critical agents of change who understand the systems of power operating on their lives. Based on this student's reflection, the Reparations Won curriculum allows educators to do just that.

Perhaps ironically, a demand for curriculum was not in the original draft of the reparations ordinance. The final inclusion of curriculum was inspired by teachers who were already teaching about the torture and had submitted syllabi to the "Opening the Black Box" exhibit.[17] Alice Kim said that the curriculum was the one part of the ordinance that she thought "would never get passed." She stressed that now that the curriculum exists, if we fight to make sure that it is taught and continues to be taught, Chicago students will be better equipped to confront and work to end the violence of policing.

> Only in naming racism and how it operates can students lead us in undoing it.

I am proud to be a member of a teacher union that has not shied away from racially charged issues. CTU members recently voted to add language to our Constitution to declare that one of the union's purposes is "to promote racial, economic, and social justice in order to achieve educational justice and build community and labor coalitions to achieve that objective."[18] It is the right thing to do, but it is also in our interest. We have to do more political education with our members to help ensure that the curriculum is implemented responsibly, effectively, and consistently in all CPS schools. Other teacher unions and members have and are promoting teaching racial justice as demonstrated by the large national participation, including CTU's, in Black Lives Matter at School Week. Where unions have not supported these efforts, members themselves must reject the argument that teaching our country's racist past or supporting current anti-racist movements is divisive. Educators must seize these opportunities to be on the right side of history and not wait for history to play out. The Burge torture survivors waited long enough for justice. ■

Jennifer (Jen) Johnson is the chief of staff for the Chicago Teachers Union. Before coming to work full time for the CTU, she taught high school history for 10 years at Lincoln Park High School, a north side Chicago public school.

TO ACCESS THE CURRICULUM, GO TO:

Middle school: https://blog.cps.edu/wp-content/uploads/2017/08/ReparationsWon_MiddleSchool.pdf

High school: https://blog.cps.edu/wp-content/uploads/2017/08/ReparationsWon_HighSchool.pdf

TO ACCESS THE CHICAGO CITY COUNCIL ORDINANCE ON THE CURRICULUM:

https://www.chicago.gov/content/dam/city/depts/dol/supp_info/Burge-Reparations-Information-Center/ORDINANCE.pdf

ENDNOTES

[1] DNA Info Staff. Nov. 26, 2015. "Teachers Union to Join Black Friday Mag Mile Laquan McDonald Protest." *DNA Info Chicago*. https://www.dnainfo.com/chicago/20151126/streeterville/teachers-union-join-black-friday-mag-mile-laquan-mcdonald-protest

[2] CTU Communications. Dec. 3, 2015. "CTU Endorses New Police Oversight Body." Chicago Teachers Union. https://www.ctulocal1.org/posts/ctu-endorses-new-police-oversight-body

[3] CTU Communications. Jan. 7, 2016. "Chicago's Teachers Vote Overwhelmingly to Officially Call for the Resignations of Emanuel and Alvarez." Chicago Teachers Union. https://www.ctulocal1.org/posts/chicagos-teachers-vote-overwhelmingly-to-officially-call-for-the-resignations-of-emanuel-and-alvarez

[4] Bauer, Kelly. March 16, 2016. "How Did Anita Alvarez Lose So Badly to Kim Foxx? (TIMELINE)." *DNA Info Chicago*. dnainfo.com/chicago/20160316/downtown/how-did-anita-alvarez-lose-so-badly-kim-foxx-timeline

[5] Belsha, Kalyn. Dec. 19, 2017. "Thousands of Black Students Leave Chicago for Other Segregated Districts." *Chicago Reporter*. chicagoreporter.com/black-cps-student-migration

[6] Chicago Public Schools. SY 2019–2020. "CPS Stats and Facts." cps.edu/SchoolData/Pages/SchoolData.aspx

[7] "History." 2013. Chicago Torture Justice Memorials. chicagotorture.org/history

[8] Conroy, John. Feb. 3, 2005. "Tools of Torture." *Chicago Reader*. chicagoreader.com/chicago/tools-of-torture/Content?oid=917876

[9] Cannon, Darrell. May 13, 2015. "Darrell Cannon: Surviving Chicago Police Torture." Praxis Center. kzoo.edu/praxis/torture-survivor-darrell-cannon

[10] Moore, Natalie. Jan. 6, 2016. "Victims of Chicago Police Torture Paid Reparations Decades Later." *Morning Edition*. npr.org/2016/01/06/462114331/victims-of-chicago-police-torture-paid-reparations-decades-later

[11] Taylor, Flint. June 26, 2015. "How Activists Won Reparations for the Survivors of Chicago Police Department Torture." *In These Times*. inthesetimes.com/article/18118/jon-burge-torture-reparations

[12] Kim, Alice. May 13, 2015. "Opening the Black Box: Reparations and the Power of Radical Imagination." Praxis Center. www.kzoo.edu/praxis/reparations-and-the-power-of-radical-imagination

[13] Coates, Ta-Nehisi. June 2014. "The Case for Reparations." *The Atlantic*. theatlantic.com/magazine/archive/2014/06/the-case-for-reparations/361631

[14] Berlatsky, Noah. Nov. 17, 2014. "At the United Nations, Chicago Activists Protest Police Brutality." *The Atlantic*. theatlantic.com/national/archive/2014/11/we-charge-genocide-movement-chicago-un/382843

[15] City of Chicago. "Burge Reparations Information." chicago.gov/content/dam/city/depts/dol/supp_info/Burge-Reparations-Information-Center/BurgeRESOLUTION.pdf

[16] Hartman, Saidiya V. 2008. *Lose Your Mother: A Journey Along the Atlantic Slave Route*. Farrar, Straus and Giroux.

[17] Kim, Alice. May 13, 2015. "Opening the Black Box: Reparations and the Power of Radical Imagination." Praxis Center. kzoo.edu/praxis/reparations-and-the-power-of-radical-imagination

[18] Chicago Teachers Union. January 2018. "Chicago Teachers Union Constitution and By-Laws." ctunet.com/for-members/constitution

Teacher Unions for Climate Justice

BY BILL BIGELOW

As the climate crisis announces itself with greater ferocity, it has become more urgent for teachers to reflect on our responsibility to act—in our classrooms, in our communities, and in our unions. *Our* unions. The organizations that teachers own. The organizations where we can articulate the kind of workplaces we deserve, the kind of education our students deserve, and where organizing for a stable climate can support our struggle for an economic justice agenda. No doubt, we are still in the early stages of these efforts.

In Portland, Oregon, where I taught for almost 30 years and was a longtime teacher union activist, members of the Portland Association of Teachers (PAT), along with retired teachers, students, parents, and activists with the local affiliate of 350.org, met through the winter of 2015–16 to draft a comprehensive climate justice education policy for the school district.

When we introduced it at a school board meeting in May 2016, the teacher union was one of more than 30 organizations to endorse it. The resolution called for increased professional development, more curriculum devoted to climate justice, abandoning textbooks that lie about the causes of the crisis and its severity, encouraging student climate activism, establishing a vision for career education that would create training opportunities for "living wage jobs in the just transition away from fossil fuels," and making sure that school buildings themselves teach lessons in environmental responsibility. The school board, seven members elected citywide, passed the resolution unanimously. (That summer, the Representative Assembly of the National Education Association, meeting in Washington, D.C., called for NEA state and local affiliates to use the Portland resolution as a model to draft their own climate justice resolutions.)

Since 2016, the teacher union in Portland and others around the country and in Canada have offered glimpses of how unions can work for climate justice. This is still a work in progress, but with a ticking climate time bomb, teacher unions need to become more audacious in their advocacy.

It may be obvious, but a discovery we've made in Portland is that the more students study about the causes and consequences of the climate crisis, the more they want to take action. Curriculum matters. And our unions can play a key role in seeding exemplary classroom practice. In cooperation with the Portland Public Schools Climate Justice Committee, PAT has sponsored full-day and after-school "Teach Climate Justice" workshops.

One of the most powerful of these was with the Marshall Islands activist/poet Kathy Jetñil-Kijiner, who in the fall of 2016 spoke to more than 80 teachers and community members at the PAT office in Portland, and performed spoken word poems like "Dear Matafele Peinam," "History Project," and "Tell Them," which concludes:

> tell them about the water
> how we have seen it rising
> flooding across our cemeteries
> gushing over the sea walls
> and crashing against our homes
> tell them what it's like
> to see the entire ocean__level___with the land
> tell them
> we are afraid
> tell them we don't know
> of the politics
> or the science
> but tell them we see
> what is in our own backyard
> tell them that some of us
> are old fishermen who believe that God
> made us a promise
> some of us
> are more skeptical of God
> but most importantly tell them
> we don't want to leave
> we've never wanted to leave
> and that we
> are nothing without our islands.

A key piece of Portland's climate justice resolution is the centering of voices of people from frontline communities, those hit first and hardest by the climate crisis, and finding ways to expose our students to these perspectives. On a stormy fall afternoon, sitting in the packed basement of the union offices, with teachers and community members brainstorming ways to engage students with Kathy Jetñil-Kijiner's poems, I glimpsed how our unions can play a leadership role in nurturing climate justice curriculum.

PAT has continued to offer a home for our "Teach Climate Justice" afternoons, where teachers demonstrate exemplary lessons, launch curriculum work groups, watch student-friendly films to discuss teaching strategies, and find other teachers of conscience to collaborate with on this crucial work.

But the union has also been an ally of climate justice work when the school district has dragged its feet. For example, in the days leading up to the Sept. 20, 2019, global strike for the climate, our Portland Public Schools Climate Justice Committee had secured the school district's promise that student participation in the strike would be considered an excused absence, and the district office sent a forceful memo to all building administrators announcing this policy. The district also sent home an excellent letter to all parents in our 50,000-student-strong school system, indicating that climate justice is a part of the "core curriculum," and citing the school board's 2016 resolution. But strangely, the district delayed and delayed sending a letter to its own teachers announcing its position and offering teaching resources on the climate crisis. So the union did it instead—sending our letter out through its own distribution channels, announcing that: "September 20 is a day when PPS students can stand in solidarity with global youth and see themselves as activists and leaders for the planet, channeling anger and fear into hope and action," and linking to a host of teaching materials, including the Zinn Education Project's Teach Climate Justice site.

> It may be obvious, but a discovery we've made in Portland is that the more students study about the causes and consequences of the climate crisis, the more they want to take action.

Other unions have been similarly full-throated in support of student activism. In the lead-up to the September strike, Teri Mooring, president of the British Columbia Teachers' Federation, expressed "enthusiastic support for the School Strike for Climate movement and the climate strikes on the worldwide days of action," and urged boards of education to make participation an excused absence and to support teachers planning to take students to the demonstrations. Mooring wrote: "Youth in Canada and around the world are deeply alarmed by our political leaders' limited efforts to address the climate emergency. The BCTF wholeheartedly support the efforts of youth to have their voices heard on this critical issue."

Merrie Najimy, president of the Massachusetts Teachers Association (MTA), organized a statewide conference call to discuss ways the union could support the student walkout: "Our legal department wrote an advisory where the gist was to say you have this right to participate, and as an organizer you can push your principal, your superintendent, to make this a field trip day."

The Green New Deal

In our summer 2019 editorial, "The Green New Deal and Our Schools," *Rethinking Schools* editors urged teacher unions to aggressively promote the Green New Deal, launched in the streets by groups like the Sunrise Movement and in Congress by Rep. Alexandria Ocasio-Cortez and Sen. Edward Markey. The Green New Deal would commit the United States to a rapid "just transition" from a fossil fuel-based economy to clean and renewable energy, cutting carbon emissions by 50 percent by 2030, and becoming net zero by 2050.

First, our unions need to educate members about the Green New Deal and initiate conversations about what it could mean in their school district and how it can be supported politically. They can insist that politicians seeking union endorsement announce their support for the Green New Deal, for climate justice education, and refuse to accept fossil fuel contributions. Unions can join with other unions to articulate and work for a Green New Deal social vision—one that also includes schools.

In *In These Times*, Rachel M. Cohen describes some early efforts to get teacher unions to push beyond their traditional arenas of activism. Kurt Ostrow, an English teacher in Fall River, Massachusetts, an MTA board member, and a member of the Sunrise Movement, successfully introduced a resolution putting the MTA on record favoring a teacher strike to support the Green New Deal. Ostrow suggested that one tactic might be taking collective sick days. "If you can take off to take care of your kids, well the fact is Mother Earth is sick," he told Cohen.

In March 2019, shortly after the Green New Deal was introduced in Congress, the 120,000-member California Federation of Teachers passed a wonderful, farsighted resolution in support of the Green New Deal, to "address the two great issues of our age—historic economic inequality and climate change," building off an earlier 2016 resolution on climate justice. The comprehensive resolution calls for educating students about climate change, economic inequality, and potential solutions such as the Green New Deal; infrastructure development to respond to climate-related changes like rising sea levels; expansion of clean energy industries, with high wages and collective bargaining agreements; new apprenticeship programs; prioritizing projects in working-class and low-income communities, and communities of color that have been disproportionately affected by environmental and economic crisis; equitable "just transition" measures for workers who might be hurt in the short term by a new carbon-free economy; and greatly increased taxation on the wealthy, including a wealth tax, to pay for Green New Deal measures.

> "What good is it to negotiate the assignment of overtime when the sky is on fire?"

The California Federation of Teachers resolution launches exactly the kind of conversation that teacher unionists need to be engaged in right now: How can we simultaneously work to address the climate crisis and the crisis of economic inequality? How can our work in schools and classrooms contribute to this project of radical social transformation? What kind of alliances do we need to nurture with other unions, community organizations, and historically marginalized communities to fulfill the promise of the Green New Deal?

Bargaining for the Common Good

"What good is it to negotiate the assignment of overtime when the sky is on fire?" Nato Green asks in "Why Unions Must Bargain Over Climate Change," in *In These Times*. As teacher unions join the broader movement to "bargain for the common good," we need to ask what exactly that looks like with respect to confronting the climate crisis and using collective bargaining as a way to effect some of the vision articulated in the Green New Deal.

> Now is the time when we must dare to "dream big, out loud, in public, together."

Matt Reed, a social studies and American Sign Language teacher at Portland's Lincoln High School and activist with PAT, took the teacher contract and began to imagine ways that a new contract might promote a web of climate justice goals:

- Dedicated professional leave time to collaboratively create climate justice curriculum with colleagues.
- Increased professional development trainings to learn more about the climate crisis and climate justice and ways we can apply it within our own classrooms.
- District-sponsored and district-supported student climate justice summits in order to deepen and facilitate more equitable student participation and engagement.
- District partnership with local, national, and international organizations that support climate justice education, with particular focus on frontline communities most impacted by the climate crisis, to support student and educator curriculum.
- The creation of a commission of students, educators, community leaders, and the district charged with identifying and recommending ways the district can reduce carbon emissions.
- Ensuring that future district construction and facilities upgrades are at least carbon neutral.
- Ensuring health and safety of students and staff as climate-related weather and natural disaster risks increase.

Looking toward upcoming contract negotiations, Reed went through his union-school district contract with a fine-tooth comb, finding specific articles and sections where alternative climate-forward language could be inserted. As Reed told me, "Too often, contract bargaining starts from the question of 'What can we win in our next contract to make work better?'—avoiding broader social justice questions like 'What do we want to see changed in our society and world?' By focusing on what seems winnable in the short term, workers accept the prevailing political, economic, and social thinking that got us into the climate/inequality crisis in the first place." Reed is working with other teacher unionists to begin to turn the aspirations of the climate justice movement into the legal documents that govern our work lives.

*   *   *

As Naomi Klein writes in her foreword to *A Planet to Win: Why We Need a Green New Deal*, now is the time when we must dare to "dream big, out loud, in public, together." We are in the early stages of this work. Thanks to the lies of the fossil fuel companies and their propagandists like the Heartland Institute, who distributed tens of thousands of misleading climate change textbooks to elementary and high school teachers, we still have school curricula that sow doubt about the causes and severity of climate change. But things are changing quickly. Despite schools' late arrival to climate reality, today's climate strikes are filling streets across the country, and around the world, with young people demanding the right to a future.

Teacher unions need to be in the thick of this struggle for a new world. ▪

Bill Bigelow taught high school social studies for 30 years. He is an editor of Rethinking Schools, co-editor of A People's Curriculum for the Earth *(Rethinking Schools, 2014), and co-director of the Zinn Education Project.*

For a comprehensive list of books, lessons, films, and organizations, go to zinnedproject.org/campaigns/teach-climate-justice.

Books and Curricular Guides on the Labor Movement and Labor History

Editors' note: Look online for more in-depth summaries and reviews of these works. Many are listed at zinnedproject.org. Keep in mind that picture books can be appropriate for a wide range of students up through middle and high schools. Encourage education union members to use these books not only with students, but also with their own children and colleagues.

Picture Books, Nonfiction

Kids on Strike
By Susan Campbell Bartoletti
(HMH Books, 2003)
Describes the conditions and treatment that drove working children to strike, from the mill workers' strike in 1834 and the coal strikes at the turn of the 20th century to the children who marched with Mother Jones in 1903. Grades 4–8.

Kid Blink Beats the World
By Don Brown
(Roaring Brook Press, 2004)
The story of an 1899 strike by the children who sold newspapers on the street. Grades K–4.

Side by Side/Lado a lado
By Monica Brown; translated by Carolina Valencia; illustrated by Joe Cepeda
(HarperCollins Español, bilingual edition, 2010)
The life stories and activism of Dolores Huerta and Cesar Chavez, the two founders of the United Farm Workers (UFW), written and illustrated for young children.

Strike: The Bitter Struggle of American Workers from Colonial Times to the Present
By Penny Colman
(Millbrook Press, 1996)
An oversized book with illustrations summarizing U.S. labor history. Good for upper elementary and middle and high school.

Which Side Are You On? The Story of a Song
By George Ella Lyon; artwork by Christopher Cardinale
(Cinco Puntos Press, 2011)
Tells the story of the classic union song of 1931 and the harsh conditions under which it was written. Grades 4 and up.

Brave Girl: Clara and the Shirtwaist Makers' Strike of 1909
By Michelle Markel; illustrated by Melissa Sweet
(HarperCollins, 2016)
The struggle of early 20th-century female garment workers is brought to life in this biography of labor leader Clara Lemlich, who successfully instigated a citywide strike that led to a life of union activism.

That's Not Fair! Emma Tenayuca's Struggle for Justice/¡No Es Justo! La lucha de Emma Tenayuca por la justicia
By Carmen Tafolla and Sharyll Teneyuca; illustrated by Terry Ybáñez
(Wings Press, 2008)
Bilingual (Spanish and English) biography of labor activist Emma Tenayuca. Grades K–2.

Picture Books, Fiction

Joelito's Big Decision/La Gran Decisión de Joelito
By Ann Berlak; illustrated by Daniel Camacho
(Hard Ball Press, 2015)
Joelito, a 4th grader, faces a big decision when he and his family go to a fast-food restaurant and see a labor action by workers, including members of his friend's family. One of the few children's books that deals so directly with the struggle of low-wage workers. Grades 2–5.

¡Sí, Se Puede! Yes, We Can! Janitor Strike in L.A.
By Diana Cohn; illustrated by Francisco Delgado
(Cinco Puntos Press, bilingual edition, 2005)
A children's book based on the true story of the Justice for Janitors strike. Grades K–2.

Click, Clack, Moo: Cows That Type
By Doreen Cronin; illustrated by Betsy Lewin
(Atheneum Books, 2000)
A barnyard struggle where the cows go on strike and the farmer is forced to negotiate. Available in Spanish as Clic, Clac, Muu: Vacas escritoras. Grades preschool–3.

Memphis, Martin, and the Mountaintop: The Sanitation Strike of 1968
By Alice Faye Duncan; illustrated by R. Gregory Christie
(Calkins Creek, 2018)
A fiction picture book that presents the story of 9-year-old Lorraine Jackson, who in 1968 witnessed the Memphis sanitation strike. Grades 4–7.

The Bobbin Girl
By Emily Arnold McCully
(Dial Books, 1996)
Historical fiction based on a true story about the Lowell textile workers. Grades 2–5.

The Carpet Boy's Gift
By Pegi Deitz Shea; illustrated by Leane Morin
(Tilbury House Publishers, 2003)
This fictional story honors the legacy of Iqbal Masih, who escaped from bonded labor to become an international leader against child labor. Excellent read aloud for elementary and middle school students.

Chapter Books/Young Adult Fiction (Upper Elementary Through Middle School)

Iqbal
By Francesco D'Adamo
(Aladdin, 2005)
A fictionalized account of a Pakistani child who escaped from bondage in a carpet factory and went on to help liberate other children like him.

Fire in the Hole!
By Mary Cronk Farrell
(Clarion Books, 2004)
Based on the true story of a silver miners' strike in Coeur d'Alene, Idaho, the book shows the desperate conditions of miners' lives and how the striking miners were detained illegally in a late 19th-century version of Guantanamo.

Lyddie
By Katherine Paterson
(Puffin Modern Classics, 2004)
When Lyddie and her younger brother are hired out as servants to help pay off their family farm's debts, Lyddie is determined to find a way to reunite her family once again. Hearing about all the money a girl can make working in the textile mills in Lowell, Massachusetts, she makes her way there, only to find that her dreams of returning home may never come true.

Bread and Roses, Too
By Katherine Paterson
(Clarion Books, 2006)
Moving young adult historical fiction novel based on a major strike in Lawrence, Massachusetts, in 1912.

Missing from Haymarket Square
By Harriette Gillem Robinet
(Atheneum, 2001)
Dinah, a 12-year-old African American girl, works long hours in a factory while her father helps organize workers in the midst of the famous Haymarket labor struggle and massacre in Chicago. A good book for introducing young readers to issues of race, immigration, labor, and the strategies used to oppress and divide workers and their resistance.

Dragon's Gate
By Laurence Yep
(HarperCollins, 1995)
The story of a teenage boy who migrates to the United States following the U.S. Civil War to work on the transcontinental railroad. A spellbinding story that weaves in issues of racism and class struggle, culminating in a massive strike by Chinese workers.

Middle/High School/College/Adult
Nonfiction

"They're Bankrupting Us!" And 20 Other Myths About Unions
By Bill Fletcher Jr.
(Beacon Press, 2012)
Fletcher takes on some of the most common contemporary myths about organized labor. This book is ideal for use in member education programs for unions and in high school civics and social studies classes.

A History of America in Ten Strikes
By Erik Loomis
(The New Press, 2018)
"A brilliantly recounted American history through the prism of major labor struggles, with critically important lessons for those who seek a better future for working people and the world." —Noam Chomsky

Journey for Justice: The Life of Larry Itliong
By Dawn Mabalon and Gayle Romasanta; illustrated by Andre Sibayan
(Bridge and Delta Publishing, 2018)
An engaging story of a Filipino labor leader and co-founder of the United Farm Workers, one of the most significant American social movements of its time. Readers will learn of the key role Filipinos played in the farmworkers' movement.

Bread & Roses: The Struggle of American Labor, 1865–1915
By Milton Meltzer
(Replica Books, 2001)
Original documents with overview for high school students. Key primary sources.

Household Workers Unite: The Untold Story of African American Women Who Built a Movement
By Premilla Nadasen
(Beacon Press, 2015)
Through stories of African American domestic workers, this book resurrects a little-known history of domestic worker activism from the 1950s to the 1970s, offering new perspectives on race, labor, feminism, and organizing.

Big Annie of Calumet: A True Story of the Industrial Revolution
By Jerry Stanley
(Crown Publishers, 1996)
This oversize book tells the true story of an amazing woman unionist, most famous for her support of the 1913 copper workers' strike in Calumet, in Michigan's Upper Peninsula. Great photos. Can be used with Woody Guthrie's song "1913 Massacre."

Why Unions Matter
By Michael Yates
(Monthly Review, 2009)
A clear introductory book about why unions are important, their weaknesses and potential, and their connections to the broader progressive political movements.

A People's History of the United States
By Howard Zinn
(Harper Perennial Modern Classics, 2005)
The best single-volume history of the United States. A must for any teacher of social studies of any kind. *A Young People's History of the United States* is appropriate for upper elementary through high school.

Labor Films with a Conscience

For a listing and reviews of powerful films about labor struggles, go to zinnedproject. org/materials/films-with-a-conscience/#labor

Golden Lands, Working Hands video and supplemental materials
By the California Federation of Teachers
This powerful 10-part video series brings the hidden history of California working people to light.

Teaching Guides

A People's History for the Classroom
By Bill Bigelow
(Rethinking Schools, 2008)
Multiple engaging teaching activities that correspond to several of the chapters in Howard Zinn's *A People's History of the United States*. (Published in cooperation with the Zinn Education Project.)

The Power in Our Hands: A Curriculum on the History of Work and Workers in the United States
By Bill Bigelow and Norm Diamond
(Monthly Review Press, 1988)
Role plays and writing activities project high school students into real-life situations to explore the history and contemporary reality of employment (and unemployment) in the U.S.

Rethinking Globalization: Teaching for Justice in an Unjust World
By Bill Bigelow and Bob Peterson, editors
(Rethinking Schools, 2002)
An extensive collection of readings and source material on critical global issues, plus teaching ideas, lesson plans, and rich collections of resources for classroom teachers. Issues of sweatshops, child labor, organizing, and much more are covered.

Labor Matters Teaching Activity
By Teaching Tolerance
Introduces students to the role of the labor movement in securing contemporary benefits such as the 40-hour workweek, the minimum wage, and workplace safety regulations. For information, see zinnedproject.org/materials/labor-matters.

On the Banks of Deer Creek
A play by 5th graders from La Escuela Fratney in Milwaukee Public Schools, about the 1886 general strike in Milwaukee for the eight-hour day. Script and teaching materials available at rethinkingschools.org/TUSJ. Video available at bit.ly/2J7K7o6.

Labor and Climate Justice Education Committee of the California Federation of Teachers
cft.org/curricula
The committee has a variety of labor education publications, including *The Yummy Pizza Company*, a role play on work and unions for elementary school children, a comic book on farmworkers, a booklet on the history of the labor movement, and their video *Golden Lands, Working Hands* (see above) on labor history in California. Many of their items are available free as PDFs. Several publications are available in Spanish and one in Chinese.

Zinn Education Project
zinnedproject.org
The Zinn Education Project offers a wide variety of teaching activities for free, including several role plays on important conflicts in labor history. The Zinn Education Project is coordinated by Rethinking Schools and Teaching for Change, and many of the activities were originally published in the *Rethinking Schools* magazine.

For additional books on teacher unions and social justice unionism, see p. 428.

A NURSE IN EVERY SCHOOL EVERY DAY!

FOR THE SCHOOL STUDENTS DES

CHICAGO PUBLIC

ON STRIKE for MY STUDENTS

STOP STARVING OUR SCHOOLS

ON STRIKE MY STUDENTS

ON STRIKE

A NURSE EVERY SCHOOL EVERY DAY

STOP STARVING OUR SCHOOLS

LOCAL 73 SEIU

CHICAGO TEACHERS UNION · ORGANIZE · UNITE · EST. 1937 · DEFEND · AFT LOCAL 1 ·

SOL

SECTION SEVEN

RESOURCES

ADOLFO VALLE

The Schools All Our Children Deserve: The Principles That Unite Us

BY THE ALLIANCE TO RECLAIM OUR SCHOOLS

The Alliance to Reclaim Our Schools was founded in 2014 as a national labor-community coalition fighting to strengthen public education. In a yearlong process that engaged individual parent, educator, and community members, the alliance developed the "Principles That Unite Us" to guide the coalition's work.

We are parents and caregivers, students and community members. We are educators and school staff.

We have come together around a common commitment to public education. We believe that the only way to give every child the opportunity to pursue a rich and productive life, both individually and as a member of society, is through a system of publicly funded, equitable, and democratically controlled public schools.

We have not reached this goal as a nation—particularly for poor children and communities of color.

We are not satisfied with an institution that finds the resources to provide some students with the most experienced and well-trained teachers, advanced technologies, expansive course options, and state-of-the-art facilities, while other students languish in substandard buildings and are taught in overcrowded classrooms by teachers lacking the basic supports they need to do their jobs.

We are not satisfied, but we believe in strengthening, not dismantling, public education in the face of these challenges.

The divide between rich and poor in the United States is vast and growing. Millions of children grow up in oppressive poverty while the super-rich advocate for policies that increase *their* wealth at others' expense. For the past 20 years, we have watched as corporate interests attempt to dismantle public education and create a new, market-based system of schooling. Their strategies include ever-expanding regimes of high-stakes tests, attacks on the collective bargaining rights of educators, and aggressive school closures that pave the way for privately managed schools. The first targets for this approach have been African American and immigrant communities. Yet despite dismal educational results, those advocating a corporate agenda are now also targeting rural and suburban school districts with their disruptive interventions.

They insist that poverty doesn't matter, as if hunger, unemployment, substandard housing, and epidemic violence have no impact on young bodies and minds. In our work in schools and communities, we confront these shameful challenges daily. Meanwhile, some of those who claim to be "saving" public education by tearing it down also oppose healthcare reform and increases in the minimum wage. Deep-pocketed entrepreneurs who created the home mortgage crisis and advocacy groups that support barriers to voting are interested in public education, not because they understand and want to nurture young minds. Their interests are their own.

Our interest is in public schools that serve *all* children. We need schools that are rooted in communities, that provide a rich and equitable academic experience, and that model democratic practices. We want schools where those closest to the classroom share in decision-making and policymaking at all levels. We need schools where students feel safe, nurtured, and empowered to become productive adults—schools that provide an alternative to the prison pipeline that too many of our children are caught in. We believe that the only way to achieve these schools is by *strengthening* the institution of public education. We are not there yet, but we can imagine no other path.

We are parents, students, and educators who have come together to fight for our schools. No longer will we allow ourselves to be divided. Now, more than ever, access to good public schools is a critical civil and human right. We are committed to working together to reclaim the promise of public education as our nation's gateway to democracy and racial and economic justice.

The Principles That Unite Us
Public schools are public institutions. Our school districts should be providing *all* children with the opportunity to attend a quality public school in their community. The corporate model of school reform seeks to turn public schools over to private managers and encourages *competition*—as opposed to *collaboration*—between schools and teachers. These strategies take away the public's right to have a voice in their schools, and inherently create winners and losers among both schools and students. Our most vulnerable children become collateral damage in these reforms. We will not accept that.

- A public school system serves all students—those with special needs or disabilities, English language learners, homeless kids, and troubled children. Creating schools that keep or push these students out in the name of efficiency or higher achievement for a few is not education reform but a return to segregation and inequality.
- We oppose the creation of charter schools for the purpose of privatization. Charter schools can serve as incubators of innovation, but they must be fully accountable to the public, part of a unified educational system, and regulated and funded for equity and accessibility.
- School closures have become a strategy to transfer students from

public to privately operated schools. No research has shown that the switch from public to private management of schools improves student learning.

- Public education should not be a source of profit.

Our voices matter. Those closest to the education process—teachers, administrators, school staff, students, and their parents and communities—must have a voice in education policy and practice. Our schools and districts should be guided by *them*, not by corporate executives, entrepreneurs, or philanthropists. Top-down interventions rarely address the real needs of schools or students.

- We oppose mayoral control and state takeovers of our school districts. Experience has taught us that these takeovers, usually justified with words like "urgent" and "crisis," too often simply spell the end of democratic ownership of our schools.
- Our districts and our schools should be governed with multiple structures for genuine input and decision-making by parents, educators, and students.
- We reject disingenuous strategies—like "parent trigger" laws and community hearings offered only after decisions have been made by others—that put profits before students and alienate communities from their neighborhood schools.

Strong public schools create strong communities. Schools are community institutions as well as centers of learning. While education alone cannot eradicate poverty, schools can help to coordinate the supports and services their students and families need to thrive. Corporate reform strategies ignore the challenges that students bring with them to school each day, and view schools as separate and autonomous from the communities in which they sit.

- "Community Schools" that provide supports and services for students and their families, such as basic health care and dental care, mentoring programs, English language classes, and more, help strengthen whole communities as well as individual students.
- Expanded learning time can offer students additional opportunities for academic and social enrichment and offer teachers additional time to collaborate and plan. It should always be implemented as part of whole-school reform, and with all stakeholders at the table.
- We support high-quality early childhood programs that nurture learning and social development. These programs have been shown to improve student outcomes.
- School closures should be a last resort. Closing a school harms both students and the surrounding neighborhood. Closing schools is not an education strategy and should not be used as such.

Assessments should be used to improve instruction. Assessments are critical tools to guide teachers in improving their lesson plans and framing their instruction to meet the needs of individual students. We support accountability. But standardized assessments are *misused* when teachers are fired, schools are closed, and students are penalized based on a single set of scores. Excessive high-stakes testing takes away valuable instructional time and narrows the curriculum—with the greatest impact on our most vulnerable students.

- All children deserve a well-rounded and rich educational experience, with a culturally relevant and comprehensive curriculum that includes the arts, world languages, the sciences, social studies, and physical education.
- Excessive testing has narrowed the content and skills our students are taught. In some districts, students lose a full month or more of instructional time due to preparing for and taking tests. We must end excessive testing and teaching to the test and focus instead on a rich and rigorous curriculum that keeps our children engaged in school and helps them succeed in college, careers, and civil society.
- Teachers need to have the training, the time, and the tools to evaluate their students' progress through multiple measures. Appropriate student assessment information includes documentation and evaluation of ongoing work, observations, and discussions with students themselves.
- Assessments used for public reporting and accountability should include these multiple types of assessment information, gathered over time and reflecting clear standards and learning goals.
- Assessments must be administered and reported in a timely manner, and both students and teachers should have access to individualized results so that the assessments can inform and guide instruction.
- No single exam should be used as a stand-alone hurdle to determine classroom funding or a student's course placement, grade promotion, or eligibility to graduate.
- Assessment results alone should not be used to rate and rank teachers, administrators, or schools, or be linked to financial rewards, bonuses, or penalties.

Quality teaching must be delivered by committed, respected, and supported educators. Today's corporate reformers have launched a war on teachers. We believe that teachers should be honored. Teaching is a career, not a temporary stop on the way to one. Our teachers should be well trained and supported. They should be given the opportunity to assume leadership roles in their schools. Highly qualified teachers and school staff are our schools' greatest assets. Let's treat them that way.

- Teacher preparation should be comprehensive and include significant student-teaching time in the classroom under the supervision of a highly skilled and experienced educator.
- Districts must address disparities in the distribution of experienced teachers. All of our students deserve access to high-quality teaching, as well as a teaching staff that reflects their cultures.
- Alternative teacher credentialing programs should not be targeted exclusively at low-income schools or our most vulnerable students.
- Professional development should be school-based and tailored to the individual needs of the teachers and school staff in the building. It should include opportunities for teachers and community partners and parents to work and learn together to strengthen the quality of student academic experiences.
- Collective bargaining must be defended to ensure that educators feel free to advocate for their students and for fair working conditions and compensation.
- Class size matters. Particularly in the most struggling schools, class size must be kept low enough that teachers are able to differentiate their instruction and provide individualized support to their students.

Schools must be welcoming and respectful places for all. Schools should be welcoming and inclusive. Students, parents, educators, and community residents should feel that their cultures and contributions are respected and valued. Schools that push out the most vulnerable students and treat parents as intruders cannot succeed in creating a strong learning environment. Respectful schools are better places to both work and learn.

- School offices should be accessible to families whose primary language is one other than English. School enrollment forms and other materials should be available in languages that are significantly represented in the community.
- All schools should strive to provide the services and support needed by students to succeed in a diverse classroom. Practices that deny services to students with disabilities or high needs, or that segregate or disproportionately punish or push out these students, have no place in our public schools.
- Respect between administration and staff is a crucial component of a strong and healthy school climate.
- Respect for students includes elimination of zero-tolerance and other policies that push students out of school. Students should play a role in creating and enforcing discipline policies that are grounded in restorative practices.
- As workplaces, schools must be safe and secure, as well as resourced for the purposes of teaching and learning.

Our schools must be fully funded for success and equity. More than 50 years ago, in *Brown v. Board of Education*, the U.S. Supreme Court acknowledged that African American students were being denied their constitutional right to an integrated and equitable public education. We have not come far enough.

Today our schools remain segregated and unequal. When we shortchange some students, we shortchange our nation as a whole. It is time to fund public schools for success and equity, for we are destined to hand off the future of our nation to all our young people.

- We must end the practice of funding our schools based on local property wealth. Only when we take responsibility for *all* our schools, and *all* our children, will schools succeed for *all* our society.
- School and district budgets should be developed through a transparent and democratic process that is guided by a commitment to equity.
- Corporations, Wall Street, and the wealthy must pay their fair share of taxes at the local, state, and national levels so that our schools have the resources they need to succeed. Wealthy corporations and individuals should not be allowed to "privatize" their contributions to public education through the use of tax write-offs or credits in lieu of payments that support all schools.
- Education funding should reflect the real costs of supporting and nurturing our young people, rather than budgetary convenience or economic circumstances. The devastating state and local budget cuts to our schools must stop. If we can find the money to support new stadiums and offer tax breaks to the wealthy, we can find the money to educate our children.

A Call to Action. Our schools belong to all of us: the students who learn in them, the parents who support them, the educators and staff who work in them, and the communities that they anchor. No longer will we allow ourselves to be divided. We have developed these principles and are committed to working together to achieve the policies and practices that they represent. Corporate-style interventions that disregard our voices and attempt to impose a system of winners and losers must end. None of our children deserve to be collateral damage.

We call on our communities, and commit the power of the organizations that we represent, to pursue these principles in our schools, districts, and states. Together, we will work nationally to make this vision of public education a reality.

Reclaimourschools.org

Building Racial Equity Teams

An excerpt from the 2019 Seattle Education Association Contract with Certificated Non-Supervisory Employees

See Drew Dillhunt's article (p. 129) on Seattle's work to develop a series of supports to strengthen professional growth. One component was the establishment of Racial Equity Teams at every school.

Collective Bargaining Agreement Between Seattle Public Schools and Seattle Education Association Certificated Non-Supervisory Employees 2019–2022

ARTICLE II: PARTNERSHIP FOR ENSURING EDUCATIONAL AND RACIAL EQUITY

   . . . 6. Building Racial Equity Teams/Program Racial Equity Teams

   a. Vision Statement: The commitment to institutionalizing racial equity is essential for the success of all learning communities; therefore, all committees must commit to make racial equity the core of their charge. This commitment requires the understanding and utilization of racial equity analysis tools, materials, and resources to support convening, planning, and action.

   We must ensure that all work is focused on implementing School Board Policy No. 0030 – Ensuring Educational and Racial Equity. . . .

   SEA and SPS will co-lead and implement the following:

   1) Racial Equity Literacy trainings for school sites and teams.

   2) The district will convene all Racial Equity Teams at least twice per school year for training and collaboration on a regional or districtwide basis. The Partnership Committee will oversee the planning of these meetings. in conjunction with the SPS (Seattle Public Schools) Department of Racial Equity Advancement and SEA (Seattle Education Association) Center for Racial Equity.

   3) The district will provide five trainings for the induction phase of newly established teams. SEA Center for Racial Equity and SPS Department of Racial Equity Advancement will jointly plan these trainings.

b. For purposes of eliminating disproportionate discipline; promoting stronger relationships between schools, their staff, parents, and students; and supporting student learning and the closing of achievement and opportunity gaps, each building and program that is selected by the Partnership Committee will establish its own Racial Equity Team (RET) that meets a minimum of once per month.

c. The Racial Equity Team will consist of at least:

1) A building administrator/program supervisor, and
2) At least four (4) SEA-represented staff. One of the four (4) seats will be designated for classified SEA-represented staff. Schools are encouraged to include staff members from Special Education and English Language Learning Departments. If the team exceeds seven (7) SEA members, representation of classified staff should at a minimum be two, ideally one Paraprofessional and one SAEOP (Seattle Association of Education Office Professionals).

Because one of the shared beliefs is that those impacted by recommendations must be given an opportunity to be involved, the parties recognize that extra effort may be required to provide opportunity for representatives of the paraprofessional and office professional staff to participate in the work of the Racial Equity Team. Buildings/programs will examine the possibilities of altered workweek scheduling, shared office coverage, limited use of voicemail coverage, and other strategies that encourage and enable the participation on behalf of paraprofessional and office staff representatives.

Certificated and classified staff will be paid equal shares of the Racial Equity Team stipend. Classified staff will submit a time sheet for hours equivalent to their share of the stipend.

3) The Building Leadership Team (BLT) team may also appoint a parent and/or student representative with consent of the Racial Equity Team. Other staff members may also be invited to participate in the Racial Equity Team meetings in a non-voting capacity. To the extent possible, the Racial Equity Team will reflect the racial and ethnic diversity of the school/program staff and school community.

d. Building/Program Racial Equity Teams are chaired by a SEA-represented member or co-chaired by a SEA-represented member and a building administrator/program supervisor.

e. The work of the Racial Equity Team may be combined with other school or program committees.

f. The responsibilities of the Racial Equity Team are to:

1) Support the analysis of individual, institutional, and structural racism that is contributing to schoolwide disproportionality.

2) Review the district's recommendations on best practices and recommended initiatives.

3) Review school/program data on disproportionality in discipline and other areas.

4) Create and lead discussions on how to reduce disproportionality in educationally supportive ways.

5) Facilitate problem-solving around identified issues of disproportionality or inequity, especially pertaining to race.

6) Work with the BLT on the CSIP (Continuing School Improvement Plan), budget, and professional development plan to incorporate strategies to reduce disproportionality and inequity.

7) In collaboration with the BLT, facilitate a review of the CSIP as it pertains to Eliminating Opportunity Gap goals.

8) Participate in and coordinate with district-level efforts to address disproportionality and inequity.

9) BLT and RET will collaborate to review the CSIP, budget, professional development plan, and other whole school initiatives.

10) Program growth for RETs.

a. SEA and SPS commit to expanding Racial Equity Teams to all school sites and programs.

b. SPS will provide $260,000 for RET program growth.

c. Within the funding, DREA/CRE will determine the annual number of teams that can be supported based on their capacity, to include non-school-based programs.

d. Current and new teams in good standing will continue to be funded for the duration of the contract in order to sustain the investments of Board Policy No. 0030 – Ensuring Educational and Racial Equity . . .

seattlewea.org/file_viewer.php?id=27081

Teacher Home Visit Project

An excerpt from the 2017 St. Paul Association of Educators Contract

See Nick Faber's article (p. 138) about how the St. Paul Association of Educators won district support for Teacher Home Visits.

Agreement between the Saint Paul Board of Education and the Saint Paul Federation of Teachers

2017–2019
SAINT PAUL PUBLIC SCHOOLS Independent School District No. 625
TERMS AND CONDITIONS OF PROFESSIONAL EMPLOYMENT

ARTICLE 22. PARENT AND FAMILY ENGAGEMENT
SECTION 1. HOME VISIT PROJECT

Parent/Teacher Home Visits (PTHV) was developed by parents in Sacramento, California, where it has been successfully implemented since 1998 and brought to Saint Paul by SPFT in 2010. The goals of Parent/Teacher Home Visits are to build a stronger partnership between teachers and parents, to promote Saint Paul Public Schools, and to work with parents to eliminate racial predictability of student outcomes. Parent/Teacher Home Visits operates on a model where parents are seen as an asset to the educational process. By meeting parents in an area of their comfort, teachers have more success in working with them in partnership around academics.

Subd. 1. Teacher participation in Parent/Teacher Home Visits requires the following commitments:

1. Attendance at four-hour Parent/Teacher Home Visit training;
2. For the first year a teacher participates: completing at least one visit with a minimum of three families;
3. For all additional years a teacher participates: completing at least one visit with a minimum of eight families;
4. Attendance at fall and spring debrief session;
5. Document visits on project visit tracker;

6. An agreement to conduct visits that follow the model outlined in the training:

- voluntary for teachers and parents
- conducted in pairs
- not solely targeting a particular group of students
- relation-based, focused on the hopes and dreams of the family

7. The district shall meet with the project's local training/leadership team at the team's December and June meetings for the purpose of evaluation and leveraging home visiting work to promote common SPPS/SPFT parent engagement goals.

Subd. 2. Compensation. Teachers who participate in Parent/Teacher Home Visits shall be paid an additional $50 stipend for each home visit conducted by the teacher. Payment of the stipends shall be made after the fall and spring debrief sessions.

The total amount of payments shall not exceed $175,000 during each school year. In addition, no one teacher in grades pre-K–4 can earn in excess of $2,500 during each school year. No one teacher in grades 5–12 can earn in excess of $3,000 during each school year.

spfe28.org/wp-content/uploads/2019/11/F-C-Teacher-17-19-FINAL.pdf

Restorative Practice

An excerpt from the 2018 Boston Teachers Union Contract

CONTRACT EXCERPTS

The Boston Teachers Union won language regarding restorative practices in their contract. See Leigh Dingerson's article (p. 158) about the efforts underway to build restorative practices in Howard County, Maryland.

Boston Teachers Union 2018–2021 Contract Book

23. Restorative Practice

IN SY 2017–2018, the BPS will hire and maintain, after consultation with the BTU president or her designee, a districtwide Restorative Practice Coach in a BTU position that shall oversee Restorative Practice Implementation and support school-based coordinators in the district.

The coach will organize a minimum of 12 hours of compensated professional development for school-based Restorative Practice coordinators, in partnership with the BTU Restorative Practice Organizing Committee.

Alternatively, the 12 hours can be arranged into two all-day sessions, with release time provided. The coach shall work the regular teacher workday and work year plus 18 days, and shall be compensated in accordance with the BTU salary grid plus a differential of 10%. All compensation paid shall be retirement worthy.

In addition, the BTU and BPS shall collaboratively determine three schools to hire educators for the purpose of implementing Restorative Practices across the school. These positions may be either Community Field Coordinators or hybrid teacher roles, where teachers are released from classroom duties to coordinate Restorative Practices across the schools where they teach.

From the Boston Teachers Union 2018–2021 Contract Book. btu.org/wp-content/uploads/2020/01/Corrected-BTU-2018-2021-Contract-Book-Text.pdf

Pilot Program—Exemption from Administrative Searches

An excerpt from the 2019 United Teachers Los Angeles Contract

See Arlene Inouye's "Lessons from the Los Angeles Strike (p. 252) to learn about Students Deserve and their demand for an end to random searches.

Memorandum of Understanding Between United Teachers Los Angeles and Los Angeles Unified School District
Pilot Program—Exemption from Administrative Searches

Schools are faced with instances of violence, including the use of weapons on or adjacent to school campuses. The district strives to provide a safe environment for students to learn, explore, and create, and for teachers and administration to be able to focus on teaching and providing students with these opportunities. The district school safety measures include random metal detector searches, locker searches, and other measures under the settled principles of constitutional construction, which permits reasonable application of metal detectors in schools. Bulletin 5424.2 focuses on random searches, metal detector searches, and locker searches.

As part of the district's efforts to ensure an effective learning environment by maintaining a safe and secure campus, secondary schools are authorized to implement random metal detector searches. These are administrative searches. This policy does not include searches conducted by law enforcement.

For the 2019–20 school year, schools may apply to be exempt from administrative searches—i.e., "wanding"—for the length of the MOU and 14 schools will be selected. This application may be sent from the Local School Leadership Council or similar governance council to their Local District review by March 15, 2019. The Local District shall submit the applications to District Operations for final approval.

For the 2020–21 school year, schools may apply to be exempt from administrative searches—i.e., "wanding"—and 14 additional schools will be selected. This application may be sent from the Local School Leadership or School Site Council to District Operations for review by March 15, 2020. The Local District shall submit the applications to District Operations for final approval.

The city of Los Angeles and the district shall work together to add services such as the LA City Gang Reduction and Youth Development (GRYD) programming to schools participating in the proposed "wanding" pilot program as well as select schools with traditional random searches. It is not the intention of both parties to add additional police presence as part of the programming on campuses.

The district may terminate a school's participation in this MOU, if it determines it is necessary to do so to preserve the safety of the students and staff at that school(s). Prior to making a final decision, the district will provide notice to the school that it is considering terminating the school's participation in the MOU, including its concerns, and provide the school with the opportunity to respond to the district's concerns. The school will have five calendar days from receipt of the district's notice to respond. Once the school has responded or the five calendar day period has elapsed, the district will provide written notice of its final decision to the school.

This MOU will terminate on June 30, 2021.

From "2019—2022 Agreement Between Los Angeles Unified School District and United Teachers Los Angeles." utla.net/sites/default/files/2019-2022_utla-lausd_collective_bargaining_agreement.pdf

Structure Tests

From Jane McAlevey's *A Collective Bargain: Unions, Organizing, and the Fight for Democracy* (2020). Reprinted with permission from the author. (See Inouye, p. 252 and Schirmer, p. 227.)

UNIONWIDE STRUCTURE TEST	DATE	IMPLEMENTATION OF STRUCTURE TEST
Each of these was done by hand, face-to-face, across 900 schools. They were carried out by teacher leaders under the guidance of staff organizers. Each test helps the leadership understand where they are strong and where they are weak, which helps to prioritize their efforts.		
Regional rallies in the contract that had expired in 2011	November 2014	Used an "I'll be there" sign-up sheet in the weeks before these smaller regional rallies, as they planned their first big citywide rally set for early 2015. This was the contract the new leadership inherited: the people who lost the election had been negotiating it for more than three years.
Organizing for February 2016 Stand Up citywide rally for the 2011 contract	January 2015	Launched a campaign-commitment card with check boxes of what people were willing to do: school-site picketing, parent outreach, attend a downtown rally in February 2015, boycott faculty meetings, protest testing, and strike if necessary.
Stand Up rally at Grand Park, escalating to citywide	February 2015	15,000 union members attended, making it the largest action since the 1989 strike

The teachers win big, a 10 percent raise (the first raise in 10 years), finally settling the 2011 contract and demonstrating to members that the new methods of organizing work.

UNIONWIDE STRUCTURE TEST	DATE	IMPLEMENTATION OF STRUCTURE TEST
Launch I'll Vote Yes to Build the Future, Fund the Fight	Fall 2015	More than half of the members of the union signed a public petition saying they would vote yes to increase their dues, which they framed as Build the Future, Fund the Fight.
Membership-wide union election to allow the rank-and-file members to vote to increase dues	February 2016	A majority of members actually participate in the ballot, with 83 percent voting yes. Like most union elections, as with most American elections, traditionally only a minority vote. But UTLA was determined to have real union democracy, with an important question going to the members, and they achieved more than 50 percent turnout.
School site-based rallies for health insurance	Fall 2017	Health benefit negotiations took place parallel to the overall contract bargaining (with a coalition of LAUSD unions), because nonteachers and teachers alike negotiate insurance benefits at the same time.
All In launches and ratification of healthcare contract	February 2018	Because the union anticipated that the right wing would prevail in the *Janus* Supreme Court case, it planned ahead and had the entire membership sign new cards with language the court would stipulate.
4 Questions petition launch	April 2018	This petition asked members about their willingness to take four actions, indicated by hand checks on boxes and their signature.
All-In for Respect rally	May 2018	12,000 members turn out at Grand Park rally
Strike vote	August 2018	84 percent turn out and participate, 98 percent vote yes.
I Will Strike petition	Fall 2018	More than 75 percent sign.

Labor and Educational Justice Organizations

Advancement Project *advancementproject.org*
The Advancement Project works at both the national level and on the ground with community partners—including young people—to examine, expose, and reform practices that lead to the criminalization of students.

The Albert Shanker Institute *shankerinstitute.org*
The Albert Shanker Institute promotes discussions and sponsors research to explore innovative structures, services, and roles for unions as they work to meet the challenges of a changing economy and workforce.

ALEC Exposed *ALECexposed.org*
A website dedicated to exposing the American Legislative Exchange Council. Check out their page on school privatization.

The Alliance to Reclaim Our Schools (AROS) *reclaimourschools.org*
An alliance of parent, youth, community, and labor organizations that coordinates national strategies to strengthen public education. See their platform, "The Principles That Unite Us," on p. 409.

American Federation of Teachers (AFT) *aft.org*

Black Lives Matter at School *blacklivesmatteratschool.com*
The Black Lives Matter at School movement started as a day of action in Seattle during the fall of 2016, when thousands of educators in Seattle came to school on Oct. 19 wearing shirts that said "Black Lives Matter: We Stand Together." Today, Black Lives Matter at School is a national coalition organizing for racial justice in education.

Coalition of Labor Union Women *cluw.org*
Formed in 1974, the Coalition of Labor Union Women (CLUW) is America's only national organization for union women.

Dignity in Schools Campaign (DSC) *dignityinschools.org*
Dignity in Schools is a national coalition that challenges the systemic problem of pushout in our nation's schools and works to dismantle the school-to-prison pipeline. DSC builds power among parents, youth, organizers, advocates, and educators to transform their own communities; to support alternatives to a

culture of zero-tolerance, punishment, criminalization, and the dismantling of public schools; and to fight racism and all forms of oppression.

Education International (EI) *ei-ie.org*
EI is a global union federation that represents organizations of teachers and other education employees. It is the world's largest, most representative global, sectoral organization of unions, with more than 32.5 million trade union members in 384 organizations in 178 countries and territories. Check out their campaign against school privatization at unite4education.org.

Education Law Center (ELC) *edlawcenter.org*
The ELC serves as a leading voice for New Jersey's public school children and is one of the most effective advocates for equal educational opportunity and equitable school funding in the United States. See their national report card: "Is School Funding Fair?"

In the Public Interest *inthepublicinterest.org*
A research and policy center on privatization and responsible contracting, it has issued several reports on the dangers of school privatization. Subscribe to their e-newsletter "Cashing in on Kids."

Journey for Justice (J4J) *j4jalliance.com*
An alliance of grassroots community, youth, and parent-led organizations in 21 cities across the country, pushing back on school closings and racism in education and demanding community-driven alternatives to the privatization of public school systems.

Labor Notes *labornotes.org*
A media and organizing project that since 1979 has been the voice of union activists who want to put the movement back in the labor movement. It promotes organizing and social justice through its monthly magazine, website, books, conferences, and workshops. Subscribe to their monthly publication.

National Day Laborer Organizing Network *ndlon.org*
NDLON improves the lives of day laborers, migrants, and low-wage workers. It builds leadership and power among those facing injustice so they can challenge inequality and expand labor, civil, and political rights for all.

National Education Association (NEA) *nea.org*

The Network for Public Education (NPE) *networkforpubliceducation.org*
An advocacy group whose mission is to preserve, promote, improve, and strengthen public schools. Check out their NPE Toolkit: School Privatization Explained.

Opportunity to Learn Network (OTL) *schottfoundation.org/our-work/otl-network*
The OTL unites a nationwide coalition of Schott Foundation for Public Education grantees and allied organizations working to secure a high-quality public education for all students.

Public Funds Public Schools *pfps.org*
Public Funds Public Schools is a national campaign supported by the Southern Poverty Law Center, SPLC Action Fund, Education Law Center, and Munger, Tolles, & Olson LLP that strives to ensure that all public funds for education are used to maintain and support public schools.

Rethinking Schools *rethinkingschools.org*
A nonprofit publisher and advocacy organization dedicated to sustaining and strengthening public education through social justice teaching and education activism. Its magazine, books, and other resources promote equity and racial justice in the classroom and in school policy. Subscribe to their magazine.

United Caucuses of Rank and File Educators (U-CORE) *ucore.org*
A network of social justice educators and union activists working together to advance economic and racial justice and democracy, U-CORE works to transform unions at the local, state, and national levels into militant, democratic organizations capable of leading the fight against corporate control and for equitable, fully funded public schools.

Zinn Education Project *zinnedproject.org*
The Zinn Education Project promotes and supports the teaching of people's history in classrooms across the country, with a special emphasis on issues of class, race, gender, and other areas of oppression. At their website there are free teaching activities about labor struggles and other social movements. The Zinn Education Project is a joint project of Teaching for Change and Rethinking Schools.

Worth the Read

Books about teacher unions and social justice unionism

....

COMPILED BY BOB PETERSON

A Fight for the Soul of Public Education: The Story of the Chicago Teachers Strike
By Steven Ashby and Robert Bruno
(ILR Press, 2016)
An analysis of the contested terrain of educational "reform" in Chicago that was the context for the CTU's unprecedented 2012 strike.

Red State Revolt: The Teachers' Strike Wave and Working-Class Politics.
By Eric Blanc
(Verso 2019)
An in-depth analysis of the largest teacher strike wave in this century.

Secrets of a Successful Organizer
By Alexandra Bradbury, Mark Brenner, and Jane Slaughter
(Labor Notes, 2016)
An excellent organizers' handbook.

How to Jump-Start Your Union: Lessons from the Chicago Teachers
By Alexandra Bradbury, Mark Brenner, Jenny Brown, Jane Slaughter, and Samantha Winslow
(Labor Notes, 2014)
Lots to learn from the CTU, and reading this is one of the best ways to do it.

Strike Back: Using the Militant Tactics of Labor's Past to Reignite Public Sector Unionism Today
By Joe Burns
(Ig Publishing, 2014)
"A clear roadmap to what type of unionism it will take to get working people engaged with communities." —Karen Lewis, former CTU president.

55 Strong: Inside the West Virginia Teachers' Strike
By Elizabeth Catte, Emily Hilliard, and Jessica Salfia, editors.
(Belt Publishing, 2018)
Photos and writings by the educators who sparked the 2018 strike wave.

Solidarity Divided: The Crisis in Organized Labor and a New Path Toward Social Justice
By Bill Fletcher Jr., and Fernando Gapasin
(UC Press, 2019)
Using concrete examples, the authors argue that "class struggle and trade union struggle are not necessarily the same thing." They also maintain that "race and gender are not just grafted onto class divisions." They call for social justice unionism and describe what that would look like for the entire labor movement.

The Newark Teacher Strikes: Hopes on the Line
By Steve Golin
(Rutgers University Press, 2002)
Golin explores Newark teachers from World War II to the 1971 strike looking at educational reform and union democracy.

Beaten Down, Worked Up: The Past, Present, and Future of American Labor
By Steven Greenhouse
(Knopf, 2019)
Former *New York Times* labor reporter recounts the rise and fall of labor unions in the U.S. by describing pivotal episodes that built the union movement up through the #RedforEd teacher strikes.

United Mind Workers: Unions and Teaching in the Knowledge Society
By Charles Taylor Kerchner, Julia E. Koppich, and Joseph G. Weeres
(Jossey-Bass, 1997)
An in-depth explanation of professional unionism. Unfortunately, it makes no mention of racism or segregation.

"All Labor Has Dignity"
King, Martin Luther Jr.
(Beacon Press, 2012)
A moving collection of King's speeches, statements, and writings about the importance of labor and unions.

A Collective Bargain: Unions, Organizing, and the Fight for Democracy
By Jane McAlevey
(HarperCollins, 2020)
McAlevey argues that strong unions are the key to fighting the corporate takeover of our society, highlighting nurses in Pennsylvania, tech workers in Silicon Valley, and teachers in Los Angeles.

No Shortcuts: Organizing for Power in the New Gilded Age
By Jane McAlevey
(Oxford University Press, 2016)
McAlevey describes organizing in the context of nursing homes, a pork factory, and the Chicago Public Schools. Her lessons can be universally applied.

Blackboard Unions: The AFT & the NEA 1900–1980
By Marjorie Murphy
(Cornell University Press, 1992)
This single volume provides an overview of the long histories of the AFT and NEA

Uncivil Rights: Teachers, Unions, and Race in the Battle for School Equity
By Jonna Perillo
(University of Chicago Press, 2012)
Well-researched and clearly narrated account of the tensions between teacher unions and communities of color in New York City since the Great Depression.

Transforming Teacher Unions: Fighting for Better Schools and Social Justice
Edited by Bob Peterson and Michael Charney
(Rethinking Schools, 1999)
Articles and interviews on social justice teacher unionism, including a description of the failed merger attempt in the 1990s between the NEA and AFT.

Citizen Teacher: The Life and Leadership of Margaret Haley
By Kate Rousmaniere
(State University of New York Press, 2005)
The story of the amazing elementary school teacher and fighter who took on Chicago's corporate moguls as well as the male-dominated NEA leadership.

Teacher Strike! Public Education and the Making of a New American Political Order
By Jon Selton
(University of Illinois Press, 2017)
A provocative analysis of key teacher strikes in the 1960s and 1970s and how they opened the door to neoliberal attacks on urban school systems. The racial divide between unions and communities of color overshadows these strikes.

Reds at the Blackboard: Communism, Civil Rights, and the New York City Teachers Union
By Clarence Taylor
(Columbia University Press, 2011)
A detailed history of the remarkable work of the Teachers Union in New York City and the right-wing campaign to destroy it.

The Future of Our Schools: Teachers Unions and Social Justice
By Lois Weiner
(Haymarket Books, 2012)
 A clear analysis of neoliberal education "reforms" and the multiple ways teacher unions are fighting back.

For additional books about labor unions, including those that can be used to teach people of all ages about labor history, see p. 399

Meet the editors

Michael Charney taught social studies in the Cleveland Public Schools for more than 30 years. He served as vice president of the Cleveland Teachers Union, where he led efforts to motivate teachers and paraprofessionals to change their schools. He developed anti-racist initiatives, innovative strategies to engage parents and the community, and edited the CTU and the Ohio Federation of Teachers newspapers. He also organized students for racial cooperation during school desegregation, to show solidarity with the students in South Africa, and to develop and organize for a statewide Ohio Youth Agenda. He successfully worked with the leading education state lawmaker to reduce class size, oppose private school vouchers, and to obtain more state funding for low-income students. Contact him at MichaelCTU@aol.com.

Jesse Hagopian teaches ethnic studies and English language arts at Seattle's Garfield High School, and is a member of the Seattle Education Association and of the social justice caucus Social Equity Educators (SEE). He is an editor for *Rethinking Schools* magazine, a writer for the Zinn Education Project, and the director of the Black Education Matters Student Activist Award. Jesse is the co-editor of several books including *Black Lives Matter at School: An Uprising for Educational Justice* and *Teaching for Black Lives*, and editor of the book *More Than a Score: The New Uprising Against High-Stakes Testing*. He is the recipient of the Seattle NAACP Youth Coalition's 2019 "Racial Justice Teacher of the Year." Contact him at hagopian.jesse@gmail.com.

Bob Peterson taught 5th grade for more than 25 years in the public schools in Milwaukee. He is a founding editor of *Rethinking Schools* magazine, and is a frequent writer, speaker, and workshop presenter. He was a founder of La Escuela Fratney, Wisconsin's first two-way bilingual school. He has co-edited several books, including *Rethinking Columbus: The Next 500 Years*, *Rethinking Mathematics*, *Rethinking Elementary Education*, *Rethinking Globalization: Teaching Justice in an Unjust World*, and and the third edition of *The New Teacher Book*. He is a former president of the Milwaukee Teachers' Education Association and currently serves as the city-wide representative on the Milwaukee Board of School Directors. Contact him at bob.e.peterson@gmail.com.

Index

Note: Page numbers in italics indicate illustrations, and those followed by a t *indicate a table.*

A

ACCE (Alliance of Californians for Community Empowerment), 109, 111, 257

achievement gap, 152–53, 305, 312–14

ACLU (American Civil Liberties Union), 167, 242, 249, 299

ACRE (Action Center on Race & the Economy Institute), 112

Advancement Project, 425

advocacy, overview of, 248, 250, 251t

AEA (Arizona Education Association), 191–93

AEU (Arizona Educators United), 190–96

AEU (Australian Education Union), 346, 347

AFL (American Federation of Labor), 26–27, 30, 45, 59

AFL-CIO, 27–28, 50, 56, 252

Afrocentric teaching, 378–79

AFT (American Federation of Teachers)

  advocacy for gay workers, 48

  aid to Puerto Rico, 336

  anti-discrimination/desegregation efforts of, 47

  on the Baltimore Teachers Union election (2019), 205, 208

  community engagement prioritized by, 15–16, 119

  formation of, 59

  as internationally active, 352

  at NCEA conference, 239

  NEA's proposed merger with, 74, 75

  Reconnecting McDowell initiative of, 286–87

  social justice teaching encouraged by, 368

  social justice unionism urged by, 16

  UTLA supported by, 260–61

AFT local (New York City), 47–48

AFT Local 212 (Milwaukee), 321–22

AFT Massachusetts, 356

AFT New Mexico, 331–32

Albert Shanker Institute, 425

ALEC (American Legislative Exchange Council), 78–79, 108, 228, 425

Allen, Robert, 32

Alliance for Quality Education, 337

Alliance of Californians for Community Empowerment (ACCE), 109, 111, 257

Alliance to Reclaim Our Schools (AROS), 229, 246–47, 292, 305–11, 425

  "The Schools All Our Children Deserve," 409–14

American Civil Liberties Union (ACLU), 167, 242, 249, 299

American Federation of Labor (AFL), 26–27, 30, 45, 59

American Federation of Teachers. *See* AFT

American Legislative Exchange Council. *See* ALEC

Ansari, Zakiyah, 337

Arizona

  as a "right-to-work" state, 191, 193, 195

  school privatization in, 84–85

  teacher salaries in, 83

  teachers strike (2018), 87, 189–96

Arizona Education Association (AEA), 191–93

Arizona Educators United (AEU), 190–96

AROS. *See* Alliance to Reclaim Our Schools

art builds, 17, 294, 297–301

Art Build Workers collective, 299–300

Asante, Molefi, 379

Ashby, Steven: *A Fight for the Soul of Public Education*, 428

Asociación de Maestros de Puerto Rico, 336

assessment. *See* standardized testing; teachers, evaluation of

Au, Wayne, 209–18, 333

Austin (Texas), 152–53

Australian Education Union (AEU), 346, 347

auto workers strike (2019), 81

B

Bacchus, Natalia, *204*, 205–6, 208

Bafia, Glenn, 275

Baker, Charlie, 353–54, 356, 360–61

Baker, Ella, 230

Baltimore Movement of Rank-and-File Educators (BMORE), 204–8

Baltimore Teachers Union (BTU), 205–8

Barber, William, II, 227, 229

Barbuto, Jay, 195

Bargaining for the Common Good (BCG), 15, 107–12, 154, 287–88, 397–98

Barrett, Tom, 78, 320

M

Mabalon, Dawn: *Journey for Justice: The Life of Larry Itliong*, 403

MacLean, Nancy: *Democracy in Chains*, 319

Madeloni, Barbara, 174–75, 246, 362, 364–65

Malden Education Association (MEA), 358

Mamula, Amanda, 301

MAP (Measures of Academic Progress) test, 17, 186, 280, 325

March for Our Lives, 87, 294, 299

Markel, Michelle: *Brave Girl: Clara and the Shirtwaist Makers' Strike of 1909*, 400

Martin, Trayvon, 385

Martinez, Mercedes, 338–39

Maryland, 86

Massachusetts, 353–61

Massachusetts Consortium for Innovative Education Assessment (MCIEA), 333

Massachusetts Education Justice Alliance (MEJA), 356–57, 359–60

Massachusetts Teachers Association. *See* MTA

mass incarceration, 14, 243, 384, 389

May Day, 57

McAlevey, Jane, 222, 248–50, 251t, 423–25t
A Collective Bargain, 429
No Shortcuts, 429

McCarthyism, 27, 46, 61–62, 371

McCully, Emily Arnold: *The Bobbin Girl*, 401

McDonald, Laquan, 384–85, 389

McDowell County (West Virginia), 286–87

McMahon, Kelly, 4

MCIEA (Massachusetts Consortium for Innovative Education Assessment), 333

MEA (Malden Education Association), 358

Measures of Academic Progress. *See* MAP test

Megel, Carl, 47

Meier, Deborah, 49

MEJA (Massachusetts Education Justice Alliance), 356–57, 359–60

Meltzer, Milton: *Bread & Roses: The Struggle of American Labor, 1865–1915*, 403

Memphis sanitation strike (1968), 401

Men Teachers Union (MTU; Chicago), 60–61

Metropolitan Milwaukee Association of Commerce (MMAC), 242, 320–22

Mills, Tia, 364–65

Milwaukee
authorization to run charter schools, 321
Martin Luther King Jr. writing and speech contest in, 376
school privatization in, 321
teacher activists in, 239
voucher program in, 238, 246, 317, 321

Milwaukee Center for Teaching, Learning, and Public Education, 244

Milwaukee Education Association, 370

Milwaukee Federated Trade Council, 371

Milwaukee Teachers' Education Association. *See* MTEA

Miner, Barbara: *Lessons from the Heartland*, 319

minimum wage, 14, 322, 356–57

Missing from Haymarket Square (Robinet), 402

Mississippi Freedom Democratic Party, 28

Mizialko, Amy, 320–23

MMAC (Metropolitan Milwaukee Association of Commerce), 242, 320–22

mobilizing, overview of, 248–50, 251t

Mobley, Mamie Till, 62

Montgomery County Education Association, 131

Mooney, Tom, 121, 283–84, 288

Mooney Institute, 102

Moore, Michael, 81

Mooring, Teri, 395

Moral Mondays, 117, 229

Morris, Colleen, 159–64

Movement for Black Lives, 385

MPS (Milwaukee Public Schools), 244–45, 290–94, 321–23

MTA (Massachusetts Teachers Association), 14, 174, 356, 395–96

MTEA (Milwaukee Teachers' Education Association)
art builds of, 299–300
Black Lives Matter protest co-sponsored by, 373
community schools promoted by, 155
database of members and supporters, 293
Facebook used by, 290–95
goals of, 243–44, 323
growth of, 244
immigrant rights supported by, 243
Instagram used by, 292
memes created by, 290–91
school takeovers opposed by, 293, 321–23
social media used by, 290–95
in solidarity with strikers in other cities, 294
as staff-led, 240
successes of, 244–45
transformation to a social justice union, 14, 17, 38, 240–41
Twitter used by, 291–92

MTU (Men Teachers Union; Chicago), 60–61

Murdoch, Rupert, 326–27

P

Pahomov, Larissa, 219–25

ParaPower, 224

paraprofessionals, 142–43, 224

PARCC exams, 331

Parent Teacher Home Visits (PTHV), 138, 140–45, 418–19

Parr-Sanchez, Mary, 330–32

PASS (People Against the Standardization of Students), 328, 330–31

PAT (Portland Association of Teachers), 374, 392, 394–95, 397

Paterson, Katherine
Bread and Roses, Too, 402
Lyddie, 401

PEAC (Progressive Educators for Action Caucus), 254–55

Pearson, 326, 346, 347–50

Peer Assistance and Review (PAR), 130–36, 243

People Against the Standardization of Students (PASS), 328, 330–31

Perillo, Jonna: *Uncivil Rights*, 430

Perlstein, Dan, 16, 42–53

Peterson, Bob, 431
on Act 10, 238
on anti-racist, social justice teaching, 368–77
on charter schools' enrollment bribes, 291
on the Colombian teacher union movement, 341–45
on the history of the labor movement, 31–33
as MTEA president, 237, 240
on the MTEA's transformation and work, 240–45
on rank-and-file militancy of teacher unions, 238–39
Rethinking Globalization, 347, 372, 404
on social justice unionism, 99–101, 239–40, 246
Transforming Teacher Unions, 430
on the Wisconsin Uprising, 237–38

PFPS (Public Funds Public Schools), 319, 427

PFT (Philadelphia Federation of Teachers), 55–56, 220–25

PHENOM (Public Higher Education Network of Massachusetts), 356

Philadelphia Federation of Teachers (PFT), 55–56, 220–25

Philadelphia school-remediation campaign, 222–24

Philippines, 348–49

Pittsburgh Federation of Teachers, 287

Playground Teachers Union (PTU; Chicago), 60

police violence, 210–12, 217–18, 373, 376, 384.

See also Cannon, Darrell; McDonald, Laquan

Portland Association of Teachers. See PAT

Portland Public Schools Climate Justice Committee, 394–95

Potter, Jackson, 70–73

poverty
in Austin, 152
of Black families, and white supremacy, 313–14
corporations' dismissal of, 410
education funding that discriminates against low-income communities, 310–11
funding for high-poverty school districts, 86, 307–9
and the G.I. Bill, 313
home visits in high-poverty school districts, 144 (*see also* PTHV)
in New Mexico, 328, 332
public schools' role in fighting, 308

Pritzker, Penny, 64

private school tuition, income tax deductions for, 238

privatization. *See* school privatization

Professional Growth and Educator Support System (PGES), 133–37

Professional Growth System, 131–33, 136

Proffitt, Bryan, 227–33, 228

Progressive Caucus, 207–8

Progressive Educators for Action Caucus (PEAC), 254–55

PROMESA (Puerto Rico Oversight, Management, and Economic Stability Act; 2016), 334, 339

Proposition 13 (California), 263

PTU (Playground Teachers Union; Chicago), 60

Public Funds Public Schools (PFPS), 319, 427

Public Higher Education Network of Massachusetts (PHENOM), 356

public sector
attacks on, 337–38
organizing in defense of, 34–41
public schools as public institutions, 410–11 (*see also* schools)
reform of, 35

public sector unions, 34–41, 78–80, 108, 238, 240, 322. *See also* teacher unions

Puerto Rico, 317, 334–40

Puerto Rico Oversight, Management, and Economic Stability Act (PROMESA; 2016), 334, 339

Q

Quinn, Lauren, 17, 263–73

R

race
  and the achievement gap, 152–53, 305, 312–14
  and class, 38, 44
Race to the Top, 83, 130, 322
Racial Equity Teams (Seattle), 186, 275, 326, 415–17
Racial Justice Committee, Philadelphia, 221
racism. *See also* white supremacy
  advancing Black freedom via working-class
    solidarity, 44, 47, 49–50
  among Seattle parents, 217
  anti-racist, social justice teaching, 368–77
  in Australia, 351
  and desegregation, 47–48, 53–54
  in HCPSS, 158–59
  in high school textbooks, 371
  institutional, 14–15, 211–14, 216, 326–27, 389
  lynching of Black people, 387
  need for examining history of, 37–38
  professional unionism as anti-racist work, 136
  racist "intelligence" tests, 370
  right-wing attacks, 210–11
  segregation, 45, 50, 162–63, 166, 211–12, 307
  "separate but equal" schools, 307
  suspensions of students of color, 211, 326
  systemic, 223–24, 313–14
  teacher strikes as fighting, 165–69
  torture of Black men by Chicago police, 383,
    384–86, 388–90
  TU's anti-racist campaigning, 45–46
  by unions, 30, 32
  used to divide white and Black workers, 29–30
  "zero-tolerance" discipline policies, 167–68
Raise Up Massachusetts, 356–57, 360–61
"random" searches/frisking of students, 165–67,
  169, 258, 421–22
Ravitch, Diane, 174, 288, 291, 319, 325
Reagon, Bernice Johnson, 242
Reams-Brown, Angela, 364–65
Reclaim Our Schools Los Angeles. *See* ROSLA
Recovery School District (Louisiana), 322
recruitment of teachers of color, 37, 181–82
#RedForEd movement, 16, 73, 85, 190–96, 232,
  252, 267, 352
Reparations Won curriculum, 376, 383–84,
  386–90
Republicans, 77, 84–85, 196, 227–29, 246, 293, 321
resources
  books about teacher unions and social justice
    unionism, 428–30
  on community schools, 157

  labor and educational justice organizations,
    425–27
  labor movement books and curricular guides,
    399–405
  on school privatization, 319
  restorative justice, 158–64, 169, 212, 221, 265,
    339, 420
Restorative Justice Partnership, 160, 163
Rethinking Columbus, 370, 381
Rethinking Our Classrooms, 370, 381
Rethinking Schools
  founding/purpose of, 100, 368–69, 427
  on the future of teacher unionism, 102
  union activists connecting via, 239
Rhodes, Ginger, 121–22
Ricker, Mary Cathryn, 113–19, 141
right-to-work states, 82, 191, 193, 195, 232–33,
  287, 350
right-wing conservatism, 77–78, 216, 228.
  See also ALEC
Rizzo, Frank, 56
Roat, Amy, 176–77
Robinet, Harriette Gillem: *Missing from
  Haymarket Square*, 402
Rogers, John, 153, 156
Romasanta, Gayle: *Journey for Justice: The Life of
  Larry Itliong*, 403
Rooks, Noliwe: *Cutting School*, 319
ROSLA (Reclaim Our Schools Los Angeles), 107,
  109, 154–55, 257–58
Rosselló, Ricardo, 334, 338
Rousmaniere, Kate: *Citizen Teacher*, 59, 430
Ryan, John, 55–56

S

Saint Paul Federation of Educators. *See* SPFE
Saint Paul Federation of Teachers. *See* SPFT
Sanchez, Adam, 4, 81–87
sanctuary schools, 73
#SayHerName, 211, 218
Schirmer, Eleni, 4, 76–80, 226–33, 247–50
school privatization. *See also* charter schools;
  vouchers
  arguments for, 36
  in Arizona, 84–85
  in Colombia, 343
  vs. community schools (see community schools)
  and disproportionate firing of teachers of color,
    181
  fighting against, 35–36, 51, 65, 82, 101, 108, 242,
    246–47, 347–50 (*see also* Schools &

U

UCORE (United Caucuses of Rank and File Educators), 173–74, 205–6, 221, 427

UFT (United Federation of Teachers; NYC)
  Civil Rights Movement supported by, 48–49
  Guild roots of, 44–47
  labor movement's support of, 47, 50
  Ocean Hill-Brownsville strike, 16, 32, 48, 50, 53
  on professional control over the curriculum, 372
  women excluded from, 44
  union caucuses. *See also* CORE; SEE; UCORE
  BMORE, 204–8
  CEDE, 206–8
  challenges for, 176–77
  Organize 2020 for Racial and Social Justice, 227–33
  PEAC, 254–55
  principles and workings of, 173–74
  unions transformed to social justice unionism by, 175–76
  WE, 220–25

Union Power (Los Angeles), 246, 255
  unions. *See also* collective bargaining; labor movement; social justice unionism; teacher unions; *and individual unions*
  activism by, 239, 276, 341–45
  advocacy by, 248, 250, 251t
  on affirmative action, 99–101
  BLM movement role of, 148–49
  community-labor partnerships, 339
  discrimination/racism by, 26, 30–33, 37, 99–100
  industrial unionism, 100, 102, 103–6t, 173–75
  member education in, 39–40, 350
  mobilizing by, 248–50, 251t
  obstacles to unionizing, 26–27
  organizing by, 248–50, 251t, 275
  percentage of workforce unionized, 26–27
  professional unionism, 48, 100, 102, 103–6t, 121, 131–32, 136, 175, 371–72
  public sector, 34–41, 78–80, 108, 238, 240, 322
  rank-and-file workers' participation/leadership in, 36, 79–80, 183–84, 189–96
  resources on history of, 399–405
  size/spread of, 343
  Supreme Court's weakening of, 50, 80, 108, 238
  transformation into social justice unions, 40
  violence toward labor activists, 341–45

Union We Deserve, 207–8

United Auto Workers, 33, 47, 73

United Caucuses of Rank and File Educators. *See* UCORE

United Federation of Teachers. *See* UFT

United States Department of Education, 211, 311, 326

United Teachers Los Angeles. See UTLA

UTLA (United Teachers Los Angeles)
  BCG used by, 108–9, 154
  Chapter Action Teams (CATs), 256–57
  contract negotiations with LAUSD (2017), 107–9, 264, 266–67, 271–72
  CTA, NEA, and AFT support of, 260–61
  escalating actions by, 258–59
  member engagement in, 256–57
  "Our New Deal for Public Schools," 261
  parent/youth/community organizing by, 257–58
  restructuring of, 255, 258
  and ROSLA, 107, 109, 154–55, 257–58
  social media use/communications by, 259–60
  structure tests by, 258–59
  Union Power's leadership in, 246, 255
  vision of, 254–55

UTLA strike (2019), 82, 85, 95, 109, 165–69, 187, 252–61, 263–73

V

Vélez, Luis Felipe, 341–42

Voces de la Frontera, 243, 299

vouchers, 245
  in Arizona, 84
  corporate promotion of, 51, 84, 108, 371
  forms of, 317
  in Milwaukee, 238, 246, 317, 321
  in North Carolina, 228
  in Puerto Rico, 336
  in Wisconsin, 317, 321–22

W

Walker, Scott, 72, 77–80, 238, 241, 320–22, 376

Walker Kelly, Tamika, 228, 232–33

Walker-Henry, Ingrid, 4

walk-ins, 92, 117–18, 193–94, 196, 229, 292–93, 323

Walton Family Foundation, 85, 108, 174, 316

WEA (Washington Education Association), 275, 279, 282, 374, 376

wealth. *See also* poverty
  concentration of, 82–83, 108, 305–6, 313, 327
  inequality in, 14, 18, 72, 108, 409
  and institutional racism, 327
  standardized testing as measuring, 325
  tax breaks for the wealthy, 84, 310, 414

tax on, 396

of vulture philanthropists, 174

and white supremacy, 313

We Charge Genocide (WCG), 385

Weeres, Joseph G.: *United Mind Workers*, 429

Wegela, Dylan, 190–92

Weiner, Lois: *The Future of Our Schools*, 430

Weingarten, Randi, 285–86

West Virginia, 83, 86

West Virginia Public Employees United, 94

West Virginia teachers strike (1990), 90–91

West Virginia teachers strike (2018)

  causes of, 82–84

  food for students during, 92

  goals and scope of, 82, 87

  illegality of, 90–91

  influence/importance of, 81–82, 84, 89–90, 232, 287

  media coverage of, 287

  parents' and students' involvement in, 92

  rank-and-file educators' support for, 93–94

  rank-and-file militancy of, 238

  social media used in, 90, 93–94

  success of, 82, 90–94, 189–90

  support staff's participation in, 91–92

  and Trump voters, 38–39

  union membership increase during, 93

  walk-ins, 92, 193

  walkouts, 94

white supremacy

  and the achievement gap, 313

  and Black Lives Matter, 14, 210, 216, 218

  defined, 313

  dismantling/disrupting, 136, 218, 360

  growth of, 351

  and the poverty of Black families, 313–14

  in trade unions, 38

  and Trump, 38–39

  and wealth accumulation by whites, 313

Winslow, Samantha, 165–69, 206

  How to Jump-Start Your Union, 428

Wisconsin

  budget cuts following the Great Recession, 77–78

  collective bargaining in, 72, 77, 322, 376

  labor history in, 77, 240

  progressive history of, 238

  vouchers in, 317, 321–22

Wisconsin Act 10 (Budget Repair Bill; 2011), 77–80, 238, 240, 243

Wisconsin Uprising (2011), 14, 16, 38, 79–80, 237–38

women

  early teacher union activism of, 33

  equality for, 370

  exclusion from unions, 32, 44

  leadership by, 182–83

women's suffrage, 59. *See also* suffragists

Woodson, Carter G., 45, 371

World Bank, 334, 348, 350

World War I, 27, 30, 59

World War II, 27, 29, 47–48, 61, 254

Wykle, Mary, 91–92

X

X, Malcolm: *The Autobiography of Malcolm X*, 378

xenophobia, 14, 351

Y

Yates, Michael: *Why Unions Matter*, 403

Yep, Laurence: *Dragon's Gate*, 402

Youth Empowered in the Struggle, 243, 245

Youth on Board, 356

Z

"zero-tolerance" discipline policies, 167–68

Zimmerman, George, 385

Zinn, Howard, 25

  on anti-racist, social justice teaching, 372

  interview with, 16, 25–30

  A People's History of the United States, 403

  on teaching unionism, 245, 350, 369, 377

Zinn Education Project, 405, 427

Zuckerberg, Mark, 348

The New Teacher Book
Edited by Linda Christensen, Stan Karp, Bob Peterson, and Moé Yonamine

Teaching is a lifelong challenge, but the first few years in the classroom are typically the hardest. This expanded third edition of *The New Teacher Book* is the only book for new teachers that talks about the importance of teacher unions and offers practical guidance on how to flourish in schools and classrooms and connect in meaningful ways with students and families from all cultures and backgrounds.

Paperback • 352 pages • ISBN: 978-0-942961-03-4

$24.95*   STUDY GUIDE AVAILABLE FOR DOWNLOAD.

A People's Curriculum for the Earth
Teaching Climate Change and the Environmental Crisis
Edited by Bill Bigelow and Tim Swinehart

Engaging environmental teaching activities from *Rethinking Schools* magazine alongside classroom-friendly readings on climate change, energy, water, food, pollution.

Paperback • 433 pages • ISBN: 978-0-942961-57-7

$24.95*

Teaching for Black Lives
Edited by Dyan Watson, Jesse Hagopian, and Wayne Au

Teaching for Black Lives grows directly out of the movement for Black lives. Throughout this book, we provide resources and demonstrate how teachers can connect curriculum to young people's lives and root their concerns and daily experiences in what is taught and how classrooms are set up. We also highlight the hope and beauty of student activism.

Paperback • 368 pages • ISBN: 978-0-942961-04-1

$29.95*

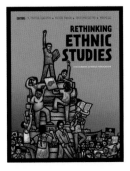

Rethinking Ethnic Studies
Edited by R. Tolteka Cuauhtin, Miguel Zavala, Christine Sleeter, and Wayne Au

Built around core themes of indigeneity, colonization, anti-racism, and activism, *Rethinking Ethnic Studies* offers vital resources for educators committed to the ongoing struggle for racial justice in our schools.

Paperback • 368 pages • ISBN: 978-0-942961-02-7

$24.95*

Use discount code RSBK20 for a 10% discount on your next order.
* Plus shipping and handling

Unions and school districts across the country buy these books in bulk for educator professional development. Email marketing@rethinkingschools.org for bulk rates and special discounts.